TOPOGRAPHIC MAP OF THE UNITED STATES

W9-DDR-440

Lake Superior

Lake Michigan

Lake Huron

Lake Ontario

Lake Erie

St. Lawrence River

Lake Champlain

Connecticut R.

Mt. Washington 6,288 ft.

CAPE COD

Mississippi R.

CENTRAL

PLAINS

Illinois R.

Wabash R.

Ohio R.

River

Allegheny R.

APPALACHIAN MOUNTAINS

Monongahela R.

Delaware R.

Hudson R.

Susquehanna R.

Potomac R.

James R.

Chesapeake Bay

CAPE
HATTERAS

OZARK HILLS

LOWER

MISSISSIPPI

VALLEY

Cumberland River

Tennessee R.

Mt. Mitchell 6,684 ft.

PIEDMONT

ATLANTIC COASTAL PLAIN

Savannah R.

Red

Mississippi River

Alabama R.

COASTAL PLAIN

MISSISSIPPI
DELTA

GULF   OF   MEXICO

FLORIDA PENINSULA

ATLANTIC   OCEAN

FLORIDA
KEYS

45°

40°

35°

30°

25°

75°

70°

90°

85°

80°

0   100   200   300   400

Miles

ATLANTIC OCEAN

PUERTO RICO

18°

0   50   100

Miles

65°

A MORE PERFECT UNION

INTRODUCTION TO AMERICAN GOVERNMENT

Samuel C. Patterson
The Ohio State University

Patterson received his undergraduate education at the University of South Dakota, and in 1959 he received his Ph.D. from the University of Wisconsin. He has been a visiting professor at the University of Wisconsin, the University of Oklahoma, and the University of Essex in England. He served as editor of the *American Journal of Political Science* and the *Legislative Studies Quarterly* before becoming managing editor of the *American Political Science Review* in 1985. From 1961 to 1986, he was on the political science faculty of the University of Iowa, where he was designated Roy J. Carver Distinguished Professor. During 1984 and 1985, he was a John Simon Guggenheim Memorial Foundation Fellow and a visiting fellow at the Brookings Institution in Washington, D.C. His works include *The Legislative Process in the United States* (4th ed., 1985); *Comparative Legislative Behavior: Frontiers of Research* (1972); *Representatives and Represented* (1975); and *Comparing Legislatures* (1979).

Roger H. Davidson
University of Maryland, College Park

Davidson received his B.A. from the University of Colorado and earned his Ph.D. from Columbia University. He recently served as senior specialist in American government and public administration at the Congressional Research Service, where he conducted research and advised members and committees concerning congressional operations. In the mid-1970s, he served as special research consultant to the U.S. Senate's Select Committee on Committees and played a similar role with its House counterpart. His teaching career began at Dartmouth College and continued at the University of California, Santa Barbara, as department chairperson and associate dean of letters and science. His works include *Congress and Its Members* (3rd ed., 1988) and *Governing: Readings and Cases in American Politics* (1987), both with Walter J. Oleszek; *The Politics of Comprehensive Manpower Legislation* (1972); and *The Role of the Congressman* (1969).

Randall B. Ripley
The Ohio State University

Ripley received his B.A. from DePauw University in Indiana and his M.A. and Ph.D. from Harvard University. He served as an intern in the office of the majority whip in the U.S. House of Representatives in 1963. From 1963 to 1967, he was on the staff of the Brookings Institution in Washington, D.C. He became a faculty member at Ohio State University in 1967 and has served as a chairperson since 1969. He has also been a faculty associate for public policy research at the Mershon Center of Ohio State University since 1967. He has served as a consultant to the Department of Labor, the Department of Housing and Urban Development. He is the author of numerous articles and books including *Congress: Process and Policy* (4th ed., 1988); *Congress, the Bureaucracy, and Public Policy*, with Grace A. Franklin (4th ed., 1987); *Policy Implementation and Bureaucracy*, with Grace A. Franklin (2nd ed., 1986); and *Policy Analysis in Political Science* (1985).

Fourth Edition

A MORE PERFECT UNION

INTRODUCTION TO AMERICAN GOVERNMENT

Brooks/Cole Publishing Company
Pacific Grove, California

Cover illustration: Steve Jones
Part Photograph: © Weinberg-Clark/Image Bank

Brooks/Cole Publishing Company
A Division of Wadsworth, Inc.

Sponsoring editor: Leo A. W. Wiegman and Cynthia C. Stormer
Developmental editor: Marlene Chamberlain
Project editor: Joan Hopkins
Production manager: Carma W. Fazio
Designer: Keith J. McPherson/Maureen McCutcheon/Michael Warrell
Artist: Jill Smith
Compositor: The Clarinda Company
Typeface: 10/12 Serif
Printer: R. R. Donnelley & Sons Company

Library of Congress Cataloging-in-Publication Data

Patterson, Samuel Charles, 1931-
  A more perfect union: Introduction to American government/ [Samuel C.
Patterson, Roger H. Davidson, Randall B. Ripley]. —4th ed.
     p.   cm.
  Bibliography: p.
  Includes index.
  ISBN 0-534-11078-9
  1. United States—Politics and government. I. Davidson, Roger H.
II. Ripley, Randall B.   III. Patterson, Samuel Charles, 1931-   More
perfect union. IV. Title.
JK31.P34 1989   88-28179
320.973—dc19   CIP

Printed in the United States of America
1 2 3 4 5 6 7 8 9 0 D

*I*n the spring of 1789, newly selected representatives and senators made their way by horseback, stage, or ship to New York City, the first seat of the new government. Many were delayed by spring rains, flooding, even a shipwreck. By early April, the House and Senate achieved their quorums of members. Two weeks later, Vice President John Adams appeared, and on April 30, George Washington—whose trip had turned into a triumphal procession with crowds and celebrations—was inaugurated as president. The new government was in place.

The year 1989 marked the bicentennial of workable national government in the United States. The first attempt at a nationwide governmental apparatus in 1781, the Articles of Confederation, was a notable failure, lacking the "energy" that Alexander Hamilton held was a government's most prized attribute. The newly drafted Constitution in 1787 was a promising sign; equally impressive was the achievement of getting the document ratified by suspicious state legislatures the following year. Yet the ratification struggle showed how fragile was the consensus in favor of a vigorous national government; reasonable observers, in fact, doubted the new scheme would survive more than a few years. Moreover, although many portions of the Constitution had historical precedents, the overall plan was untried and unknown—little more than a series of ideas on paper.

COMPLETING THE FOUNDERS' DESIGN

The achievements of the First Congress (1789–1791) were every bit as noteworthy as the events that led up to it. For the Constitution, despite its stately design and practical wisdom, contained few specifications for the internal structure of the legislative, executive, or judicial branches, much less the day-to-day relationships between these branches. Soon, however, the two houses of Congress got down to business, choosing their officers and laying out rules and precedents, some of which are still used today. The executive branch took form with the creation of its three component entities: the State, Treasury, and War departments. Federal courts were established by the Judiciary Act of 1789—still the cornerstone of judicial structure, though the Marshall Court invalidated a tiny portion of it in asserting the power of judicial review in the celebrated case of *Marbury* v. *Madison* (1803). Another accomplishment of the First Congress was drafting a Bill of Rights for ratification by the states.

No one in 1789 knew what "a more perfect union" would ultimately look like. The founders realized that the compact of 13 independent states, only loosely banded together under the earlier Articles of Confederation, had utterly failed to "establish justice, insure domestic tranquillity, provide for the common defense, (or) promote the general welfare. . . ." They intended the new government to forge a stronger unity among the states and among their people. They did not want to destroy the states—far from it. Rather, they tried to invent a system in which strong and active states would work in harmony to create a new balance between states and nation.

The founders understood better than most of their contemporaries—indeed, better than many of today's professed constitutionalists—that forming a more perfect union is a never-ending process, not something that was conceived in a moment or born full-grown. Indeed, the founding generation of leaders were intensely practical politicians with a mature understanding of the difficult, frustrating tasks that lay ahead. No one understood this more keenly than shrewd old Benjamin Franklin, who spoke briefly to the delegates at the close of the Constitutional Convention. "I agree to this Constitution with all its faults," Franklin declared. Although he doubted whether any other convention of political leaders could "make a better Constitution," he did not think it was perfect:

> For when you assemble a number of men to have the advantage of their joint wisdom, you inevitably assemble with those men all their prejudices, their passions, their errors of opinion, their local interests and their selfish views. From such an assembly can a perfect introduction be expected? It therefore astonishes me . . . to find this system approaching so near to perfection as it does.

So, concluded Franklin, "I consent . . . to this Constitution because I expect no better, and because I am not sure it is not the best."

ADAPTING TO THE THIRD CENTURY

As we enter the third century of this government—viewed so guardedly by its founders—we do well to take stock of the adequacy of their handiwork. Our reference point must be the 21st century, not the 18th. We face many challenges that were unanticipated, or only dimly perceived, by the architects of our governmental framework. They of all people would expect us to apply our own standards, geared to contemporary questions that we must resolve.

The Constitution has endured in part because of its flexibility and pliability in the face of unforeseen conditions. Indeed, the development of our government would have been inconceivable without elements that were neither specified nor contemplated by the founders. Political parties, the cabinet, legislative

investigations, universal adult suffrage, intricate legislative-executive arrangements, judicial review of congressional and administrative acts—none of these matters were addressed directly by the Constitution.

Many Americans today question whether changes in our Constitutional structure would not foster more effective government. Should members of Congress be allowed to serve in the president's cabinet in order to bring the legislative and executive branches more closely together? Should the president be permitted to dissolve Congress and call new elections if there were a stalemate between the two? Should Congress be allowed to remove a president or other officers more easily than present impeachment procedures makes possible? Should candidates for president and for Congress be required to run as a political party slate to ensure closer ties between them? Should the terms of office of president and members of Congress be longer? Should the president have the power of the "item veto" to annul specific provisions of legislation without vetoing it entirely? These are the kinds of questions that stimulate a healthy and constructive debate as we mark our entry into a third century of national government.

The Constitution's preamble, its opening words, comprises a statements of goals and ideals. It also establishes that the governmental charter, whatever its virtues, must ultimately be judged by its capacity to satisfy its citizens' needs. Regardless of the elegance of its design or the vitality of its precedents, a government is doomed if it cannot satisfy its citizens' basic demands and expectations.

THE AUTHORS' APPROACH TO AMERICAN GOVERNMENT

In this spirit we began in the mid-1970s to think about this textbook. While we respect constitutional structures and understand the vagaries of institutional behavior, we realize that government's ultimate output is going to dispose citizens to take pride in it or to turn their backs on it. "What have you done for me, lately?" is the persistent question democratic voters pose to their leaders. When *A More Perfect Union: Introduction to American Government* appeared in 1979, it was one of the very first American government texts based upon a full-dress analysis of policy consequences of government structures and political processes. A number of other authors subsequently followed our lead.

Subsequent editions of *A More Perfect Union* retained this orientation toward policy making but explored other subthemes in greater detail. We are especially proud of our emphases upon such topics as the nation's political culture, the role and structure of communications media, congressional behavior, and implementation of public policy. As we delivered this manuscript to the publisher, we realized as authors and editors that the book was a more substantially revised manuscript than even our initial and ambitious revision plan had called for. Every paragraph had been improved in some manner of style or context; many new sections, four new chapters, and a political atlas had been added; the order of chapters had been rearranged; the illustration program had been rebuilt.

The present volume, although substantially revised, still reflects our concern for the policy context of government and politics. While we have reshaped and condensed our policy treatment to conform more precisely with what instructors are likely to cover in one- and two-semester treatments of the subject, we continue to stress policy consequences and policy content as major variables for understanding and evaluating our governmental system. We endeavor to present comprehensive coverage of political processes and governmental institutions, with emphasis on the interaction between these and the content of public policy.

Our perspective is further that of professional political scientists: we endeavor to stress analytic (rather than purely descriptive) propositions, political scientists' theoretical concerns, research perspectives, and historical perspectives. We recognize a student's need to master the descriptive details of our political system; but we want to place these facts in broader conceptual and theoretical contexts.

In 1979, when the initial version of this book appeared, we were able to take full account of what *New York Times* correspondent Hedrick Smith has called the reform "earthquake" that swept over our political system in the 1960s and 1970s. This reform period served to open up citizen participation in party nominations, voting, interest group activities, congressional operations, executive decision making, and even court proceedings. Subsequent editions refined this picture as new developments and research findings became apparent.

By the late 1980s, however, a new set of conditions conspired to alter our political structures once again. Economic uncertainty, coupled with fiscal policies detrimental to national government, produced a new policy climate, which in turn forced political leaders to rethink their policy assumptions and adjust their ways of doing business.

NEW FEATURES

This fourth edition of *A More Perfect Union* reflects this shift in the political agenda. New chapters on "A Changing Federalism" (Chapter 3) and "Economic Policies, Spending, and Taxing" (Chapter 18) are major additions which, we feel, bring fresh perspectives to these important topics. Two chapters each are devoted to Congress and the president—confirming our initial instincts in devoting two chapters on these subjects in 1979. The Congress chapters (10 and 11) follow generally the well-known formulation of the "two Congresses": the Congress of individual politicians tending their careers in contrast to the Congress of lawmakers working collectively to make public policy. The subject of the presidency (chapters 12 and 13) divides roughly between the office's traditional constitutional duties and the newer "public presidency" of popular support and media exploitation.

Many other portions of *A More Perfect Union* are substantially reorganized, rewritten, and updated. Chapter 1, "A First New Nation," is largely new to this edition, providing in-depth background for considering the creation of the Constitution. The discussion of political parties (Chapter 6) has been thoroughly recast to take account of new research on party organization and current developments in party structure and alignment. Treatment of the judiciary (Chapter 15) has likewise been reorganized to convey a broader picture of the courts' growing roles as educated policy makers. As always, we have made every effort to devote attention throughout the book to the roles that women and minorities play in our politics.

New pedagogical aids appear in *A More Perfect Union*. These include detailed chapter outlines, chapter introductions that highlight problems of governance, lists of key words, and a glossary. In all chapters, boxed materials have been organized into three consistent categories: Words and Ideas, Historical Perspectives, and Practice of Politics. Remembering from our own student days the power of illustrations to convey ideas, we have carefully selected materials of historic and contemporary interest that tell their stories, and we have written detailed captions to enhance the stories.

A new full-color Political Atlas tells a different set of stories about American politics. We are especially pleased with the series of maps examining changing political demographics in the United States (maps 1–4), those portraying the historical evolution of the United States, and those describing the nation's place in contemporary global politics (maps 27–34).

A comprehensive package of excellent instructional materials is available for instructors and students. Again we are pleased to offer a companion Study Guide, authored by Grace Franklin of the Ohio State University. An Instructor's Manual and Test Manual with summaries, outlines, explanations, lecture ideas, and hundreds of examination ideas has been prepared by Gary Copeland of the University of Oklahoma. Computerized test banks are available for use with Apple and IBM-compatible personal computers.

We gratefully acknowledge the wise advice and counsel of the following scholars for their help in making this a better teaching text:

Calvin J. Mouw, University of Missouri-St. Louis

James F. Sheffield, Jr., Wichita State University

Mark E. Rushefsky, Southwest Missouri State University

Walter B. Mead, Illinois State University

Fred A. Kramer, University of Massachusetts at Amherst

Paul M. Heisig, Bradley University

Joseph A. Pika, University of Delaware

Paul S. Herrnson, University of Massachusetts at Amherst

Harvey J. Tucker, Texas A&M University

Samuel B. Hoff, SUNY College at Genesso

Richard A. Loverd, Villanova University

Stephanie L. Bellar, Texas Tech University

Ryan J. Barilleaux, Miami University

Michael W. McCann, University of Washington

Samuel C. Patterson
Roger H. Davidson
Randall B. Ripley

Contents

This text has to do with governing—with the institutions, processes, and policies that provide effective government in the United States. The broad objective of democratic government in this country has been to forge "a more perfect union." This has been a historic and continuing purpose of the American Constitution.

The Constitution of the United States was first put into practice just 200 years ago. In April 1789, the first session of Congress achieved a working quorum and George Washington was sworn in as the first president. In about a month, President Washington had signed into law the first legislation passed by Congress. In less than two months, Congress created the first cabinet department, the Department of State. From these beginnings, the governing institutions of the United States have evolved into today's large, complex national government.

This book portrays in detail the governing processes that grew from the Constitution and still take their basic authority from it. The Constitution is reprinted in Appendix B of this book. Read it carefully. The founders, 55 men who participated in the Constitutional Convention, which met in Philadelphia from late May until mid-September 1787, crafted the document with great care and thorough deliberation. To justify the Constitution's provisions, they wrote this Preamble to its seven articles:

> We, the People of the United States, in order to form a more perfect Union, establish Justice, insure domestic Tranquility, provide for the common Defense, promote the General Welfare, and secure the Blessings of Liberty to Ourselves and our Posterity, do ordain and establish this Constitution of the United States of America.

In this single sentence, the Preamble clearly and eloquently expresses the purposes of government. It declares those purposes to be the establishment of justice, the guarantee of domestic peace, the defense of the nation from aggression, the advancement of the people's welfare, and the protection of the blessings of liberty both for the generation living then and for future generations. The Preamble provides ideals for governing America.

Before the Constitution was written and ratified, the national government consisted of a loose confederation of states on the Atlantic seaboard, each retaining a great deal of independence. The founders strongly desired a system of national government that would be grounded in the loyalty, support, and consent, not merely of the state governments, but of the people themselves.

No one knew in the late 1780s what "a more perfect union" would be like. However, the delegates to the Constitutional Convention did recognize that functioning as 13 largely independent states, only recently freed from British colonial rule, was not working very well. They intended the new Constitution to fashion a stronger unity among the states and their people. They sought to invent a system under which strong and vibrant states could work together with a strong national government.

The founders surely understood better than any of their fellow Americans that forming a more perfect union was going to be an ongoing process, not something that would be conceived in a moment or born full-grown. Indeed, these people of practical political sense showed a deeply mature perception of the difficult and often frustrating experience that lay ahead for the new union. As the historian Henry Steele Commager has said, "The Constitution did make a more perfect union. Not pefect—that will never be achieved—but more perfect than any previous experiment in federalism: one in which power came from 'the Peole' from the bottom up, not from the top down.''

The Constitution has lasted a long time, longer than any democratic constitution in world history. Will it endure as the basis for governing in the 21st century? It may be that the Constitution has endured more because of its flexibility than because of its inventors' prescience. Political parties, judicial review of congressional and administrative acts, intricate legislative-executive arrangements, the presidential cabinet, universal adult suffrage— these political phenomena, commonplace today, were simply not addressed in the Constitution.

Now some Americans wonder whether changes in the Constitution would foster more effective government. Should members of Congress be allowed to serve in the president's cabinet so as to bond the legislative and executive branches more closely together? If there is a stalemate between the president and Congress, should the president be allowed to dissolve Congress and call new elections? Should Congress be allowed to remove a president more easily than is possible under the present impeachment process? Should candidates for presidential and congressional candidates be required to run as a political party slate so as to build in closer ties between the president and Congress? Should the terms of office of the president and members of the House of Representatives be lengthened. Should the president be given the "item veto" power so that he or she can annul specific provisions of a legislative measure without vetoing the entire measure? Such questions about governing America under the Constitution stimulate a healthy and constructive debate today.

The Constitution's opening words are a statement of goals and ideals. As ideals, the purposes of the new nation were not likely to be realized quickly or easily. Because the founders understood that it would take time to achieve the ideals of the Preamble, they created a Constitution not just for the people living in the late 18th century but for people who would be born long afterward. Debate about the contemporary meaning of the Constitution and discussion of constitutional change are invaluable as we search for better ways to make government work.

In *A More Perfect Union: Introduction to American Government,* we explain how the social, political, and economic environment of American government helps shape the political beliefs of individuals, participation in political life, and governing processes. We carefully analyze American political institutions— the electoral system, political parties, Congress, the presidency and the bureaucracy, the courts—because good government depends on these institutions. The governing processes matter; how things are done and how they are seen to be done are often as crucial as what is done. Abraham Lincoln's reference to "government of the people, by the people, for the people" is an eloquent testimony to this reality.

Governing Americans would be impossible if political institutions and processes were unable to create public policies responsive to public needs and effective in grappling with public problems. Accordingly, we carefully analyze public policies by showing how they are made, how they can be assessed, and what the major public policy arenas are. After having examined how American government works and taken stock of the public policies that unfold from the governing process, we speculate about governing toward a more perfect union in the coming decades, decades in which you, the reader, will play a critical role.

A MORE PERFECT UNION

INTRODUCTION TO AMERICAN GOVERNMENT

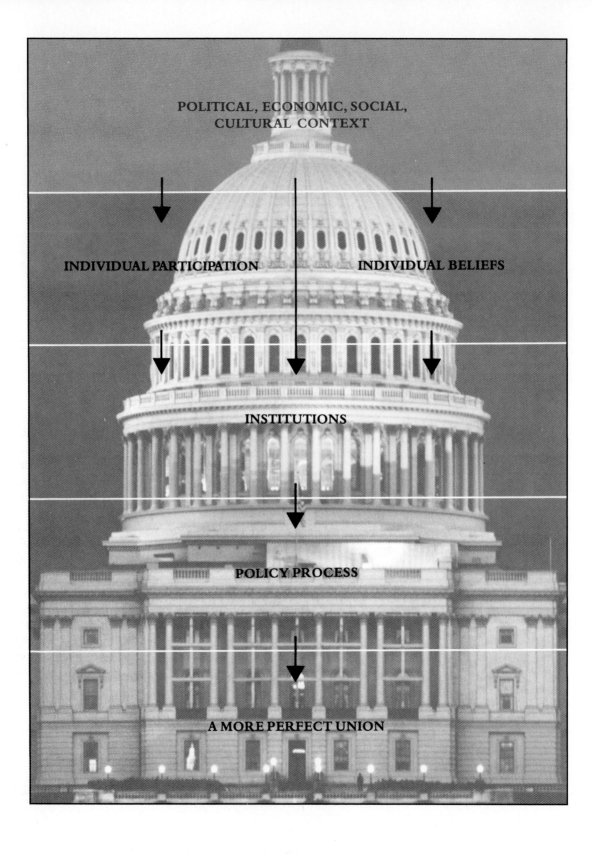

Part One

THE CONTEXT OF AMERICAN POLITICS

Alexis de Tocqueville, a young French visitor to America, thought of our nation as a natural laboratory experiment in democracy as he traveled about in the 1830s. He was curious to find out how democracy worked, so he looked for answers to basic questions about governing: Can men and women govern themselves? Can liberty be reconciled with order? Can a democracy avoid the tyranny of the majority? Must liberty degenerate into tyranny? Can a multiracial, multiethnic, multireligious society maintain democracy? Can democracy survive?

The young Frenchman found "the social condition of the Americans . . . eminently democratic." In *Democracy in America* (1835), he wrote that "in America . . . , I sought the image of democracy itself, with its inclina-tions, its character, its prejudices, and its passions, in order to learn what we have to fear or to hope from its progress." Today democracy in America remains an experiment, but we can look back on the experience of a century and a half to assess its successes and failures.

The context of American democracy embraces the full fabric of our historical, social, economic, and cultural life. The chapters in Part One portray the backdrop for our governing system: patterns of interrelationships stemming from the formative years of the first new nation, the forging of the U.S. Constitution, the establishment of governing through a federal system, and the emergence of characteristic political values, attitudes, and beliefs.

Chapter One

THE FIRST NEW NATION

The United States was the first country to break away from a colonial power—Great Britain—and establish independence. The American Revolution succeeded: The colonists vanquished the British army and navy and sent the royal administration of the colonies packing. Like many countries of the Third World today (in Africa, Latin America, and Asia), the North American colonies faced the problem of forging a new nation when they won independence. What resources could the citizens of the first new nation bring to bear on the problem of developing successful governing capacity? What role was played by the development of unity and national identity? How could effective government be established, avoiding anarchy with its lack of authority at one extreme and monarchy with its excessive authority at the other?

The first new nation was very fragile. Its economy had been decimated by revolution; its people's loyalties were still divided by parochial attachments to Virginia, or South Carolina, or New Hampshire; its security was easily threatened by outside powers, as when the British burned the Capitol in the War of 1812; its governing institutions were only beginning to take shape and develop strength. Today we take our governmental system for granted, but in its early years our nation's ability to govern itself was uncertain. The United States of America took time to develop as a strong and viable polity.

*I*n this chapter, we analyze the broad features of colonial America to show how political ideas and traditions, and practical experience with representative government, helped shape the new nation. We discuss the causes of the American Revolution and explain its main consequences for the development of a new system of government. We investigate American political development along lines worked out by scholars who today study the developing countries of the Third World. Finally, we take stock of the ways in which the major national political institutions—Congress, the presidency, the courts, the bureaucracy—developed over the years. This background lays the foundation for understanding the formation of the U.S. Constitution and the processes of government under it.

THE NECESSITY OF GOVERNMENT

Americans are often heard to complain about "the government." We do this because we don't like the people running it, because we find its policies distasteful, or because we don't like to be bothered. But the fact is that **government** in some form has been around a long time. One reason for the existence of government everywhere is that societies need it to protect themselves. One of the fundamental things that government does is to provide us with security. Governments try to protect their people from external threats by establishing means of national defense, such as an army or a navy. And they try to maintain order within a country through laws, regulations, or court decisions enforced, if necessary, by police. Of course, governments may do many other things for the welfare of their people—they may provide educational or social services; build bridges, buildings, roads, or dams; or explore outer space. And we know that governments sometimes have too much power, which they may use to oppress people.

Authoritarian systems of government have few limits on what they can do to control people. In these systems, the masses of people may have very little to say about how they are governed and the police or the armed forces may have great power to order people around or imprison them. In one such authoritarian system, the Soviet Union, government decisions are made by a small number of leaders in the top ranks of the Communist party, with the result that thousands have been detained in prison camps— the "Gulag Archipelago" described so vividly by Soviet author Aleksandr Solzhenitsyn. In **democracies,** the powers of government are circumscribed, citizens can participate in governing themselves, and **human rights** are protected. A democratic government is one that particularly emphasizes **free elections** and **individual liberty.**

Government is necessary; it is not just a necessary evil. Government can be an instrument for good, as those who founded the United States of America assumed. They wrote the purposes of government into the Preamble to the Constitution. The first job of government, they said, was to bring about "a more perfect union." They had in mind bringing the states and the people together in security, harmony, well-being, and freedom. Then, they said, government should "establish justice, insure domestic tranquility, provide for the common defense, promote the general welfare, and secure the blessings of liberty to ourselves and our posterity." There are many nations in the world today that aspire to such high purposes and look to the example of American democracy for guidance.

The American example of democracy grew up over a long period of time, beginning back in the 17th century, when England started to establish colonies in North America. Colonial Americans enjoyed a considerable measure of liberty and practiced democratic government in many quarters—especially so in contrast to the Europeans of the day. When the Americans threw off English rule in 1775, they became the first major colony to escape colonialism. As a result, the United States became the "first new nation." Abraham Lincoln said it best, speaking in Gettysburg, Pennsylvania, in 1863: "Four score and seven years ago our fathers brought forth on this continent, a new nation, conceived in Liberty, and dedicated to the proposition that all men are created equal." American democracy today is the end product of fully two centuries of experience following independence.

EUROPE AND AMERICA

Who Came, and Why

Like such other colonial peoples as the Spanish and Portuguese in Latin America, the Dutch in South Africa, the French in Canada, and the British in Australia, the British people who first settled the American colonies were a **fragment society** (Hartz, 1964). They brought with them a host of cultural assumptions, fears, and desires that were deeply rooted in European society.

The first English settlements were established by merchants who developed joint-stock companies, chartered by the king. These merchants raised enough capital to colonize in America by selling shares to investors among the aristocracy and landed gentry. Their joint-stock companies were sometimes called "companies of merchant-adventurers." After several failures, the Virginia Company of London in 1607 finally succeeded in establishing a permanent colony at Jamestown, Virginia. Later the Massachusetts Bay Company invested in the settlement of New England. But colonists did not come to America merely for commercial purposes. In addition to the company settlers, many religious dissenters (most notably the Puritans) fled to the colonies. The first of these refugees were the Pilgrims, led by William Bradford, who established Plymouth Colony in Massachusetts in 1620.

The life in Britain that the colonists escaped was often savage and unpleasant. Here is how a British historian has described it:

> The placid countryside and sleepy market towns witnessed rick burnings, machine-smashing, hunger-riots. The starving poor were run down by the yeomanry, herded into jails, strung up on gibbets, transported to the colo-

nies. No one cared. This was a part of life like the seasons, like the deep-drinking, meat-stuffing orgies of the good times and bumper harvests. The wheel turned, some were crushed, some favoured. Life was cheap enough. Boys were urged to fight. Dogs baited bulls and bears. Cocks slaughtered each other for trivial wagers. . . . Death came so easily. A stolen penknife and a boy of 10 was strung up at Norwich; a handkerchief, taken secretly by a girl of 14, brought her the noose. Every six weeks London gave itself to a raucous fete as men and women were dragged to Tyburn to meet their end at the hangman's hands. The same violence, the same cruelty, infused all ranks of society. . . . Jails and workhouses resembled concentration camps; starvation and cruelty killed the sick, the poor, and the guilty. . . . Vile slums in the overcrowded towns bred violent epidemics; typhoid, cholera, smallpox ravaged the land. (Plumb, 1963: 9–10)

The poor had little to lose if they abandoned England. And the middle class and aristocracy saw America as a ripe field for new profits in trade.

People left England to settle the Atlantic seaboard for a variety of reasons. Some sought to improve their economic condition, lured by the prospect of cheap land and a good business venture. Some were laborers recruited by businessmen who saw that colonial development could add to the power of the mother country. Such recruits often shared their employers' vision of building a great colonial empire, or they viewed a few years of labor as a fair trade for eventual possession of their own land. Some sought freedom from religious persecution. The Puritans who migrated to Massachusetts were among them; they were filled with religious zeal and unhappy with the restrictions that England placed on their religious practices.

The English philosopher John Locke (1632–1704) greatly influenced political thinking in the United States. In the first part of the Declaration of Independence, Thomas Jefferson drew heavily on his ideas. Locke's Letter Concerning Toleration *(1689) fostered support of religious toleration. His* Two Treatises of Government *(1690) laid the basis for government based on the consent of the governed.*

The Roots of American Political Ideas

American political ideas were shaped in the ferment of political philosophizing in the 17th and 18th centuries. In those centuries, belief in the God-given right of the king or queen to **absolute rule** dwindled. **Social contract** theories of government replaced the idea of the **divine right** of kings. The thinking of such philosophers as Thomas Hobbes, John Locke, and Jean Jacques Rousseau attracted wide currency. These social contract theorists contrasted the advantages of a governing community with the disadvantages of a "state of nature," a hypothetical condition in which there was no governing authority. This comparison convinced them that government was useful and that people entered into a social contract establishing government in order to protect their rights and guide their obligations. These ideas seemed especially relevant to people faced with the necessity of establishing government in a wilderness.

The main theme of British political thought that the settlers brought with them was the **liberal tradition.** This was a bundle of political ideas advanced by the 17th-century English philosopher John Locke (Hartz, 1955). Locke was well read in philosophy and politics, but he also acquired plenty of practical political experience. He spent a good deal of his time advising British officials, and he helped draft a constitution for the colony of Carolina. He also wrote essays in support of religious toleration and civil liberties and against the "divine right" of kings to rule as absolute monarchs.

HISTORICAL PERSPECTIVE

The Mayflower Compact, 1620

The Pilgrims were a group of English religious dissenters living in exile in Holland who decided to transplant their colony to the New World, where they hoped for greater freedom to practice their religion. The leaders of the Pilgrims were able to get permission from the Virginia Company to establish a colony at Plymouth, Massachusetts. En route, the leaders agreed to the famous Mayflower Compact, named after the ship in which the Pilgrims had sailed to America. This compact, which served as the constitution for Plymouth Colony, exemplified the colonists' belief in government as a contract limiting governmental power and providing for the general welfare.

IN The Name of God, Amen. We, whose names are underwritten, the Loyal Subjects of our dread Sovereign Lord King *James,* by the Grace of God, of *Great Britain, France,* and *Ireland,* King, *Defender of the Faith,* &c. Having undertaken for the Glory of God, and Advancement of the Christian Faith, and the Honour of our King and Country, a Voyage to plant the first colony in the northern Parts of Virginia; Do by these Presents, solemnly and mutually in the Presence of God and one another, covenant and combine ourselves together into a civil Body Politick, for our better Ordering and Preservation, and Furtherance of the Ends aforesaid; And by Virtue hereof do enact, constitute, and frame, such just and equal Laws, Ordinances, Acts, Constitutions, and Offices, from time to time, as shall be thought most meet and convenient for the general Good of the Colony; unto which we promise all due Submission and Obedience.

Locke developed his political ideas most fully in his *Two Treatises of Government,* first published in 1690. In this book, he made three central, interconnected arguments that deeply influenced the founders of the American republic. First, Locke argued that human beings in a natural state—without government—have inalienable rights to life, liberty, and property but that in the "state of nature" there is no way to protect the rights of the weak against infringements by the strong. These views came to be called the doctrine of **natural rights.**

Second, Locke argued that people instinctively establish government to protect their inalienable rights. For the sake of self-preservation, people band together and draw up a governing contract. This contract, or constitution, would spell out the rights and duties of members of the polity; it would set forth both the responsibilities of the governments and its limits. Locke believed in the idea of a **written constitution** that would provide for a government of **enumerated powers.** He believed in **limited government,** one bound by the strictures of the constitution and laws.

Third, Locke believed that government must be strong enough to protect the rights of citizens but not so strong as to threaten their freedoms. He favored a constitution of liberty in which government would be based on the **consent of the governed,** that government should be held accountable to the nation's citizens. He thought that the people could rightly overthrow their government if it failed to protect and defend their natural and inalienable rights.

No group of British settlers better anticipated Locke's ideas than the Pilgrims. Seeking to practice their religion freely, they left England on the ship *Mayflower* in 1620. After a very rough voyage of about three months, they landed at Plymouth in Massachusetts. Before they left the ship, their leaders drew up an agreement that would be the basis for their self-government. This document, the Mayflower Compact, became the model of basic constitutional government for several other New England colonies. Moreover, the Pilgrims' experience seemed to give historical validity to Locke's concepts of governing.

Individual freedom and equality seemed very natural in the New World, where newness, abundance, and a fresh start gave a sense of practicality to Locke's political ideas. And to the Americans of the 18th century, Locke's ideas seemed consistent with American colonial experience. His vision of a constitutional government with limited powers directly influenced Benjamin Franklin, Thomas Jefferson, James Madison, and other colonial leaders. The liberal tradition became the basis both for America's claim to independence and for the constitution of the new nation.

POLITICAL LIFE IN THE COLONIES

Three political trends stood out during colonial times. One of these trends was the emergence of **representative government.** The English settlers brought ideas about parliamentary government with them to America. The colonial charters provided for legislative assemblies that either represented citizens directly or allowed each town to send a representative. So influential did these legislatures become that on the eve of the American Revolution they were in control of most of the colonies.

Another important political trend of the colonial era was persistent political conflict, especially between the executive and the legislature. The colonial governors directly appointed by the king—in the so-called royal colonies—were in the most heated conflict with their assemblies. And the third trend was the growth of a sense of national community among the colonists, so that they came to think of themselves more as "Americans" than as "British."

The fragment society of colonial America was detached at a time when Europeans, particularly the British, were starting to strongly assert and put into practice the ideals of individual freedom and liberty. Most of the

American colonists brought with them British ways of thinking and political values. But they faced very new experiences in settling a wilderness far from the strong reach of British authority.

Representative Government Takes Hold

Representative government was a part of everyday political life for Americans long before the Revolution. The first representative assembly in America, the Virginia House of Burgesses, first met in 1619, one year before the Pilgrims landed and only 12 years after the colony of Virginia was founded at Jamestown. The House of Burgesses and other colonial assemblies were set up on the initiative of authorities in London who assumed that these assemblies would add to political stability.

The colonial legislatures were remarkable for their time. First, they were much more democratically apportioned than legislatures anywhere else. While these colonial bodies would not meet present-day equal population—"one person, one vote"—**apportionment** standards, towns and counties were substantially represented in them. The ties between constituents and their colonial legislators were close. And "it became generally the custom to require representatives to be residents of and property owners within their constituencies, to instruct the deputies, and subsequently to check upon their actions as delegates" (Kammen, 1969: 6). Government by the consent of the governed in the colonies quickly came to mean government by the representative assemblies. Massachusetts provided an early example. In 1634, only six years after the founding of the colony, the General Court (then, as now, the name of the Massachusetts legislature) met in Boston to declare "that none but the Generall Court hath power to make and establishe lawes, nor to elect and appoynt officers, as Governor, Deputy Governor, Assistants, Treasurer, Secretary, Captain, Leiuetenants, Ensignes, or any of like moment, or to remove such upon misdemeanor, as also to sett out the dutyes and powers of the said officers."

Second, a kind of **two-party politics** gradually developed in the American colonies. A "country" party drew inland farmers, and a "commercial" party attracted businessmen in the coastal towns. By the time of the Revolution, there were two well-developed voting blocs in every colony. The country party of mainly inland and frontier farmers ultimately emerged as the Jeffersonian Republican party, the forerunner of the modern **Democratic party.** And the commercial party, drawing support mainly from the mercantile interests in the coastal towns, evolved as the Federalist party of the post-Revolution period, the forerunner of the present-day **Republican party** (Main, 1973).

Third, people voted in numbers unequaled by any standards of the time. As in European nations, voting was limited to white males who owned property and paid taxes. But because so many men in America owned land, between 50 and 75 percent of adult white males were eligible

Public education is vital to American democracy. In this 18th-century Pennsylvania schoolroom, children recited their lessons from a chalkboard. One child sits on a high stool wearing a dunce cap, presumably as punishment for a poor recitation.

to vote, a much higher percentage than in England. The democratic spirit of the colonists was confirmed in their relatively high level of participation in the political life of the town and colony.

Finally, the colonial assemblies had and exercised important **legislative powers.** Pressures for rapid development to claim the wilderness and establish communities required positive government action. Since the assemblies had the **power of the purse,** they were able to expedite development without the delays that would have been required if the Parliament in London had to approve expenditures. So the assemblies passed laws regulating land distribution, paid for the construction of public facilities (such as wharfs, roads, ferries, and public buildings), established towns and schools, and governed inheritance. Thus, the assemblies took an active role in local and colonial government. They vigorously debated and resolved many issues that in "old England" had been settled quietly and gradually over several centuries.

The legislators and the landowners who elected them were for the most part loyal to England. They admired the British contitution and the British system of **mixed government,** which in theory divided power among the king, the nobility represented in the House of Lords, and the citizenry represented in the House of Commons. They shared the British belief in a representative government that protected liberty and individual freedom. However, the colonists saw themselves as full British citizens, whereas Parliament saw them as residents of colonies whose business and trade must be controlled to suit British needs (Henretta et al., 1987: 152–77). By 1760, Parliament had passed over 100 laws to regulate colonial affairs. Although many of these laws benefited the colonists, some were regarded as arbitrary and restrictive. The colonists particularly disliked trade restrictions requiring that goods shipped to and from the colonies pass through British ports. Widespread evasion of British economic regulations fostered a spirit of independence and disobedience in the colonists.

The colonists' independence showed up forcefully in challenges to executive power. Major political conflicts in the colonies came to revolve around the governors appointed by officials in London. British officials thought of colonial government as a mixed one like their own. In their view, the Crown was represented by the governor, the **aristocracy** by the upper house, or council, and the people by the popular house of the legislature. In practice, this system worked out much differently in the colonies. The governors were a long way from their patrons in London, and turnover among them was frequent. There was little in the way of a colonial aristocracy to support **gubernatorial power.** And the assemblies, able to claim that they represented the colonists, vigorously opposed the weak governors. This meant that leadership in the colonies was uncertain, factional, and often highly contentious. The governors had wide authority, but they lacked the influence needed to enforce it. This uncertainty of authority meant that the colonies did not become stable political systems. Rather, colonial governments "bred belief that faction was seditious, a menace to government itself, and the fear . . . that the government was corrupt and a threat to the survival of Liberty" (Bailyn, 1968: 105).

Admiration of the British constitution was widespread among 18th-century Americans. But so was the belief that the British constitution was being subverted by the excessive growth of power and the taint of corruption. The colonists widely accepted the idea that political power was, by nature, likely to be used to suppress liberty. They believed that "threats to free government . . . lurked everywhere, but nowhere more dangerously than in the designs of ministers in office to aggrandize power by the corrupt use of influence, and by this means ultimately to destroy the balance of the constitution." Political corruption "was as universal a cry in the colonies as it was in England, and with it the same sense of despair at the state of the rest of the world, the same belief that tyranny, already dominant over most of the earth, was continuing to spread its menace and was threatening even that greatest bastion of liberty, England itself" (Bailyn, 1968: 56–57). Political instability and the belief that the established government was corrupt meant a climate congenial to demands for change.

alter or to abolish it, and to institute new government, laying its foundation on such principles, and organizing its powers in such form, as to them shall seem most likely to effect their safety and happiness.

John Locke's political philosophy and the liberal tradition of the colonies were never better stated. Because the Declaration so cogently captured basic American ideals, Jefferson is credited with the "invention of America" in his own special way (see Wills, 1978). It is certainly true that the signers of the Declaration did not believe that women, blacks, or Indians had inalienable rights, at least not in the same sense that white men had them. That was more than the belief system of the late 18th century could manage. In its own time, however, the Declaration was a ringing statement of freedom. Rights for women, blacks, native Americans, and others required time and struggle as the meaning of the Declaration came more and more to embrace all persons.

The First New Nation

Unlike the great revolutions in France and Russia, the Revolutionary War did not bring sweeping social and economic changes. But it did replace one set of political authorities with another. The Crown-appointed governors and administrators and their loyal supporters fled the colonies. They returned to England or emigrated to British Canada. In their stead were authorities chosen by the citizens of the new little republics of the independent states. The former colonies became self-governing.

The revolutionary conflict, the disruption of normal life, the fighting, and the destruction of property brought by the war between the colonists and the British served to unify the new Americans. They could cling together against a common British enemy. That "long, straggling, often disruptive, and sometimes atrocious war," as one historian called it, had the effect of politicizing communities and individuals. "After the fortunes and pressures of war had destroyed his other alternatives, each member of a large majority could claim his tiny but concrete share in the creation of the United States" (in Kurtz and Hutson, 1973: 155). As a unified people, Americans came to feel a larger stake in the new nation, which was now under their own control.

The most tangible results of the American Revolution were the independent American governments that quickly formed in its wake. The new state governments were much like the colonial ones, but most of them did away with the office of governor. Late in 1777, the Continental Congress approved the final draft of a national constitution called the **Articles of Confederation.** These Articles created a confederation of states, affirmed the Continental Congress as the national representative body, and gave it quite a bit of national power (including the power to conduct foreign policy and war). But they stressed in no uncertain terms the independence of the states, and they made no provision for a national court system or a

General George Washington viewing the battle at Yorktown, Virginia. On October 9, 1781, the British forces at Yorktown were surrounded by American and French troops. General Cornwallis, their commander, surrendered 10 days later, virtually bringing the American Revolution to an end.

chief executive. Our first constitution did little more than legalize what the Continental Congress had been doing. Congress did gain the power to create executive departments; it promptly set up departments of foreign affairs, finance, war, admiralty, and post office.

The Revolution and the adoption of the Articles of Confederation did not put an end to discontent. Hard economic times after the Revolution, especially for farmers, led to protests against mortgage foreclosure and to jailing when people could not pay debts and taxes. The most serious of these protests was Shays' Rebellion in Massachusetts in 1787. The prevailing discontent led many to believe that the federal government should be strengthened.

Meanwhile, in order to improve the flow of trade, Virginia and Maryland signed an agreement dealing with commercial traffic on the Potomac River. The arrangements worked out so well that the Virginians proposed holding a general commercial conference in Annapolis, Maryland. The Annapolis Convention did not have great success. But its moving spirits— Alexander Hamilton and James Madison—used the occasion to urge the convening of another conference of state delegates; this conference would deal with pressing constitutional and economic problems. A number of state legislatures endorsed this proposal. Congress then passed a resolution calling for a meeting to consider needed changes in the Articles of Confederation. The meeting was to be held in Philadelphia in 1787.

This Philadelphia conclave became the Constitutional Convention. The delegates to the conclave soon determined that the Articles of Confederation could not be patched up—that there would have to be an entirely new constitution. They formulated the Constitution of the United States, which was ratified and put into effect in 1789. In the 1980s, we have been celebrating its bicentennial. The basic ideas of the Constitution have lasted two centuries; we explain the foundations of our constitutional system in Chapter 2.

When the first federal census was taken, in 1790, there were fewer than 4 million people in the 13 states, approximately the present-day population of Minnesota. Most of these people were preoccupied with the protection of their lives and property under hard conditions. Many of them lived on the frontier, in some danger of life and limb. If their lives were unsettled, all the more frail and fragile was the new national government that the Constitution had set up. It is hard now to imagine how experimental the government was; no federal, **republican government** had ever worked on such a large scale. George Washington, the first president, told a friend that he faced "an ocean of difficulties, without that competency of political skill, abilities, and inclinations which is necessary to manage the helm" (in Morison, 1965: 317).

Most successful revolutionaries inherit governmental machinery that can be turned to the aims of the new regime. This was true of France in the 18th century and of Russia in the 20th. In the first new nation, the apparatus of the central government had to be built virtually from scratch. Most important, the new government had to establish its authority as an effective instrument and provide the basis on which Americans could identify themselves as a nation.

In its early days, the new government's authority flowed mainly from two springs: the personal role of George Washington as our first chief executive and the government's success in dealing with key economic and political problems.

Washington's role as "the father of his country" has often been overdrawn. But his part in establishing national political authority was of the highest importance. Because of his great prestige, Washington could command the loyalty both of the leaders of the different political factions and of the public at large. Americans rallied around him, and he personally provided a basis for national unity. Firmly wedded to the principles of constitutional government, he was able to guide the creation of the machinery of government along constitutional lines. He was an influential leader for a number of years, first as commander of the revolutionary army, then as the leader of those who created the new federal constitution,

Alexander Hamilton (1755–1804). After the Revolution, Hamilton, an officer in the revolutionary army, fervently supported a strong national government. He played an active part at the Constitutional Convention and then coauthored The Federalist *papers to aid ratification of the Constitution in New York. George Washington appointed him the first secretary of the Treasury. Hamilton was killed in a pistol duel by his longtime political enemy, vice president Aaron Burr.*

and finally, for eight years, as President of the United States. His influence was lasting enough to allow diverse political factions to crystallize into organized political parties. Finally, he set an example that for many years resolved the problem of leadership succession. He voluntarily retired from the presidency after two terms despite the fact that he was in good health and could have been reelected easily (see Lipset 1963: 22–23).

Equally important, the new government was fairly successful. Under Alexander Hamilton's leadership as the first secretary of the Treasury, a sound financial plan was put into effect. The plan drew the support of state governments; their confidence in the new regime was won by the plan's provisions for federal assumption of state debts and for the refinancing of debts owed to foreign countries, such as France. The Bank of the United States provided a means for national investment in economic development. More and more in the 19th century, the federal government (as well as the states) intervened in the economy to foster rapid economic growth.

The new system proved successful politically as well. Thomas Jefferson's election as president in 1800 was the first case of the succession of one party (the Democratic-Republicans) over another (the Federalists). This election showed that peaceful succession in party control of the government was workable. It also showed how two national parties competing for office could bring politics to the grass roots, providing a link between ordinary citizens and the nation's leaders.

The new nation emerged from a revolution to throw off British colonialism. After experimentation within the independent state governments and then with the Articles of Confederation, the constitutional order that marks its 200th birthday in 1989 took its shape. The new nation began its struggle to succeed, to develop, and to grow. Once the new national governing institutions were in place, how well did they function? What tests did the nation undergo, and how have things changed?

Our political system took a long time to develop, and it is still changing. The United States began as a rural and agricultural society and became a mixed, mostly urban, technologically advanced, and industrialized society. Until the 1900s, it was not much involved in world affairs—it pursued mainly **isolationist** policies. But in this century, it has become an awesome military and industrial power. Its people were at first mainly British, but it now comprises a highly diverse population. From 13 sparsely populated territories clinging to the eastern seaboard, Americans settled a large continent. In the 1800s, they left their tracks across the prairies of the West; in this century, they left their tracks on the moon.

A country is considered politically developed when its political institutions have proven able to govern. **Political development** always involves change; as our country grew and society became more complicated, governmental institutions became differentiated and specialized. For example, the functions of Congress, the executive, and the judiciary became increasingly distinct, and each acquired special ways of conducting its business. As a nation's political institutions differentiate and specialize, they govern more effectively. Political development also involves changes in national identity and in the use and distribution of political power.

In the remainder of this chapter, we will study America's political development by asking a series of questions that political scientists use to analyze the development of nations today.

1. How does a nation develop its own identity?
2. How do political institutions gain legitimacy?
3. How does government keep control as the nation grows?
4. How does political participation change over time?
5. Who benefits or suffers as the political system changes?

Developing National Identity

New nations confront the problem of arousing a sense of national awareness in their citizens and winning their citizens' commitment to the political system. How does a country develop a national identity?

POLITICAL DEVELOPMENT AND SOCIAL CHANGE

The nation's Capitol—symbol of national authority. This portrayal of the Capitol, painted in 1835 by an unknown artist, was acquired by the White House in the early 1960s.

National symbols

One way in which national identity develops is through symbols. These symbols may be political abstractions, as was the case in the years before the Revolution, when Americans united in their demands for freedom, independence, and justice against British authority. The stars and stripes of the American flag and the national anthem arouse national identity, and many other symbols do the same. As such symbols increased in numbers, deepened their hold on citizens, and became more widely experienced, national identity grew (see Henretta et al., 1987: 279–305).

National identity was strengthened through political leadership. George Washington, the nation's first president, symbolized the new nation to many of its people—he was "first in peace, first in war, and first in the hearts of his countrymen." His leadership and that of such other early nationalists as John Adams, James Madison, and Thomas Jefferson helped firm up our sense of being a nation.

The national capital is a center for the exercise of national authority, and it can symbolize the meaning of a nation. The early American government was not highly visible. It did not have a fixed site until it was settled in Washington, D.C., in 1800. At that time, the states of Virginia and Maryland ceded part of their land to the national government in order to form a federal district for the new capital. Previously, Congress had met in Philadelphia and New York (and before that in other towns). Even with a fixed capital, for a long time the government was not a vital center of national political life or a major focal point of identification with the na-

The modern U.S. Capitol building in Washington, D.C., as seen through trees.

tion. Small and remote, it had very little impact on the everyday lives of most citizens. In our own time, we are used to big government and large bureaucracies, so it is hard for us to imagine how small the early government was. Two years after it had been settled in Washington, it consisted of a mere 291 officials. At the end of the Jefferson era, 27 years later, the "headquarters establishment" had only a little more than doubled in size (Young, 1966: 28).

How did the United States survive its slowness in developing national identification? The answer lies partly in the fact that its citizens, mostly farmers and small-town merchants, were very busy growing crops, developing trade, clearing land, and pushing the frontier westward. Preoccupied with their own problems, Americans acquired a national identity as they went along. A better answer may be that time and the environment were very advantageous. Because there was only moderate urgency about national mobilization, national identity could be allowed to grow slowly. The country was isolated from outside forces and influences, and it could therefore safely develop on its own.

"Americanizing" the immigrants

Beginning in the 1830s, immigration to the United States began to grow rapidly, with new Americans coming mostly from Europe. Before long, the country became a "land of immigrants" and needed to absorb people of diverse races and nationalities. In fact, the United States has absorbed large tides of immigrants and many racial and ethnic groups. Just look at the portrayal of this in Figure 1–2, which shows the waves of immigrants coming to this country over the years. While native Americans (including

FIGURE 1–2   Immigration into the United States, 1820–1980

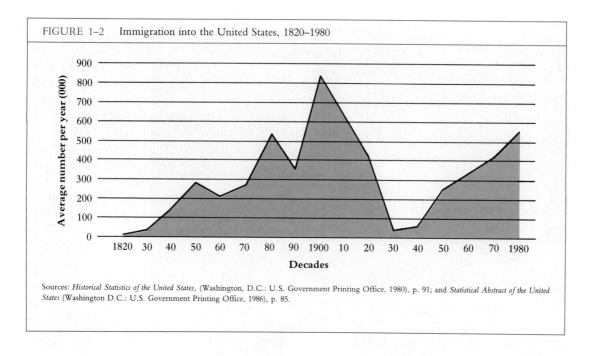

Sources: *Historical Statistics of the United States*, (Washington, D.C.: U.S. Government Printing Office, 1980), p. 91; and *Statistical Abstract of the United States* (Washington D.C.: U.S. Government Printing Office, 1986), p. 85.

Eskimos and Aleuts) now number about 1.4 million, more than ever before, most U.S. citizens have come here from somewhere else, mostly Europe. Several hundred thousand slaves were brought to America from Africa, most before 1820. In the last decade, thousands of Hispanics have come to America (from Cuba, Central America, and Mexico), flowing mostly into Florida, Texas, and California. These very new immigrants have created anew the problem of instilling an American national identity in the hearts and minds of newcomers.

When the nation was founded, its people were mainly British. Today the United States is a multiracial, very diverse country. About 500,000 new immigrants enter it legally each year. More than 10 million people came to this country between 1951 and 1980: 33 percent were Europeans, 19 percent were Asians, and 46 percent (including 1.8 million Mexicans and Cubans) were from the Western Hemisphere. Although many European immigrants have kept an ethnic identity over a long time, blacks are today the largest single ethnic group in the United States. They comprise about 12 percent of the population.

The absorption of immigrants did not mean assimilation. To be sure, most immigrants did become "Americanized." They learned to speak English, qualified for citizenship, got jobs, and were accepted into the community. But much ethnic diversity was preserved. Nevertheless, pressure on immigrants to Americanize shows the strength of our national identity and our mixed feelings about cultural pluralism.

Still a nation of immigrants. In September 1984, 9,706 people were sworn in as citizens of the United States in a mass ceremony at the Orange Bowl in Miami, Florida. Like many other Cubans, Artime and Elvira Veloso came to the United States seeking freedom and opportunity.

Political party identity

In today's politics, people often identify themselves as part of the political process through their loyalty to political parties. Indeed, it is now hard to see how a large-scale democracy could operate without party loyalties and the competition that parties give to elections. But the framers of the Constitution did not appreciate this. They included not one word about political parties in the Constitution. They assumed that the president would be elected on a nonpartisan basis, much as Washington had been elected in the first two presidential elections. Such leaders as Hamilton, Washington, Madison, and Jefferson felt that **political parties** (they called them "factions") would be destructive, divisive forces that would frustrate the public interest (see Ranney, 1975). A large portion of Washington's Farewell Address warned against "the baneful effects of the Spirit of Party."

Because of their haphazard parentage, our parties have been dubbed "the unplanned institution of organized partisanship" (Holcombe, 1950:

107). Ironically, it was Madison and Jefferson who started the first opposition political party in the history of democratic governments. Ostensibly on a botanical expedition, the two traveled all over the United States in the 1790s to mobilize support for "democratic societies" in communities. They aimed to form a popular political party that could win elections and thus wrest control of government from the Federalists (led by Washington, Hamilton, and John Adams). They succeeded. Jefferson became president in 1801, and he was followed in the White House by Madison in 1809. So it is true that "the one major political institution invented in America is . . . the political party" (Huntington, 1968: 130).

Once the new nation had broken formal ties with England, it faced some crucial, divisive issues: How centralized should the government be? What should its stance be toward such powers as England and France? How should it handle such economic issues as war debts and coinage? The struggle over centralization continued. In the 1790s, rival groups in the new Congress argued over policy questions. Factions clustered around issues and leaders.

Although Washington struggled to stay above the fray, his secretary of the Treasury, Alexander Hamilton, became the intellectual leader of the Federalists. The Federalists espoused what Hamilton called "energetic government"—strong central direction and national solutions to public problems. They tended to be **elitists.** They feared widespread democratic participation, and they protected commercial interests. In 1793, war broke out in Europe between revolutionary France and a coalition of old regimes that included England. The Federalists sided with the dependable (and commercially profitable) British against the French "party of humanity."

The rival Republican faction (later to be called the "Democratic-Republicans" and then the "Democrats") looked to Thomas Jefferson as its spiritual leader. It attracted those who opposed the policies of Washington and Adams. These Democratic-Republicans favored local autonomy, weaker national government, lower-class and debtor interests, and "French principles."

From these beginnings, the party system evolved over the 19th century. More and more people identified themselves with one party or the other. And the parties changed. The Federalists, unable to survive their original leaders, disappeared after 1816. Subsequently, their place was taken by the Whig party and then by the modern-day Republicans. The party of Jefferson and Madison evolved into the modern Democratic party.

The basic pattern of **party identification** today dates back to the 1930s. The New Deal coalition was forged in the critical election of 1932, when Franklin D. Roosevelt, a Democrat, was elected president by a landslide. The Democratic party took on a progressive role. It was sworn to strong, positive government and social welfare programs. Roosevelt's progressivism appealed to the working class in the industrial North, and northern urban centers were transformed into Democratic bastions (see Sundquist, 1983: 215). Immigrants such as the Irish were pushed into the

Democratic ranks by urban machines. Mainly urban dwellers such as Jewish voters, most of whom had formerly supported the Republicans, switched their loyalties to the Democrats. Blacks who had been loyal to the Republican party of Abraham Lincoln also joined the Roosevelt coalition. And the Democratic party retained the loyal support of the "solid South" until the 1960s.

The Republican party shriveled in strength during the heyday of the New Deal, clinging to support in the northeastern states and in the small towns of the Middle West. But in the 1960s, the volatility of the **New Deal coalition** became apparent. Since then, there have been startling shifts in the presidential successes of the parties. The Republicans have made gains in the South, which had been a Democratic base. Republican growth has been spectacular in the Sunbelt states of the South and Southwest. With an attractive candidate such as Ronald Reagan, the Republican party has been able to win wide support in the country, resting on a strong base in the West. By the 1980s, Americans were about equally divided nationally in their attachments to political parties.

Gaining Legitimacy

We can think of a government as "legitimate" if its decisions are accepted and obeyed because people think they are made in a right and proper way by those in authority. In our country, more than anything else the Constitution establishes **legitimacy.**

The founding generation of Americans accepted the idea of the "rule of law," which had grown up in British constitutional practice. Moreover, they laid the foundation for an enduring belief in the idea of government based on the consent of the people. That consent was given in a "written constitution," in which the power of government would be laid down and provision would be made for the proper institutions of government. And this prescription for a written constitution was not limited to the national government. All of the 50 states have written constitutions as well, many of which are much longer than the national constitution. For both state and nation, Americans adopted a commitment to a "government of laws, not men." Not long after the federal Constitution was ratified and made official, it came to be especially revered, accepted as a "higher law" that could not be changed by ordinary politicians. Government could legitimately take action or do things in a certain manner only if this was permitted by the Constitution.

It is remarkable how firmly Americans have been committed to their national constitution. The stability of our constitutional experience is especially obvious if we compare that experience with the experience of other democratic countries, whose constitutions have often been subject to drastic changes. The main exception to the stability of our constitutional system came in the middle of the 19th century. The rift between the North and the South over slavery caused a breach in the legitimacy of

HISTORICAL PERSPECTIVE

Lincoln's Gettysburg Address

On November 19, 1863, President Abraham Lincoln delivered an address at the federal cemetery in Gettysburg, Pennsylvania, where many Union and Confederate soldiers had died in a huge battle the previous July. In this "Gettysburg Address," Lincoln said, in part:

> Four score and seven years ago our Fathers brought forth on this continent a new nation, conceived in liberty and dedicated to the proposition that all men are created equal.
>
> Now we are engaged in a great civil war testing whether that nation or any nation so conceived and so dedicated can long endure. We are met on a great battlefield of that war. We have come to dedicate a portion of that field as a final resting place for those who here gave their lives that that nation might live. . . .
>
> . . . we here highly resolve that these dead shall not have died in

> vain—that this nation under God shall have a new birth of freedom—and that government of the people, by the people, for the people shall not perish from the earth.

the Constitution. A long, bloody Civil War finally restored the Union. As President Abraham Lincoln told Congress in 1862, "That portion of the earth's surface which is owned and inhabited by the people of the United States is well adapted to be the home of one national family, and is not well adapted for two or more." Reconstruction after the war, restoring the "national family," was slow and painful. Lincoln's beliefs about the Civil War's significance for the political legitimacy of the nation are encapsulated in his famous short speech commemorating the Union war dead at the bloody battlefield of Gettysburg.

After the Civil War, the Constitution was amended in several important ways, the first changes in the Constitution since 1804. The 13th Amendment (1865) abolished slavery. The 14th Amendment (1868) said that no state could "deprive any person of life, liberty, or property without due process of law; nor deny to any person within its jurisdiction the equal protection of the laws." The 15th Amendment (1870) banned racial discrimination in voting rights. These were historic changes, but the Constitution's basic provisions remain largely intact. The lasting character of the Constitution demonstrates that our system of government has generally had a very high degree of legitimacy.

The Politics of an Expanding Nation

All governments face a very fundamental problem: How can government control and administer the territory for which it is responsible? We see this problem of governing today in the practical difficulties that the Third World countries of Africa, Asia, and Latin America have in "penetrating the countryside." In many of these countries, governmental authority is limited to the urban centers—guerrillas, private armies, or local overlords may control large parts of the countries. This problem developed differently for the United States than for present-day new nations because of its peculiar circumstances.

Winning the West

Much of the U.S. history concerns expanding territory and incorporating new people into the citizenry. In 1803, the Jefferson administration negotiated the so-called **Louisiana Purchase,** which more than doubled the geographic size of the country. This presented the national government with the huge problem of integrating the vast wilderness of the West into the national fold. Much of the history of the United States in the 19th century is the story of "how the West was won." The opportunity and **egalitarianism** of the western frontier helped shape the political ideas and practices that we have inherited. Frontier life was dangerous, hard, and individualistic, and day-to-day democracy prevailed where governmental authority was distant and uncertain.

How did the American government manage to penetrate the countryside? Two important political processes contributed mightily to this success—federalism and the political party system. The American political system marched into the West by first creating territories complete with an administration appointed in Washington and then, when settlement reached a certain minimum, establishing new states. The vast continent was conquered by leapfrogging states; with one North-to-South tier of states in place, the process moved another notch to the West. The federal system of the Constitution provided the means of expansion.

Along with the establishment of "law and order"in the West came democratic political institutions, accompanied by an emerging political party system that shaped national politics and pulled the system together. Grass-roots competition for public office linked people and government together and mobilized people in a national constituency. In short, "the party system linked men and groups from region to region and state to state, providing a national framework for political expression within

HISTORICAL PERSPECTIVE

Territorial Growth of the United States

An important part of the political history of the United States is the westward movement. As the map shows, vast territories of the American West did not become part of the United States until the middle of the 19th century. The newest states, Alaska and Hawaii, did not achieve statehood until 1959. The Commonwealth of Puerto Rico, acquired after the Spanish-American War in 1898, might someday become a state. The year in which a state shown in the map achieved statehood is given under its name. When did your state enter the Union?

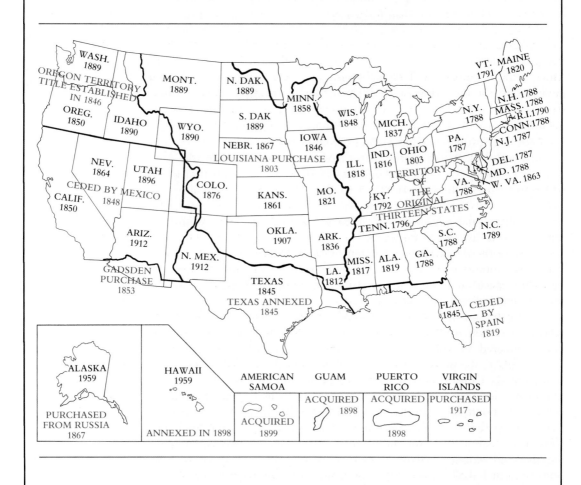

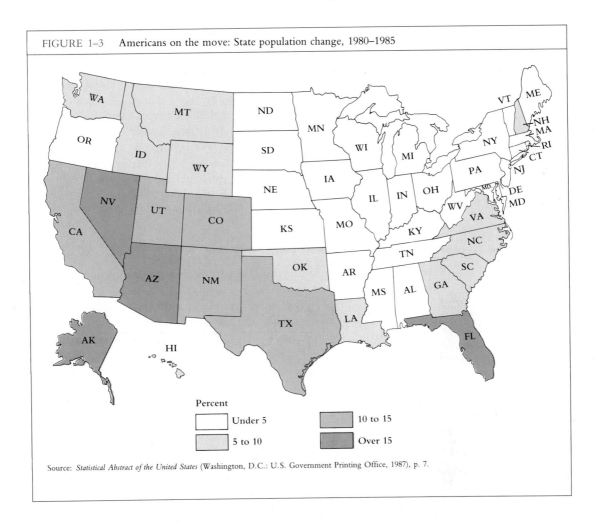

FIGURE 1–3   Americans on the move: State population change, 1980–1985

Percent

Under 5

5 to 10

10 to 15

Over 15

Source: *Statistical Abstract of the United States* (Washington, D.C.: U.S. Government Printing Office, 1987), p. 7.

from its 1970 peak of 18.2 million to 17.6 million in 1980, and between 1980 and 1985 the number of New Yorkers grew by only 225,000.

This shift in population growth brings about an important change in the regional basis of political power. Changes in state populations have direct consequences for state representation in Congress, whose members are reapportioned among the states after every census. Between 1970 and 1980, the Sunbelt states gained representation in Congress as a reward for their population growth, while the "rustbelt" states of the Northeast lost representation. This happened, of course, because the number of representatives that a state has in the House of Representatives is based on its population as counted every 10 years by the federal census.

Urban growth means government growth. In rural areas or small towns, people can do much for themselves. Urban dwellers need more government. They cannot get rid of the garbage, get water, walk to work, or provide their own fire protection. The interdependence and complexity of urban life require government help in many areas: housing, health, sanitation, fire and police protection, poverty, unemployment, traffic and parking, urban renewal, water supply, treatment of the elderly and minorities, and so on. Urban growth has greatly expanded government activities and programs at all levels. Since 1960, the role of the federal government in handling urban problems has grown rapidly.

Because the policies of government have become so important in our daily lives, it is especially important to make a two-pronged effort to understand them in this book. First, we must get a good grasp of how our political institutions work to make public policies. Second, we must understand how public policies are actually formulated and put into effect.

Removing Obstacles to Participation

Participation refers to those who take part in choosing political leaders and influencing government decisions. In a democracy, it is often assumed that a large majority of eligible citizens will take part in political life. In practice, many Americans are **apolitical,** devoid of political interest and unwilling to participate in politics. The electoral history of the United States has shown an increase in the proportion of potential voters, but actual participation in politics falls short of this potential. This gap between democratic expectations and political reality is bothersome. For a time, participation was low because people were prohibited from involvement.

The first major extension of political participation was the elimination of property and taxpaying qualifications for voting. These were all but abolished by the mid-1840s. The second major extension was the granting of voting rights to blacks. These rights were assured by the 15th Amendment but were not fully effective until the passage of the Voting Rights Act of 1965.

Voting by aliens and electoral corruption were major participation issues between the Civil War and the 1920s. To counteract widespread fraud in elections and prevent newly arrived immigrants from being manipulated, states passed reforms under which voting was restricted to people who could prove they intended to become citizens. Today all states permit only citizens of the United States to vote. After the Civil War, states also passed laws to counter electoral corruption. These laws required voter registration, a secret ballot (the so-called **Australian ballot),** and regulation of election practices to ensure honesty. At the same time, poll taxes and other devices to restrict black voting were used in the South to discourage black participation. In 1964, the 24th Amendment to the Constitution was ratified. It prohibited payment of a **poll tax** as a condition for voting.

A third major extension of political participation was the granting of women's right to vote. After a long struggle dating back to the 1840s, the 19th Amendment was ratified in 1920. It prohibited the denial of the right to vote on account of sex. Finally, after World War II, the issue of voting

---

WORDS AND IDEAS

The Poll Tax

The word *poll* is derived from the Old English word *polle,* which meant "a head." Thus, a poll tax was a uniform payment made by each person, or "head." This kind of tax was used in England from the 14th to the 17th centuries to raise money.

In this country, poll taxes have been levied mainly as a way to keep black people from voting. In southern states, a person had to pay a $1 to $2 tax to qualify to vote. This amount was enough to keep many blacks and poor whites from voting. In some states, a person had to pay not just this year's poll tax but unpaid poll taxes for all previous years.

In 1937, the U.S. Supreme Court upheld the constitutionality of the poll tax in Georgia. By the 1950s, several southern states had abolished the poll tax, but it remained in force in Virginia, Arkansas, Texas, Alabama, and Mississippi. By 1960, the $1 or $2 poll tax probably did not disenfranchise many people. It was, however, a lingering symbol of discrimination against blacks.

In 1964, the 24th Amendment to the Constitution was ratified. This amendment prohibited the requirement of a poll tax for federal elections. Then, in 1966, the Supreme Court held that a poll tax requirement for voting in any election, including state and local elections, violated the "equal protection" clause of the 14th Amendment. At long last, the poll tax was dead.

---

rights for 18- to 20-year-olds arose. In 1971, the 26th Amendment gave voting rights to all citizens 18 years of age or older.

Changes in the Constitution and laws have expanded political participation. As we will see in Chapter 5, many factors affect how much people participate in politics. Eligibility to vote in elections has changed dramatically. By the 1840s, all white males in the United States could vote; by 1971 almost all people over 18 could vote. And participation in elections has also grown in the long run. Figure 1–4 shows what proportions of the total population have voted in presidential elections since 1824. Note the effect of granting women the right to vote for the first time in the presidential election of 1920.

But if the number of potential voters has grown since the early 1800s, actual voter turnout has declined (Burnham, 1965). Figure 1–5 shows what proportions of eligible people have voted in presidential elections. Sharp declines in voter turnout beginning in the 1890s reflect the wholesale denial of voting rights to blacks in the South and the enactment of state residency and ballot reform laws aimed at reducing corruption. Although

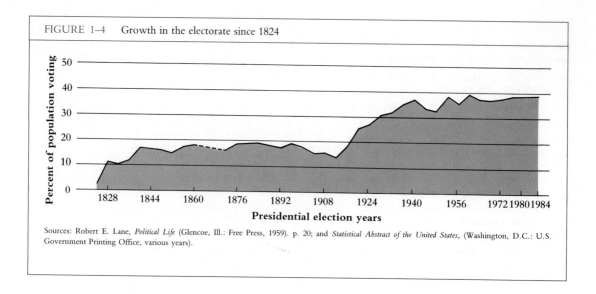

FIGURE 1–4   Growth in the electorate since 1824

Sources: Robert E. Lane, *Political Life* (Glencoe, Ill.: Free Press, 1959). p. 20; and *Statistical Abstract of the United States,* (Washington, D.C.: U.S. Government Printing Office, various years).

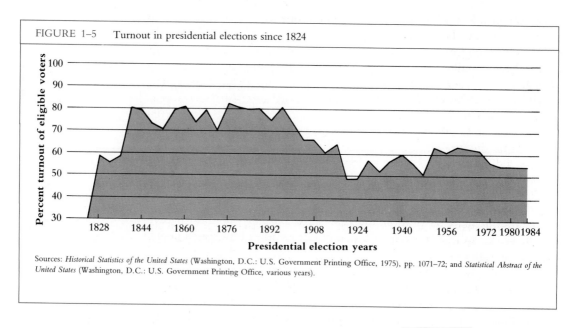

FIGURE 1–5   Turnout in presidential elections since 1824

Sources: *Historical Statistics of the United States* (Washington, D.C.: U.S. Government Printing Office, 1975), pp. 1071–72; and *Statistical Abstract of the United States* (Washington, D.C.: U.S. Government Printing Office, various years).

women's suffrage greatly increased the number of potential voters, its immediate effect was to drastically reduce the percentage of eligible people who voted (especially in 1920 and 1924). Only since the 1970s has the percentage of female voting been about the same as that of male voting. Finally, the inclusion of 18-year-olds beginning with the 1972 presidential election mainly accounts for the subsequent drop in **voter turnout** (Converse, 1972).

Although the decline in the proportion of eligible voters who cast ballots has resulted from changes in election laws and increases in population, other factors have also been involved. Politics was more entertaining in the later 1800s than it is today. Voter turnout is stimulated by certain candidates and issues (for example, colorful Al Smith in 1928 and heroic Dwight Eisenhower in 1952). Sometimes certain events (such as the Vietnam War or the Watergate crisis of 1973, which precipitated President Nixon's resignation) cause political apathy, indifference, and estrangement.

Who Benefits, Who Suffers?

A famous political scientist once defined politics as "who gets what, when, how" (Lasswell, 1958). He meant that political systems are naturally involved in distributing or redistributing benefits (and, perhaps, deprivations). In the last chapters of this book (Chapters 16 through 20), we explain how national public policies are formed and implemented. In doing so, we deal in detail with distributive and redistributive policies.

But the problem of "distribution" is an old one for human society, and governments have been confronting this problem for a long time. In the early 1800s, Congress spent money to spur economic development. That money helped build roads and canals whose purpose was to stimulate trade and spur private economic enterprise. More important, federal land policies in the 1800s distributed vast tracts of land, first to private speculators and then to homesteaders. The Homestead Act of 1862 gave 160 acres of free land in the West to anyone who would settle on and improve them within five years. This huge land giveaway drew thousands of poor farmers and their families. Also in 1862, Congress gave land grants of up to 100 million acres to help build transcontinental railroads.

If handing out western land played a vital role in the physical development of the country, education helped develop the American character. Public schools have been the hallmark of our educational system since colonial times. In the 1830s, the French observer de Tocqueville said, "It is by the attention it pays to public education that the original character of American civilization is at once placed in the clearest light." Public education has grown remarkably, especially in the 20th century. Now almost all children attend school, mainly public school. In the 1860s and 1870s, the distribution of public lands was invoked to aid higher education. The Morrill Act provided federal land to the states for the establishment and support of the "land grant" universities. In the last generation, the proportion of adults with a college degree has doubled, so that today about 16 percent of Americans 25 years old or older have finished college. Now most state spending and a large part of federal spending go to education.

Just as those who get high school diplomas or college degrees, unlike those who do not, are rewarded by status (better jobs, political influence, and so forth), so too income and wealth distribution helps some and hinders others. As a country grows, political power may be used to distribute economic resources among the people. The problem of distribution comes up when the government is pressured to change the way in which the economic system works.

In our early days, a large amount of personal wealth was in land and many people owned land. The increased practice of political equality during the 19th century is often attributed to the relative equality of economic condition. Government policies that regulated inheritance helped distribute property more widely; the open frontier in the West made cheap land abundant.

As time passed and an industrial economy replaced subsistence agriculture, money became more important than land. In the 1800s, there were alternating times of prosperity and depression. But even so, affluence has usually prevailed. In recent years, the family incomes of Americans have grown steadily. Despite inflation in the 1970s and 1980s, average family income continues to rise in constant dollars (correcting for inflation). Still, there is a gap in the average incomes of whites and blacks.

Disparities in the incomes of whites and blacks illustrate a range of inequalities that separate racial and ethnic groups. The extent of such disparities between whites, on the one hand, and blacks and Hispanics, on the other, is shown in Table 1–1. Despite the distributive social programs of the last half century and the "war on poverty" launched in the mid-1960s, great gaps remain. The unemployment rate for Americans of Spanish origin is nearly double that for whites, and the unemployment rate for blacks is more than double that for whites. And in other respects (income, poverty level, home ownership), social and economic disparities are, on the average, very large among the major American racial and ethnic groups.

A mobile society, racially and ethnically diverse, urban and industrial, with growing, more difficult governing problems, can erupt in violent conflict. Over the course of American experience, violent conflicts have been a frequent part of our politics. Sometimes the violence was started by challenging groups, sometimes by the governing authorities.

One study of U.S. political violence showed that between 1890 and 1970 2,861 incidents involving such violence were recorded. They lasted for 3,393 days and resulted in 18,985 arrests and 1,180 deaths. About one fourth of them were started by the government or dominant political groups; about 15 percent were started by antisystem groups; and about 60 percent were "clashes" in which it could not be determined who started the violence. More than half of these incidents were radical. Another 29 percent involved labor-management relations (Stohl, 1976: 80–87).

Most American violence has not been particularly political, and political violence has rarely challenged our political system or the Constitution. American violence has largely involved immediate grievances or long-term complaints against social or economic conditions. Seldom has it become an attack against constitutional order. Ironically, the great stability

TABLE 1-1   Socioeconomic disparities in 1984: Whites, blacks, Hispanics

Race and ethnic origin	Completed college	Unemployed	Married couple with own children	Median family income	Below poverty level*	Owner-occupied housing
Whites	19.8%	6.5%	40.2%	$25,757	12.1%	67.3%
Blacks	10.4	15.9	28.1	14,506	35.7	45.5
Hispanics	8.5	11.3	48.0	18,833	28.4	41.1

*Noncash benefits not included.

Source: *Statistical Abstract of the United States* (Washington, D.C.: U.S. Government Printing Office, 1986), pp. 30,32.

of our political system has often made it hard to change the conditions that produce dissatisfaction. Witness the passage of 100 years before blacks got effective voting rights. The system is so stable that it is sometimes slow to change and beyond the reach of small, deprived groups.

The Constitution was supposed to prevent the tyranny of the majority. But it was not enacted in Heaven. The men and women who created our constitutional ideals were imperfect. Thus, the black minority suffered from white oppression. The business class and its many supporters successfully blocked trade union efforts, especially early in this century. As one political scientist shrewdly observed:

> The history of the United States is not merely one of mutual accommodation among competing groups under a broad umbrella of consensus. The proper image of our society has never been a melting pot. In bad times, it is a boiling pot; in good times, it is a tossed salad. For those who are *in,* this is all very well. But the price has always been paid by those who are *out,* and when they do get in, they do not always get in through a process of mutual accommodation under a broad umbrella of consensus. (Lowi, 1971: 53)

In the main, political violence has resulted from impatience over failure to carry out policies or programs or from strong grievances about specific wrongs or evils. It has not been a result of general alienation, frustration, or weakness. Violence has been a political act "aimed at furthering the purposes of the group that uses it when they have some reason to think it will help their cause" (Gamson, 1975: 81). More often than not, violent protest has given new advantages to challenging groups and brought them into the political mainstream.

Much of the texture of American politics has been a struggle between the "haves" and the "have nots" over wealth, well-being, and power. In the 20th century, the government has been a major arena for this struggle. The evolution of the modern welfare state is testimony to the role that the government plays in "equalizing" the harsher realities of life through distributive or redistributive public policies.

DEVELOPING
INSTITUTIONS
OF
GOVERNMENT

Ample time was a real advantage in our political development. Nowhere is this clearer than in the evolution of our basic institutions. Today in developing nations, such as those of Africa and Asia, pressures on government force the quick establishment of authority. In the United States, in contrast, institutions evolved more slowly. Although all branches of the U.S. government were helped by having time to develop, Congress was helped the most. The history of the world's parliaments shows that they, more than any other governmental agencies, take time to grow.

The Growth of Congress

Congress, which we aim to analyze in its modern form in Chapters 10 and 11, got its start as the Continental Congress of revolutionary times. Although it had roots in British parliamentary practice, it was mostly homegrown. It was born and grew up as an unusually independent and democratic legislative body. What were the main lines of its growth?

Under the new Constitution, Congress, a frail and fragile institution in many ways, began its work with a certain optimism and zeal. A quorum (the majority of members needed to conduct business) was finally present on April Fools' Day, 1789. The House then chose Congressman Frederick A. C. Muhlenberg, a Federalist from Pennsylvania, as its first Speaker. Shortly afterward, it adopted rules of procedure and began its legislative business. Legislation was needed to establish executive departments (such as War, Treasury, and State), the judicial system, and government for the Northwest Territory. Taxes had to be levied, and appropriations had to be made. Congress passed laws regulating patents and copyrights, governing bankruptcies, controlling harbors, punishing crimes, and regulating naturalization, the importation of slaves, and relations with Indians. It also offered the first constitutional amendments—the Bill of Rights—to the state legislatures for ratification.

As Congress became a better-established political institution, its evolution took two main tracks. First, it developed a system of committees to help cope with its workload. Second, it acquired political parties and party leadership to provide bases for decision making among like-minded legislators. Strong legislative bodies have well-developed committee systems, which allow them to deal with legislative issues in depth and to make decisions expertly. Because the U.S. Congress developed a sturdy committee system early in its life, it emerged as a powerful legislative body.

The first few Congresses were so small that committees were not seen as necessary. Some temporary committees were appointed, but the House conducted most of its business without committees. The standing, permanent committees of Congress grew up over the years. The House Committee on Interstate and Foreign Commerce, formed in 1795 (and now called the House Committee on Energy and Commerce), was the first major standing committee. Between the creation of the commerce committee and the Civil War, new committees were created as they were needed—including Ways and Means, Post Office, Judiciary, Agriculture, the military services committees, and Foreign Affairs. With the industrialization of the country during and after the Civil War, new committees came into being—Appropriations, Banking and Currency, Merchant Marine and Fisheries, and Education and Labor. It took the Senate a little longer to create a committee system, probably because it was a much smaller body than the House. But by the 1820s, the Senate had established many standing committees that paralleled those of the House. The establishment of congressional committees over the course of the 19th century provided the division of labor needed to cope with ever-growing demands for new legislation and allowed members of Congress to specialize and become experts.

Although political parties are nowhere mentioned in the Constitution, party divisions arose fairly early in Congress. Policies advocated by Secretary of the Treasury Alexander Hamilton—those providing for the payment of federal and state debts and for the creation of a national bank—gained the warm support of business and commercial interests. These policies also stimulated the opposition of congressmen speaking for the interests of farmers. James Madison became the key House leader opposing the legislative programs of Washington and Hamilton. In 1800, Democratic-Republican Thomas Jefferson was elected president and his followers captured a majority of both the House and the Senate from the Federalists. Partisanship became a central feature of congressional life by the end of the 19th century. At this point, Congress, especially the House, was dominated by unified parties with strong leaders. Such speakers as Thomas B. Reed and Joseph G. Cannon, both Republicans, had so much influence that they were called "czars." Beginning in the 1920s, congressional party battles came to be less fierce, but party cleavage remains the most persistent, fundamental division in congressional policy-making.

By roughly 1900, Congress had a modern form and had become an autonomous body. It had a complex committee system and party leadership, and it was able to operate independently of the president in many ways. Traditions evolved concerning the conduct of members. There were settled rules of the game, written and unwritten. These rules permitted effective lawmaking and gave an air of dignity and formality to the process. The well-developed committee system and the stable two-party structure gave coherence to many of the major policy questions facing Congress and the country. Congress had proven to be a durable, resilient, adaptive political body (Jewell and Patterson, 1986; Davidson and Oleszek, 1985: 15–44; Ripley, 1988). Today Congress is a large, highly complex organization. There are 435 members of the House of Representatives and 100 senators. Congress has more than 300 committees and subcommittees; its members, committees, and research agencies employ nearly 24,000 staff people; and it is deeply and innovatively involved in formulating and enacting the laws of the land.

Institutionalizing the Presidency

Under its first constitution, the Articles of Confederation, our government had no chief executive. That did not work very well. A large nation requires the leadership and direction that a chief executive can give it. Advocates of a new constitution believed that a "vigorous executive" was needed. Alexander Hamilton defended the presidency in No. 70 of *The Federalist*, a series of newspaper articles advocating ratification. Here, he argued that "energy in the executive is a leading character in the definition of good government," so "a feeble executive implies a feeble execution of the government."

George Washington had great stature as the first president, and he had no models to follow. He and the other early presidents were not always the center of attention, as presidents are today. Thomas Jefferson walked to his inauguration. Cabinet members and legislators often outshone the president in fame and social prominence. Like a pendulum, influence and leadership swung between "weak" and "strong" presidents.

The first of the strong presidential leaders after the founding period was Andrew Jackson (1829–37). Jackson was the first presidential candidate selected at a national nominating convention. Under his leadership, the Democratic party initiated the noise and hoopla of the modern political campaign, responding to the mushrooming size of the electorate in the late 1820s. Jackson used the constitutional and political powers of the presidency in impressive ways. He used the **spoils system (patronage)** to reward the party faithful. The Jacksonian system of **rotation in office** gave loyal partisans government jobs and turned out opponents. Jackson was the first president to make extensive use of the **veto** to get Congress to accede to his wishes. He used the cabinet more effectively than his predecessors. His able informal advisers, known as the **kitchen cabinet,** were the forerunners of today's White House advisers.

Abraham Lincoln (1861–65) was the next person to leave a substantial imprint on the presidency. No president before or since confronted the crisis of civil war; few presidents managed the presidency as forcefully or as shrewdly. In the midst of the national emergency, Lincoln demonstrated the outer reaches of the president's "war powers." He took a more forceful role as commander in chief than any other president. He used the president's power to "take care that the laws be faithfully executed," as the Constitution commands, justifying drastic steps to save the Union.

After a nearly 40-year eclipse, Theodore Roosevelt (1901–09) brought life back to the presidency. He was probably the most popular president since Jackson. He was strong and vigorous, a sometime cowboy, big-game hunter, and war hero (the Battle of San Juan Hill during the Spanish-American War). In domestic politics, Roosevelt stood for checking the power of the giant monopolistic corporations (called *trust-busting*), wages and hours laws, conservation of natural resources, and government regulation of packinghouses, railroads, and other industries. In foreign affairs,

HISTORICAL PERSPECTIVE

The Institutionalized Presidency from Roosevelt to Reagan

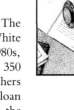

The institutionalizing of the presidency is no better exemplified than in the growth in the size and importance of the president's staff. Washington had only one assistant, a nephew whom he paid out of his own pocket. Jefferson managed with a messenger and an occasional clerk. More than 100 years later, Wilson led the country through World War I with only seven assistants. In 1939, Franklin D. Roosevelt established the Executive Office of the President to provide effective staff support. The graph below shows how the White House staff has grown. By the 1980s, the budget provided for about 350 White House staff people, and others worked at the White House on loan from executive agencies such as the Secret Service, Department of the Treasury.

Source: *Washington Post,* January 22, 1986, p. A17.

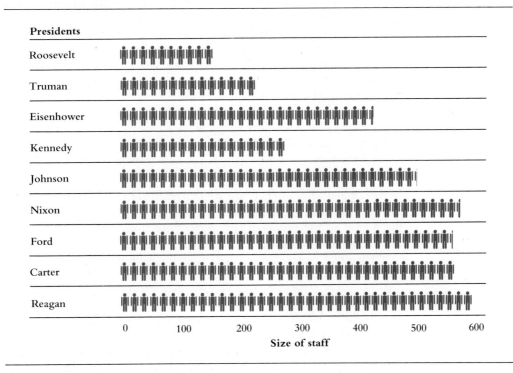

Presidents

Roosevelt

Truman

Eisenhower

Kennedy

Johnson

Nixon

Ford

Carter

Reagan

| 0 | 100 | 200 | 300 | 400 | 500 | 600 |

Size of staff

he was an unabashed nationalist; his motto was that the United States should "speak softly and carry a big stick." To back up his wide conception of presidential powers, he espoused the so-called **stewardship theory.** In his autobiography (1927: 357), he argued that "executive power was limited only by specific restrictions and prohibitions appearing in the Constitution or imposed by the Congress under its constitutional powers."

The modern presidency owes its greatest debt to Franklin Delano Roosevelt (1933–45), a distant cousin of Theodore Roosevelt. FDR served in a challenging period that encompassed the Great Depression and World War II. FDR's administration is called the New Deal because it was a bold experiment with public policies designed to improve the economy and the well-being of citizens. FDR's program laid the foundations of today's welfare state. It included social welfare measures (such as social security) and legislation to curb the abuses of industrial society. Roosevelt's firm leadership throughout World War II and his postwar planning (including the creation of the United Nations) were the framework for America's activist role in world affairs.

Since the New Deal, presidents, whatever their politics, have followed the Roosevelt model. The public expects presidents to be strong, to exert leadership, to range widely, and to resolve public problems. Ronald Reagan, a Republican president who had at one time been a New Deal Democrat, often claimed that he had patterned his presidency after precedents set by FDR. One precedent that FDR set was categorically rejected: his breaking of the **two-term tradition** when he ran for a third term in 1940 (and for a fourth term in 1944). In 1951, the 22nd Amendment limited presidential tenure to two terms.

Today the office of the President of the United States is a very substantial institution. It embraces the work of the president in the Oval Office, to be sure, but it also includes the staffs of the Domestic Council and the National Security Council, the cabinet, the vice president's staff, and various other agencies and advisory offices. When we speak of the President of the United States today, we are not referring merely to a lonely figure toiling away in the White House. The institutionalized presidency involves the person of the president, of course. But it also includes the advisers, cabinet officers, and staff specialists who constitute the presidential office. In Chapters 12 and 13, we will describe how the modern presidency works.

Establishing Courts

The federal judicial body has always been fairly small. The Supreme Court was provided for in Article III of the Constitution. It first met after the passage of the Judiciary Act of 1789. Of the six justices appointed, one turned down the post and one resigned without attending a session. The other four met in the Royal Exchange Building in New York City as the

FIGURE 1–6   Growth of the judiciary: Cases in U.S. Courts

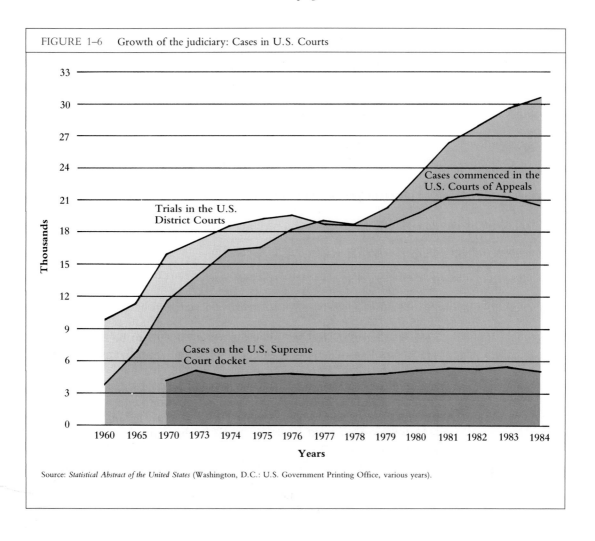

Source: *Statistical Abstract of the United States* (Washington, D.C.: U.S. Government Printing Office, various years).

first Supreme Court. They started what came to be a very potent part of our constitutional system. They took on the role of interpreting the meaning of a constitution that was brief, ambiguous, and unclear in many particulars (McCloskey, 1960).

Today there are nine Supreme Court justices (A chief justice and eight associate justices), and that number has not changed for many decades. But the federal court system as a whole has grown a great deal in numbers of appellate judges, trial judges, and staff assistants and in volume of work. The growth in the judicial workload illustrates the development of the judicial system very well (see Figure 1–6); the federal courts employed well over 17,000 people by 1984, and demands on the courts have grown quite steadily for the past 20 years.

Historically, courts have played an important role in this country. The Supreme Court's power of **judicial review** (the power to declare whether or not laws are constitutional) gives it a part in adjusting the meaning of the Constitution as historical circumstances change. More broadly, in a society governed by law and insistent on equality, many will bring their grievances to court. Ours is a litigious society. Citizens are prone to sue, to take an adversary to court. A society like ours has great need of courts—we even dramatize courtroom events and show make-believe courts on television. In Chapter 15 we explain how our judicial system works, and in Chapter 19 we put the spotlight on civil rights and liberties, an important province of the American courts.

The Burgeoning Bureaucracy

An excellent litmus test for the growth of government is the expansion of the **bureaucracy.** The federal government's bureaucracy has mushroomed in size and scope since the Departments of War, Treasury, and State were first set up in 1789. Most of its expansion occurred in the 20th century. In 1821, for example, there were fewer than 7,000 federal civilian employees; their number exceeded one-half million by the 1920s; and today there are nearly 3 million federal civilian employees. The initial growth in the federal bureaucracy came around the turn of the century (1890–1910) as a response to industrialization and the public's demand that the government regulate economic development, facilitate economic expansion, and control abuses (see Skowronek, 1982). The second great burst of growth in federal bureaucracy came with the New Deal, as the government initiated new, large-scale welfare programs and expanded its regulatory activity.

Today the executive branch of the federal government is enormous; we dissect it in some detail in Chapter 14. The federal bureaucratic establishment now includes 13 cabinet departments; 60 major agencies, boards, and commissions and 100 smaller units of these types; 850 interagency committees; hundreds of citizens' advisory groups; and dozens of presidential commissions, committees, and task forces. One of the largest federal executive agencies is the U.S. Postal Service. With more than 680,000 employees, it alone is far larger than was the whole federal bureaucracy before the 1890s and larger than nearly all private corporations.

It is important to have a clear understanding of where recent growth in government has occurred. In fact, the federal bureaucracy has not grown very much since World War II. The real burgeoning of bureaucracy has been at state and local levels of government, as Figure 1–7 shows. State and local bureaucracy is, as a whole, much larger than the federal bureaucracy, and it has been growing at a faster rate. Over 13 million people work for state and local governments (more than half of whom are in public education). And these people make up over 82 percent of all government workers. State and local agencies have grown by more than 220

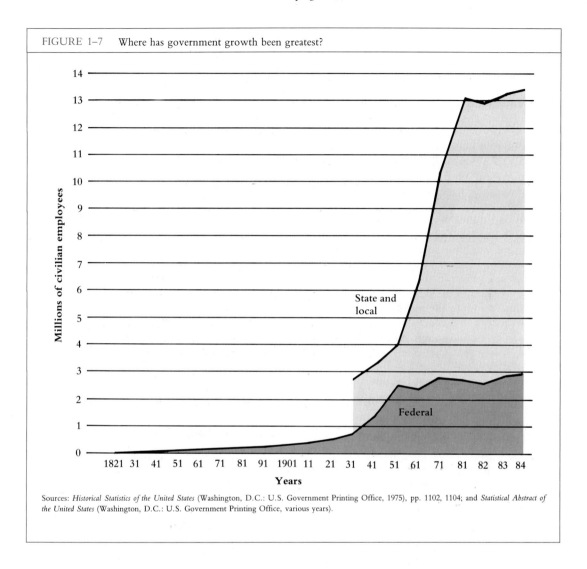

FIGURE 1–7   Where has government growth been greatest?

Sources: *Historical Statistics of the United States* (Washington, D.C.: U.S. Government Printing Office, 1975), pp. 1102, 1104; and *Statistical Abstract of the United States* (Washington, D.C.: U.S. Government Printing Office, various years).

percent in the last 30 years. This has occurred both because states and localities have administered new federal programs and because they have expanded their own services.

The governing institutions that evolved under the Constitution over the 200-year history of our nation have changed in many ways. They have become larger in scale, and they perform more complex functions. Today the party system and the system of congressional politics are still engaged in adapting to the bureaucratization of government. Considering the enormousness of change in modern life, it is remarkable that our governing institutions have retained so much of their original form and substance.

CONCLUSIONS

It is hard to imagine today how feeble and uncertain the national government was at its birth two centuries ago. For a few years, the new government even lacked a home, since the national capital in Washington, D.C., was not ready for use until 1800. The early federal government was itinerant, meeting now in Philadelphia, now in New York. George Washington was inaugurated as the first president in New York City.

The present-day nations of the Third World—in Africa, Asia, and Latin America—face excruciating problems and difficulties. They suffer wrenching economic turmoil, incredible poverty and immiseration, civil war, and sometimes heavy pressure from stronger nations. When the United States was emerging as a nation in the 18th century, it was beset by problems, to be sure. The American Revolution had an especially negative effect on the economy because it involved great costs, brought about large debts, and created economic uncertainties and hardships. The countries of the Old World, the European countries from which the early American settlers came, had developed as nations over many years and had long and tradition-filled histories. The United States was really the first new nation, the first nation to be created in a relatively short span of time. Carved out of the vast virgin territory of the New World, the United States was "a nation of immigrants."

The basic processes of national political development are markedly similar across time and space. Still, the building of the American nation took place under conditions very different from those that face emerging new nations today. The United States occupied a large continent, affording ample opportunity for territorial expansion to accommodate a growing population. There was no feudal tradition, and no aristocracy, to prevent democratic experimentation or produce gross inequalities in income or wealth. The abundant resources of the new land could be exploited by ambitious people and their governments. And the new nation was insulated from outside influences by a large ocean to the east and vast, largely uninhabited territory to the west. So Americans were left to develop a nation largely on their own initiative.

The new nation did not begin life on the day of its independence in 1776. Europeans began settling the New World in the 17th century, and the English colonies were in existence about as long as the United States has been a free nation. Since all political systems are rooted in their pasts, knowing something about the past history of the new nation is important. Many of our political beliefs and practices grew out of our colonial experience. We cannot understand American politics today without reflecting on some of this experience.

In this chapter, we have dealt with important aspects of the background of our political system and its institutions. We can draw the following conclusions:

1. The American colonies as a "fragment society" developed a political tradition that was grounded partly in British ideas of rights and freedoms of the individual on which government could not infringe and partly in the experiences of Americans with their emerging, democratic, representative politics.

2. The colonial experience permitted the development of representative assemblies in America and created the conditions for national independence and national community.

3. The American Revolution politicized and nationalized the colonial people. Independence gave them the luxury of a unique experiment in representative government on a larger scale than had previously been thought possible.

4. An unmistakable national identity emerged early in the history of the republic. It remained a marked feature of political life except for the major breach brought about by the Civil War. An unprecedented flood of immigrants was absorbed by the American political system. These new Americans embraced a national identity while often keeping a distinct cultural and ethnic identity.

5. The new American regime gained legitimacy almost at its start. The Constitution was widely accepted. The governing establishment in Washington, centering on Congress, began very modestly but became complex and extensive. The major governing bodies—Congress, the

presidency, the bureaucracy, and the courts—grew in size and in the scope of their powers. But they retained the basic forms set forth for them in the Constitution.

6. Our political system was the first experiment in running democratic government over such a large area. The government reached the countryside because from the start it actively fostered commerce and industry. In creating new states, the federal government was able to add new territory to the union.

7. In modern terms, the republic was hardly democratic at its founding. Constant struggle, even violence, was needed to make it more democratic. But our political system became more and more participatory. The invention of a competitive political party system brought ordinary citizens into politics and promoted orderly political change.

8. In an environment rich in resources, shrewd people were able to spur rapid economic growth and gain material affluence. Although the benefits of economic growth were not equally distributed, they were widely distributed. The main distributive principle, equal opportunity, emphasized private initiative and individual productivity. Those who did not share the general wealth—factory workers in the early 1900s and many blacks in recent years—often protested to improve their condition. Because equality was a widely held principle, demands for equality in social, economic, or political benefits have always been on the governing agenda.

FURTHER READING

CHAMBERS, WILLIAM NISBET, and WALTER DEAN BURNHAM, eds. (1975) *The American Party Systems*. 2nd ed. New York: Oxford University Press. Various authors analyze the role of political parties in the development of the American political system and identify major stages of its development.

HEALE, M. J. (1977) *The Making of American Politics*. London: Longman. A British historian's story of the early political development of the United States, in which that nation's British inheritance is contrasted with its own brand of government.

HOLLINGSWORTH, J. ROGERS (1978) "The United States." In *Crises of Political Development in Europe and the United States,* ed. Raymond Grew. Princeton, N.J.: Princeton University Press. A unique, if brief, analysis of the importance of "crises" in the political development of the United States.

LIPSET, SEYMOUR MARTIN (1963) *The First New Nation*. New York: Basic Books. An inquiry into the conflicting values of achievement and equality in America, with an excellent analysis of American character as it emerged from our early national experience.

SKOWRONEK, STEPHEN (1982) *Building a New American State*. Cambridge: Cambridge University Press. An account of the expansion of the administrative arm of the national government between 1877 and 1920.

WILLS, GARRY (1987) *Inventing America*. Garden City, N.Y.: Doubleday. A detailed dissection of the origins of the Declaration of Independence as it was formulated by Thomas Jefferson.

WOOD, GORDON S. (1969) *The Creation of the American Republic, 1776–1787*. New York: W. W. Norton. The most exhaustive and distinguished history of the early formative years of the American nation.

YOUNG, JAMES S. (1966) *The Washington Community, 1800–1828*. New York: Columbia University Press. A fascinating portrayal of life in the nation's capital in its infancy, including an interesting and controversial analysis of the development of national government beginning with the Jefferson administration.

A CONSTITUTIONAL DEMOCRACY

$\mathcal{H}$ow can a democratic society find workable and lasting ways for people to govern themselves in peace? The solution to this broad problem of governing is the establishment of a fundamental law, or constitution, that provides for the basic institutions of government and sets limits on what government can do.

When the founders wrote the Constitution of the United States in 1787, they well understood that they were laying down the ground rules for a free society, rules that would both give the national government adequate powers and protect the freedom of Americans. Their handiwork has often been admired. The great British statesman William Gladstone wrote of it: "The American Constitution is the most wonderful work ever struck off at a given time by the brain and purpose of man." This assessment may seem extravagant, and some critics disagree. The Constitution evolves as a foundation for governing. Because it makes room for "a more perfect union" to grow over the years, the Constitution has endured a remarkably long time.

A new nation desperately needs to acquire political legitimacy and find ways to hold itself together. A constitution is an essential formulation of basic governing policies. Properly formulated and agreed to by the people, a constitution can give a new government the acceptance, or legitimacy, it needs to govern effectively. And a constitution can help hold a changing nation together by providing institutions capable of governing.

*T*his chapter focuses on the formation of the Constitution and describes the main principles in our fundamental law. First, we tell the story of the drafting and ratification of the Constitution, a process filled with drama, great debates, and compromises. Then, we explain the enduring principles that are written into the Constitution—popular sovereignty, representation, limited government, separation of powers, federalism, national supremacy, individual liberty, and judicial review. Finally, we consider how the Constitution can be changed in order to adapt it to a changing world, to new realities, and to changing ideas about the relationship between society and governing.

THE DURABLE CONSTITUTION

The government of the United States grew up from the Constitution, and it still takes its basic authority from the Constitution. Our Constitution has been remarkably durable. Its core is basically the same today as it was two centuries ago. If prizes were given to constitutions for lasting a long time, ours would deserve a large championship trophy.

Symbols of law and justice. During the bicentennial of the U.S. Constitution, celebrated throughout 1987, the communications media stimulated an interest in various constitutional and national symbols. In this example, a facsimile of the Constitution and the scales of justice were presented as "bright images of the nation's system of government."

What is more, the Constitution has come to be revered by Americans; it has even become a national icon. Those who drafted it were not so sure it was satisfactory. One of the drafters, Benjamin Franklin, made a brief speech to the delegates as the Constitutional Convention finished its work. "I agree to this Constitution with all its faults," Franklin said. Although he doubted whether any other convention of political leaders of his time could do better, he did not think that the new constitution was perfect. So, said Franklin, "I consent . . . to this Constitution because I expect no better, and because I am not sure it is not the best."

Thomas Jefferson was not a delegate to the Convention, which may help account for his skepticism about the new basic law that was being touted so enthusiastically by the nationalist leaders—John Jay, James Madison, and Alexander Hamilton. Jefferson thought that Americans would be lucky if the constitution lasted a generation. That constitution endured, and it acquired deep-seated admiration, respect, and even reverence among Americans. Indeed, the original document drafted by the founders has come to be treated like a religious relic—kept under glass, pickled by special gas in a glass case, and exhibited in the National Archives in Washington, D.C.

Today the American Constitution is the object of much fascination. How did this unusual, extraordinary, long-lasting instrument get formulated and adopted? What are the main ideas about governing that the founders wrote into the Constitution? How has this Constitution worked out in practice over the years, and what are its prospects?

COMPROMISE POLITICS AT THE PHILADELPHIA CONVENTION

It was a hot and humid summer in Philadelphia, then America's largest city, in 1787—the worst since 1750, many said. Fifty-five delegates chosen by the state legislatures met in the Pennsylvania State House, now called Independence Hall, to hammer out a new plan of government.

The delegates included such famous Americans as George Washington and James Madison from Virginia, Alexander Hamilton from New York, and Benjamin Franklin from Pennsylvania. Some who played an important role at the Convention—such as James Wilson and Gouverneur Morris of Pennsylvania—are less well known today. Elbridge Gerry and Rufus King were there from Massachusetts. Oliver Ellsworth, later to be an important leader in the U.S. Senate, represented Connecticut. The governor of New Jersey, William Livingston, and the governor of Virginia, Edmund Randolph, were delegates. From Delaware came John Dickinson; from Maryland, Daniel Carroll; from Georgia, William Pierce; from the Carolinas, William Blount and Charles Pinckney.

These were extraordinary people, mostly successful plantation owners, lawyers, and merchants and mostly college graduates. They were men of exceptional political experience—as state legislators or governors, signers of the Declaration of Independence, leaders in the Revolution, drafters of the Articles of Confederation, or members of the Continental Congress.

The Convention Meets

The Convention membership reached a quorum on May 25, 11 days late. But in the interim, the Virginia and Pennsylvania delegates had been caucusing every day. James Madison's pre-Convention strategy was to develop solid support among the early arrivers for provisions that would substantially strengthen national power. More than any other member, Madison was the architect of the Constitution. On opening day, the delegates unanimously elected General Washington, the most famous and respected person among them, as presiding officer, and the Convention was under way.

Outside the Convention hall, the state of the union was not very good. National government under the **Articles of Confederation** was not very effective. The Articles, said Madison, were "nothing more than a treaty of amity and alliance between independent and sovereign states." They were a constitution that provided no chief executive and no national courts. Each state had only one vote in the Continental Congress, and Congress had limited power to govern. There was a serious economic depression, and much talk of war between the states. George Washington, who had led the revolutionary army, sadly remarked in 1785 that "the wheels of government are clogged."

The delegates had been sent to the Philadelphia Convention merely to revise the Articles of Confederation so that they would serve as a more workable constitution for the nation. But they almost immediately agreed that this was impossible and that they must write a new basic law of the land. Convention debate dwelt both on broad questions of constitutional design and on the specific decision rules that would determine the distribution of authority under the new government (see Jillson, 1988: 1–17). For the first couple of weeks of the Convention, the delegates discussed general issues of governmental philosophy. Then, they got down to the business of writing a new constitution.

The most contentious and vexing policy issues that the Convention dealt with concerned political equality. First and foremost, the delegates grappled with the issue of **representation** in the new Congress. Should the states be equally represented there, as was the practice of the Articles of Confederation? Or should the people of the states be equally represented? Then, the Convention dealt with the problem of slavery. Legal in every state but Massachusetts, slavery was practiced mainly in the southern states. Should black slaves be counted equally in determining representation? Finally, the delegates considered the issue of political equality, and specifically debated the question "Who should be qualified to vote in national elections?"

A Reform Caucus in Action

James Madison, a brilliant 36-year-old Virginian, came to the Convention with a plan for a new national government in mind. He had discussed his

James Madison (1751–1836). Behind-the-scenes caucus leader at the Constitutional Convention in 1787 and architect of the Virginia Plan which the delegates accepted, Madison later fought for ratification of the Constitution as an author of the Federalist papers, engineered the adoption of the Bill of Rights amendments to the Constitution after the Constitution was ratified and a new government was formed, and served as the fourth president under that government—from 1809 to 1817.

proposal with the other Virginians and the Pennsylvania delegation in the days before the Convention achieved a quorum. Madison's so-called **Virginia Plan,** presented to the convention by Edmund Randolph, governor of Virginia, provided for strong national power that would be divided into three parts: the executive, legislative, and judicial branches. Most important, the plan provided for a **bicameral,** or two-house, Congress in which state delegations in both the House of Representatives and the Senate would be based on population.

The Convention readily accepted the idea of three governmental branches, and it agreed to a bicameral Congress. What came into dispute was the role of the states in the new federal scheme of things. Some of the delegates thought that the Virginia Plan went too far from the provisions of the Articles of Confederation and feared that the new government envisaged by the Virginia Plan might ride roughshod over the small states. In time, these "federalist" delegates offered the so-called **New Jersey Plan** to the Convention. This proposal actually changed the Articles of Confederation very little, remedying some of the major complaints against the Articles and providing for a one-house, or **unicameral,** Congress in which all of the states would be equally represented.

The two competing proposals prompted several days of intense debate. On one side were the "nationalists" (Washington, Madison, Hamilton, Charles Pinckney, Franklin, James Wilson, Gouverneur Morris), who shared a vision of a strong nation able to promote economic expansion and enforce equal rights across the land. On the other side were the "federalists" (William Paterson, John Dickinson, Luther Martin, Elbridge

HISTORICAL PERSPECTIVE

Virginia and New Jersey Plans Compared

The Virginia Plan to strengthen the national government, advocated by James Madison and proposed to the Constitutional Convention by Edmund Randolph (both of whom were from Virginia), was the first plan to be debated. Randolph's resolutions provided the main agenda for the first nine weeks of the Convention. Many of these proposals were adopted. The New Jersey Plan, offered late in the Convention by William Paterson of that state, sought only to modify the Articles of Confederation and retain state sovereignty, rather than make a wholly new constitution as the advocates of the Virginia Plan proposed. The central provisions of these two competing programs for constitution making are presented below.

Source: David G. Smith, *The Convention and the Constitution* (New York: St. Martin's Press, 1965), pp. 38–39.

The Virginia Plan (Randolph resolutions): Summary of provisions

1. A National Legislature of two branches (houses) with representation proportioned either to the quotas of contribution or to the number of free inhabitants.

   The members of the second branch to be elected by the first from persons nominated by the state legislatures, to receive such salary and hold term for such times as will ensure their independence, and to be ineligible for any office established by a state (except legislative office).

   Congress to have the power to legislate where "the separate States are incompetent" or where "the harmony of the United States may be interrupted by the exercise of individual legislation," to negative any laws contravening the articles of union, and to call forth the "force of the Union" against any recalcitrant member.

2. A National Executive to be elected by the legislature for a fixed term of years and to be ineligible for reelection.

3. A Council of Revision composed of the executive and members of the judiciary to review acts of the National Legislature and particular state legislatures and to exercise a suspensive veto over these acts.

4. A National Judiciary to include a "supreme tribunal" and inferior tribunals chosen by the legislature but to serve during good behavior and to have jurisdiction over admiralty, diversity of citizenship cases, cases involving collection of the national revenues, impeachment of national officers, and "questions which involve the national peace and harmony."

5. Provision to be made for the admission of new states; a guarantee of the territory of each state and of a republican government to each state.

6. The legislative, executive, and judiciary officers in each state to be bound by oath to support the articles of union.

The New Jersey Plan (Paterson resolutions): Summary of provisions

1. The Congress to consist of one house in which representation would be by states.

   Congress to have the power, subject to the concurrence of a number (unstated) of states, to levy duties on foreign goods, impose stamp taxes and postal fees, and make rules and regulations for their collection; to regulate foreign and interstate commerce; to make requisitions in proportion to the number of white inhabitants and "three-fifths of other persons" except Indians not paying taxes; and to devise provisions for collection from noncomplying states.

2. A plural Executive to be elected by Congress for a term of years and to be removable ei-

(Continued)

HISTORICAL PERSPECTIVE

(Concluded)

ther by Congress or by application of a majority of the executives of the states.

The Executive to have the power to appoint federal officers and direct military operations (provided that no member of the Executive personally take command of any troops).

3. A supreme tribunal (no inferior federal tribunals) appointed by the Executive and holding office during good behavior.

The supreme tribunal to have jurisdiction over the impeachment of federal officers, cases involving the law of nations, treaties, regulation of trade, or collection of federal revenue (jurisdiction in the latter two categories only in the last instance).

4. All laws or treaties of the United States to be the law of the respective states and the judiciary of the states to be bound by them; the federal Executive authorized to "call forth the power of the Confederated States" to compel obedience.

5. Provision to be made for the admission of new states, for a uniform rule of naturalization, and for a fair trial within each state of offenses committed by citizens of other states.

Gerry, David Brearley, Gunning Bedford), concerned that the national government would swallow up the states and fearful that the states would reject a new constitution along the lines of the Virginia Plan (see Jillson and Eubanks, 1984: 440–45). These federalists contended (as James Madison recorded in his *Journal*) that if "in the second branch [the Senate] . . . each state has an equal vote, there must be always a majority of states, as well as a majority of the people, on the side of public measures, and the government will have decision and efficacy" (Madison, 1893: 308).

After more than two weeks of deadlock, the delegates reached the first of the great political compromises of the Convention. The delegates at last supported a resolution under which members would be elected to the House of Representatives in proportion to the populations of the states, but every state would have an equal voice, two senators, in the Senate. Because this resolution was originally proposed by Roger Sherman of Connecticut, it was dubbed the **Connecticut Compromise.** "This is," says constitutional historian Max Farrand, "the great compromise of the convention and of the constitution" (Farrand, 1913: 105).

With the adoption of the Connecticut Compromise, the issue of equality of representation was resolved and the basic outlines of the new constitution took shape. But it remained for the Convention to resolve a range of issues of economic development for the new republic. What powers would the new government have to regulate commerce? What taxing powers would it have? Who would control the admission of new states into the federal union? How would slavery, a part of the economic system of the South, be handled? The nationalists won in their effort to grant economic and taxing powers to the new national government, but at the expense of compromise over slavery.

The Convention agreed to prohibit the importation of slaves, but not until 1808. And slaves would be counted for purposes of determining state representation in the House of Representatives and of levying direct taxes—but only at three fifths of their total number. The new Constitution provided that "representatives and direct taxes shall be apportioned among the several states . . . according to their respective numbers, which shall be determined by adding to the whole number of free persons . . . three fifths of all other persons." Although this **three-fifths compromise** resolved differences at the Constitutional Convention, the problem of slavery festered until the 13th Amendment, adopted after the Civil War, repealed it and gave black Americans full rights as citizens.

The Convention struggled with vexing disagreements about political equality. The delegates understood that popular elections were the heart of democratic government, but universal suffrage was far from the actual practice of the times. In most states in the 1780s, property ownership was required to hold office and vote in elections. The delegates kept property qualifications out of the Constitution. But they dodged the wider issue of **suffrage** by allowing the states to determine voter qualifications. Those eligible to vote in elections for state offices could vote in national elections.

The political skills of the Convention delegates were shown in the shrewd compromises and the new things found in the constitution they drafted. These delegates have been called a "**reform caucus** in action" because of the political imaginativeness and sensitivity that they displayed. They framed a constitution reflecting both their shared political experience and many compromises among different points of view. If they could not compromise on an issue, as was true for the issue of slavery, they did not confront it directly. They resolved other issues, such as the scope of the executive's powers, by using language that could be understood in more than one way. Yet other issues were resolved by straightforward compromise, as was the case with the great Connecticut Compromise over representation in Congress.

The Convention sought to fashion a new system of government that would be grounded in the loyalties and support of, and dependent on the consent of, the people generally, not merely the state governments. During the drafting of the new constitution, the delegates determined to put aside the language of the Articles of Confederation, which referred to an agreement "between the States of New Hampshire, Massachusetts, Rhode Island," and the others, and instead to begin with these words: "We the People of the States."

In September 1787, the Convention chose a committee on style to polish up the language of the draft document, so as to make it ready for final approval. One of the committee members, Gouverneur Morris, insisted that the first words of the new constitution be changed to read "We the People of the United States." The delegates agreed. The Convention had created a national government. "It appears to me," said Convention chairman George Washington, "little short of a miracle that the delegates from so many different states . . . should unite in forming a system of national government so little liable to well founded objections" (quoted in Bowen, 1966: xvii).

A miracle, perhaps. But hardheaded political compromises made it possible. The new constitution "was a patchwork sewn together under the pressure of both time and events by a group of extremely talented democratic politicians" (Roche, 1961: 815). These politicians did not create a centralized national government based on the principle of **legislative supremacy** for the very good reason that the people would not have accepted it. But they did greatly strengthen the national government because they were convinced that the existing government was a failure. In the words of a close student of the Constitutional Convention (Roche, 1961: 815–16): "For over three months, in what must have seemed to the faithful participants an endless process of give-and-take, they reasoned, cajoled, threatened, and bargained amongst themselves. The result was a Constitution which the people, in fact, by democratic processes, did accept, and a far better national government was established."

Getting the New Constitution Adopted

The Philadelphia Convention completed its job when it recommended a draft of the new constitution to Congress for approval by the states. The first hurdle in the **ratification** process was to get Congress to submit the proposed constitution to the state legislatures without amending it in any way. Opening the draft to changes would have undone the enterprise, so delicate and carefully crafted were the compromises entered into at the Convention.

The Convention had adjourned on September 17, 1787. On September 20, the official draft of the new constitution along with a Convention resolution of approval and a letter of transmittal reached Congress, which was meeting in New York. More than half the members of Congress came up from Philadelphia, having been Convention delegates. Congress readily voted to send the draft constitution out to the states, whose legislatures would schedule elections of delegates to state ratifying conventions. If conventions in nine states ratified, the new basic law would go into effect.

But the decisions of the state legislatures to call convention elections came quickly. By the end of January 1788, all the states but Rhode Island had issued convention calls. The ratification process was in motion. "But these were only battles, not the war" (McDonald, 1965: 212). The real

George Washington presiding over the Constitutional Convention. From May 25 until September 18, 1787, a new U.S. constitution was hammered out in Philadelphia by 55 delegates from the various states. On the last day, Benjamin Franklin told his fellow delegates that he was astonished to find the result of their efforts "approaching so near to perfection as it does."

struggle would come as debates developed in each of the state conventions.

Newspapers everywhere printed the draft constitution as soon as they could get copies. Then, in the country at large, there was a repetition of the debates that had preoccupied the Philadelphia Convention. Commentators, such men as Elbridge Gerry, Richard Henry Lee, and Patrick Henry, printed their reservations and objections—the Convention had been convoked only to revise the Articles of Confederation, not to draft an entirely new constitution; there was no bill of rights; the president had no executive council; the House of Representatives would be weak; the office of vice president was unnecessary.

George Washington, James Madison, Alexander Hamilton, and John Jay defended the new constitution and skillfully maneuvered for ratification. Their chief propaganda tool was a series of newspaper articles, together called the *Federalist* **papers.** Patiently and with tenacity, Madison, Hamilton, and Jay (writing as Publius) argued the case for the Constitution.

WORDS AND IDEAS

The Federalist, No. 51

In this issue of the Federalist papers, James Madison advocated ratification of the Constitution by defending its provision for the separation of powers and checks and balances. Madison maintained that separating power into three branches of government—executive, legislative, and judicial—would help prevent tyranny. He said that it was essential to give "those who administer each department the necessary constitutional means and personal motives to resist encroachments of the others." Then, he argued:

> Ambition must be made to counteract ambition. The interest of the man must be connected with the constitutional rights of the place. It may be a reflection on human nature that such devices should be necessary to control the abuses of government. But what is government itself but the greatest of all reflections on human nature? If men were angels, no government would be necessary. If angels were to govern men, neither external nor internal controls on government would be necessary. In framing a government which is to be administered by men over men, the great difficulty lies in this: you must first enable the government to control the governed; and in the next place oblige it to control itself. A dependence on the people is, no doubt, the primary control on the government; but experience has taught mankind the necessity of auxiliary precautions.

Separation of powers was the constitution-makers' way of "contriving the interior structure of the government as that its several constituent parts may, by their mutual relations, be the means of keeping each other in their proper places."

State by state, the ratification fights were tough (for a colorful, blow-by-blow account, see McDonald, 1965: 209–36). At the Pennsylvania ratification convention, James Wilson and Dr. Benjamin Rush labored long and hard to get the delegates to ratify. After five weeks, they succeeded by a vote of 46 to 23. In the meantime, Delaware had ratified unanimously, and New Jersey followed 10 days later. Georgia, "with the Indians on its back and the Spaniards on its flank," as Washington said (Bowen, 1966: 277), ratified next, by a vote of 128 to 42. Then Connecticut ratified, then Massachusetts, Maryland, South Carolina, New Hampshire, Virginia, and New York. By August 1788, 11 states had ratified the Constitution. In due time, North Carolina and Rhode Island also ratified. A new constitutional system had been established. Benjamin Rush, that redoubtable Philadelphia physician and patriot, wrote, "'Tis done. We have become a nation" (Bowen, 1966: 310).

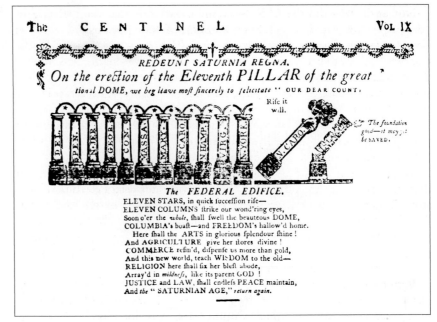

ELEVEN STARS, in quick fucceffion rife—
ELEVEN COLUMNS ftrike our wond'ring eyes,
Soon o'er the *whole*, fhall fwell the beauteous DOME,
COLUMBIA's boaft—and FREEDOM's hallow'd home.
  Here fhall the ARTS in glorious fplendour fhine !
And AGRICULTURE give her ftores divine !
COMMERCE refin'd, difpenfe us more than gold,
And this new world, teach WISDOM to the old—
RELIGION here fhall fix her bleft abode,
Array'd in *mildnefs*, like its parent GOD !
JUSTICE and LAW, fhall endlefs PEACE maintain,
And the " SATURNIAN AGE," *return again.*

Ratification of the Constitution occasioned patriotic celebration. This cartoon was printed in the Centinel, *a Massachusetts publication, to celebrate New York's ratification of the Constitution on July 26, 1788. The Constitution went into effect after New Hampshire ratified, but the importance of Virginia and New York made their approval essential. The new government was elected in the fall of 1788, though North Carolina did not ratify until 1789 and Rhode Island did not ratify until 1790.*

REPRESEN-TATIVE, LIMITED GOVERNMENT

The United States is the first nation to have a *written constitution*. This seems commonplace today, but 200 years ago it was remarkable. That ours is the oldest written constitution in the world is extraordinary even today. Despite sharp debate over ratification, the new Constitution was widely accepted after the ratification fight was over and implemented forthwith. So pervasive and long-standing are the requirements of the Constitution that it is impossible to understand American politics without understanding its basic principles.

The Constitution contains the principle of **popular sovereignty.** This means rule by the people, government based on the consent of the governed. The pro-Constitution spokesmen in the ratification fight argued that it was a sovereign people who established by a written constitution the proper limitations on governmental power. The Declaration of Independence proclaimed that governments derive "their just powers from the consent of the governed." No such language appears in the Constitution. But the Preamble does say, "We the people of the United States . . . do ordain and establish this Constitution for the United States of America." James Fenimore Cooper reached the conclusion in 1838 that these words were "a naked and vague profession" (Cooper, 1956: 18). But popular rule in the Constitution does not stand or fall on the language of the Preamble. Article I requires that members of the House of Representatives be "chosen every second year by the people of the several states." It was the founders' intent that direct popular participation be limited to the election of members of the House.

Not until 1964 did the U.S. Supreme Court rule that the meaning of "the people" in Article I includes the notion of "one person, one vote" in elections for the House. In this court case, *Wesberry* v. *Sanders* (1964), the Georgia legislature was required to draw congressional district lines so that the districts would be as equal in population as possible. Justice Black, who gave the opinion of the Court, said that "it would defeat the principle solemnly embodied in the Great Compromise—equal representation in the House of equal numbers of people—for us to hold that [state] legislatures may draw the lines of congressional districts in such a way as to give some voters a greater voice in choosing a congressman than others."

Senators were chosen indirectly by the state legislatures until 1913. In that year, the 17th Amendment, which provides for direct election of senators, was approved. The president is officially elected by electoral votes; these are cast by electors chosen in a popular election. The president appoints federal judges and officials of the federal administrative departments with the advice and consent of the Senate. Thus, the role of the people is not pervasive, though it is clearly present.

Representative government is a fundamental principle of the Constitution. Although direct rule by the people, as in New England town meetings, may be possible in small communities, it is not feasible on a large scale. A vital part of our concept of governing is that the people rule through representatives who are chosen in free elections and are accountable to the voters. These representatives meet in a legislative assembly; there, they deliberate, debate, and compromise to make laws for all—laws that, ideally, are in the public interest. In an imperfect world, there will always be debate and strife over what laws are in the interest of the general public and over how well elected representatives enact such laws.

Our concept of representation includes the belief that a legislature is representative of the people only if the members of its houses have an equal number of people in their districts. The Senate is exempted from this requirement because of its special federal character—the Constitution gives each state two senators no matter what the state populations. **Malapportionment** is the term for a situation in which the populations of legislative districts are grossly unequal. In the 1960s, many state legislatures were malapportioned—some districts were far too large, some far too small. For instance, the Tennessee legislature had not been reapportioned for 60 years despite the fact that the state constitution required representation based on the number of qualified voters in each county. A county with 2,340 voters chose one representative, while another county with 312,245 voters chose only seven. Because of this kind of gross malapportionment, a number of urban residents including the mayor of Nashville and county judge Charles W. Baker brought suit against Tennessee's secretary of state, Joe C. Carr. They claimed that their constitutional rights had been violated. In the case of *Baker* v. *Carr* (1962), the U.S. Supreme Court held that boundary lines must be drawn so that state legislative districts are reasonably equal in population.

Reenacting the Constitutional Convention. Dressed in colonial attire, "delegates" arrived at Independence Hall, Philadelphia, on May 23, 1987, to reenact the convening of the Constitutional Convention 200 years earlier. On their way, they passed a statue of George Washington, chairman of the 1787 Convention.

Fundamental to the founders' vision of American government was the view that political power should be limited. They wrote the principle of **limited government** into the heart of the Constitution. This principle simply means that the powers that government can exercise are limited by the provisions of the Constitution. The founders thought that both by setting down the powers of the national government and by spelling out the things that the government could not do, a written constitution would keep the government within its proper bounds. So basic is the principle of limited government to a written constitution that this principle is sometimes called **constitutionalism.**

The Constitution sets limits on governmental power by granting specific powers to the national government. In Article I, Section 8, for example, the powers of Congress are listed: "The Congress shall have power to lay and collect taxes . . . , borrow money . . . , regulate commerce . . . , establish post offices . . . , declare war," and so forth. Moreover,

confederations of localities or states, where most power remained at the local level. In the debates over the adoption of the U.S. Constitution, those who favored a strong national government appropriated the appellation **Federalists.** They seem to have believed that this label would give their cause credibility among those who were suspicious of giving power to a national government. Although we may speak of the "federal" government in Washington, this is but a form of shorthand; we often use the terms *federal* and *national* interchangeably to refer to the central government with its home in the nation's capital. In actuality, a **federal system** is a system of government in which two levels, national and state, have governing authority over the same territory and citizenry. People who live in Ohio, for example, are governed under the authority of both the constitution of Ohio and the U.S. Constitution.

Federal versus Unitary Government

In a federal constitution, governmental power is divided between a national government and some number of subnational units, usually called states or provinces. The subnational units have an independent basis for governing authority in their own constitutions. Federalism is not espe-

India, like the United States, has a federal constitution. India's constitution provides powers for the central government, 17 states, and a number of territories. Here, presiding over a 1985 Congress party conference, Indian Prime Minister Rajiv Gandhi leads a brief period of silence in memory of his mother, Indira Gandhi, a former prime minister.

PRACTICE OF POLITICS

How Are State and Local Governments Organized?

What Is the Constitutional Basis of State Government?

Each of the 50 states has its own state constitution, which lays down the basic legal framework for the state. All of the state constitutions embrace the principle of separation of powers and checks and balances. Accordingly, each state has executive, legislative, and judicial branches of government. State action—by the state executive, the state legislature, or the courts—must conform to the U.S. Constitution.

How Are State Governments Organized?

The executive The governor is the chief executive officer in each state. State governors are elected for four-year terms, except in the New England states of New Hampshire, Rhode Island, and Vermont, where the governors serve only a two-year term. In half of the states, governors are limited to two consecutive terms in office.

State governors exercise the power to develop and recommend the state's budget and manage the state administration. In many states, however, the governor must share administrative management with other independently elected officials (such as the attorney general, the auditor, or the secretary of state). The governor in all states but one (North Carolina) has the power to veto laws passed by the legislature, and in 43 states the governor wields the **item veto,** with which he or she may reduce or strike out line items in state budget bills.

The legislature All but one of the state legislatures are **bicameral**— they are made up of a house of representatives and a senate. The lower house is called the Assembly in California, Nevada, New Jersey, New York, and Wisconsin, and in Maryland, Virginia, and West Virginia it is called the House of Delegates. In all
(Continued)

cially rare in national constitutions. Both Canada and Mexico have federal constitutions. Australia, India, the Federal Republic of Germany, Switzerland, Brazil, and a dozen other countries are also federal systems.

Most countries of the world, however, have constitutions that vest all governing authority in the national government. These countries are said to be **unitary systems** because the national government has the authority to monopolize governmental power. It may delegate authority to cities or other local administrative units, but under a unitary constitution it can reclaim any of the authority that it grants to such subnational units. France, Great Britain, Italy, and Japan are examples of unitary systems. Within their own terms, the American states are also unitary systems. Un-

PRACTICE OF POLITICS

(Concluded)

the states, the upper house is called the Senate. Nebraska has a one-house, or unicameral, legislature, called the Legislature, whose members are called senators.

In each state, the districts in which legislators are chosen must be equal in population; in the bicameral states, this is true for both house and senate districts. The house and senate are organized along party lines, except in nonpartisan Nebraska. State houses of representatives vary in size from 40 in Alaska to 400 in New Hampshire; state senates vary from 20 in Alaska to 67 in Minnesota.

The courts Since most of the laws affecting ordinary Americans are state laws (regulating professions; defining crimes; validating marriages, divorces, and deaths), the state courts are important. Although the state court systems vary in detail, all of them include municipal or local courts, general district trial courts, courts of appeal, and a state supreme court. The state supreme court and appellate court judges are popularly elected in about half of the states; in the others, judges are appointed or chosen by methods that combine appointment and election.

What Is the Constitutional Basis of Local Governments?

Local governments, including all counties, townships, towns, and cities, are creatures of the states. These units of government are established under the authority of the state constitution and laws. In general, local governments may be altered by the states that created them. A state can, for instance, change or abolish its existing counties. A state can also confer measured independence on localities; this is done in about half of the states, where municipalities can achieve "home rule."

The states have prescribed independence and autonomy within the terms of the federal constitution. But the states are themselves unitary systems, so counties and cities do not have an independent constitutional status comparable to that of states in the federal union.

der each of the state constitutions, all of the governmental power that the state may properly exercise is vested in the state. The state governments may delegate power to counties, cities, towns, or special districts, but their constitutions also permit them to take away such power.

Comparison with Other Democracies

If we were to distribute the nations of the world on a continuum from unitary systems at one end to federal systems at the other end, we would notice at once that most countries—more than 80 percent—have unitary governments. The 20 countries that are federal systems include countries that are federal only in the most formalistic sense. For instance, the Soviet Union—with its 15 union republics and other "autonomous" territories—has a formally federal constitution. But practically, the Soviet Union is unitary, controlled at the national level by a highly centralized Communist party.

The federal democracies vary in the way they allocate governmental powers to the national government and the subnational units. Federalism has a long tradition in Brazil and is an important part of its constitution, but military-authoritarian regimes in the country often make federalism a formality. Similarly, federalism has become something of a facade in Mexico, where the constitution has permitted concentration of political power.

In some federal systems, the constitution spells out the powers of the national government, with powers not mentioned residing with the states; this is true of Switzerland, West Germany, and the United States. In other federal systems, the constitution enumerates the powers of the subnational units, leaving the remainder to the national level; examples include India and Canada. These differences in allocating governmental powers mean that in democratic countries there are variations in the "federal formula"—in what is appropriate for the national government to do and in what the states can do. Among the federal democracies, such countries as the United States and West Germany lie at the more centralized end of the scale, while such countries as Canada and Switzerland are located at the more decentralized end of the scale.

Historically, federalism has been a means mainly for countries large in size and ethnically diverse to establish governmental authority over their territories. In such cases as the United States, Australia, and Brazil, federalism provided a method for expanding across a continent. It also enabled national unity to coincide with ethnic diversity, permitting a Mormon Utah to cohabit with a French Louisiana or a French-speaking Quebec to remain in a federation with an Ontario of British heritage.

But China's unitary regime is evidence that a federal structure is not the only answer for large territories with an ethnically diverse population. And federal constitutions do not resolve all disagreements over where political power should be exercised—by the nation or by the states. In federal systems, conflicts between national and state exercise of power are usually managed by courts or intergovernmental councils (such as the U.S. Supreme Court), according supremacy to the national governing authority.

STATES AS POLITICAL ENTITIES

In federal democracies, the national government typically has the power to conduct foreign relations, make war, regulate the economy, and establish welfare programs. The subnational units have the power to maintain order, regulate the local economy, and provide welfare, education, and social services directly to citizens. Typically, some powers, such as taxa-

Governor Jimmy Carter mingles with constituents. In 1970, when Carter was governor of Georgia, citizens at Jekyll Island, Georgia, thanked him for stopping developers from filling in marshes. The sign reads, "Thanks for Saving Our Marshes."

tion, can be exercised by both the nation and the states. In all democratic federal systems, there has been a tendency toward centralization.

The U.S. state capitals are lively centers of governmental activity. The 50 states permit a fairly wide diversity of political participation and action. Under a unitary system, Americans might elect only four national government officials directly: the president, two U.S. senators, and a member of the House of Representatives. Federalism extends direct political participation: under a federal system, voters choose literally thousands of state and local officials. The ordinary citizen is likely to feel a closer affinity with officials of the smaller units of government and to feel that state and local authorities are more accessible. Because a federal system decentralizes political authority, it fosters democracy by keeping citizens active and responsible.

Moreover, a federal system permits diversity of governmental organization, political structure, and public policies. Nebraskans decided back in the 1930s to have a one-house, or **unicameral,** legislature, and the federal system permitted that experiment. Historically, New York has had a three-party system, with Democrats, Republicans, and Liberals on the ballot; many states have only two competitive political parties, a few have

WORDS AND IDEAS

Tocqueville on the Importance of the States

Alexis de Tocqueville, a French aristocrat, came to the United States in the 1830s seeking to understand why, in a world of despotisms, democracy had grown up in America. He traveled the country widely and was a perceptive observer of the life and politics of the time. His book *Democracy in America,* first published in 1835 and subsequently published in many editions, is a classic still worth reading.

It is incontestably true that the love and the habits of republican government in the United States were engendered in the townships and in the provincial assemblies. In a small State, like that of Connecticut for instance, where cutting a canal or laying down a road is a momentous political question, where the State has no army to pay and no wars to carry on, and where much wealth and much honour cannot be bestowed upon the chief citizens, no form of government can be more natural or more appropriate than that of a republic. But it is this same republican spirit, it is these manners and customs of a free people, which are engendered and nurtured in the different States, to be afterward applied to the country at large. The public spirit of the Union is, so to speak, nothing more than an abstract of the patriotic zeal of the provinces. Every citizen of the United States transfuses his attachment to his little republic in the common store of American patriotism. In defending the Union he defends the increasing prosperity of his own district, the right of conducting its affairs, and the hope of causing measures of improvement to be adopted which may be favourable to his own interests; and these are motives which are wont to stir men more readily than the general interests of the country and the glory of the nation.

only one effective party, and some state and local offices are nonpartisan. Automobiles sold in California, where environmental laws have strong support, must have special emission control equipment intended to prevent air pollution. Such diversity makes for flexibility and helps give citizens a sense of control over their destiny.

A federal system is especially well suited to a large country like the United States because it helps hold the society together, contributing to political integration, as we suggested in Chapter 1. Americans' loyalty to the nation is fostered by their attachment to their state and their local community. To be a Californian, an Ohioan, a New Yorker, a Michigander, an Okie, or a Mississippian is part of what it means to be an American. And so de Tocqueville was surely right a century and a half ago when he said that "every citizen of the United States transfuses his attachment to his little republic in the common store of American patriotism."

Powers of the States

In the United States, the states perform many governmental functions largely by themselves. Public education, though federally subsidized and run in accordance with some federal standards, is largely a state function. Laws concerning birth, death, marriage, and divorce are state laws, and most of the criminal and civil law of the United States is state law. Running elections is a state function, though the electoral rules are affected by federal regulations. The states are solely responsible for setting up local governments. The hundreds of cities, counties, and special-purpose districts, the governmental units that most directly affect our lives, operate under mainly state laws. Finally, the states wield so-called police powers—powers to protect and nurture the health, safety, welfare, and morals of their people.

Americans themselves sharply distinguish which levels of government—federal, state, or local—should provide and pay for public services. Figure 3–1 shows the results of a recent survey of Americans' beliefs about which level of government should have primary responsibility for various public functions. Unsurprisingly, the vast majority of Americans think that the national government should handle national security programs. A majority think that the states should be mainly responsible for building and maintaining roads and bridges. And a very large proportion think that police and fire protection should be primarily in the hands of local officials.

The **supremacy clause** of the national Constitution (which we discussed in Chapter 2) requires that the states (or their creatures, the local governments) give way to the national government when conflicts arise between national and state exercise of concurrent powers. National-state conflicts are normally resolved by legislation passed by Congress, but the umpire of the federal system is the U.S. Supreme Court. Just as the states may not use their taxing power to cripple or inhibit activities of the national government, so the national government may not use its enormous taxing power to destroy the states or make them ineffective.

The Constitution prohibits both the national government and the states from exercising certain powers, provides guarantees that protect the states, and sets forth rules governing relations among the states. For instance, the national government may not violate the Bill of Rights, the states may not deny individuals the right to vote because of their sex, the states may not coin money, a state may not be broken up into two states or more without its consent, and states must give **full faith and credit** to the official acts of other states, such as court decisions.

Today the American states retain remarkable vitality. In recent decades, they have become more important in the federal system and more viable. The state capitals are important centers of governmental activity. Indeed, most of the contacts that Americans have with government are with states and local governments. Most of the states have recently rewritten or re-

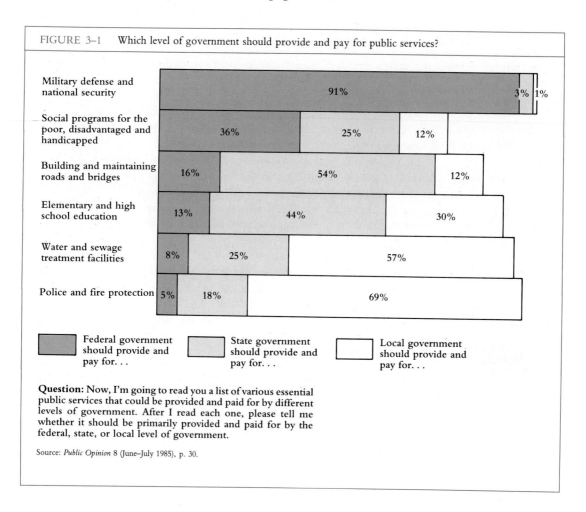

FIGURE 3–1   Which level of government should provide and pay for public services?

Military defense and national security: 91% | 3% | 1%

Social programs for the poor, disadvantaged and handicapped: 36% | 25% | 12%

Building and maintaining roads and bridges: 16% | 54% | 12%

Elementary and high school education: 13% | 44% | 30%

Water and sewage treatment facilities: 8% | 25% | 57%

Police and fire protection: 5% | 18% | 69%

Federal government should provide and pay for. . .

State government should provide and pay for. . .

Local government should provide and pay for. . .

Question: Now, I'm going to read you a list of various essential public services that could be provided and paid for by different levels of government. After I read each one, please tell me whether it should be primarily provided and paid for by the federal, state, or local level of government.

Source: *Public Opinion* 8 (June–July 1985), p. 30.

vised their constitutions to make them more effective. In all of the states, there have been pervasive actions to modernize and streamline governmental institutions and processes. When the Associated Press erroneously reported in 1897 that Mark Twain had died, he wired from London that "the reports of my death are greatly exaggerated." The American states, similarly, are alive and vigorous, and reports of their demise are greatly exaggerated.

State Political Cultures

Population migrations in the 18th and 19th centuries brought peoples with various cultural heritages to different parts of the United States—the Irish to Massachusetts, the German and Dutch to Pennsylvania, the Mormons to Utah, Hispanics to Texas and New Mexico. Forced migration concentrated the American Indians in the West and Afro-Americans in the South.

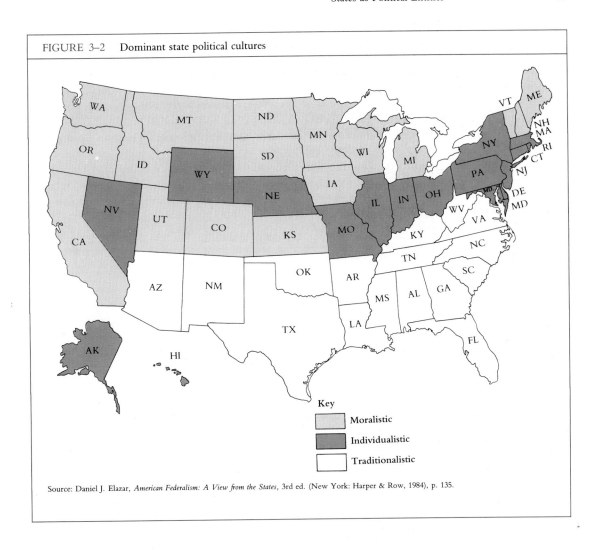

FIGURE 3–2   Dominant state political cultures

Key

Moralistic

Individualistic

Traditionalistic

Source: Daniel J. Elazar, *American Federalism: A View from the States,* 3rd ed. (New York: Harper & Row, 1984), p. 135.

Diverse cultural heritages have made for abundant diversity in the **political cultures** and political traditions of American states and regions. Political scientists have identified three analytically distinct political subcultures in the United States. These have come to be called the **individualistic,** the **moralistic,** and the **traditionalistic** political cultures (Elazar, 1984: 109–49). Some American states strongly reflect one of these cultural types, and some show characteristics of two types in combination, as Figure 3–2 shows.

Individualistic

The individualistic political culture conceives politics as a marketplace ruled by the politically competitive interests of individuals, rather than the common interest. It regards private concerns as central to the political process, which emphasizes compromise and limitations on governmental intervention in everyday life. In this environment, politics is rather like a business and can be best conducted by professional politicians. The individualistic culture encourages competitive party politics, and politicians tend to seek public office more as a method of controlling and distributing governmental favors and rewards than for the sake of carrying out particular policies. Politics has little to do with ideology; politicians and voters commonly see politics as a dirty, though necessary, business. The individualistic political culture is especially well illustrated in Illinois, with its long tradition of political patronage and the old-fashioned **machine politics** of Chicago.

Moralistic

The moralistic political culture emphasizes the public interest and is epitomized by "good government" orientations. Honesty, civic sacrifice, duty, and commitment to the general welfare are both its political watchwords and its common practice. People with this outlook view government as important to all citizens, political participation as highly desirable, and political office as a public service that carries weighty moral obligations. The moralistic culture places a high premium on the role of the amateur in politics. Although politics may be competitive, party loyalty is relatively unimportant. **Nonpartisanship** may characterize elections in the moralistic culture, and the merit system prevails in its public bureaucracy.

An excellent example of a moralistic political culture is Oregon, with its long and hardy tradition of political reform, honest politics, and innovative policies. Oregon shares with Minnesota, Utah, and other moralistic states both unusually competitive politics and high levels of voter activity. And these states make greater efforts to provide excellent education, highway, and welfare services than would be expected from their economic resources alone.

Traditionalistic

The traditionalistic political culture is conservative and elitist, thriving in states with a tradition of a hierarchical social order. To preserve the established order of social relations, leaders from the established social and political elite control the course of government. The elite group is often self-perpetuating, inheriting public office through family ties or social position. Thus, personal and family connections are more important than political parties and political competition is usually conducted through factional politics within what is ordinarily a one-party system.

This pattern of state politics has a legacy in the southern states. These were historically the poorest states, retarded by racial policies inhibiting both blacks and whites. Dominated by a white **power elite** in statehouse, courthouse, and city hall, voter turnout was lower in the states of the South than elsewhere. Louisiana exemplifies the traditionalistic political culture very well. The Long family has dominated Louisiana politics for 50 years—since Huey Long, the "kingfish," was elected governor in 1928. His brother Earl and his son Russell followed him as governor and U.S. senator, respectively. Rivalry within the Democratic party has typified Louisiana politics throughout this period. In the last two decades, the politics of the South has changed. With the success of the southern Republican party, its politics has become more competitive. So the southern "peculiarity," though it remains, is much less notable than it used to be.

Cultural variations among the American states are easily detectable, though cultural distinctiveness exists in bolder relief in some states than in others (Gastil, 1975). Because the imprint of the national political culture is profound, interstate and interregional variations appear as *subcultural* variations. Nevertheless, the states retain considerable cultural distinctiveness. In general, the states in the middle part of the country, stretching from Massachusetts through Illinois, are predominantly individualistic political cultures. The states of the most northern tier and the West are primarily moralistic political cultures. The southern and southwestern states, particularly the states of the Deep South, are largely traditionalistic political cultures. These politico-cultural differences among states affect how state governments perform and how they respond to federal government inducements, encouragement, programs, or financial incentives.

Political Laboratories

The government in Washington, D.C., gets so much attention and is engaged in so many activities that state actions are often overlooked. In fact, the states historically have been laboratories for testing the workability of laws and programs. Because the states are smaller, more homogeneous units than the nation as a whole, it has sometimes proven easier to get agreement at the state level to initiate new policies. The demand for policy change has been brisker in some states than in others—for instance, rapidly urbanizing states felt a sharper demand for education and welfare services than did rural states. In the moralistic political cultures, civic insistence on government responsiveness led these states to be more innovative. In the last century, the states have pioneered in such areas as **women's suffrage, civil service** systems, election reforms, and educational programs. Wyoming first opened voting to women in the late 19th century. Wisconsin initiated the **direct primary** as a way to clean up elections, and this was copied in other states. Today the states continue to develop innovative policies. These are but a few examples:

1. Beginning with Montana in 1985, a handful of states have required that automobile insurance rates be the same for men and women.

PRACTICE OF POLITICS

Who Governs in the States?

These two maps show which political party controlled the governorships and the state legislative houses circa 1987. Look your own state up.

Does the same party hold the governorship and the legislature in your state?

(Continued)

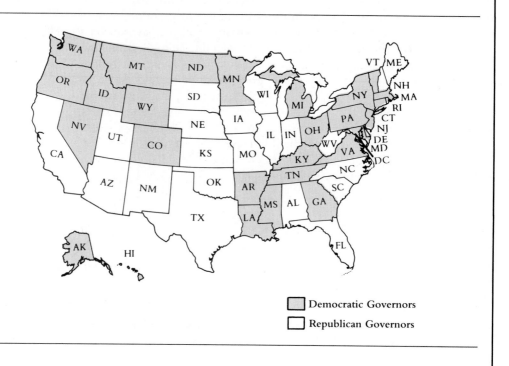

☐ Democratic Governors
☐ Republican Governors

Congress has considered requiring unisex insurance policies, but it has not enacted such a law.

2. A number of states have been investing millions of dollars in new programs to protect endangered wildlife and restore certain species to their natural habitats. Such efforts, mostly financed from state funds, have brought bighorn sheep back to the mountains of Oregon, restored beavers to rivers in Ohio, and allowed falcons to fly the skies of California.

PRACTICE OF POLITICS

(Concluded)

Divided party control, in which the governor belongs to one political party and one or both legislative houses are in the hands of the other party, is not unusual in the states. In fact, this condition prevailed in 46 states between 1965 and 1988.

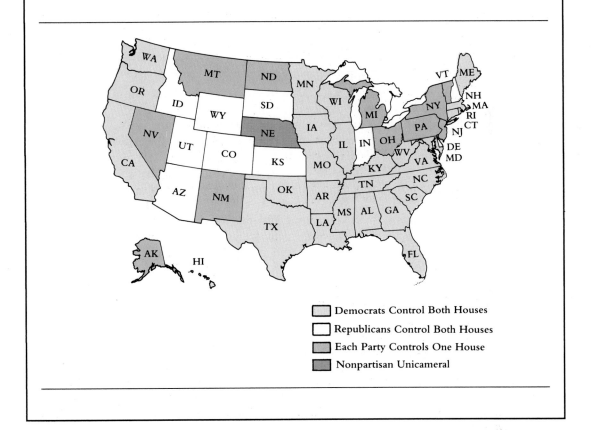

☐ Democrats Control Both Houses
☐ Republicans Control Both Houses
☐ Each Party Controls One House
☐ Nonpartisan Unicameral

3. Several states have developed innovative information systems. The Nebraska Natural Resource Data Bank, for instance, provides computer access to information on soil and water resources. In Colorado, an information management system provides computerized data on oil and gas activities in the states.

4. In 1985, Florida's legislature passed pioneering land use management legislation designed to manage growth, protect wetlands, and preserve the seacoast.

5. Illinois has pioneered in coordinating activities to cope with hazardous wastes and is promoting new research efforts to cope with the 2 million metric tons of hazardous wastes generated in the state each year.

A federal system encourages innovativeness by the subnational units. The states' autonomy in policy-making and their budgetary independence allow much diversity and initiative. But state autonomy and independence involve costs. Until the passage of national civil rights legislation in the 1960s, state inaction and discriminatory laws in southern states made blacks second-class citizens. When the oil crisis of the 1970s required national conservation of fuels, the federal government threatened to withhold highway construction money from states that refused to pass speed limits of 55 miles an hour. State objection continued, especially in the West, until 1987, when Congress permitted states to allow a 65-mph speed limit on some highways.

The states are powerful because they function effectively, because they are innovative in public policies, and because the national government must rely heavily on them to administer federal programs or carry out policies determined to be in the national interest. That the states are working better is evidenced by (1) modernized constitutions in 40 states since the 1960s; (2) reforms of state executive branches, legislatures, and court systems; (3) better revenue systems and financial management, allowing expansion of state government operations; and (4) greater interstate cooperation, fostering more rapid diffusion of policy innovations among the states. The resurgence of the states has encouraged the national government to consider greater reliance on the states in the future.

FROM FEDERALISM TO INTERGOVERN-MENTAL RELATIONS

Until at least the mid-1930s, it was conceivable to think of the American system of government as one in which distinct functions were performed by two levels of government, national and state. The national government had its specific powers and obligations, prescribed by the U.S. Constitution. The states performed separate and independent governing functions under their own constitutional authority or on account of the powers *reserved* to them in the Constitution. This pattern of national-state relations was called **dual federalism** to denote the separate roles of federal and state authority.

The March of Centralization

It is important to recognize the continuing importance of the states, but there can be no doubt that the American governmental system has become more centralized. Two centuries of practice under the Constitution have brought important changes in federal-state relationships (see Table 3–1).

Both federal and state governments manage crises. In 1987, when more than 8 inches of rain produced heavy flooding in Lawrence, Massachusetts, looting occurred in a flooded neighborhood. Members of the National Guard military police were then sent to Lawrence to back up local police officers.

The rudimentary theory of federalism—a division of powers between a national government and subnational units—is too simplistic to apply to the American political realities of the last 50 years.

During the Great Depression of the 1930s, the states were not able to deal with the trauma of economic and social problems. The New Deal program of President Franklin D. Roosevelt brought new national agencies and solutions into existence. The great financial and economic powers of the national government were mobilized to subsidize the states, and along with financial aid came federal regulation. The courts interpreted the **commerce clause** of the U.S. Constitution so as to extend the potential control of the national government over the movement of goods and services, even within the states. Decisions by Congress and the U.S. Supreme Court greatly enlarged the role of the national government in education, the regulation of elections, and civil rights.

TABLE 3–1   Changes in the centralization of the United States

Governmental functions	Years				
	1790	*1850*	*1910*	*1960*	*1987*
External affairs (e.g. military, diplomatic)	2	5	5	5	5
Public safety	1	2	2	2	2
Property rights	1	1	2	2	2
Civic rights (e.g. liberties, voting)	1	1	1	3	4
Morality (social values and norms)	1	1	1	1	2
Patriotism (the instilling of allegiance and pride)	3	3	3	3	3
Money, credit and banking	3	2	3	5	5
Transport and communication	2	2	4	4	4
Utilities (services and regulation)	1	1	1	2	3
Production and distribution	1	1	2	4	4
Economic development (e.g., subsidies)	3	2	3	4	4
Natural resources	—	—	4	4	4
Education	—	1	1	2	2
Indigency (e.g., aid to the handicapped)	1	1	1	4	4
Recreation and culture	—	2	2	3	3
Health (services and regulation)	—	—	2	3	4
Knowledge (research, patents, copyrights, etc.)	5	5	5	4	4
Average	1.9	2.0	2.5	3.2	3.5

Note: The ratings in the table range from 1 to 5; a score of 1 means that the states perform the function, while a score of 5 means that the national government does. Here are the details of the rating system:

1   The function is performed exclusively or almost exclusively by the state governments.

2   The function is performed predominantly by the state governments, though the national government plays a significant secondary role.

3   The function is performed by national and state governments in about equal proportions.

4   The function is performed predominantly by the national government, though the state governments play a significant secondary role.

5   The functions is performed exclusively or almost exclusively by the national government.

—   The function was not recognized to exist at the time.

Sources: William H. Riker, *Federalism: Origin, Operation, Significance* (Boston: Little, Brown, 1964), p. 85; and Advisory Commissions on Intergovernmental Relations, *The Federal Role in the Federal System: The Dynamics of Growth*, Report A–77 (Washington, D.C.: Advisory Commission on Intergovernmental Relations, 1980); p. 90.

The founders of the constitutional system recognized that a **compound republic,** an admixture of national and state power, built in potential instability. James Madison could see by 1828 "it will be fortunate if the struggle should end in a permanent equilibrium of powers" (quoted in Derthick, 1986: 33). Madison hoped that the handiwork of the Constitutional Convention would prove to have a national bias, and it did. The supremacy clause and the sweeping interpretations of the meaning of the commerce clause (giving Congress the power to regulate interstate commerce) by the Supreme Court have served as potent tools for those advancing nationalizing policies.

HISTORICAL PERSPECTIVE

Landmarks in Intergovernmental Relations

Over a period of 200 years, the relationship between the national government and the states has changed greatly. Much of this change has come about because of laws enacted by Congress or decisions made by the Supreme Court. Here are some of the most important developments in national-state relations:

1824 *Gibbons* v. *Ogden*. Supreme Court says that Congress has broad power to regulate "commercial intercourse"; strikes down New York law granting steamboat monopoly to a private company operating between New York and New Jersey.

1870 *U.S.* v. *DeWitt*. Supreme Court strikes down federal law prohibiting intrastate sale of certain inflammable petroleum products; says that Congress cannot regulate the "internal trade" of a state.

1887 Congress creates the Interstate Commerce Commission to regulate railroads.

1895 Sugar trust case. Supreme Court says that Congress does not have the power to regulate manufacturing even if the products manufactured later enter interstate commerce; holds that manufacturing is subject to state regulation.

1914 Shreveport rate case. Supreme Court upholds federal regulation of intrastate rail rates because of their effect on interstate commerce.

1918 *Hammer* v. *Dagenhart*. Supreme Court strikes down federal child labor law on the ground that it invades an area reserved for state regulation.

1937 *National Labor Relations Board* v. *Jones & Laughlin Steel Corporation*. Supreme Court says that Congress can regulate labor relations at a big steel plant because a work stoppage would have "a most serious effect upon interstate commerce."

1942 *Wickard* v. *Filburn*. Supreme Court says that Congress may control a farmer's production of wheat for home consumption because the cumulative effect of such production by many farmers would influence the national supply and price of wheat.

1964 Congress invokes the "commerce power" in passing the Civil Rights Act; forbids discrimination in public accommodations.

1976 *National League of Cities* v. *Usery*. Supreme court says that Congress lacks the power to regulate the wages and hours of key state and local government employees; emphasizes "state sovereignty."

1985 *Garcia* v. *San Antonio Transit Authority*. Supreme Court overrules 1976 decision; holds that federal wage and hour laws apply to state and local governments.

Source: *New York Times*, November 16, 1986; based on material from Domestic Policy Council's Working Group on Federalism and on Supreme Court decisions.

National, state, and local police cooperate in a "war against drugs." A 1986 drug raid in Yonkers, New York, yielded 5 pounds of crack, 45 pounds of cocaine, $713,000 in cash, and a money-counting machine. Showing the evidence are a U.S. special agent, the chief of the New York City Police Department, and a captain of the New York State Police.

Moreover, as historian Garry Wills once pointed out, "the Constitution is not itself a theoretical statement, but a practical instrument of rule" (Wills, 1981: ix). In practice, constitutional principles have been shaped by the great technological, economic, and social changes that have taken place. The Great Depression of the 1930s underscored economic changes beyond the control of any state; the airplane and television make use of airways that cannot be regulated effectively by a state; the national security requirements of the modern world require technically sophisticated national armed forces, not state militias. Especially in the last half century, technological, economic, and social changes have served as powerful stimuli for governmental centralization.

Yet the United States is far from a fully centralized system. Although the national government has grown greatly in power, the states have grown in power as well. The defining feature of modern federalism has become *cooperation*. The national government cannot govern the United States alone. It needs the cooperation of the states. Two of the leading students of American federalism have summed it up well: "Old-style federalism is a legal concept, emphasizing a constitutional division of authority and functions between a national government and state governments. . . . New-style federalism is a political and pragmatic concept, stressing the actual interdependence and sharing of functions between

In the United States, fighting fires is mainly a job for local governments. Fire departments and fire districts are established under local ordinances and state laws. In 1985, there were 317,000 firefighters in the nation's towns and cities.

Washington and the states and focusing on the leverage that each actor is able to exert on the other" (Reagan and Sanzone, 1981: 3).

The Web of Intergovernmental Relations

The old system of dual federalism is far from reality today. Twenty-five years ago, a leading student of federalism said it bluntly: "Federalism—old style—is dead. Yet federalism—new style—is alive and well and living in the United States. Its name is *intergovernmental relations*" (Reagan and Sanzone, 1981: 3). The term **intergovernmental relations** refers to the complex web of interrelationships among governments—the national government, the 50 state governments, and thousands of local governments. These interrelationships embrace contacts among national, state, and local governmental officials, mutual obligations, federal rules and guidelines, lateral cooperation, and financial transactions (Wright, 1982).

Local governments, providing the public services closest to the people, come in several forms—counties, municipal corporations, townships, school districts, and special districts. Although local governments are established by state laws and their powers and functions are controlled by the state goverments, the governmental system is highly pluralistic. From the citizen's-eye view, the state governments are often preferred to the federal government for performing various jobs. Figure 3–3 provides a good example. Most of us think that the state governments would run social programs more effectively than the federal government. Nearly half of us think that there is little difference between the two levels of government in "caring about the poor," though more of us rate the state government as "caring more" than rate the federal goverment as "caring more." And nearly three fourths of us think that "state and local officials are more sensitive than federal officials in knowing who deserves food stamps and welfare."

Sometimes jurisdictions overlap and the delivery of public services is made very complicated by the multiplicity of governments controlling the same area. One solution to this complexity has been city-county consolidation. For example, the city of Lexington and Fayette County, Kentucky, merged into a single government, as did the city of Columbus and Muscogee County, Georgia, and these consolidated governments proved more efficient and responsive than the multiple governments they replaced. Since the 1960s, the effective provision of public services by local governments has been enormously enhanced by direct support from the national government to localities. Such national-local intergovernmental relations have been mainly financial and have often involved bypassing the state governments.

In recognition that the growing maze of relations among governments was poorly coordinated and lacked direction, Congress enacted legislation in 1959 creating an Advisory Commission on Intergovernmental Relations (ACIR). Composed of members of Congress, federal executive branch officials, state governors and legislators, mayors, and county officials, the 26-member ACIR monitors how well the federal system seems to be operating and recommends improvements in intergovernmental relations.

The growth of national government activities and the even more dramatic growth of state and local government programs have heightened and amplified relations among levels of government. National, state, and local governments interact far more frequently than before, and the striking increase in national regulatory policies has resulted in the intergovernmentalization of almost everything. One pair of political scientists even speak of "galloping intergovernmentalization" (Glendening and Reeves, 1984: 86).

The Federal Aid Explosion

A sizable part of the transactions between governments involves money. The national government began extending **grants-in-aid** to the states early in the nation's history. This involved using the economic resources, especially the taxing power, of the national government to provide the funding for state or local governmental programs or services. In the early 19th century, this was done by giving the states proceeds from the sale of national land that they could use as an endowment for public schools. The New Deal brought a great upsurge in national aid in the 1930s, and another burst of growth occurred in the 1960s.

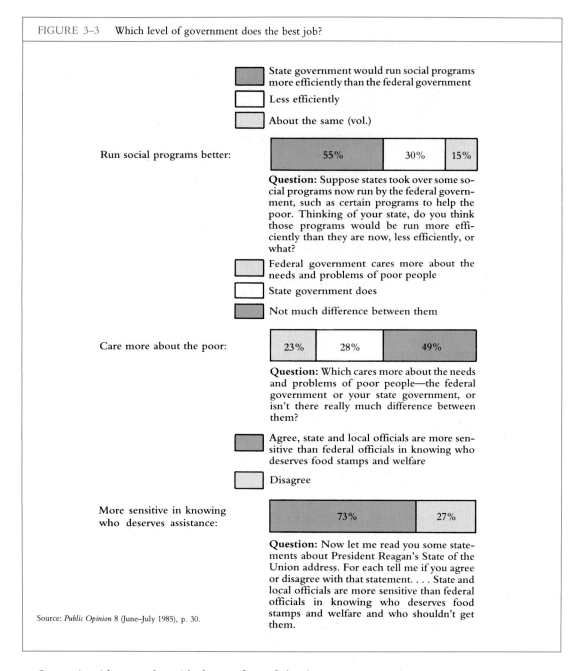

FIGURE 3–3   Which level of government does the best job?

State government would run social programs more efficiently than the federal government

Less efficiently

About the same (vol.)

Run social programs better:

| 55% | 30% | 15% |

Question: Suppose states took over some social programs now run by the federal government, such as certain programs to help the poor. Thinking of your state, do you think those programs would be run more efficiently than they are now, less efficiently, or what?

Federal government cares more about the needs and problems of poor people

State government does

Not much difference between them

Care more about the poor:

| 23% | 28% | 49% |

Question: Which cares more about the needs and problems of poor people—the federal government or your state government, or isn't there really much difference between them?

Agree, state and local officials are more sensitive than federal officials in knowing who deserves food stamps and welfare

Disagree

More sensitive in knowing who deserves assistance:

| 73% | 27% |

Question: Now let me read you some statements about President Reagan's State of the Union address. For each tell me if you agree or disagree with that statement. . . . State and local officials are more sensitive than federal officials in knowing who deserves food stamps and welfare and who shouldn't get them.

Source: *Public Opinion* 8 (June–July 1985), p. 30.

Grants-in-aid seemed an ideal way for a federal system to work. It is easy to see why a system of federal grants-in-aid to states and localities was so attractive to policymakers. If state and local governments needed more money for desirable governmental programs and services, the greater taxing power of the national government could be used to provide

States work together through interstate compacts. In 1921, New York and New Jersey established the Port of New York Authority by such a compact. The Port Authority operates bridges, tunnels, airports, and port and terminal facilities serving New York City and other communities in New York and New Jersey. In 1977, after the first landing of a Concorde at Kennedy Airport, this Port Authority police car stood vigil over the aircraft.

the money. And if there were gross and undesirable inequalities among the states in the provision of public services, then direct grants could be used to equalize the availability of those services. New York is a rich state, able to provide adequate welfare services to its less fortunate citizens; Mississippi, a very poor state, receives large amounts of federal aid to help it provide a welfare program for its citizens (though a more modest one than that of New York).

The increases in federal grants-in-aid to state and local governments have been important in providing services that Americans demand of their governments today. But it would be a mistake to think that the national government now finances everything. The state and local governments in this country still bear the major financial burden for providing nondefense services to their publics. In fact, state and local governments together spend more than 2½ times as much as the national government for civilian governmental services. It is still true that "education, roads, welfare, public health, hospitals, police, sanitation are primarily state and local responsibilities, and their cost falls mainly on state and local sources of revenue" (Aronson and Hilley, 1986: 1).

A growth industry

Federal grants-in-aid to state and local governments grew continuously from the 1960s through the 1980s, from $7 billion in current dollars in 1960 to more than $100 billion in the 1980s. The figures in Table 3–2 give some of the details for this pattern of growth. Federal grants grew in the

TABLE 3–2   Federal grants-in-aid to state and local governments

Years	Average annual grants-in-aid in current dollars (billions)	As a percentage of:			Grants in constant (1982) dollars (billions)
		State-local receipts from own sources	Total federal outlays	Gross national product	
1955–59	$ 4.5	13.5%	5.6%	1.0%	$ 16.4
1960–65	8.1	16.6	7.7	1.5	27.8
1965–69	15.6	20.3	10.0	2.0	46.0
1970–74	34.3	25.8	14.7	2.9	75.7
1975–79	67.6	30.8	16.2	3.6	100.7
1980–84	92.9	22.9	12.8	3.0	94.8
1985–88*	108.6	19.5	11.0	2.6	90.8

*Amounts for fiscal year 1988 are estimated.
Source: Advisory Commission on Intergovernmental Relations, *Significant Features of Fiscal Federalism, 1988 Edition* (Washington, D.C.: Advisory Commission on Intergovernmental Relations, 1987), p. 15.

1960s to nearly a third of the funds that state and local governments raised on their own and then subsided to about a fourth of state and local receipts. From the mid-1950s to the end of the 1970s, federal grants nearly tripled as a proportion of total federal fiscal outlays, and then their share of federal fiscal outlays ebbed in the 1980s. And over the same period, federal assistance to state and local governments grew from 1 percent of the **gross national product** (GNP) to more than 3 percent; then, such federal aid subsided to somewhat below 3 percent of GNP. In constant (1982) dollars, correcting for the ravages of inflation, federal aid to states and localities showed significant growth, increasing sixfold from the 1950s to the 1980s.

The administration of President Ronald Reagan was determined to cut the amount of federal aid to the states. Beginning in 1981, it initiated systematic reductions in federal assistance, especially in the **entitlement programs.** These programs provide cash or benefits in kind (such as food stamps) to persons whose incomes are below a certain level and who meet various other requirements. The reductions sought by President Reagan stemmed from two objectives: (1) to generally cut back the size of the domestic national budget and (2) to devolve governing responsibilities from the national government to the states. "At the national level," say two students of Reagan federalism, "programs that are most highly redistributive to politically vulnerable groups among the poor were most likely to be cut" (Nathan and Doolittle, 1987: 355). Among the entitlement programs, only Medicaid was protected from deep cuts, largely because of the political strength of the Medicaid constituency (middle-income elderly people) and the resistance of the states.

But the twin objectives of the Reagan administration, retrenchment of social programs and devolution to the states, worked at cross-purposes. Many of the states found funds to replace the federal aid cuts and otherwise protect social programs. This "paradox of devolution" meant that "to the extent that state and local governments responded to Reagan's devolutionary initiatives by increasing their own support for programs cut at the federal level, the Reagan goal of social program retrenchment was undercut" (Nathan and Doolittle, 1987: 357).

Varieties of federal aid

In 1963, there were 181 federal grant programs. The number of such programs grew to 534 by 1981, in response to a growing demand for government regulation and services. From the viewpoint of state and local officials, the national government became an increasingly important source of money, but the grant programs became increasingly complex and diverse. The Reagan administration sought to consolidate grant programs and to cut down the growth rate of federal grants. This effort succeeded in cutting the number of federal grant programs to 405 by 1984, more by consolidating programs than by eliminating them. What is more, the Reagan administration succeeded in slowing down the growth rate of aid programs, putting a greater burden on states to pay for their own programs, as Table 3–2 shows.

More than 80 percent of federal aid goes for four major categories of assistance: transportation, education, health, and income security. Most of the transportation grants have been for highways, but federal aid also goes to airports, railroads, and urban mass transit. The national government channels aid to education for a variety of purposes, including education of the disadvantaged, human development, employment training, elementary and secondary education, and various special programs. The lion's share of health aid is spent for Medicaid, but there are also alcohol and drug abuse programs and programs for mental health. The income security programs include food stamps, child nutrition, housing assistance, and payments to the old, the blind, and the disabled. Beyond these major programs, the national government provides grants-in-aid for environmental protection, energy conservation, agriculture, community and regional development, veterans' benefits, and the administration of justice.

In 1972, President Richard M. Nixon proposed a new relationship between the national government, on the one hand, and the state and local governments, on the other. At his recommendation, Congress passed legislation providing **general revenue sharing.** Under this legislation, the national government shared billions of dollars with the states and the 39,000 local governments. Localities used revenue sharing funds for all kinds of purposes, from paying firefighters' salaries to constructing roads. When the revenue sharing program ended in 1986, state and local govern-

Federal aid for highways enables the states to build and maintain roads. This stretch of a New York road is being rebuilt.

ments had received about $82 billion in general revenue sharing funds. The Reagan administration ended the program on the grounds that there was a deficit in the national coffers, while state and local governments enjoyed budget surpluses. Revenue sharing was intended to enhance state and local autonomy and provide fiscal equalization. But many local governments became dependent on it for ordinary operating expenses. When it was discontinued, some mayors asserted that this would cause municipal services to decline. But, in fact, the effects of revenue sharing were quite modest, since the amounts involved were small in relation to overall government spending levels.

Most federal grants-in-aid are **categorical grants.** For such grants, there exists a well-defined national purpose and states and local governments are given aid for a specific purpose—for health research, or beautification, or recreation, or community development. Since the mid-1960s, the federal government has created **block grants** for general programs, giving the states and localities considerable discretion in the spending of grant funds—for law enforcement, manpower training, transportation, or housing assistance.

President Ronald Reagan convinced Congress to enact, in the Omnibus Budget Reconciliation Act of 1981, a consolidation of a number of categorical grants into block grant programs. But categorical grants continue to be the basis of the grant-in-aid system. Categorical grants foster centralization because they entail national performance standards. And the established bureaucratic network administering categorical grant programs institutionalizes a centralizing bias. One political scientist put it this way:

PRACTICE OF POLITICS

How the Federal Government Regulates the States

Here is a list of the major national statutes that regulate what state and local governments can do:

Age Discrimination in Employment Act, amended in 1974 Prevents discrimination on the basis of age in state and local government employment.

Architectural Barriers Act of 1968 Makes federally occupied and funded buildings, facilities, and public conveyances accessible to the physically handicapped.

Civil Rights Act of 1964 Prevents discrimination on the basis of race, color, or national origin in federally assisted programs.

Civil Rights Act of 1968 Prevents discrimination on the basis of race, color, religion, sex, or national origin in the sale or rental of federally assisted housing.

Clean Air Act Amendments of 1970 Establishes national air quality and emissions standards.

Coastal Zone Management Act of 1972 Assures that federally assisted activities are consistent with federally approved state coastal zone management programs.

Davis-Bacon Act of 1931 Assures that locally prevailing wages are paid to construction workers employed under federal contracts and financial assistance programs.

Education Amendments of 1972 Prevents discrimination on the basis of sex in federally assisted education programs.

Education for All Handicapped Children Act of 1975 Provides a free appropriate public education to all handicapped children.

Equal Employment Opportunity Act of 1972 Prevents discrimination on the basis of race, color, religion, sex, or national origin in state and local government employment.

Fair Labor Standards Act Amendments of 1974 Extends federal minimum wage and overtime pay protection to state and local government employees.

Family Educational Rights and Privacy Act of 1974 Provides student and parental access to educational records while restricting access by others.

Federal Insecticide, Fungicide, and Rodenticide Act of 1972 Controls the use of pesticides that may be harmful to the environment.

(Continued)

A vast intergovernmental bureaucracy nurtured by federal funds supports centralization. This particular bureaucracy, representing the interests of federal grant beneficiaries—many of whom had been powerless in state and local politics—presents subnational politicians with a serious dilemma. Those politicians can support a centralized federalism, or they can mediate the political conflicts among subnational program beneficiaries and taxpayers

PRACTICE OF POLITICS

(Concluded)

Federal Water Pollution Control Act Amendments of 1972 Establishes federal effluent limitations to control the discharge of pollutants.

Flood Disaster Protection Act of 1973 Expands coverage of the national flood insurance program.

Highway Beautification Act of 1965 Controls and removes outdoor advertising along major highways.

Marine Protection Research and Sanctuaries Act Amendments of 1977 Prohibits ocean dumping of municipal sludge.

National Energy Conservation Policy Act of 1978 Establishes residential energy conservation plans.

National Environmental Policy Act of 1969 Assures consideration of the environmental impact of major federal actions.

National Health Planning and Resources Development Act of 1974 Establishes state and local health planning agencies and procedures.

National Historic Preservation Act of 1966 Protects properties of historical, architectural, archaeological, and cultural significance.

Occupational Safety and Health Act of 1970 Eliminates unsafe and unhealthful working conditions.

Public Utilities Regulatory Policies Act of 1978 Requires consideration of federal standards for the pricing of electricity and natural gas.

Rehabilitation Act of 1973 Prevents discrimination against otherwise qualified individuals on the basis of physical or mental handicap in federally assisted programs.

Resource Conservation and Recovery Act of 1976 Establishes standards for the control of hazardous wastes.

Safe Drinking Water Act of 1974 Assures the purity of drinking water.

Surface Mining Control and Reclamation Act of 1977 Establishes federal standards for the control of surface mining.

Water Quality Act of 1965 Establishes federal water quality standards for interstate waters.

Wholesale Poultry Products Act of 1968 Establishes systems for the inspection of poultry sold in intrastate commerce.

Source: Advisory Commission on Intergovernmental Relations, *Regulatory Federalism: Policy, Process, Impact, and Reform* (Washington, D.C.: Advisory Commission on Intergovernmental Relations, 1984).

if Washington's role is reduced. Until now, those politicians have usually supported centralized federalism. (Chubb, 1985: 292)

Altogether, today there are 392 categorical grants, 12 block grants, and general revenue sharing, bringing the total number of federal grant-in-aid programs to 405. Many of these programs include formulas that require

Regulatory federalism in action. In 1974, Congress passed a law under which states risked losing federal highway grants if they did not adopt a 55-mile-per-hour speed limit.

matching—that is, the grants are awarded on the condition that states or local governments pay part of the program costs.

By the 1980s, it was clear that "federal financial aid has created a nationally dominated system of shared power and shared functions" and that "the basic relationship between the nation and the states today, whatever the theory or practice of federalism may have been earlier, is one of interdependence rather than independence" (Reagan and Sanzone, 1981: 157). Recent efforts have been made to return government functions, and the funding for them, to the states in order to restore "states' rights." Moreover, the struggle to reduce the federal budget deficit has precipitated cuts in grant-in-aid programs. But ideological disputes and fiscal pressures are unlikely to bring about a fundamental change in the existing basic framework of intergovernmental relations (Golonka, 1985).

Regulatory Federalism

Federal grants to states (and, for that matter, state grants to local governments) have a way of coming with strings attached. In the last 25 years, as federal aid proliferated, federal regulation became much more extensive.

The 55-mile-per-hour speed limit

One highly publicized example is the 1974 National Maximum Speed Act, which withheld 10 percent of highway grants from states whose legislatures did not pass a 55-mph speed limit. Proponents of this act argued that

Regulatory federalism in action. In 1987, Congress relented somewhat in requiring a 55-mile-per-hour speed limit, allowing a 65-mile-per-hour speed limit on some stretches of the interstate highway system.

the mandatory 55-mph limit would conserve precious oil and reduce death on the highways. Because the states were highly dependent on the national government for highway funds, the state legislatures complied with the new speed limit, many of them grudgingly.

Polls showed that (depending on when the poll was taken) half or more than half of Americans favored the 55-mph limit, but many state legislators felt that they had been blackmailed by the government in Washington, D.C. There was controversy over the alleged benefits of the speed limit, some arguing that fuel consumption and highway deaths were not affected by the limit, but rather by safer and more efficient automobiles. Many argued that the interstate highway system was suited to faster speed limits. Finally, in 1987, Congress passed a highway funding bill over the veto of President Reagan that allowed states to raise the speed limit to 65 mph on parts of the interstate highway system lying outside urban areas of 50,000 people or more. But the 55-mph federal restriction continues to apply to other roads, including state turnpikes.

The 21-year-minimum drinking age

More recently, a threat was made to cut federal highway construction money if states did not adopt a minimum drinking age of 21. Under pressure from members of Congress, Secretary of Transportation Elizabeth Dole, and a lobbying group called Mothers Against Drunk Driving (MADD), in 1984 President Reagan endorsed a bill requiring a 21-year minimum drinking age and Congress quickly passed it. In signing the bill, the president said, "The problem is bigger than the states." He added, "With the problem so clear-cut and the proven solution at hand, we have no misgivings about this judicious use of federal power" (quoted in Golonka, 1985: 9).

Again, the threat for states failing to comply was the federal highway fund—states that failed to require a minimum drinking age of 21 by 1987 stood to lose 5 percent of their highway grant. The penalty increased to 10 percent in 1988 and to 15 percent thereafter. Many state officials were outraged by the drinking age requirement, arguing that it violated states' rights, upset the federal balance, and blackmailed the states. But advocates of national uniformity in the drinking age argued that raising the drinking age reduced automobile fatalities involving teenage drivers.

When the Uniform Minimum Drinking-Age Law was passed, 23 states had a minimum drinking age of 21. By the 1987 deadline, 19 additional states had adopted the 21-year minimum age. The remaining eight states refused to comply. They were Colorado, Idaho, Louisiana, Montana, Ohio, South Dakota, Tennessee (for military personnel only), and Wyoming. Louisiana fell into line in time to avoid a penalty, but the other states temporarily lost 5 percent of their fiscal 1987 highway allocations. One by one, these states eventually came into compliance. One of them, South Dakota, had a 21-year age minimum for the purchase of hard liquor but permitted persons 19 and older to buy low-alcohol 3.2 beer.

South Dakota took its case to the U.S. Supreme Court. It argued that the federal law was an unconstitutional intrusion into an area reserved to the states under the 21st Amendment (which repealed Prohibition). South Dakota's case was supported by the National Conference of State Legislatures, the U.S. Conference of Mayors, the National Governors' Association, and the National Association of Counties. But in June 1987, the Supreme Court upheld the drinking age law in the case of *South Dakota* v. *Dole*. By a 7-to-2 vote, the Court held that Congress, under its spending power, could impose conditions on the states for receiving funds, including a minimum drinking age.

The minimum drinking age law and the speed limit requirement are dramatic illustrations of the national government's ability to use the threat of withholding federal aid as a means of regulation in realms formerly considered the exclusive province of the states.

Regulatory federalism in action. In 1984, Congress passed a law requiring the states to set a 21-year-old minimum drinking age or else lose part of their federal highway money. Grudgingly, the states complied. This bartender is carding a customer under state drinking laws required by the national government.

Forms of regulatory federalism

There are four common forms of regulatory federalism. First, the national government may give states and localities **direct orders.** For instance, the Equal Employment Opportunity Act of 1972 flatly prohibits job discrimination by state and local governments on the basis of race, religion, sex, or national origin.

Second, **crosscutting requirements** may be included in grant legislation. That is, recipients of federal financial assistance may be required to comply with certain standards. For example, the Civil Rights Act of 1964 prohibited racial discrimination in federally assisted programs. Subsequent legislation protected other groups, including the handicapped, the elderly, and women.

Third, federal grant-in-aid programs may incorporate **crossover sanctions.** Federal sanctions may be imposed in one program area in order to get state and local governments to comply in some other area. The 55-mph speed limit and the 21-year minimum drinking age illustrate this strategy.

Fourth, the technique **partial preemption** may be used. Here, the federal government lays down the basic policies to be followed in a program but gives the state or local governments responsibility for administering the program if they meet certain standards. The Clean Air Act Amendments of 1970 set federal air quality standards but required the states to devise ways to implement and enforce those standards.

State and local government officials and the Advisory Commission on Intergovernmental Relations have taken a very dim view of the rapid escalation of regulatory federalism. In 1984, the ACIR conducted a full-scale study of federal regulation of the states and local governments. The commission concluded that "federal intergovernmental regulation is warranted only when a clear and convincing case has demonstrated both the necessity of such intervention and a marked inability of state and local governments to address the regulatory problem involved" (ACIR, 1984: 259). Despite such objections, federal regulation of states and localities appears likely to continue, and even to increase, in the future.

CONCLUSIONS

The debate goes on over what functions the national government should perform and what functions should be performed by the states. Today there is little left of the constitutional claim that the states have sovereign powers beyond the minimum needed to preserve their existence. But the prudence of national versus state performance of governmental functions is a matter of continuing discussion. Some advocate strengthening national power, arguing that centralization is needed to cope with the problems of the environment, poverty, health, and the economy. Others urge that the system be decentralized through national legislation reallocating governmental functions to the states. President Ronald Reagan proposed a "new federalism," recommending a transfer of services from national to state control, but such a program was not pressed by the White House or debated in Congress. Some have even suggested that a constitutional convention be held every few years to reconsider the national-state division of powers and functions. In the meantime, the states and their progeny, local governments, have grown stronger as a result of effective state and local leadership, institutional reform, economic development, and federal aid.

State and local governments have grown in size, strength, and bankroll. These days they have the muscle to demand a larger share of authority and governmental programs. They have organized lobbying groups (such as the National Governors' Association and the U.S. Conference of Mayors), opened offices in Washington, D.C., and sent lobbyists to influence Congress. Federal largess has grown and become a more attractive target for grantsmanship by state and local officials. On the other side of the coin, the national government has found that its own concept of the national interest can be fostered by attaching strings to its very attractive grants-in-aid. The push and pull between officials at different levels of government continues with only small changes one way or another in a system that may have reached an equilibrium. Two recent presidents—Jimmy Carter and Ronald Reagan—were state governors before they moved to the White House. President Carter served as governor of Georgia, and President Reagan served as governor of California. Both came to Washington with intentions of improving federal-state-local relations. Neither had the successes he had hoped for.

In this chapter, we have stressed the following major points about American federalism:

1. A federal constitution divides governmental powers and functions between a central government and some number of constituent subnational units. The U.S. Constitution assigns governing powers to the national government and reserves other powers to the states. The founders also intended to ensure national preeminence by means of the supremacy clause in the Constitution, but they could not have foreseen the extent to which the verdict of history would enhance national power.

2. The United States has become a more centralized system. But the state and local governments have also become more important, more

A rough idea of the nature of religious belief in the United States is given by public opinion surveys. A 1971 Gallup poll showed that about 9 percent of Americans were agnostics, that 11 percent were atheists, and that 77 percent believed in God. Recent Gallup polls show that 9 out of 10 Americans believe in God or a universal spirit. In 1981, about 70 percent of those polled said that they believed in the existence of a Heaven. In 1983, 7 out of 10 Americans claimed to be members of a church or synagogue; 40 percent said that they had attended a house of worship in the past seven days. In a 1978 survey, 40 percent said that they had "been 'born again' or had a 'born again' experience, that is, a turning point in your life when you committed yourself to Christ." In 1985, 83 percent said that they "feel close to God most of the time," with only 16 percent saying they were "not close" or were nonbelievers.

Prayer is an important part of many public events in this country. Every day when they are in session, meetings of the U.S. Senate and House of Representatives are opened with a prayer given by a member of the clergy. In 1954, Congress added the words *under God* to the Pledge of Allegience. The words *In God we trust* appear on our coins. Polls show that most Americans believe both in the separation of church and state and in the basic religious character of our political tradition. Many Americans think that their country has moral commitments grounded in religious belief, commitments requiring humanitarian policies.

Religious beliefs can play a direct political role when churches, clergy, or fervently religious individuals get involved in politics. In the 1984 presidential election, for instance, black churches provided an important locale for the Reverend Jesse Jackson's campaign to capture the Democratic presidential nomination. More recently, the "new Christian Right" has become politically active, establishing political action committees (PACs), raising millions of dollars, and campaigning for political offices (see Liebman and Wuthnow, 1983).

The major Christian evangelical organizations played an important part in the 1984 reelection of President Ronald Reagan. Highly visible in this effort was the Moral Majority, an organization founded in 1979 by the Reverend Jerry Falwell, pastor of a huge Baptist church in Lynchburg, Virginia. The evangelical political movement has been stimulated by popular radio and television evangelists, whose fund-raising and political appeals became more intense in the mid-1980s. TV evangelist and broadcaster Marion G. "Pat" Robertson, the son of a former Virginia U.S. senator, became active in presidential politics in 1986. He headed the Christian Broadcasting Network (CBN) and hosted the "700 club" religious talk show. Robertson took an active part in Republican party politics during the early stages of the 1988 presidential election, seeking the support of Republican national party convention delegates for the presidential nomination.

Television evangelist and broadcaster Marion G. "Pat" Robertson on the campaign trail in 1988. Although Robertson failed to win the Republican presidential nomination, he and his supporters were influential in national Republican politics.

Rights of property

The framers of the Constitution thought that human freedom depended on the sanctity of property because citizens would feel that they had a stake in the preservation and protection of the nation only if they were guaranteed the right to their own property. The framers themselves defended the Constitution because it established legal principles that would protect their property. Under the Constitution, government cannot take private property for public use without fair payment to the owner. The 5th Amendment provides that "no person shall be . . . deprived of life, liberty, or property without due process of law; nor shall private property be taken for public use without just compensation.

Americans' beliefs about property are shown in diverse ways. For one thing, we strongly believe in the system of private property. For years, polls have shown that there is overwhelming opposition to government ownership or operation of the basic industries. The classic definition of **socialism** is that it is a society in which the government owns and runs the major industries—steel, transportation, energy production. Few Americans favor government ownership of industries; most of us prefer private ownership, or "free enterprise." Along with this preference for private property, our feelings about property are shown by our emphasis

on making money and by the high value that we give work and its rewards.

The government routinely and properly takes part of our property in
the form of taxes. Personal income taxes are, at least in name, **progressive;** that is, the percentage of income paid in taxes goes up as income
goes up. In contrast, property taxes and sales taxes are **regressive;** that is,
such taxes take more from low-income people than from high-income
people. Because of this, one might expect low-income people to favor
income taxes and high-income people to favor property and sales taxes.
Surveys concerning forms of taxation do lean very slightly in these directions. But, strangely, Americans' attitudes toward the fairness or unfairness of different forms of taxation do not differ much by income levels.

For at least the last 20 years, we have complained about high taxes.
Starting in the 1970s, discontent about taxes arose in several states, which
passed laws limiting state and local taxes. The most famous of these "tax
revolts" was Proposition 13 in California, which limited property taxes.
Public opinion polls consistently show that most Americans consider our
taxes unreasonable and that many Americans actually favor lower taxes
while advocating more government spending. The strongest objection to
the income tax comes from those in the higher-income groups.

To say that our political culture is one in which beliefs in equality,
freedom of expression, religious liberty, and rights of property are widely
shared does not mean that America is a democratic paradise. In everyday
use, we often see disagreement about who is equal to whom or about
what freedoms should be allowed in practice. The protection of rights
depends heavily on the willingness and ability of government officials to
enforce them, and sometimes these officials have been unwilling or unable
to do so. Organized bigotry, such as that of the Ku Klux Klan or the
American Nazi party, persists in this country and is free to do so. Democratic values require that we permit dissension and ideological diversity.
Moreover, rights often conflict with one another. Social welfare may conflict with the drive of individuals to make money. Busing to promote
equality of education for blacks limits the right of parents to choose the
schools their children attend. When cities force renters or homeowners to
clear out so that a new highway can be built, the public need for transportation may seem to violate the right to private property.

Priorities among these basic political beliefs are changing. Property
rights have become more regulated as government has sought to cope
with the growth and influence of business corporations. The civil rights
movement of the last generation brought liberty to the forefront and gave
it high priority. Some think that our society now values liberty and equality over achievement, complaining that the social welfare system stifles
incentive. Since the New Deal of the 1930s, tax and welfare policies have
changed the value of equality. Still, in both their constancy and their
changes, equality, liberty, religion, and property are at the core of our
political beliefs.

WHAT AMERICANS KNOW ABOUT POLITICS

Americans are not true political animals. They do not have much interest in or concern for politics and government in their daily lives. We live in a country where most people feel politically secure and think that they need to be concerned about what the government is doing only when there is a crisis. In general, Americans simply know little about political events, officials, or institutions. Most of us know who Madonna is, or that Columbus discovered America, or that the Lone Ranger shouted "Hi Ho, Silver," without knowing much about political goings-on and without knowing the name of our congressman or the difference between executive, legislative, and judicial branches of government.

In fact, the political awareness of Americans is mixed. Most of us know who the president is, or who the state governor is, but many of us cannot recall the name of our congressman or state legislator. For instance, polls regularly show that less than half of us know the names of both the U.S. senators from our state. And we are not very aware of the details of governmental organization, the specifics of political party control, or the intricacies of public policy debates. Yet Americans show remarkable attentiveness to political affairs on many occasions. For example, during the 1987 Senate hearings on the support of the Nicaraguan rebels (the "Contras") with money obtained from the secret sale of weapons to Iran, an astonishingly large television audience watched the gavel-to-gavel coverage on C-Span. When political conflict becomes highly visible, the political awareness of Americans can be impressive.

The political attentiveness of Americans may often run in neutral, but the brute fact is that we compare pretty favorably with citizens in other democratic countries. According to public opinion surveys, American politicians are generally more visible to the public than the politicians of many other countries, including most of the European democracies. A major exception is Britain. A study directly comparing the visibility of U.S. congressmen and British members of Parliament (MPs) shows incumbent MPs are about twice as visible as U.S. representatives (Cain, Ferejohn, and Fiorina, 1987: 28). About a third of the Americans polled could recall the name of their representative, while two thirds of the British polled could do this. At the same time, about four fifths of Americans know something about their representative and recognize their representative's name when shown it. Interestingly enough, the same study also shows that Americans are in more frequent contact with their legislator than are British constituents and that U.S. representatives are viewed more positively by their constituents than British MPs are by theirs.

It is all too easy, but it may be misleading, to use public opinion polls to find Americans politically unaware and ignorant. We do not go overboard on politics, but neither are we found lacking as citizens. In short, Americans may not be political animals, but they can be aroused to political attentiveness and they are not fools.

Americans show very strong pride in the **regime** under which they are governed—the constitutional system, the people of the political community, and the historic political institutions of the nation. This kind of patriotism—national pride—is often uncovered by pollsters who are told by average citizens that they are proud to be Americans and proud of the liberties and freedoms they enjoy.

But Americans have always distrusted political authorities, and they still do. **Political trust** refers to the confidence that people have in the way the government is run and in the integrity of the people who run it. In research on political attitudes, such trust has come to be measured by asking five questions:

1. How much of the time do you think you can trust the government in Washington to do what is right—just about always, most of the time, or only some of the time?

2. Do you think that the people in the government waste a lot of the money we pay in taxes, waste some of it, or don't waste very much of it?

3. Do you feel that almost all of the people running the government are smart people who usually know what they are doing, or do you think that quite a few of them don't seem to know what they are doing?

4. Do you think that quite a few of the people running the government are a little crooked, that not very many of them are crooked, or that hardly any of them are crooked?

5. Would you say that the government is pretty much run by a few big interests looking out for themselves or that it is run for the benefit of all the people?

When these questions were first asked of Americans in the 1950s, large majorities gave trusting responses, saying that they trusted the government in Washington at least most of the time, that the government did not generally waste tax money, that the people running the government were smart and that not many of them were crooks, and that the government was run for the benefit of all.

In the 1960s and 1970s, levels of political trust declined sharply. This decline in the 1960s is usually associated with the growing public disenchantment with the Vietnam War. A precipitous drop in trust in the early 1970s appears to have been due to the effects of the so-called **Watergate** affair, the 1972 burglary, sanctioned by the Nixon White House, of Democratic party offices in the Watergate building in Washington, which resulted in Senate hearings and President Nixon's resignation.

Because the political trust survey questions have been asked for three decades, we can easily plot how citizens' political trust has changed over the years. Similar trajectories were followed by the replies to all five of

TRUST IN
THE SYSTEM

The benevolent leader. American children often have an idealized image of the president's role. President George Washington is depicted here as a sacred, godly figure, in the hands of the angels. In his own time, Washington was highly respected by his political associates and revered by the public; later generations viewed him as more than human.

the trust items, so in Figure 4–2, for the sake of illustration, we show changes in the percentages of those who say that the government is "run for the benefit of all the people." The figure dramatizes the high levels of political trust at the beginning of Lyndon B. Johnson's presidency and the marked decline in political trust that has occurred since then. However, political trust took an upturn in the 1980s, perhaps largely due to confidence in President Ronald Reagan and favorable economic conditions.

Research on political attitudes has demonstrated that the extent of trust in government is closely tied to class differences. Distrust is highest among the working and lower classes. Trust is highest among the middle and upper-middle class. Also, there is a marked difference between whites and blacks. Since the mid-1960s, distrust has grown much more among blacks than among whites (Abramson, 1983: 193–238). Finally, Ameri-

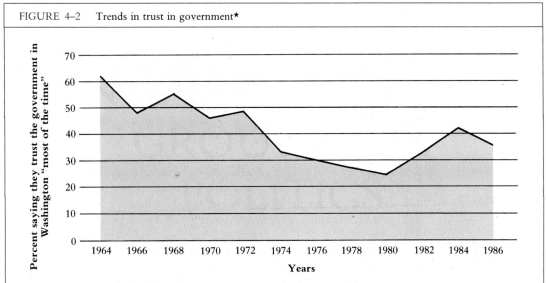

FIGURE 4–2   Trends in trust in government*

Percent saying they trust the government in Washington "most of the time"

Years

*Respondents were asked: "How much of the time do you think you can trust the government in Washington to do what is right—just about always, most of the time, or only some of the time?" The figure shows the percentage saying that they trust the government most of the time.

Sources: The data for 1964 to 1978 come from Warren E. Miller, Arthur H. Miller, and Edward J. Schneider, *American National Election Studies Data Sourcebook* (Cambridge, Mass.: Harvard University Press, 1980). The data for more recent years come from the codebooks for the University of Michigan National Election Studies.

cans' trust in government may depend on their economic outlook; people trust in government more when it produces economic conditions favorable to their lives.

People with extremely low trust in the system are said to be **alienated.** Highly alienated persons may become so disgusted with the system that they emigrate—to Canada, or Australia, or Mexico. Not very many Americans choose to do this. What effects do the alienated have on our politics? Apparently not much. James Wright, a political sociologist, draws two conclusions from his research on the impact of political alienation. First, he notes a connection between the actual use of political influence and the belief that one *can* be influential. He concludes that "the alienated are drawn from social groups whose members characteristically participate little in politics, are inactive in political or other voluntary associations, and have little of the money, time, or resources that effective politicking requires." These politically alienated people probably have little effect on the political system. Wright portrays the typical alienated person as aging, poorly educated, and working class, unlikely to attend church, inattentive to the mass media, probably not interested or involved in much of anything outside the family, work, and perhaps a close circle of friends. The common suggestion that political alienation represents a "threat" to democratic regimes seems farfetched in light of these results. (Wright, 1976: 165)

Second, he shows that such alienation is not strongly related to other political feelings or actions. Because of the political isolation of the alienated, it would be very hard to group them into a mass political movement. Thus, Wright feels that they pose little threat.

The decline in trust in government traced in Figure 4–2 could be repeated for most of the major institutions in the country. It was not only public confidence in government that declined after the mid-1960s. So, too, did public confidence in business, labor, education, religion, the military, and the press. This general decline in trust in major institutions seemed to reflect loss of confidence in those running the institutions, rather than a crisis of legitimacy for the system as such (Lipset and Schneider, 1983: 375–412).

Because the tumbling of political trust has focused on politicians and government officials, it has effected changes in personnel rather than demands for changes in the system itself. Even those who distrust the government often express national pride, and few of them advocate major changes. An interesting study conducted in 1972, when political trust was plummeting, showed that strong pride in our form of government was expressed not only by almost all of those with "high" trust in government but also by fully three fourths of those with "low" political trust (Citrin, 1974: 975). The lesson seems to be that our political culture is not monolithic. Many who express pride in our system of government are apt to complain, criticize, and distrust. We are cynical about the system and about our role in it. In juggling such feelings, we show, on the one hand, that we are proud of the strength and effectiveness of our constitutional system and, on the other hand, that, like our colonial forebears, we distrust power and those who have it.

CYNICISM ABOUT POLITICIANS

Politicians are often the butt of jokes and cynicism. They are said to be immoral, crooked, incompetent, and weak. Negative attitudes about politicians have been characteristic of American life for a long time. The 19th-century writer Artemus Ward said on one Fourth of July: "I am not a politician, and my other habits are good." In 1944, e. e. cummings wrote a poem called "One Times One" in which he said, "A politician is an arse upon which everyone has sat except a man." In *Pudd'nhead Wilson,* Mark Twain wrote: "It could probably be shown by facts and figures that there is no distinctively native American criminal class except Congress." Many Americans share this kind of cynicism.

One edge of our **political cynicism** is ambivalence about political power. On the other hand, we may view power as protective, self-sacrificing, and benevolent. Uncle Sam is one of our symbols of national security and paternalism. Public opinion polls show that substantial pluralities believe that men and women in political life are deprived of their privacy, are often unfairly criticized, and make real sacrifices for public service. We often admire highly visible politicians and give high prestige to political occupations. The Gallup poll regularly asks which men and women are admired most, and public officials usually dominate. And research on occupational prestige has shown for decades that a number of political offices are considered among the most prestigious occupations. Of more than fourscore occupations that have been looked at, those of Supreme Court justice, state governor, cabinet secretary, congressman, and big-city mayor are among the most highly regarded.

On the other hand, we are often negative about politicians and about politics as a vocation. The polls indicate that at least 8 out of 10 Americans think that "most elected officials promise one thing at election time and do something different once in office." And many Americans believe that a lot of politicians take **graft** (money acquired dishonestly by taking advantage of one's official position). The majority view is that politicians are apt to be corrupt and crooked. Few parents aspire to a political career for their children. Polls asking "If you had a child, would you like to see him or her go into politics as a life's work?" have never shown fewer than two thirds who say no.

These mixed feelings toward politicians may occur because we expect more than we can get. On the one hand, we believe that political leaders should be honest, hardworking, competent, and subservient to the public interest. But on the other hand, graft and corruption, poor judgment, and stupidity among politicians arise often enough to make us suspicious and distrustful. Cynicism toward politics and politicians may help protect us against excesses of power. But cynicism has its drawbacks. For one thing, public opinion really does not treat politicians very fairly; far fewer politicians are crooked than most people think. For another, cynicism about politicians and the belief that politics is immoral surely discourage civic participation.

Another edge of political cynicism is belief in **conspiracies.** We often believe that the many are controlled by the few for evil and immoral reasons (Hofstadter, 1965). Our political history is filled with examples of widespread belief in conspiracies about political movements and events. We are not saying that conspiracies never exist; for instance, there was surely a well-planned conspiracy to kill President Lincoln in 1865. What we are saying is that Americans often believe that public affairs are manipulated by conspiracies, whether or not this is true.

Behind every church door is a Freemason bent on undermining orthodox Christian virtue! The cause of the evils of the welfare state is the labor unions! Strikes are fomented by the communists! War efforts are undermined by "subversives"! The economic difficulties of the nation are caused by the international bankers! Behind every door in the State Department

McCarthyism

Joe McCarthy was America's most successful national demagogue. In the early 1950s, the Cold War between the United States and the Soviet Union made many Americans fear the threat of communism. Joseph R. McCarthy, elected to the U.S. Senate from Wisconsin in 1946, became nationally prominent because of his crusade against communism between 1950 and 1954.

McCarthy claimed that the State Department had been infiltrated by Communists. He accused many people in government of being "fellow travelers" and charged leading army officers and civilian officials of the army with communist sympathies. Many innocent people were falsely accused. Their reputations were destroyed, and many of them lost their livelihoods as well.

Public fear of communism, some-times hysterical, made McCarthy's charges seem credible. He was feared by senators, government officials, and many media people. Even President Eisenhower could not find an effective way to curb McCarthy's reckless and unsupported charges. McCarthy created a climate of fear. Many people were afraid to express opinions, especially about our policies toward Russia or about his assaults on freedom. Finally, McCarthy was brought down by the Senate itself. In 1954, it condemned him for conduct "contrary to Senate traditions."

Herbert Block, the cartoonist for the *Washington Post* who signs himself "Herblock," coined the term *McCarthyism*. It has become a synonym for mudslinging and for baselessly defaming a person or a class of people.

U.S. Senator Joseph McCarthy [left front] and his chief aide, Roy Cohn [center].

lurks a communist ready to betray us! President Kennedy's assassination was planned and carried out by pro-Castro Cubans who hated him! Behind all acts of terrorism or skyjacking are Libya's Colonel Qaddafi or the fanatic Iranian followers of the Ayatollah Khomeini! Conspiracy theories provide quick, easy, and simple answers to frightening, worrisome events.

In the 1820s, it was widely believed that Freemasons had infiltrated the U.S. government. People thought that this alleged Masonic conspiracy planned to subvert orthodox Christian beliefs. A political party, the Anti-Masons, became a strong movement in the 1820s and 30s. In the 1880s and 90s, the Populist movement was built around the "widespread Populist idea that all American history since the Civil War could be understood as a sustained conspiracy of the international money power" (Richard Hofstadter, in Curry and Brown, 1972: 100).

Fears of a communist conspiracy accompanied the growth of labor unions at the turn of the century. A "red scare" followed the Great Steel Strike of 1919. After the Japanese attacked Pearl Harbor in 1941, many feared a subversive conspiracy among Japanese-Americans on the West Coast; 120,000 Americans of Japanese descent, most of them native-born citizens, were interned in camps called "relocation centers." This was one of the most glaring deprivations of citizens' rights in our history.

In the 1950s, Senator Joseph McCarthy of Wisconsin led and symbolized what has come to be known as **McCarthyism.** He and his supporters attacked what they thought was a communist plot to subvert the government. In the 1960s, "corporate imperialism" was a concern of the New Left, which thought that democratic institutions had been perverted by a power elite led by a "corporate directorate." When President Kennedy was killed in 1963, many believed that the alleged assassin, Lee Harvey Oswald, could not have killed the president alone. No hard evidence of a plot has been found, though massive investigations have been conducted. But periodic efforts to rekindle the probe into Kennedy's assassination have had an effect. In 1983, 20 years after Kennedy's assassination, fully 80 percent of Americans told the Gallup pollsters that they thought there had been a conspiracy.

POLITICAL IDEOLOGY IN AMERICA

Americans rarely voice strong opinions on political issues, and it is often said that our politics is not very ideological. We can take **ideology** to mean a set of beliefs that is a tightly organized, logical, and consistent program of action. We may speak of the ideology of socialism, communism, fascism, or nazism. In that strict sense of the term, there are few ideologues in American politics. Many people hold inconsistent attitudes toward political issues. One of the most common is favoring the raising of government spending and the reduction of taxes in the same breath! Yet a distinct and important minority of Americans adhere to the tenets of particular systems of beliefs. The most common are **liberal** ideology and **conservative** ideology.

TABLE 4–1   How Americans identify themselves ideologically (percent)

Ideological self-designation	1976	1978	1980	1982	1984	1986
Conservative	25	31	34	27	29	30
Middle-of-the-road	25	27	20	22	23	27
Liberal	16	20	14	15	18	18
Don't know	33	27	32	36	30	25
Total	100	100	100	100	100	100

Sources: Warren E. Miller, Arthur H. Miller, and Edward J. Schneider, *American National Election Studies Sourcebook, 1952–1978* (Cambridge, Mass.: Harvard University Press, 1980), p. 95. The data for 1980 to 1986 are from the codebooks of the American National Election Studies, University of Michigan Center for Political Studies.

Liberals and Conservatives

There are liberals and conservatives in American politics, and there are some **libertarians** and **populists** as well. What do these ideological labels mean? This question can be answered in various ways. One way to answer it is historically. *Liberalism* and *conservatism* are terms with hoary and dignified lineages. We will not try in this book to unravel all the historical complexity of the ideological labels.

Another approach is to say that these labels mean what people think they mean. The Center for Political Studies at the University of Michigan has its interviewers ask people to identify themselves as conservative, liberal, or middle-of-the-road, and about two thirds of Americans can do this. The results are shown in Table 4–1. These ideological categories obviously have some meaning for Americans, though those who can be grouped together as self-styled liberals or conservatives hold remarkably divergent views on policy issues. Nevertheless, ideological self-placement is correlated with party identification: liberals tend to be Democrats, and conservatives tend to be Republicans.

Yet another approach is to define ideological tendencies in the light of their main features. Two such features commonly separate ideological groups: attitudes toward governmental intervention in the economy and attitudes toward the expansion or protection of personal freedoms. We can combine these two dimensions to define four ideological tendencies, as Figure 4–3 shows. Defined in this shorthand manner, a liberal is one who generally favors the intervention of the government in economic affairs (i.e., regulating business) and supports the expansion of personal freedoms (i.e., civil liberties). Senator Edward "Ted" Kennedy, Democrat of Massachusetts, is an exemplar of the liberal in American politics today. Conservatives tend to oppose government intervention in the economy and favor constraints on personal behavior to preserve traditional values. For many years, Senator Barry Goldwater, Republican of Arizona, exempli-

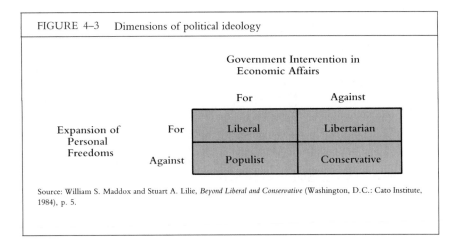

FIGURE 4–3   Dimensions of political ideology

Source: William S. Maddox and Stuart A. Lilie, *Beyond Liberal and Conservative* (Washington, D.C.: Cato Institute, 1984), p. 5.

fied the modern conservative; he ran as the Republican presidential candidate in 1964.

Liberals and conservatives make up the largest and most familiar numbers of those who are ideologically oriented. But ideological politics, when it arises, is often too complicated to fit perfectly on a liberal-conservative continuum. Populists and libertarians share the ideological stage and make political discourse diverse.

Populists agree with liberals that the government should intervene in the economy to benefit the average citizen, but they have also favored using governmental power to enforce their own beliefs about personal moral behavior (e.g., prohibition of the manufacture and sales of alcoholic beverages). Populist politicians are often found in the South—for example, Huey Long of Louisiana, who served both state governor and as U.S. senator in the 1920s and 30s and left a legacy to that state's politics.

Finally libertarians favor expanding individual freedoms, but they generally oppose government regulation of the economy. A diverse group both in adherents and in issue stands, libertarians basically favor free market mechanisms in the economy (a view they share with conservatives), but they vociferously oppose the intrusion of government in the area of personal freedoms and civil liberties. Libertarian belief is highly individualistic. A Libertarian party began to run candidates for president in 1972. It has established state and local party organizations, and its candidates have appeared on the ballot in all 50 states.

Few Political Ideologues

Despite their widespread use, the labels *liberal* and *conservative* do not have strong meaning to most people. Those who say that they are "liberal" or "conservative" often cannot explain what this means in terms of public policies. Many Americans are liberal on some things and conservative on others. Only a small minority of Americans are hard-core **ideologues**—that is, they adhere consistently to the tenets of a particular system of beliefs, have a clear idea what the labels *liberal* and *conservative* mean, and directly connect their beliefs on issues with their partisan choices in elections. In these terms, about a fifth of Americans qualify as ideologues (Flanigan and Zingale, 1983: 108).

The fact that only a small group of Americans are political ideologues does not mean that we are adrift politically. Few of us have the sophisticated, coordinated attitudes that would qualify as a full-blown ideology. Many of us, however, have deep-seated conceptions of our democratic rights. As two keen observers of ideology in U.S. politics point out, "To say that the large public does not consist of ideologues is not to say that it is feckless." On the contrary, "the American public demonstrably has a strong sense of its own basic democratic rights and has no reluctance to assert itself with respect to those rights" (Lipset and Raab, 1970: 430).

Most of us have beliefs about freedom and equality. We have ideas about what the government should do and about our roles as citizens. Some citizens, and a lot of our political leaders, not only believe strongly in democratic principles but also practice them. The concrete application of democratic principles

> calls for conceptual skills, historic perspective, and wide-based integrated belief systems which for the most part do not exist. . . . massive numbers of Americans who presumably have a ritual attachment to the concept of free speech and would reject any gross attempts to subvert it do not understand or have a commitment to the fine points of that concept when hard-core dissenters intrude upon their sensibilities. The American people would reject any gross attempt to subvert religious freedom, but almost half of them say that if a man does not believe in God, he should not be allowed to run for public office. And a majority of them, while jealous of due process, would throw away the book and resort to the whip when dealing with sex criminals. In short, . . . abstract and complex democratic institutions and practices have stood and flourished in America because some people understood them and most of the rest were loyal to them. This loyalty was based on an inertia of investment in the country, the system, and the traditional political structure. (Lipset and Raab, 1970: 431)

An eminent political scientist once said: "Democracy is an odd system. It requires that most men tolerate freedom and that some men hold it dear" (Lane, 1962: 39). The primitive political beliefs of most people are not an ideology in the programmatic sense. But being nonideologues does not keep Americans from meaningful citizenship.

ACQUIRING A POLITICAL SELF

We know that people are not born with a full set of political beliefs. Men and women acquire political beliefs—a political self—as they mature. The political self is molded and shaped by the values of family, friends, schoolmates, the community, TV, schools, and major political events. At the

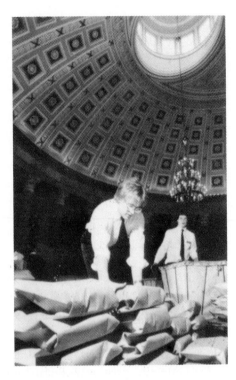

Learning firsthand about politics. These two teenagers serve as pages in the U.S. House of Representatives. Here, they begin the delivery of budget documents to House and Senate committees.

core of the political self are basic loyalties and attachments and often strong feelings toward the nation and its institutions. The political self includes important kinds of political knowledge and evaluation. These consist of some knowledge of how government works, some feeling for the rights and duties of citizens, some preferences regarding public policies, and judgments about parties and leaders.

Children usually form notions about politics before they go to school. In preschool, their most common civic learning deals with basic views about the nation and its symbols, such as the flag. Children also identify with parties to a great extent. Probaby half of them learn to be little Democrats or Republicans by the fourth grade. At first, these ties to nation and party are just labels without much content. Later young people become much more sophisticated.

These identifications develop at a time when other kinds of social awareness are also forming. A child gains racial awareness, a religious bent, and a sense of social class identity along with political ties. Thus, a young child becomes aware that he or she is a black, Baptist, working-class Democrat; a white, Anglo-Saxon, Protestant Republican; or a middle-class Jewish independent. Other views form along with such social and political identification. The child starts to develop attitudes and views about political leaders and what they do. The first public figure that most children know about is the police officer. But they think the president is important too.

Later in childhood, from about the ages of 9 through 13, children move away from notions of politics based largely on feelings and vague ideas. They become more sophisticated and know more about what leaders do and how governments work. By the early teens, young people understand politics in much the same way as most adults. But this does not mean that teenagers do not change their beliefs. At this point, young people spend less time with their parents and are swayed more by their peers. They leave home, perhaps to attend college in an area quite different from the one they were used to. They work in a service station, a grocery store, or a factory. At work, they may meet people whose political beliefs differ greatly from those of the people they knew as children. And teenagers gain political knowledge and understanding, usually in school, and often get involved in some kind of political activity.

The process of acquiring political beliefs, attitudes, loyalties, or values is **political socialization.** Studies by social scientists allow us to make various generalizations about this interesting process (adapted from Dawson, Prewitt, and Dawson, 1977: 59–60):

1. Political learning begins early and continues through early childhood, late childhood, and adolescence.

2. Different types of political learning take place at different points over the preadult years.

3. Basic attachments and identifications, those orientations identified as the core components of the political self, are among the first political outlooks to be acquired.

4. Early orientations toward political authorities seem to be indiscriminately positive and benevolent, and become less so as the child moves through late childhood and into adolescence.

5. Early conceptions of politics and government are highly personalized. The government, the president, the mayor, and so on are understood initially in personal terms. By late childhood and early adolescence, this personalization fades and more abstract perceptions replace it.

6. Affective orientations or feelings about political objects seem to be acquired before information or knowledge. One has feelings about the nation and the president before one has much understanding of what they are.

7. During late childhood, the child acquires information and knowledge about the political world. He or she begins to distinguish between different political roles and to acquire the basic factual information needed to map out the political world.

8. During adolescence, the individual increases his or her capacity to deal with abstractions and to engage in ideological thinking and

ends-means analysis. He or she becomes more involved in partisan and electoral politics.

9. Because different types of political learning occur at different points over the preadult years, it is difficult to specify any particular period as the crucial or most important point. If one places importance on the ability of the maturing citizen to understand political roles and relationships, the end of late childhood and early adolescence might be regarded as the most significant period—roughly the period between ages 11 and 15.

10. Political learning seems to coincide with other types of social learning. Political identities are formed during the same period when other social identities are acquired. The development of political thinking follows the capacity of the individual to handle abstractions and engage in the types of thinking necessary for understanding social and political relationships.

11. By the end of the preadult years, the political self is well developed. Then, most of our basic orientations and knowledge about the political relationships, are acquired or developed as far as they are likely to be.

Early political socialization greatly affects the kinds of citizens we become. But early learning can be changed. Adult experiences, such as an active role in politics or the effects of such events as war and economic depression, may cause changes in political beliefs. Despite this possibility of change in values, in fact many attachments and values acquired early in life have a lasting effect on our political behavior.

IMAGES OF NATION AND LEADERSHIP

A British social psychologist asked an 11-year-old in Glasgow, "What is Britain?" and "What is Scotland?" The lad replied, "Scotland is a country. Britain is a lot of different countries—Glasgow, London, France" (Jahoda, 1963: 58). Young children often have an imperfect idea of their nation. In Britain, which takes in the separate "countries" of England, Scotland, Wales, and Northern Ireland, confusion about country and nation is easy to understand.

You would expect American children to have an easier time. But even here, most children do not have a clear idea of nation until about the fifth grade. One student of political socialization interviewed more than 800 schoolchildren in Philadelphia. One of the questions he asked was, "What is the name of our country?" Sixty-eight percent of the third graders did not know the right answer; about half said "Philadelphia," and another large group said "Pennsylvania." The vast majority of the children in the seventh to ninth grades knew the right answer (Greenberg, 1969: 478).

One of the first political ideas that children learn is a sense of their country, a **national identity,** a sense of being part of a political community. This is shown in their ability to identify national symbols—such as the flag and the national anthem, or Uncle Sam and Lady Liberty. These symbols give them "tangible objects toward which feelings of attachment can be socialized" (Hess and Torney, 1967: 28).

Such symbols are only vaguely understood by very young children. But even they often connect the symbols and the values that go with them. A second-grade boy in Chicago was asked, "What does the Statue of Liberty do?" He replied, "Well, it keeps liberty." "How does it do that?" "Well, it doesn't do it, but there are some guys that do it." "Some others guys do it for the Statue of Liberty?" "The statue is not alive." "Well, what does it do?" "It has this torch in its hand, and sometimes they light up the torch. If the statue was gone, there wouldn't be any liberty" (Hess and Torney, 1967: 29). Over the grammer school years, American children acquire a sharply defined notion of their country and the meaning of its major symbols.

Very young children have a simple notion of their country's **government,** and that notion is highly personal. As children mature, however, their ideas become more complex and realistic. Their view includes giving Congress a central place in the government and such activities as voting. As people grow up, they gain a better understanding of how government works and a better notion of its structure. Many children in the early grades think that the president makes the laws on his own. By seventh grade, most students know that Congress plays a major part in lawmaking. By the time children leave grammar school, they have some idea of the structure of political leadership.

The Role of the President

Because the president is a central, highly visible political figure, he plays an important role in political socialization. Both adults and children know more about the president than about any other public official. Studies show that by teenage, young people know as much as adults about the president and vice president. But they are not very aware of any other politicians. By the end of grammar school, almost all children know who the president is.

Earlier in this chapter, we described the mixed feelings of adults toward political authority. We noted that Americans often see politics as crooked and dirty. Yet they accord great prestige to high political offices. Do we learn negative attitudes toward political leaders early in life?

Much evidence shows that, in the main, we do not. Most children have a very positive image of the president, whom they see as a benevolent leader and as extremely important and powerful. During early childhood, feelings about the president are both very personal and highly idealized. As children get older, their positive feelings about the president erode. By adolescence, their attitudes are much like those of adults (see Delli Carpini, 1986: 84–90). And like adults, children are capable of holding negative attitudes toward a particular president while harboring idealized notions of the presidency as a high office (Greenstein, 1975: 1390).

Why are young children so positive about the president when adults are often so cynical? In our culture, honesty, trustworthiness, helpfulness, and caring are highly valued. Children expect the president to act like good adults in general. But it is also probable that "highly positive pre-adult views of the president . . . result from a combination of adult tendencies to cushion children from the more negative aspects of adult perceptions of the political world, and from pre-adult tendencies to perceive selectively the kindly, supportive aspects of a central figure in the wider environment" (Greenstein, 1974: 130). Parents shield their children from negative and hostile assessments of political leaders, and especially from such assessments of the president.

Reactions to the President's Assassination

One event that dramatizes the importance of the president in our political world is his assassination. The assassination of John F. Kennedy in Dallas on November 22, 1963, deeply affected both young and old (Crotty, 1971). Shock and disbelief followed the event. People grieved as if a close friend or relative had died (Greenberg and Parker, 1965). A typical reaction came from a seventh-grade boy in New York.

> I was walking into my homeroom class when I heard that the President of the United States was shot. I just didn't want to believe it. I walked home from school wondering if it was true. Then, I heard another bulletin when I got home. It went "Ladies and Gentlemen, the President is dead." I was dumbfounded. When I heard the bulletin I couldn't believe it, yet it was true. He died in a Dallas hospital. I never thought I would ever live to hear about an assassination of a President that really happened. I just couldn't believe it. I just couldn't bear the thoughts of having someone take the life of the heroic John Fitzgerald Kennedy. He was so living at first, and then "poof" he's dead. I was thinking that it isn't even safe to take a walk anymore. I hope I will never have to witness anything like that again. (Wolfenstein and Kliman, 1965: 224–225)

Adults reacted in the same way that children did. Television and radio quickly spread the news of the president's death, and the nation grieved together, almost instantaneously. The media made the Kennedy assassination different from previous assassinations, at least in the magnitude and speed of the public response.

The way parents explained the Kennedy assassination to their children reinforced the children's idealized view of the president. How parents shield their children from the seamier side of politics or from their own cynicism toward politics was shown in how they explained the assassination. Many adults thought that there had been a conspiracy, that a lone gunman could not have killed Kennedy, but they apparently kept this view from their children (Orren and Peterson, 1967: 399).

Presidential assassins. Lee Harvey Oswald [top left] shot President John F. Kennedy in Dallas in November 1963; Oswald, in turn, was murdered by Jack Ruby in the Dallas police station. Leon Czolgosz [top right] shot President William McKinley at the Pan American Exposition in Buffalo, New York, in September 1901; he was executed in the electric chair after a brief trial. Giuseppe Zangara [bottom left] attempted to assassinate President Franklin D. Roosevelt in Miami in 1932, but he missed, killing Mayor Anton Cermak of Chicago instead; he died in the electric chair. Lynette "Squeaky" Fromme [bottom right] tried to shoot President Gerald Ford in Sacramento, California, in 1975; she is serving a life sentence in a federal prison.

The assassination of President Kennedy in 1963 was not a unique event. Presidents Abraham Lincoln, James Garfield, and William McKinley were also assassinated, and attempts were made on the lives of Andrew Jackson, Theodore Roosevelt (who was wounded), Franklin D. Roosevelt (the assassin's shot missed FDR but killed Mayor Anton Cermak of Chicago), Harry S Truman, Gerald R. Ford (who was attacked twice but not hurt), and Ronald Reagan (who was wounded). Two prominent leaders were assassinated in 1968—presidential candidate Robert Kennedy and civil rights leader Martin Luther King, Jr. (Clarke, 1982).

Although too little is known about how presidential deaths affect attitudes toward political figures, we do know that many patterns are repeated again and again. Deeply felt grief is widespread. The fallen president is immortalized, and however ordinary he was in life, he becomes a heroic figure. Policies not likely to be passed in more normal times may

John W. Hinckley, Jr., shot and wounded President Ronald Reagan outside the Washington Hilton Hotel on March 30, 1981. He may have been motivated by a bizarre desire to impress a teenage movie star he had never met. Doctors removed a bullet from President Reagan's left lung. James Brady, the president's press secretary, was shot in the head and permanently injured; one Secret Service agent and one local police officer were also wounded. Hinckley, 25 years old at the time, did his shooting with a .22-caliber "Saturday night special."

be adopted as part of his legacy. Since assassination is an extreme and violent act, it can raise levels of suspicion and distrust of government, perhaps even of political life generally. The killing of the president creates an atmosphere of despair and fosters the belief that a good political society is futile. The murders of President John Kennedy, Senator Robert Kennedy, and the Reverend Martin Luther King, Jr., in the 1960s surely contributed to the political apathy and alienation of the 1970s.

The Effects of Scandal

Scandal is a recurring feature of our politics, all the more prominent in this day of instant television coverage and a public obsession with impropriety. Corruption or improper actions in high places are bound to have a negative effect on the images of political leaders. Fraud and corruption in the 1870s, when Ulysses S. Grant was president, are the most remembered aspects of his presidency. This is so even though Grant was never personally implicated. More devastating scandal struck the presidency of Warren G. Harding in the 1920s. His cabinet secretaries took bribes in connection with developing the Teapot Dome oil reserve in South Dakota. Harding, like Grant, was not personally involved, but his incompetence made corruption by his underlings easier.

There were no studies of political socialization during Grant's presidency or after the Teapot Dome scandal. However, the effects of corruption during the presidency of Richard M. Nixon have been studied. Acts of political chicanery and corruption during the 1972 presidential election—the Watergate affair—drastically discredited Nixon among adults. Watergate deeply influenced children's feelings about the president, but the Nixon scandal failed to crush their idealizing of the presidency. Even in the post-Watergate era, children had benevolent attitudes toward the president and their views of national leaders were more idealized than those of children in other Western countries (see Greenstein, 1975: 1384).

In 1986, President Ronald Reagan was immersed in talk of scandal—the so-called Iran-Contra affair. Despite administration policy precluding the sale of arms to Iran, weapons had been sold to that country, putatively in exchange for its help in recovering hostages held by terrorists in Lebanon. Money from the arms sale was used to support the Nicaraguan rebels—the Contras—in the face of congressional prohibitions on government support for them. Televised congressional hearings held during nine months of 1987 sometimes attracted a large audience. President Reagan's popularity in the polls plummeted between October 1986 and February 1987, but then returned to the levels reached in 1982 when it became clear that he could not be personally implicated in wrongdoing. Although the "scandal" seemed to underscore the dictum that "affairs are the stuff by which presidencies are made or broken," there is no evidence that the Iran-Contra affair made a lasting impact on images of the president (Ceaser, 1987: 7).

AGENTS OF POLITICAL SOCIALIZATION

The acquisition of political values, ties, and attitudes is affected by many factors. No easy formula accounts for all aspects of political socialization. But we do know that important consequences result from the social influences that people experience as they grow up. Among these influences are the family, the school, peer groups, and the mass media.

The Political Role of the Family

The family plays a crucial role in political socialization. This is partly because some political learning takes place very early. The early years are especially important for children's growth in every respect, including the political. The family is also central to political socialization because of the

TABLE 4–2 Party identification of children and parents

Percent of children who are	Parents are		
	Democrats	Independents	Republicans
Democrats	66	29	13
Independents	27	53	36
Republicans	7	17	51
Total	100	100	100

Source: M. Kent Jennings and Richard G. Niemi, *The Political Character of Adolescence: The Influence of Families and Schools* (Princeton, N.J.: Princeton University Press, 1974), p. 41. Copyright © 1974 by Princeton University Press. Reprinted by permission of Princeton University Press.

strong bonds that exist within it. Learning, including political learning, is more likely to be swayed where there are strong personal ties, such as the ties between parents and children.

The influence of the family is most important in transmitting norms of behavior and beliefs, including basic political identifications. National identity and loyalty are well formed at an early age, and this development takes place almost wholly within the family. In addition, children gain many loyalties and beliefs early. These include ties to and views toward political leaders, which we discussed earlier in this chapter.

Americans tend to adopt the political loyalties of their parents. Studies based on interviews with high school students and their parents have found, as Table 4–2 illustrates, that Democratic parents tend to have Democratic children, that Republican parents tend to have Republican children, and that independent parents tend to have independent children. Why do party loyalties pass from parents to children?

Party loyalty makes it possible for many people to join in the political process without taking the time to master all of its complexities. Children hear a lot of political talk in their families. They may pick up their parents' attachments to political parties (or their parents' independence), just as they may acquire their parents' religious, ethnic, or class identity. In most American families, the husband and wife have the same party allegiance. Where this is so, children strongly tend to adopt their parents' party attachments. But the passing of party loyalty is far from perfect. In the 1970s, although not many young people took a partisan allegiance opposite that of their parents, a growing proportion were attracted to the "independent" label (Jennings and Niemi, 1981: 89–93).

The family plays a smaller role in transmitting specific opinions and preferences. Parents are much more likely to teach children their party ties than their views on issues or candidates. The same is true for nonpolitical values. Children tend to acquire the religious identifications of their par-

PRACTICE OF POLITICS

The Kennedy Family Dynasty in Politics

A new generation from a highly politicized family. Two children of Robert Kennedy—presidential adviser, attorney general, senator, and candidate for president—entered the political fray in 1986. Kathleen Kennedy Townsend (left) was an unsuccessful Democratic congressional candidate in Maryland. That same year Joseph P. Kenedy II (right), her brother, won the Massachusetts congressional seat long held by former Speaker Thomas P. "Tip" O'Neill. The same district had once been represented by his uncle, President John F. Kennedy.

ents, but they are much less likely to adopt their parents' exact religious beliefs, attitudes, or practices. It is easy to see why family socialization is strong in regard to party loyalties but relatively weak in regard to specific views and preferences. Party loyalty is acquired early in life, when family influence is at its peak. However, people arrive at political opinions over their lifetime, in response to changing events, experiences, and political figures.

In highly politicized families, where parents are highly interested in politics, actively participate in it, talk about it a lot at home, and perhaps even get their children involved, parental political socialization will naturally be greater than in nonpolitical families. But in general, parents probably care less about what their children's political views are than about whether those views are what the parents consider socially and culturally appropriate. Because families differ in their social, cultural, and political views, family socialization helps maintain diverse loyalties, attitudes, and perspectives. But children tend to be shaped by their parents' values and to model themselves on their parents, and family political learning therefore has a conservative effect on the system. Each new generation will, in many ways, reflect the old.

Education and Schools

Education has a dramatic effect on political behavior because it profoundly affects people's outlook and awareness. Educated people read and travel. They have many opportunities to gain political knowledge, information, and interests. Their skills and habits make them better organizers than those with less education. They are, therefore, better prepared to take part in civic affairs. Educated people tend to think that they can control events and social processes, that their efforts can help human progress. So educated people are more confident that their involvement in public affairs can produce desired results or achieve goals. Finally, educated people are relatively high in social and economic status. This gives them reason to think that political outcomes will affect them personally. These attributes of educated people—feelings of effectiveness, confidence, sense of purpose, ability to influence the political process, and belief in a responsive political system—are together called a sense of **political efficacy.** Educated people have a strong sense of political efficacy. They are likely to be more active in politics because they believe that their own well-being is at stake.

The effects of education on political involvement are huge. The strong relationship between education and interest in politics is illustrated by the findings shown in Figure 4–4. Note that interest in politics tends to grow with age, regardless of the level of education. At the same time, at all ages the interest of the more educated is greater than that of the less educated. Although middle-aged high school graduates are at least as interested as younger, college-educated people, the interest of college-educated people remains highest for all age cohorts.

Education also trains people in what it means to be a citizen. Although the United States, unlike the Soviet Union, does not coordinate civic training on a national basis, nearly all of our schools include courses in civics. Our schools also inculcate political values indirectly. Patriotic rites in the lower grades, such as reciting the Pledge of Allegiance and singing the national anthem, reinforce and symbolize children's basic national ties. In grammar schools, children learn about the duties of citizens to the extent that the school, the classroom environment, and the teachers stress

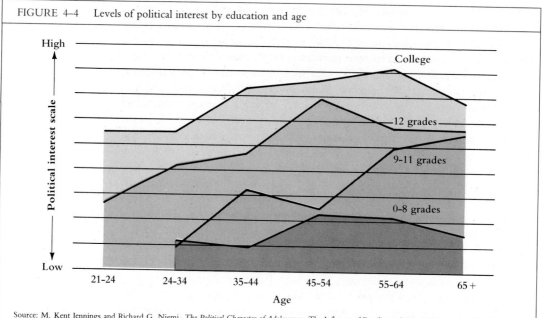

FIGURE 4–4   Levels of political interest by education and age

Source: M. Kent Jennings and Richard G. Niemi, *The Political Character of Adolescence: The Influence of Families and Schools* (Princeton, N.J.: Princeton University Press, 1974), p. 257. Reprinted by permission of Princeton University Press.

compliance with authority and rules. Teachers serve as role models for pupils. Political socialization studies show that in many ways children's political views are like those of their teachers.

Much political socialization is established by the end of grammar school. Thus, you might think that civic education in high school or college would have less influence on students. This is largely true. Although high schools stress civic education, the high school civics program normally does little to change students' political identifications or values. The main effect of civics courses at this point is to transmit knowledge about political processes and public affairs, not to alter basic attachments or beliefs.

Peer Groups and Political Learning

Most people's beliefs and behavior are shaped by their social environment. And most people search out others whose views reinforce their own. "Birds of a feather flock together" in politics as elsewhere. As a result, people's opinions are both shaped and strengthened by the social groups to which they belong.

Families tend to live in neighborhoods of like-minded people. They live with people of the same general social class, racial or ethnic background, and political leanings. As a result, the school, and especially the grammar school, is likely to strengthen the socialization that takes place in the family. Also, since children's friends tend to be from the same neighborhood, peer groups are likely to share the same outlooks. Thus, many children are socialized in a web with a high degree of sharing and reinforcement of political beliefs (Huckfeldt, 1986).

But we know that American families are quite mobile. When children grow up, they tend to leave the family and move to a different area. They also tend to move several times, especially during early adulthood. This mobility, as well as adulthood itself, brings them into contact with a wide range of social groups and circumstances. The more socially and geographically mobile people are, the more they are influenced by social groups with different views. For instance, if a person raised in a Republican family and town (say, Delaware, Ohio) moves to a strongly Democratic town in the South (say, Plains, Georgia), there is a pretty strong chance that he or she will become a Democrat.

Peer groups in which people meet face to face have important socializing effects. At the same time, these influences are not overpowering among high school–age students. Teenagers' political party and voting choices are much more affected by the family than by peer groups. But the stance of teenagers on issues is swayed more by peers than by the family.

Media Socialization

Many claims are made about the influence of the mass media, especially television. No one could deny that the media are important in many ways. But there is not much evidence that they play a big part in political socialization. Children use the mass media (TV, newspapers, magazines, radio) more and more as they go through the lower grades. But at these ages, the media, especially TV, are probably more a source of entertainment than of political information. The use of the media as a news source increases after high school. High school students do use the media for news, but far less so than their parents. Parents frequently select the political TV programming (and also the newspapers, magazines, and radio broadcasts) that their children consume. Thus, they indirectly control the effects of the media on their children.

Research on the impact of the media in politial socialization has been sparse. However, it does show that the media (1) play a big role in providing political information but (2) have little independent influence on the development of political opinions or political activity. There is serious concern about the media's potential for a kind of mass political thought control. But the media mainly reinforce the beliefs that children get from other sources, mostly from the family.

GROUP VARIATIONS IN POLITICAL SOCIALIZATION

Social class, racial, ethnic, and sex differences among Americans can show up as differences in political socialization. Social class differences in political learning loom larger in the advantage of middle-class children in acquiring political interests, knowledge, and skills than in differences in basic class orientations toward political authorities. Middle-class children grow up in more highly politicized families than lower-class children. Thus, they acquire stronger tendencies to participate in politics. As a result, class differences in adult participation persist from one generation to the next.

Gender Differences

Theoretically, the traditional male control of political offices in the United States might stem from sex differences in childhood political socialization. If, in the process of political learning, children think that females have a subordinate role, then the political beliefs of boys and girls will be quite different. This may have once been true. But research of the last two decades shows that there are now only small differences in the political socialization of girls and boys. In early childhood, girls have slightly more positive feelings toward government and its leaders but are less politically active. Girls seem to be more influenced than boys by their immediate environment. In high school, girls are more apt to agree politically with their parents and friends. But gender differences in political participation do not last into the high school years (Jennings and Niemi, 1974: 325–26).

Levels of political interest, efficacy, and trust are not the same for all women, of course. Women employed outside the home show higher levels of political interest and efficacy than homemakers. And the political beliefs of women are influenced by marriage and motherhood. One perceptive student of gender differences has concluded that "women's roles no longer exclude them from politics at the mass level, but the remains of traditional women's roles still inhibit the development of the woman citizen" (Sapiro, 1983: 108).

So-called gender-role stereotyping is real enough. Many women do learn that, though they can participate in politics, only men can hold office. Many men agree. Many women think that their role in society is at home raising children and that public office demands more than this maternal role can permit. Now that most women are working outside the home, the double burden of work and family may simply keep them from the kinds of political party and campaign experiences that are essential to a high level of political participation. In no country do women seek public office as actively as men. But women who are elected are every bit as effective as men (Kirkpatrick, 1974).

The women's movement of the 1960s and 70s brought many reforms. Such groups as the National Organization for Women (NOW) have raised the consciousness of both women and men about sex discrimination and have carved a place for women's issues in national politics. These include economic discrimination (women receiving less than equal pay for work

Raising women's consciousness, seeking power. Delegates to a convention of the National Organization of Women (NOW) listen intently to a speech by their new president, Eleanor Smeal.

equal to that of men), maternity leave, child care, education, political participation, the Equal Rights Amendment, and foreign and defense policy. A women's vote had become detectable in presidential elections by 1972, and it continued to be important throughout the 1980s. According to one student of gender politics, "sex differences in policy options and candidate preferences on campaign issues form part of the basis for a women's vote." A degree of distinctiveness in voting by women "grows out of different priorities and values from those that influence men's decisions," so that "the women's vote is based on issues rather than party allegiance" (Klein, 1984: 163).

Racial Differences

Students of electoral behavior note that "political differences between blacks and whites are far sharper than any other social cleavage" (Abramson et al., 1986: 134). In the 1984 presidential election, for instance, the polls consistently showed that Democrat Walter Mondale was chosen over Republican Ronald Reagan by about 90 percent of voting blacks, compared to only a third of whites. Racial differences in political socialization are not so large as to foreshadow the enormous black-white cleavage in partisan attachment.

Studies comparing the political orientations of black and white children indicate that, if anything, black children are slightly more positive toward government than white children. Black children also differ from white children in their feelings toward the president. Black children felt more positive about Presidents Kennedy and Johnson than white children; they

Black mayors lead American cities. In the 1970s and 1980s, black politicians were elected mayors of several cities, including Chicago, Birmingham, New Orleans, Los Angeles, Philadelphia, Detroit, and Gary, Indiana. These large-city mayors are Andrew Young of Atlanta [top left], Tom Bradley of Los Angeles [top right], W. Wilson Goode of Philadelphia [bottom left], and Eugene Sawyer of Chicago [bottom right].

had more negative feelings about President Nixon (see Orum and Cohen, 1973). More recently, black attitudes have been negative toward President Reagan and highly positive toward President Jimmy Carter. These and other differences come largely from long deprivation and from discrimination against blacks as they tried to exercise their civil and political rights. Blacks have felt that Presidents Kennedy, Johnson, and Carter were highly supportive of black rights but that President Nixon and Reagan were not.

Major black-white differences exist in learning party attachment, in the effect of school socialization, and in feelings about political efficacy. Since at least the 1960s, black adults have generally agreed that the Democratic party serves black interests better than the Republican party. They feel that the Democrats, unlike the Republicans, will improve the economic condition of blacks and enforce their rights. Yet parental transmission of party ties has been far weaker among blacks than among whites. The Democratic party has attracted young blacks regardless of their parents' party attachment. Since the 1960s, family socialization has had much less impact on party loyalty for blacks than for whites. In their party attachments, black children seem to respond more to the larger political arena and to racial consciousness.

On average, black children score lower than white children on questions of political knowledge. Black children come to high school with much less political knowledge than white children. So the high school civics course (which has little impact on whites) has a greater effect on black students than on white students. "Because of cultural and social status differences," black students "are more likely to encounter new or conflicting perspectives and content" in civics courses. For white students, the civics program "is a further layering of familiar materials which, by and large, repeat the message from other past and contemporary sources" (Jennings and Niemi, 1974: 206). School socialization has a greater impact on blacks than on whites.

Feelings of political effectiveness and of trust in politicians are much weaker in black children than in white children. Children's sense of political efficacy is shown by asking them how much they agree or disagree with five statements:

1. My family doesn't have any say about what the government does.
2. Citizens don't have a chance to say what they think about running the government.
3. What happens in the government will happen no matter what people do.
4. There are some big powerful men in the government who are running the whole thing, and they don't care about us ordinary people.
5. I don't think people in the government care much what people like my family think.

Children's responses to these statements make it possible to set up an "index of political efficacy."

This index was used in a study of black and white students in Rochester, New York. The results are shown in Figure 4–5. Note (1) that black and white children in third and fourth grades show little difference in their sense of political efficacy; (2) that after fourth grade, white children feel more effective and black children feel less effective; and (3) that the gap between white and black children generally grows with each grade level.

Differences between blacks and whites in political trust have fluctuated in the last three decades. Generally, the trust of blacks in political leaders has been less than that of whites. This black-white gap was especially large in the early 1970s. Because trust declined steadily among whites and increased among blacks, the racial gap did not appear in 1978 or 1980. But the gap reappeared in 1982 and widened in 1984, reflecting black disenchantment with Reagan administration policies. In Figure 4–6, these trends are shown for one representative entry in the trust scale (spelled out earlier. This figure shows the total "always" and "almost always" responses to the statement "The government in Washington can be trusted to do what is right." Black distrust is tied mostly to political events, developments in the black community, and a realistic appraisal of the black

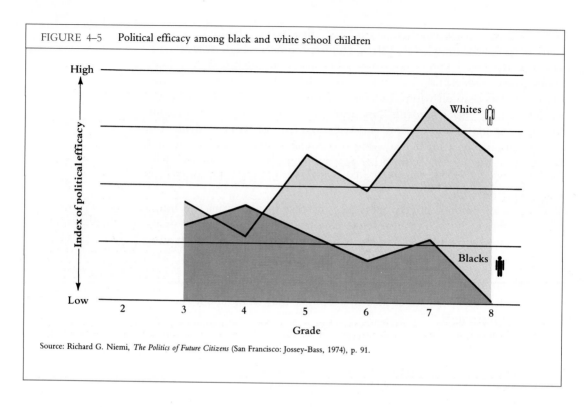

FIGURE 4–5   Political efficacy among black and white school children

Source: Richard G. Niemi, *The Politics of Future Citizens* (San Francisco: Jossey-Bass, 1974), p. 91.

political condition. The data in Figure 4–6 are for adults, but similar trends are reported for black school children. Young blacks are not hostile to politicians because their parents are. They feel that way because both young and adult blacks have less reason than whites to trust politicians.

Ethnic Differences

Little is known about the political socialization of white ethnic groups, such as the Irish, the Poles, or the Italians. Scattered evidence suggests that "Americanization" was the major socializing experience for immigrants. It is possible that white ethnic groups have a stronger tie to national politics than do Americans in general. By and large, these groups were accepted into the mainstream of American life and politics, sometimes after a struggle. Other ethnic groups—American Indians, Orientals, Hispanics—have suffered serious discrimination. Mexican Americans, or Chicanos, make up the largest such group. An in-depth study of the political socialization of Chicanos in California gives us some data (Garcia, 1973).

FIGURE 4–6   Political trust among black and white adults

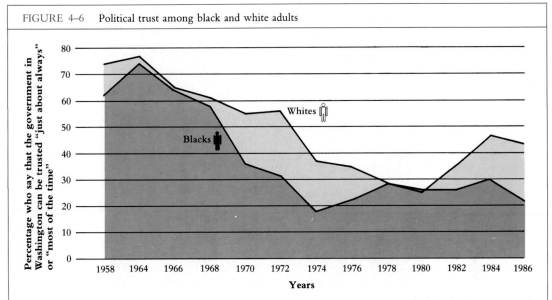

Sources: Paul R. Abramson, *Political Attitudes in America* (San Francisco: W. H. Freeman 1983), p. 230. Copyright © 1983 by W. H. Freeman and Company. All rights reserved. The data for 1982 to 1986 are drawn from the National Election Studies conducted by the Center for Political Studies, University of Michigan.

This study was based on interviews with Chicano and "Anglo" school-children. The majority of Chicanos have a lower class status than Anglos and a long history of discrimination. Yet there are very few differences in the socialization of Chicano and Anglo children. Chicano children show a very strong attachment to the political community and remarkably positive feelings toward the government—feelings that are often more positive than those of Anglo children. When social class differences are taken into account, there are no differences between Chicano and Anglo children in these basic political attitudes. Also, Chicano children support democratic procedures and values as much as Anglo children do. In addition, the two groups have very similar ideas about the duties of citizenship.

The one striking difference between the Chicano and Anglo children in the California study is in their feelings of political efficacy. The Anglo children's levels of political efficacy gradually grew from third grade to ninth grade. The Chicano children's feelings of political efficacy, unlike those of black children (see Figure 4–5), did not decline. Rather, as shown in Figure 4–7, their levels of political efficacy increased over the grammar school years, although at a much slower rate than those of the Anglo children. Note that this figure shows the same widening gap between the

Mayor Henry Cisneros of San Antonio, Texas, working with aides at city hall. San Antonio is the third-largest city in Texas, a Mexican-American city with a Hispanic majority. Mayor Cisneros, first elected in 1981, has been called "one of the brightest young Democrats in the country." In 1987, he received more favorable ratings in a statewide poll than any other Texas politician tested.

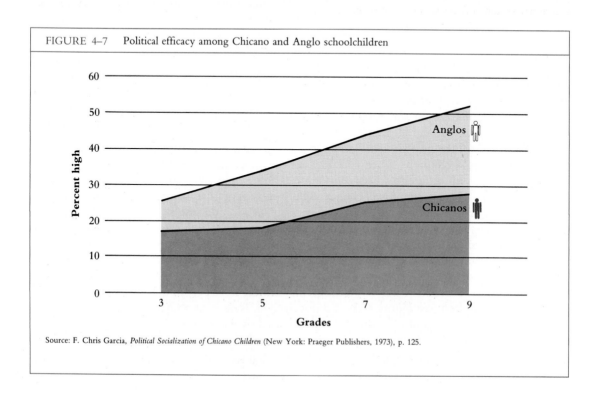

FIGURE 4–7   Political efficacy among Chicano and Anglo schoolchildren

Source: F. Chris Garcia, *Political Socialization of Chicano Children* (New York: Praeger Publishers, 1973), p. 125.

Part Two

MOBILIZING INDIVIDUALS AND GROUPS FOR POLITICS

James Madison advocated ratification of the U.S. Constitution in the *Federalist* papers. He believed that the new Constitution provided governing processes well suited to a society with a multiplicity of groups, or "factions," with divergent interests. In *The Federalist,* No. 10, he wrote: "The most common and durable source of factions has been the various and unequal distribution of property. Those who hold and those who are without property have ever formed distinct interests in society. . . . A landed interest, a manufacturing interest, a mercantile interest, a monied interest, with many lesser interests, grow up of necessity in civilized nations. . . , actuated by different sentiments and views."

Madison thought that governing a diverse society required the mobilization of people, groups, and interests so as to assure a proper balance among conflicting interests. He saw that political parties and interest groups could *mobilize* citizens to participate in governing themselves. Today we understand that people do not always get into politics spontaneously. Americans need to be aroused by politicians, political parties, and the election campaigns themselves to take part in free elections. As we discover in the chapters of Part Two, our endemically low voter turnout presents us with the continuing challenge of involving citizens in the politics of democracy.

Chapter Five

GETTING INTO POLITICS

*P*olitical participation does not make most Americans into celebrities, even in their hometown or neighborhood. They are like Stimson Bullitt, a Seattle lawyer and businessman, who has been politically active all his life. Bullitt wrote a widely read book in which he gave political advice to those who contemplated going into politics. Here are a few good examples of his advice, as valuable now as it was over a decade ago:

> To enjoy politics, one must enjoy people; it helps if one likes them as well. A politician wants and tries to like people. He must be with them, and a friendly relationship makes it easier for him to satisfy and please.

> An able politician is neither an amateur nor a specialist. He is a general practitioner.

> Most American citizens are given better government than they realize, and most politicians are better public servants than many people think.

> To enter politics at the bottom is easy and good sense. Competition is mild, and one may practice in an arena where mistaken judgment is not fatal.

> To succeed in American politics, one must win the acceptance of many people and the approval of some, but compared to what other fields require, the approval needs to be more widespread and need not be as strong.

> To enter politics costs a person little in his vocational progress. (Bullitt, 1977: 3–22)

*F*or Stimson Bullitt, politics has been a fascination. He has been very active in state politics, and he was twice an unsuccessful candidate for Congress. For him, politics is a calling—not a vocation but a summons to be involved. Politics do not call as loudly to many of us. Yet we have a sense that as citizens we have some duty to take part in the democratic process.

In a democratic society, getting into politics is easy. For some, politics is a vocation, a way of life, and a livelihood. Some Americans are full-time politicians, making their living as professional legislators, executives, political party officials, and so forth. For others, politics is an avocation—not a full-time job but an activity that commands their time and interest. Many Americans are active in politics, working in political campaigns, contributing money, or running for and serving in a part-time office. These "amateur" politicians often show impressive political savvy. Then, there are those whose involvement in politics is minimal—whose political activity is confined, for the most part, to voting in elections. Finally, some Americans are apolitical. They take advantage of living in a country where they are free not to participate in politics. These "free riders" may, of course, benefit from politics and government without contributing to public well-being.

This chapter focuses on how people take part in politics. The standard wisdom holds that active, participating citizens are important to the political process. What would happen if we had elections and no one voted? Or if it were possible everywhere, as in Nevada, to vote "none of the above," and everyone did that?

Taking part and making choices are essential in a democracy. However, no one knows for sure how many citizens must be politically active to keep a democracy healthy. If the reach of such involvement must include every adult, or even all but a few, then no nation could be called fully democratic. It is not realistic to say that a country can be called a democracy only if all or most of its people are highly active politically. But we do expect a large amount of rank-and-file involvement in such a system.

We must know what the record shows about political involvement in this country to take stock of its democratic makeup. What are the various ways in which people take part in our political process? How active are these people in politics? What are the traits of the highly active, compared to the traits of those who are only somewhat active or inactive? Under what conditions are people most and least apt to take part in politics? These are the main questions that we address in this chapter. We analyze political participation in this chapter with the individual citizen in mind. In Chapter 9, we will consider elections and electoral processes in greater depth.

VOTING IN ELECTIONS

In a political system as diverse, large scale, open, and equal as ours, there are many ways to take part. Voting is the way most often discussed. It is, though, only one kind of political activity.

Dedicated voters. Newlyweds make a stop at the North School in Abington, Massachusetts, to vote in town elections after exchanging wedding vows. After voting, the couple went on to their wedding reception in Holbrook, Massachusetts.

The Act of Voting

Americans vote in more elections than people in any other country. The political demands on us as citizens are very heavy indeed. Every four years, we pick a president and a vice president. Every two years, all 435 members of the House of Representatives and a third of the members of the Senate are elected. Governors, state legislators, county and city officials, school board members, and other local officials are elected periodically, often in different elections. Candidates for many offices are picked in primary elections. Moreover, beyond electing public officers, we regularly vote on state constitutional amendments, referenda, and school or municipal bonds to finance public projects. In this country, elections are so frequent that they are large items of public expense and require a large bureaucracy.

Americans vote for many reasons. Many vote as an act of loyalty or patriotism and out of a sense of civic duty. In a 1984 national survey, Americans were asked about the obligations that they thought citizens owed their country. Fully 80 percent said that voting in elections was a "very important obligation of citizenship," and another 16 percent said that voting was "somewhat important" (*Public Opinion* 8, October–November 1985: 32).

Many find the act of voting satisfying and enjoyable. A classic survey showed that 71 percent felt a sense of satisfaction in voting and that 66 percent found election campaigns pleasant and enjoyable (Almond and Verba, 1963: 146). Most people know that one person's vote, by itself, has little effect on the outcome of elections. But together with the votes of like-minded people, that vote can help decide who is elected.

The act of voting requires little knowledge or motivation, compared to other forms of political activity. Many politically uninvolved people vote regularly, and many people who are very active in politics may not bother to vote. There is the story of the lady in her 80s who was to baby-sit on the night of the first Kennedy-Nixon TV debate in 1960. She urged the parents to pick her up on time so that she would not miss any of the debate. When asked why she was so interested, she replied that she had been fascinated with presidential campaigns since Grover Cleveland ran against Benjamin Harrison in 1892 and had followed them ever since with great interest. When she was settled in front of the TV set well before the debate, she was asked how she planned to vote. "Why, I've never voted," she said. "I could never bring myself to vote against one of those nice boys."

The act of voting requires something from everyone who goes to the polls. In the first place, it requires some effort: voters have to be registered; they have to take time to go the polls; they may have to stand in line to vote; and they must have confidence in their ability to make choices. To some people, voting can be intimidating. They may be confused by the often long and complicated ballot, or they may be unable to cope with a voting machine. Second, voting requires some kind of a decision. Voters must make a choice—either between parties or between candidates. Third, going to the polls requires a modicum of social consciousness on the part of the voter. He or she must at least know that election day is *this* Tuesday and where the polling place is. Fourth, voting requires the play of at least some emotion. That emotion could be an urge to conform, a wish to show party loyalty, support for policies or a program, or ties to a certain candidate. And finally, the act of voting is an affirmation; it expresses a belief that "democracy is not a sham," that voting makes a difference (Lane, 1959: 47).

Voter Turnout

In the United States, **voter turnout** usually refers to the percentage of persons of voting age who cast votes in an election. That percentage is rather low in this country. The average in presidential elections has been about 60 percent over the last 25 years, whereas in many European countries, turnout in national elections is between 75 and 90 percent. This kind of comparison is tricky, though. In Europe, as in the United States, people must be registered to vote, but Europeans are registered automatically by the government. European election turnout figures are based on the number of registered voters, not on the total voting-age population. And the total voting-age population may include aliens, illiterates, the mentally

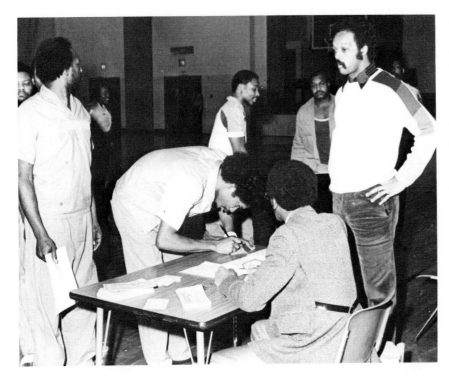

Getting out the vote. During 1983 and 1984, many efforts were made to register voters so that they would be eligible to vote on election day. In Chicago, mobile registrars went to unusual places to find prospective voters. Here, Democratic presidential candidate Jesse Jackson looks on as registrars sign up voters in the Cook County jail!

disabled, prisoners, and other ineligibles. The European turnout figures may therefore be deceptively high.

In contrast, registration is voluntary here. Those who do not want to take part in elections are free not to register. Also, registration requires personal initiative. Going to the appropriate office to register can be inconvenient.

Even taking into account only those who are registered, Americans simply do not turn out to vote in national elections in the same measure as registered voters in other democracies. The exception is Switzerland, a very model of **grass-roots democracy,** whose voter turnout is lower than that of the United States (Glass, Squire, and Wolfinger, 1984).

Voter registration

Sixty-two percent of those interviewed by the University of Michigan Survey Research Center before the 1984 presidential election said they were registered. A smaller number really were; more people think they are registered than in fact are. Of those who thought they were registered, 51 percent said they were registered Democrats; 36 percent, registered Republicans; and 13 percent, registered with no party preference.

The main purpose of registration has been to prevent fraud in elections. Registration is now required by law in every state except North Dakota.

PRACTICE OF POLITICS

"People Don't See a Need to Vote"

A May 1987 public opinion survey by *The New York Times*/CBS News Poll gives us some clues about Americans' attitudes toward voting on election day. We seem to be reluctant to make it too easy to vote. For instance, the poll showed that most Americans oppose a more open voting process—62 percent think that new people in a community should not be able to register to vote on election day. Only three states—Minnesota, Wisconsin, and Maine—now allow election day registration.

A majority of us think that people should be allowed to vote at 18 years of age, as is prescribed by the 26th Amendment to the U.S. Constitution. But more than a third of us believe that voters ought to be 21 years old or older. A majority think that voters should be residents of a community for a year or more before being allowed to vote, and most seem to favor literacy as a voting qualification.

Research on the impact of registration requirements indicates that easier registration rules would boost turnout by about 9 percent. But political analyst Kevin Phillips argues, "If people don't care, the easy of regis-

Public Opinion Survey

How old should people have to be to vote for the president and Congress?

Under 18	3%
18	53
19 or 20	4
21	35
Older than 21	3

How long should people have to live in a place before they can vote there for the president and Congress?

No limit	14%
180 days or less	22
181 days to a year	31
One year	30
More than one year	24

If all voters had to be able to read and write, would they elect better officials?

Yes	59%
It wouldn't make a difference	37

Poll conducted by telephone May 11–14, 1987, with 1,254 respondents. The poll has a margin of sampling error of plus or minus 3 percentage points. Those with no opinion are not shown.

tration isn't going to get them to the polls on election day. People don't see a need to vote."

Source: *New York Times*, May 31, 1987, p. E4.

Without it, a dishonest person could easily vote several times in different precincts. One person wrote to ask his congressman for a favor, saying that he was a loyal supporter who had voted for the congressman several times. "The several times I voted for you were in the election of 1966," he explained.

State **voter registration** laws always involve residence requirements of some kind. By federal law, these may not exceed 30 days' residence for presidential elections or 50 days' residence for state and local elections. Also, federal law forbids the states to use literacy or "good character" tests for registration. Otherwise, all U.S. citizens who are at least 18 years of age and not mentally incompetent or in prison are generally eligible to vote.

The registration requirement and the qualifications to register disenfranchise many persons of voting age. In 1985, more than 9.6 million nonimmigrant aliens resided in the United States. And there is good reason to think that many more resident aliens fail to report, though they are required to. Over 2 million people are institutionalized in prisons, mental hospitals, homes for the mentally retarded, or homes for the aged and dependent. Many of these people are part of the voting-age population, but under most state laws they are for the most part not eligible to be registered voters.

Residence rules are designed to permit proper personal identification of voters and to prevent voting fraud. But they **disenfranchise** many people who might have registered and voted had they not moved just before election day. No one knows for sure how extensive this problem is. It is easy, though, to forget how mobile our population is. The Census Bureau found that, on the average, Americans make 12 moves in their lifetimes. Between 1980 and 1985, almost 40 percent of the nation's people moved to a different house or apartment—over 86 million people! In short, voter registration without doubt keeps highly mobile people from voting. Also, many people do not register because it is too much bother and they are not interested.

Some effects of registration and population mobility on voter turnout are illustrated in Table 5–1. (The figures are for a congressional election, not a presidential election.) Notice that the proportion of adults registered to vote is very low among people whose length of residence is less than a year and higher for people with longer residence. Of those with less than one year of residency, many were not eligible to register. Voter turnout in general was low. But high proportions of those registered went to the polls, regardless of their length of residence.

Registration requirements have stirred much controversy (Crotty, 1977: 72–100). Some favor ending voter registration completely. North Dakota has no registration. But vote fraud has been rare there, and its voter turnout is among the highest of all the states. North Dakota is hardly typical. Would eliminating registration invite trouble in states or localities with long histories of corruption? Some states have retained registration but have made it more convenient. Registration by mail has been adopted in 22 states; door-to-door registration campaigns are conducted in some states. On the whole, these devices appear to have distressingly little effect on how many voters take part (Phillips and Blackman, 1975: 14–22).

Three states—Minnesota, Wisconsin, and Maine—adopted election day registration. In Minnesota and Wisconsin, which adopted such registration

TABLE 5–1   Residence, registration, and voter turnout

Length of residence	Percent of population	Percent registered to vote	Percent of voting-age population who voted in 1974	Percent of registered who voted in 1974
Less than one year	17	38	22	60
One–two years	16	52	36	69
Three–five years	16	66	47	71
Six years or more	48	78	58	75
Total	97★	62	45	72

★Not reported for 3 percent.

Source: *Statistical Abstract of the United States* (Washington, D.C.: U.S. Government Printing Office, 1977), p. 468.

after the 1972 election, voter turnout was 1 or 2 percent higher in 1976. But the costs of this system can be large. Experiences in these states suggest that voters are encouraged to wait until election day to register. This causes confusion and long waiting lines at the polls, and it may result in registration errors that allow hundreds to vote in the wrong place. It also opens the door for vote fraud in states where the honesty of elections is not taken for granted (Smolka, 1977).

Many elections

Voter turnout is usually discussed in relation to presidential elections. But there are many elections in the country. Voters are called on regularly to vote on referenda issues and for candidates for Congress, governor, state legislator, and county and local offices. If we limit analysis of turnout to the presidential contests, we understate voting participation. Surveys conducted from 1972 to 1976, some of whose results are shown in Figure 5–1, disclose that during this period the average adult voted 3.4 times and the average registered voter voted 4.5 times. On the one hand, only about 25 percent of all Americans, and 5 percent of registered voters, failed to vote in any election. On the other hand, 33 percent of all adults and 45 percent of those registered voted in five elections or more. So voting is much more intense among Americans than it seems to be from presidential turnout alone.

Variations in turnout

Figuring voter turnout on the basis of the voting-age population gives a low estimate. The voting-age population includes many who are ineligible or unable to vote. Although a higher proportion of those able and eligible to vote did so in 1980 and 1984, the total voting for president was only

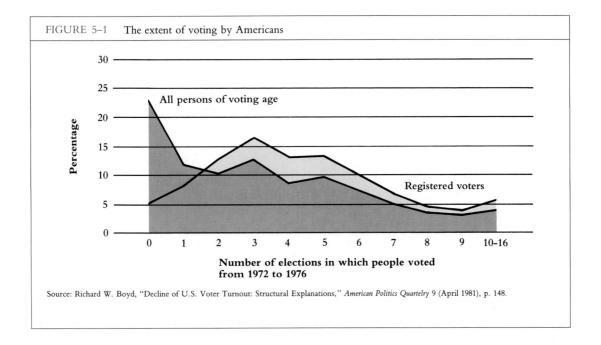

FIGURE 5–1   The extent of voting by Americans

**Number of elections in which people voted
from 1972 to 1976**

Source: Richard W. Boyd, "Decline of U.S. Voter Turnout: Structural Explanations," *American Politics Quarterly* 9 (April 1981), p. 148.

53 percent of the voting-age population. However, voter turnout has been lower since 1976 than in any presidential election since Truman ran against Dewey in 1948. One cause of this was the addition of 18-to-20-year-olds to the electorate. This age group is noted for low turnout. Also, disenchantment with politics and loss of interest in elections have contributed to lower turnout.

The national average of 53 percent voter turnout for presidential elections in the 1980s covers up wide variations among states (see Table 5–2). In 1984, more than 60 percent of those of voting age voted in 10 states—Connecticut, Iowa, Maine, Minnesota, North Dakota, South Dakota, Wisconsin, Montana, Oregon, and Utah. Nine states and the District of Columbia had a turnout rate below 50 percent. Most of the low-turnout states are in the South. But the South is the only region in which voter turnout has been growing—from 45 percent in 1972 to about half of the voting-age population in the 1980s.

For any one election, voter turnout varies across presidential elections and among the states. There are also large turnout differences for presidential and congressional races. Figure 5–2 shows the pattern of these differences. Voter turnout is usually lower in congressional elections than in presidential elections. From 1952 to 1986, the average turnout was 58 percent for presidential contests and 47 percent for congressional races. But, as Figure 5–2 shows, congressional turnout has a "sawtooth" pattern. The midterm turnout is much lower than the turnout when congressional

TABLE 5–2   Presidential election turnout in the states

Region and state	Percent of voting-age population	
	1980	1984
East:		
Connecticut	61	61
Delaware	55	56
District of Columbia	36	44
Maine	65	65
Maryland	50	51
Massachusetts	59	58
New Hampshire	57	54
New Jersey	55	57
New York	48	51
Pennsylvania	52	54
Rhode Island	59	56
Vermont	58	60
West Virginia	53	51
South:		
Alabama	49	50
Arkansas	51	52
Florida	49	49
Georgia	41	42
Kentucky	50	51
Louisiana	53	54
Mississippi	52	52
North Carolina	44	48
Oklahoma	52	51
South Carolina	41	41
Tennessee	49	49
Texas	45	47
Virginia	48	51
Midwest:		
Illinois	58	57
Indiana	58	56

choices are made at the same time as presidential choices. This difference results from lower voter interest in **midterm elections**. In such elections, there are no presidential candidates to attract national attention through wide media coverage. The high visibility of the presidential contest greatly increases voter turnout.

Presidential election turnout has declined since 1960 among almost all groups. But there have been two important exceptions. The voting rate has increased among southern blacks and southern white women. Voting by blacks in the South shot up strikingly from 1952 to 1968. Their voting

TABLE 5–2   (Concluded)

Region and state	Percent of voting-age population	
	1980	*1984*
Iowa	63	62
Kansas	57	57
Michigan	60	58
Minnesota	70	69
Missouri	59	58
Nebraska	57	56
North Dakota	65	63
Ohio	55	58
South Dakota	68	64
Wisconsin	67	63
West:		
Alaska	58	60
Arizona	45	47
California	49	50
Colorado	56	55
Hawaii	44	45
Idaho	68	60
Montana	65	65
Nevada	41	42
New Mexico	51	52
Oregon	61	63
Utah	64	61
Washington	57	59
Wyoming	53	52
Nation	53	53

Source: *Statistical Abstract of the United States* (Washington, D.C.: U.S. Government Printing Office, 1985), p. 255.

rate more than doubled between 1960 and 1968, spurred by the Voting Rights Act of 1965. This act outlawed discrimination in registering voters, such as literacy tests; strengthened by Congress in 1970, 1975, and 1982, it brought millions of blacks onto the voting rolls. And the traditionally large gap in the voting rates of southern men and women was, by 1976, nearly closed (Cassel, 1979).

On occasion, issues or candidates in state or local elections spur voter turnout. When in February 1983, black Congressman Harold Washington ran in Chicago's Democratic mayoral primary, nearly 78 percent of Chicago's eligible voters went to the polls. Turnout exceeded 80 percent in the white ethnic wards on Chicago's northwest and southwest sides. But Washington captured the nomination because of huge increases in black registration and the solid support of black wards (Green, 1983).

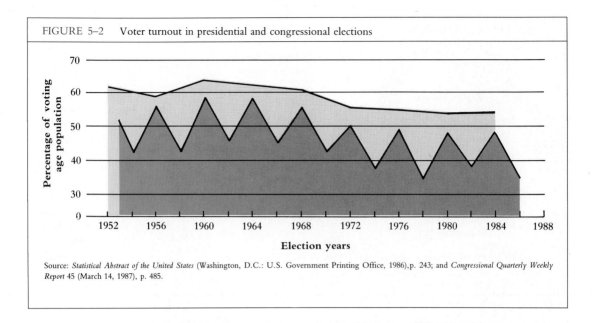

FIGURE 5–2   Voter turnout in presidential and congressional elections

Source: *Statistical Abstract of the United States* (Washington, D.C.: U.S. Government Printing Office, 1986),p. 243; and *Congressional Quarterly Weekly Report* 45 (March 14, 1987), p. 485.

Many commentators on American politics bemoan the low turnout levels in our elections. The causes and remedies are controversial. If all people of voting age had to be registered, turnout would rise. But American policymakers hesitate to remove the voluntarism in elections. Vigorous competition between Republicans and Democrats and efforts by parties to "get out the vote" increase turnout levels. This suggests that strengthening party organizations might be useful (Patterson and Caldeira, 1983).

The Voting Situation

The voting situation itself may affect elections. Voter turnout may be influenced by the number of polling places available per 1,000 voters. The polling station may be distant, hard to find, or otherwise inadequate. If so, people may be discouraged from voting.

Bad weather on election day affects voter turnout. Onetime Denver mayor Ben Stapleton knew how to turn bad weather to his benefit on election day. When heavy snowstorms threatened to keep voters away, he made sure that friendly precincts were well plowed but was slow about cleaning the streets in unfriendly precincts.

In addition, interest in voting is apt to be low if there is no contest, if candidates are unopposed, or if races are very one-sided.

Campaign workers for Mike Dukakis. Campaign headquarters work is engrossing for these activists working for Massachusetts Governor Michael Dukakis in the 1988 presidential primaries.

as candidates or, with luck, as officeholders. How much do Americans engage in these kinds of participation?

Party and Campaign Activity

Even in the age of television, elections involve thousands of people in party organizations and campaign work. These are the precinct committeemen and women who serve as grass-roots party workers. They are the delegates to county and state party conventions, as well as the delegates and alternates to national party conventions. In addition to these activists, campaigns enlist many volunteers. These workers handle mailings, ring doorbells, work at the polls, make telephone calls, and pass out leaflets, posters, and bumper stickers. This work requires more information and motivation than does the mere act of voting. Campaign workers are the "gladiators" who do most of the political work. Most people sit in the "spectator grandstands" and decide the outcome of elections by voting for the candidates of their choice (Milbrath and Goel, 1977: 13).

Community Activity

Political activity is not confined to elections. After all, elections occur only at fixed intervals. For instance, a president is elected only in November of every fourth year. Yet thousands of people are active in ongoing public affairs in their communities. They work for bond issues for new schools. They concern themselves about school policies and programs through participation in parent-teacher associations. They work for community beautification through garden clubs. They fight against rezoning the property across the street for use as a service station.

Political issues and problems are often not raised or resolved by elections. Thus, it is common for us to work together in our communities to grapple with public needs that are of direct and immediate concern to us.

Contacting Officials

We take part in politics by contacting public officials when we are concerned about some issue that affects us directly. In general, public officials are highly accessible to ordinary citizens.

The University of Michigan's Center for Political Studies took a poll after the 1982 congressional elections. Seventy-nine percent of the respondents said that they had had some contact with their congressman, but only 14 percent said that they had met their congressman personally. Two thirds said that they thought their congressman would help them if contacted about a problem.

Many government services are provided directly to us. Therefore, millions of us have contact with administrative workers. A 1973 study of this kind of contact focused on seven service agencies and showed that 58 percent of citizens had contacted a government office. Almost three fourths of them said that their "bureaucratic encounter" had been helpful (Katz et al., 1975).

A number of studies in the United States and other countries point to the wide practice of contacting as a mode of political participation. These studies indicate that about half of American adults have contacted government officials and other political leaders. Americans are substantially more prone to contact public figures than citizens of other democratic countries. One study of citizen contacting shows that people who have political ties—especially to political parties—are more likely to contact officials. Without this political connection, the extent of such contacting generally follows the socioeconomic structure—that is, the probability of contacting officials increases with wealth and education (Zukerman and West, 1985).

Millions of people contact public officials by mail, and this kind of contact has grown dramatically in recent years. Those who write to officials are also likely to be politically involved in other ways.

Congressional representatives are prominent targets of letter writers. Handling this great volume of mail is a big part of the work of a represen-

---

PRACTICE OF POLITICS

Amateur and Professional Politicians

In his book *The Amateur Democrat,* James Q. Wilson distinguishes deftly between amateur and professional politicians. Here are some excerpts (pp. 2–4):

> By amateur is not meant a dabbler, a dilettante, or an inept practitioner of some special skill. . . . Nor does amateur here mean a person who is in politics for fun or as an avocation, rather than for money or as a career.
>
> An amateur is one who finds politics *intrinsically* interesting because it expresses a conception of the public interest. The amateur politician sees the political world more in terms of ideas and principles than in terms of persons. Politics is the determination of public policy, and public policy ought to be set deliberately rather than as the accidental by-product of a struggle for personal and party advantage. . . . He is not oblivious to considerations of partisan or personal advantage in assessing the outcome, but (in the pure case) he dwells on the relation of outcome to his conception, be it vague or specific, of the public weal. Although politics may have attractions as a game of skill, it is never simply that.
>
> The professional, on the other hand—even the "professional" who practices politics as a hobby rather than as a vocation—is preoccupied with the outcome of politics in terms of winning and losing. Politics, to him, consists of concrete questions and specific persons who must be dealt with in a manner that will "keep everybody happy" and thus minimize the possibility of defeat at the next election.
>
> The principal reward of politics to the amateur is the sense of having satisfied a felt obligation to "participate," and this satisfaction is greater the higher the value the amateur can attach to the ends which the outcomes of politics serve. The principal reward of the professional is to be found in the extrinsic satisfactions of participation—power, income, status, or the fun of the game.

---

tative's office. In 1986, more than 130 million pieces of mail flowed into congressional offices. Some senators received as many as 10,000 letters a week. In the 1980s, mail sent out from Capitol Hill has averaged more than 656 million pieces per year.

Protesting

Protest marches and demonstrations are historic forms of political participation in this country. Even before the Revolution, Americans had developed the art and strategy of the demonstration. Conflicts over states'

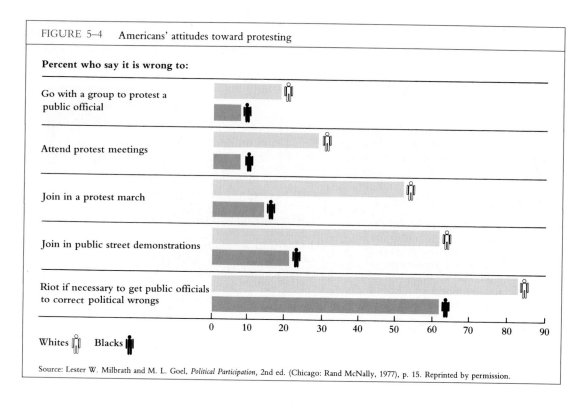

FIGURE 5–4   Americans' attitudes toward protesting

Percent who say it is wrong to:

Go with a group to protest a public official

Attend protest meetings

Join in a protest march

Join in public street demonstrations

Riot if necessary to get public officials to correct political wrongs

Whites   Blacks

Source: Lester W. Milbrath and M. L. Goel, *Political Participation,* 2nd ed. (Chicago: Rand McNally, 1977), p. 15. Reprinted by permission.

rights, the abolition of slavery, women's rights, the tariff, the gold standard, the unionization of labor, and war (to name only a few) have historically caused public protests. Public protest has become a potent political technique. Witness the protest marches of the 1960s for civil rights for blacks, demonstrations on college campuses in the early 1970s, and more recently, protests by environmentalists against such practices as killing whales or constructing nuclear power plants.

Various forms of protesting are aimed at mobilizing support for policy demands. The more drastic forms include boycotts, sit-ins, picketing, demonstrations, and riots. Among the tamer but no less effective forms are mass meetings in neighborhoods, petition drives, mass turnouts at meetings, and highly publicized press conferences.

Most people feel it is all right to go with a group to protest to a public official. But many take a dim view of street demonstrations. An interesting study done in Buffalo, New York, gives some clues to our feelings about protests (see Figure 5–4). One of its notable findings is that blacks are much more in favor or protests than whites. This stands to reason. Blacks have suffered greater deprivations than whites, and their protests have more often succeeded in bringing about change. But one should also note that the majority of both blacks and whites think that it is wrong to riot.

*Wheelchair demonstration
in Washington, D.C.
Here, citizens urge
legislation favorable to
handicapped Americans as
they wheel past the
Lincoln Memorial.*

Research in 10 California cities has shown that protesting by blacks and Hispanics reached a crescendo in the late 1960s and that it had its greatest lasting effect where it was coupled with effective mobilization of the minority group to support political candidates or capture elective office. The authors of the California study conclude:

> We know that protest is not enough. Protest alone is not sufficient for representation and the stronger forms of access and responsiveness. Something more is needed, and electoral effort is the key. Protest must be translated into electoral organizing, the traditional political activity of recruiting candidates, controlling the number who run, and developing support and coalitions. (Browning, Marshall, and Tabb, 1984: 263)

Although protesting is not enough, traditional political activity alone would probably not have brought about the increased political representation that blacks and Hispanics have achieved since the 1960s.

Protest through marches and demonstrations has become both sport and serious business in recent years. A large number of people take stands on one issue or another. But the number who actually protest is small, only 2 to 3 percent. At the same time, in some locales—especially black urban ghettos—a large percentage may engage in protests. The protesting minority has visibility and intensity. Thus, protests tend to have an impact well beyond the number of those involved. Also, as many as a fifth of Americans are potential protesters. They are willing to protest if necessary (Barnes and Kaase, 1979: 155).

Rigors of campaigning. In North Providence, Rhode Island, a candidate for the town council tries to persuade a potential voter to come to her door. When this effort failed, he left one of his campaign pamphlets on the front step.

Running for Public Office

Few of us try to gain public office—either by election or by appointment. Seeking office may involve deciding to invest much time, money, and energy in public affairs. Some political families, such as the Kennedys of Massachusetts, have huge personal wealth and fame that support generations of political prominence. But most public officeholders are not wealthy or famous, and campaigning for most offices does not require a lot of money. Moreover, the large number of elective offices—there are about 526,000 elected public officials in this country—provide a fair amount of opportunity to run.

HOW MUCH DO AMERICANS PARTICIPATE?

Many American engage in some kind of political activity. But the number varies from one activity to another. Our best estimates of the extent of political activity are shown in Figure 5–5. The most widespread activity is voting. Nearly two thirds of us vote in national and local elections with some regularity, while other kinds of political activity draw smaller numbers.

Political Activities

The University of Michigan Survey Research Center has conducted National Election Studies since 1952. These surveys regularly include questions asking about election-related poltical activities. One indicator of political activism is whether respondents "talked politics." (They are asked,

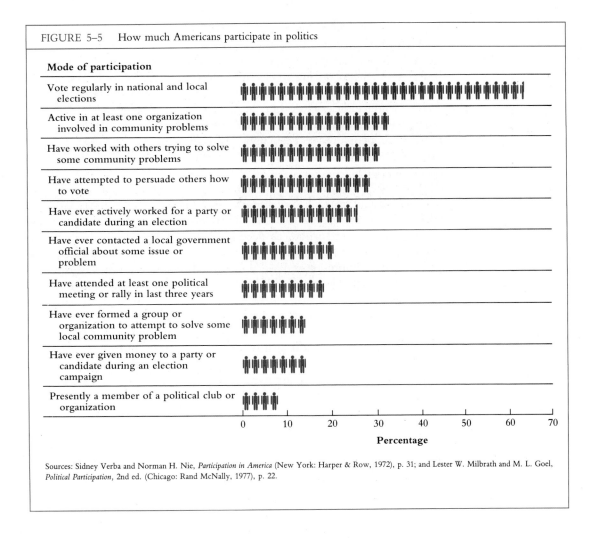

FIGURE 5–5   How much Americans participate in politics

Mode of participation

Vote regularly in national and local elections

Active in at least one organization involved in community problems

Have worked with others trying to solve some community problems

Have attempted to persuade others how to vote

Have ever actively worked for a party or candidate during an election

Have ever contacted a local government official about some issue or problem

Have attended at least one political meeting or rally in last three years

Have ever formed a group or organization to attempt to solve some local community problem

Have ever given money to a party or candidate during an election campaign

Presently a member of a political club or organization

0   10   20   30   40   50   60   70

Percentage

Sources: Sidney Verba and Norman H. Nie, *Participation in America* (New York: Harper & Row, 1972), p. 31; and Lester W. Milbrath and M. L. Goel, *Political Participation,* 2nd ed. (Chicago: Rand McNally, 1977), p. 22.

"During the campaign, did you talk to any people and try to show them why they should vote for one of the parties or candidates?") Since 1960, about a third of the respondents have reported this kind of activity in presidential years. This is a greater proportion than reported such activity in the 1950s. In 1976 and 1980, record proportions of Americans reported that they "talked politics" (37 percent in 1976 and 36 percent in 1980). But 1984 was a less talkative election: only 28 percent said that they talked to people and tried "to show them why they should vote for one of the parties or candidates." Since 1952, 6 to 10 percent have reported attending political meetings, rallies, and the like. The incidence of such activity has barely changed over the years.

In recent election years, party or candidate work has been twice as high as it was in the 1950s. Nevertheless, the proportions have been small—4 to 7 percent have reported working for a party or candidate in any one election. Fewer people have worn a campaign button or put a bumper sticker on their car during an election campaign. The figure is less than 10 percent, fewer than did so in the 1950s and the 1960s. These Survey Research Center indicators do not, of course, show, as Figure 5–5 does, the extent of participation in particular activities. Neither do they indicate how much people have been involved over a period of years. Instead, these election-by-election indicators show involvement for a single election campaign.

Is political participation in the United States high or low? The answer requires a comparison. Comparing levels of political activism today with levels in the past suggests that the overall level is higher today. As we saw in Chapter 1, voter turnout in elections has waxed and waned. But other kinds of political activity may well have increased. This could be because such activity is highly correlated with education. As the ranks of the educated have grown, levels of political activity may have also gone up.

A more precise contrast can be made between political participation in the United States and political participation in other democratic countries. Voter turnout is lower here than in Europe. But this does not seem to stem from greater political apathy among Americans. In party and campaign activity, we compare favorably with Europeans. In community activity, we are clearly more involved than Europeans (Nie and Verba, 1975: 24–25).

A study of political activity in the United States and four European democracies focused on action other than voting (see the comparison in Figure 5–6). Because European democracies have far fewer elections, each of which tends to draw a higher voter turnout than the many local, state, and national elections in the United States, this comparative study excluded voting. The results showed participation to be fairly high in this country. The authors note that "political apathy, by a wide margin, is lowest in the United States." They conclude that "the United States can be characterized as a fully developed participant political culture" (Barnes and Kaase, 1979; 168–69). In political involvement other than voting, their study found Americans more willing than Europeans to engage in a wide range of political activities, including protests and boycotts as well as conventional actions.

It seems paradoxical that Americans are more politically involved and aware than citizens in other democratic countries and yet go to the polls in elections in proportions well below the average for other democracies. This seeming paradox can be largely resolved when we consider the environmental inhibitions to U.S. voter participation. The electoral system, registration requirements, and loosely organized party system contribute mightily to depressing voter turnout in the United States. In European democracies, the system calls on voters to participate less frequently, the governments see to it that all voting-age citizens are registered, and the

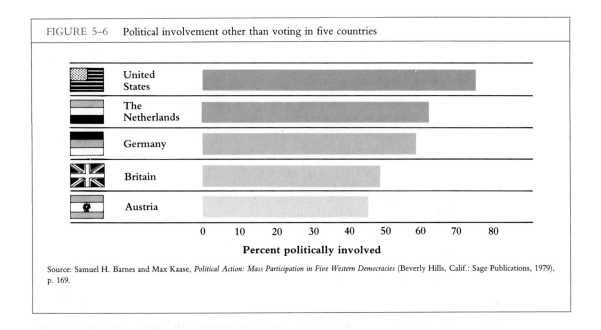

FIGURE 5–6   Political involvement other than voting in five countries

Percent politically involved

Source: Samuel H. Barnes and Max Kaase, *Political Action: Mass Participation in Five Western Democracies* (Beverly Hills, Calif.: Sage Publications, 1979), p. 169.

political parties fervently mobilize voters on a national scale. These comparisons between the turnout in the United States and in Europe are confirmed by very careful research, which political scientist Bingham Powell summarizes as follows:

> Americans do possess political attitudes that encourage their voting activity. If citizens in other democracies possessed the American configuration of attitudes, their voter participation would on average increase. However, the American attitudinal advantage is only a marginal enhancer of voting . . . because voting is so powerfully shaped by institutional context. In comparative perspective, the American registration rules, electoral system, and party system inhibit voter participation, outweighing by far the attitudinal advantage. (Powell, 1986: 17)

It appears likely that further relaxation of the state voter registration laws so as to encourage more Americans to register to vote would do more than anything else to help bridge the gap between levels of voter turnout in the United States and other democracies.

Types of Political Activity

For a long time, political scientists thought that political activity formed a hierarchy. Members of political clubs also engaged in community work, contacted public officials, engaged in party and campaign work, and voted in elections. Now we know that there are distinct types of politically active people. Involvement in one aspect of politics does not always mean involvement in another (Verba and Nie, 1972: 79–91).

Some Americans, 20 to 25 percent by the best estimate, are completely inactive. They take no part in political affairs. These inactives do not participate in community action or in party and campaign work; they do not contact public officials; and most of them do not vote. They are "out of it." They add very little to the political life of the nation, and they have very little effect on the course of public affairs.

The **voting specialists** are another group. They are not very active politically, but they do vote regularly. About one fifth of us are in this category. Although this is a fairly large group, note that it is not the case that most people, as often claimed, vote and do nothing else. Voting specialists are far from being a majority.

Community activists engage heavily in community work but are not much involved in partisan political activity. They make up about a fifth of the people. These activists are found in every community. In contrast, the political **campaigners**, about 15 percent of us, are little involved in community affairs but are heavily engaged in campaign work.

About 1 person in 10 is a **complete activist**. Complete activists engage in all kinds of political activity. They provide much of the personnel and leadership for politics, and doubtless their influence far exceeds their proportion of the population. Of all the types of politically active people, they rank highest in psychological involvement in politics, political skill, partisanship, issue awareness, and civic-mindedness.

In our country, people are free *not* to be active in politics and public affairs. A democracy may prefer that citizens be politically active but does not demand this. For many, being informed and active in public and civic life does not seem to pay off. As one observer of the politically inactive has written, they "cling tenaciously to ignorance of public affairs" partly because being unaware helps them avoid conflicts. Like the Communist who reads only Marxist tracts, these people may avoid politics so as not to threaten their sense of well-being. They may avoid political activity because they do not see it as meeting any of their needs. Politics seems far from the concerns of their daily lives. They may also avoid political activity because they fear that it might threaten their social environment; such activity might alienate customers, friends, neighbors, or employers (Lane, 1959: 113–114).

WHO ARE THE POLITICALLY ACTIVE?

The truly active people in politics, such as Stimson Bullitt, stand out. They have been called the "active minority" or the "politically active subculture." As we have seen, they take part in politics well beyond just voting. They also work in party organizations; they are active in the community; they contact public officials in person and by writing letters; they give money for election campaigns; and some of them become candidates for public office. Who are these highly active people?

FIGURE 5–7   Socioeconomic status and political participation

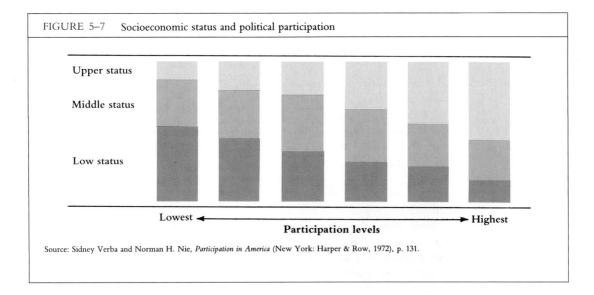

Source: Sidney Verba and Norman H. Nie, *Participation in America* (New York: Harper & Row, 1972), p. 131.

Socioeconomic Status

Politically active people tend to be well educated and to have high-status occupations and high incomes. These three traits—education, occupation, and income—indicate a person's **socioeconomic status**. The strong relationship between socioeconomic status and political activity is shown in Figure 5–7. In the lowest-participation group (at the far left of the figure), about 60 percent have low status, about a third have middle status, and only about 10 percent have high status. In contrast, in the highest-participation group (at the far right of the figure), 57 percent have high status, 29 percent have middle status, and 14 percent have low status.

One group stands out for its high rate of action in politics—the college educated. Most public officeholders and most of the people who occupy the higher positions at state and national levels have college degrees. Similarly, among those involved in politics, the college educated dominate. A 1975 Harris survey underscored the role of the college educated in the **politically active subculture**. About 38 percent of those 18 and over are college educated, but they make up 46 percent of the people most likely to vote and 57 percent of the most politically active.

Age and Participation

The rate of political involvement grows sharply from youth to middle age. The young usually have not established themselves in a community. They are apt to move often and to be deeply involved in finding an occupation. For the most part, they have relatively little stake in local affairs.

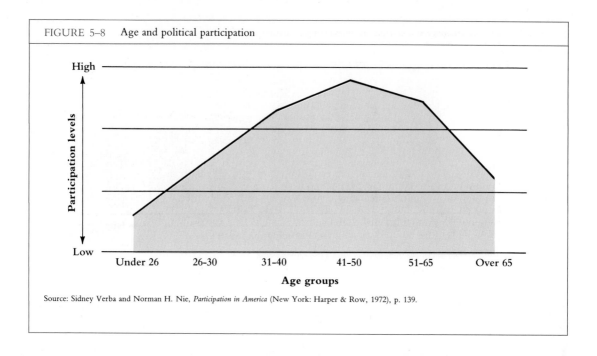

FIGURE 5–8   Age and political participation

Source: Sidney Verba and Norman H. Nie, *Participation in America* (New York: Harper & Row, 1972), p. 139.

A larger stake comes with extended residence, owning a home, forming a family, sending children to school, and taking part in community and job-related groups.

Figure 5–8 tells the story. It shows that participation levels are lowest among those aged 18 to 26. These levels go up smartly with increasing age to the group in their 40s. Though showing lower levels of involvement than people aged 41 to 50, those in their 50s participate in politics at relatively high levels. Participation drops off for those over 65, undoubtedly partly because of aging itself. People over 65 may lose some of their social interests. Some become physically infirm and unable to take part, and others withdraw after retirement.

Part of the surge in participation through middle age surely occurs because older groups have higher average socioeconomic status, for higher status enhances the likelihood of political activism. Much of the decline shown in Figure 5–8 occurs because, at present, people over 50 have relatively less education and income. They were raised in an era when education was less available than it is today, when job opportunities were meager, and when income levels were lower.

Political Participation by Minorities

Few political changes are more striking than the closing of the gap in the political participation of blacks and whites. Traditionally, the participation of blacks was much lower than that of whites. This is not hard to under-

LA ESPERANZA
DEL FUTURO

Nuestros hijos merecen una vida
mejor. Registrese y vote.
SU VOTO ES SU VOZ.

Drive to register Hispanic voters. This poster says, "The hope of the future . . . Our children deserve a better life. Register and vote. Your vote is your voice."

Gender and Political Activity

Studies in the 1950s showed men to be more politically active than women. This was largely because the average education level of women was lower than that of men. Since then, the education gap between men and women has closed, and so has the gap in political participation. Men still participate more than women, but in most respects not much more. The remaining differences are shown in Table 5–5. Although the participation of women is now about the same as that of men, they exercise much less political influence. Women constitute slightly more than half of the adult population, but far fewer women than men run for public offices or are elected. There seem to be four main reasons why women are less active than men:

1. General social values and norms discourage women from highly active political roles; their socially set roles as housewives and mothers do not encourage them to run for office.

TABLE 5–5   Political participation of women compared to that of men

	Women	Men
Are definitely registered to vote	77	80
Always vote in presidential elections	48	51
Try to influence others on political issues	26	35
Write public officials	25	29
Wear political buttons or stickers	14	14
Contribute money to campaigns	9	12
Have worked for a candidate	6	4

Source: John W. Soule and Wilma E. McGrath, "A Comparative Study of Male-Female Political Attitudes at Citizen and Elite Levels," in *A Portrait of Marginality: The Political Behavior of the American Women*, ed. Marianne Githens and Jewel L. Prestage (New York: Longman, 1977), pp. 178–95. Reprinted by permission.

2. Female socialization discourages political activity. Thus, women's motivations for political careers are not as strong as those of men.

3. Political careers are not felt to particularly fit women's family duties.

4. Men discriminate against women.

Exactly what part each of these reasons plays in reducing the number of highly active women in politics is not certain. The explanations of those who are highly involved provide some clues.

Jeane Kirkpatrick, former ambassador to the United Nations, studied delegates to the 1972 national party conventions. Her intensive interviews with large samples of delegates included questions about sex roles in politics. Some results of this study are shown in Table 5–6. It gives answers to this question: "In general, there have been fewer women candidates for political office than men. Why do you think this has been the case?" The answers of men and women were about the same. Most of the respondents said that social values were the main reason. The fewest blamed male discrimination.

The study gave other evidence about attitudes toward women's failure to seek public office. Most of the respondents agreed that "men prevent women from seeking political careers." Nearly half disagreed with the claim that "women have just as much opportunity as men to become political leaders." At the same time, many said that local party leaders encouraged women to run for political office. As many women respondents reported preferential treatment as reported discrimination. Most of these respondents denied ever being discriminated against. The political experiences of women differ in different areas and different partisan circumstances, so that it is hard to generalize. Most of the women respondents still believed men were more suited for political office than women. The best conclusion now seems to be that "women's low participation in

TABLE 5–6   Why women rarely run for public office

There are fewer women candidates for public office because of	*Percentage of*	
	Women	*Men*
Society in general	45	47
Lack of motivation	25	21
Family responsibilities	22	25
Male discrimination	8	7

Source: Jeane Kirkpatrick, *The New Presidential Elite: Men and Women in National Politics* (New York; Russell Sage Foundation and Twentieth Century Fund, 1976), p. 455.

power today derives from relatively low political ambition *and* from male prejudice" (Kirkpatrick, 1976: 455, 458, 488).

Careful research on the aspirations and experiences of women politicians is beginning to grow beyond Kirkpatrick's pioneering work. For instance, a systematic study based on interviews of 1,212 women who ran for state legislatures in 1976 indicated that at that level women were about as ambitious as men. The author concluded that "the number of women among elective officeholders has been kept low partly, and perhaps primarily, by systematic limitations in the structure of political opportunity" (Carroll, 1985: 157). Some features of the opportunity structure—access to financial backing and the advantage of previous office-holding experience—affect female candidates more than males. In many other ways, however, political offices are available to men and women in about the same measure. But "because far fewer women than men presently hold elective office, the barriers in the political opportunity structure work against women as a group to a far greater extent than they work against men" (Carroll, 1985: 158).

Organizational Involvement

When Alexis de Tocqueville observed our politics in the 1830s, he concluded that a key feature of our democracy was our tendency to be joiners. He thought democracy depended on people with an active voluntary organizational life. His conclusion, reached without the help of modern survey research methods, seems largely correct. There is now much evidence to support his observation that "a rich political participant life" rests on "a rich associational life." Taking part in all kinds of groups is one of the strongest predictors of active political involvement (Verba and Nie, 1972: 175). Americans are not more prone to join groups than people in other societies, but those Americans who are group members are more active than people in other industrial countries.

Jeane Kirkpatrick, political science professor and former UN ambassador, testifies before the U.S. Senate Armed Services Committee on the INF treaty in January 1988. She testified that she favored the treaty even though it left "Europe somewhat vulnerable, the Soviet Union somewhat less vulnerable, and the alliance somewhat weaker." Some Republicans favored Kirkpatrick as the vice-presidential candidate in 1988.

About two thirds of Americans belong to some social, religious, economic, or professional group; about 40 percent are active members. Active group members are much more politically involved than nonmembers. In Figure 5–11, the effects of socioeconomic status, age, sex, and race have been removed to show the "pure" effect of group membership on participation. The direct relationship between group membership and political participation is clearly evidenced in the curve's steady rise. Group involvement has an independent effect on political activism. It also enlarges the gap between high and low socioeconomic status. High-status people are more apt to be active in organizations.

Merely being a member of a group does not foster political action. One must also be *active*. Inactive members participate no more in politics than nonmembers. In addition, though blacks are no more active in groups than whites, their participation is more apt to spark political activism. Involved members of such groups as the Elks Club, League of Women Voters, NAACP, American Legion, National Farmers' Union, PTA, or American Medical Association learn group-related skills. They mix with like-minded people who may come to share their concerns. They learn about public affairs and about how to use available resources to reach their goals. Perhaps their sense of civic duty is aroused. The participant, democratic person is clearly one who becomes actively involved in organizations.

Membership in American political parties is unique. Most Americans identify themselves as Republicans or Democrats, but few are members of these parties in a strict sense. Being a Democrat is different from being a

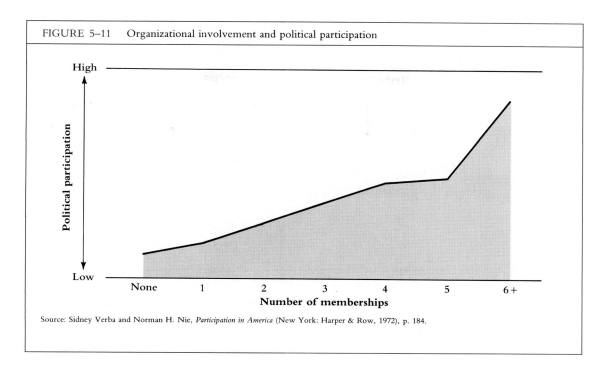

FIGURE 5–11   Organizational involvement and political participation

Source: Sidney Verba and Norman H. Nie, *Participation in America* (New York: Harper & Row, 1972), p. 184.

member of the Rotary Club or Lambda Chi Alpha. In those organizations, membership means paying dues, attending meetings, taking part in activities, perhaps even carrying a membership card. Few of us are card-carrying, dues-paying, meeting-attending party members.

There are some organized political clubs in our country, but fewer than 10 percent of Americans belong to such clubs. Membership in other kinds of groups is not very great either. Americans are about as apt to belong to strictly political clubs as they are to belong to veterans', youth, or professional groups. Many more belong to sports, fraternal, school service, or labor groups. However, members of political clubs are usually quite active.

Partisanship

Political parties are, for most people, not membership groups in the strict sense. Yet millions of us identify with a party. We think of ourselves as Democrats or Republicans (or Communists, Socialists, Libertarians, or whatever). **Party identification** indicates psychological involvement in politics, and about 80 percent of us are so involved. Does identifying with a party, and the strength of that identification, foster political action?

The short answer is that partisanship does foster political activity. Those who identify with a party are far more politically active than those

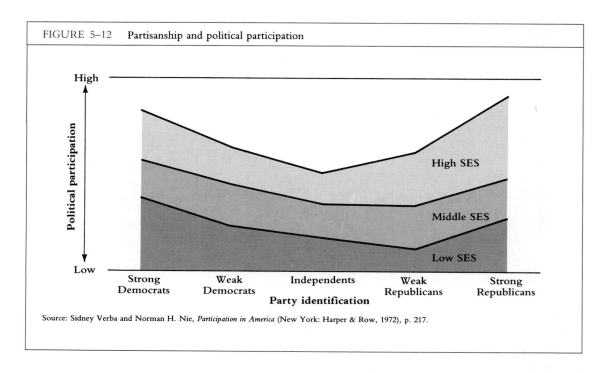

FIGURE 5–12   Partisanship and political participation

Source: Sidney Verba and Norman H. Nie, *Participation in America* (New York: Harper & Row, 1972), p. 217.

who do not. What is more, though those of higher status are more apt to identify with a political party than those of lower status, both groups take part in politics more than do independents, regardless of status. Also, political action rises with how strongly partisan people are. This is shown in Figure 5–12. "Strong" Democrats and Republicans are more active politically than are "weak" ones or independents in each major socioeconomic status (SES) category.

Notice in Figure 5–12 that Republicans, especially high-status ones, participate more than Democrats. This Republican "hyperactivity" is very large if one looks only at differences between parties. Much of the difference arises because there are more high-status Republicans, yet even when that difference is factored out of the comparison, the hyperactivity of Republicans persists. Also, Republicans hold political beliefs more strongly than Democrats. The higher social status Republicans and their more intensely held beliefs help explain why their rate of political activity is higher than that of Democrats.

Such factors as socioeconomic status, maturity, group involvement, and partisanship tend to raise political involvement. People also take part more if their environment is conducive to it. Political activism depends partly on who people are. But it also depends partly on where they live. We would expect, for example, to find levels of political activity higher in areas where political parties are competitive.

TABLE 5–7   Electoral competition and political participation

Winner's share of the popular vote in district (1972)	Percent of average voting participation
Competitive	
Under 55 percent	65
55–59.9 percent	62
60–64.9 percent	59
Uncompetitive	
65 percent and above	50

Source: Kevin P. Phillips and Paul H. Blackman, *Electoral Reform and Voter Participation* (Washington, D.C.: American Enterprise Institute for Public Policy Research, 1975), p. 37.

Competition and Participation

Political participation is greatest when rival parties and candidates compete strongly for public offices. This is easy to show. Thus, another reason for the low levels of activism in the South is that large parts of the area are politically stagnant. One-party, noncompetitive politics breeds citizen inertia.

The tie between competitive environments and involvement is well illustrated by checking voter turnout in a congressional election against the tightness of contests for congressional seats, as shown in Table 5–7 with data from the 1972 election. In competitive districts (those where the winner got less than 55 percent of the vote), about 65 percent of voters went to the polls. In uncompetitive districts (where the winner got more than 65 percent of the vote), voting participation fell to 50 percent of the voting population.

Why is this so? If an election contest is lopsided, its outcome is a foregone conclusion. Ordinary citizens are unlikely to get interested in it. This also holds true if candidates from two parties do not differ on any issues or present voters with any other meaningful choice. Where politics is "Tweedledee and Tweedledum," voter reaction is apt to be "ho hum." Another consideration is the degree of organized party activity. Where parties do not compete vigorously for office, grass-roots party work is likely to be sparse. Workers will not contact voters, proselytize, stimulate interest, or work to get voters to the polls. People who are contacted by party workers in election campaigns are more likely to vote than people who are not contacted. Thus, in noncompetitive environments with little or no campaigning, low participation is likely.

CONCLUSIONS

In the United States, politics is not the foremost concern of many citizens. People are free to take part in politics or not; many choose to have little to do with it. Legal restrictions, such as registration for voting, may discourage some. The extent of political inactivity is far greater, however, than could result from legal limitations alone.

Political participation makes a difference. Those who are active in politics have more access to political leadership than those who are not active. The policy positions and attitudes of leaders are more likely to coincide with those of politically active people than with those of inactives. Political and governmental decisions are very responsive to the beliefs and preferences of people in the politically active subculture. And decisions about who is nominated and elected to public office are greatly influenced by politically active people. "Government for the people" may well involve accounting for the opinions and needs of the politically inactive; inactives may be represented because of their social and economic needs. But "government by the people" is very largely government by the politically active.

In this chapter, we have explored the key elements of political activity in the United States. We have shown that

1. People may take part in politics in many ways. They may vote; engage in party and campaign activity; involve themselves in community affairs; contact public officials; take part in marches, demonstrations, and other protests; run for political office; or be active party members. Those who are active in politics are likely to have more influence over the course of public affairs than those who are not active.

2. Voter turnout varies in several important ways. In the presidential elections held since 1960, national levels of voter turnout have declined. There are sizable differences in the levels of voter turnout in the states, with very high levels in some states notably Minnesota and Montana, and very low levels in others, such as Nevada and South Carolina. Turnout also varies among elected offices. For example, more people vote in presidential contests than in congressional contests. While relatively low turnout in a presidential election does not seem to have much effect on the outcome—since nonvoters, were they to vote, would probably distribute their votes in about the same ways that voters do—nonvoting may have serious effects on many elections that are less competitive and visible.

3. Those who take part in politics are by no means a random sample of the general adult population. They form an elite in the sense that they are better educated and have higher incomes and higher-status occupations than nonparticipants. Thus, ironically, those who need the greatest public or government help are the least active in politics.

4. Political activity is fostered by several factors. The most important factor is probably organizational involvement. The people who are most involved in social, economic, religious, civic, and other groups are also most likely to take part in politics. Political participation grows with age. This is partly because increasing age is accompanied by increasing involvement in organizations. But psychological factors such as group consciousness and partisan ties can also foster political activity. This is well illustrated by the political activism of blacks whose racial consciousness has been raised and by the heightened political involvement of persons who have strong ties to a political party.

5. Where politics is competitive, people take a more active part in it. Competition sparks interest in politics. It also creates incentives for parties and their leaders to organize and mobilize people for political involvement.

FURTHER READING

BROWNING, RUFUS P.; DALE ROGERS MARSHALL; and DAVID H. TABB (1984) *Protest Is Not Enough: The Struggle of Blacks and Hispanics for Equality in Urban Politics*. Berkeley: University of California Press. A study of electoral mobilization and protesting by blacks and Hispanics in 10 California cities that attempts to account for variations among cities in the effectiveness of protest politics. The authors conclude that protest can make a difference but that "protest is not enough."

LANE, ROBERT E. (1959) *Political Life: Why People Get Involved in Politics*. Glencoe, Ill.: Free Press. A classic study explaining the social, political, and psychological factors that influence people to participate in politics.

MILBRATH, LESTER W., and M. L. GOEL (1977) *Political Participation*. 2nd ed. Chicago: Rand McNally. An examination of the factors affecting political participation that draws its evidence from a large number of countries.

VERBA, SIDNEY, and NORMAN H. NIE (1972) *Participation in America*. New York: Harper & Row. Based on sample survey data, this study distinguishes various ways of participating in politics, examines why people participate in different ways and to different degrees, and assesses the consequences of participation.

THE PARADOX OF OUR POLITICAL PARTIES

$\mathcal{P}$olitical parties: now you see them, now you don't. "The Party's Over," proclaimed the noted political reporter David S. Broder (1971) nearly a generation ago. This country's parties, he argued, were in decline, probably for good; candidates and campaigns had become independent and even antiparty. Subsequently, many pundits wrote the parties' obituaries. But in the mid-1980s, two respected political analysts announced that "The Party Goes On." After the upheaval of the 1960s, they explained, a new party system of professional, Washington-based organizations had arisen to finance campaigns and even select candidates (Kayden and Mahe, 1985). Then, Larry J. Sabato, a political scientist, joined the book title war with *The Party's Just Begun* (1988). Though conceding that party loyalty had eroded, Sabato believed that if people considered parties valuable, they could revive partisan spirit through changes in law and practice.

Confusion over political parties flows partly from the fact that parties mean different things to different people. The political journalist Broder saw parties through the eyes of the candidates he covered. The party professionals Kayden and Mahe assessed parties in organizational terms. The political scientist Sabato examined partisan loyalties among the mass electorate. These are all partial sketches of the parties—which embody candidates (and other activists), organizations, and voter attitudes. ∞

*P*olitical parties in the United States have been paradoxical and many-faceted from their very beginnings. Although the founders feared their rise and did not mention them in the Constitution, they were practically an American invention when they burst on the scene full-blown in the 1830s. Many scholars credit the parties with making possible a "more perfect union" by joining politicians in the country's far-flung parts and by linking the branches of government that the Constitution separates. Yet despite their longevity, our parties are weaker and more loosely organized than those of any other advanced democracy. And although critics and commentators have consigned them to the graveyard, their organizations are now flourishing. Overpraised and underestimated, our parties are a unique kind of organization that is worth examining in detail.

In this chapter, we describe and analyze parties, their forms and functions. Because parties are varied and elusive creatures, we opt for describing them as tripartite social structures. First we explore the so-called parties in the electorate—partisan attitudes and loyalties among voters. Then, we describe parties as organizations: how they are structured to choose and promote candidates, mainly at the national level. Finally, we consider "parties in the government," the cadres of partisan officeholders at the local, state, and national levels.

WHAT ARE POLITICAL PARTIES?

Political parties are defined in many ways; no definition is universally accepted. Edmund Burke, the 18th-century English conservative, defined a party as a body of people "united for promoting by their joint endeavors the national interest upon some particular principle in which they are all agreed." This idealistic definition does not fully apply to our own diverse parties. Other definitions stress the organizational side of parties, their ideologies, or their stands on issues. Still others begin, as we will, with the various ways in which parties reveal themselves in everyday political life.

The goal of capturing control of government is the nub of the parties' functions. Thus, a political party can be defined as "any group, however loosely organized, seeking to elect governmental officeholders under a given label" (Epstein, 1967: 9). In pursuing this goal, parties perform a number of tasks: they nominate candidates, contest elections, shape voters' attitudes, organize the branches of government, build broad coalitions out of issues and factions, and provide citizens with a way to control the course of public affairs. Political parties have many guises. Their components range from

> the weakly committed voter who usually supports the party's candidates to the dedicated activist with an ideological commitment who volunteers time and treasure; from the party boss seeking to run a disciplined patronage dispensing organization to the public official who, while elected on a party label, seeks to project an image independent of party. (Bibby, 1987: 4)

For most of us, political parties are synonymous with such traditional broad-scale parties as the Democrats and the Republicans, which have dominated national and state elections for most of our history. These parties began with the start of mass elections in the 1800s. They have developed complex structures for recruiting, promoting, and unifying office-holders. For well over a century, they virtually monopolized the voting process in this country.

American parties differ sharply from parties in other democratic regimes. They have always had less coherent policy programs than their counterparts in parliamentary systems. Their organizations tended to be state and local rather than national. Instead of relying on masses of dues-paying members, our parties were built on **patronage**—the appointment of loyalists to government jobs. After the turn of the 20th century, American parties began to lose control of their own affairs, as state-run primaries increasingly determined which candidates would run in their name. As Epstein has pointed out (1986: 4), our parties' weaknesses did not appear overnight. "The fact is that American party organizations have not, at least in this century, dominated election campaigns in the manner of European parties both before and during the television age."

The hold of our parties over electoral politics has, however, weakened still further over the last generation. Party leaders do not have free rein to name those who run for office under their party's label. Candidates have to recruit followers—or hire firms—to run their campaigns, raise funds, and contact voters. Advertising, media, and direct mail consultants help mobilize voters. Interest groups—labor unions, professional associations, and industry organizations, to name a few—play important and growing roles in electoral politics. (The special roles of interest groups and the communications media in American politics will be explained in the next two chapters.) Although a majority of Americans call themselves Democrats or Republicans, these Americans no longer cast their votes simply out of party loyalty.

How are parties different from other types of political groups? The differences are not always easy to demonstrate—especially because interest groups nowadays invest heavily in electoral politics. However, parties remain the primary organizational entities that contest elections; they are the only groups that run candidates under their own labels. Moreover, the concerns of parties are typically much broader than those of interest groups—which of necessity voice the needs of an industry, or a cause, or a special class of people. Finally, unlike most private associations, parties are quasi-public organizations that are heavily regulated by federal and state laws. As Frank J. Sorauf summarizes, "The American party is an open, inclusive, and semi-public political organization composed of its own clientele, a tangible organization, and personnel in government. As such it stands alone and unique in the American political system" (1984: 10).

Two party leaders. Democratic National Committee Chairman Paul G. Kirk [left] chats with Republican National Committee Chairman Frank J. Fahrenkopf, Jr. before their appearance on a 1988 TV interview program. The two were chosen by their respective national party committees to serve as the chief administrative officers and spokesmen of their parties.

Two Parties—with Variations

The most obvious fact about our parties is that there are normally two, and only two, of them. For most of our history, our elections have been dominated by two broad coalition parties: Federalists versus Anti-Federalists; Democrats versus Whigs; Republicans versus Democrats.

Yet there is nothing sacred about two-party politics. Many countries have multiparty systems. In other countries, one-party governments (military juntas or ideological or nationalist movements) control political life. Why, then, has the two-party system been such a fixture in the United States?

The prevalence of two-party competition is not easy to explain. Some people think that there is a basic dualism in politics based on personality, character, or ideology: optimists versus pessimists, extroverts versus introverts, reformers versus traditionalists. But if this is so, why don't all countries have two-party systems? It may be that American history embodies a tradition of debating major issues from two (and only two) sides. Some think that the battle over the Constitution reflected the conflict that pitted eastern financial and commercial interests against western frontiersmen and that this shifted to a conflict of North against South and then urban against rural or rich against poor (Key, 1964: 229 ff.). Other cleavages—along religious or ethnic lines or even economic class—did not congeal into consistent partisan divisions.

The best explanation for two-partyism lies in the electoral rules of the game. Our **winner-take-all elections** ensure that there will be only one victor for each office. Our executives are **unitary,** elected individually rather than as part of a council or commission. Our legislators are each chosen from **single-member districts**—only one for a given geographic area. (Although two senators represent each state, they run singly, in separate years.)

Countries with more than two major parties usually have multiple-member districts. In these countries, minority parties can hope to gain offices somewhat in proportion to their overall electoral strength (Duverger, 1954). But to wield influence in the United States, a splinter party must either replace one of the existing major parties or force a major party to adopt its objectives.

Once a two-party pattern has been established, powerful forces keep it going. Politicians have a vested stake in the system that put them into power. They pass election laws designed to entrench the major parties and erect barriers against third-party intrusion. Laws discourage minor parties from getting on the ballot. Voting machines and ballots are sometimes designed to encourage citizens to vote a straight party ticket rather than selecting individual candidates. But two-partyism is not simply a matter of legal manipulation. As we will see, many voters have long-standing party preferences that are quite firm and stable over time.

Presidential competition between the two parties has been close over the past 100 years. In the 25 presidential elections from 1892 through 1988, the Republicans won 13 and the Democrats won 11 (see Table 6–1). Since World War II, several presidential elections have been very close, especially those in 1948, 1960, 1968, and 1976. Yet there have been long stretches of one-party dominance—periods more like "one and a half parties" than strict two-party competition. Realignment in the critical election of 1896 enthroned the "Grand Old Party," or GOP, and threw the Democratic party into temporary eclipse; Franklin Roosevelt's coalition did the same thing to the GOP in the 1930s.

Below the national level, strict two-party competition has been even less the norm. Many congressional districts have nearly always been "safe" in the Democratic or Republican column. Indeed, the number of truly competitive districts (called "marginal districts") has dwindled in our era (Mayhew, 1974). At the state level, Austin Ranney (1976) has developed an "index of competitiveness." This index, drawn from election results, serves as a "snapshot" of shifting party balances. Applying the index to the period from 1974 through 1980, a team of political scientists classed 8 states (most of which were southern) as one-party Democratic, 20 states as either modified one-party Democratic or modified one-party Republican, and 22 states, or fewer than half, as two-party competitive (see Figure 6–1). During the 1970s, the Democratic party strengthened its position in

TABLE 6–1   Shifting national party fortunes (partisan control of the White House and Congress)

	Presidential elections		House of Representatives		Senate	
	Democrats	Republicans	Democrats	Republicans	Democrats	Republicans
1861–1931 (37th–71st Congress)	4	14	12	23	5	30
1931–1988 (72nd–100th Congress)	8	6	27	2	23	5

12 states. Such indexes, based on past election results, do not always reflect current partisan balances: since the most recent compilation, for example, Democratic fortunes have fallen in some of the states. How would you rate your state today on such a scale of partisanship?

The smaller the electoral unit, the less competitive it is likely to be. Local constituencies may be too small to have a balanced mix of social, economic, and population ingredients. Thus, the features that strongly favor one party may prevail. Studies have shown that a "typical" Democratic district tends to have mostly working-class people, ethnic groups, Catholics, Jews, blacks, Hispanics, or ethnic groups from southern or eastern Europe. A "typical" Republican district tends to have executives and professionals, higher-income groups, Protestants, and English or German ethnic stocks.

Another barrier to local competition may be poor media coverage of local elections. National and statewide elections draw much press coverage. Thus, all contenders have a chance to gain public attention and support. In local races, however, traditional patterns may prevail because media coverage is scanty or confusing. Many states are listed as one-party in Figure 6–1 on the basis of local elections. But these same states swing back and forth between parties in presidential, senatorial, and gubernatorial contests.

However widespread the two-party system, then, it is by no means a monopoly. Two-partyism is a broad concept that ignores many variations. Truly balanced competition between the parties is fairly rare. Try to think of two-partyism as a model or norm that describes the overall picture but not every specific election or electoral district.

Minor Parties

Two-party dominance is also challenged by minor-party factions or movements. Since the 1830s, some 100 minor parties have participated in the presidential races. Sometimes they have affected the outcome. Histor-

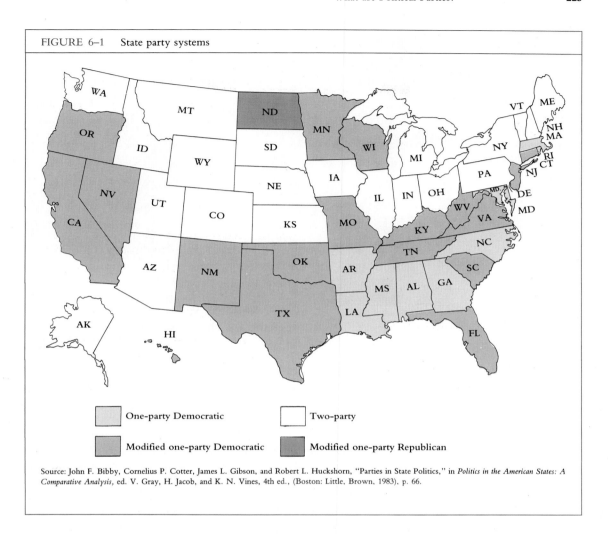

FIGURE 6–1   State party systems

One-party Democratic

Two-party

Modified one-party Democratic

Modified one-party Republican

Source: John F. Bibby, Cornelius P. Cotter, James L. Gibson, and Robert L. Huckshorn, "Parties in State Politics," in *Politics in the American States: A Comparative Analysis,* ed. V. Gray, H. Jacob, and K. N. Vines, 4th ed., (Boston: Little, Brown, 1983), p. 66.

ically, the average vote for minor-party presidential candidates has been a little more than 5 percent of the total. In the 1980 presidential election, John B. Anderson, a former Illinois congressman, pulled 7 percent of the vote as an independent who appealed to people dissatisfied with the two major candidates, Jimmy Carter and Ronald Reagan.

Minor parties differ sharply in their aims and in their likelihood of success. Some are narrow and sectarian, formed around a single ideology, issue, or leader. Parties of this kind may be fleeting or durable. Without exception, they are small and have no chance of winning office or even of wielding much influence over the major parties. They enter elections

Eugene V. Debs [left] (1855–1926) founded the Socialist Party of the United States and ran for president five times between 1900 and 1920. George Wallace [right] was the standard-bearer for the American Independent party, which won nearly 14 percent of the vote in 1968.

mainly to publicize their goals. Examples of such parties are the Socialist Labor, Socialist Workers, Prohibition, Libertarian, and Communist parties.

Occasionally, however, broad-based third-party movements form around a charismatic candidate or around a burning issue that the major parties have put aside. Such movements may throw an election one way or the other. They may also reflect major unresolved issues that can become the basis for party realignment (Rosenstone, Behr, and Lazarus, 1984). (See Table 6–2.) In the 1860s, a splinter party, the Republicans, merged the antislavery movement with long-standing regional concerns (tariff protection and cheap western land) and became the dominant major party. In 1912, the GOP was split by Theodore Roosevelt's progressive Bull Moose faction, helping to send Democrat Woodrow Wilson to the White House.

Minor parties are constant reminders of our diverse politics. They germinate new ideas. The abolition of slavery, women's suffrage, direct election of senators, regulation of monopolies, farm price supports, social security, and the progressive income tax were all first proposed by third parties. In advancing such proposals, minor parties convey a warning to the major parties: If you ignore emerging public concerns, you risk defeat or obsolescence.

Third-party candidates run for president. John Anderson [left] won 7 percent of the 1980 presidential vote with his Independent party. Sonia Johnson [center] was a 1984 Citizens party candidate for president, and Ed Clark [right] carried the Libertarian party banner in 1980.

Lenora Fulani. Independent presidential candidate in the 1988 election, Fulani is shown here with homeless activist supporters.

TABLE 6–2   Third-party ventures*

Candidate (Party)	Year	Percent of popular vote	Electoral votes
William Wirt (Anti-Masonic)	1832	8	7
Martin Van Buren (Free Soil)	1848	10	0
Millard Fillmore (Whig-American)	1856	22	8
John Bell (Constitutional Union)	1860	13	39
John C. Breckinridge (Southern Democrat)	1860	18	72
James B. Weaver (Populist)	1892	9	22
Theodore Roosevelt (Progressive)	1912	27	88
Eugene V. Debs (Socialist)	1912	6	0
Robert M. La Follette (Progressive)	1924	17	13
George C. Wallace (American Independent)	1968	14	46
John B. Anderson (Independent)	1980	7	0

*Based on third-party candidates receiving 5 percent or more of the popular vote.

PARTIES IN THE ELECTORATE

Although few of us are card-carrying party members, most of us are attracted to or repelled by one or both of the major political parties. And we tend to assess the parties, positively or negatively, in reaching our conclusions about issues and candidates. That is why social scientists regard the parties as **reference groups**—groups that give cues or reference points to people who may have little or no formal connection with the parties. Thus, party "membership" may be seen as a psychological attraction to one or another party.

A majority of people, of course, register with a party for the purpose of elections. Party registration can be a misleading indicator, however, because it may mask the registrant's true partisanship. For example, many people register with a locally dominant party to gain social acceptance or to be able to vote in its primaries. Social scientists therefore focus their attention on attitudes and behaviors that indicate partisanship—for example, feelings of closeness to one party or the other, favorable or unfavorable evaluations of the parties, or consistent voting patterns.

Party Identification

The most commonly used measure of partisanship, **party identification,** is gathered from public opinion surveys. "Generally speaking," the interviewer asks, "do you usually think of yourself as a Republican, Democrat, Independent, or what?" Respondents who name a party are probed on the strength of their ties; those who claim to be independents are asked whether they lean toward one party or the other. The result is a scale of party ties indicating both the strength and the direction of partisanship.

The donkeys symbolizes the Democratic party. A pair of donkey dolls are attached to the Montana delegation marker on the floor of the 1984 Democratic National Convention in San Francisco.

Devised in the 1940s, this scale continues to be used in major opinion surveys.

Political scientists thus conceive of partisanship as "a positive sense of affect toward one of the parties"—a sense of belonging (Wattenberg, 1986: 10). This psychological attachment is learned early in life, from one's parents or peers, and it usually grows stronger with age (see Chapter 5). Researchers have found that in the United States this attachment, rather than legal membership or contact with party organizations, determines party loyalty, or *partisanship*.

Party loyalties have been remarkably stable since the 1930s (Niemi and Weisberg, 1984). Yet significant shifts have taken place in recent years (see Figure 6–2). In the 1960s and 1970s, there was a surge in the number of those who called themselves independents. Some present-day "independents" are true independents; others admit to being closer to one party than to the other. Analysts differ on how to treat such people, but the prevailing view is that the "leaners," at least, are really closet partisans who should probably be lumped with the Republicans or the Democrats.

FIGURE 6–2   Political party identification, 1981–1987

Question: Generally speaking, do you usually consider yourself a Republican, a Democrat, an Independent, or what?

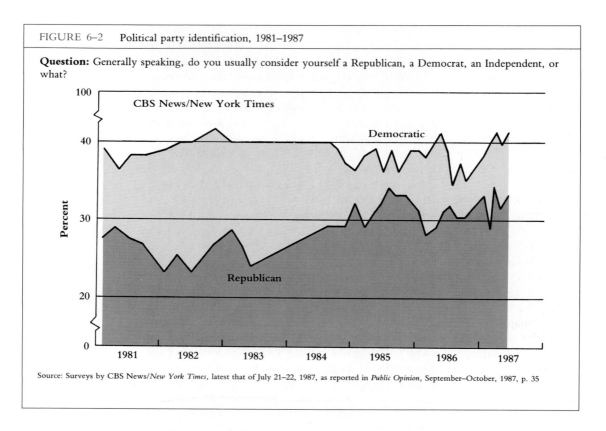

Source: Surveys by CBS News/*New York Times*, latest that of July 21–22, 1987, as reported in *Public Opinion*, September–October, 1987, p. 35

Several other shifts have taken place in party loyalty patterns. The proportion of whites claiming to be strong Democrats has declined in the South, a traditional Democratic stronghold, and elsewhere. The failed presidential candidacy of Senator Barry Goldwater (R–Ariz.) in 1964 and President Nixon's resignation in 1974 were setbacks for the Republican party. By the 1980s, however, the GOP had staged an impressive comeback, reaching virtual parity with the Democrats. In recent years, citizens coming of voting age have been less likely to be Democrats and more likely to be independent or Republican. Older age groups, in contrast, have been reporting stable patterns of party identification over the last 40 years.

Party loyalties are not everything. National and statewide elections often veer away from the overall party balance. From 1952 through 1984, Republican presidential candidates won six elections, four of them by wide margins, and Democratic presidential candidates won three times, only once by a landslide (in 1964, against the hapless Goldwater). Yet Democratic congressional candidates captured more than half of the two-party vote in virtually every election year.

The social groups associated with each party help explain the difference between party loyalty and election results. The Democrats tend to attract lower socioeconomic groupings, whose members as a rule vote less often than the average. The Republicans, on the other hand, have the allegiance of higher socioeconomic groupings, whose members are more faithful in going to the polls. Moreover, the Republicans today hold a sizable advantage in organization and funding. This means that they are better able than the Democrats to mobilize their supporters.

In other words, party identification figures need to be discounted by the likelihood that partisan voters will or will not go to the polls on election day. Prior to the 1980s, when the Democrats commanded about a 60–40 edge in party identification, their typical proportion of votes in presidential elections was only 53–55 percent nationally—a figure pretty close to the two-party margin of votes in House and Senate contests nationwide (Converse, 1966). With the closer partisan balance of the 1980s, the results became even more unpredictable.

Moreover, party identification fails to account for swings in presidential elections. Even in the post–World War II period of Democratic ascendancy, the "minority" Republicans captured the presidency twice as often as the "majority" Democrats. Long-term loyalty can be temporarily deflected by such short-term forces as candidates or issues. Many Democrats, for example, voted for Eisenhower in the 1950s without altering their basic party allegiance, just as many Republicans deserted their party to support Lyndon Johnson over Goldwater in 1984.

Many analysts go further and contend that party identification is a misleading indicator of citizens' voting preferences, especially in highly visible nationwide and even statewide contests. The indicators preferred by these analysts are actual voting records (which may depart from underlying party loyalties) or views about which party is best able to cope with the leading problems of the day. These indicators yield an even more fluid picture of citizens' partisan attachments.

Average people today—better educated and bombarded by media and interest group appeals—wear their party mantles lightly. In one study (Dennis, 1966), more than 8 out of 10 people thought that "the best rule in voting is to pick the candidate regardless of party label." A majority thought that the parties confused issues more than they clarified issues. They felt that government would work better without party conflict and that parties caused needless conflicts.

Voters' loyalties are weaker than they once were. "Perhaps the most dramatic political change in the American public," a team of voting analysts writes, "has been the decline of partisanship" (Nie, Verba, and Petrocik, 1976: 47–48). These analysts summarize the decline as follows:

1. *Fewer people have strong, steady ties with a party.* From 1952 to 1964, election studies found that about three fourths of the electorate identified themselves as either Democrats or Republicans and that

The elephant symbolizes the Republican party. A Michigan delegate to the 1984 Republican National Convention in Dallas wears a Detroit Tigers baseball cap complete with elephant earmuffs.

roughly half of these voters regarded themselves as strong partisans. After 1964, the proportions of party identifiers and strong partisans both declined by about 10 percentage points.

2. *Party affiliations are less often a guide to voting.* The number of straight-ticket voters has declined significantly. Nearly 60 percent of all voters report that they voted for different parties in presidential elections, and about half of that proportion split their party votes between presidential and congressional candidates or between House and Senate candidates.

3. *Parties are less often used as standards of evaluation.* The correlation between voters' ratings of parties and their ratings of the parties' candidates has declined over the years.

4. *Parties are less often objects of positive feelings.* The long-term decline of partisanship reflects not so much hostility toward the parties as rising feelings of neutrality or indifference toward them.

5. *Partisanship is less likely to be passed from one generation to another.* While older generations have clung to their party labels—acquired when parties meant more to voters than they do now—those labels no longer have the importance that they once had.

Partisanship made something of a comeback in the 1980s. After building gradually over decades and surging between the mid-1960s and the mid-1970s, the proportion of voters outside the parties has remained steady and even declined somewhat. The main beneficiary of this decline

to the North; an influx of Yankee Republicans, especially in urban areas; a new generation of native-born Southerners who could be dislodged from the region's Democratic past; and the conversion of some older voters. Among the last were millions of Christian fundamentalists who opposed liberalism on social issues. While racial tensions have subsided in the South, racial electoral divisions have become sharper. White Southerners are the most Republican regional grouping in the nation; yet 9 out of 10 southern blacks voted for Walter Mondale in 1984.

3. Republican performance on the issues galvanized support from diverse groups. President Reagan's seemingly vigorous leadership, his aggressive anticommunism, and his prodefense stance appealed to many citizens. The Republicans' position on potent social issues—for example, crime and violence, abortion, school prayer, and traditional family values—won over such groupings as evangelical Protestants, mainstream Catholics, ethnics, and even many union families. Economic issues less clearly favored the Republicans, given the 1982–1983 recession and the uneven recovery thereafter. But general prosperity in the 1980s added to the Republicans' image of competence and success.

Does all of this add up to the long-anticipated realignment? In some respects, the answer to that question must be yes. Major social groupings have altered their voting patterns, and the partisan balance of power has shifted. These trends have bolstered the Republicans, bringing the partisan balance closer to the tipping point than at any other time within the memory of most living Americans.

One viewpoint, associated with conservative columnist Kevin Phillips, holds that a **split-level realignment** has already taken place. At the presidential level, there seems to be a normal Republican majority. The GOP has won six of the last nine presidential contests, four of them by landslides. At the congressional level, the Senate is competitive for both parties, while the House of Representatives favors the Democrats.

Other analysts argue that **dealignment** will overpower any realignment that takes place. They hold that the increasingly independent stance of today's well-educated, skeptical voters means that any partisan gain is temporary and subject to mercurial swings. Recent events underscore the instability of party identification. If the 1984 elections marked the high-water mark of Republican fortunes, what followed can only be called a receding tide. The 1986 elections restored the Senate to Democratic hands after six years; subsequent revelations about the Reagan administration's Iran-*contra* arms dealings cast doubt on the substance of Reagan's leadership. By 1987, the Democrats again registered a plurality in party identifiers: 40 percent, to 30 percent Republican and 30 percent independent.

Some commentators conclude that party identification no longer char-

FIGURE 6–4   The fragmented electorate, 1987

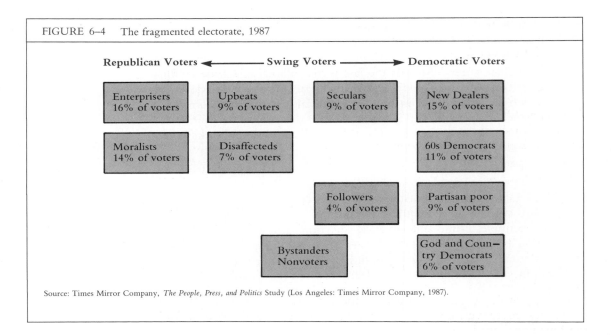

Source: Times Mirror Company, *The People, Press, and Politics* Study (Los Angeles: Times Mirror Company, 1987).

acterizes the political orientation of American citizens. A massive study conducted in 1987 by the Gallup Organization for the Times Mirror Company identified 11 distinct "typology groups" in the American electorate—10 of which vote in varying degrees and one of which hardly votes (Times Mirror, 1987). These groups were defined by combinations of basic values and orientations—religious faith, tolerance, social justice, anticommunism, alienation, America's capacities, financial pressure, and attitudes toward government and business. The groups differ in their partisanship and in their attitudes toward political issues.

As portrayed in Figure 6–4, 6 of the 11 groups fall into one of the two party camps. The Democratic party claims four of the six groups, which are partly defined by age and class and which are divided over the values of tolerance and militant anticommunism. The *New Dealers,* the largest of the four Democratic groups, are older, more traditional, less tolerant, and more anticommunist than the other Democratic groups. The *Sixties Democrats* tend to be upper-middle-class people in their 30s and 40s who are tolerant and concerned about peace and social justice. The *Partisan Poor,* mainly blacks and financially pressured people, are very politicized and very loyal to the Democrats. The *God and Country Democrats,* also low-income people, are less active politically and less critical of American institutions and their own lot than the Partisan Poor.

The Republican party claims two groups. *Enterprisers* are traditional Republicans who are driven by free enterprise economic issues. *Moralists* are less affluent and more populist people driven by moral concerns and militant anticommunism.

Four independent groups exist, two leaning toward the Republicans and two toward the Democrats. The two Republican-leaning groups, about equal in size, differ dramatically in outlook. *Upbeats* are young, optimistic, and fervently patriotic; the *Disaffecteds* are middle-aged, pessimistic, and distrustful of business and government. The two Democratic-leaning groups are also quite different. *Seculars* are affluent, well informed, tolerant, peace oriented—and lacking in religious beliefs. *Followers* are young, poor, and uninformed; though displaying little faith in their country, they are surprisingly uncritical of its institutions.

The final group, *Bystanders,* is largely uninvolved in public affairs and politics. Mainly young, white, and poorly educated, Bystanders have no interest in politics, no history of voting, and no desire to participate in other ways.

This map of the American electorate emphasizes its fragmentation and fluidity. While 6 of the 11 groups are loyal to one party or the other, these groups are driven by diverse passions and their support is fickle. Within the parties, moreover, loyalist groups can pull in opposite directions. And the four nonaligned groups may be pulled by candidates or issues to one party or the other. Presidential races, especially, are "up for grabs."

If party loyalties are so volatile, they may well shift with events rather than shape people's perceptions of those events. Today's elections look more like isolated skirmishes than like battles in a long-running struggle of stable party loyalties. "Candidate images have become so paramount . . . that each election breaks the mold of the one that preceded it" (White and Morris, 1984: 48).

Activists versus Followers

Adherents of the two parties are by no means carbon copies of one another. Basic issues of priorities and the government's role in national life divide Republicans and Democrats at all levels. Democrats are readier than Republicans to use government to achieve economic and social goals. Republicans would limit government's welfare functions but are more apt than Democrats to condone "big government" in defense, intelligence, law enforcement, and personal morality.

Democratic and Republican activists diverge on these issues more sharply than do party followers. Party leaders and activists tend to be more committed to issues and ideologies than ordinary voters. Democratic convention delegates, for example, are to the left and Republican convention delegates are to the right of their parties' rank-and-file voters (Plissner and Mitofsky, 1981). This is shown strikingly in Figure 6–5, which compares the leanings of convention delegates with those of party voters and

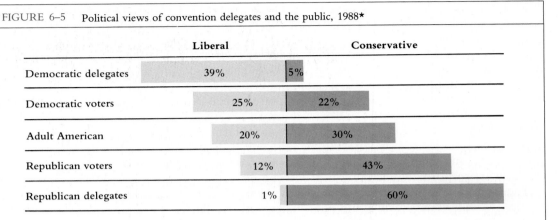

FIGURE 6–5   Political views of convention delegates and the public, 1988*

	Liberal		Conservative
Democratic delegates	39%	5%	
Democratic voters	25%	22%	
Adult American	20%	30%	
Republican voters	12%	43%	
Republican delegates	1%	60%	

*Figures represent respondents who described their views as "liberal" or "conservative." (Other responses were permitted, so figures do not add up to 100%.) Delegates' views were surveyed in telephone interviews with samples of 1,059 delegates to the Democratic National Convention and 739 delegates to the Republican National Convention, conducted just prior to the opening of the conventions in the summer of 1988. Views of total adults and each party's registered voters are based on telephone interviews conducted earlier in the year as part of New York Times–CBS Polls.

Source: *New York Times*, August 14, 1988, p. 32.

the electorate as a whole. (The percentages shown in this figure are virtually the same for other years.)

As we will see, opening up the presidential nominating process in the 1970s brought in waves of issue- and candidate-oriented activists. These activists were initially described as "amateurs" or "purists." Among the Democrats, they included "new politics" advocates—antiwar activists, feminists, environmentalists, spokespersons for minority rights and proponents of all manner of other causes. After 1972, the Democratic activists who remained were relatively stable in attitudes and values—still committed to insurgent values but increasingly tolerant of the traditional party elites (such as union leaders) and worried about the party's fortunes. The newer delegates tended to be loyal to candidates and somewhat less committed to liberal causes (Miller and Jennings, 1986). Among the Republicans, there was a gradual infusion of "movement conservatives," who viewed the party as a channel for a variety of right-wing social, moral, and economic causes. At the same time, many of the more liberal GOP activists drifted away from the party. Those who remained drifted rightward, responding to the party's ever more conservative atmosphere and the 1980 nomination of Ronald Reagan.

Thus, the elites of the two parties are often at odds with themselves. To consolidate disparate interests and appeal to independents, they blur many divisive issues. The result is the "something for everyone" character of party appeals (Downs, 1957). Watering down these appeals, however, may cause an intellectual backlash among the parties' most loyal and dedicated adherents. This internal tension plagues both of the major parties.

American political parties are a paradox. Virtually all observers describe them as weak and elusive; and some observers claim that they are dying or that they are already dead. Yet the parties are extensively organized—and have become more so over the last generation. In their formal structures, in the reach of their rules and services, and in the legal underpinnings, the political parties are stronger than ever.

Membership

Voters in most states can register themselves as Republicans, Democrats, independents, or adherents of a minor party. In 38 states, voters must declare themselves members of a party before voting in that party's primary election to choose candidates for the general election. Party registration numbers for the 28 states maintaining permanent records are given in Table 6–3. In other states with primaries, voters just ask for the ballot of the party in whose primary they wish to vote.

Most people take a casual view of party registration. Such registration does not require them to support the party, add to its coffers, or even vote for its candidates. In one-party areas, many people register with the leading party just to vote in its all-important primaries, even when their sympathies lie elsewhere. Some states permit people to register as independents—or as "unaffiliated," "nonpartisan," "undeclared," or "decline to state." As Table 6–3 shows, independents are numerous in states permitting such designations. These people consider it a privilege to be loyal to no party and to renounce all of them.

State and Local Parties

The organizations and leaders of state and local parties are the building blocks of electoral politics. Structurally, the parties are creatures of state laws. These laws specify how parties and their candidates get on the ballot, how people become party members through registration procedures, how the parties are to function, and how they are to finance their activities. As creatures of state law, "the parties have increasingly become adjuncts of state government" (Bibby et al., 1983: 75). Thus, grass-roots party structures vary from state to state.

Local party structures parallel elective offices and voting districts (see Figure 6–6). Sorauf (1984: 66) says that these structures "form great step pyramids of the myriad, overlapping constituencies of a democracy committed to the election of vast numbers of officeholders." At the bottom are ward and precinct committees and their members. Then, there are committees for city, county, state legislative, and congressional offices. These committees often overlap because no uniform method is used to establish the boundaries for the various districts. The various organizational levels are independent of one another—no chain of command goes from one to another. This is a condition that Eldersveld (1982: 133) has

TABLE 6–3   Party registration in 28 states

State	Republican	Democrat	Independent	Total
Alaska	21.8%	23.1%	55.1%★	282,226
Arizona	45.5	43.1	11.4	1,596,079
California	39.1	51.9	10.0[+]	12,555,205
Colorado	33.1	31.0	35.9[‡]	1,817,370
Connecticut	26.7	40.1	33.2[‡]	1,672,008
Delaware	43.7	56.3	—	234,571
Florida	38.8	61.2	—	5,253,584
Iowa	31.2	35.3	33.5[§]	1,621,538
Kansas	58.6	41.4	—	824,720
Kentucky	29.6	70.4	—	1,933,495
Louisiana	14.7	85.3	—	1,998,560
Maine	30.4	34.0	35.6[‡]	773,966
Maryland	25.1	67.4	7.5	2,139,690
Massachusetts	13.3	46.6	31.2[‡]	2,933,464
Nebraska	54.8	45.2	—	794,570
Nevada	43.0	50.2	7.8★	366,812
New Hampshire	36.7	30.4	32.9[‖]	551,257
New Jersey	20.4	34.3	45.3[‡]	3,773,266
New Mexico	34.0	60.1	5.9[†]	632,787
New York	32.2	47.3	20.5[‖]	8,078,779
North Carolina	28.4	71.6	—	2,951,262
Ohio	18.7	32.0	49.3[‡]	5,882,085
Oklahoma	31.1	68.9	—	1,965,204
Oregon	44.6	55.4	—	1,315,331
Pennsylvania	43.6	56.4	—	5,550,650
South Dakota	53.1	46.9	—	393,655
West Virginia	31.7	68.3	—	925,746
Wyoming	63.7	36.3	—	212,633
Total	32.6%	52.1%	15.3%	69,030,413

Note: The states shown are those that compile state party registration data.
★Nonpartisan.
[†]Decline to state.
[‡]Unaffiliated.
[§]No party preference.
[‖] Undeclared. In New York, includes minor-party registrations amounting to about 2.5 percent of the registrants.
Source: Compiled by Royce Crocker, Congressional Research Service, from data produced by Election Data Service, Inc.

called **stratarchy:** "a series of layers of organization, or strata, superimposed . . . one on the other but with no indication that it is a neat pyramid of authority."

At the state level, each party is led by a state chairperson and a central committee. The latter may vary from 20 members to nearly 1,000. The members are elected by county committees, state conventions, or party primaries. Typically, the party is directed by an executive committee drawn from the central committee. Day-to-day leadership is in the hands

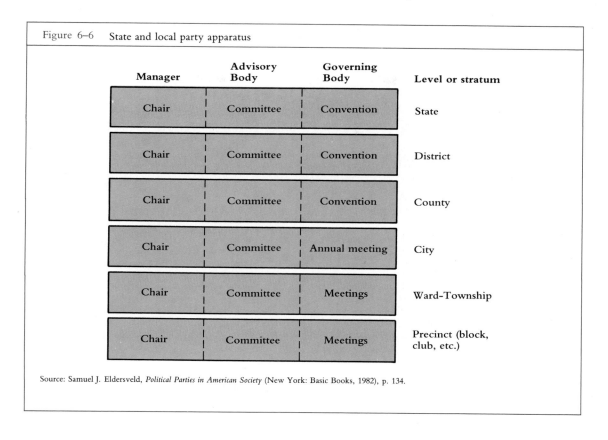

Figure 6–6   State and local party apparatus

Manager	Advisory Body	Governing Body	Level or stratum
Chair	Committee	Convention	State
Chair	Committee	Convention	District
Chair	Committee	Convention	County
Chair	Committee	Annual meeting	City
Chair	Committee	Meetings	Ward–Township
Chair	Committee	Meetings	Precinct (block, club, etc.)

Source: Samuel J. Eldersveld, *Political Parties in American Society* (New York: Basic Books, 1982), p. 134.

of a state chairperson elected by the central committee or the state convention.

County, city, ward, district, and precinct units parallel the state structure. That is, they are usually controlled by an elected committee headed by a chairperson. Each party level is responsible for calling caucuses or conventions, conducting campaigns, raising campaign funds, and mobilizing voters.

Most of the state party organizations have headquarters in the state capital or another major city. These headquarters are staffed by at least a handful of full-time salaried employees. A survey conducted in 1979 and 1980 found that the average state party staff had about 7 members and that in a quarter of the states the state party staff had 10 or more members (Bibby et al., 1983: 77). State party expenditures range from the $14,000 that the Vermont Democrats spent one year to outlays in excess of a million dollars a year (the figure for several state GOP organizations). As a rule, Republican party state organizations are stronger than those of the Democratic party—a pattern that is also displayed in the national party organizations. In budgets and staffs, the state party organizations have

TABLE 6–4   Where House and Senate candidates got their campaign funds, 1974–1986

Receipts	1973–74	1975–76	1977–78	1979–80	1981–82	1983–84	1985–86
From individuals	73%	59%	60%	56%	51%	47%	48%
From PACs	17	22	24	28	30	37	36
From political parties★	4	8	7	6	6	7	4
From all others†	6	11	9	10	12	10	12
Total receipts (in $ millions)	$45.7	$65.7	$93.6	$127.1	$189.9	$204.9	$235.0

★Includes both direct contributions and indirect ("coordinated") expenditures on behalf of the party's candidates.

†Includes the candidates' own contributions (and unrepaid loans), interest on previous campaign funds, and campaign refunds.

Sources: Richard P. Conlon, "The Declining Role of Individual Contributions in Financing Congressional Campaigns," *Journal of Law and Politics* III:3 (Winter 1987), p. 491. The 1985–86 data were compiled by Royce Crocker of the Congressional Research Service on the basis of Federal Election Commission data (press release, May 10, 1987).

grown over the past generation. The increase has been rapid for the Republicans, slower for the Democrats. This trend belies the widespread notion that party organizations have been withering on the vine (Gibson, Cotter, and Bibby, 1983: 206).

What functions are performed by these party organizations? A recent canvass of 54 state party organizations by Cotter and his colleagues (1984) identified two kinds of functions: *institutional support* and *candidate support*. Five types of party activities fall into the first category: raising funds, conducting registration and get-out-the vote programs, sponsoring public opinion surveys, developing and promoting issue positions, and publishing newsletters.

The state parties support candidates by contributing financially to candidates, providing candidates with services, helping to recruit candidates, influencing the selection of national convention delegates, and making preprimary endorsements (see Table 6–4). The average state party apparatus enters most of these areas, although activity levels vary from state to state. Most of the state parties, for example, offer such candidate support services as advertising and media help, research, public opinion polling, seminars, fund raising, and advice on organization and bookkeeping. Stress on primaries to select candidates may blunt the influence of the state parties, but half of the state party leaders make some kind of preprimary endorsement. In most of the areas mentioned, state parties are substantially more active today than they were two decades ago.

Less is known about local party structure than about state party structure. Moreover, local organizations are so diverse that it is hard to generalize about them, beyond saying that they usually boast officers but little staff or financial support.

Still, many local party organizations are quite active, especially during

Machine politics, Chicago style. Mayor Richard Daley of Chicago (1902–76) was one of the last of the old-time big-city political bosses.

campaigns. A survey of local party organizations disclosed that a majority conducted the following campaign activities: distributing literature, arranging fund raising and campaign events (such as rallies), contributing money, mounting telephone and mail campaigns, buying newspaper ads, distributing posters or lawn signs, coordinating countywide efforts, and preparing press releases. About 7 out of 10 local party organizations took part in recruiting candidates, but only about half of these organizations worked with candidate organizations in mapping strategy (Gibson et al., 1982). Overall, local parties do not seem to have withered as organizations. Yet some of the most spectacular cases of party decline have been at the local level.

In our major cities, there once flourished unique and potent political organizations—**urban machines.** These entrenched and disciplined organizations were usually led by a "boss" who controlled the city and by a group of ward or precinct "bosses." They did many things to win support from rank-and-file voters. Machine-controlled patronage jobs—in police, fire, transit, sanitation, and other city departments—were given to the faithful. Precinct and ward officials helped their people find jobs; aided those in trouble with the law; assisted merchants in getting city contracts,

HISTORICAL PERSPECTIVES

The Strenuous Life of a New York Political Boss

One of the most colorful political bosses of the golden age of the urban machines was George Washington Plunkitt (1842–1924). Ward boss of the 15th Assembly District in lower Manhattan, Plunkitt was a power in Tammany Hall, as New York City's Democratic organization was known. His life as a ward boss and his colorful views on machine politics were recorded by William L. Riordon, a newspaperman who published Plunkitt's *Very Plain Talks on Very Practical Politics* in 1905. In this book, Plunkitt revealed how he had made the most out of politics by "honest graft" ("I seen my opportunities and I took 'em"). The following excerpts are taken from Plunkitt's diaries and Riordon's observations of the daily life of a Tammany leader.

> The life of the Tammany district leader is strenuous. . . . As a rule, he has no business or occupation other than politics. He plays politics every day and night in the year, and his headquarters bears the inscription, "Never closed."
> Everybody in the district knows him. Everybody knows where to find him, and nearly everybody goes to him for assistance of one sort or another, especially the poor of the tenements. He is always obliging. He will go to the police courts to put in a good word for the "drunks and disorderlies" or pay their fines, if a good word is not effective. He will attend christenings, weddings, and funerals. He will feed the hungry and help bury the dead.
> A philanthropist? Not at all. He is playing politics all the time. . . .
> This is a record of a day's work by Plunkitt:
> 2 A.M.: Aroused from sleep by the ringing of his doorbell; went to the door and found a bartender, who asked him to go to the police station and bail out a saloonkeeper who had been arrested for violating the excise law. Furnished bail and returned to bed at three o'clock.
> 6 A.M.: Awakened by fire engines passing his house. Hastened to the scene of the fire, according to the custom of the Tammany district leaders, to give assistance to the fire sufferers, if needed. Met several of his election district captains who are always under orders to look out for fires, which are considered great vote-getters. Found several tenants who had been burned out, took them to a hotel, supplied them with clothes, fed them, and ar-

(Continued)

licenses, and police protection; and dispensed a variety of personal and social services. Such machines as New York's Tammany Hall also sponsored social activities, ranging from baseball teams and singing groups to clambakes and picnics. For the waves of unschooled immigrants who flooded the cities at the turn of the century, the machines offered protection, help, participation, and a sense of identity. In exchange for their

---

HISTORICAL PERSPECTIVES

(Concluded)

ranged temporary quarters for them until they could rent and furnish new apartments.

8:30 A.M.: Went to the police court to look after his constituents. Found six "drunks." Secured the discharge of four by a timely word with the judge, and paid the fines of two.

9 A.M.: Appeared in Municipal District Court. Directed one of his district captains to act as counsel for a widow against whom dispossess proceedings had been instituted and obtained an extension of time. Paid the rent of a poor family about to be dispossessed and gave them a dollar for food.

11 A.M.: At home again. Found four men waiting for him. One had been discharged by the Metropolitan Railway Company for neglect of duty, and wanted the district leader to fix things. Another wanted a job on the road. The third sought a place on the Subway, and the fourth, a plumber, was looking for work with the Consolidated Gas Company. The district leader spent nearly three hours fixing things for the four men, and succeeded in each case.

3 P.M.: Attended the funeral of an Italian as far as the ferry. Hurried back to make his appearance at the funeral of a Hebrew constituent. Went conspicuously to the front both in the Catholic church and the synagogue, and later attended the Hebrew confirmation ceremonies in the synagogue.

7 P.M.: Went to district head-

quarters and presided over a meeting of election district captains. Each captain submitted a list of all the voters in his district, reported on their attitude toward Tammany, suggested who might be won over and how they could be won, told who were in need, and who were in trouble of any kind and the best way to reach them. District leader took notes and gave orders.

8 P.M.: Went to a church fair. Took chances on everything, bought ice cream for the young girls and the children. Kissed the little ones, flattered their mothers, and took their fathers out for something down at the corner (pub).

9 P.M.: At the clubhouse again. Spent $10 on tickets for a church excursion and promised a subscription for a new church bell. Bought tickets for a baseball game to be played by two nines from his district. Listened to the complaints of a dozen pushcart peddlers who said they were persecuted by the police and assured them he would go to Police Headquarters in the morning and see about it.

10:30 P.M.: Attended a Hebrew wedding reception and dance. Had previously sent a handsome wedding present to the bride.

12 P.M.: In bed.

Source: William L. Riordon, *Plunkitt of Tammany Hall* (New York: E. P. Dutton, 1963), pp. 90–98.

---

votes, confused and often illiterate immigrants could get a job, a helping hand in case of trouble, and even a sense of belonging.

Strong party organizations linger in a few large cities. But few, if any, of them could be called "machines" in the old sense. Some, such as Chicago's once proud Democratic organization, are torn by ethnic and racial factionalism.

The machines broke down because the things that fueled them—votes, jobs, services—slipped from their grasp. Civil service reforms have insulated most jobs from party control. Even when patronage is available (as in federally subsidized jobs for the hard-core unemployed), it does not build strong local parties (Johnston, 1979). Welfare services, once dispensed by party ward bosses, now flow from state and federal agencies. Most of today's voters do not want party bosses telling them how to vote. And they are less tolerant of the corruption that pervaded the machines.

The old-style urban machines were the peak in party organization. Today's state and local party organizations, as we have seen, are much more genteel and muted. Yet they are far from breathing their last. As we have seen, the organizational trappings of the parties seem to be enjoying a significant revival.

National Parties

Organizational growth has been even more dramatic in the national party structures. At the same time that voters' party loyalties have wavered, the parties themselves have built impressive organizations and expanded their activities (Longley, 1980). President Eisenhower once remarked that national parties did not really exist in America. Today his name graces the Republican party's stately Capitol Hill headquarters. Nearby, the Democrats now occupy their first national headquarters building.

The parties' ongoing business is in the hands of national committees, chairpersons, and headquarters staffs, whose functions are quite diverse; they do not focus only on presidential contests. The organizational features of the national Democratic party are shown in Figure 6–7.

The Republican and Democratic national committees consist of people from each state and territory who meet at intervals. National committee representatives from the states may be chosen at state conventions, by the state's delegation to the national convention, by the state's central committee, or in a primary election.

The national committees are quite varied and very large (Republicans, 176 members; Democrats, 397). They reflect geographic, factional, and candidate groupings. In a bargain struck between Michael Dukakis and Jesse Jackson, for example, the Democrats in 1988 added 20 new at-large seats to their national committee—12 of them from the Jackson campaign. Democratic Chairman Paul G. Kirk, Jr., hailed the result as "the most expansive diversity in our history." Predictably, the national committees have little collective identity; their occasional meetings are largely for show and newsmaking.

Day-to-day direction of the national parties is in the hands of the national chairpersons. They direct the headquarters staff, make public statements on the party's behalf, and try to fuse intraparty factions into an effective force. If the party controls the White House, the president handpicks the chairperson. In 1983, Reagan chose his close friend Senator Paul

FIGURE 6–7   Organization of the National Democratic Party

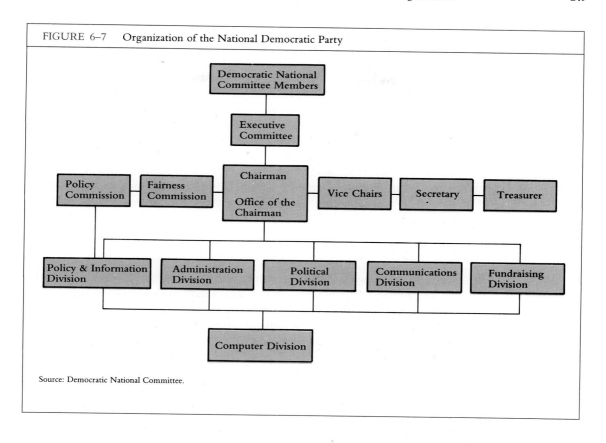

Source: Democratic National Committee.

Laxalt (R–N. Mex.) to the newly created post of GOP "general chairman" (a role that ended when Laxalt left the Senate in 1987). Laxalt in turn designated Frank J. Fahrenkopf, Jr., former Nevada party chairman, to assume operating leadership as chairman of the Republican National Committee. This arrangement underscored the White House stake in the party's organization while leaving detailed direction in the hands of a professional. Few presidents have lent as much support to the party apparatus. The strongest chairs have been those who have grasped the reins of a defeated party and worked to pull its factions together into a winning coalition. The most notable party chairs have been the Republicans' Ray Bliss (1965–69) and William Brock (1977–80) and the Democrats' Paul Butler (1955–60), Robert Strauss (1972–76), and Paul G. Kirk, Jr., who campaigned for and won the DNC post in 1985.

The GOP's challenge in the 1970s was to break out of its minority status and the stigma of Watergate (Cotter and Bibby, 1980). Funding was no barrier, because in recent years the Republican finance committees have brought in far more than Democratic counterparts. With their backs to the wall in the mid-1970s, the Republicans poured money and talent into developing a truly sophisticated national campaign support system. They provided computer services, extensive polling, television studios, speech outlines, candidate recruitment and training, issue analyses, fund-raising assistance, and a host of other services not matched by the Democrats. They encouraged local candidates and gave them financial and technical help. The GOP even ran a series of nationwide TV ads urging people to "Vote Republican. For a change." They did so well that seasoned political analysts credit a number of GOP victories to their organizational superiority.

The task confronting Democratic strategists is how to hold together the party's scattered racial, ethnic, regional, and issue factions without perpetuating the impression that they run the party. The Democrats continue to play catch-up with the Republicans in terms of finances and technical campaign support. Under Kirk's low-key leadership, the party apparatus firmed up discipline in the ranks, reined in the special-interest caucuses, avoided a brawl over the 1988 nomination rules, and launched groups to develop party policy along moderate, mainstream lines.

The parties' role in identifying and supporting candidates is substantial. Party staff members work with would-be candidates at the local level, encouraging them to make the race and supplying them with campaign advice, issue briefs, and other aids.

THE PARTIES CHOOSE THEIR CANDIDATES

The most important aspect of partisan organization is the way the parties choose their candidates for public office. After all, the parties' only path toward controlling the government is putting up an attractive candidate or slate of candidates. The candidates are the parties' best (or worst) advertising in an election; as we have seen, they have become the main standard by which voters judge the parties' credentials.

Historically, there has been a trend toward more open nominating procedures, with more and more people taking part. The oldest nominating device, the **party caucus,** is simply a meeting of party loyalists. With the advent of mass parties in the 19th century, the nominating caucus was enlarged into the **nominating convention,** made up of delegates representing various localities or factions. The 20th century has seen the spread of **primary elections,** or primaries, which are public elections for choosing candidates. The more people who take part in nominating, of course, the less leverage party leaders can wield.

Party Caucuses

Caucuses are simply meetings of party members to discuss and decide on candidates, politics, or strategies. Parties used caucuses to conduct business when they were little more than factions of elected officials. Through 1824, members of Congress caucused to name presidential candidates. In that year, the Jeffersonians (then called Democratic Republicans) passed

Citizen enthusiasm at the Iowa caucuses. Democrats vote their presidential choices in a Des Moines, Iowa, precinct caucus.

over the immensely popular Andrew Jackson for a candidate who eventually was runner-up to him in the electoral college. No candidate captured an electoral college majority; the House of Representatives then chose John Quincy Adams as president over Jackson, whose supporters condemned the choice as a "corrupt bargain." Thus discredited, the congressional caucus for choosing presidential candidates was soon abandoned.

Parties still use caucuses to conduct party business, though rarely for actual nominating. Party members in legislatures caucus to choose leaders and debate issues and strategies. Local caucuses often discuss issues or pick delegates to state and national conventions. In the 1988 presidential nominating process, precinct, town, or county caucuses were used by one or both parties in 26 states—as part of two- or three-tier processes leading to statewide conventions for selecting delegates.

Caucuses are the most party-centered nominating devices because they entail the most old-fashioned face-to-face campaigning among party activists. They place a premium on organization and on loyalists who (as was said of George McGovern's 1972 supporters) are "the kind of people who stay until the end of the meeting."

Most of the party identifiers in the electorate, on the other hand, are mere spectators to such proceedings. Participation in politics tends to be lower in states choosing delegates through caucuses and conventions than in states using primary elections. In a highly touted caucus system such as Iowa's, no more than 15 percent of the party's voters turn out.

Nominating Conventions

An American invention, nominating conventions were adopted in the 1830s to replace congressional caucuses for choosing presidential candidates. They soon spread to the states and localities. Depending on how the delegates are chosen, these conventions can broadly represent all party factions. Moreover, they are public spectacles. They draw attention to party activities and arouse excitement among party workers and voters. Most familiar to citizens are the presidential nominating conventions, which every four years bring together under one roof the party's state, local, candidate, and issue factions.

Nominating conventions soon displayed the same drawback as caucuses: They could be manipulated by party bosses who controlled the selection of delegates. So the state legislatures began to regulate convention procedures. And the parties themselves set up detailed rules for delegate selection.

Local party workers prefer large numbers of delegates and alternates. This gives them a better chance of being picked. The 1988 presidential conventions were the largest in history: the Democrats had 4,161 delegates and 1,170 alternates; the Republicans had 2,278 delegates and 2,278 alternates. The parties use complex formulas to allocate delegates among the states. They want to stress broad geographic representation, but they also have to reward their most loyal supporters.

In view of their large size and short duration, presidential nominating conventions are hardly deliberative bodies. The delegates tend to ratify and rally rather than debate or choose. Because of the national character of presidential politics, not to mention the 1970s reforms that led to the selection of most delegates by primaries, conventions themselves no longer choose the nominees in anything but the most formal sense. After 1952, writes Byron E. Shafer (1988: 18), "without formal decisions by anyone, the nomination left the convention hall, and it has remained outside ever since." Of course, the conventions remain what Shafer calls "the nominator of last resort." If no front runner emerges in the primary season, there is always the possibility of a "brokered convention," that is, a convention that actually serves to choose the nominee.

Yet national conventions remain public spectacles and news events. Under pressure from the TV networks, the conventions have streamlined their schedules down to several prime-time evenings. The nominee and party officials work at "orchestrating the convention to set out the themes of—and effectively to launch—the general election campaign" (Shafer, 1988: 228).

And important party business is conducted at these conventions. While floor debates may be formal and sometimes tedious, they serve to ratify, alter, or reject the recommendations of various party committees.

The *Platform Committee* hears the views of party leaders and interest groups and figures out how the party stands on issues. Hearings are held to allow all of the party's voices to be heard; but the platform declarations themselves are phrased cautiously to reflect the balance of views within the party. An incumbent president, or a dominant candidate or faction, may control the drafting.

The *Rules Committee* recommends procedures for conducting convention business. Many of the rules have already been set and are merely readopted. Others may be changed to give one candidate the advantage or to accommodate the TV networks (for example, changes in the number and length of speeches).

The *Credentials Committee* compiles the official delegate list and checks the credentials of delegates and alternates. Disputes sometimes break out between rival delegates or slates. The qualifications of delegates may be challenged. Such contests are often fought on the floor, the outcome giving an early hint of the relative strength of rival candidates.

Finally, the *Committee on Permanent Organization* recommends people for permanent convention posts, including that of chairperson. The work of this committee is normally not disputed.

At conventions, much politicking takes place in meetings behind the scenes, out of the range of TV cameras. For the delegates, these infrequent meetings offer an opportunity to meet fellow partisans from other areas, to compare ideas and try out arguments, to assess candidates and their organizations, and to learn about new developments. Like convention-goers everywhere, the delegates use party conventions to further personal interests and common goals. The local functions of these conventions, then, are quite different from the images that the media convey to outside observers (Shafer, 1988).

Primary Elections

Primary or nominating elections were pushed by turn-of-the-century reformers. These reformers thought that primaries would neutralize political bosses and ensure popular control over nominations. First used in Wisconsin in 1903, the primary spread rapidly. Primaries have loosened the grip of party leaders on the nominating process, transferring control and influence to candidates and the media.

Because primaries are creatures of state law, moreover, they are supervised by state officials. States have differing rules about who can take part in primaries.

Primaries are usually classed according to the degree of partisanship required to vote in them. In the **closed primary,** voters must affirm their party preference in order to vote. This system is used in 38 states. In some states, voters must register their party affiliation before the primary. In others, voters merely have to declare their party at the polls to establish party registration. Thus, some primaries are more "closed" than others. In certain states, voters can be challenged if they have not supported the party in the past; but such challenges are rare and almost impossible to prove. What sets closed-primary states apart is that party affiliation, however established, restricts participation in primaries and is considered permanent until the voter goes through the process of changing it. The rules vary from state to state, but they clearly discourage casual crossing of party lines.

Nine states conduct an **open primary.** Instead of registering by party, voters are allowed to vote in either party's primary (but not in both primaries). Most open of all are the **blanket primary** (Alaska, Washington) and the **nonpartisan primary** (Louisiana). In the former, voters can take part in the primary of more than one party by moving back and forth from office to office on the ballot. In the latter, all of the candidates for the same office are grouped together on the ballot, with no party affiliation listed.

Party leaders usually favor strict primary rules that reward party loyalty and help leaders shape the outcomes. An exception was Connecticut's badly outnumbered GOP, which wanted to broaden its base by allowing registered Independents to vote in its primaries. The state's strict closed-primary law, which the Democratic legislature and governor were not about to change, proved a barrier to this procedure. In a 5-to-4 decision (*Tashjian* v. *Republican Party of Connecticut,* 1986), the U.S. Supreme Court ruled that Connecticut's primary law violated the state Republican party's freedom of association. While the Constitution grants states the power to prescribe the "times, places, and manner" of holding elections, wrote Justice Thurgood Marshall, "this authority does not extinguish the state's responsibility to observe limits established by the First Amendment rights of the state's citizens." Advocates of strong parties had mixed reactions to the Supreme Court ruling. On the one hand, it was hailed as protecting the parties against aggressive state regulation. On the other, it confirmed the Connecticut GOP's right to open its primaries—a procedure generally thought to dilute a party's control over its nominating process.

All 50 states use primaries to select candidates for some offices. In most of the states, primaries are used exclusively; in other states, conventions are used to select candidates in certain races. Four southern states (Alabama, Georgia, South Carolina, and Virginia) let the parties decide whether to hold conventions or primaries.

Several states combine conventions and primaries. Utah and Colorado, for example, hold **preprimary conventions** to endorse candidates. Typically, the convention's choice wins the primary; candidates carrying the convention overwhelmingly (70–80 percent of the votes) are deemed nominated. Other states (for example, Connecticut, Delaware, and New York) hold primaries only if candidates receive a specified share of the convention's delegate vote (from 20 to 35 percent, depending on the state). Conventions tend to bolster party organizations and inhibit "outsider" candidates. As one study found, "The principal effect of the convention system, even if it is only one step in the overall nominating process, is that it permits a greater party influence on candidate selection" (Bibby et al., 1983: 73).

Most of the southern states require a **runoff primary** between the top two candidates if no candidate gets a majority in the first primary. Historically, runoffs were aimed at giving coherence to Democratic selections. Because of the party's dominance in the South, nomination has been (in the common phrase) "tantamount to election." Therefore, the value of the nomination, combined with the party's own factionalism, draws a horde of candidates who lack broad support. The two-tier primary gives candidates a chance to build that support.

Primaries have been something of a disappointment to reformers. Although they open the door to wider participation in nominations, they normally attract far fewer voters than general elections. (Exceptions occur in one-party areas where primaries are more important than general elections.) Primaries are less publicized than general elections. They tend to attract voters who are older, richer, better educated, and more politically aware. Primary voters are also more committed to issues and more loyal to the party than general-election voters (Ranney, 1976). Even in highly touted presidential contests, voting in primaries has not been impressive: only 36 percent of the eligible voters in primary states voted in 1980, when there were lively contests in both parties. The much-publicized New Hampshire primary, which is a media event, brought all of 101,000 Democrats to the polls in 1984—14 percent of the state's voting-age population.

State registration laws and other primary election rules do not seem to affect the extent of primary voting. Neither does the competitiveness of the contests. But factors that do seem to influence primary voting are (1) campaign spending by the candidates (for publicity draws attention to the contest) and (2) the general level of education. Primary turnout is much higher in states with well-educated populations (Ranney, 1977: 26–35).

Most politicians and many political scientists blame primaries for speeding the decline of political parties. Certainly, primaries have weakened party control over nominees. Party leaders can influence the results of primaries by endorsing certain candidates, but it is harder to control an election than a caucus or convention.

With the rise of the mass media, would-be nominees can appeal to the public over the heads of party leaders. Indeed, candidates nowadays build networks of personal support separate from those of other party officeholders. For this reason, primaries are costly. Unless candidates start with commanding advantages, they must mount almost the same kind of campaign in the primary as in the general election, using the same techniques—personal appearances, direct mailing, canvassing, and media advertising. Thus, the spread of primaries has helped boost the costs of running for office.

Some reformers have tried to do away with party labels altogether.

Nebraska elects its legislators on a nonpartisan basis. In many states, local officials (mayors, school boards, judges, councils, and the like) are picked in the same way. There are no party labels on the primary ballot. The top two candidates from the primary face each other in the general election. (If the winner has an absolute majority in the primary, he or she may be declared elected.)

Some say that getting rid of party labels insulates local elections from divisive national issues. When the parties keep their hands off, other factors—newspaper endorsements or civic-group sponsorship—may serve as party substitutes in helping voters sort out competing claims. Still, without party labels, voters often cannot figure out what, or whom, the candidates really stand for. They may then grasp at trivial things (if all else fails, the candidates' last names will do), or they may throw up their hands in despair and not vote. No doubt this helps explain why turnout is lower in local elections than in national ones.

A Special Case: Presidential Nominations

The presidential nominating process is the nation's longest-running road show. It attracts nonstop attention from politicians and the press. It is also unbelievably complex. As one commentator said, "In America the presidential nominating game is played under by far the most elaborate, variegated, and complex set of rules in the world. They include national party rules, state and local party rules, state statutes (especially those governing presidential primaries), and a wide variety of rulings by national and state courts" (Ranney, 1974: 72).

Although presidential nominations are uniquely visible, they reflect the same historic trend that we observed for nominating politics generally: toward ever broader participation. The nominating process is today an amalgam of all forms—caucuses, conventions, and primaries, with the final choice made by a national convention. Accordingly, the process embodies an unresolved tug-of-war between those elements that favor party activists (caucuses, conventions) and those that favor public opinion and the media (primaries). It also forces candidates to decide how to balance their appeals to party leaders (which might be called an *insider strategy*) and their bids for public image and media attention (which might be called an *outsider strategy*).

The insider strategy

Before the 1970s, when primaries became dominant, would-be candidates treated the national convention as a sort of large-scale caucus. They tried to win support by gaining favor with bosses who controlled blocs of delegates. This "insider strategy" regarded the party as a bundle of leaders and factions that had to be appeased. The strategy assumed that candidates had little control over the choice of delegates. Rather, they had to win

"Insiders" Hubert Humphrey and Edmund Muskie, 1968 running mates, appealed to traditional Democratic groups. Humphrey, a U.S. senator from Minnesota, was the presidential candidate; Muskie, a U.S. senator from Maine, was the vice-presidential candidate. Nominated by their party to run, they lost to the Republican ticket of Richard Nixon and Spiro Agnew.

favor with the delegates (and their leaders) after the delegates had been picked.

Candidates lacking broad first-ballot support resorted to a variant of the insider strategy known as the **dark horse:** combining with other forces to knock off the front-runners while trying to stay in everyone's good graces. When the front-runners faded, the dark horse's name was put forward, maybe in some smoke-filled room. That was exactly what happened in 1920, when the Republicans chose Ohio Senator Warren G. Harding, and again in 1940, when they settled on Wendell Willkie. Today's early nomination candidacies and lengthy delegate selection campaigns, however, have made the dark horse a thing of the past.

The insider strategy, modern style, has been a springboard for candidates who have a lot of support from party leaders, financial backers, and interest groups allied with the party. Incumbent presidents or candidates who are hands-down front-runners are most likely to be in this situation. Recent insider campaigns have been run by Hubert Humphrey (1968), Gerald Ford (1976), Jimmy Carter (1980), Walter Mondale (1984), and George Bush (1988).

With so many delegates chosen in open contests and with such a diffuse party in the electorate, no candidate can today sweep to victory solely on the support of party influentials. So in addition to the inside campaign (behind-closed-doors maneuvering over endorsements, money, and strategy), there is the public campaign, conducted by and for the media and their mass audience.

The "outsider strategy"

Although presidential primaries had been around since the early 1900s, politicians long scoffed at them. (Harry Truman, no political novice, called them "eyewash.") After 1968, however, there was an upheaval among the Democrats and, to a lesser degree, among the Republicans. That year, backers of the Democratic senators Eugene McCarthy and Robert F. Kennedy, seeking delegates after President Lyndon Johnson quit the race, found to their dismay that many delegate slots were already locked up. The convention was months away and the candidates had not all been identified, yet delegates had already been chosen. Rules and procedures were chaotic, irregular, and often secret. Candidates with minority support got few delegates, if any; certain groups (blacks, women, and youth, in particular) were underrepresented. A Commission on Party Structure and Delegate Selection (the McGovern-Fraser Commission) was named by the 1968 convention to suggest reforms. According to the commission, "Meaningful participation of Democratic voters in the choice of the presidential nominee was often difficult or costly, sometimes completely illusory, and, in not a few instances, impossible."

Since 1968, the Democrats have tinkered with their nominating rules every four years (see Table 6–5). The guidelines of the McGovern-Fraser Commission, largely adopted for 1972 and modified through 1980, opened up the delegate selection process. Delegates were to be chosen in a "timely manner," with certain safeguards. Each state was urged to include blacks, women, youth, and ethnic minorities in its delegation. Within the states, delegates had to be fairly apportioned. Afterward, statewide winner-take-all primaries were banned. Also banned were "winner-take-more primaries," in which candidates could capture all the delegates from individual congressional districts by winning only a plurality of the vote.

The post-1968 reforms transformed the nominating process, especially in the Democratic party. "From a system in which primaries played a supporting rather than a leading role," Polsby concluded, "the United States rapidly moved toward a nominating system in which primaries dominated the process" (1983: 63).

The GOP nominating process underwent similar but far less spectacular changes. The Republican party tried to open up its nominations and broaden the groups represented. But it started from a narrower base than the Democrats, and its internal rifts have been less deep. Thus, it has held back from nationalizing its selection rules. It retains a confederational structure; states take the first step toward changes (Bibby, 1980). The GOP never banned winner-take-all primaries. Still, where state electoral

TABLE 6–5   Changing Democratic party rules*

	Year					
Rule	*1972*	*1976*	*1980*	*1984*	*1988*	*1992*
Timing Restricts delegate selection events to a three-month period (the "window")			✔	✔	✔	✔
Conditions of participation Restricts participation in delegate selection events to Democrats		✔	✔	✔	✔	✔
Proportional representation Bans all types of winner-take-all and winner-take-more contests				✔		✔
Delegate loyalty Gives candidates the right to approve delegates identifying with their candidacy		✔	✔	✔	✔	✔
Binds delegates to vote for their original presidential preference at convention on first ballot				✔		
Party and elected officials Expands each delegation by 10 percent to include pledged party and elected officials				✔	✔	✔
Further expands each delegation to include uncommitted party and elected officials ("superdelegates")				✔	✔	✔†
Demographic representation Encourages participation and representation of minorities and traditionally underrepresented groups (affirmative action)	✔	✔	✔	✔	✔	✔
Requires delegations to be equally divided between men and women				✔	✔	✔

*The check marks indicate the years in which major rule changes were in effect. Source: *Congressional Quarterly Weekly Report* 41 (August 6, 1983), p. 1612. Updated by the authors.

†"Superdelegates" in 1992 will be cut back by about one third, to just under 10 percent of the total delegates.

laws were changed in response to Democratic party turmoil, the GOP often had to shift its practices.

Opening up the delegate selection process has yielded a long, tedious, and scattered ordeal. The formal process starts no less than 14 months before the election itself, when the Michigan GOP elects committees, which in turn choose their convention delegates. The Iowa caucuses are in late February; the New Hampshire primary is in early March. Even before this, the candidates are in full cry; the media are busy pronouncing winners and losers. Across the country trek the candidates, advance crews, and reporters. The climax is the giant California primary in early June.

Because so many delegates are chosen in open primaries or caucuses, the leading candidate typically comes to the fore long before the convention convenes. The delegates ratify a popular choice that has already been made in full public view; since 1956, *all* nominees have been named on the first ballot. (Past conventions, in contrast, were often marathon affairs. This was especially true for the Democrats, who had a two-thirds rule for nominations. In 1924, 103 ballots were needed to pick the Democratic nominee, John W. Davis.)

Highly publicized early primary and caucus victories not only produce delegates. They also give some candidates **momentum**—"Big Mo," as George Bush once put it. In a game of expectations, candidates' promoters and the press often distort the results to establish "front-runners" and "also-rans." A candidate might win with 40 percent of a state's vote. Is this an impressive victory or a fatal setback? It all depends. It is a victory if the candidate is a long shot whose bid has been dismissed by the pros. It is a setback if the candidate is a front-runner who was expected to do much better. Victories or defeats, especially very early in the campaign or near its climax, exert a powerful pull.

Even when no delegates are at stake, the nomination race runs full tilt in the media. Frequent opinion surveys and straw polls—of doubtful significance early in the game—provide fodder for stories touting this or that candidate as "the one to beat."

Reporters and pundits are eager to declare big winners and big losers, even if the results fall somewhere in between (Weaver, 1976). Such publicity can spotlight obscure candidates or tarnish the image of well-known ones. In turn, the results affect the candidate's name recognition among the public, the zeal of the workers, and the generosity of financial backers. In 1972, Senator George McGovern was the clear front-runner when the convention began. Yet he got only about 30 percent of the primary votes and caucus-convention support. Jimmy Carter, with about 39 percent of voter support in the various states, blew away his rivals and dominated the 1976 convention. Michael Dukakis received 42 percent of the primary votes cast in 1988, which gave him a majority of the delegates and allowed him to dominate the Democratic convention in Atlanta that year.

All candidates today must in some sense mount "outsider" campaigns. They must look beyond the party leaders to demonstrate their popular appeal through media exposure and favorable poll standings. Only by taking the outside route can candidates lacking special ties with party inner circles force party leaders to take them seriously. John F. Kennedy in 1960 used his public appeal as leverage to gain the support of party bosses. In 1984, contenders as diverse as John Glenn and Jesse Jackson bid for public support to bolster their quest for the party nomination.

The partisans versus the reformers

The "reformed," primary-oriented nominating process has certain defects. The biggest losers were the party organizations themselves, including their leaders and elected officials. The debate on this point raged mainly among the Democrats. The party's Commission on Presidential Nomination (the

Hunt Commission), authorized by the 1980 convention, eventually summarized the predicament (Democratic National Committee, 1982: 3):

> Primaries have proliferated, removing decision-making power from party caucuses and conventions. Our national convention has been in danger of what one critic has called a "rubber stamp electoral college." To an alarming extent our party's public officials have not participated in and thus have felt only a limited responsibility for our recent national conventions.

The estrangement of party leaders also hindered successful candidates' efforts to forge effective governing coalitions with other officeholders. Candidates are led to mobilize factions at the expense of building broad coalitions that will enable them to govern (Polsby, 1983: 65). Jimmy Carter ran for president apart from party leaders; once elected, he lacked the contacts he needed to win party support for his programs.

Under pressure from officeholders and regulars, the Democrats adopted the Hunt Commission's recommendations for the 1984 nominating season. Taken together, these recommendations represented a substantial reversal of the post-1968 reforms. Major changes included:

1. Reserving about 22 percent of the convention seats for **superdelegates,** mostly party and elected officials, unpledged to any candidate.
2. Relaxing proportional representation—allocating delegates to candidates strictly according to their share of the primary or caucus vote—to aid top vote getters.
3. Shortening the nominating process by five weeks—early March through early June.

The new system took a step in the direction of restoring the influence of party leaders. Elected officials played a bigger part in the 1984 convention than they had played in years. So did key groups such as the major labor unions (the AFL-CIO boasted some 600 delegates). The new system also boosted the chances of an "insider" candidate like Walter F. Mondale who had close ties with party officials, labor leaders, and key interest groups allied with the party. Mondale drew less than 40 percent of the primary votes but entered the convention with a majority of delegates and the nomination wrapped up. The unpledged superdelegates backed him overwhelmingly, even in states where his rivals won the primary or caucus (Southwell, 1986).

The "outsider" candidates of 1984, Gary Hart and Jesse Jackson, charged that the system had shortchanged them. Jackson, the black activist who entered the contest in December 1983, claimed that the rules were stacked against outside or later-entering challengers. Both of these unsuccessful contenders attacked the rule denying delegates to candidates with less than 20 percent of a primary's votes. They asked that the 1988 rules be changed to reduce the number of unpledged superdelegates, lower the threshold for winning delegates in a caucus or primary, and open up the caucuses in certain states.

When the report of the "Fairness Commission"—the fifth such panel in as many nomination cycles —was adopted in 1986, however, it turned out that the party regulars had given little ground. The number of uncommitted superdelegates was even enlarged slightly. The threshold level—the vote share that a candidate had to win to get any delegates—was lowered from 20 percent to 15 percent. Most party leaders wanted to retain a threshold because they believed that this would shrink the field of candidates during the spring caucus and primary season.

In 1988, the nominating rules helped to winnow the candidates— dubbed "the seven dwarfs" at the start of the primary season. Well before the Atlanta convention convened, Massachusetts Governor Michael Dukakis had wrapped up the nomination and had a majority of the delegates; his only challenger was Jackson, whose persistent campaigning and growing following had netted him 30 percent of the delegates.

While Democratic party leaders had reason to be pleased that the rules had yielded a clear winner with broad appeal, Jackson's supporters continued to feel their candidate, as the outsider, had been shortchanged in delegates. The issue is seen in Figure 6–8, which compares the primary votes and delegate share received by the two candidates in various types of primaries. (The chart excludes delegates won from other candidates or from the uncommited ranks.) Dukakis won four of the five states that held direct-election primaries in which voters balloted directly for district delegates, making possible a winner-take-all result. He won 6 of 10 states with bonus systems—"winner-take-more" systems where the winner in each district won a bonus delegate. In direct-election primaries, moreover, Jackson's delegate count was less than half his vote totals. In other words, primaries resembled other U.S. elections in that victors took most, and sometimes all, of the delegates at the expense of the also-rans.

Jackson's forces pressed a series of rules changes that would enhance their place in the Democratic party and move toward proportional representation in allocating delegates won in the primaries. Not all of Jackson's demands were accepted, but on two crucial points Dukakis yielded in the interests of party unity. First, the number of superdelegates for 1992 would be reduced by about 250 from the 1988 level of 644. Second, all systems that gave a primary winner bonuses in delegates would be banned. This includes both "winner-take-all" and "winner-take-more" schemes. While the compromises prevented a convention fight (which the Dukakis forces could have won) in order to placate the Jackson forces, some party leaders wondered what the long-term costs would be. Would it be harder for a front-runner to emerge from a field of contenders? Would it lead to a "brokered" convention, in which several candidates with sizable delegations negotiated for the nomination? Would the changes, as Jackson contended, widen participation and lead to a freer convention choice?

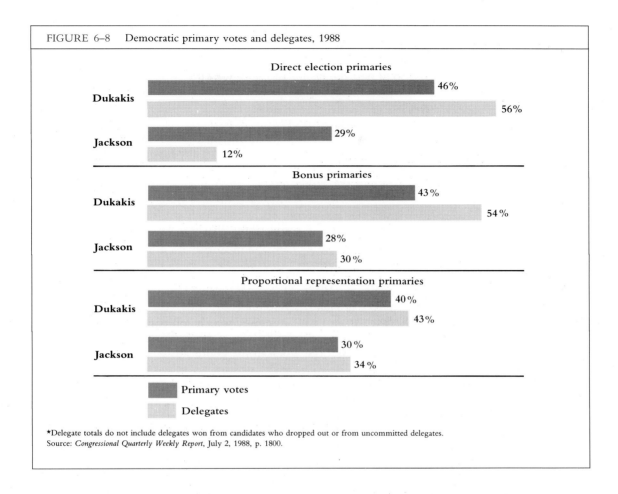

FIGURE 6–8   Democratic primary votes and delegates, 1988

Direct election primaries

Dukakis — 46%
Dukakis — 56%

Jackson — 29%
Jackson — 12%

Bonus primaries

Dukakis — 43%
Dukakis — 54%

Jackson — 28%
Jackson — 30%

Proportional representation primaries

Dukakis — 40%
Dukakis — 43%

Jackson — 30%
Jackson — 34%

■ Primary votes
▢ Delegates

*Delegate totals do not include delegates won from candidates who dropped out or from uncommitted delegates.
Source: *Congressional Quarterly Weekly Report*, July 2, 1988, p. 1800.

The wild card in the 1988 process was the March 8 regional primary that 20 states adopted to enhance their role in candidate selection. Because states are free to set their own primary dates within the three-month window set by the Democratic National Committee, this move occurred outside the party's rulemaking. The idea was that the winner of this **Super Tuesday**—presumably a moderate acceptable to southern voters—would get a boost from media attention, like the winners of the Iowa caucuses or the New Hampshire primary.

Like most of the tinkering with nomination rules, the superprimary led to unintended results that defied the reformers' intentions. For one thing, the Super Tuesday states were too numerous and too scattered geographically for the candidates—and the media following them around—to mount a focused effort. Nor was there a single Democratic candidate, much less one clearly in the moderate mold foreseen by Super Tuesday's designers, to win the primaries in all those states. (Jackson and Tennessee

Senator Albert Gore, Jr., did well on Super Tuesday, but other candidates won delegates, too. On the GOP side, Vice President George Bush's superior organization allowed him to tighten his grip on the his party's nomination.) So at best the results of the superprimary experiment were mixed and inconclusive.

Pitfalls of choosing publicly?

Today's nominating politics are more open than the old smoke-filled rooms. But they are prolonged and costly. They favor candidates who are unemployed (unless they are incumbent presidents): that is, those who have the time and the single-minded passion to devote to running for office.

Should potential presidents be put through the ordeal of our present nominating process? Some people think that this grueling process exposes candidates to realistic pressures. It puts them in contact with the public and the press, and it exposes misjudgments made under pressure. Others think the process is a joke. They feel that it shows little about someone's ability to serve in the White House. As Alan Ehrenhalt, a veteran political reporter, wrote: "Virtually every aspect of this year's Democratic marathon—the 'cattle show' public appearances, the pledges to special interest groups, the thousands of fund-raising phone calls, the courtship of the press—has brought out the worst in the good candidates as well as the bad ones" (1984: 167).

Some reformers would replace the present nominating process with a series of multistate regional primaries or even one national primary. This would shorten the nomination campaign and reduce wear and tear on candidates. Defenders of the current system say that it provides a variety of settings for candidates to prove themselves. "As long as there are many things we demand of a president—intelligence as well as popularity, integrity as well as speaking ability, private virtue as well as public presentability," argue Polsby and Wildavsky, "we ought to foster a selection process that provides a mixture of devices for screening according to different criteria" (1984: 226). Some contend that such candidates as McGovern and Carter could have emerged only from a disjointed chain of individual contests. Others counter that the success of such candidates proves that the current system is defective.

For the time being, Republicans are "staying the course," as Democrats still tinker with their rules. There is no consensus on how to alter the parties' jerry-built nominating systems. Conflicts between party leaders and the broader electoral party will continue to make wholesale solutions difficult, if not impossible. Democratic party leaders were able to recapture some of their lost control for the 1984 and 1988 races. But the inevitable cost was exposure to attacks from "outsider" candidates, who charged that the system was rigged to exclude certain segments.

Factors more fundamental than rules changes, moreover, affect nominating politics and will make it difficult to go back to the smoke-filled rooms. Among these factors are the role of the mass media, profound shifts in campaign funding patterns, and the popularity of broad participation norms. These factors point toward weaker party control of nominations and suggest that modern nominating trends cannot easily be reversed.

Parties are not only voter loyalties and electoral coalitions, though these are their main reasons for being. Their job does not stop once the votes have been counted and the winning candidates take office. Officeholders retain their partisan goals and link up with like-minded people to develop, pass, and implement the policies and programs they favor. At the same time, they reach out to cultivate and strengthen grass-roots linkages with partisan supporters.

PARTIES IN THE GOVERNMENT

Parties and Policy-Making

It is trendy to belittle party rhetoric. Many contend that people running for office cannot be believed and that parties, like "Tweedledee and Tweedledum," are no different from each other. Of course, it would be risky to stake your life on party promises. But if you listen to politicians, you will gain insight into current issues. Patterson and McClure (1976) even contend that voters are apt to learn more about the issues from campaign advertising than from TV network news.

Parties differ significantly over policies; they also strive to implement their preferences. In a revealing study, a political scientist examined **platforms** of the major parties and then determined what the parties had done to make good their promises (Pomper, 1980: 158–76). He found that the platforms of the two parties were quite different—they either stressed different issues or made opposing promises. He also found that the parties in power eventually kept at least 7 out of every 10 promises.

What do partisans do once they are elected? Often they seem more dedicated to career advancement than to policies or principles. But they do use party ties to fulfill their duties. Party platforms can be blueprints for executives and legislators. Party caucuses and meetings help officeholders exchange information and support. They can then form coalitions to enact and carry out policies.

In state and national legislative chambers, party loyalties are the most notable feature of day-to-day life. (Nebraska's nonpartisan legislature is the one exception.) Democrats sit on one side, Republicans on the other. Party caucuses pick presiding officers, chairpersons, and members of committees. Majority-party leaders preside over sessions, control the agendas, and use parliamentary rules to their advantage. Party leaders help teach new members the traditions and procedures. They work up partisan support for bills and resolutions. And in spite of the parties' weaknesses, party membership is still the best way to predict how legislators will vote (Mayhew, 1966).

For more than 150 years, presidents have been expected to serve as party leaders. The early presidents, from Washington through John Quincy Adams, regarded their office as one that represented the whole citizenry. Andrew Jackson and his successor, Martin Van Buren, introduced the view that party loyalists should be rewarded with government posts (Ketcham, 1984). Subsequent 19th-century presidents were not chief executives so much as principal patronage agents of their parties. They were deluged with what Grover Cleveland called "this dreadful, damnable office-seeking [which] hangs over me and surrounds me—and makes me feel like resigning" (Tourtellot, 1964: 166). When James A. Garfield was murdered by a disappointed office seeker in 1881, the stage was set for civil service reform, which gradually narrowed the chief executive's patronage role.

Presidents now lead their parties through speeches and public appearances designed to promote party policies. They serve as symbolic heads of their parties, act on their popular mandate, and name loyal partisans to posts in their administrations. Presidents cannot ignore the needs of their party without impairing their program or their legacy. "No president, it seems to me, can escape politics," asserted President Kennedy:

> He has not only been chosen by the nation—he has been chosen by his party. And if he insists that he is president of all the people and should, therefore, offend none of them—if he blurs the issues and differences between the parties—if he neglects the party machinery and avoids his party's leadership—then he has not only weakened the political party. . . . he has dealt a death blow to the democratic process itself. (Ketcham, 1984: 226)

Thus, the president's fate is intertwined with that of his party. Especially in an age of loose party ties, strong and visible incumbents help solidify loyalties and motivate party workers.

Groups with the best access to decision makers are typically more prominent in the party ranks. For the Republicans, this means businesspeople and conservative activists; for the Democrats, it means union officials, leaders of ethnic and racial groups, and intellectuals. As we have seen, there are marked and lasting differences among the groups that the parties draw on for electoral support; these same groups provide personnel and policy advice for the winning party.

Party Government

Many scholars and politicians advocate **party government,** a system in which each party puts forth united programs and has the clout, if elected, to carry them out. "At their best, American political parties are a great deal more than mechanisms for filling offices," asserted an American Assembly study group.

They can be—and frequently have been in the past—robust institutions which both facilitate social change and preserve public consensus. . . . [they] provide a means of attracting, nourishing, testing, and assessing new public leadership from and for oncoming generations. . . . At their fullest potential, political parties are mediating institutions that provide some measure of continuity, stability, and orderliness in politics. (American Assembly, 1982)

People who back stronger parties favor some or all of the following reforms: less emphasis on primary elections to choose national convention delegates and better convention representation for party officials and officeholders; the use of state caucuses or conventions to endorse candidates in party primaries; the channeling of funds, public or private, through the parties; and strengthened party organizations that actively cultivate issues and support candidates. In some of these respects (mainly in their national organizations and rule-making efforts), the parties are stronger today than they ever were (Cotter and Bibby, 1980).

THE STATE OF THE PARTIES

The last generation has not comforted advocates of stronger, more responsible parties. The parties no longer control nominations. The campaign help they offer is no better, and often less reliable, than what can be coaxed from friendly interest groups or bought from consultants. Jobs and welfare services, once provided by party machines, are now in government hands.

The parties once fulfilled social functions: they provided entertainment, fellowship, and a sense of belonging. These are no longer needed in an era of TV, pro sports, movies, and other escapes. Old-fashioned party clambakes and torchlight parades, once a highlight of local life, are today tame stuff indeed. In short, the parties' social functions, so important in the 1800s and at the turn of the century, today have a hazy future.

Today the parties present a puzzling paradox. Party organizations are vigorous and active, perhaps more so than in earlier days. Yet party loyalties have never been thinner; voters seem to view parties as irrelevant to most of their pressing concerns. In government, officeholders often forsake their partisan loyalties to set their own policy course. This leads to a serious question: How long can party organizations remain robust if there is no solid support from either officeholders or the electorate?

Some observers think that in the future party alignments will depart from past patterns. Long-standing party ties and groups, they note, are withering away. And they point to evidence that the virtual party monopoly over the electoral process is crumbling.

Other observers think that political parties will revive. They argue that the antiparty spirit of the 1960s and 1970s was a passing phenomenon, fueled by the cynicism and alienation that came with social unrest, the Vietnam War, and the Watergate scandal. The nonpartisan surge occurred mainly among younger people who entered the system during this period of unrest and disillusionment. Are these people developing more traditional party ties as they grow older? Will the parties regain their control over the leadership recruitment process? No one knows for sure.

CONCLUSIONS

In this chapter, we have described the workings of political parties and how they evolved. The following points are especially important:

1. The major goal of parties is to elect candidates or slates of candidates to public office. They do this by choosing candidates and mobilizing voters.

2. Political parties emerged and thrived in the 1800s and early 1900s. At that time, liberalized voting laws for the first time created a mass electorate.

3. Americans think in terms of a two-party system, dominated by Democrats and Republicans. In fact, party coalitions have shifted repeatedly during our history. Many areas are dominated by one party, and splinter parties are not unknown.

4. Party loyalties are part of citizens' basic political attitudes and are still the strongest predictor of voting. However, party loyalties may be fading as candidates and issues grow in importance.

5. Party alignment is a crucial factor in electoral results, and party realignment is a matter of constant investigation. Many analysts, however, believe that dealignment is more likely than realignment.

6. Party organizations are surprisingly vigorous at all levels. State and federal laws increasingly regulate party operations, and the parties themselves have formulated many rules and regulations.

7. Candidate selection has evolved from caucuses to conventions to primary elections. A series of reforms has widened the circle of potential participants and loosened the grip of traditional party leaders.

8. Party loyalties tie officeholders together. The average citizen does not seem to take the parties too seriously, but many commentators remain impressed with their potential for organizing the government and promoting responsible policy-making.

FURTHER READING

BIBBY, JOHN F. (1987) *Politics, Parties, and Elections in America.* Chicago: Nelson-Hall. An up-to-date text by an important scholar who knows parties inside and out.

CROTTY, WILLIAM J. (1984) *American Parties in Decline.* 2nd ed. Boston: Little, Brown. A thoughtful analysis of the declining influence of American political parties among the voters, in campaigns, and in Congress.

EPSTEIN, LEON D. (1986) *Political Parties in the American Mold.* Madison: University of Wisconsin Press. This thoughtful appraisal of the state of U.S. parties argues that many of their alleged weaknesses are of long standing and that they have shown their adaptability by seizing on several new functions.

SABATO, LARRY J. (1988) *The Party's Just Begun.* Glenview, Ill.: Scott, Foresman/Little, Brown. A readable assessment of partisan loyalties among the mass electorate and an activist's appeal for laws and practices designed to protect party autonomy and strengthen the parties' control over their own affairs.

SHAFER, BYRON E. (1988) *Bifurcated Politics: Evolution and Reform in the National Party Convention.* Cambridge, Mass.: Harvard University Press. A fresh, thoughtful analysis of the two faces of national political conventions: the TV spectacle to ratify the standard bearer, and the gathering of partisans to advance their own careers and concerns.

SORAUF, FRANK J. and PAUL A. BECK (1988) *Party Politics in America*. 6th ed. Boston: Little, Brown. A basic textbook on political parties that examines their organization, their relationship to voters, their role in contesting elections, and their impact on government.

SUNDQUIST, JAMES L. (1983) *Dynamics of the Party System*. Rev. ed. Washington, D.C.: Brookings Institution. A penetrating historical analysis of shifting party coalitions in America.

WATTENBERG, MARTIN P. (1986) *The Decline of American Political Parties, 1952–1984*. Cambridge, Mass.: Harvard University Press. Survey and voting evidence for the party decline thesis.

Chapter Seven

THE POWER OF INTEREST GROUPS

$\mathcal{D}$o you see political interest groups as shadowy "special interests" that bend government policies to their purposes? Do you think that lobbyists are always "other people" who promote their own goals at the expense of the rest of us? If so, then consider the following.

Not long ago, Ann Landers, the nationally syndicated advice columnist, answered a letter about psychological therapists who abused their patients and got away with it. In her reply, she endorsed a bill for the creation of a national computer system that would track unfit health-care providers and bar them from taking part in federal health programs. She exhorted her readers:

> I urge every reader who is in therapy, was in therapy, or has a friend or relative in therapy (this includes just about everybody) to clip this column and send it to your senators and representatives. Write across it, "SUPPORT THIS BILL!"

To make sure that her readers knew where to send their messages, she spelled out the addresses of senators and representatives. Thousands of readers complied with her request.

In this example, a single-purpose lobby group was created by a popular advice columnist. Not all spontaneously organized groups have such powerful backing, but thousands of groups seek to influence public policy in one way or another. Differing widely in size and visibility, many of these groups aim to bend the instruments of government in their direction. Taken as a whole, interest groups account in large measure for what our government does and how it is done. Interest-group power raises serious questions of policy-making: Are groups too influential? Are their methods of influence fair and open? Are competing groups on an equal footing? Do unorganized people get the same respectful hearing that is given to groups? Is the public interest simply the sum total of what all the groups want, or is it something beyond that? $\mathcal{O}$

*I*n this chapter, we explore what some have called "the group basis of politics." First, we define interest groups and distinguish them from political parties. Then, we outline the major types of groups and analyze their resources and liabilities in political arenas. Next, we explain the techniques used by groups to influence policy. Finally, we ponder the effects of groups on our politics: Do they represent the public interest, or do they thwart it?

GROUPS, POLITICAL AND OTHERWISE

People join together to form groups for many reasons—to make friends, to share ideas or promote common interests, to seek intellectual or spiritual betterment, to spread their ideas and press their demands on government.

The groups that concern us here are involved in politics. Our focus will be on such groups as labor unions and trade associations, not on sewing circles or motorcycle clubs. It should be understood, however, that groups often cross the line between political and nonpolitical purposes. A motorcycle club, for example, exists because like-minded people want to get together, socialize, and engage in joint activities, including recreation. Such a club may also seek to obtain permission for off-road riding facilities from public officials or may lobby against laws requiring cyclists to wear helmets. If it does, it has entered politics. Similarly, churches and religious sects, though not political groups, are repeatedly drawn into politics. They may mobilize their members on issues of world peace, criminal justice, pornography, or abortion. And they lobby for tax-exempt status and for tax deductions for charitable giving.

By the same token, political groups can fulfill personal, nonpolitical needs. Labor unions and retirees' associations, for example, sponsor social events, sell life insurance, and arrange group vacation tours. Fulfilling such individual needs cements the ties of their members and helps motivate their members to engage in broader political activity.

Because it is virtually impossible to say that a group is always political or always nonpolitical, we will call a group political when it functions politically. In other words, a group becomes a political **interest group** when it seeks to press its claims on other parts of society through political action and influence (Truman, 1971: 33).

How do political parties differ from interest groups? As we have seen, the main aim of parties is to win elections. An interest group, however, is "an association that tries to bring about the adoption and execution of certain policies without nominating candidates for the great offices, without fighting election campaigns, and without attempting to get complete control of government" (Schattschneider, 1942: 187). This distinction has blurred in recent years, as we will see; but it provides a workable definition.

Organized women. At this demonstration, 200 women picketed the 1984 Reagan-Bush headquarters in Boston to protest what they called the "disastrous effects" of President Reagan's policies on women. The demonstration was organized by the National Organization for Women (NOW).

HOW WIDESPREAD ARE INTEREST GROUPS?

Everyone who has glimpsed our society has been impressed by the number and variety of its organized activities. The French social critic Alexis de Tocqueville wrote in the 1830s that "in no country in the world has the principle of association been more successfully used or applied to a greater multitude of objects than in America."

Few would dispute this statement. Associations of all kinds have always flourished in our country. Large national groups whose names are known to everyone are merely the tip of the iceberg. The numbers of regional, state, and local groups are beyond counting. This is true not only because these groups are so numerous and varied, but also because they come and go so rapidly.

Why So Many Interest Groups?

The large number of organized activities flows from the diversity of modern life. Like other industrialized nations, ours is economically, socially, and culturally diverse. Our highly specialized activities and relationships demand specialized organizations to represent and link them.

WORDS AND IDEAS

James Madison on the Causes of "Faction"

The latent causes of faction are . . . sown in the nature of man; and we see them everywhere brought into different degrees of activity, according to the different circumstances of civil society. A zeal for different opinions concerning religion, concerning government, and many other points . . . ; an attachment to different leaders ambitiously contending for preeminence and power; or to persons . . . whose fortunes have been interesting to the human passions, have, in turn, divided mankind into parties, inflamed them with mutual animosity, and rendered them much more disposed to vex and oppress each other than to cooperate for their common good. . . . But the most common and durable source of factions has been the various and unequal distribution of property. Those who hold and those who are without property have ever formed distinct interests in society. . . . A landed interest, a manufacturing interest, a mercantile interest, a moneyed interest, with many lesser interests, grow up of necessity in civilized nations, and divide them into different classes, actuated by different sentiments and views. The regulation of these various and interfering interests forms the principal task of modern legislation.

Source: *Federalist*, No. 10 (1787).

If diversity stimulates the formation of groups, legal protection of freedom helps groups to flourish. James Madison put it well in the *Federalist*, No. 10: "Liberty is to faction what air is to fire, an element without which it instantly expires." Essential to the formation and functioning of groups are such Bill of Rights guarantees as freedom of speech, freedom of association, and freedom to petition the government. Nonprofit groups also enjoy a wide range of statutory aids—for example, tax exemptions and low-cost postal rates.

Our highly decentralized government reflects and fosters the diversity of our nation. Authority and responsibility are spread among 50 states and thousands of counties, cities, and special districts—nearly 100,000 government bodies in all. This decentralization causes people to organize on a great many levels, to wage battles over public policy on a variety of fronts (Truman, 1971: 519). A narrow, specialized interest that has little chance of affecting the national government may influence or even control a local community. Conversely, small local minorities may join like-minded groups to wield great power.

Decentralized government, as we have seen, leads to a decentralized party system—"more *pluribus* than *unum,*" as one scholar put it. The lack of unified, disciplined parties gives interest groups more leeway to influence government action. The parties no longer control sufficient funds or voter loyalties to ensure the success of their officeholders—executives and legislators. Thus, the hold of the parties on these officeholders is loose enough to give lobbyists the possibility of shaping government policies.

Groups continue to proliferate. Students of politics have been startled by the explosion of interest groups in recent decades. No one really knows how many groups there are; one recent study found that a majority of the sampled groups had been formed since World War II, especially since the early 1960s (Walker, 1983). In the 1980s, there were nearly 15,000 national nonprofit associations of one kind or another—40 percent more than in 1968 (Salisbury, 1986: 149–50). Two political scientists recently declared that "a 'participation revolution' is occurring in the country as large numbers of citizens are becoming active in an ever-increasing number of protest groups, citizens' organizations, and special interest groups. These groups often are composed of issue-oriented activists or individuals who seek collective material benefits" (Cigler and Loomis, 1986: 9). Growth has been especially notable among groups that are not primarily economic—those with social, ethical, or ideological goals.

Why has this group explosion occurred? While no single cause can be isolated, a combination of the following factors can explain the trend:

1. Ours is an increasingly educated populace, linked by ever more sophisticated and specialized communications media. Along with the traditional bread-and-butter issues of jobs and income, we are now animated by a variety of "quality of life" issues. Some of these issues have given rise to powerful broad-scale movements—civil rights, environmental protection, consumerism, opposition to the Vietnam War, and moral concerns.

2. Few of the issues listed above sharply divide the Democrats from the Republicans (as we noted in Chapter 6). Thus, activists have had to move outside the parties to push their causes most effectively.

3. Today's interest groups are assisted by new techniques and technologies that extend their reach. Examples include grass-roots organizing, computerized mailings, fund-raising appeals and candidate funding.

4. Partly in response to citizen activism, our political and governmental structures have become more open and accessible. Recent trends that have fostered such openness and accessibility include the broadening of political party leadership, campaign financing laws, decentralization in Congress and the executive branch, open-door decision making, and the passage of laws encouraging or even sponsoring interest-group inputs.

Joiners and Nonjoiners

The multiplicity of groups has led some writers to assume that, as a whole, all citizens are equally represented. Some writers even feel that a kind of natural balance results from the open marketplace in which interests can freely be organized into groups.

However widespread, groups are not universal. Not all parts of our society are equally prone to join groups. The sheer number of groups does not mean that they fairly represent people's interests. Some people—the "joiners"—belong to many clubs and associations; other people, the "nonjoiners," belong to none.

How many of us are joiners? In a nationwide survey, 62 percent of those polled belonged to at least 1 of 16 types of voluntary groups (Verba and Nie, 1972: 41–43). These ranged from labor unions, to recreational groups, to religious organizations. About two thirds of these members said that they were active in some way. Thus, about 4 out of every 10 adults are active members of at least one group. However, only about 8 percent of the adult population takes part in groups that are mainly political—partisan groups, political action groups, and voters' leagues.

Group membership does not faithfully mirror the total population. As with other forms of participation, those who join and take part tend to be richer and better educated than those who do not (Milbrath and Goel, 1977: 110–13). More men than women take part in groups, more middle-aged people than young or old people, and more of those with strong community ties than newcomers or transients. Thus, the characteristics of the people who seek membership in interest groups are about the same as the characteristics of those who participate politically in other ways.

Group involvement sparks political activity. The more groups you belong to, the more apt you are to become politically active. This is because groups publicize and stimulate action. They spread information on issues affecting their members, begging or shaming their members into taking part.

ECONOMIC GROUPS

Interest groups are not new to the American scene. The founders knew well the causes and effects of group activities; they were themselves skilled organizers. James Madison, in No. 10 of the *Federalist,* defined **faction** (not yet something different from parties or other types of groups) as "a number of citizens, whether amounting to a majority or minority of the whole, who are united and actuated by some common impulse of passion, or of interest." The most common and lasting sources of faction, Madison said, are economic interests caused by unequal distribution of property.

Today, as in Madison's time, the vast majority of interest groups work to achieve economic betterment. Their members are mainly producers or people in a given occupation, profession, or job category. (Not all of these groups are in the private sector. Public sector unions and professional groups actively pursue many policy fields.)

The Business Community

The most common business organizations, corporations, have never been shy in dealing with government. A corporation's "interest" is profit, and its "members" are its managers, workers, and stockholders. In many firms, a busy public relations department encourages members of the corporate family to speak out on issues affecting the firm's well-being.

Business firms inevitably affect the politics of local communities where they have facilities. At the federal level, many large firms use Washington offices to maintain contact with officials. Smaller firms call on lobbying consultants, law firms, or trade associations to speak for them. Today's corporate giants are the **multinational corporations,** whose affairs cross national boundaries and whose agents deal with officials in many countries.

Trade associations are made up of business firms in the same field. They are business's chief way of influencing government. As early as 1741, a New York City bakers' guild was embroiled in a dispute over an ordinance fixing the price of bread. Today's trade associations are among the most visible lobbying groups in Washington. There are probably 40,000 trade associations in the United States, counting local chapters and independent or regional groups. Their size varies widely. The Motor Vehicle Manufacturers Association, for example, has only 12 members—mostly huge enterprises. But the National Automobile Dealers Association includes 22,000 companies. Thousands of other trade groups, embracing almost every type of business or industry, deal with legislators and bureaucrats (Bauer, Pool, and Dexter, 1963). They dispense information and other services to their members. They wage public relations campaigns to win praise and support for their industry. And, of course, they lobby for legislation to protect and enhance the industry.

The business community also has many **umbrella groups** that speak for the overall interests of business. The U.S. Chamber of Commerce and the National Association of Manufacturers (NAM) stand out. The Chamber is a federation of local chambers of commerce, firms, individuals, and trade and professional groups. The NAM, with 13,000 corporate members, speaks mainly for big business.

Big business tends to define the business viewpoint in Washington. Yet small firms also have vocal lobbies; more important, they get a warm reception on Capitol Hill. Small-business representatives are conspicuous and wield influence in small and medium-sized towns. They are courted by legislators who covet seats on congressional small-business committees.

Organized Labor

Local trade unions date from the nation's beginnings. Indeed, the first strike in the country is thought to have occurred in 1786, when a group of printers in Philadelphia sought a minimum weekly wage of $6. Large-scale unions, which employers fiercely resisted, remained disorganized and short-lived until 1886, when the *American Federation of Labor* (AFL) was formed. This alliance of skilled **craft unions** grew to more than 1 million members by the turn of the century. The AFL stressed economic bargaining with employers, and favored voluntarism—the right of skilled workers to control their own workplace conditions. It negotiated directly with employers for higher wages and better working conditions, shunning the political arena.

After a while, the AFL stepped up its political activity. But it remained a group for skilled laborers. Semiskilled or unskilled workers in mass-production industries could not protect their jobs because they lacked the control wielded by the craft unions. Therefore, these workers formed more militant political groups, the **industrial unions.** In 1935, these unions fused into what later became the *Congress of Industrial Organizations* (CIO). The CIO's most eloquent spokesman was the head of the United Mine Workers, John L. Lewis (1880–1969).

The AFL–CIO, which resulted from the merger of the two labor groups in 1955, now embraces nearly 100 unions. Their members range from teachers to plumbers, from meat cutters to government workers. With 14 million dues-paying members speaking for some 50 million people, the AFL–CIO is labor's loudest voice. Yet several strong unions are outside its ranks.

Bargaining over wages and work conditions is left largely to individual unions. But political action is directed by the AFL–CIO and the large international unions. Political arms, such as the Committee on Political Education (COPE), are financed by union contributions and carry out registration and campaign drives.

The voice of unions is firmest on economic issues that directly touch their members. These include labor-management relations, job safety, minimum wages, plant closings, and social security. Unions often lobby on such issues as welfare, antipoverty, federal aid to education, and trade policy.

Politically, organized labor is badly divided. It has long been aligned with the Democrats, but its Democratic leanings flagged as New Deal issues faded and union members blended into the nation's middle class. In 1980 and 1984, most of the AFL–CIO leaders stood firmly with the Democratic presidential candidates; however, some labor groups, such as the International Brotherhood of Teamsters and the building trades unions, made no secret of their GOP leanings. In 1984, about 45 percent of all the votes from labor families went to Reagan.

Organized labor. Lane Kirkland, president of the American Federation of Labor and Congress of Industrial Organizations (AFL–CIO), and other AFL–CIO leaders at the organization's national convention wait for the tabulation of votes to endorse a presidential candidate in 1984. The Democrat Walter Mondale received 96.5 percent of the votes cast.

Reagan's presidency, however, eventually galvanized the opposition of most labor leaders and strengthened their determination to remain allied with the Democrats. But labor resolved to have a place at the party's table, rather than to watch from the sidelines during the nominating phase. In 1984, AFL–CIO leaders mounted an expensive drive to see that the pro-labor candidate Walter F. Mondale got the Democratic nomination. No candidate won organized labor's pre-nomination nod four years later: union leaders were found in the camps of several contenders, and 27 percent of the Democratic delegates were union members.

Organized labor's political troubles reflect its decades-old economic slide. Its share of the nation's work force has been dwindling, with less than one fifth of all workers now counted as union members. Union strength is highest in older industries that are declining in importance, such as the steel and automotive industries. Indeed, competitive pressures in such industries have led unions to accept settlements that limit labor costs; the unions hope that doing this will keep the industries alive. Labor's future rests in part on organizing new generations of service and public sector workers; but these workers are less wedded to the union ideal than were their parents or grandparents.

Organized labor's weaknesses were reflected in the 1981 walkout of 13,000 members of the Professional Air Traffic Controllers Organization (PATCO). This tight-knit union had a string of grievances against the

Professional Air Traffic Controllers Organization (PATCO) on strike. An air traffic controller and his family picket at John F. Kennedy Airport in New York. As a result of the strike, which took place in 1981, 12,000 PATCO air controllers were dismissed and five union officers were jailed. The air control towers were staffed thereafter by nonunion air traffic controllers.

Federal Aviation Administration (FAA). But strikes by federal workers are forbidden by law, and President Reagan's fiscal plans left him little leeway to meet the controllers' demands. The FAA declared that the striking workers had quit. It improvised a scaled-down flight schedule with supervisors and military controllers, and set about rebuilding the air traffic control system. The public tended to support the president in this conflict, and the labor leaders themselves were divided. The failure of the PATCO walkout heralded harder times for labor, both at the bargaining table and in the court of public opinion.

Agriculture

Farm producers have plowed deep furrows in American politics since the founding of our nation. Until the Civil War the number of farmers exceeded that of all other workers, and until the 1960s rural areas dominated many state legislatures and congressional delegations. The U.S. Department of Agriculture (USDA) was, not surprisingly, the first cabinet de-

Protesting farmers. The American Agriculture Movement sponsored a "tractorcade" in Washington, D.C., to protest low farm incomes.

partment explicitly formed to serve a "clientele" economic sector. Federal research and education programs have helped make American farmers the most productive in the world.

Some of the most powerful farm organizations arose in response to governmental programs. With government help, the American Farm Bureau Federation grew as an organization of the people served by the local farm bureaus set up under the Smith-Lever Act of 1914. The National Rural Electric Cooperatives Association is a federation of local rural electric co-ops that through federal loans provide cheap power for rural areas.

Protest has been a perennial element of farmers' political activity, for small farmers have always been vulnerable to exploitation by outside interests. The Grange, founded in 1867, fought the tyranny of the railroads that got their crops and livestock to market. Modern groups fighting for family farms include the National Farmers Organization (1955) and the American Agriculture Movement (1977), both of which have led middle-class farmers' revolts against declining farm revenues. The rash of failures of family-sized farms in the 1980s yielded not only tales of personal tragedy but political reprisals in the form of defeats for officeholders.

Although agriculture is essential and farm products are the nation's biggest export, fewer people live on farms than ever before. According to the 1980 census, only 2.5 percent of the nation's people (5.6 million persons) lived on farms, barely a sixth of the number 30 years earlier.

Despite the fact that there are fewer farm voters than ever, political clout is today wielded by the large farmers and corporate food firms that manage increasing portions of our farm acreage. For example, dairy associations contributed more than $1.8 million to House campaigns in the 1980s. Not surprisingly, the industry succeeded in maintaining high price-support programs. Other agricultural producers—tobacco and sugar producers, for example—maintain prices, ward off competition, or receive subsidized water or reclamation through legislative means. They do this through strong regional ties, lavish contributions to legislators' campaigns, friendly congressional committees, and a clientele agency, the U.S. Department of Agriculture.

Professional Groups

Professional associations are related to unions but tend to represent higher-status occupations. Their membership is limited to persons formally trained for specific careers (Zeigler and Peak, 1972).

Professional associations patrol the standards of admission to the professions they represent. Thus, they maintain close ties with professional schools and often help in licensing practitioners. Having locked up the profession's exclusive status, they protect the economic well-being of their members and defend them against outsiders, including nonprofessionals or paraprofessionals (McConnell, 1967; Lowi, 1969).

Strategic position, not numbers, gives professional groups their clout. The nation's 650,000 lawyers, for instance, earn more per capita than those of any other industrialized society. Their influence derives not from their numbers, but from their singular role in shaping, interpreting, and implementing laws at the local, state, and national levels. Among the members of virtually all elected assemblies, from city councils to the U.S. Congress, lawyers are the most numerous profession. Bar association panels screen candidates for judgeships—a practice that, though informal, often determines who sits on the bench. The upshot is that citizens must approach the legal system largely on the legal profession's terms.

Physicians make effective use of their unique prestige in our culture; their major organization, the American Medical Association (AMA), speaks loudly and often decisively in their behalf. For many years, the AMA led the fight against federal health insurance, depicting "socialized medicine" as a violation of the intimate doctor-patient relationship. The AMA lost this fight in 1965, when medicare was enacted; but it made sure

Organized teachers. Members of the American Federation of Teachers (AFT) in Baltimore, Maryland, discuss campaign strategy. The AFT has a membership of about half a million.

that its members profited handsomely from medicare-medicaid business. And the AMA has lobbied to deter the government from cutting doctors' costs or regulating fees. Pressed by rival health groups, the AMA now enrolls less than half of all the country's physicians, but it remains active on such fronts as fees, drug legislation, medical research, and federal health support. Using physicians' financial resources, the AMA's Political Action Committee (AMPAC) ranks high among lobby groups in spending.

Many other professionals have associations—real estate agents, contractors, veterinarians, barbers, and beauticians, for example. In many states professions are regulated by state licensing boards consisting largely of association members. These boards work under state laws that regulate the dispensing of professional services as well as entry into and exit from the profession.

In the last decade or so, the rights of professionals to define services and set the conditions for dispensing them have met with increasing public resistance. But most professions are well organized and lobby vigorously with legislative and administrative bodies to preserve their monopoly positions.

NONECONOMIC GROUPS
Groups not directly linked to production or economic interests have flourished since the 1960s. Some of these noneconomic groups are well known to the general public: the Sierra Club, the Moral Majority, People for the American Way, and "right to life" groups are examples. Indeed, they represent the fastest-growing type of group; according to one survey, more than half of them have formed since 1960 (Walker, 1983).

Such a group, says Berry, is "one that seeks a collective good, the achievement of which will not selectively and materially benefit the membership or activists of the organization" (1977: 7). Groups of this kind do not represent the interests of people as producers or wage earners but as pursuers of ideals, consumers, taxpayers, and users of goods, services, and the nation's resources.

Noneconomic groups flourish despite Olson's (1965) assumption that groups pursuing "collective" benefits—received by everyone in a class or segment of society regardless of group membership—would be very difficult to form and maintain. The problem, according to Olson, is *free riders*. That is, "rational" individuals in such broad groups—consumers, for example—should balk at bearing the costs (time, dues, membership) of participating, because they can reap the benefits of the group (favorable legislation, for instance) whether or not they join. The free-rider problem plagues large groups in particular; the larger the group, the less likely it is that an individual will see his or her contribution as affecting success.

Nonetheless, noneconomic interest groups are the fastest-growing class of groups, comprising perhaps a fifth more of all active political associations. As Walker (1983: 397) observes, "The political system is beset by a swarm of organizational bumblebees that are busily flying about in spite of the fact that prevailing theories cannot explain how they manage it."

Such groups can overcome the free-rider problem in several ways. First, they may find sponsors—wealthy individuals or foundations—that will bankroll the group and reduce its dependence on members' contributions. Second, they may avail themselves of the huge pool of potential group organizers and supporters among educated, affluent people with leisure time—people seeking symbolic rather than material benefits. Third, they may make use of contemporary technologies—media appeals and targeted mailing, for example—that make it easier than ever for groups to seek out their constituencies. Finally, government itself can initiate or sponsor group activity. We have already seen, for example, that government services inevitably create "clienteles," which in turn often create groups dedicated to continuing or expanding the services. In other cases, the government sets up a policy-making procedure that encourages people to organize so as to participate effectively.

Representing large and scattered constituencies has its good and bad points. Broad, spread-out noneconomic groups are hard to mobilize, especially when their goals are diffuse and their resources meager. But because they don't have overt economic motives, these groups are often regarded as fair and impartial. Of course, such groups are not the only ones that wrap their demands in the mantle of the "public interest."

Environmentalists

The first environmental groups were the Sierra Club (1892) and the National Audubon Society (1905). They were formed by people who wanted to preserve the country's natural beauty. Later the post–World War II economic boom brought smog alerts, nuclear fallout, and pesticides. It also produced a new wave of environmental groups, including Friends of the Earth, the Environmental Defense Fund, and the Natural Resources Defense Council.

The high-water mark of environmentalism came in the early 1970s. Two new government bodies, the Environmental Protection Agency (EPA) and the Council on Environmental Quality (CEQ), were created during the Nixon years. In the decade following 1969, Congress passed 37 antipollution laws, including the National Environmental Policy Act of 1969 and the 1970 Clean Air Act. Environmentalists saved the brown pelican and the bald eagle from pesticides; they obtained sweeping changes in waste disposal; and they pushed through auto pollution limits that added perhaps $800 to the price of the average car.

Most environmental groups are small and have scant member funding. Their best resource is publicity; they can shape and mobilize public opinion by dramatizing threats to health and natural resources. The high point was Earth Day, April 22, 1970, a massive demonstration to defend the environment. One group targeted the "dirty dozen" antienvironmental legislators and the "filthy five" allegedly polluting companies. As one legislator said, "You can't build a highway now without some group telling you that it will be harmful to a ladybug colony or an ant heap."

In the 1980s, the environmental movement experienced both reverses and resurgence. Adverse reaction to the cost and the red tape of the government's environmental programs resulted in a stalemate over renewing many of them (Cook and Davidson, 1985). The Reagan administration's antienvironmental thrusts were typified by the stormy careers of Interior Secretary James G. Watt and EPA Administrator Ann Gorsuch Burford, both of whom promoted policies that favored business interests over environmental protection. But these threats also helped revitalize environmental groups and reactivate their members. Environmental regulations are complex and beg for simplification; but surveys show that the public wants continued environmental protection, even at the cost of higher consumer prices and reduced productivity.

*"Free at last . . ." Dr
Martin Luther King, Jr.
(1929–68), is shown
addressing 200,000 people
at the Lincoln Memorial
in Washington, D.C., in
1963. King's March on
Washington for Jobs and
Freedom helped pass the
historic civil rights laws of
the 1960s. King was
assassinated in Memphis,
Tennessee, on April 4,
1968; his assassin, James
Earl Ray, was sentenced
to 99 years in prison.
King's birthday, January
15, was made a national
holiday in 1983.*

The Civil Rights Community

Since World War II, the civil rights bloc has been a potent political force.
Civil rights groups sway public attitudes and mobilize constituencies at
the grass-roots level; they also exert direct pressure on government.

The earliest civil rights groups led the fight for black rights. The National Association for the Advancement of Colored People (NAACP),
founded in 1909, sponsored actions that led to the Supreme Court's 1954
school desegregation decision *(Brown* v. *Board of Education).* Another civil
rights group, the National Urban League, stands behind more than 100
local groups and runs an active national lobbying program.

During the 1960s, civil rights activists gained results through petitions and mass protests. The March on Washington for Jobs and Freedom brought 200,000 to the Lincoln Memorial in 1963 and featured a stirring speech by the Reverend Martin Luther King, Jr. This protest demanded tougher enforcement of antibias laws and helped pass historic civil rights laws in 1964 and 1965.

Today's civil rights organizations represent a wide range of concerns. There are groups that speak for Hispanics, Asian Americans, children, the handicapped, women, gays, and lesbians, as well as blacks. In addition, there are allied church, union, and civil liberties associations. About 165 groups belong to the Leadership Conference on Civil Rights, an umbrella organization founded in 1950 that coordinates groups in the civil rights movement.

The civil rights community is now broader and more scattered than it was in the 1960s. Its groups can still rally impressive support for basic civil rights laws. But its interests today run the whole gamut of government policy—from insurance and pension guarantees to the rights of children and families. Like the environmentalists, these groups have been revitalized by the policies of the Reagan administration—in this case, by its alleged departures from civil rights goals. They have mustered broad bipartisan support for their efforts to preserve their earlier gains, and they have battled the Reagan administration over renewal of the Voting Rights Act, control of the U.S. Commission on Civil Rights, creation of a holiday commemorating the birthday of Martin Luther King, Jr., sanctions on the South African government, and withholding federal funds from firms or institutions found to discriminate.

Women's Groups

Women's political action is no new phenomenon. Women's organizations trace their origins to the late 1860s, when two groups organized separately to win the right to vote for women. Two decades later, the two groups merged to form the National American Woman Suffrage Association (NAWSA). For the next 30 years, this organization lobbied Congress and state legislatures to extend the vote to women. The result was the 19th Amendment to the Constitution (1920). Ethel Klein (1984: 16) describes NAWSA's tireless efforts:

> This victory came after 56 referendum campaigns, 480 efforts to get state legislatures to allow suffrage referenda, 47 campaigns at state constitutional conventions for suffrage, 277 attempts to include woman suffrage in state party programs, and 19 campaigns to get the 19th Amendment through Congress.

Once suffrage was achieved, center stage was taken by the League of Women Voters, a group that encouraged political participation and disseminated information on pressing national issues.

In the mid-1960s, a more militant women's movement came to the fore. At issue was equal treatment for women in the marketplace and in society and adoption of the Equal Rights Amendment (ERA), which specified that "equality of rights under the law shall not be denied or abridged . . . on account of sex." The ERA fell short of the 38 states required for ratification, in part because its opponents were able to raise fears among men (and among women who adhered to traditional social values) that it would eradicate social differences between the sexes.

The most conspicuous group of the new women's movement was the National Organization for Women (NOW). NOW adopted an aggressive, confrontational approach to lobbying. In one of its first press releases, NOW proclaimed its advocacy of "a militant program of action toward full equality for women in equal partnership with men" (Costain and Costain, 1983: 192). Along with other civil rights organizations, it took part in protest actions and public demonstrations.

Women's groups scored important legislative victories in the 1970s. Among these were getting Congress to approve the ERA and to revise the 1964 Civil Rights Act to protect pregnant workers from job discrimination. These gains were made possible by the large number of women in the electorate and by their higher levels of voting and political activism.

By the 1980s, the goals of the women's movement—like those of other civil rights groups—had spread to a wide variety of public goals. Women played pivotal roles in campaigns for nuclear disarmament, children's rights, and tough treatment of drunk drivers. Growing numbers of women held posts in Congress and at the state and local levels. "State government is where women have the most political clout" (Steinbach, 1987). Nearly 1,200 women were serving as state lawmakers in 1987; women also served in the cabinet and on the federal and state bench; and in 1984 a woman ran as the vice presidential candidate of a major party. The ranks of women among public officeholders are bound to swell.

Public Interest Groups

A bewildering variety of groups purport to voice the concerns of average citizens. Their original self-description, **public interest groups,** aroused resentment from other lobbyists, who protested that they were every bit as devoted to the public's concerns as any of the so-called citizen's groups.

One of the most notable of these groups is Common Cause, founded in 1970. It professes two major goals: "Change political structures so they will be more responsive to social needs and . . . produce a major reordering of national priorities." Common Cause is bipartisan, but it is often seen as left of center. Its large Washington staff unabashedly lobbies government officials. Its campaigns have aimed at ending the Vietnam War, granting the vote to 18-year-olds, changing the congressional seniority system, reducing restrictions on voter registration, strengthening legal

Ralph Nader (1934–), citizens' lobbyist. The preeminent advocate of consumer rights, Nader was the effective founder of the modern consumer movement in the United States. He has championed auto safety, publicized the dangers of certain food additives, and warned of the hazards of radiation from TV sets. Here, he is speaking on the risks of nuclear power stations at a meeting in Beverly Hills, California.

controls over lobbying and campaign spending, and streamlining the structure of government. Common Cause takes credit for the passage of post-Watergate campaign finance reforms; it has declared war on the clout of big contributors in political campaigns.

The best-known citizens' lobbyist is Ralph Nader, a consumer advocate and lawyer. He burst on the scene in 1965, when a Senate inquiry found that he had been harassed by a giant automaker after writing a book critical of auto safety standards. Nader built on this publicity and on single-minded absorption in his work. He turned his advocacy into a lobbying industry, employing swarms of young, idealistic, low-paid workers to research and write reports on public issues. These reports form the basis for lobbying efforts by Nader's groups, Congress Watch and Public Citizen. Nader and his aides have examined a wide variety of issues, mainly consumer protection and the dangers of nuclear power.

Two ideological citizens' groups are Americans for Democratic Action (ADA) and Americans for Constitutional Action (ACA). ADA is "an organization of progressives, dedicated to the achievement of freedom and economic security for all people everywhere, through education and democratic political action." ACA, founded to counter ADA, supports constitutional conservatism. Each year, both groups rate members of Congress, using an index based on selected lists of key votes. Naturally, the scores of the two groups' indexes are virtual opposites.

Religious Groups

Churches and religious groups have long been a powerful force in American politics. They were a key element in the 19th-century movement to abolish slavery, and at the turn of this century conservative Protestant groups backed the "antisaloon movement" to ban alcoholic beverages. The 18th Amendment made this ban national policy between 1919 and 1933 (when it was rescinded by the 21st Amendment). In the 1960s, religious groups bolstered efforts to enact civil rights law protecting blacks and other minorities.

Religious groups, now extensively organized, give voice to diverse visions of morality and differing ways of embodying these visions in public policy. Many religious bodies, including some mainline Protestant and Catholic organizations, are linked to such liberal causes as racial and minority rights, social and economic equality, liberalized refugee policies, and human rights around the globe. More recently, a number of evangelical groups, such as Moral Majority, have voiced a distinctly right-wing version of public policy, including prayer in schools, heavier military spending, and opposition to abortion, gays, and the Equal Rights Amendment. These groups buttressed Ronald Reagan's drive for the White House and his call for a return to traditional values. Some of their leaders, such as TV evangelists Jerry Falwell and Pat Robertson, became better known for their political views than for their theology.

In recent years, the National Conference of Catholic Bishops has launched efforts to sway national policy. It has issued statements opposing abortion and advocating economic justice and the control of nuclear weapons. Needless to say, church involvement in such issues can mobilize voters. Yet each foray into politics risks dividing church members and exposes church leaders to rough-and-tumble political clashes.

Government Lobbyists

Not only private groups seek to influence public policies. Some lobbyists represent elected and appointed officials of other governments—mainly states, counties, and municipalities. Crucial portions of these governments' budgets hinge on decisions made in Washington. Thus, their representatives have become more vocal. These representatives, many of whom have offices in the "Hall of the States" near Capitol Hill, have natural affinities with state delegations and regional caucuses in Congress.

The National Governors Conference provides state governors with a national platform. The conference, originally an extension of periodic governors' meetings, expanded its activities in the 1960s. It remains a loose group because its members are highly visible, partisan figures. "It consists of an alliance of 50 prima donnas, the highest elected officials within the states, leaders and rarely followers" (Haider, 1974: 24). Lobbying is only a sideline for the National Conference of State Legislatures.

Its main aims are to conduct research and to serve as a clearinghouse for information on state problems.

Cities are represented by two groups, the National League of Cities and the U.S. Conference of Mayors (USCM). The missions of the two groups intertwine; for four years (1970 to 1974), their staffs were merged. But differing views and styles have kept them apart. The USCM, representing the largest cities, tends toward liberal views on civil rights, housing, transportation, and federal programs. The National League represents smaller cities, has a more complicated structure, and tends toward a moderate course.

The National Association of Counties (NACO) has more than 2,000 county governments as members. Its annual conferences attract thousands of elected and appointed officials. NACO reflects disparate interests, because counties vary widely in population and organization. It stands behind both large and small counties and thus tends to avoid controversial issues. NACO members supported the Reagan administration's early efforts to cut federal domestic spending; when local grants were threatened, however, county officials followed city officials in opposing further cutbacks.

Federal money is the prime target of government lobbyists. They have fought to continue revenue sharing, model cities, mass transit, Urban Development Action Grants (UDAGs), and tax exemption for municipal bonds. These lobbyists also argue for more freedom in using federal funds and making policies. For example, they want to decentralize and decategorize program grants and they want fewer strings on federal moneys.

The state and local government representatives constitute a kind of "third house" of officials at the national level. They "provide another form of political representation at the national level, one founded not on functional lines or shifting congressional boundaries but on representation of interests based essentially on geopolitical units—states, counties, and municipalities" (Haider, 1974: 306).

Single-Interest Groups

Many noneconomic interest groups organize around a single cause or issue. They bend their efforts toward realizing one goal, against which they measure all politicians. Such single-interest groups are not new. The antislavery crusade of the mid-19th century was a very successful single-interest drive. The Anti-Saloon League's drive in the early 20th century to prohibit alcohol was another.

What is novel about today's single-interest groups is not their flamboyant publicity or their meticulous cultivation of grass-roots support. ("At the start of the century, without so much as a microchip to aid it, the Anti-Saloon League had a mailing list of more than half a million people" [Schlozman and Tierney, 1983: 363]). It is the number and variety of these groups that are novel. Groups of this kind range from animal rights advocates to anti–nuclear power activists, from proponents of gun control to opponents of abortion. Many of these groups urge their members to vote on their issue without regard to other considerations. More than one politician has been defeated because group members—gun owners or anti-abortionists, for instance—cast their votes solely on such an issue.

Needless to say, politicians tend to frown on this approach. They argue that public stewardship mixes many ingredients and should not be reduced to simplistic formulas, no matter now persuasive. But to adherents of single-interest politics, their particular goals take on paramount importance.

And Many Other Groups

The number and scope of political interest groups are truly staggering. Nearly any organization can turn into a political group if its interests are at stake. This includes organizations of women, Hispanics, senior citizens, professors, consumers, federal employees, and judges, as well as all kinds of ideological and social groups.

It is tempting to condemn such groups as "special interests" when they enter the political arena. Yet all of us sooner or later try to put pressure on the government on issues we care deeply about.

This does not imply that everyone is equally represented by interest groups. As noted, organized interest groups have a definite class bias. Middle- and upper-income groups are better organized than lower-income groups. Surveys consistently show that group membership varies with income, occupation, and education. "The poor and the unemployed," Olson points out, "like consumers and taxpayers, are still without organization everywhere; the picket lines and other selective incentives needed for collective action are not feasible for them" (1987: A23).

To some, such as E. E. Schattschneider, this means that "large areas of the population appear to be wholly outside of the system of private organization" (1960: 30). There is considerable truth to this view: many categories of people—nonunion workers, consumers, mental patients, and the poor—are politically underorganized. Yet the proliferation of groups has aided such people. Even those who belong to no groups may actually be represented by groups with related interests. Moreover, people can compensate for lack of schooling, money, or status by joining groups. To see how this works, we must examine how a group's characteristics affect its political style and influence.

GROUP RESOURCES

Let us consider two contrasting organizations: the Carlton Group and the National Education Association (NEA). These are two of the thousands of groups that try to shape public policy; they illustrate the wide range of resources and techniques that are open to interest groups.

The Carlton Group is small and informal. It consists of a dozen or so men and two women who meet every other Tuesday for breakfast in a private salon of Washington's Sheraton-Carlton Hotel, three blocks from the White House. The group's objective is to shape America's tax code to the advantage of business. Its great triumph was the Economic Recovery Tax Act of 1981. This act, in addition to incorporating President Reagan's three-year, across-the-board tax cut, adopted an accelerated depreciation scheme for which business had been lobbying for several years. Business firms stood to save $158 billion in taxes in the act's first five years; labor charged that the act virtually repealed corporate income taxes. Since its passage, the Carlton Group has fought new business taxes while urging other steps to cut federal deficits.

In structure, Carlton is a **catalytic group** (Riggs, 1950): it exchanges information and coordinates other groups. Its members are top lobbyists, lawyers, and economists from such major business groups as the U.S. Chamber of Commerce (200,000 members), the American Business Conference (100 midsize companies), the National Federation of Independent Business (500,000 small firms), and the Business Roundtable (chief executives of some 200 major companies). A few key law firms and corporations with large Washington offices regularly send representatives. Over the breakfast table, Carlton Group members discuss why they should support or oppose certain policies. By tapping their organizational bases, they can mobilize support for key legislation from almost every major segment of the business community, ranging from the largest corporations to small unincorporated firms and local chambers of commerce.

The Carlton Group has few organizational trappings and few resources of its own. Its members avoid the limelight and were distressed at stories written about the group following the 1981 tax cut. "Getting the Carlton Group out of the headlines" was how its organizer described his role.

The National Education Association (NEA), in contrast, could not escape headlines even if it wanted to. It is an organization of nearly 2 million teachers. Its annual budget approaches $50 million, and its Washington staff exceeds 500. As a large and varied organization, the NEA commands a variety of resources for affecting public policies. Its lobbyists are familiar in the corridors and offices on Capitol Hill and in agencies downtown. Its ads and bumper stickers ask citizens to "support your schools." It makes the most of its numbers and wealth by rating legislators' votes and rewarding its friends with campaign funds.

Like the Carlton Group, the NEA has had its political triumphs. The most notable was the creation of the Department of Education in 1979, a long-held NEA goal that President Carter pushed to gain NEA support for his reelection. More recently, the NEA has been under siege for its liberal leanings and for its defense of teachers in the wake of widespread demands for teacher testing, certification, and merit pay. The NEA has been a prominent target of Reagan administration officials seeking to lay blame for the ills of the public schools.

Both business leaders and teachers are forces to be reckoned with. But the differences in their characteristics affect their resources, their techniques, and their effectiveness. These differences focus our attention on group attributes.

Group Size

The most obvious attribute of groups is their size. Some, like the Carlton Group, have only a handful of members. Others, like the NEA, have millions. Some groups enroll members directly; others, such as federations of local groups, enroll them indirectly; still others have few members but gain money and support through direct mail soliciting.

Large groups can, of course, be impressive. Leaders of such groups can rightly assert that they speak for millions of people. But groups of this kind are hard to organize and maintain. Individuals who support the goals of a large group may reason that they can reap benefits from its successes without incurring the cost of joining (Olson, 1965). Because of their diversity of views, such groups are hard to mobilize for achieving concrete political objectives.

Large groups can overcome such organizational barriers through shrewd strategies. Many of them offer their members basic services, turning to politics incidentally to further their members' interests. Union locals, for example, attract members by representing them in negotiations with employers; members seek out the American Automobile Association (AAA) for its accident insurance and travel aids. Both union locals and the AAA offer services to gain members and to collect funds for their political efforts. Other groups gain members by monopolizing a valuable resource—access to a government board or commission, for example. Still other groups—most notably ideological and single-issue groups—gain members by compiling huge mailing lists and using targeted mailings to solicit funds.

Status and Money

Another attribute of groups is the socioeconomic status of their members. Some groups, like those of doctors and judges, have an enviable public image; others, like those of truck drivers and stevedores, lack that advantage. The AMA uses its image as the voice of a respected profession, along with generous funding, to shape the nation's health-care system.

A group's strategic position is related to its status. Does it command indispensable information or services? A prime example is the Air Line Pilots Association. Its views on safety and flight-crew size are heeded not just because of pilots' prestige but also because of the fear of work stoppages.

Some groups seem to command endless funds for political action; others have little to spend. A large group can pool its members' resources through dues or gifts. Many such groups are, like labor unions, well financed by masses of middle-income members.

Lack of funds is not necessarily fatal to a group. Any group with a credible cause or candidate and a little seed money can mount an extensive direct mail campaign. A direct mail firm will supply its services for part of the proceeds. Low-status groups may find that gaining public attention and sympathy for their cause serves as a substitute for funds. Lacking virtually all resources save enthusiasm, groups can stage protest demonstrations to make their point (Lipsky, 1968).

Political Skills

A group's political resources or skills affect its political actions. The legal profession, for instance, has a "special relationship" with the political world. Lawyers' skills—advocacy and negotiation—easily convey into the coin of political influence, and flexible work schedules make lawyers relatively free to engage in politics. This helps explain why so many lawyers become legislators and key government managers.

In contrast, look at doctors or engineers. They enjoy higher status than lawyers, but their skills are not closely linked to politics and their heavy work schedules discourage the socializing that marks politically active people.

Differences in resources and skills also exist among lower-status groups. Printers, air controllers, or maritime workers are together on the job for long stretches and form easy and sometimes garrulous relationships. They readily join together in organizations. Tuna fishermen or farm laborers, in contrast, tend to work alone. They are hard to bring together, much less organize; political skills are not relevant to their daily routines. If they lack middle-class leaders or sponsors with technical and organizational know-how, they are likely to be ignored. Any group of people has a unique mix of skills and resources that will help push it into the political realm or keep it apart.

Distribution of the Group's Members

How a group's members are distributed among the population affects its makeup and its approach to government. Is the group spread throughout the nation, or is it concentrated in certain places? Is its leverage more likely to be at the local level or at the national level?

Because legislators are picked geographically, concentrated groups are more likely to influence them. Politically active college students, for instance, can sway legislators when they can affect elections in certain districts. The high concentration of the maritime industry in seaport towns and cities magnifies its impact on the local economy and thus its importance to area legislators. Groups that are more evenly scattered throughout the nation, such as professionals, exert less impact on legislators.

Groups differ in whether they seek access at the local, state, or national level of government. Early in the civil rights movement, for instance, blacks and other minorities were often shut out in the very areas where they were most numerous, especially in the South. By contrast, racial and ethnic groups were pivotal in determining the outcome of elections in northern industrial states (and in turn in the electoral college)—a fact that made civil rights issues a strong factor in presidential politics. So civil rights groups turned to the national government, and especially to the president, to redress discrimination by local communities.

By the same token, groups that are disadvantaged at the national level may seek to guard their interests at the local or state level. This is the meaning of "states' rights" versus "federal intervention": groups with divergent bases of power always turn to the governmental level most friendly to them (McConnell, 1967: 91–118).

The Organizational Factor

Whatever the outward appearance of groups, internal organizaton is part of their life. In a small group, such organization may be as simple as informal habits or norms. In a larger group, it may be a "private government"—a structure with officers, legislative councils, referenda (sometimes formally monitored), constitutions, and bylaws.

Leaders and followers emerge in all groups. The noted sociologist Robert Michels (1959) termed this the "iron law of oligarchy": In all associations, power tends to gravitate to a few strong members. Not all groups operate in the same manner. Some are free and lively, with many members taking part; others are dictatorships of the few. **Oligarchy** is most common in large groups with low-status, geographically diffuse members. Democracy is more feasible in small groups with high-status members (or members of relatively equal status) who have frequent face-to-face contact (Lipset et al., 1956). A group may seem oligarchic, yet its internal dynamics may give followers subtle controls over its leaders (Moe, 1980).

The degree of popular control concerns people outside as well as inside the group. The political demands that a group makes in a labor contract, an import quota agreement, or a law conferring benefits may impose costs on citizens, taxpayers, or consumers who had no part in the bargaining.

Whether a group's demands really reflect its members' views is sometimes open to question. Few groups regularly poll their members. (Common Cause is a conspicuous exception.) Some groups have only the most haphazard ways of finding out what their members want. Many groups are guided by tiny cliques of activists; the largely inactive members may not know or care what their leaders are doing. In some groups, dissent is bullied into silence.

People should question the claims of those who speak in the name of their group. Politicians learn to look critically at the statements of group spokespersons. Alert public officials learn which groups can be trusted to reflect their members' real concerns.

All political groups try to influence government policy-making. The typical paths of group influence are set forth in Figure 7–1. Truman (1971) pointed out that one prerequisite for influence is **access:** reaching one or more key decision points in the government. Cultivating access points is common to almost all collective political activity. This activity occupies much of the time and energy of group leaders.

TECHNIQUES OF INFLUENCE

Group leaders prize access for a personal reason: It helps demonstrate their usefulness. They often seem as interested in having their day in court as in actually getting results. In communicating to their members or supporters, they constantly stress their contacts with government officials—for example, at meetings, formal hearings, and social events.

The type of access and the means used to achieve it depend on the group attributes we have discussed: size, socioeconomic status, political resources and skills, distribution of membership, and organization. Not all groups have equal resources for gaining access. And different groups employ different tactics to gain access.

Groups and Agenda Setting

When we think of interest group influence, the image that leaps to mind is that of lobbyists wheeling and dealing to induce officials to decide a certain way. Long before policies are decided on, however, the matters they address have to be considered genuine problems deserving of solution (Kingdon, 1984). Agenda setting—getting its concerns put on the public agenda—is therefore the first job of an interest group and its representatives.

In working to shape the public agenda, interest groups supply the ideas and information that policymakers must have to formulate and justify their actions. Most interest groups therefore have active research staffs that compile facts and statistics to buttress their policy stands. The job of these groups' lobbyists is not to twist arms but to transmit information and arguments, mainly to supporters, but also to those on the fence, so that they, in turn, will be able to make convincing speeches and appeals to others.

In this country, a unique kind of research organization provides many of the ideas and arguments that propel the policy-making process on Capitol Hill and in executive agencies. **Think tanks** are nonprofit research organizations, not really interest groups in the traditional sense; they do much of the thinking that finds its way into politicians' speeches, legislative hearings, and government reports.

FIGURE 7–1   Paths of interest group influence

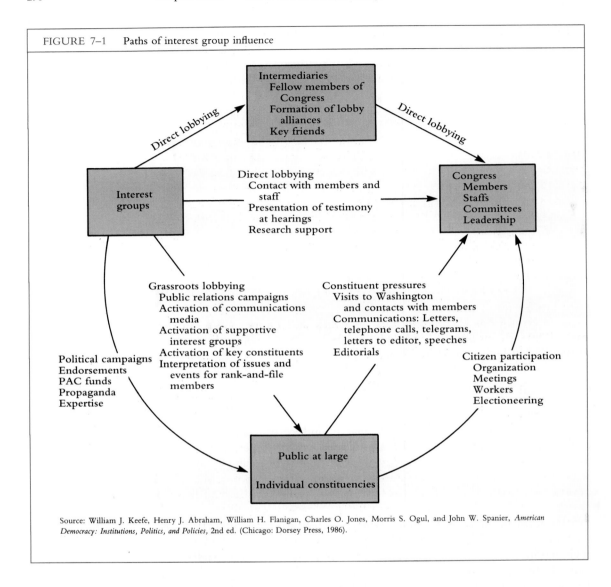

Source: William J. Keefe, Henry J. Abraham, William H. Flanigan, Charles O. Jones, Morris S. Ogul, and John W. Spanier, *American Democracy: Institutions, Politics, and Policies,* 2nd ed. (Chicago: Dorsey Press, 1986).

The traditional think tanks work much like academic faculties, with individuals conducting research and disseminating their findings in books, articles, and public appearances. Well-known examples are the Brookings Institution and the American Enterprise Institute, which are located three blocks apart in Washington, D.C. Although Brookings is regarded as liberal and AEI as conservative, both are in fact respected mainstream scholarly enterprises whose experts in economics, policy studies, and foreign affairs move easily between government, universities, and research posts.

In the 1970s, more ideological think tanks came on the scene. Rather than doing original research, these organizations began with ideological premises and whipped up arguments and policy proposals that conformed to those premises. Examples are the left-wing Institute for Policy Analysis and the right-wing Heritage Foundation. The mandate of such think tanks is to promote their distinct viewpoints and supply information to their friends.

More recently, there has been a proliferation of think tanks linked to a given candidate or an ideological faction. Gary Hart's "Center for New Democracy," for example, enlisted policy specialists in his candidacy for the Democratic presidential nomination and provided him with elements of his "new ideas" campaign. Groups of this kind testify to the degree to which we now expect political discourse to have, or at least appear to have, research underpinnings.

Such groups—and scores of them are now at work—help push issues onto the political agenda and shape the content of public debate. Although some dismiss the power of ideas in politics, it is a mistake to do so. For example, "deregulation"—removing many of the regulations governing such businesses as airlines and trucking—gained momentum in the 1970s because economists touted this idea (Derthick and Quirk, 1985). In the early 1980s, the notion of "industrial policy"—government policy aimed at promoting high-growth industries—was first promoted and then killed by idea merchants whose views found their way into politicians' speeches and deliberations. Research and promotion of such policy ideas are an enormous enterprise that fuels the debate over public issues.

Lobbying

Lobbying has been a staple of interest groups ever since the rise of legislative assemblies. In the early 1800s, lobby agents swarmed in the anterooms and cloakrooms of legislative chambers, seeking personal favors; the term *lobby agent,* shortened to **lobbyist,** has come to refer to anyone who tries to influence government officials through personal contact.

Although the term *lobbying* had not been yet coined, the right to lobby was set forth in the Bill of Rights. The First Amendment provides that "Congress shall make no law . . . abridging the freedom of speech or of the press; or the right of the people peaceably to assemble and to petition the government for redress of grievances." Thus, lobbying is constitutionally protected; steps to regulate or limit it must take this into account.

Who are the lobbyists?

Several thousand individuals and groups register each year as lobbyists with the clerk of the U.S. House of Representatives and the secretary of the Senate. One directory counts more than 10,000 "Washington representatives" under the broad definition of "persons working to influence government policies and actions to advance their own or their client's inter-

Washington representatives working the Hill. In a Capitol Hill hallway, Representative James R. Jones (D–Okla.) speaks with lobbyists opposed to the MX missile, including Fred Wertheimer (right), the president of Common Cause.

ests." The largest component—about 4,000 representatives—consists of officers of 1,500 unions and trade and professional associations with Washington offices. Another 1,250 representatives handle government relations for individual corporations. An equal number are advocates of noneconomic causes—ranging from handgun control to school prayers, from saving whales to saving the unborn. Finally, 2,500 or so are lawyers and consultants who represent clients (including foreign governments) on Capitol Hill or before administrative agencies.

There are more lobbyists in Washington now than ever before, for at least two reasons. First, as noted, there has been an explosion in the number of interest groups, especially noneconomic advocacy groups. Second, groups have migrated to Washington to be near the seat of government. One survey found that since the 1970s an average of 2.7 associations moved to Washington *every week;* by 1975, Washington replaced New York as the most popular headquarters for interest groups (Pika, 1986: 304).

Some organizations recruit lobbyists from within. Others turn to "hired guns," people with inside knowledge of government processes—former legislators, Capitol Hill staffers, or executive managers. Such people can earn far more as consultants than they could working for the government, though not without a measure of criticism. In 1986, Michael Deaver, a former White House public relations aide, drew angry comments for allegedly using his inside contacts to gain lucrative lobbying contracts from foreign governments. This case was widely reported, but Deaver's behavior was hardly unique for a former official.

Remember, though, that lobbyists are not always "other people." They often include average citizens who are disturbed enough over an issue to express concern by writing or contacting elected officials. According to a 1976 House survey, 8 percent of those polled had seen or talked with their representative about some matter. And 29 percent had written a letter, sent a telegram, or signed a petition about some problem or issue (U.S. House of Representatives, 1977: 835). In short, lobbying is not a remote activity of a few shady people; it is constitutionally guarded free speech and petition. Everyone can engage in it, and many of us actually do.

Contacting officials

"Classic" lobbying involves directly contacting legislators (or bureau chiefs, cabinet members, or White House aides). In Washington and in state capitals, lobbyists are judged on the basis of their skill in giving information and persuading others. This means buttonholing legislators, giving testimony, supplying technical information, or making informal social contacts (see Table 7–1).

How do lobbyists approach legislators or other officials? Contrary to folklore, such contacts are usually open, even routine. The lobbyist's chief job is to give information to the decision maker. In a legislature, lobbyists start with members who serve on key committees or subcommittees or members who already support the aims of the lobby group. Such members, in turn, relay the lobby group's point of view to their colleagues (Bauer, Pool, and Dexter, 1963).

Lobbyists thus play an *informational* role: they spread information among legislators and aides who are too busy to obtain it on their own. Lobbyists become known for the quality of their information; those who are ill-informed or whose statements prove unreliable are not likely to be effective.

Contacting decision makers is not as simple as it once was. Power is now widely dispersed on Capitol Hill and throughout executive agencies. Members of Congress who are not on the committees that are concerned with a specific topic can still shape the policy in question. As one executive branch lobbyist said, "It used to be that all one had to do was to contact the chairman and a few ranking members of a committee; now all 435 members and 100 senators have to be contacted."

A favorable hearing

Many techniques are open to the lobbyist seeking a favorable hearing from a committee or subcommittee. Some legislative committees owe their very existence to group pressures; committees on veterans' affairs, small business, and aging are examples. A lobbyist's group may try to stack a committee's membership in its favor. In fact, committees attract members with constituents who gain from what these committees do. Farm belt legislators are on agriculture committees; Westerners are on natural resource committees; legislators from areas of military or aerospace concentrations are on armed services committees; and so forth. This self-selection helps interests dominate a particular field by allowing them to capture control of the committee most crucial to them. Lobbyists for weaker interests have a tougher task; they must persuade their friends to accept what may be an unrewarding, frustrating assignment. Thwarted by one committee, a group may turn to another that promises to be more compliant.

TABLE 7–1   Techniques used by 174 sampled interest groups (1982)

Technique	Percent of groups using it
Testifying at hearings	99%
Contacting government officials directly to present your point of view	98
Engaging in informal contacts with officials at conventions, over lunch, etc.	95
Presenting research results or technical information	92
Sending letters to members of your organization to inform them about your activities	92
Entering into coalitions with other organizations	90
Attempting to shape the implementation of policies	89
Talking with people from the press and the media	86
Consulting with government officials to plan legislative strategy	85
Helping to draft legislation	85
Inspiring letter-writing or telegram campaigns	84
Shaping the government's agenda by raising new issues and calling attention to previously ignored problems	84
Mounting grass-roots lobbying efforts	80
Having influential constituents contact their congressman's office	80
Helping to draft regulations, rules, or guidelines	78
Serving on advisory commissions and boards	76
Alerting congressmen to the effects of a bill on their districts	75
Filing suit or otherwise engaging in litigation	72
Making financial contributions to electoral campaigns	58
Doing favors for officials who need assistance	56
Attempting to influence appointments to public office	53
Publicizing candidates' voting records	44
Engaging in direct-mail fund-raising for your organization	44
Running advertisements in the media about your position on issues	31
Contributing work or personnel to electoral campaigns	24
Making public endorsements of candidates for office	22
Engaging in protests or demonstrations	20
Average number of techniques	19

Source: Kay Lehman Schlozman and John T. Tierney, "More of the Same; Washington Pressure Group Activity in a Decade of Change," *Journal of Politics* 45 (May 1983), p. 377.

Lobbyists often appear as witnesses at hearings to air their views and "get them on the record." They may sit in on committee meetings convened to work on the details of a bill. Information generated by a lobby group may form a key part of the committee report that comes with the bill. Such reports often frame the issues for debate and present the case for the committee's recommendations.

A new technique used by lobbies to gain a favorable hearing is to sponsor or support an informal caucus of senators or representatives. More than 100 such caucuses, many inspired by interest groups, now exist in the two chambers. The Textile Caucus, the Steel Caucus, and the Tourism Caucus work closely with their respective industry groups. Regional caucuses such as the Northeast-Midwest Coalition cooperate with city and state officials.

Coalitions

Most public issues touch more than a single interest group. Lobbyists for a particular group can profit by cooperating with counterparts from like-minded groups. Pooling information and contacts works to the advantage of all. Not surprisingly, lobbyists closely watch one another's actions and look for chances to collaborate.

Sometimes groups coalesce to form a new organization. This catalytic group coordinates work in a common cause. Catalytic groups coordinate lobby efforts in many fields. Their work helps primary groups exchange information and focus efforts. A leading example is the Leadership Conference on Civil Rights, a coalition of labor, religious, and ethnic groups that coordinates lobbying for civil rights bills.

Lining up the votes

When a bill is being argued in the House or Senate, lobbyists talk to members to shore up support, gain last-minute commitments, and find out how the voting will turn out. Congressional leaders often rely on lobbyists to help take an accurate "whip count" of the members. This in turn helps decide parliamentary strategy. If there are enough votes for passage, legislators can press for a quick vote; if passage is in doubt, they can stall to bring around the undecided.

Last-minute campaigns to pass or defeat bills on the chamber floor can be spectacular. When the House considered the 1987 trade bill, for example, fierce lobbying broke out over an amendment submitted by Representative Richard A. Gephardt (D–Mo.) that would have restricted imports to assist ailing domestic industries. Union lobbyists swarmed Capitol Hill to plead for protecting workers' jobs; on the opposite side were the Reagan administration and several large business groups, which argued against trade restrictions. The amendment passed by only three votes. This stage of the legislative process is most visible to the public. At this stage, direct lobbying can best be supplemented by a flood of mail, telegrams, phone calls, or delegations of constituents. Such last-minute efforts often bring results. But they may be too late to change the basic thrust of the measure.

Effective lobbyists are in on the bill from the start. They help shape the measure as it comes from a committee or subcommittee. Once its basic shape has been fixed, an opposing group is faced with a vexing choice. It can try to amend the bill on the floor or go all-out to kill it.

Clout with Congress. The National Rifle Association (NRA) has influenced legislation regulating firearms and prevented effective gun control.

Grass-roots lobbying

Most of the lobbying on major issues includes broad efforts to spark favorable public attitudes. This **grass-roots lobbying** assumes that constituents' attitudes will sway politicians more than the efforts of well-paid lobbyists.

Large groups, like labor unions, have the built-in advantage of numbers, so they can create huge floods of sentiment. However, a group that has few members but a big bank account can stir grass-roots support through costly ads or public relations campaigns. Groups that are neither large nor well financed may get free publicity through media events.

One example of stunningly successful grass-roots lobbying was the all-out campaign of the National Rifle Association (NRA) for passage of the Firearm Owners Protection Act in 1986. The bill (S.49), which relaxed rules for gun sales, registration, and transport, had to overcome several hurdles: a hostile House Judiciary Committee, skeptical members in both chambers, and opposition from law enforcement agencies and gun control groups. Determined lobbying by gun owners overcame all of these hurdles, and the measure was signed into law.

Founded shortly after the Civil War by a group of National Guard officers who wanted to improve citizens' marksmanship, the NRA wraps itself in the Constitution's Second Amendment (construed as the right of individuals to keep and bear arms) and describes itself as an organization whose members "share a commitment to safe and responsible firearms use" (Corrigan, 1986). Its 3.1 million members include Vice President George Bush and John D. Dingell (D–Mich.), chairman of the House En-

Lobbying for gun control. Police officers from around the country, members of the Fraternal Order of Police, visited the U.S. Capitol to lobby members of Congress in behalf of gun control legislation. Their efforts were vigorously opposed by the National Rifle Association (NRA), the nation's strongest opponent of such regulation.

ergy and Commerce Committee. Its Washington headquarters staff numbers 300, of whom 78 constitute a "legislative action" group.

To polish its public image, the NRA sponsored a series of "I'm the NRA" ads featuring well-known people who told why they supported the organization. Another program sold "I'm the NRA—And I Vote" bumper stickers. A voter registration program (100,000 new registrants claimed in 1984), a PAC, and the NRA Victory Fund ($1.6 million in the 1983–84 election cycle) underscored the organization's political muscle. For the 1986 act, the NRA magazines contained appeals with blank petitions to be signed and sent to members of Congress:

> This is it. For years you have asked us for a quick, easy way to tell if your Congressman really supports the right to keep and bear arms in America. You've wanted a way to tell whether your Congressman will stand up and be counted when it really matters. . . . It's time now for your Congressman to fight for your gun and hunting rights and sign the discharge petition (to extract the bill from the House Judiciary Committee). Don't let your Congressman "take a walk." . . . THIS IS THE LITMUS TEST.

Faced with this ultimatum, members of Congress meekly fell into line.

Used at the right moment, grass-roots campaigns—sometimes called "hot-button" tactics—can be strikingly effective. But such campaigns must be used sparingly. Legislators are accustomed to mass letter-writing campaigns, and they suspect floods of letters and telegrams. Seasoned lobbyists reserve the grass-roots technique for big issues. Not even large and wealthy groups, moreover, can charge up their troops simply by passing orders down the line. If members are not directly touched by an issue, they are apt to ignore the efforts of leaders. Grass-roots mobilization demands large-scale organization, effective communication, and precise timing.

Regulating the lobbies

Lobbying is linked to the cherished right of free speech. Yet it has a bad reputation with the public, and it has sometimes deserved that reputation. Until the turn of the century, lobbyists often bribed or bullied officials. In the 1830s, when Congress sought to recharter the Bank of the United States over President Andrew Jackson's objections, word got around that Daniel Webster, a Massachusetts senator, had been hired by the bank to plead its cause. During the Grant administration, 12 members of Congress were alleged to have received stock in Crédit Mobilier, a construction company. In return, they won approval for sizable grants to build the Union Pacific Railroad, whose owners controlled Crédit Mobilier.

Today vote buying is usually subtler. It may involve contributions from the interest group's campaign funding arm, or **political action committee (PAC).** For the interest group, such contributions are a solid investment that will yield dividends in access to lawmakers. Because incumbent lawmakers tend to get reelected, they are a better investment than challengers and hence get the lion's share of PAC money. From the lawmakers' viewpoint, interest group money helps cover skyrocketing election costs. Indeed, some legislative committees—for instance, those handling taxes, banking, or regulatory laws—are especially lucrative targets of PAC money; seats on such committees are valued partly for that reason. Another form of payment is an honorarium, a sum of money (now limited to $2,000 by congressional ethics codes) that is paid appearing at an interest group's meeting. Such payments involve tacit understandings that those who make them will have access to lawmakers and will receive a respectful hearing.

Occasionally, though, bribes are directly offered and taken. In the **Abscam** (a combination of the words *Arab* and *scam,* or con man's trick) probe of the late 1970s, FBI agents posed as representatives of an Arab sheikh who wanted to pay for favorable action on immigration and other matters. This "sting" operation resulted in the conviction of seven members of Congress for criminal wrongdoing, proving that at least a few legislators were willing to trade votes for cash.

The federal government and most of the states have lobbying laws. Most of these laws require some form of registration and disclosure to throw "the antiseptic light of publicity on the lobby." The 1946 Federal Regulation of Lobbying Act, the basic statute, requires paid lobbyists to register with the clerk of the House and the secretary of the Senate and to file quarterly financial reports.

The act does not seriously hamper lobbying activities. Large loopholes exempt many interest groups from even registering. The act applies only to those groups whose principal purpose is to influence legislation. Some large groups decline to register because, they claim, lobbying is not their main purpose but incidental to other activities. Because lobbying is defined by the act as direct dealings with members of Congress, such techniques as grass-roots lobbying and electronic communications are also exempted from its provisions.

House and Senate codes of ethics place further limits on lobbying. They ban members of Congress from taking gifts above a certain value; they also limit members' outside income to 15 percent of their salary and restrict their lecture fees.

Periodic exposés of lobbying abuses underscore loopholes in the lobbying laws. For example, the revelations regarding Michael Deaver's activities led to cries for curbs on "revolving-door lobbying," in which high-level government officials leave office and exploit their access to represent private clients doing business with the government. A bill considered by the Senate Judiciary Committee would have barred former officials from representing, advising, or assisting foreign clients for 10 years; former members of Congress from lobbying for 5 years; and former staff members of Congress or executive agencies for 1 year.

The problem with such proposals is that they are almost certainly unconstitutional. Under the Constitution, laws must not infringe on the rights of free speech, press, assembly, and petition. Thus, no laws can interfere with the flow of information from specialized interests to lawmaking bodies, nor can they have a "chilling effect" on legitimate group activities. These restrictions dictate caution on the part of lawmakers and judges.

None of these periodic efforts to plug loopholes in lobby laws have succeeded. Proponents of restrictive lobby laws cloak such efforts with the goals of "curbing misuse of influence and access" and "restoring public confidence and integrity" to government. But their proposals raise the issue of balancing the public's right to know about lobbying with the lobbyists' right to free speech and petition.

Backing Candidates in Electoral Contests

Campaign funding, mainly through political action committees, enables interest groups to take part in the electoral process. Both incumbents and challengers know that they must appeal to various PACs to finance their political careers. Interest groups may not nominate or elect candidates, but they sponsor and sustain candidates' campaigns in important ways.

Many groups give money directly to friendly candidates; others launch registration or get-out-the-vote drives; still others tell their members to reward friends or punish enemies at the polls. As might be expected, groups with money or large memberships are most apt to use these techniques.

Campaign funding is limited by complex rules. Corporations and labor unions, for instance, may not, under federal law, contribute directly to campaigns for federal office. But they are allowed to contribute indirectly; they may set up PACs like the AFL–CIO's Committee on Political Education (COPE) or Tenneco's Employees' Good Government Fund, and these PACs may make direct contributions to candidates (up to $5,000 per candidate per election). Corporations and unions may also spend any amount to inform their own members, personnel, or stockholders about issues of interest. And they may use their own funds to pay administrative and fund-raising costs.

Union members and corporate employees are often pressured into PAC giving. "I know it isn't mandatory to give," said a corporation executive. "But the word around the water cooler is that if you don't give or if you give less than the amount expected based on your salary, you're liable to be called in for a pep talk from the divisional president" (Sansweet, 1980: 1).

PACs are flourishing. Though all types of PACs have grown in numbers, corporate PACs have grown the most. Their number increased from 89 in 1974 to more than 1,800 in 1988. The number of labor PACs nearly doubled over the same period (see Figure 7–2).

PAC funds flow directly to favored candidates or help such candidates indirectly by being used to educate the public, turn out the vote, or provide volunteer campaign help. Such efforts, called **independent expenditures,** are supposed to be separate from the candidates' own efforts, but this restriction is hard to enforce. During presidential campaigns, labor's efforts are often hard to distinguish from those of the Democratic National Committee; similarly, many groups work hand in glove with the Republicans.

Most PACs, however, are strictly nonpartisan, spreading their donations where they will do the most good. This means making sure that incumbent legislators are taken care of. According to compilations made by the Federal Election Commission, during the 1985–86 congressional election cycle, PACs gave incumbent senators and representatives more than three times as much money as they gave to challengers. Given the high reelection rates of incumbent members of Congress, such a distribution of donations is smart politics. As an official of a business PAC remarked in explaining a large contribution to one liberal Democrat, "It's more fun to back a winner than a loser."

The clout that groups lacking size and wealth may obtain through publicity can affect elections. Disclosing scandals and making candidates' views public are methods of getting such publicity.

A common technique of groups is compiling voting records and scor-

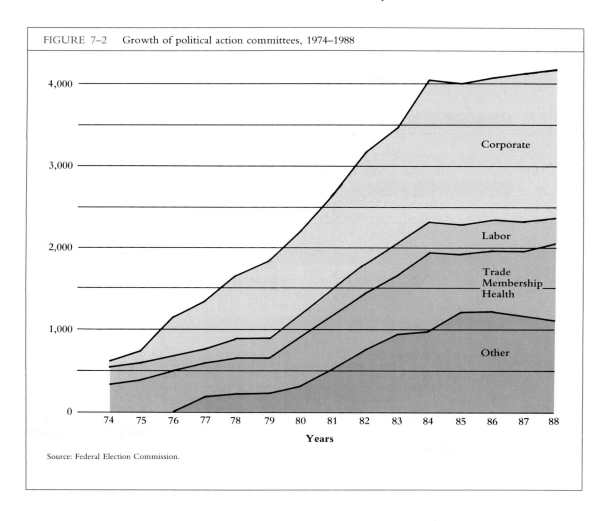

FIGURE 7–2   Growth of political action committees, 1974–1988

Source: Federal Election Commission.

ing legislators by the group's standards. Members of Congress are rated by nearly 100 groups. These range from the American Bakers Association to the National Taxpayers Union.

There are great differences in these group ratings. Figure 7–3 gives the 1986 ratings of senators gathered by a leading labor group (the AFL–CIO), a leading business association (the U.S. Chamber of Commerce), and two ideological groups, one liberal (Americans for Democratic Action) and one conservative (American Conservative Union). The two political parties split fairly neatly on these scales: the Democrats lean toward labor and liberalism, while the Republicans lean toward business and conservatism. Not all of the voting indexes reveal such clear-cut party lines.

The voting indexes help interest groups mobilize their members. They show whether legislators vote "right" or "wrong" on issues affecting the

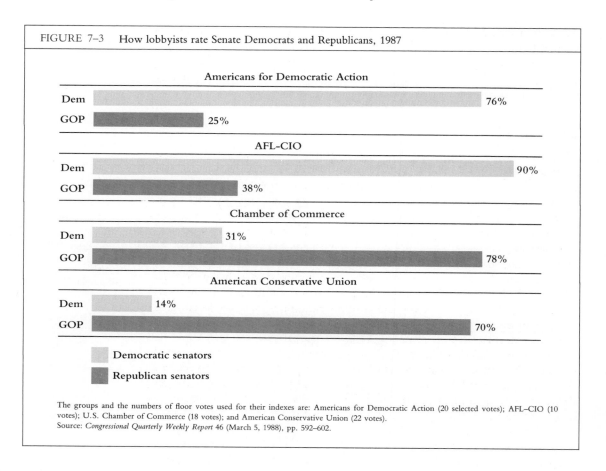

FIGURE 7–3   How lobbyists rate Senate Democrats and Republicans, 1987

Americans for Democratic Action

Dem — 76%
GOP — 25%

AFL–CIO

Dem — 90%
GOP — 38%

Chamber of Commerce

Dem — 31%
GOP — 78%

American Conservative Union

Dem — 14%
GOP — 70%

Democratic senators

Republican senators

The groups and the numbers of floor votes used for their indexes are: Americans for Democratic Action (20 selected votes); AFL–CIO (10 votes); U.S. Chamber of Commerce (18 votes); and American Conservative Union (22 votes).
Source: *Congressional Quarterly Weekly Report* 46 (March 5, 1988), pp. 592–602.

given interest group. They also provide a basis for independent campaigns for or against certain legislators by giving people a shorthand way of judging how incumbents perform.

Ratings of this kind are not always correct, though. Voters should beware of taking them literally. For one thing, the votes used in the indexes may be carelessly chosen. The indexes may confuse procedural votes with substantive stands. Such indexes may also ignore the complex factors that cause members to vote in a certain way. Many angry legislators have spoken on the House or Senate floor denouncing groups for distorting their records. (In 1984, a religious group awarded a 100 percent "report card" to a legislator who had admitted sexual misconduct with a 17-year-old female page. At the same time, this group gave zero ratings to legislators with unblemished records.)

Groups are also sometimes accused of targeting legislators who are already in trouble at the polls. If the beleaguered incumbents lose, the groups then claim credit for having hit their targets.

The lesson to be learned is this: Let the voter beware! Ratings may simplify one's choice at the polls, but they can also distort an elected official's overall record.

Executive and Judicial Lobbying

"Merely placing a program before Congress is not enough," declared President Lyndon Johnson—probably the shrewdest former legislator ever to serve in the White House. "Without constant attention from the administration, most legislation moves through the congressional process at the speed of a glacier" (Johnson, 1971: 448). Ever since George Washington dispatched Secretary of the Treasury Alexander Hamilton to consult with congressional leaders, chief executives have been trying to influence the course of legislative activity.

At present, most executive agencies have congressional liaison offices. The function of these offices is to meet requests for information and assistance. They also try to convey the administration's viewpoint to congressional committees and legislators. Especially in final negotiations on legislation, administration lobbyists can play a critical role.

Interest groups also take part in the judicial process. Here their participation is less obvious than in the legislative process or electoral campaigns. Groups sometimes lobby to have certain types of persons picked as judges. Recently women and minorities have pressed for broader standards in judicial selection, criticizing the preponderance of white males on the bench.

President Reagan's mid-1987 nomination of the conservative Judge Robert Bork to replace the moderate Supreme Court Justice Lewis Powell triggered unprecedented interest-group campaigns for and against Bork. As soon as Bork's selection was announced, a broad coalition of groups—racial, women's, civil liberties, and the like—rallied to oppose him. The rallying point for the anti-Bork forces was the Leadership Conference on Civil Rights, led by Ralph Neas, its executive director. (The pro-Bork forces, though slower to mobilize, were also led by an umbrella group.) Senator Edward M. Kennedy (D–Mass.) quickly denounced the nominee—to prevent liberal groups from giving up the fight as hopeless—and persuaded group leaders to mobilize their memberships. The anti-Bork campaign sold the idea that the nominee would upset the Court's delicate liberal-conservative balance and recruited witnesses to counter his testimony before the Senate Judiciary Committee. The final vote was 58–42 against confirmation.

Groups often sponsor court fights. Courts decisively shape public policy; but they are not equally accessible to all. Litigation takes time and is very costly. The legal trail blazed in the 1940s and 1950s for black civil rights was largely subsidized by the National Association for the Advancement of Colored People (NAACP). The NAACP brought carefully chosen test cases to courts at the best moment and under the best conditions. After winning a long line of rulings against discrimination in education, it challenged the concept of "separate but equal" schools. In *Brown* v. *Board of Education* (1954), a landmark decision, the Supreme Court struck down that concept. The NAACP's chief counsel, Thurgood Marshall, argued the *Brown* case before the Supreme Court and later became a Supreme Court justice himself.

Groups that are not litigants can enter court contests by filing ***amicus curiae*** ("friend of the court") briefs giving their views and showing their concern. This was done in the 1978 *Bakke* case, which challenged special admissions programs for racial minorities. In that case scores of groups filed briefs, most of which favored special admission programs and opposed Bakke's stand.

INTEREST-GROUP INFLUENCE

Everyone concedes that interest groups are important in politics. But just how important are they? Newspaper accounts of politics sometimes convey the idea that a legion of all-powerful groups buys legislative votes. Such accounts make it seem that policymakers are controlled by a shadowy underground of influence peddlers.

The Limits of Influence

Sometimes the notion of vast interest-group power is correct. The American Medical Association succeeded in stalling national health insurance for a generation; the civil rights movement produced victories in the 1960s; environmentalists won many new statutes in the 1970s.

Yet none of these groups could have reached its goals without a social and historical setting that supplied the raw materials for influence. The AMA used physicians' prestige and popular fears about "socialized medicine." Civil rights activists gained attention from years of protests and outrages in the segregated South; they gained political clout from the support of concerned blacks in the urban North. Environmentalists were helped by widespread alarm over pollution. Also, these groups succeeded within a narrow range of fairly clear-cut issues. For example, none of them tried to alter major foreign policy, tariffs, or tax laws.

Finally, the strength of these groups ebbed as conditions changed. After a while, exploding medical costs and public discontent with the medical establishment overrode the AMA's pressure against health insurance. Widespread resistance to busing and affirmative action slowed the civil rights movement. Worries over productivity, red tape, and energy supplies halted the extension of environmental protection. The groups in question do not lack resources or influence; but they, like other strong groups, are limited by issues, circumstances, and time.

Segmented Power

Interest-group power is limited by our complex, multilevel, multistage political system. Not all organized interests at all levels, local to national, get involved. More often, decision making is segmented into thousands of distinct but overlapping networks of power. It makes little sense to talk about political power in sweeping terms. It is more correct to talk about political arenas, such as military contracting, employment and training programs, resource conservation, cotton subsidies, housing, banking regulations, municipal schools, local planning and zoning, and thousands of similar segments. Some arenas are highly competitive; most have a few key players (Hayes, 1981).

At the national level, **subgovernments** strive to dominate policy in a given field. Bureaucratic agencies, congressional subcommittees, and interest groups are linked together, as is shown schematically in Figure 7–4. They work in numerous policy fields—for example, milk pricing, sugar quotas, oil production, and weapons system contracting. If the groups in such governments agree on public policy, they can control the outcomes that affect policy. This is not really the result of a conspiracy. It just shows that those most directly affected by a policy can have their own way as long as the general public is looking the other direction.

Events sometimes break open these "cozy triangles" of power. A scandal over a drug with disastrous side effects for pregnant women and their babies pressured legislators in the 1960s to set strict drug-testing standards. But the public's attention span is brief. After such upheavals, the subgovernments may slip back into a stable pattern. At best, a new balance of power is imposed by the brief crisis and public outcry. Not all public policy can be explained in terms of segmented arenas. But much of it, especially in the domestic sphere, can be.

Some writers stress the complexity and fluidity of the links between interest groups and government. They claim that the cozy triangles notion is too simple and rigid and that a broader term, such as *issue networks,* would be more accurate (Heclo, 1978). There is much truth to this view. With the rise of citizen groups, not to mention the popularity of investigative journalism, the links between interest groups and government can be exposed to public criticism. Moreover, the multiplicity of groups makes it harder for a few to monopolize policy-making.

Groups often seem effective in pressing their demands. But the fact is that usually they do not have to win over the whole political system in order to do so. The United States has many specialized policy arenas. Thus, groups can generally attain their goals by capturing a relevant body of decision makers. This shows why people must organize. It also shows the vastness of our politics and the difficulty of watching all that is going on.

Today interest groups seem to have supplanted political parties as the

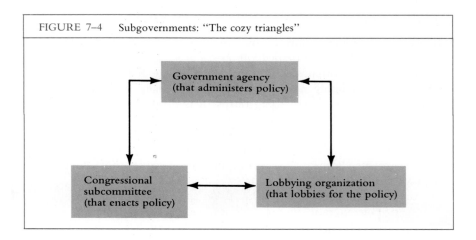

FIGURE 7–4   Subgovernments: "The cozy triangles"

chief channels for conveying citizen opinion to the government. In fact, groups represent people's views with a variety and richness that parties cannot match. Groups cannot produce broad governing coalitions, but they can, and do, reflect the factionalism that pervades modern America.

CONCLUSIONS

Several conclusions can be drawn from our discussion of interest groups in this chapter:

1. Our society contains a vast number of groups, few of them wholly political. Most of these groups, however, can and do enter the political arena under certain circumstances. Group activity is protected by the Constitution and has marked our entire history.

2. Americans are not equally represented by interest groups. The educated and rich are better represented than the uneducated and poor. Segments of the population are politically underorganized.

3. To influence political decisions, groups draw on many resources. These include size, status, money, relevant political skills, geographic distribution of members, and organization. Groups

short on some resources (such as money) can substitute other resources (such as numbers or publicity) to make an impact.

4. Lobbying is a leading technique of group influence. Groups seek more than just access to officials. They seek public acceptance through grass-roots techniques and legal victories through group-sponsored court cases.

5. Interest groups are becoming more and more active in the electoral arena. Their tools include political action committees (PACs), independent spending, and the publicizing of officials' voting records.

6. Group influence varies with the issue, arena, and time. Subgovernments are one example of the segmented nature of political influence in this country.

FURTHER READING

CIGLER, ALLAN J., and BURDETT A. LOOMIS (1986) *Interest Group Politics.* 2nd ed. Washington, D.C.: Congressional Quarterly Press. A collection of up-to-date studies by leading students of interest groups.

HAYES, MICHAEL T. (1981) *Lobbyists and Legislators.* New Brunswick, N.J.: Rutgers University Press. An intriguing and stimulating analytic study, summarizing the literature and proposing new approaches.

LOWI, THEODORE J. (1969) *The End of Liberalism.* New York: W. W. Norton. A critical treatment of the theory and practice of interest-group politics since the New Deal.

SCHLOZMAN, KAY LEHMAN, and JOHN T. TIERNEY (1986) *Organized Interests and American Democracy.* New York: Harper & Row. The most comprehensive of a new generation of texts on interest groups and their techniques.

TRUMAN, DAVID B. (1971) *The Governmental Process.* 2nd ed. New York: Alfred A. Knopf. A landmark study of interest groups that develops a general theory of group action and applies it to various political arenas.

MASS MEDIA IN POLITICS

$\mathcal{M}$ost of us remember the precise moment in January 1986 that we learned of the explosion of the space shuttle *Challenger*. People who have reached a certain age remember exactly where, and under what circumstances, they learned in 1963 that President John F. Kennedy had been shot in a Dallas motorcade.

For political events to have any impact, they must be communicated. How do we learn about such events? For most of us, the answer is obvious. Whether it is the election of a president, the passage of a bill in Congress, or the progress of a grass-roots political movement, we learn about a political event through one of the media of mass communications. Although political leaders are direct participants in such events, they too rely on the media for information, and they also use the media to convey their messages to potential audiences. Thus, the communications media are a political force that is every bit as crucial as interest groups or elected officials.

Communication is vital to politics. Some call it the nervous system of the body politic, transmitting messages between the various parts (Fagan, 1966). The modes we know best are the so-called **mass media:** newspapers and magazines, radio and television. But other media—personal conversation, for example—carry important political messages.

*T*he media are something of a puzzle to students of politics. Their influence on our lives is immediate and pervasive. But their political impact is still not well understood. In this chapter, we examine the structure of the news media, emphasizing the contrasts between print and electronic media organizations. Then we profile newsgatherers, giving special attention to the Washington press corps. We consider how "news" is defined by those who collect and disseminate it and how their definitions reflect the peculiar characteristics of their medium—again contrasting print and electronic media. We turn next to the difficult question of assessing the effects of the media on our political system. Finally, we explain how the news business is limited and regulated—by the federal government (in the case of electronic media), by court rulings (in the case of print media), and by public attitudes and reactions (in the case of all the media).

In the United States, the mass media are as much a part of governing as the formal institutions of government. Indeed, citizens in a democracy would be unable to function without communications to inform their votes or other political activities. And public officials in a democracy could not perform their duties without communications—from voters, from other elites in the society, from other policymakers. And yet the process of communications distorts reality, magnifying certain facts or events, ignoring or minimizing others that may be equally important. Such distortion complicates the task of governing, or at least of governing effectively. Our discussion of the communications media reflects a paradox: We cannot live without the media, but we must not ignore their effects on our politics, both for good and for ill.

WHAT IS COMMUNI-CATION?

A straightforward framework for looking at communication is offered by the political scientist Harold D. Lasswell (1948: 37–51): "Who Says What, in Which Channel, to Whom, with What Effect?" In other words, communication includes a source, a message, a medium (or channel), an audience, and an effect.

The Source and the Audience

Many levels of communication can be categorized in terms of *who* (the source) is speaking to *whom* (the audience).

Politicians, for instance, communicate with masses of people. Presidents, party leaders, and interest-group spokespersons spend much time spreading ideas among the masses. Conversely, people send messages to leaders in many ways—letters and phone calls, audience reactions, votes, and so on. One means of classifying governments is to look at the communication between elites and masses. In dictatorships, messages flow mostly from the top down; in democracies, the flow is two-way.

Leaders want to transmit their ideas to concerned **attentive publics.**

Members of politically active groups such as trade unions are swamped with speeches, newsletters, and pamphlets outlining issues that affect working people. The same is true for corporate executives, gun owners, civil libertarians, and members of other special groups. Such information can influence policy in particular fields even though little of it reaches the media.

In complex societies, sources and audiences often interlock. Parts of a news briefing may reach the general public on the network news; the rest may be seen only by the press or TV producers. Reporters sift and shape the material before passing it on to the next audience: their editors and producers. It is like the game of gossip-chain: A news event passes through many hands before we encounter it in a newspaper or newscast.

Certain people play a key role in transmitting information to friends and neighbors. These **opinion leaders** are alert to media accounts, relaying information to friends and coworkers who watch the media less. This "two-step flow of communication" is a crucial link in spreading political information (Katz, 1957: 61–78).

The Medium and the Message

Students of politics tend to stress the formal messages of politicians: for example, speeches, press releases, government reports, and party platforms. Just as important are informal messages, such as off-the-cuff remarks, leaks, or private conversations. The "informed source" is a staple for reporters. Clues from an unnamed informer, "Deep Throat," helped reporters Robert Woodward and Carl Bernstein unravel the Watergate scandal in the mid-1970s. Politicians as diverse as Henry Kissinger and Jesse Jackson have been embarrassed when their private or personal remarks became public.

Communication channels include the mass media. These are the *print* media (newspapers, magazines, special journals) and the *electronic* media (radio and TV). There are a vast number of media organizations in our country. Table 8–1 shows the major categories and the number of outlets in each.

An outlet's character and limitations affect how it sends messages. At the very least, this means that certain messages are more easily sent by one medium than by another. Complex arguments can best be stated in print, through books and articles. The emotional and personal aspects of an event are most powerfully conveyed by TV, the fastest and most intimate medium. Before TV, the horrors of war had been reported by many talented people. Notable examples are Matthew Brady's Civil War photographs, Wilfred Owen's bitter World War I poems, and Edward R. Murrow's historic radio broadcasts from World War II London. But the film clips that were shown on TV news programs in the late 1960s proved more effective than any nonvisual account in causing revulsion against the

*Political information in
newsmagazines comes in
many varieties.*

Vietnam War. "The medium is the message" was the thesis of Marshall
McLuhan (1964). This thesis overstates things, but it contains a kernel of
truth.

The Effects

The impact of communication is in one sense total and pervasive. This is
because we need communication to inform, to persuade, and even to conduct social life. But it is hard to isolate the effects of the communications
process on politics. Social philosophers and commentators are well aware
that the media exert an irresistible pull on politics. But what is the direction of that pull? Studies on this matter are far from conclusive. We will
have more to say about it after we discuss the communications process in
detail.

ORGANIZA-
TION OF THE
MASS MEDIA

Every medium of communication springs from technological and social
advances. Language was spoken when it was invented, and then it was
written. Later printing presses and cheap paper made mass culture possible. Then came the telegraph, the telephone, and in this century, radio,
TV, and advanced forms of data transmission. Each advance affected social organization. Organized communication has many outcomes: knowledge becomes more organized; institutions are formed just for communicating; and a collective memory forms for the body politic (De Fleur and
Ball-Rokeach, 1975: 1–14).

| TABLE 8–1 | Major media outlets in the United States |

Newspapers		Radio stations	
Daily	1,861	Commercial AM	4,856
Semiweekly	591	Commercial FM	3,936
Weekly	8,188	Noncommercial FM	1,254
Less frequent	343		10,046
	11,034		
Periodicals		Television stations	
Daily	82	Commercial VHF	547
Semiweekly	43	Commercial UHF	435
Weekly	941	Noncommercial VHF	111
Semimonthly	320	Noncommercial UHF	192
Monthly	4,505		1,285
Bimonthly	1,733	Cable television systems	7,800
Quarterly	2,414		
Other	2,271		
	12,309		

Sources: *Gale Directory of Publications,* vol. 2 (Detroit: Gale Research, 1988), p. viii; *Broadcasting-Cablecasting Yearbook* (Washington, D.C.: Broadcasting Publishing, 1987), pp. A–2, D–3.

The Print Media

Newspapers

About 11,000 newspapers are printed in the United States. Although this is by far the largest number of any nation, it is one fourth fewer than our all-time high around World War I. Most U.S. newspapers are weeklies, but the 1,800 or so dailies boast the most readers and the most political clout. (See Table 8–1.)

Modern newspapers are often vast enterprises. They involve thousands of employees and equipment worth millions of dollars. Competition for readers and ad revenues is keen; many of the weaker papers cannot compete. Other media have shattered the print media's monopoly over the mass dispersion of information.

Newspaper formation has not kept pace with population growth. As noted, there are about 25 percent fewer daily papers today than there were at the outbreak of World War I. In 1880, 9 out of 10 "urban places" (towns of 2,500 people or more) had their own dailies; by 1961, this figure had fallen to less than 1 in 3.

Newspapers are constantly being forced to close their doors or merge with other papers. New York City had 14 general newspapers in 1920; now it has 3. Philadelphia once had 13 papers; now it has 1. Today only

27 U.S. cities have competing newspapers, compared with 609 cities at the turn of the century. Fierce competition and rising costs squeeze the smaller papers especially hard. The Newspaper Preservation Act of 1970 allows rival papers to share printing plants to cut costs—an unusual exemption from antitrust rules.

Large chains—Gannett, Newhouse, Knight-Ridder, Cox, and others—account for three fourths of all daily papers and 80 percent of their circulation. Almost all papers rely on syndicated features and the giant wire services—mainly the Associated Press (AP)—for all but local news and ads.

Although more and more U.S. newspapers are centrally owned, they are still locally produced and distributed (Bagdikian, 1971). Only recently have national newspapers been available daily across the whole country at newsstands and by subscription. These newspapers include *USA Today, The Wall Street Journal,* and the *Christian Science Monitor.*

The local media persist for both political and economic reasons. There are half a million local government units of one sort or another in the United States, most of which have an immediate impact on citizens. Schools, police and fire protection, land use and zoning, local highway routes, and property tax rates are all decided by local bodies. No national paper could ever cover the doings of all these local governments; local papers specialize in hometown news.

Advertising is the lifeblood of the local media, and indeed of all the mass media. Most personal income is spent at some 1.7 million local retail stores. Suburban papers, the "underground press," and shoppers' weeklies are successful because of local advertising.

Other publications

The number of daily papers has been declining, but an increasingly diverse variety of other publications has become available. There are newsmagazines, such as *Time, Newsweek,* and *U.S. News and World Report.* There are journals of opinion, such as the conservative *National Review,* the neoconservative *Public Interest,* the neoliberal *Washington Monthly,* and the liberal *Nation* and *New Republic.* For nearly every specialized taste or interest, some publication now communicates news of political or governmental developments. *Oil and Gas Weekly, Aviation Week and Space Technology,* and *Today's Health,* for example, air issues that affect, respectively, the petroleum, aerospace, and health-care industries.

The labor press exemplifies this specialized journalism. Some 800 union journals have a combined local, national, and international circulation of more than 30 million. "Most union newspapers are long on flattery for the incumbent officers and short on comment for the rank and file," according to one labor editor (Nader, 1977). A small but growing number of labor papers give lively coverage to union elections and other controversies.

The Electronic Media

U.S. commercial broadcasting was born in 1920. That year, KDKA in Pittsburgh aired the Harding-Cox presidential election returns, the first major news event that was covered electronically.

Radio quickly became an entertainment medium, but it also became a powerful political instrument. Many politicians in the 1930s and 1940s (from FDR to Adolph Hitler) grasped its importance and used it to mobilize support. Radio reporting, especially during World War II, brought home the drama of world events. Modern politicians as diverse as Richard Nixon and Jimmy Carter used radio to deliver their messages; Ronald Reagan scheduled brief weekly radio talks throughout his years in the White House.

Despite the rise of TV, radio is a growing business. Its recent growth is largely in the FM sector, because of FM's superior sound quality. Americans own some 500 million radios, more than ever before. Radio reaches almost every American home; the average family has more than five radios. About 125 million radios are in cars, trucks, and boats.

Radio, like print, must specialize to compete with other media. Today's stations stress formats that appeal to certain audience segments. Major formats include all-news, country-and-western music, popular music (including top 40, middle-of-the-road, rhythm and blues, and album-oriented rock), classical music, ethnic, and educational programming. Specialized programming allows advertisers, commercial or political, to pinpoint the audiences they want to reach. Campaigners therefore buy ad time to reach intended audiences at prime listening times.

Television, developed in the 1930s, burst on the scene after World War II and spread like wildfire. Today 98 percent of all households have at least one TV set; about half have more than one.

Until quite recently, TV was wildly profitable. In 1983, the television industry brought in about $21.3 billion in revenues. National TV ads are expensive (the average is $100,000 for 30 seconds of prime time, $200,000 for a top-rated series). Indeed, most aspects of the industry are costly.

Because of its costs, television was tightly centralized until quite recently. Three fourths of all commercial stations are affiliated with one of the three national networks. In the top 50 markets, where 75 percent of the people live, the three networks (NBC, CBS, ABC) and one noncommercial network (PBS) capture most of the audience, especially in prime evening hours. A former FCC chairperson said that local stations "throw the network switch or open a syndicated film package as they would a can of beans." During prime evening hours, about 95 percent of broadcast material comes from the networks.

To pursue huge audiences and support high production costs, commercial TV has become a homogenized, middle-of-the-road medium. With its safe format of sports, adventures, sitcoms, and variety and talk shows,

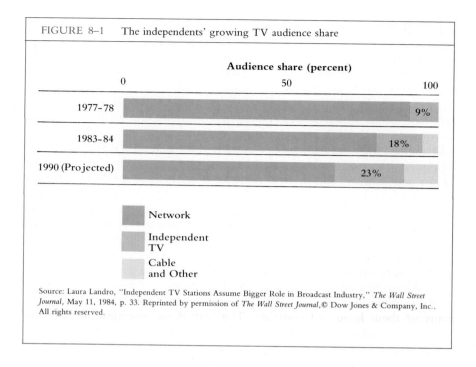

FIGURE 8-1   The independents' growing TV audience share

Audience share (percent)

Source: Laura Landro, "Independent TV Stations Assume Bigger Role in Broadcast Industry," *The Wall Street Journal*, May 11, 1984, p. 33. Reprinted by permission of *The Wall Street Journal*,© Dow Jones & Company, Inc., All rights reserved.

TV eats up talent and program ideas as fast as they appear. Recently viewers have become increasingly restive over the quality and selection of network programs; the networks' share of the TV audience has declined more than 10 percent in the last five years (see Figure 8–1). This has further eroded the standing and budgets of network news departments—long regarded as stepchildren of the more profitable sports and entertainment operations. "The audience for network news appears to be growing older and smaller as a larger percentage of viewers stray to cable, videotapes, or more active pursuits" (Randolph, 1987).

At the same time, local TV outlets, including network affiliates, have been expanding local news programming. Cheaper technologies such as video recording and microwave transmission have enhanced local newscasts. Presidential candidates now gear their schedules to appear on local news programs—a free and noncommercial forum; local stations do their own stories on Washington events or national conventions, often giving them a hometown slant. Thus, as the networks cut back their political coverage, local outlets have taken up a bit of the slack.

TV is now ripe for the kind of diversification that has already overtaken radio and the print media. In the 1950s, cable systems, linked by satellite transmissions, began to extend TV reception to remote areas and to help big-city reception. Now about 4 out of every 10 TV homes are served by cable, and the number is growing. The largest cable system (in San Diego) boasts 235,000 subscribers; some systems have fewer than 100. Cable itself may be overtaken by newer technologies that offer the same benefits without costly wiring.

The effects of diversified "narrowcasting" can already be seen. The Cable News Network (CNN) built a respectable audience with an all-news format; C-SPAN (Cable-Satellite Public Affairs Network) has an audience of at least 3 million for its broadcasts of House and Senate sessions, as well as committee hearings, speeches, and public affairs discussions. Other public affairs ventures are likely at the local and state levels. Private sector groups such as the U.S. Chamber of Commerce, the AFL–CIO, and religious associations have already launched extensive cable-TV efforts. The new technologies may promote cultural pluralism and end the monopoly of the commercial TV networks; but their potential impact on political information is less clear.

As products of technology, the communications media are driven by their technical characteristics—as transmitters of written words, or speech, or pictures. The media as we know them are also human organizations, many of them large and complex. The way these organizations are put together can affect the types of messages that are transmitted, just as the technology of the medium does. And so we need to know about the jobs and relationships within media organizations in order to understand what is reported and how.

THE STRUCTURE OF THE NEWS MEDIA

Reporters and Editors

The image of the crusading reporter lends journalists a certain glamour. But journalism is at best an unformed profession. There are, for instance, no universal standards for becoming a journalist. Although there are more than 100 accredited journalism schools, many news executives prefer to hire liberal arts graduates or those with a flair for writing and dealing with people.

Journalists tend to come from the middle class. They are also well educated. One study found that 98 percent of the Washington press corps had attended college (Hess, 1981). Some assume that journalists are left-wingers; others charge that they are unwitting lackeys of the business interests that own media outlets. In a recent survey, 59 percent of the journalists questioned said that they were middle-of-the-road and so were the organizations for which they worked (Friendly, 1983). Most journalists consider themselves independent progressives—open-minded, nonpartisan, and suspicious of all authority.

The vast majority of journalists cover local news for one of the nation's 11,000 newspapers. A medium-sized paper (40,000 circulation) will boast a news staff of 35-40 people and will spend more than $1 million a year on its news operation. Full-time reporters usually cover special beats for

Investigative journalists. Carl Bernstein [left] and Bob Woodward, then metro reporters for the Washington Post, *dug out the story of a lifetime—the Watergate burglary cover-up by the Nixon White House. Their book, about this investigation,* All the President's Men, *was the basis for a movie starring Dustin Hoffman as Bernstein and Robert Redford as Woodward.*

local news—for example, city hall, the courts and police, business, society, sports, or outlying communities.

The average paper rarely assigns its reporters to cover national politics. Most papers cover national and world news with syndicated articles or with wire service copy from the Associated Press (AP) or the United Press International (UPI); with stories written by reporters who work for other papers in their chain; or occasionally with material provided by **stringers** (people who contract to write for a "string" of papers).

Fewer journalists are found in radio and TV than in the print media. Networks hire specialists on the White House, Congress, diplomacy, and the courts; beyond that, there is little specialized reporting. The average radio or TV station draws most of its news from its network or from AP or UPI, which offer shortened versions of stories sent to the print media. The rest of the news is local, often borrowed from local newspaper leads. News staffs are small. One or two people may report for a smaller radio or TV station; a handful may work for larger outlets. Almost all are on general assignment; that is, they handle any news story that comes along.

The Washington press corps

Much of the nation's political news and analysis comes from the Washington press corps. This is a diverse group of 4,000 or so journalists who cover our national government. At the top are those whom Timothy Crouse (1973) called the heavies. These are the correspondents, columnists, and editors with so much clout that they have personal access to public officials. Many of their names are familiar—David S. Broder of the *Washington Post,* Sam Donaldson of ABC News, Tom Wicker of the *New York Times,* Jack Nelson of the *Los Angeles Times,* and columnists George Will and James J. Kilpatrick.

Most members of the Washington press corps are either specially assigned reporters for one of the major papers or members of a chain's Washington bureau. AP and UPI support the largest news offices in the city. Although wire-service reporters have beats, they also write stories on request from the thousands of wire-service clients around the world. An Omaha editor may call for a story on the Department of Agriculture's relief plans for a midwestern drought; some reporter must then drop what he or she is doing and dig out the story. Writing for a wire service, one harassed UPI reporter complained, "is like having a thousand mothers-in-law."

The specialized press also maintains bureaus in Washington. It channels news to businesspeople, trade associations, and other special groups. *Women's Wear Daily,* the *Chronicle of Higher Education,* and the *Army Times* all have alert reporters in Washington. Such reporters rarely show up at White House press conferences or in congressional press galleries. But they busily follow bills and policy statements in committee rooms or agency offices to gather information required by their organizations' attentive publics.

Gatekeepers

If reporters are the front lines of the news system, editors and producers are the traffic cops. The term **gatekeeper** is used to describe the obscure but essential people who decide what appears in print or on the air. Their function is the same, whether their title is "news editor," "film editor," or "executive producer."

Every news operation gets a flood of potential stories—from reporters, wire services, news syndicates, and press releases. Only a small number of these stories can be squeezed into a paper or newscast. The available space for news stories—the **news hole**—varies with the medium. For newspapers, it is about one fourth of the total space; the rest is used for ads. Radio and TV outlets use less than 10 percent of their airtime for news or news-related matters. (The one exception is the all-news station.) A half-hour network news show boils down to about 22 minutes of news—10 or 15 stories.

The gatekeeper has a vexing task: fitting news items into the tight space, or time, supplied by the medium. One study (Bagdikian, 1971) found that the average gatekeeper scanned five times as many stories as could be used. For listeners or readers, it is as if 80 percent of the world's events never happened.

What makes gatekeepers decide as they do? Why do news outlets trumpet some stories and ignore others? These questions are guaranteed to ig-

PRACTICE OF POLITICS

A Political Media Event

In 1984, Navy Lieutenant Robert O. Goodman, Jr., was reunited with his family via satellite on the network morning news programs. It was a total marriage of political event and media theater.

Goodman, an American flier, had been captured by the Syrians after engaging in raids over Lebanon. In a political gamble, Democratic presidential candidate Jesse Jackson traveled to the Middle East and persuaded Syria's President Hafez Assad to release Goodman. The news was relayed by satellite to millions of early-morning TV viewers. The first live pictures of Goodman and Jackson were carried by "The CBS Morning News." Then, also through live transmissions, the young flier was united with his father on ABC's "Good Morning, America" and with his mother and brother on NBC's "Today" show. One of Goodman's first questions on learning of his release was, "Does that mean I get to talk to Bryant Gumbel [cohost of the "Today" show]?"

The Goodman rescue was a perfect union of political and media reality (Shales, 1984). And it turned out to be one of those "instant" media events: within four months, only 1 percent of the public listed it as a memorable public event (Robinson and Clancy, 1984: 15).

nite arguments among readers and viewers, among newsmakers, and among journalists themselves. The questions bring us to the core issue in the process of gathering and disseminating news: What *is* news anyway?

What Is News?

News is, to put it bluntly, what the news media report. People disagree sharply over what is newsworthy—that is, over what the news media should report. Newspeople themselves differ over just what and how they should report.

News deals with current events that we need or want to learn about. To be classed as news, events must be *recent* (or at least recently disclosed), *quickly conveyed,* and *relevant* to the audience. Timeliness and immediacy are qualities of newsworthiness. When everyone knows about an event, it ceases to be news. Even though an event may be momentous, it is not newsworthy if it is remote from the public's interests and lives.

The central debate over the nature of news is whether *surface events* or *underlying conditions* should be stressed (Roshco, 1975). This reflects the ancient debate over what reality is. Is it things that can be seen or heard or touched? Or is it basic concepts that can be understood but not directly sensed? If the first definition prevails, then news need only be described as correctly as possible. If the second definition prevails, then news must be explained and interpreted.

Most of the time, the media adhere to the first definition—they assume that news is mainly made up of concrete events. The following rules of thumb reflect this bias:

1. The news media tend to focus on surface events—such as wars, summit meetings, speeches, and press conferences.

2. One theory says that "names make news." Reporters thus focus on celebrities—highly visible people who, they assume, fascinate the public.

3. Surprise or strangeness heightens newsworthiness. An old journalistic cliché puts it this way: "When a dog bites a man, that is not news; when a man bites a dog, *that's* news."

4. Bad news is more intriguing than good news. Danger creates suspense and rivets our attention. Thus, the oft-heard complaint that "you never print any good news" has some merit. When bad news is the norm, however, a sudden flow of good tidings will be newsworthy.

5. Finally, conflict is newsworthy. It creates suspense over the outcome; it makes summing up the event easier. Thus, all kinds of contests—from football games to election campaigns—are news staples.

The news media simplify reality to fit these criteria, inevitably distorting the true complexity of things. Reported facts are the tip of the iceberg of reality. To be reported, that reality must assume an easily recognizable form: a fire, a wreck, an arrest, a speech, a vote, a price change, a proposal to build a road. Subtle events—a shift in social values or the decline of a world power—are harder to report. They demand more space (or time), and they require painstaking and thoughtful analysis. Thus, such stories are usually left to historians or social analysts. As the distinguished journalist Walter Lippmann once said about the Russian Revolution, "The hardest thing to report is chaos, even if it is evolving chaos."

The medium shapes the message

The technical structure of a medium—whether it relies on printed words, spoken words, or visual images—shapes not only what newspeople prefer to report but also how they report it.

A medium's limitations affect how messages are conveyed. This means that some messages are more easily sent by one medium than another. Editors in the print media favor unusual stories with color, conflict, and personalities. Radio news must be brief and fast moving; radio reporters use background sounds and short taped statements or interviews, sometimes procured by phone, to add interest and variety to their stories. Television producers look for stories with visual appeal. Pageants, crowd scenes, and natural disasters are ready-made for TV cameras. An in-depth story may take twice as much time as a news piece (say, two minutes rather than one); so brief quotes, or "bites," are favored. Thus, the simple and direct tends to drive out the complex and abstract.

Critics often fault radio and TV for superficial news coverage. The average paper, of course, contains far more news. The transcript of a nightly network TV news show would not fill half the front page of the *New York Times*. Electronic news also shies away from complex background stories and focuses on glib comments and colorful, fast-breaking events. The average TV "sound bite" (quoted material from a source) is about 12 seconds—hardly enough time to complete a thought, much less analyze an issue.

The speed and impact of the electronic media make up for what they lack in depth. When people want the latest bulletins, they turn to radio or TV. A page of print cannot have the unique impact of, say, 30 seconds of film showing Lt. Col. Oliver North parrying congressional questions or bloody rioting in a South African township. Each medium, in short, is best suited for certain types of stories, tending to emphasize those stories at the expense of others. In this sense, the medium surely shapes the message.

Counting costs and paying the piper

Economics dictate many aspects of news gathering and dissemination. Once a story has been assigned, it is likely to be used. Once a reporter has used time and energy to research and write a story, an editor does not want to "kill" it—even if it is dull. Coverage costs are even higher in the electronic media than in the print media. So producers send film crews only to the most promising news events and are apt to use the film once it has been shot. (In small cities, TV reporters may double as camera operators; in large cities, union contracts usually require multiperson crews for every story.)

Cost-conscious gatekeepers do not like to send well-paid reporters or camera crews to wait for something to happen. They prefer to cover scheduled "events," such as speeches or press conferences. These events are in turn planned to attract just such notice. "This town runs on non-events," explained a Washington press aide. "Their sole purpose is to create a perception that defies reality. They oversimplify and overdramatize" (Tolchin, 1985) Thus, the president sometimes delivers "speeches" in the White House's East Room to an "audience" of staff members. And House Democratic leaders once staged an elaborate "bill signing" on the Capitol steps—just as President Reagan was vetoing the bill.

Most of the media organizations are big, costly enterprises. Advertising, which pays the bills for news operations, dictates the size of the news

Lt. Col. Oliver North, a former staff member of the President's National Security Council, testifies before the congressional Iran-contra investigating committee. In defending the White House policy of support for the Nicaraguan contras, North described photographic slides to the committee. The so-called Iran-contra affair arose in 1986 when it was revealed that the Reagan administration had secretly sold weapons to Iran and illegally used the money from the weapons sales to finance the anti-Sandinista rebels (called contras) in Nicaragua.

hole—that is, the amount of time or space available for news. Advertisers have been known to sway editorial decisions, especially those of small-city outlets, which place a premium on being cordial with Main Street merchants. Larger enterprises can, and often do, assert their independence when news coverage jeopardizes the goodwill of advertisers.

The muckraking tradition

The news media cherish their right to uncover scandal and to comment freely on events. Early papers in this nation were savagely partisan, usually allied with a political party or faction. Even after standards of objectivity took hold, there remained a crusading tradition of investigative journalism. At the turn of the century, **muckrakers** exposed inhuman working conditions, unhealthy products, and backroom politics. In the "new journalism" of the 1960s, reporters told readers their biases, often recording in detail their personal reactions to what they were covering. The investigative tradition received new life with prizewinning reporting of the Vietnam War by such reporters as David Halberstam and Seymour Hersh and with the exposure of President Nixon's role in the Watergate scandal by Robert Woodward, Carl Bernstein, and others. Thus, while most stories are delivered straight, the exposure and reformist urge remains vibrant and is often honored by journalism's highest awards.

Today's newspapers and newsmagazines tend to relegate outright opinions to their editorial pages. Although most of these publications style

Media heavies. Top row, from left: *David Broder, national political reporter; Georgie Anne Geyer, syndicated columnist; James J. Kilpatrick, conservative columnist;* Middle row: *Joseph Kraft, late foreign affairs columnist; Mary McGrory, liberal columnist; Jack Nelson,* Los Angeles Times *Washington bureau chief;* Bottom row: *Carl Rowan, liberal columnist; George Will, conservative columnist; Ellen Goodman,* Boston Globe *commentator.*

themselves as "independent," they still devote much thought and craftsmanship to their editorials. Most editorial pages include letters to the editors and syndicated columns by such writers as David S. Broder, Mary McGrory, George Will, and Ellen Goodman.

Editorial cartoons are a special form of political commentary that dates from the earliest days of newspapers. The cartoonist Thomas Nast (1840–1902) invented the Democratic donkey and the Republican elephant. His vicious cartoons ruined the career of one of the strongest political bosses, New York Tammany Hall chief William Marcy Tweed. Nast's tradition flourishes in the work of such modern cartoonists as Herbert Block of the *Washington Post,* Tony Auth of the *Philadelphia Inquirer,* Paul Szep of the *Boston Globe,* and Paul Conrad of the *Los Angeles Times.*

The electronic media have a hazier editorial tradition. As users of publicly owned airwaves, radio and TV stations must give access to varying points of view. They also risk offending segments of their broad audience. Still, editorials are occasionally aired. The high point of electronic commentary occurred in the 1950s and 1960s, when "CBS Reports" and "NBC White Papers" brought distinguished commentary on many topics. Edward R. Murrow of CBS produced notable exposés of McCarthyism and the plight of migrant workers. Networks rarely show such boldness today, but local stations often run editorials and opposing viewpoints. Such commentators as Bill Moyers, John Chancellor, and David Brinkley enliven regular newscasts.

The newsmagazine concept came to TV in CBS's highly successful "60 Minutes" and its imitators. Strictly speaking, this program is more interpretive journalism than commentary. PBS pioneered several successful shows, among them "Washington Week in Review" and "The Lawmakers." As the major networks decline and cable TV airs more varied programs, we can expect more specialized news and commentary.

Is objectivity possible?

The very earliest newspapers were wildly unreliable, printing all manner of rumors, self-serving reports, and partisan criticism masking as news. With the rise of the mass-audience press in the 19th century, however, journalists developed the standard of *objectivity* to vouch for the truth of their work. The American Society of Newspaper Editors' Canons of Journalism, written in 1923, expressed the norms of objective and impartial reporting: "Sound practice makes a clear distinction between news reports and expressions of opinion. News reports should be free from opinion or bias of any kind. This rule does not apply to so-called special articles unmistakably devoted to advocating or characterized by a signature authorizing the writer's own conclusions and interpretations." The 1947 report of the Commission on Freedom of the Press, the so-called Hutchins Commission, emphasized this concept: News should be truthful, complete, and intelligent accounts of the day's events in the context that gives them meaning. If people are given facts as raw material, the argument runs, they can make up their own minds about what the facts mean.

The canons of objectivity are not, however, universally accepted. Journalists quarrel over the degree to which they ought to be, or can be, objective recorders of concrete events. Recently a fascinating trial in Concord, New Hampshire, probed federal labor standards for "professionals" and posed this question: Are reporters classed as skilled, creative professionals or as nonprofessionals who merely transcribe what they observe? One journalism dean argued that most newspaper writing was "creative";

another testified that reporters were not professionals and that they relied more on "observed reality" than on creativity or imagination *(New York Times,* 1986).

Thoughtful reporters admit that judgments are unavoidable in picking and editing stories. Many stories have an "angle" or **spin** (as in the spin of a baseball): how the reporter interprets or embellishes the story, imparting a tone that goes beyond the hard news. Now that print journalists rarely "scoop" radio and TV in fast-breaking stories, they have sought new interpretive roles. Newsmagazines such as *Time* and *Newsweek* show that how stories are presented can be as striking as the facts themselves; witty phrases and colorful descriptions help make their news stories entertaining. The press is sometimes charged with ideological bias. In fact, studies have detected little, if any, overt ideological slanting of the news (Clancey and Robinson, 1985). What has been found, rather, is the more subtle kind of "biases" we have noted: for the concrete over the abstract, for the anecdotal over the analytic, for the glib over the thoughtful, and for tried-and-true formulas over the unconventional.

The debate over how factual reporting can be embraces two issues. The first issue, as we have seen, is how much space should be given to *interpretation* as opposed to *concrete events.* Most reporters and editors think that readers need some interpretation to put the facts into context. The amount varies with the occasion: Wire-service stories on breaking news events have little interpretation; newsmagazines and many papers often run background stories or opinion pieces.

The second issue is *objectivity* versus *bias.* Reporters' norms stress objectivity, and most stories in print or on the air reflect that stress. But there is a place for crusading journalism; the highest awards, like the Pulitzer prizes, are often given to those who go beyond the everyday canons.

Sources of Political News

Most news doesn't just happen: it is arranged. Reporters rely heavily on *sources* for their stories—people who have special information or who can express themselves succinctly.

Relationships with sources are usually formal—an interview, a press conference, or a press release. Hess (1981: 17–18) found that Washington reporters conducted about five interviews for every story but that they rarely used documents or other written sources.

Reporters and sources are locked in a love-hate relationship. Each has what the other wants: sources have information; reporters have the power to create publicity, the lifeblood of political careers. Whatever their private feelings, reporters sense that they cannot disclose certain things if they want future interviews. Sources, for their part, know that getting friendly with key press corps members can pay off in good publicity. Correspondent David S. Broder (1987: 171) describes President Jimmy Carter as "sending Indian arrowheads from his farm to the children of one corre-

Informal press conference. Franklin D. Roosevelt, who was elected president in 1932 and served until his death in 1945, presided over economic reforms and social welfare legislation that he called the "New Deal." Because he liked reporters and had close ties with them, he held twice-a-week press conferences around his desk in the Oval Office of the White House.

spondent, dropping a note to the parents of another on their 50th wedding anniversary" in an effort to win press corps favor.

Scheduled events, such as press conferences or news releases, are the bread and butter of day-to-day news gathering. Such devices enable sources to control the timing and format of the information they give out. Reporters find them a great convenience in sidestepping the time-consuming task of tracking down stories. In a news-conscious place such as Washington, D.C., reporters' daily schedules are easily filled up by attending press conferences and reading documents and press releases. Though such practices are scorned as spoon-feeding, nearly all reporters rely on them.

Press conferences

Presidential press conferences are the most visible public exchanges between a news source and reporters. Dating from Theodore Roosevelt's regular meetings with friendly correspondents, begun in 1901, they have since become an institution. The press now expects them to be held periodically. Franklin Roosevelt, who had a warm relationship with reporters, held them twice a week; Harry Truman held one every 10 days; Dwight Eisenhower and John Kennedy held them about every two weeks, as did Lyndon Johnson until his ratings in the polls began to dive. Nixon, who hated journalists as a class, held few press conferences, preferring off-the-cuff interviews with friendly journalists. So did Ronald Reagan, who often performed poorly in formal press corps encounters.

Articulate presidents use press conferences to capture public attention and build support. Presidents prepare for them thoroughly; their press aides compile briefing books and sometimes plant questions with friendly reporters. For their part, reporters (according to one White House correspondent) "go in there memorizing our own little question and barely pay attention to the other questions." *Washington Post* veteran Haynes Johnson (Washington Post Writers Group, 1976) explained some of the drawbacks of the press conference:

> Questions are often self-serving, or occasionally obsequious. There are all too few sharp exchanges, or pointed follow-ups, or relentless pursuits of the sort that provide fresh insights into the president's thinking, or help to explain his actions. Important topics are often ignored or glossed over. . . . Style, not substance, wins acclaim and builds reputations. Some of the questions are, in reality, speeches or personal points of view. The press, like other professions, is not wthout its prima donnas.

The results of these encounters were not only unenlightening; they played into the president's hands. "The press conference had become a form of political theater," Broder (1981) observed, "played by the president to the TV audience, in the presence of an obstreperous and distracting mob of reporters."

To quell the clamor that marked post-Watergate press conferences, President Reagan's advisers instituted several reforms. Reporters remained seated and raised their hands for recognition, instead of leaping and shouting to gain the president's attention. Reporters were assigned seats, to help the president call them by name and to segregate the tough questioners from those who could be counted on for softer queries. Amplifiers hidden inside the president's bulletproof podium helped him hear the questions. "Reagan's press conferences are not nearly the spontaneous encounters the average television viewer might suspect," one White House reporter (De Frank, 1982: 27) explained. "On the contrary, they have evolved into elaborately choreographed exercises in damage control."

When presidential press conferences are few and far between, reporters resort to shouting questions during other events. During the late Reagan years, a ritual evolved: as the president arrived or departed (often with the roar of the presidential helicopter in the background), questions would be shouted and brief answers (planned in advance) would be shouted in return. The brief encounters served the White House's purpose by producing brief newsworthy quips without the risk of cross examination.

Radio and TV networks typically accept White House requests for free airtime to make announcements or give major speeches. As government-licensed outlets, stations do this in the public interest. This "free use of an expensive commodity" allows presidents to choose when they appear (Minow, Martin, and Mitchell, 1973). Occasionally, however, White

Media event. Reporters clamored for attention at the White House press conferences held by President Ronald Reagan, but these press conferences were formal, structured events.

House requests for airtime are turned down because the purpose is deemed too partisan. The networks sometimes grant opposition leaders equal time to reply to the president—for example, to counter the annual State of the Union address.

Off the record

A step removed from formal press conferences are off-the-record comments that officials make to help journalists prepare their stories. Reporters are flattered by such comments because they have an air of confidentiality and provide the makings of a "scoop" without legwork. Off-the-record comments are just as useful for officials, who can use them to shape news coverage without risking personal exposure.

Informal rules of the game set three categories of off-the-record comments: the *not-for-attribution* quote ("a senior White House official said . . ."); the **backgrounder** ("the administration is worried that . . ."); and the *deep backgrounder,* used only on the reporter's own authority.

Backgrounders are controversial. The AP code is not clear-cut: "News sources should be disclosed unless there is a clear reason not to do so. When it is necessary to protect the confidentiality of a source, the reason should be given." Reporters publicly deplore the use of backgrounders, but most of them use confidential sources. A Washington correspondent once started a group called the Frontgrounders, which held only on-the-record interviews. The group soon disbanded because few officials would grant such interviews.

Off-the-record comments may cause friction between sources and reporters. When the comments are tantalizing, the media are apt to use them, even at the risk of angering the source. President Reagan once made an offhand jest while testing his microphone before a radio broadcast. "My fellow Americans," he said, "I am pleased to tell you I have just signed legislation which outlaws Russia forever. The bombing begins in five minutes." The networks had agreed that informal remarks made prior to the president's radio talks would be off the record; thus, although the remark had been recorded, the networks hesitated to use it. Written reports of the remark filtered out, however, and caused an uproar abroad. The networks then aired the tapes. Eventually, they announced that they would no longer conceal off-the-record or off-the-cuff remarks made by presidents or political candidates.

Much off-the-record information is voluntarily and deliberately "leaked" to the press. **Leaks** have various uses. They may test the political waters, air a view that cannot be expressed officially, or seek public sympathy for a position that has lost out in bureaucratic infighting (Hess, 1984). Usually they tell the source's side of the story. Sources often say, "If you quote me, I'll deny I said it." Administrative managers frequently denounce leaks and sometimes launch efforts to "plumb" them (investigate their sources); a Nixon White House "plumbers" group was assigned the job of covering up details of the Watergate affair and concealing them from the press.

THE MEDIA'S POLITICAL IMPACT

The media intrude on every phase of public life. Yet their precise impact is a matter of keen debate. To round out our survey of political communications, we will focus on three areas of media influence: (1) political socialization and learning, (2) campaigns and elections, and (3) the conduct and performance of government.

The Media as Teachers of Politics

As providers of information about politics and government, the media help socialize people into politics. Media images of politicians are among the first political things to which children are exposed. Such exposure is reinforced through a lifetime of viewing and reading.

Children take their media in huge doses. Grade-school children spend about 27 hours a week watching TV—nearly as much time as they spend in school. Studies show that television rivals parents and teachers as a source of political information (Kraus and Davis, 1976). Moreover, those who teach children—mainly parents and teachers—rely on media-based information.

The average adult American spends nearly three hours a day watching TV; but that "watching" may be casual and offhand. He or she also spends two hours listening to radio, 20 minutes reading a paper, and 10 minutes reading magazines. Time spent with the mass media has risen by 40 percent since the advent of TV. It comes mostly at the expense of other leisure activities (John P. Robinson, 1977).

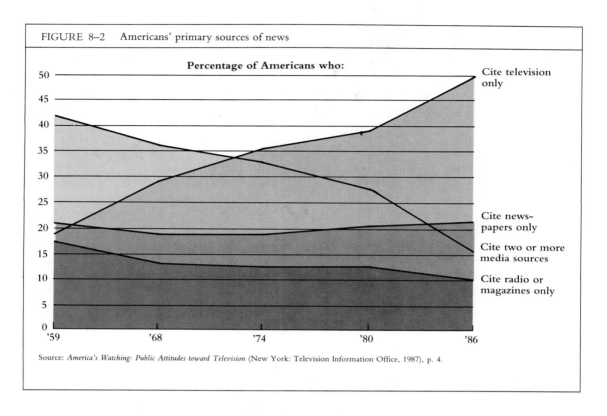

FIGURE 8–2   Americans' primary sources of news

Percentage of Americans who:

- Cite television only
- Cite news-papers only
- Cite two or more media sources
- Cite radio or magazines only

Source: *America's Watching: Public Attitudes toward Television* (New York: Television Information Office, 1987), p. 4.

Television is the broadest source of information. Since the early 1960s, it has been Americans' chief source of news; today about 65 percent of all Americans rely chiefly on TV for their news (see Figure 8–2), and 4 out of every 10 get *all* of their news from TV. More than half rate TV as the most believable news source (see Figure 8–3).

People who get their news from a mixture of sources are not only better informed than people who do not; they are also more interested and active in politics. They are the so-called attentive publics. In contrast, people who lean wholly on TV are apt to be passive spectators. They are an "inadvertent audience"—they just happen to be in front of the set when political news is broadcast and don't take the trouble to tune it out. Few people seek out political news on TV. "No matter how much some critics may deplore the sketchiness of television's political coverage," Ranney (1983: 11) observes, "the fact is that television gives considerably more attention to politics than most viewers feel they need or want."

Subtle values—transmitted through movies, popular songs, comic strips, and TV and radio programs—affect our approach to politics. An old Ronald Reagan film portrayed Knute Rockne inspiring his team to "win one for the Gipper"—a theme that resurfaced in such later films as

FIGURE 8–3   Which media report is most credible?

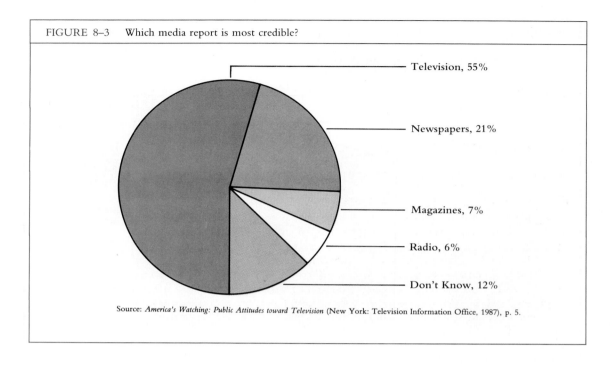

Television, 55%

Newspapers, 21%

Magazines, 7%

Radio, 6%

Don't Know, 12%

Source: *America's Watching: Public Attitudes toward Television* (New York: Television Information Office, 1987), p. 5.

Television news anchors are media gatekeepers. The content of broadcast news depends a great deal on what information they regard as important and newsworthy. Here, President Ronald Reagan holds an interview in the White House's Oval Office with the main network TV news anchors. From left: Tom Brokaw of NBC, Bernard Shaw of CNN, President Reagan, Dan Rather of CBS, and Peter Jennings of ABC.

WORDS AND IDEAS

The Game of Politics, According to Television News

[According to television news] politics is essentially a game played by individual politicians for personal advancement, gain, or power. The game is a competitive one, and the players' principal activities are those of calculating and pursuing strategies designed to defeat competitors and to achieve their goals (usually election to public office). Of course, the game takes place against a backdrop of governmental institutions, public problems, policy debates, and the like, but these are noteworthy only insofar as they affect, or are used by, players in pursuit of the game's rewards. The game is played before an audience—the electorate—which controls most of the prizes, and players therefore constantly attempt to make a favorable impression. In consequence, there is an endemic tendency for players to exaggerate their good qualities and to minimize their bad ones, to be deceitful, to engage in hypocrisies, to manipulate appearances; though inevitable, these tendencies are bad tendencies . . . and should be exposed. They reduce the electorate's ability to make its own discriminating choices, and they may hide players' infractions of the game's rules, such as those against corruption and lying.

Source: Paul H. Weaver, "Is Television News Biased?" *Public Interest* 7 (Winter 1972), p. 69.

Rocky and *The Karate Kid*. Films of that kind, while not labeled political, tell citizens as much about waging campaigns or fighting wars as about football or boxing or karate.

What exactly do people learn from the media? How does that knowledge shape their behavior? The conclusions are tentative. The media's strongest role is **agenda setting,** 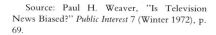 giving visibility or importance to a problem or personality. People may or may not learn facts from the media. But they take cues from the media about what and who should be taken seriously (Shaw and McCombs, 1977).

As for specific information, the picture is less clear. It seems that people gain only limited facts from the media; they recall little, but they can remember details mentioned to them (Graber, 1984: 157–59). Their factual learning from the media is greatest if they have little prior knowledge. The most important things that people gain from the media are general feelings about events: apathy, cynicism, fear, trust, acquiescence, or support.

FIGURE 8–4

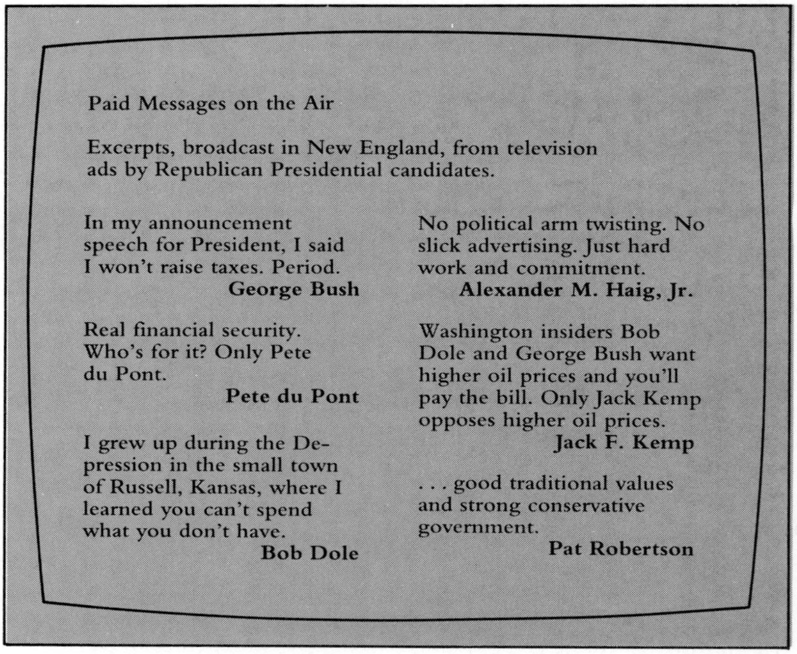

Paid Messages on the Air

Excerpts, broadcast in New England, from television ads by Republican Presidential candidates.

In my announcement speech for President, I said I won't raise taxes. Period.
George Bush

No political arm twisting. No slick advertising. Just hard work and commitment.
Alexander M. Haig, Jr.

Real financial security. Who's for it? Only Pete du Pont.
Pete du Pont

Washington insiders Bob Dole and George Bush want higher oil prices and you'll pay the bill. Only Jack Kemp opposes higher oil prices.
Jack F. Kemp

I grew up during the Depression in the small town of Russell, Kansas, where I learned you can't spend what you don't have.
Bob Dole

. . . good traditional values and strong conservative government.
Pat Robertson

Source: *New York Times*, February 2, 1988, p. A14.

The Media and Electoral Contests

Campaigns and elections cannot help but be media events. After all, they are efforts to communicate and persuade. Some campaign communications—ads, brochures, and billboards—are controlled by the campaigners themselves. Other campaign communications—such as media coverage—lie outside the campaigners' control. Campaigners want to turn media coverage to their advantage: it is free, and it is more believable than paid advertising.

Campaign communication has passed through at least five distinct stages (Heard, 1966). At first, candidates engaged in little public campaigning, leaving things in the hands of supporters and the partisan press. Andrew Jackson's election ushered in the "torchlight era" of stump speeches, parades, and costly entertainment. An era of campaign literature—ads and mass mailings—began about 1880. This approach was displaced in 1928 by radio campaigning, which in turn was displaced by TV campaigning in the 1950s (see Figure 8–4). (Eisenhower, in 1952, was the

TABLE 8–2   Top five stories of the presidential primaries, 1988

Subject of coverage	Number of stories
"Horse race"	537
Campaign issues	312
Campaign strategy, tactics	280
Policy issues	215
Candidate politics	88

SOURCE: Center for Media and Public Affairs, election news coverage on ABC, CBS, and NBC (February 1987–June 1988). Cited in S. Robert Lichter, "How the Press Covered the Primaries," *Public Opinion* 11 (July–August 1988), p. 45.

first presidential candidate to employ TV ads.) At each stage, politicians aimed their messages past the immediate audience and at the press, which held the key to the larger audience.

Covering the horse race

Political contests are ready-made for today's mass media. They meet the basic tests of newsworthiness: they are full of fast-breaking events that can be quickly conveyed and are relevant to a broad audience. They also satisfy the rules of thumb for what makes news: concrete events, famous names, conflict, and surprise.

Campaign reporting tends to stress the "game" or "horse race" rather than issues or policy positions (see Table 8–2). "In virtually every campaign waged in the television era, the most frequent evening news story has been the on-the-road, horse-race piece—the reporter covers the day's campaign events and then assesses the candidate's motives and/or the electorate's possible response" (Clancey and Robinson, 1985; 51). One exception was the 1984 presidential campaign, in which issues made up 40 percent of the coverage, surpassing traditional **horse-race coverage**. This happened because there was really no horse race to cover: Reagan was virtually assured of reelection.

Whatever the odds, reporters try to heighten the sense of competition. The media are eager to name winners and losers in primaries, caucuses, or straw polls; if there are no clear winners, the press tries to declare them anyhow. Before the caucuses and primaries begin, this means relying on candidate-preference surveys—notoriously unreliable at this early stage.

Once the balloting begins, the press starts calling the race. Carter's 1976 campaign took off when he won the Iowa caucus votes. (Actually, "uncommitted" won with 37 percent of the vote to Carter's 28 percent.) Four years later, George Bush gained credibility in Iowa. As Bush's press secretary confessed (Bonafede, 1980: 1134), "The ride we got out of Iowa gave us an enormous boost—probably undeserving. It projected us into the front-running status we did not deserve. It seemed to indicate that we were in a two-man race. Our expectations became too high . . . . But there is no doubt about it: a ride by the press makes a lot of converts." The Iowa caucuses proved pivotal for Gary Hart's 1984 drive. Although Mondale won impressively, Hart came in second with 15 percent (all of 12,600 votes). The press announced that Hart had bumped John Glenn as the leading alternative to Mondale, and seven days later that prophecy was fulfilled in New Hampshire's primary.

When reporters are unsure how to interpret events, they sometimes follow the lead of influential reporters. After R. W. "Johnny" Apple wrote in the *New York Times* that Senator McGovern had made a surprisingly strong showing in the 1972 Iowa caucuses, other reporters were prompted to take up the theme. This also happened in 1976, after Apple reported that Carter was doing well in Iowa; the story itself became a political event. Crouse (1973) dubbed this **pack journalism.**

Early nominating contests, or those competing with few other news events, get extra attention from reporters. The Iowa caucuses, the New Hampshire primary, and even the Michigan precinct primaries held more than a year before the election, are hyped as bellwethers. (For the Democrats, Iowa and New Hampshire are ill-chosen indicators: neither state is found in the party's presidential column very often.) A study of the 1976 primaries found that the New Hampshire results received 170 times as much network news time per Democratic vote as the outcome in New York (Michael J. Robinson, 1977: 80–81). The result of this extra attention is **front-loading** the selection process: candidates who surge ahead in the early contests are "front-runners" who hold "commanding leads"; they may be pressed by "leading challengers" who emerge from the pack to be taken seriously by the press. Two reasons for the southern states' Super Tuesday primary in March 1988 were to combat front-loading and focus media coverage on the region.

Another preoccupation of the press is candidates' mistakes: character flaws, misstatements, slips of the tongue, or other errors are given undue attention. In 1972, Democratic front-runner Edmund Muskie was sidetracked by the "crying incident"; he allegedly broke down while answering vicious personal attacks by the right-wing *Manchester* (New Hampshire) *Union-Leader*. An anti-Jewish slur made allegedly by Jesse Jackson was taken up by reporters in 1984. The press dogged Gary Hart in 1984 because he had changed his name early in his career and had issued conflicting information about his age. Four years later, accounts of an affair with a young model forced him out of the presidential campaign. Another candidate, Delaware Senator Joseph Biden, was forced out of the 1988 race by plagiarism charges. In all of these cases, reporters seized on events to dramatize traits that they had seen in the candidates— Muskie's temperament, Jackson's arrogance, Hart's irresponsibility, Biden's carelessness with facts. A fierce debate ranges over whether the

Exposure. Former U.S. Senator Gary Hart (D–Colo.) dropped out of the 1988 presidential race for several months when the press exposed the fact that he had had an affair with Donna Rice, a young model. In 1987, the National Enquirer, *a tabloid newspaper whose specialty is exposing the private lives of the rich and famous, published a front-page photograph showing Rice on Senator Hart's lap and carried a story describing their "fun-filled weekend in the Bahamas." Rice complained that the media had victimized her by putting her face "on the cover of every magazine in America."*

press has any business dogging candidates on such "personal character" issues.

Candidates and their managers, for their part, strive to mold the view of reality conveyed by the media. They try to foster the picture of victory against great odds, no matter what the real situation. As Elizabeth Drew noted (1976: 89), "A classic problem for candidates is how to inflate their prospects in order to attract allies and followers without creating a standard against which they can be measured unfavorably."

Candidates are judged on whether they meet, exceed, or fall short of their expected showing in a given contest. A candidate who surprises everyone and does better than expected in a primary may be boosted to the status of a major contender. A front-running candidate who does poorly will face reports that his campaign is "running out of steam." So candidates and their managers try to shape expectations before the vote and to influence the "spin" of the story once the votes are in. At stake is not just the candidate's public image; campaign contributions, loans, professional advisory services, and recruitment of volunteer workers come easier for "winners" than for "losers."

Televised debates

Candidate debates are the most conspicuous use of TV to bring campaigns to the people. Though the direct effect of debates on nomination and election results is mixed, their impact on campaign strategy and activists' opinions is considerable.

Modern presidential debates began in 1960 with four televised encounters between John Kennedy and Richard Nixon. Most of the observers (including the candidates) thought that the crucial first debate turned the tide in Kennedy's favor. It showed him as vigorous, well spoken, and capable—fully the equal of Vice President Nixon (who was tired, ill, and badly made up for the cameras). Actually, according to polls, little overall opinion shift resulted from the debates (Katz and Feldman, 1962). But Kennedy's impressive showing excited many Democrats who had worried about his youth and inexperience.

Since 1960, debates have become a campaign staple, even if few have been as influential as the Kennedy-Nixon encounters. During the next debates, in 1976, a misstatement President Ford made about Eastern Europe fostered the view that challenger Jimmy Carter had won the encounter. The single 1980 debate, held only a week before the balloting, probably helped fuel a last-minute surge for Ronald Reagan. President Carter tried to depict Reagan as a dangerous extremist, but Reagan parried these thrusts and portrayed himself as an average guy. Toward the end of the debate, he moved in with the clincher: Voters should ask themselves, he said, whether they were better off than they had been four years before. For voters worried about inflation and humiliated by the Iran hostage crisis, the answer was obvious. Since 1984, debates among contenders for the nominations of the two parties have burgeoned.

With no incumbent and few overriding issues, the 1988 debates were pivotal. Dukakis wanted four sessions; Vice President Bush's managers wanted as few as possible. Three debates were held, two presidential and one vice-presidential. Although no knock-out punches were thrown, Dukakis had a slight edge in the first outing. In the second, however, Bush appeared confident and cogent, while Dukakis failed either to press his case or display his personal appeal. The result, even if judged a tie, was not enough to help Dukakis. In the vice-presidential debate, Democrat Lloyd Bentsen scored a TKO over Dan Quayle ("You're no John Kennedy!"), solidifying doubts about the latter's suitability for national office.

Candidate debates have several effects on campaign tactics. First, reporters tend to cover these debates as they do other aspects of campaigns —as personal contests rather than as forums for airing issues. The press is eager to declare who won or lost the debate and is on the lookout for mistakes or misstatements.

*Republicans debate.
During the 1988
presidential nominating
season, contenders for the
Democratic and
Republican party
nominations participated
in many televised debates.
At Dartmouth College in
Hanover, New
Hampshire, U.S. Senator
Robert Dole (R–Kans.)
[right] answers a question
from the television
audience while Vice
President George Bush
[left] and former General
Alexander M. Haig, Jr.,
listen.*

Second, fearing missteps in such encounters, candidates and their managers try to limit the confrontational elements. Thus, the debates are often genteel affairs. There is little real clash of personalities or views, little or no dialogue between the candidates, and little real follow-up by the questioners. (Somewhat more freedom is allowed when a number of contenders are vying at the nomination stage.)

Third, such debates seem to have scant direct impact on how we vote. Indeed, the performance of the candidates tends to reinforce earlier views rather than make converts (Sears, 1977). This is important, though: a candidate's performance may, as in 1960 (Nixon versus Kennedy), fire up or dampen the enthusiasm of partisan activists and contributors.

Finally, debates are tactically more desirable for candidates who are "behind." Those who are not incumbents, who are less known or respected, or who trail in the polls need to prove themselves and are thus likely to push for debates. Front-running candidates do not want to give their challengers the exposure that debates provide.

Candidate debates help challengers by showing them on an equal footing with incumbents or front-runners. Kennedy's youth and inexperience were not an issue once he proved himself a match for Nixon, who had been vice president for eight years. Carter, relatively unknown, looked presidential by meeting toe-to-toe with President Ford in 1976. Fears about Reagan's hawkishness faded in 1980 as he turned aside Carter's attacks and showed himself a reasonable, reliable man. Smarting from his defeat in 1960, Nixon refused to debate in 1968 or 1972 when he was the front-runner. Lyndon Johnson took the same stand as an incumbent in

1964. In 1976 and 1980, challengers pressed for debates; incumbents resisted until sagging polls convinced them that it was best to gamble.

Candidate debates are now a key part of presidential campaign tactics. Whether they are actually held depends on "whether in the future both candidates will calculate that they stand to gain more than they will lose by debating" (Ranney, 1983: 28).

Media effects on results

Many people believe that the mass media shape election outcomes. But the research findings are mixed. In one of the earliest scientific studies of voting behavior, the Erie County (Ohio) study, the authors concluded that the media had little impact on voting behavior (Lazarsfeld, Berelson, and Gaudet, 1944). Later studies bear this out. One, 'of the 1972 presidential elections, concluded that TV network newscasts had little impact on voters (Patterson and McClure, 1976).

Most experts agree that the media sharpen or reinforce existing opinions rather than change them. Most people hold basic attitudes that color their assessment of anything they read or see. This is why two people can draw opposite conclusions from the same material. Also, many people suffer from what one writer calls "videomalaise"; they are cynical and distrust the press.

But the media have a unique ability to lend visibility to candidates or ideas. The media may not affect *how* something is viewed, but they do determine *whether* it is viewed at all.

This is why politicians say: "I don't care what you print about me—just spell my name right!" It accounts for politicians' constant struggle to get their names and faces before the public, to achieve name recognition. And it may help explain why more visible politicians—longtime incumbents or candidates with famous names—seem to succeed, other things being equal.

One controversial issue is whether election outcomes are affected by media announcements of results before the polls close. With sophisticated procedures, TV networks can sometimes project election winners well before the last votes have been cast. These methods include *key precinct analysis,* in which early, partial returns are compared with past voting records to predict the outcome, and **exit polls,** in which samples of voters are interviewed as they leave voting places. Politicians believe that projecting results discourages people from going to the polls. President Carter's early defeat and concession in 1980 are credited with discouraging Democratic voters on the West Coast, probably causing the defeat of some candidates in close congressional races. Media executives discount the impact of early vote projections and exit polls; but under pressure from elected officials of both parties, the major networks have agreed not to project probable presidential election winners in any state before its polls have closed. Any formal effort to limit media reporting, however, would raise First Amendment objections.

Studies of media influence in general elections yield mixed results. Most studies show little effect on voter preferences (Patterson and McClure, 1976). There is some evidence, however, that newspaper accounts, and especially endorsements, can influence voters (Erickson, 1976). More clearly, the media have influenced the processes of nominations and elections.

First, the media have diluted party influence, especially in presidential contests. Candidates no longer appeal to the public through the media only after having won their party's nomination. Today, through the media, they go over the heads of party leaders to win popular acceptance and gain nominations. Paid consultants usually give candidates more assistance in media campaigns than party officials do.

Second, the media help screen potential candidates at the nominating stage, when party labels do not separate the candidates. Reporters describe candidate behavior and personalities, try to name winners and losers in caucuses and primaries, and pinpoint candidates' errors.

Third, the media shape alternatives. Certain types of candidates are bound to do better than others in making media appeals. Franklin Roosevelt was a master at radio communication, but the fact that he was confined to a wheelchair might have impaired his impact on television. Ronald Reagan, a longtime actor, took to TV as if he had invented it. A host of lesser TV-age candidates have come on the scene sporting good looks and informal speaking styles. Other candidates have been stymied by TV's demands. "I've never really warmed up to television, and in fairness to television, it's never really warmed up to me," confessed Walter F. Mondale after his crushing 1984 defeat by Ronald Reagan. Clumsiness on TV was just one of Mondale's problems, but it sharpened the contrast between him and TV-wise Reagan.

Fourth, the media have altered the selection process itself. They have encouraged the spread of such "open" procedures as primaries; they have opened up less formal events such as caucuses and straw polls. These contests have rendered anticlimactic the nominating conventions, which themselves have been streamlined to accommodate the media.

The Media and Governing

Presidents and other chief executives are prime targets of media coverage because they are easily described, understood, and reported. Presidents are almost always in the spotlight. From Theodore Roosevelt to Ronald Reagan, presidents have exploited their unique media coverage to focus public attention and spark support. As we will see in Chapter 13, presidents and their staffs spend much of their time planning and scheduling activities for maximum media exposure.

In contrast, Congress is harder to cover. Not that Congress is ignored; studies show that it gets coverage equal to the president's, even in presidential election years (Graber, 1984: 238). Yet Congress is at a disadvantage. With more than 500 politicians and as many legislative issues, it has no single focus of attention. Its work is scattered and often dull—not the stuff of TV drama.

More than a generation of experience with television passed before congressional leaders realized that they were losing out to presidents in the battle for media attention. Closed-circuit TV coverage of floor proceedings came to the House in 1979 and to the Senate in 1986. Fearing adverse publicity, both chambers installed their own equipment and kept control over the cameras. Normally, the cameras show only speakers (so that no empty seats will appear). The proceedings are beamed to Capitol Hill offices and, via **C-SPAN** (Cable-Satellite Public Affairs Network), to cable subscribers throughout the country.

Video coverage has sharpened the public's perception of Congress as a working legislative body. While audience estimates vary, the potential viewership is enormous—some 30 million households can pick up C-SPAN broadcasts. Regular viewers, numbering in the hundreds of thousands, tend to be politically informed and active. On occasion, the audience balloons to huge dimensions. An Alaska lands bill debate in 1979 had blanket coverage throughout the state; the Senate's 1986 tax reform debate commanded nationwide attention.

Has live media coverage changed the two chambers? The effects have been subtle. More lawmakers are taking part in floor debate, usually with shorter, more carefully crafted speeches. They frame arguments and appeals with their audience in mind. Some members, including Senator Robert Dole (R–Kans.), the Senate GOP floor leader, and Representative Newt Gingrich (R–Ga.), have enhanced their national followings by effective floor speaking.

National and local press organizations diverge in covering legislative affairs. The national outlets—networks, wire services, newsmagazines, and major newspapers—cover major legislative events. The attention they pay to individual lawmakers is confined mostly to floor leaders, committee chairpersons, and a few "big names" (Hess, 1986). Coverage of individual members is left mainly to local newspapers, radio, and TV. Such coverage is increasing because of technological advances (cheaper TV transmissions) and organizational changes (expanded newspaper chains). But lacking the resources of the national media, local outlets are more dependent on the legislators themselves for information, through interviews and press releases.

Most legislators organize their offices and their schedules to provide such information. Virtually all senators and most representatives have one or more press aides. Both chambers have recording studios where members can tape radio or TV messages at costs far below commercial rates. Most legislators make use of such services. Such activities help inform constituents and aid reelection as well.

The judiciary gets the least media exposure of the three branches of government. The nature of court proceedings is partly at fault. Court decisions are complex and difficult to interpret accurately, but few news operations can afford to assign their most experienced and skilled reporters to cover the judicial beat. Thus, reporting of the courts is sketchier and less accurate than that of other government branches (Grey, 1968).

Government officials know that they need sympathetic press coverage to promote their programs and protect their jobs. Some (for example, former Secretary of State Henry Kissinger and former Special Trade Representative Robert Strauss) cultivate the press corps and are rewarded with generous publicity and friendly treatment. Agencies, too, realize that they must tend their public image to win the funding and programs they want. All have public affairs offices; highly visible agencies—the military services, the FBI, and NASA—work hard to polish their media images.

Yet officials are also wary of the press's watchful eye. The media cannot cover all government activities; but officials know that reports of "waste, fraud, and abuse" invite negative publicity. So do spectacular failures, such as the 1986 explosion of the space shuttle *Challenger,* an event that ended NASA's prolonged press honeymoon. Many agencies, however, simply lack glamour, and others are prone to bad publicity. Their main public relations goal is damage control, in which "no news is good news."

The communications media are not politically important merely because politicians and officials spend so much time catering to their needs. The media actually shape government processes and institutions, and even the content of policies. Ranney's (1983: 124–55) arguments about the effects of TV apply to other media as well. Though certainly debatable, these arguments deserve serious thought:

1. The media may compress the time available to decision makers for initiating programs and achieving results. Both television and the print media are eager for stories and action; the media world moves fast and favors neat solutions.

2. Media coverage may reduce options by spotlighting proposed solutions prematurely, inviting criticism, and eliminating alternatives from consideration.

3. By highlighting leaders who simplify policies, take extreme stands, and fight courageously, the media may weaken the less glamorous processes of compromising and building coalitions.

4. By spotlighting elected officials and ignoring bureaucratic politics, the media may have "helped the unelected officials in both the legislative and executive branches to fill the policy-making vacuums left by the declining power of the elected officials" (Ranney, 1983: 155).

Finally, the communications media tend to reinforce the traditional American distaste for government and politicians. Journalists are cynical about politics; they belittle politicians' motives, words, and actions. This may sour public confidence in government institutions. Of course, many people—including journalists—expect the press to act as a sort of fourth estate, watching over officials and keeping them responsible. How faithfully the media play this role is open to question.

"Were it left to me to decide whether we should have a government without newspapers, or newspapers without government," Thomas Jefferson observed, "I should not hesitate a moment to prefer the latter." But when Jefferson was president and received barbed criticisms from the press, he lamented that "the man who never looks into a newspaper is better informed than he who reads them; inasmuch as he who knows nothing is nearer to truth than he whose mind is filled with falsehoods and errors." Such is the ambivalent relationship between the press and government.

RESPONSIBILITIES OF THE PRESS

Democracies give wide latitude to communications media. Free speech and press were central political and philosophical issues in the Old World; in the colonies, papers and journals thrived because they could be published without royal licenses or taxes. Their privileged role was acknowledged in the First Amendment, which enjoins Congress to "make no law . . . abridging the freedom . . . of the press."

This does not mean that the media are free from government influence or control. Like all businesses, they are subject to many regulations, large and small. In addition, they are sensitive to government pressures. And since electronic media, unlike print media, operate in the publicly owned electromagnetic spectrum, they are subject to federal regulation.

The scope of press liberty inevitably breeds controversy. The Constitution gives what seems to be a total right to report and publish. But there are competing rights, both for individuals and for the government.

A Free Press versus Privacy

The First Amendment makes the press the only private industry that is expressly protected by the Constitution. Most newspeople think that this gives them almost complete freedom to gather and print news and opinions as they see fit. If a story clashes with other constitutionally protected values, the remedy is not prior restraint but after-the-fact court action.

Editors legally have complete freedom to decide what goes into or stays out of their publications, even if the result is unfair. In a unanimous decision (*Miami Herald Publishing Company* v. *Tornillo,* 1974), the Supreme Court struck down a Florida law requiring papers to give candidates free space to reply to newspaper criticisms. A paper involves a "crucial process" of editorial judgment that lies beyond government regulation, Chief Justice Warren Burger wrote for the Court. "A responsible press is an undoubtedly desirable goal," he noted. "But press responsibility is not mandated by the Constitution and like many other virtues, it cannot be

Getting the tough story. An NBC television news producer leans from a car window with his microphone [right] to get a comment from Soviet UN employee Gennadiy Zakharov as they speed along a New York City highway. The U.S. Government had caught Zakharov spying and had ordered him to leave the country.

legislated.'' Hence, editorial judgments are covered by the First Amendment.

On the other hand, people have ways of fending off the press. Private citizens can shield themselves from the glare of publicity. When a person becomes the subject of public interest, though, the courts usually allow media coverage—even when the coverage is harmful or obnoxious. A person may lose rights of privacy by becoming a public figure, by being charged with (or the victim of) a crime, or even by granting interviews. Voluntary press restraint protects most rape victims and AIDS sufferers, for example.

People whose reputations or careers have been damaged by a published story may sue for **libel**. To win such a suit, the plaintiff must prove that the material is both false and damaging. A public official suing for libel must also show that the story was published ''with knowledge that it was false or with reckless disregard of whether it was false or not'' (*New York Times* v. *Sullivan,* 1964). The Court underscored this burden of proof by cautioning judges to consider whether public figures who are plaintiffs have presented enough evidence to warrant a jury trial; it said that judges should dismiss cases where evidence of ''actual malice'' by the media was not ''clear and convincing'' (*Anderson* v. *Liberty Lobby,* 1986). In practice, it is hard to prove willful and reckless libel. Moreover, a court case guarantees that the charges will be publicized, and it can make the plaintiff seem to be bullying the press.

Faced with harassment or career threats, however, public figures have been tempted to bring suits against the press. They realize that they may win sympathy from a public (and a jury) that resents the media's arrogance, exemplified by TV crews that climbed trees outside a presidential aide's home and newspaper reporters who rummaged through an official's garbage cans. Not libel, but the way major news organizations gather and report news, was the crux of celebrated recent trials: former Israeli Defense Minister Ariel Sharon's suit against *Time* magazine and General William C. Westmoreland's suit against CBS. In both cases, the litigants claimed they had been defamed by media coverage. The suits uncovered sloppy journalism and false statements, but they did not win judgments because they could not show "reckless" falsehood.

Most plaintiffs initiate libel suits mainly to make points against the press or to deter enemies. Whether such suits attack the press or individuals who have criticized the plaintiffs, they harass the defendant and often force the defendant to incur hefty legal expenses, both of which may have a "chilling effect" on public expression; that is, the threat of libel suits may force people to think twice before speaking their mind in public.

Limited Access

Reporters may be prohibited from covering criminal trials if publicity could affect the outcome. Some convictions have been reversed because of sensational press coverage. Judges sometimes bar the press from some or all of a court case, even when the court sessions are open to the public. The press fiercely resents these "gag orders"; many dispute their constitutionality. The founders, well aware of the evils of private trials, included the guarantee of "a speedy and public trial" in the Bill of Rights. A 1976 Supreme Court ruling struck down a gag order placed on a famous murder trial and suggested other remedies. These included moving the trial to avoid local publicity and filing after-the-fact suits against unfair reporting *(Nebraska Press Association* v. *Stuart)*.

Some government dealings are privileged and beyond press freedom. Security classification is given to much government information, such as law enforcement investigations, military secrets, and federal financial decisions whose early release would cause economic chaos. In the fiscal year 1985, the federal government created 22.3 million secret documents, a jump of 14 percent over the number for the previous fiscal year. Most of these originated in the Defense Department or the Central Intelligence Agency.

Reporters and editors typically respect classified information, either from a sense of civic duty or from a desire to cultivate the goodwill of government news sources. In 1961, for instance, the *New York Times* withheld information about a planned invasion of Cuba (the Bay of Pigs invasion) for fear that advance word would doom the operation. (Ironically, the invasion failed anyway; perhaps public scrutiny would have deterred the operation.)

Certain secrecy rules have been challenged as excessive or as inconsistent with a free society. In 1971, the *New York Times* published the so-called Pentagon Papers. This 7,000-page secret Defense Department study, describing how the United States had become enmeshed in the Vietnam War, was leaked by former security aide Daniel Ellsberg. The Supreme Court ruled (*New York Times* v. *U.S.,* 1971) that the government had been overly cautious in restricting the information and that publication did not harm the nation's security.

Most government records, however, are supposed to be open to the public; no reason need be given to request them. This is the gist of the *Freedom of Information Act (FOIA)*. Enacted in 1966 and strengthened in 1974, the FOIA requires government agencies to prove that they are entitled to withhold information. Agencies have protested the cost of FOIA compliance and have been ingenious in developing reasons for not complying—often with the support of the Justice Department during the Reagan years. Although press groups originate only 5 percent of all FOIA requests, they have staunchly resisted efforts to limit the act.

Government Regulation of Electronic Media

Unlike printed publications, radio and TV have been regulated by the government almost since their inception. The present law, the Communications Act of 1934 (as amended), firmly sets the electromagnetic spectrum as a national resource that can be leased and regulated.

The Federal Communications Commission (FCC) is a seven-person board appointed by the president and approved by the Senate. It grants temporary monopolies (five- to seven-year licenses) to companies pledging to run their stations "in the public interest, convenience, or necessity." The FCC also regulates interstate and foreign transmissions by wire, cable, and satellite. It tries to curb monopolies in news outlets by banning papers from owning radio and TV outlets in their communities and by limiting the number of radio and TV outlets owned by a single firm.

The FCC cannot censor broadcast material, but it does use its licensing power to enforce certain standards. For example, it restricts indecency, which it defines as "language or material that depicts or describes, in terms patently offensive as measured by contemporary community standards for the broadcast medium, sexual or excretory activities or organs." This is derisively referred to as barring "seven dirty words" about sex and bodily functions. Stations airing programs or even music breaching these standards have received fines or warnings threatening their license renewals. However, the FCC has been more permissive in permitting such material after 10 P.M.—when children are not expected to be listening.

Another FCC standard, now abandoned, was the so-called **fairness doctrine**, obliging licensees to make reasonable efforts to discuss varied views on controversial issues of importance to the community. A chance for reply was to be given—free of charge if no paid sponsor could be found. In the case of elections, stations had to offer equal time to all candidates.

Many broadcasters believed that the fairness doctrine was so ambiguous that it caused stations to avoid controversy, defeating the doctrine's very goal. But the doctrine was upheld by the Supreme Court *(Red Lion Broadcasting Co. v. FCC, 1969)*. "It is the rights of the viewers and the listeners, not the rights of the broadcasters, which are paramount," wrote Justice Byron White for the Court. "It is the purpose of the First Amendment to preserve an uninhibited marketplace of ideas in which truth will ultimately prevail, rather than to countenance monopolization of that market, whether it be by the government itself or a private licensee."

Seized by the free market philosophy of the Reagan era, the FCC in the 1980s moved to deregulate broadcasting. While it has by no means quit the licensing business, the FCC has eased program standards and simplified reporting rules. Stations are no longer required to present a minimum amount of news or public affairs programs or to limit the number of commercials that they air each hour.

In 1987, the FCC formally abandoned the fairness doctrine as "misguided government policy" that no longer served the public interest. It argued that the original detailed program standards, designed when there were only a few general-purpose outlets, served little purpose at a time when many radio and TV stations—six times the number of daily newspapers—and other media catered to the public's specialized needs.

Yet many interest groups, both liberal and conservative, oppose deregulation. Echoing a former FCC chairman's charge that TV was a "vast wasteland," many citizens' groups seek to pressure the industry into higher standards. Citizens' groups voice complaints: programs are filled with sex and violence; children's programs are unhealthy; minorities are portrayed unfairly; and so forth. Given conflicts over the scope of government power over the electronic media, it is unclear how far the deregulation drive will go.

The federal government affects the electronic media in yet another way. It helps fund noncommercial radio and TV as an alternative to commercial outlets. The Public Broadcasting Act of 1967 formed the Corporation for Public Broadcasting (CPB) to parcel out federal money for noncommercial radio and TV. In 1969, CPB in turn set up the Public Broadcasting Service, (PBS), an "interconnection service" that schedules, promotes, and distributes shows to local stations. In 1971, CPB set up National Public Radio (NPR) as a programming and interlinking service for radio. PBS works with stations and agencies to get ideas and find funding for shows or series.

CONCLUSIONS

Several major points emerge from our study of the media's role in politics:

1. For political events to have any impact, they must be communicated. Communication is a complex process involving sources, messages, media (or channels), audiences, and effects.

2. Newsgatherers work for many news outlets, more for the print media than for the electronic media. Most of the news outlets in the United States are local; broadcast networks and wire services are national. All of the media forms are becoming more diverse.

3. Newsworthiness involves timeliness and immediacy. Two basic issues surround the concept of news: Should it interpret, or should it just report concrete events? Should (or can) news be truly objective, or is it necessarily biased?

4. News sources and reporters are locked in a mutually dependent relationship. For mutual convenience, formal contacts—such as press conferences and press releases—are favored. But there

is also a hierarchy of off-the-record contacts. This includes leaks, which serve the needs of both reporters and sources but may hamper decision making.

5. Gatekeepers determine what news will be passed on to the public. Each medium has certain advantages and disadvantages for handling different types of news.

6. Everyone agrees that the media shape our politics in key ways; but commentators disagree on the exact effects. The media are especially important in political learning, for both children and adults; in political campaigning; and in the relationships between government agencies and the public.

7. The print media are given wide protection by the First Amendment. Electronic media, as franchisees of the publicly owned electromagnetic spectrum, are subject to a measure of government regulation, though the extent of such regulation is a matter of debate.

FURTHER READING

BRODER, DAVID S. (1987) *Behind the Front Page: A Candid Look at How the News Is Made.* New York: Simon & Schuster. An honest, self-critical account of political journalism, warts and all, by a Pulitzer prize–winning political reporter who is widely regarded as the best in the business.

CROUSE, TIMOTHY (1973) *The Boys on the Bus.* New York: Ballantine Books. The events and the players are from days gone by, but the accounts of the 1972 Nixon-McGovern campaign and the press room of the Nixon White House are vivid, insightful, and often hilarious.

GRABER, DORIS (1988) *Mass Media and American Politics.* 3rd ed. Washington, D.C.: Congressional Quarterly Press. An authoritative survey of the subject by a leading political scientist in this subfield.

HALBERSTAM, DAVID (1981) *The Powers*

That Be. New York: Alfred A. Knopf. A fascinating anecdotal history of the rise of current media giants: CBS, the *New York Times*, the *Washington Post*, the *Los Angeles Times*, and Time, Inc.

HESS, STEPHEN (1981, 1984, 1986) *The Washington Reporters. The Government/Press Connection. The Ultimate Insiders.* Washington, D.C.: Brookings Institution. The volumes in this trilogy by a respected Washington press analyst contain, respectively, a survey of the Washington press corps, a description of the press offices of selected federal agencies, and an account of how the press treats U.S. senators.

RANNEY, AUSTIN (1983) *Channels of Power.* New York: Basic Books. A sensible survey and evaluation of literature bearing on the role that TV has played in shaping our current politics and government.

Chapter Nine

CAMPAIGNS, VOTERS, AND ELECTIONS

One of America's best political scientists, V. O. Key, Jr., deeply believed in democracy and in the American voter, arguing fervently that "voters are not fools."

> In his reflective moments even the most experienced politician senses a nagging curiosity about why people vote as they do. His power and his position depend upon the outcome of the mysterious rites we perform as opposing candidates harangue the multitudes who finally march to the polls to prolong the rule of their champion, to thrust him, ungratefully, back into the void of private life, or to raise to eminence a new tribune of the people. What kinds of appeals enable a candidate to win the favor of the great god, The People? What circumstances move voters to shift their preferences in this direction or that? What clever propaganda tactic or slogan led to this result? What mannerism of oratory or style of rhetoric produced another outcome? What band of electors rallied to this candidate to save the day for him? What policy of state attracted the devotion of another bloc of voters? What action repelled a third sector of the electorate? (Key, 1966:1)

Key thought that, while "many individual voters act in odd ways indeed . . . , in the large the electorate behaves about as rationally and responsibly as we should expect, given the clarity of the alternatives presented to it and the character of the information available to it" (Key, 1966:7). ✑

*F*ree elections are vital to democracy. In the United States, elections occur frequently, the opportunity to become a candidate for elective public office is widely distributed, and thousands of Americans choose to run. In our presidential elections, about 90 million citizens go to the polls to register their choices. The political campaign—with its hoopla, vigorous electioneering, and media blitzes—mobilizes voters to win elections. On election day, we find out what the verdict of the people is. The collective choices of the electorate are final, at least for the two- or four-year terms that politicians serve, and give our leaders the authority and power to govern.

Finding out about political campaigning in this country could involve a massive search for information about the struggle for literally thousands of offices in cities, towns, counties, and states across the nation. Our focus is narrower; in this chapter, we concentrate on national elective offices. There are only 537, and election to them is provided in the U.S. Constitution. We choose a president and a vice president, two senators from each of the 50 states, and 435 representatives. It is true that the center of gravity of our national politics lies in the great quadrennial choice that Americans make for president. Less dramatic but almost equally important are elections of members of Congress.

In the following pages, we deal with several central questions about political campaigns and elections. First, we ask, "How does the American electoral system work?" In this country, campaigning and elections take place according to a fairly complicated system. There are many elections and many offices. The president is elected by means of a complex electoral college system. Members of Congress are chosen in districts scattered across the land. Understanding our elections requires a good grasp of the way our electoral system works.

Our second question puts the average citizen into the electoral process: "How can citizens vote in elections?" Since we might expect Americans to partake in elections more readily if they think the results make a difference, we also ask, "Do elections matter?"

About campaigning, we raise a third question: "How are national political campaigns organized and conducted?" Here, we see interesting differences between presidential and congressional campaigning and we have a chance to explore the importance of the candidate-centered campaign versus the party-centered campaign. Because money plays a crucial role in the modern political campaign, we also want to ask about the extent of political giving and spending. In the end, we raise this question: "Does money win elections?"

Our fourth question is, "Who are the Democratic and Republican voters?" These are the people who fulfill their civic obligation by going to the polls to vote. Their role is especially important in a democracy. They determine which candidates will hold public offices. We present a profile of the voters for the two major parties in which prominent traits are high-

An invitation to vote in an election. On election day, signs saying "Vote here" accompanied by the flag go up at fire stations, schools, courthouses, and other public buildings to denote polling stations.

lighted. These traits include voters' socioeconomic status, race, ethnic and religious background, sex, age, and trade union membership.

Fifth, we ask, "What factors explain the voting behavior of Americans?" Everyone knows that it is hard to explain why people do what they do. People often do not act as they are expected to act or do what they say they will do. Human behavior is highly complex; it cannot be "explained" by any simple set of factors. If how you vote depends on what you had for breakfast, a social scientist will have trouble using data from national samples to discover that cause of your behavior. Your behavior is *idiosyncratic*—unique to you as an individual. However, certain factors that affect how people vote pertain to millions of voters and thus can be analyzed in a systematic way. These factors—party ties, candidate appeal, campaign issues—have a predictable effect on many people.

Finally, we paint the shape of our presidential elections on a large canvas. We classify elections and show that these periodic political events have different forms. Some elections have been "repeats" of previous elections. In such elections, voting patterns and the election results repeat those of the previous election. Some elections are "test patterns" for future changes. Elections of this kind show changing voter alignments that forecast changes in political leadership. Some elections reflect sharp changes in voting patterns. These "critical elections" produce new and different leaders. Every four years, with each presidential election, students of American politics have an opportunity to observe yet another electoral event and to assay its wider significance. The presidential elections of the 1980s show how these great contests can both continue and depart from past trends. We will discuss these presidential elections as case studies.

To understand why elections turn out the way they do, it is essential to know something about the "system." Many Americans think that the presidential election takes place only on election day, but it is more complicated than that. We therefore begin by unraveling the complexities of electing the president, and then we turn to congressional elections.

HOW THE ELECTORAL SYSTEM WORKS

On January 6, 1981, members of the House and Senate met in a joint session at which Vice President Walter Mondale presided. Four "tellers," two for the House and two for the Senate, publicly counted the electoral votes for president and vice president. Of the 538 votes, Ronald Reagan and his running mate, George Bush, received 489 votes; Jimmy Carter and Walter Mondale received only 49 votes. As the presiding officer, Mondale had to announce that Ronald Reagan had been elected president and George Bush had been elected vice president. That was the official election. The 538 electors had been chosen by the voters in the election of November 4, 1980. They had gone to their respective state capitals on December 15 to cast their electoral votes, and their votes had then been sent to the president of the Senate. But the president and vice president were not *constitutionally* elected until January 6, 1981. The same process took place between November 1988 and January 1989. How does this system work?

The Constitution does not provide for the *popular* election of the president. Though many of us do not realize it, we do not vote directly for the president. Rather, we choose electors who later officially elect the president. The Constitution provides that these electors be chosen in each state "in such manner as the legislature thereof may direct." Every state legislature now provides that electors be chosen by popular vote. But in the 1800s, electors were often chosen by the legislatures themselves. Today the **electoral college system** is a central feature of the "strategic environment within which the drama of a presidential election is played" (Polsby and Wildavsky, 1984:50).

Selecting Presidential Electors

Each state gets a number of **presidential electors** equal to the number of its senators and representatives. So each state gets two electors for its two senators and an added number equal to the number of its House members. Since a state's representation in the House is based on population, the states with the largest populations get the most electoral votes. California, with two senators and 45 House members, now has 47 electoral votes; the other states' electoral votes are figured in the same way. There are 435

House members and 100 senators, so the states' electoral votes add up to 535. In 1961, the 23rd Amendment to the Constitution provided three electoral votes for the District of Columbia, bringing the total number of electoral votes to 538.

Nearly all presidential electors are elected on the **general ticket system.** This means that in each state all of the electoral candidates for each party run together as a slate. Thus, when a voter votes for president, he or she is really voting for a number of electors equal to the state's congressional delegation. The one exception is Maine, which adopted a district system in 1969. Under this system, two of the state's four electors are chosen statewide and one is chosen in each of the state's two congressional districts. In the presidential elections of 1972, 1976, and 1980, the Republican candidate carried both districts. Thus, the Maine electoral vote was not divided in these elections.

Where do the electors come from? This is determined by state law. In 1980, electors were nominated by state political party conventions in 38 states. In most of the other states, electors are picked by state party committees or in primary elections. In Pennsylvania, each presidential candidate is required to choose the electors for his party. Thus, nearly all of the individuals who serve as candidates for presidential elector are chosen by political parties. Usually, they are chosen to confer a minor honor recognizing loyal service.

In the November election, voters choose among slates of presidential electors. In most states, however, the electors' names do not appear on the ballot; only the names of the presidential and vice presidential candidates appear. In 1980, only the candidates' names were listed on the ballot in 38 states and the District of Columbia; in 12 states, both the candidates' and the electors' names appeared. But whether or not the electors' names are on the ballot, the voter is choosing electors. In each state, the slate of electors with the most votes wins. Stated differently, the presidential candidate who polls a plurality (more votes than anyone else, but not necessarily a majority) of a state's popular vote wins *all* of the state's electoral votes.

Casting the Electoral Vote

Presidential electors are for the most part loyal party people. They are not expected to use independent judgment in voting. Rather, they are expected to vote for the nominees of their party's national nominating convention. Most of the time, that is what they do. Their voting is so automatic that, as we have seen, only the candidates' names are on the ballot in most states.

In 21 states, presidential electors must by law vote for the nominees of their national party convention or the presidential candidate receiving a plurality of their state's popular votes, or they are pledged to support the party nominees because this is required by the party organizations. In the other states, electors only need to follow the duties prescribed by the Constitution and the laws of the country or their state.

These conditions have brought about the so-called **faithless elector** problem, which arises because an elector can vote for a candidate other than the winner of the popular vote in his or her state. From 1820 to 1944, this never occurred; but in six subsequent elections (1948, 1956, 1960, 1968, 1972, and 1976), electors voted for a person other than the one entitled to the vote. Most recently, in 1976, a Republican elector from Spokane voted for Ronald Reagan instead of Gerald R. Ford, who was entitled to the vote since he had won the popular vote of Washington. In none of these elections did the defection change the election outcome. The faithless elector problem is more hypothetical than real.

Counting the Electoral Votes

The electoral votes are officially counted before a joint session of Congress in the January after the popular election. To win the electoral count, a candidate must receive an **absolute majority**—270 of the 538 electoral votes. If no candidate gets a majority, the House proceeds to elect a president and the Senate elects a vice president. In such a case, 50 votes are cast for president in the House, each state delegation casting one vote. Thomas Jefferson was elected president by the House of Representatives in 1801 because he and Aaron Burr each got 73 electoral votes. No candidate had a majority of the electoral vote in 1825, and the House then elected John Quincy Adams. For more than 150 years, this backup election procedure has not been required.

In the electoral college system, a candidate with a popular vote plurality can lose the electoral vote. In 1876, Democrat Samuel J. Tilden got 254,000 more popular votes than Republican Rutherford B. Hayes. But Hayes became president because he got 185 electoral votes to Tilden's 184. There was widespread fraud in the election, though, so no one can be sure that the popular votes were correctly counted.

A purer case occurred in 1888. Democrat Grover Cleveland got 91,000 more popular votes than Republican Benjamin Harrison, but Harrison got 233 of the 401 electoral votes. Harrison had won several key states by thin margins but had lost other states by large margins. President Cleveland accepted his defeat, and Harrison became president. Cleveland got his revenge in 1892 by clearly defeating Harrison.

No such peculiarity of the system has occurred for nearly a century. It is possible, however, by figuring different patterns of popular votes, to show that recent close presidential elections might have resulted in an electoral victory for the minority candidate. (This can be done easily for 1960 and 1968.)

Counting electoral votes. The president is officially elected when the electoral votes are counted before a joint session of Congress. Here, in January 1961, the official count of electoral votes for the November 1960 election is being taken in the House chamber. The count showed that John F. Kennedy won 303 electoral votes. Ironically, Vice President Richard M. Nixon [seated below the flag], Kennedy's opponent, was required to announce the result to the assembled members of Congress.

Many presidents have not received a popular majority. But they got more popular votes than their opponents and a majority of the electoral votes. In nearly two fifths of the presidential elections since 1824, the winner has won less than half of the popular vote. Lincoln was elected in 1860 with less than 40 percent of the popular vote; his closest opponent, Stephen A. Douglas, got 30 percent of the popular vote. More recently, Nixon was elected with 43.4 percent of the popular vote versus 42.7 percent for Hubert Humphrey. Because Nixon resigned, Gerald R. Ford became president in 1974 without having been elected at all!

The Impact of the Electoral College System

The electoral college system has one major impact on the election of the president: it greatly magnifies in electoral votes the popular vote of the winner and greatly diminishes that of the loser. The winner gets a manufactured majority in electoral votes. For instance, Nixon beat Humphrey in 1968 by less than 1 percent of the popular vote but received 56 percent of the electoral vote. In 1972, George McGovern got 38 percent of the popular vote (compared to Nixon's 61 percent) but won only 3 percent of the electoral vote. And Ronald Reagan received just a bare majority of the popular vote in 1980 (50.7 percent), yet he got 91 percent of the electoral vote.

The magnification of electoral majorities occurs because of the winner-take-all rule. The candidate who wins a mere plurality of a state's popular vote wins *all* of that state's electoral votes. This is called the **Matthew**

FIGURE 9–1   Democratic candidates' popular votes and electoral votes, 1880–1984

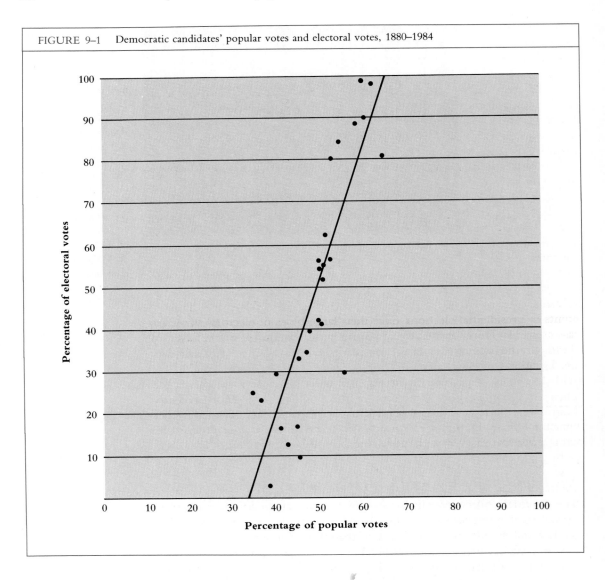

effect. In Matthew 13:12 it is written: "For whosoever hath, to him shall be given, and he shall have more abundance; but whosoever hath not, from him shall be taken away even that he hath." That is the way the electoral college system works. Presidential candidates who have many popular votes are given electoral votes in even greater proportion; candidates who have few popular votes are given electoral votes in much smaller proportion.

The relationship between popular and electoral vote percentages for Democratic presidential candidates from 1880 to 1984 is given in Figure 9–1. This figure shows that candidates who only get about 40 percent of the popular vote tend to get less than a fifth of the electoral votes; those who get about half of the popular vote tend to get about half of the electoral votes; and those who get roughly 60 percent of the popular vote are apt to get more than 80 percent of the electoral votes. Though a president may win a small victory in the popular election, he will get a decisive majority in the electoral vote.

The electoral college system also gives small but measurable advantages to the people in some states and hurts the people in other states. This happens because, despite population, each state gets two electoral votes for its two senators and because of the **winner-take-all rule.** Alaska, with a 1980 census population of 400,481, got three electoral votes in the 1984 election; Delaware, with a 1980 population of 594,338, also got three electoral votes. The "voting power" of Delawareans was not as great as that of Alaskans. But the winner-take-all rule gives the greatest influence in presidential elections to the largest states—California, New York, Pennsylvania, Texas, Ohio, Illinois, and Michigan. These states are the focal points in presidential elections since their large blocs of electoral votes are cast as units. Thus, the urbanites of the populous states of the East and West gain the biggest advantage from the electoral college system (Yunker and Longley, 1976).

Reforming the Electoral College

For many years, there have been proposals to change the method of electing the president (Sayre and Parris, 1970:69–134). These proposals include casting the electoral vote automatically, dispensing with presidential electors, which would get rid of the problem of the faithless elector; proportioning the electoral vote in each state according to the popular vote for each candidate, which would abolish the winner-take-all rule; and adopting the third and choosing electors by districts rather than on a statewide basis, which would make the electoral vote more proportional to the popular vote (Peirce and Longley, 1981: 131–80).

By far the most popular proposed reform of the electoral college has been the so-called **direct vote plan.** Under this proposal, the electoral college system would be abolished and the president and vice president would be elected by a direct popular vote. This reform was identified with former Senator Birch Bayh (D–Ind.) His plan involved a direct popular vote if the winning ticket got at least 40 percent of the popular vote; if not, a runoff election would be held between the two leading tickets. Such a reform passed the House of Representatives in 1969 but was killed in the Senate in 1970. In 1977, President Carter included the direct vote proposal in his package of election system reforms, but nothing came of it. Because

PRACTICE OF POLITICS

Rules of the Electoral College Game

Getting elected president and vice president of the United States involves the following rules of the electoral college game.

1. Each state gets the same number of presidential electors as it has members of the U. S. Congress; the District of Columbia gets three electors. Altogether, there are 538 electoral votes to be cast.

2. Presidential electors run in each state (and the District of Columbia) on a statewide basis. The electors of each party run as a slate. The slate of electors getting the most popular votes is elected in each state. This is the winner-take-all rule.

3. To be elected president or vice president, candidates must win an absolute majority, 50 percent plus one, of the electoral vote. With a total of 538 presidential electors, this means that a candidate must get at least 270 electoral votes in order to win.

4. If no candidate wins a majority of the electoral vote, the House of Representatives proceeds to elect a president and the Senate elects a vice president.

such a change requires a constitutional amendment, its adoption is difficult.

The direct vote plan would eliminate what many see as the main problems of the present system: the faithless elector, the winner-take-all rule, the two electoral votes given to each state regardless of population, and the possibility that the popular-vote winner will not get a majority of the electoral votes. But critics of this plan worry about possible undesirable effects. They fear that the two-party system, fragile enough under the present system, might be further weakened. A candidate could be elected who had great support in some parts of the country but little support in others, which would make it difficult for him to represent the whole country. The outcome of the election would be more affected by differences in voter turnout among the states. Critics of the direct vote plan also question the desirability of the runoff election, which would be expensive, and they doubt whether enough Americans would take part in a runoff election (Longley and Braun, 1975: 66–69; Best, 1975). Americans are not very prone to vote in national elections as it is.

The electoral college, though not well understood by most of us, is a controversial institution. It has a subtle yet potent impact on presidential politics. The founders wanted presidents to be chosen, not by the people at large, but by a group of people who would use their own knowledge and judgment. This hope waned with the emergence of popular candidates, nationwide campaigns, and political parties. Yet the electoral college itself remains as a reminder of the founders' intentions. It is a potential vehicle for distorting the popular will in choosing our chief executive.

The Congressional Election System

Presidential elections are dramatic, and the presidential election system is important. But the congressional election system is equally important. Its most salient features are the apportionment of members, the creation of districts, and the decision rules for election.

Seats in Congress are apportioned among the states according to the requirements of Article I of the Constitution. The Constitution prescribes equal representation of the *states* in the U.S. Senate; each state elects two senators. Moreover, the Constitution awards each state at least one member of the U.S. House regardless of population. The additional House members—from the 51st to the 435th—are apportioned among the states by population.

Apportionment takes place every 10 years, after the federal census. As population shifts, states gain or lose congressional seats. Today's shifts pit the older industrial Northeast against the growing South and West—the Frostbelt against the Sunbelt. After the 1980 census, 17 seats shifted. The big winners were Florida, California, and Texas; the big losers were New York, Illinois, Ohio, and Pennsylvania. Census results are so important to states and regions that census taking itself has become highly political. The 1980 census, for instance, was plagued by lawsuits charging that certain areas or racial groups were undercounted.

Once the census has been completed and the states have been awarded their congressional seats, congressional district boundary lines must be drawn. Here, several observations can be made. First, the so-called **single-member district** system is used: Each state is divided into a number of districts equal to the number of congressional seats to which it is entitled. This is in contrast to the **multiple-member district** system, in which each constituency chooses several representatives. The latter system is used in some European democracies and, in fact, in the election of some American state legislators.

Second, congressional districts are formed by the state legislatures. Following a change in the number of congressional seats awarded to a state, or in the state's population, the legislature must redistrict. In 1964, the U.S. Supreme Court held, in the famous case of *Wesberry v. Sanders*, that congressional districting must be done according to the "one person, one vote" principle—in other words, on the basis of equal population. Later Supreme Court decisions required congressional districts to be equal in population within each state. If a state legislature fails to meet this stan-

FIGURE 9–2   Gerrymandering–old and new

The Original Gerrymander—
Massachusetts 1812

California Congressional
Districts—Los Angeles
Area 1984

dard, a federal court is likely to order elections to be conducted in court-drawn equal-population districts.

Third, because districts must be equal in population, the time-honored practice of **gerrymandering** has been given new life. This is the art of drawing district boundary lines to gain the most partisan advantage. In the early 19th century, during the governorship of Elbridge Gerry, a Massachusetts legislative district was oddly shaped for partisan purposes. When it was suggested that the district wiggled across the landscape like a salamander, someone suggested that the district should be called a "gerrymander." In Figure 9–2, we show the original gerrymander and a modern illustration. There are two gerrymandering techniques, jokingly called *packing* and *cracking*. **Packing** a district is drawing the lines to include as many of one party's voters as possible. This limits that party's seats or makes the district safe for an incumbent. In **cracking**, an area of one party's strength is split between two or more districts to minimize that party's voting leverage.

Finally, legislators are chosen by **plurality vote.** The candidate who gets the most votes wins; he or she need not win by a majority. Thus, congressional elections have a winner-take-all feature. Since there is only one seat to win in each congressional district, the candidate with the most votes wins "all" of the seats. Consequently, there is a Matthew effect in congressional elections. Though not as sharply defined as in the presidential system, the multiplier in congressional elections rewards the majority part quite handsomely. In the 1982 congressional election, the Democrats, with 56 percent of the popular votes for members of the House, won 62 percent of the House seats and the Republicans, with 43 percent of the popular votes, garnered only 38 percent of the House seats. The electoral system persistently gives the Democrats some advantage nationally. This is partly because they tend to win in smaller congressional districts and in those with low voter turnouts. But in several states, the electoral system favors the Republicans in electing state legislators (Tufte, 1973: 543–44); it also favored the Republicans in congressional elections held prior to the New Deal, when the GOP was dominant. Of course, the partisan advantages of the Matthew effect are magnified if there has been widespread gerrymandering.

Within the electoral system, candidates vie for offices and citizens cast their votes. In so doing, they provide drama in important national events—presidential and congressional elections. Because our elections are significant events involving partisan choices by voters, we should examine patterns of voting behavior. Doing this will set the stage for summarizing the results of the most recent major electoral event—the 1988 presidential election.

Elections take place more frequently and more regularly in the United States than anywhere else in the world. They are so much a part of our everyday lives that we often take them for granted. Yet it would be impossible to have democratic government, as we understand it, without free elections.

CITIZENS IN FREE ELECTIONS

Choosing to Vote in Elections

Our Constitution does not say much about elections and, in particular, about which people are qualified to vote. In the original Constitution, all that was said about eligibility to vote was that "the electors in each state shall have the qualifications requisite for electors of the most numerous branch of the state legislature" (see Article I, Section 2 and the 17th

Amendment). Various amendments to the Constitution prohibited the states from denying the right to vote to certain classes of people.

In 1870, the 15th Amendment was adopted, protecting the right of blacks to vote; in 1920, the 19th Amendment assured the voting rights of women; in 1961, the 23rd Amendment gave residents of the District of Columbia (Washington, D.C.) the right to choose presidential electors as if they were living in one of the 50 states; in 1964, the 24th Amendment guaranteed that the right to vote could not be denied because of failure to pay a poll tax; and in 1971, the 26th Amendment extended voting rights to all persons 18 years of age or older.

Within these constraints of the federal Constitution and a few federal laws (providing for election dates, protecting the voting rights of minority citizens, regulating campaign spending), elections in this country are almost completely run by the *states*. And, in fact, elections are mainly administered by local governments under the control of state laws. The states run elections not only for state and local officers but also for national officers—the president and vice president and members of Congress.

Actually, the states administer four kinds of elections. One kind is the **primary election.** In presidential primaries, voters select delegates to the national presidential nominating conventions; in so-called direct primaries, voters choose candidates for local or state offices or for the U.S. House of Representatives and Senate. Another kind is the **general election,** in which officeholders are chosen from among the candidates nominated previously.

Yet another kind of election is called the **initiative and referendum.** Here, citizens may adopt legislation directly by voting on propositions— either initiated by petition or referred to the people by action of the state legislature. California is the state most noted for its direct legislation; the most publicized example is Proposition 13, passed by Californians in 1977, which required cuts in property taxes. Then, there is the **recall election,** in which officeholders may be voted out of office before their terms expire if they are unsatisfactory. Not all of the states have laws providing for the initiative, referendum, or recall.

Most Americans who are 18 years old or older can make themselves eligible to vote in elections if they want to do so. The emphasis in this country is on *want to*. Americans can choose to vote or not to vote. We do not, like some countries, have **compulsory voting,** a system in which citizens are fined if they fail to vote. If Americans wish to vote, they must (in every state but North Dakota) be *registered* to vote. This is not a difficult requirement, but meeting it does require some forethought on the part of would-be voters. In most of the states, prospective voters must register some number of days before the primary or general election.

State registration requirements encourage maximum participation in some states, where people can register by mail, registrars go to the workplace or the neighborhood, or people can register at the polling place on election day. In other states, would-be voters must plan ahead by getting

Voting on propositions. These enthusiastic supporters of Proposition 13, the California tax limitation initiative adopted in 1978, are celebrating their victory at a campaign headquarters in a Los Angeles hotel.

themselves registered before the books have been closed. But many Americans do not register to vote even where doing so is easy.

In most of the other democratic countries, registration of voters is a government responsibility—it is the job of a government agency to see that all eligible people are signed up. In this country, registration is voluntary. Voters must take the initiative to register, and they can decide not to be registered if they wish. Perhaps most of those who decide not to bother to register do not think that elections matter.

Do Elections Matter?

In one sense, it is easy to see that elections matter. Elections give voters control over who the officeholders are, so that they can, given a competitive choice, install one person or set of persons in office instead of another person or set of persons. The voters can "throw the rascals out" if they disapprove of them or if they prefer other officeholders. Although Americans more often return incumbents to office than throw them out, electoral defeat is always possible and challengers frequently win office. American politicians are "unsafe at any margin"—they may be ousted in an election even after having won a long string of comfortable victories. They "run scared," fearing electoral defeat and attuning their behavior to their perceptions of voters' preferences. So voters can determine which individuals will occupy elective offices.

A more difficult issue is the impact of elections on public policies. Most of the scholarly research on elections has concerned why people vote in the way they do. Students of voting behavior recognize that citizens may

Contenders for the 1988 Democratic presidential nomination vied for a "southern identity" when they competed for convention delegates in southern primaries, all of which were held on a day known as Super Tuesday. This cartoon depicts [left to right] Sen. Albert Gore, Jr., of Tennessee, Rep. Richard A. Gephardt of Missouri, Gov. Bruce Babbitt of Arizona, Rev. Jesse Jackson of Illinois, Sen. Joseph R. Biden, Jr., of Delaware, Gov. Michael S. Dukakis of Massachusetts, and Sen. Paul Simon of Illinois.

engage in **retrospective voting** (see Fiorina, 1981). They may size up the performance of incumbent candidates, assess whether they are economically better or worse off than they were before those incumbents took office, or take stock of the policy performance of the government in the realms that concern them most. Then, they may make choices in an election in accord with their dissatisfactions, their feelings of well-being, or their perceptions of the incumbents' effectiveness. Even presidential election outcomes have hinged on retrospective voting, as happened in 1980 when Ronald Reagan defeated the incumbent president, Jimmy Carter, because many voters thought that President Carter had not done a very good job as president, that he should have been able to get the American hostages in Iran released, and that he had not developed effective means for licking the twin problems of inflation and unemployment.

Political scientists have studied in only a limited way the effects that election outcomes have on public policy. Sometimes, of course, the policy effects of elections are direct and dramatic, as when Proposition 13 in California substantially reduced property taxes and, temporarily, the provision of government services. But the outcomes of ordinary elections, in which voters merely choose among candidates, are not likely to have a direct influence on governmental policies unless the candidates or parties make their policy stands clear and distinct and then carry out their promises if they win.

In many election contests, candidates deliberately avoid clear-cut stands on issues, thinking that taking a position will only alienate some group of voters. These candidates behave like the person who ran for governor in a southern state a few years ago. In his campaign, he said, "I stand with my friends on racial segregation. I have some friends who are for segregation; I have some friends who are against segregation." Sometimes candidates seek to suppress even their party label in the hope that voters will not use issues as a basis for making choices on election day.

The Democratic and Republican parties express their collective stands on issues in their **party platforms**. These are manifestos drawn up by committees of party leaders and ratified at party conventions. In recent presidential elections, the national parties have offered platforms that showed substantial differences between them on major questions of national policy.

The conventional political wisdom is that the party platforms are meaningless. In truth, however, a party's platform *is* important, "not as an inspired gospel to which politicians resort for policy guidance," but "because it summarizes, crystallizes, and presents to the voters the character of the party coalition" (Pomper and Lederman, 1980: 173). The platforms indicate the parties' past positions on major issues and their future intentions. Our constitutional system does not make it very easy for the political parties to carry out their platform promises. But when conditions are such that they could do so (when a party has, at a minimum, a majority in both houses of Congress and control of the White House), the two major parties carry out those promises pretty well. So elections in which voters decide along party lines can matter on that account.

Elections also matter when the parties and candidates offer voters a real and substantial choice. And elections seem to matter most when the parties present voters with major differences over issues at times in history when great changes in the basic loyalties of voters are under way. Election-driven policy changes seem to be at their peak after a so-called **critical election**—one in which new issues have arisen, there is a new majority party, and a realignment in the partisan attachments of voters has taken place (see Ginsberg and Stone, 1986). Although not all of these conditions were met in the 1980 or 1984 presidential elections, the Reagan election victories had important policy consequences, nonetheless, for the state of the economy and for the defense establishment. Even in a democracy like the United States, elections may be a sham, a mere popularity contest without any substance. In a more perfect union, good men and women strive to prevent their democratic institutions from becoming moribund. Elections can matter a great deal.

The political campaign is a vital part of the process of democratic elections. Through the campaign, voters are aroused, mobilized, and informed—if the campaigners are doing their jobs. But the way in which the electoral system works helps shape the focus, targeting, planning, and conduct of campaigns. Because the large industrial, urban states provide the major share of presidential electors to candidates, the campaign concentrates on those states. Because the electoral system makes voters in the big states—New York, California, Pennsylvania, Ohio, Illinois, Michigan—count for more in the final reckoning, presidential contenders concentrate their campaigns in those states.

CAMPAIGNING FOR OFFICE

Campaigns can make elections matter. When a candidate's campaign is effectively organized, sufficiently staffed, properly financed, and perceptively conducted, it can activate or mobilize support among voters. From the viewpoint of the citizens of a democracy, the campaign may be crucial. The job of the campaigner is to arouse the electorate, stimulate and educate citizens, and mobilize voters on the day of decision.

At campaign time, the proper working of the electoral process depends mightily on the candidates for office. The nominated candidate has won only half of the battle. Now comes the general election campaign with its noisy mix of personal appearances, speechmaking, advertising, and symbolic appeals. Candidates fresh from wresting the nomination in primary election contests may see the general election campaign as more of the same. Candidates who gained nomination by an easier path—say, acclamation at a party convention—are brought before the public for the first time during the election campaign. All candidates, though, now face the entire electorate, not just their own partisans. They must organize, raise money, plot campaign strategy, and conduct the campaign effectively.

Organizing for the Campaign

From the candidate's-eye view, the campaign organization is a temporary thing. The candidate's staff, war chest, agenda, and activities will wither away after election day. Moreover, the realities and uncertainties of the upcoming battle impel candidates to keep the organization flexible so that it can adapt to unexpected developments and roll with the punches.

Campaign organization involves establishing headquarters and field organizations. This means attracting a good staff. A campaigner will need a campaign manager, preferably a professional with political experience. Since much of the organization's work is fund-raising, an effective staff is needed for this purpose. Given federal and state regulation of campaign financing these days, most campaigns will need the counsel of lawyers and accountants. Fund-raising efforts may necessitate campaign personnel who are expert in direct mail drives.

Where television is required for competitive campaigning, a campaign organization will need media consultants. And relations with the media may require the services of a press secretary. More traditional activities

Working in a campaign headquarters. In this sparsely furnished office, Bethesda, Maryland, campaign workers seek potential votes for congressional candidate Constance A. Morella. A liberal Republican, Morella was elected to Congress in 1986 after having served eight years in the Maryland legislature.

dictate a need for staff to coordinate grass-roots campaigning, do research work, and provide policy advice to the candidate. Scheduling staff will be needed to keep the candidate in effective touch with voters. The candidate's schedule, strategy, or stand on issues may be determined by taking the public's pulse, so the organization may require a pollster.

Although a campaign organization's ultimate purpose is to win elections, a visit to a campaign headquarters would show you that most of its workers are not directly engaged in stimulating voters. Rather, "most of the campaign staff devotes most of its time to creating and maintaining the campaign organization"—mobilizing the resources of money and time from among the candidate's political supporters (Kayden, 1978, p. 61).

The political parties as well as the candidate's personal campaign staff are organized for campaigning. The national Republican and Democratic parties maintain substantial party headquarters in Washington, D.C., and there are counterparts in the state capitals. These party organizations provide invaluable campaign services to candidates—research, money, media advice and technical support, direct mail assistance, legal counsel, staff assistance on loan, field staff support, and even training for candidates and their staffs. Similar national party services are provided specifically to candidates for Congress by the campaign committees of the respective parties in the House of Representatives and the Senate.

Party- versus Candidate-Centered Campaigns

Students of elections have found it useful to distinguish between party-centered and candidate-centered campaigns. A **party-centered campaign** is one in which candidates are selected through the party apparatus or handpicked by the party leaders, the campaign organization is part of the party structure, the campaign appeals to voters' party loyalties, and the election system facilitates partisan choices. Accounts of American politics in the 19th century suggest that party-centered campaigning was prevalent in those days. And in more recent years, the political "machines" of some states and cities, such as that of Chicago's Mayor Richard Daley in the 1950s and 60s, have engaged in classic party-centered campaigns.

The **candidate-centered campaign** emphasizes the individual candidate who captures the nomination for an office without party support (perhaps in a freewheeling "open" primary), runs as an independent with his own campaign organization (often downplaying party labels), and raises campaign money from personal resources, friends, or political action committees (PACs). Such a candidate wants and receives little support from a party during the campaign and feels little sense of loyalty to it afterward.

The advent of the "television age," in which national and statewide political campaigns are heavily conducted on television, has fostered the candidate-centered campaign (see Salmore and Salmore, 1985). Escalation in the costs of running for office, fueled mainly by the extraordinary expense of television campaigning, has transferred the drawstrings of campaigning from party leaders and their organizations to media consultants, fund-raisers, direct mail specialists, and public relations experts.

Candidate-centered campaigning has taken politics out of the hands of party "bosses" and unrepresentative party organizations and made campaigns and elections more open, more public, more expensive, and more uncertain. The dangers of the new style of campaigning were exposed by the Watergate scandal of 1973. Richard Nixon's 1972 reelection campaign was taken out of the hands of the national Republican party and given over to the candidate's own committee—the Committee to Re-Elect the President, or CREEP. The Watergate scandal underscored the need for reform of campaign financing. But the subsequent Federal Election Campaign Act of 1974 itself encourages candidate-centered campaigning by fostering the proliferation of PACs with their contribution of money to individual candidates.

Campaign Strategy

The key decision faced by candidates and their managers is choosing a **campaign strategy**. This is the campaign's overall tone or thrust. It will determine how to deploy such resources as time, money, and personnel to produce a favorable voter response. To design a winning strategy, the candidate must first ponder these questions: What type of office am I seeking? Am I the incumbent or the challenger? Am I the candidate of the majority party or the minority party? Are my face and career familiar to the voters, or am I unknown? What images do the voters already have of me? What issues or problems are uppermost in the voters' minds? What resources—money, support, volunteer effort—will I command during the campaign?

The campaign is affected by the level of the office being sought. Candidates for president, for instance, can be sure that their name and face will reach the voters. The mass media's relentless coverage assures that. But many electoral contests attract little media attention, which leaves the task of communication more or less to the candidates themselves.

The incumbency factor

Incumbency normally, though not always, works in the officeholder's favor. Every incumbent, from a city council member to the president, has resources and privileges that can be used to draw public attention and build support. Incumbents are better known than challengers. They have built-in ways of reaching voters—speeches, press coverage, newsletters, staff help, ability to help constituents, and sheer familiarity with the issues.

Even presidential challengers, though by no means ignored, find it hard to match the pomp and circumstance that the president commands in performing official duties. Running for reelection in 1972, President Nixon visited mainland China during the New Hampshire primary and Moscow during the California primary. These publicity coups robbed Democratic contenders of valuable exposure during two critical periods. In 1980, Carter stopped campaigning altogether under the pretext that the Iranian hostage crisis demanded his full attention. This approach is sometimes known as "campaigning from the White House rose garden." It has the advantage of showing the candidate in a presidential role rather than as just another politician.

Incumbency can be a liability, though. Popular unrest, policy fiascos, or scandals can turn the table against officeholders. Faced with inflation at home and national humiliation abroad, President Carter was the target of discontent in 1980. Challenger Ronald Reagan's strategy, devised by his survey analyst, Richard Wirthlin, was twofold: first to establish Reagan's credibility as a reliable leader, not an extremist; second, to spotlight Carter's record. In his TV debate with Carter, when Reagan asked people whether they were better off than they had been four years earlier, his strategy hit home.

Majority-minority party status is often difficult to assess; states or districts vary widely and split-ticket voting is common. In one-party areas, majority-party candidates have little need to campaign; their nomination is tantamount to election. Opponents may drop campaigning for the same reason. Or they may take desperate measures to catch the voters' attention.

Democrats have been the majority choice for party identifiers since the Roosevelt realignment of the 1930s. So a typical Democratic campaign stresses party loyalty, past party achievements, and voter registration. The theory is that the higher the turnout, the better for the majority party. Republican campaigns, in contrast, aim at blurring party differences: the GOP has conducted "me-too" campaigns (1940–48), run a popular hero (Eisenhower in 1952 and 1956), or exploited splits in the majority party (Nixon in 1968 and 1972). The 1980–84 Reagan strategy was a combination of all these approaches: the candidate was a movie actor who quoted Franklin Roosevelt and wooed dissident Democrats.

What are the voters thinking?

Other questions affecting strategy can be answered by public opinion surveys. Skilled analysts can pinpoint popular views and suggest ways of dealing with them. Well-known candidates try to cash in on "name recognition"; candidates who are not well known have their names repeated over and over again in advertising. Candidates with a reputation for openness and friendliness highlight these qualities; those who are less glib may stress experience and competence. Candidates who have made tough, unpopular decisions are billed as persons of courage. And so on.

As popular moods change, so too do desired candidate images. In crises, voters prefer experience, competence, and reassurance. After the Watergate scandal, voters seemed to value honesty and openness above all other virtues.

Campaign strategy is often distilled into a single theme or slogan. John F. Kennedy in 1960 symbolized a fresh young generation. He used the theme "Get America Moving Again." In 1972, President Nixon's advisers saw that voters respected the presidency but were lukewarm toward Nixon. Hence, they adopted the theme "Reelect the President." In 1980, the Republicans' slogan "Vote Republican. For a change!" stressed that the GOP was not to blame for the country's ills.

Slogans are also employed to simplify campaign arguments and pierce through public and media indifference. In 1984, for instance, Gary Hart used the "new ideas" theme to tap voters' uneasiness about the past Democratic record. To cast doubt on Hart's theme, Walter Mondale grabbed a slogan from America's fast-food wars ("Where's the beef?"). The slogan may not have been edifying, but it was not ignored.

Conducting the Campaign

Implementing strategy is the grueling job of the candidate's organizers. Contenders used to rely on party leaders to wage their battles; in certain places, this is still done. But party organizations are typically incomplete and fragmented; they command neither the workers nor the money to mount effective campaigns. The old party pros have been replaced by new professionals, available for sizable fees.

Many campaign management firms offer a complete range of services. They can draw up strategies and use them according to the candidate's desires or pocketbook. Other firms offer special services: survey research, direct mail appeals, coordinating volunteers, advertising, and financial management and accounting (Sabato, 1981).

Helped by modern technology, these firms take on projects that dwarf the efforts of even the best-oiled old-style machines. Richard Viguerie—whose company specializes in direct mail appeals—estimated that his computers spewed out 50 million letters on behalf of conservative groups and candidates during 1977. And that was a political off year. The mailings yielded between $15 million and $20 million, which about equaled the combined take of the Republican and Democratic national committees (Shogan, 1977: 10).

Contacting voters

A key phase of campaigns is direct voter appeal, sometimes through door-to-door canvassing. In strong party areas, this was a basic duty of ward, precinct, and block captains. The political machine leaders' ability to "deliver the vote" was the ultimate test of success. In certain places, the candidates still give out "walking-around money" so that local captains can get out the vote by providing small financial inducements for voting.

Today few areas boast tight organization. So candidates must recruit workers, usually volunteers. These workers are brought in to campaign door-to-door, make sure that voters are registered, supply campaign literature, and get out the vote. Such workers may run telephone banks in central headquarters or walk the precincts. They are not only expected to get out the vote; they also have to produce large crowds for candidate appearances and party rallies.

Using the media

With TV, candidates can partially bypass face-to-face voter appeals by using ads and news programs. Ad agencies prepare radio and television "spots" that display the candidate's themes and messages.

Because TV is an expensive, broad medium, its appeal is general. The candidate's TV ads therefore embody his or her basic strategy. In the 1984 race for the Democratic nomination, front-runner Walter Mondale's ads ignored name recognition but stressed his experience and toughness. His most notable ad featured a red "hotline" telephone with the message that Mondale was the most seasoned candidate for handling international crises. In contrast, Gary Hart's TV ads stressed his new generation of leadership, offering "new ideas." Radio stations reach more specialized groups of listeners. Thus, candidates can tailor their appeals to a station's audiences.

The mix of appeals

The population of an electoral district dictates which techniques will be most effective. Heavy media campaigns are most economical if only a few newspapers or radio-TV outlets cover the entire area, with a small spillover into neighboring areas. For a congressional candidate in a huge city such as New York or Los Angeles, TV ads would be too expensive and would reach millions outside the district.

Local voter traditions also affect campaigns. Appearances at plant gates or union halls may suffice for some areas. But shopping center rallies and coffee hours are more the style elsewhere. The delicate job of the planner is to mesh the candidate's message with the voters' special traits.

A matter of resources

Techniques must suit the candidate's resources. They must mesh not only with finances but also with volunteer support, party backing, and personal skills.

Money is a must for nearly everything in a campaign. Just about any technique can be used if there is enough money to pay for it. To be sure, money is not everything in politics. But many campaigns fail for lack of it; many others expend much of their energy in trying to get it. What politicans call **early money**—money available at the start for planning and purchasing ads and radio-TV time—is most useful. With such seed money, the candidate can gain visibility and credibility that will mobilize workers and attract more money. Candidates who face stiff contests in both the primary and the general election have a really tough decision to make. Should they ration their funds and risk losing the primary, or should they spend a lot on the primary and risk running out of funds later?

Nonmonetary resources are often just as valuable as money. They give a candidate exposure that would otherwise have to be paid for. Support from a strong party machine or a powerful union may attract free publicity and volunteers. Large numbers of excited volunteers or skilled operatives are also valuable.

MONEY AND ELECTIONS

Our campaigns have become very costly. In 1984, some $700 million was spent on campaigns for federal office. Half went into the presidential race, half into the congressional races. There is no mystery surrounding the increase in campaign costs. Inflation accounts for some of it, as does population growth and a growing electorate. And many candidates use new, high-cost methods to reach the voters. The most expensive method is TV, but computer mailings and other expensive appeals are also used. Opening up the process and using nonparty campaigners have also boosted campaign costs. An old-style campaign involved a caucus or convention nomination and scores of workers for canvassing. It was obviously much cheaper than a modern campaign with large-scale primaries and media appeals.

Haves and Have-Nots

A more important issue is how money is spread among candidates. Fiscally speaking, some candidates are more equal than others. The most expensive campaign in the history of the U.S. Senate was the 1984 Senate contest in North Carolina between right-wing Senator Jesse Helms (R) and moderate Governor James B. Hunt (D). Around $20 million was spent, much of it pouring in from out of state. Two years earlier, department store heir Mark Dayton spent $7 million—nearly all his own money—in a losing bid to unseat Minnesota GOP incumbent Dave Durenberger. The average Senate campaign in a competitive state may cost millions; House races often cost $200,000 or more.

Incumbents have a double-barreled advantage over challengers: they need less, but they receive more. Since incumbents are better known and have government-subsidized ways of reaching voters, they need less money to get their message across. A few, such as Wisconsin's veteran Senator William Proxmire (D), report no contributions and no spending.

Moreover, incumbents attract more money than do challengers. Perhaps this is because they are deemed better "investments"; contributors want a return for their dollars in access or favors. In the 1982 elections, for example, House and Senate incumbents drew almost 3.5 times as much political action committee (PAC) money as did challengers. (PACs will be discussed later in this chapter.) In fact, incumbents often end up with a surplus. That money is saved for future campaigns or given to needier party candidates.

Controlling Campaign Funding

The financial inequalities that exist between incumbents and challengers, and between wealthy and poor donors, have led to demands for legal controls over campaign funding. Reforms have been urged not just to clean up campaign financing but also to shift political influence from those who rely on donations to those who rely on other resources. Several methods control the role of money in campaigns. Primary among there are (1) disclosure of contributions and expenses, (2) limits on contributions, (3) free radio and TV time for candidates, and (4) public financing of campaigns.

In the wake of the Watergate scandal, the federal government and many states passed broad laws using some or all of the above methods. The

Federal Election Campaign Act (FECA) was signed by President Ford in October 1974. A Supreme Court ruling in January 1976 upheld certain parts of the law and voided others (*Buckley* v. *Valeo*). In the midst of the confusion, Congress passed a revised act that reconciled the ruling with the original intent. The 1976 act was amended three years later to ease the paperwork for candidates and committees. Major parts of the law are as follows.

Limits on individual contributions

Individuals can give a maximum of $1,000 per candidate for presidential and congressional primaries and $1,000 more per candidate in the general elections. Such contributions can total no more than $5,000 in any one year. Primary, runoff, and general contests are considered separate elections, but all presidential primaries are lumped together as one election. Individuals may give up to $20,000 per year to a political party, and they may spend an unlimited amount independently to promote a party or a candidate. Independent spending of more than $250 must be reported. The person must declare, under penalty of law, that the expenditures were not made in secret agreement with the candidate. (Individual volunteer expenses—housing, food, personal travel—of up to $1,000 for a candidate or $2,000 for a party are not reportable donations.)

Limits on party contributions

National party committees may give directly to candidates for the House ($10,000 each) and Senate ($17,500). They may also spend a certain amount on behalf of their presidential tickets, even if their candidates have chosen public financing. And they may spend unlimited amounts on *independent* efforts not tied to specific candidates.

In addition to direct donations, there are **coordinated expenditures**. These are funds paid out by the party for services that candidates request—including polling or TV ad production. Candidates have a say in how the funds are spent. For Senate candidates, party committees may spend two cents for every voting-age person in a state. In 1982, these limits ranged from about $37,000 to about $666,000. For House candidates, party committees may spend no more than $18,440 in coordinated funds. Coordinated funds are used in general elections but not in primaries.

Contributions by nonparty groups

Labor unions, corporations, and membership groups may advocate to their stockholders, personnel, or members the election or defeat of a clearly named candidate. Expenses for this purpose are not limited. However, amounts over $2,000 must be reported. The groups must declare, under penalty of law, that the funds were not spent in secret agreement with the candidate. Such groups do not have to report expenses used to influence voters on issues or ballot propositions. Unions and corporations may spend an unlimited amount for "nonpartisan" registration and voter drives.

Corporations and labor unions may not give corporate or union funds directly to candidates. Under the 1976 campaign finance amendments, however, they may use their own funds to pay for administrative or fund-raising costs of separate, voluntary funds of **political action committees (PACs).** For some time, PACs have been a common way to channel corporate or union energies into campaign war chests. Corporations typically have PACs with such names as "Good Government Club," to which executives donate. And almost all unions have PACs. The best known of these is the AFL–CIO's Committee on Political Education (COPE). On the surface, such groups are wholly voluntary, but it does not take a cynic to suspect that subtle social pressures help keep the money flowing.

Other types of groups are also covered by the finance law. Multicandidate committees may give no more than $5,000 per election to a candidate. These committees must have more than 50 members and must support five or more candidates. Such committees may also give up to $15,000 per year to a political party.

Controls on candidates' spending

Except for presidential candidates who accept public financing, there are no restrictions on how much candidates or their supporters may spend. Nor are there restrictions on how much candidates may contribute to their own cause. But strict accounting is required. All donations of $50 or more must be recorded, and donors of more than $200 must be named. Accounting of funds must be made by a single committee for each candidate, with regular reports of receipts and expenses.

Public Financing for Presidential Candidates

The law provides public financing for presidential contenders. The money comes from income tax checkoffs. Matching public funds are available to each of the primary candidates who meet the eligibility requirement. The candidate must raise at least $100,000—at least $5,000 in 20 or more states. Only the first $250 of private donations is matched by the government. No more than 45 percent of the funds available can go to the candidates of a single party. In the general election, candidates may opt for full public campaign funding. Minor-party or independent candidates may receive a portion of full funding, based on past or current votes received. Candidates who accept **public funding** must agree to overall spending limits.

A number of groups, most notably the citizens' lobby Common Cause, have lobbied for public funding of Senate and House campaigns. Congress refused to include such a provision in the 1974 act covering public funding. No doubt, its intention was to preserve the financial edge of incumbents. However, it did set spending limits for House and Senate candidates. (Incidentally, the spending limits were way below the amount that challengers normally needed to unseat incumbents.) The Supreme Court held that these overall spending limits were unconstitutional. The main effect of the court's decision was to limit publicly funded presidential campaign spending but leave congressional contests open to unlimited spending.

To administer its complex features, the act set up a six-member Federal Election Commission (FEC). The FEC's members are appointed by the president and confirmed by the Senate. The commission may issue regulations and advisory opinions, conduct investigations, and prosecute violations. Beset by political pressures from all sides, it has had a stormy history.

Postreform Trends

Since the introduction of modern reporting methods in the early 1970s, three leading trends in campaign financing have been noted: the growth of PACs, the rise of independent spending, and shifts in the funding mix.

Political action committees (PACs) are thriving, partly because the law favors them. In 1974, there were 608 PACs; 10 years later, there were 3,700. All types of PACs have grown in numbers, but corporate PACs have grown most of all.

PACs have grown in financial clout as well as number (see Figure 9–3). PAC donations to federal candidates hovered around $100 million in 1984; the amount in 1972 was $8.5 million. PAC money forms an ever-larger portion of House candidates' election budgets; its proportional role in Senate races seems not to have changed (Malbin, 1984).

In direct giving to candidates, the most generous PACs are those of important unions or trade associations. The biggest givers to federal candidates in 1982 were the Realtors' PAC ($2.1 million), the American Medical Association PAC ($1.7 million), the United Auto Workers PAC ($1.6 million), the Machinists' Nonpartisan Political League PAC ($1.45 million), and the National Education Association PAC ($1.2 million).

Also growing has been **independent spending**—made without the cooperation or consent of candidates. According to FEC figures, $5.7 million was spent in this way for or against 81 candidates in 1982.

PACs that launch independent campaigns are usually formed to advance a philosophy or an issue. In 1982, the biggest campaign of this kind was conducted by the Congressional Club, a conservative group that spent nearly $10.5 million. Other groups that launched independent campaigns in 1982 were the Fund for a Conservative Majority and National Conservative PAC (NCPAC), and the liberal National Committee for an Effective Congress.

Such independent efforts have been devoted mainly to *negative* campaigns. These are aimed at discrediting a candidate and boosting the opponent. NCPAC in 1980 targeted six liberal Senators, four of whom were

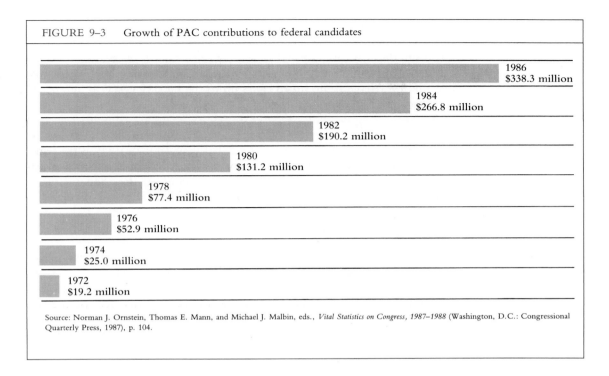

FIGURE 9–3   Growth of PAC contributions to federal candidates

1986
$338.3 million

1984
$266.8 million

1982
$190.2 million

1980
$131.2 million

1978
$77.4 million

1976
$52.9 million

1974
$25.0 million

1972
$19.2 million

Source: Norman J. Ornstein, Thomas E. Mann, and Michael J. Malbin, eds., *Vital Statistics on Congress, 1987–1988* (Washington, D.C.: Congressional Quarterly Press, 1987), p. 104.

defeated. How well such tactics work is not clear. The defeated liberals all faced uphill battles with or without NCPAC; some of the targeted liberals may even have rallied their forces by fighting "vicious out-of-state campaigns."

The level and mixture of campaign funding have shifted since the early 1970s. Gary C. Jacobson (1984: 40–41) has pinpointed the following trends: (1) money available for federal campaigns has grown steadily; (2) private individuals remain the most important source of funds; (3) nonparty PAC contributions have grown both in dollars and as a proportion of total campaign spending; and (4) though parties' direct contributions have lagged somewhat, their total contributions (including indirect and coordinated spending) are higher than ever, mainly because of GOP spending.

PAC funds seem to be more important to candidates than ever. This is certainly true for House contenders,' though the picture for Senate contenders is less clear. One source that has grown in importance is the candidates' own pocketbooks. Candidates can spend any amount of their own funds. As a result, a number of rich contenders have given generously in their own behalf. Donations from other individuals, in contrast, do not seem to have changed in importance.

Parties may also give direct or coordinated aid to candidates. Republicans have outspent their Democratic counterparts by wide margins in recent elections. This comparison includes spending by House and Senate campaign committees, as well as spending by the party National Committee. Democratic party committees have traditionally lagged in spending, and they have far to go to catch up to the GOP levels.

Unresolved Issues in Campaign Finance

The campaign funding reforms of the 1970s have not cleared up the most vexing problems. First, and most important, they have failed in their main goal of limiting the impact of big money in politics. Big money is alive and well. But now it flows through a somewhat wider range of issue and candidate groups. Many of the best-funded PACs are built on large numbers of mail-solicited donations, not a few "fat cats."

The campaign finance laws are so riddled with loopholes that money freely flows into federal elections. One problem surfaced in 1984, when more than 130 supposedly independent Mondale "delegate committees" raised and spent funds separately from the nationwide Mondale effort— which operated under legal ceilings. If the state groups had been truly separate from the Mondale effort, their actions would have been legal; but mounting criticisms, plus allegations that funds were being transferred between the delegate groups and the national campaign, forced Mondale to halt the separate fund-raising.

The flap over the Mondale delegate committees was only the tip of the iceberg. Special-purpose accounts are used by national parties to accept donations that would be illegal if given directly to campaigns. Tax-exempt foundations are used by parties and PACs to take donations in excess of legal limits. Creative accounting and "independent spending" on behalf of candidates are used to skirt the $5,000 limit on what PACs can give directly to candidates. Bankers and other monied people can lend money or extend credit to candidates under loose rules. And money has been moving underground, thwarting federal inducement and disclosure efforts.

All in all, the financing system bears an increasing resemblance to the pre-Watergate days. "You can do just about anything, as long as you take care," said one party official (Jackson, 1984).

Second, the reforms have done little to reduce inequalities between incumbents and challengers. In fact, they may really help keep incumbents in office and make it harder for challengers to raise the money they need (Jacobson, 1980).

Third, the reforms have not resolved the question of what aid should be regulated. A backer who gives time or services to a candidate makes an in-kind donation that may be every bit as valuable as cash. For example, members of unions (or other groups) donate a lot to campaigns. They use telephones, get out the vote, and do other valuable but free chores. Likewise, public figures, such as entertainers, donate talents to candidates through concerts or public appearances. How are these donations counted?

The laws emphasize money. They have not dealt with how to weigh other forms of donations.

Finally, the reforms may have sped the decline of old-style parties. There are several reasons: (1) candidates may pour unlimited funds of their own into a campaign; (2) interest groups may do the same through independent spending, thereby airing their views about candidates; (3) under present law, PACs spread funds among many candidates of both parties.

The campaign finance reforms of the 1970s have had a deep impact on the election process, as did the primaries and ballot reforms earlier in the century. For reformers, the new rules were justified by their intended goal: reduce the power of big money. Yet political scientists tend to see such reforms as shifts of influence from one set of groups to another. "Don't kid yourself that you back public financing to prevent Watergates and corruption," said a leader of Common Cause, a citizens' lobby. "You do it to change the system."

Complaints against the power of money abound; several efforts have been launched to promote changes. Common Cause has mounted a large campaign against PAC contributions. So has a blue-ribbon group called Citizens against PACs. Party leaders are not against PACs per se. But they do want to lift restrictions on party spending for candidates. Short of a major scandal, little change seems likely; incumbent legislators, who would have to approve any changes, are major beneficiaries of the present system.

Citizens interact with the election system and the campaigns for office, and then they decide whether or not to vote. Most of those who vote choose either Democratic or Republican candidates. The voters for candidates of both political parties reside in the vast middle class, but there are some differences between Democratic and Republican voters (see Table 9–1). What are these differences?

WHO ARE THE DEMOCRATIC AND REPUBLICAN VOTERS?

Socioeconomic Status

Businesspeople and professionals tend to support Republican candidates for president. More than two thirds of them voted for Nixon in 1972; well over half of them voted for Ford in 1976 and for Reagan in 1980. The poor have been a declining element in Democratic voter support. This is largely because the proportion of poor people has declined overall. Working-class people usually vote Democratic by big margins. Nixon's landslide victory in 1972 came because more than half of the Republican votes were cast by manual workers. Job differences were reflected in the 1976 election. More than half of the business and professional people voted for Ford; more than half of the manual workers voted for Carter. But in 1980, manual workers voted equally for Reagan (the winner) and Carter.

There are similar differences among the college educated, those who

TABLE 9–1   Democratic and Republican voters in 1980 and 1984

| | Percentage voting for | | | |
| | 1984 | | 1980 | |
Group	Democrat (Mondale)	Republican (Reagan)	Democrat (Carter)	Republican (Reagan)
Sex				
Male	37	61	37	54
Female	42	57	45	46
Race				
White	34	66	36	55
Nonwhite	90	9	82	14
Education				
College	40	59	35	53
High school	39	60	43	51
Grade school	49	50	50	45
Occupation				
Professional and business	37	62	33	56
White collar	40	59	42	48
Manual	46	53	46	47
Age				
Under 30 years	41	58	44	42
30–44 years	42	58	37	54
45–59 years	39	60	39	55
60 and older	36	63	40	54
Religion				
Protestant	26	73	37	56
Catholic	44	55	40	51
Politics				
Republican	7	92	11	84
Democrat	73	26	66	26
Independent	35	63	30	54
Region				
East	47	52	42	47
Midwest	38	61	40	51
South	36	63	44	51
West	40	59	35	53
Union membership				
Members of labor union families	53	45	47	44

*Less than 1 percent.

Source: *New York Times/CBS News* poll reported in Gerald M. Pomper, *The Election of 1984* (Chatham, N.J.: Chatham House Publishers, 1985), pp. 67–68.

only went to high school, and those who did not go beyond grade school. A majority of the college educated voted for the Republican presidential candidate in all but one of the recent elections. The exception was the Democratic landslide victory of 1964, in which Lyndon Johnson got a majority of the votes of almost all classes. In contrast, most of the grade-school educated usually vote for Democrats. In 1972, however, Republican Richard Nixon won a majority of their votes.

Race, Religion, Ethnics

Voters of Irish, Polish, or Italian descent have usually been Democratic presidential supporters. But blacks form the most heavily Democratic voting group. They have voted increasingly Democratic since 1952 and now comprise nearly a fifth of the Democratic vote. In 1976 and 1980, more than 80 percent of blacks voted for Carter.

Catholics and Jews have normally voted heavily for Democratic candidates. Only in 1972 and 1980 did a majority of Catholics vote for the Republican presidential candidate. Even "born again" Protestant Jimmy Carter got a large proportion of the Catholic vote in 1976. The most notable presidential year for the Catholic vote was 1960, when John F. Kennedy, a Catholic, was the Democratic candidate. Nearly half of his votes came from Catholics (Axelrod, 1972:16). In contrast, Republican voters have been mostly white and Protestant.

Sex and Age

On the whole, sex differences in voting behavior have not been very important. They emerge mainly because of sex differences in socioeconomic status and age. In 1972 and 1976, both sexes supported the Democratic and Republican presidential candidates in about the same proportions. But in 1980, a large majority of men voted for Reagan and women were about evenly divided. There was much speculation that a "gender gap" might affect Reagan's reelection, and in fact, he suffered some loss of support among women in 1984.

Younger voters usually vote more Democratic than do older voters. Voters who are middle-aged or older tend to vote Republican. This is mainly because the older generation has, over time, always been more Republican, not because people become more Republican as they get older. But in 1980, voters under 30 supported Reagan and Carter about equally. And there were more votes for John Anderson, the independent candidate (11 percent), among those under 30 than among other age groups.

Trade Union Membership

Voting is affected by the social groups to which people belong. One very compelling affiliation is membership in labor unions. For many years, labor union families have been heavily Democratic. Since 1952, union members and their families have supplied about a third of the Democratic vote for president. In 1972, there was a huge defection of union members to Nixon. But a large union majority supported Carter in 1976. In 1980,

Two delegates to the 1984 Democratic National Convention are moved by a speech of the Reverend Jesse Jackson.

Carter won more support than Reagan among union members. But his support was much smaller than it had been in 1976. However, about three fourths of all adults live in families that do not include union members. These nonunion families contribute heavily to the support of Republican presidential hopefuls.

Place of Residence

Democratic presidential candidates draw more support from the central cities than do Republicans. About 10 percent of the population lives in the central cities of 12 major urban centers. These people provide about 15 percent of the Democratic presidential vote. Voters outside the central cities are more Republican. More striking, though, are regional differences in Republican and Democratic voting.

The southern and border states have generally been Democratic. They provide about one fourth of the votes for Democratic presidential candidates. But in recent presidential elections, Republicans—Goldwater in 1964, Nixon in 1972, and Reagan in 1980—have won the electoral votes of southern states. In 1972, McGovern received only 29 percent of the southern vote but over 40 percent of the vote in other regions. Carter got his strongest support in the South in 1976, but in 1980 Reagan won more southern support than Carter. Though regional differences are on the downswing (politics has become more nationalized), they are still noticeable.

Accounting for why people vote as they do became much more effective with sample survey data. Adequate national election surveys date back only to the 1940s. Before then, election analysis depended on the study of overall official returns; it was not possible to tell how individuals voted. Sample surveys, or public opinion polls, give data on voters' attitudes and traits. They also report on how each voted. Many factors influence voting behavior. Three of them have proven to be very important. These are (1) party identification, (2) candidate appeal, and (3) the impact of issues. The influence of these three factors may change from election to election.

WHY DO PEOPLE VOTE THE WAY THEY DO?

Party Identification

One of the most persistent traits in political behavior is the distribution of **party identification** (Niemi and Weisberg, 1976: 160–438). As Table 9–2 shows, party loyalties have been very consistent since 1952.

We may assume that election outcomes are influenced by short-term and long-term forces. The short-term forces include candidate appeal and the strength of the issues. The long-term forces are those voting habits that recur and endure. Party loyalty is the most important of these. It is like a cord that ties voters to one party—a cord that is fairly inelastic for strong partisans and more elastic for weak partisans. Even very strong short-term forces will move the average strong party members only a little way; few of them will vote for the opposition party candidate. For the less strongly attached, the cord stretches more easily; short-term forces often cause defections in their voting. Independents with no sense of party tie at all are "unanchored." They are highly susceptible to short-term forces in any one election (Miller and Levitin, 1976: 34). Party identifiers are more apt to vote than independents. In 1980, for instance, more than two thirds of the strong Democrats and Republicans voted, but only 43 percent of the independents voted (Abramson, Aldrich, and Rohde, 1982: 90).

Most party members vote for the presidential candidate of their party. But in some elections, the short-term forces are so strong that defections skyrocket. In 1968 and 1972, defections to Nixon and American Independent party candidate George Wallace were great among weak Democrats and among persons with Democratic leanings. In 1964, there were marked

TABLE 9–2   Party identification in the United States

Percentage who are	October 1952	October 1956	October 1960	November 1964	November 1968	November 1972	November 1976	November 1980	November 1982	November 1984	November 1986
Strong Democrats	22	21	20	27	20	15	15	18	20	17	18
Weak Democrats	25	23	25	25	25	26	25	23	24	20	22
Leaning Democratic	10	6	6	9	10	11	12	11	11	11	10
Independent	5	9	10	8	11	13	15	13	11	11	12
Leaning Republican	7	8	7	6	9	11	10	10	8	12	11
Weak Republicans	14	14	14	14	15	13	14	14	14	15	15
Strong Republicans	14	15	16	11	10	10	9	9	10	12	10
Apolitical	3	4	3	1	1	1	1	2	2	2	2
Total	100	100	100	100	100	100	100	100	100	100	100

Sources: Warren E. Miller, Authur Miller, and Edward J. Schneider, *American National Election Studies Data Sourcebook, 1952 1978* (Cambridge, Mass.: Harvard University Press, 1980), p. 81; and Codebooks of the University of Michigan Center for Political Studies National Election Surveys.

defections from Barry Goldwater among weak Republicans. The 1976 election was more "normal" than the three previous ones. Partisan loyalists gave party candidates consistent support. But defections were again prominent in 1980.

Growth of "Independence"

Independents have been the most volatile voters both in election turnout and in support for presidential candidates. Except for the 1964 election, most independents have voted for the Republican presidential candidate since 1952 (Asher, 1988: 89). But "leaners" and independents are especially prone to split-ticket voting. Since 1952, there has been a long-run trend toward the erosion of partisan loyalties and a pointed increase in the number of independents.

The growing proportion of independents in the electorate has not come mainly from conversions of party members. More important has been the dramatic influx of young people into the electorate. These new voters are less apt than any other group to be regular party members (Converse, 1972). In 1952, before 18-year-old voting and the effect of the World War II baby boom, only about 7 percent of voters were under 25; by 1978, the proportion of such voters had risen to 19 percent. The increase in independent voters was largely due to this huge influx of younger people, most of whom had not developed firm party loyalty (Miller and Levitin, 1976: 192–99).

In the 1960s there were also major shifts away from the Democratic party in the South, especially among young Southerners. A large part of the rise in the national proportion of independents came because of these shifts. The Republicans gained few adherents. Many Southerners identified themselves as independents. They supported George Wallace's third-party movement (Glenn, 1972).

Candidate Appeal

Candidates and campaigns affect how and why people vote. At the presidential level, the major party candidates are highly visible. Their personalities, family backgrounds, physical features, and personal and political styles receive much attention during campaigns. But the impact of candidate appeal on elections varies. Eisenhower had exceptional candidate appeal in the two elections of the 1950s. He entered the White House as the nonpartisan hero of World War II in Europe. But the outcomes of the 1964, 1972, and 1980 elections were more rejections of candidates than positive appeal. Republican Goldwater in 1964 and Democrat McGovern in 1972 drew negative reactions even from their own parties. In 1980, Americans rejected President Carter for his poor performance. Figure 9–4 shows the net effect of the candidates on the vote from 1952 to 1980. Note that except for the 1964 election, Republicans have been helped substan-

FIGURE 9–4   The electoral impact of candidate appeal

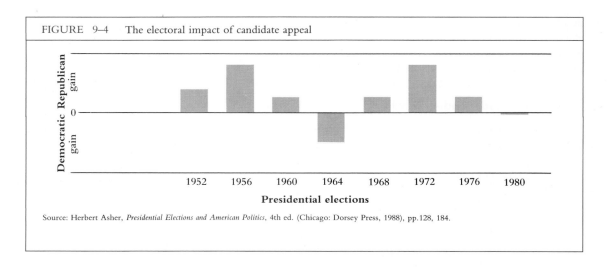

Source: Herbert Asher, *Presidential Elections and American Politics*, 4th ed. (Chicago: Dorsey Press, 1988), pp.128, 184.

During his campaign for the 1988 Democratic presidential nomination, at a rally in Tucson, Arizona, the Reverend Jesse Jackson signifies his satisfaction at his strong showing in the Colorado caucuses and the Wisconsin primary (both of which were won by Gov. Michael Dukakis) as he gets a hug from a three-year-old girl.

WORDS AND IDEAS

How to Tell Democrats from Republicans

A few years ago, an anonymous wit drew up a list of the main differences between Democrats and Republicans. A Republican congressman from California, Craig Hosmer, included this anonymous author's formulation in the *Congressional Record*. It reads as follows:

Democrats buy most of the books that have been banned somewhere. Republicans form censorship committees and read them as a group.

Republicans consume three fourths of all the rutabaga produced in this country. The remainder is thrown out.

Republicans usually wear hats and almost always clean their paintbrushes.

Democrats give their worn-out clothes to those less fortunate. Republicans wear theirs.

Republicans employ exterminators. Democrats step on the bugs.

Democrats name their children after currently popular sports figures, politicians, and entertainers. Republican children are named after their parents or grandparents, according to where the most money is.

Democrats keep trying to cut down on smoking but are not successful. Neither are Republicans.

Republicans tend to keep their shades drawn, although there is seldom any reason why they should. Democrats ought to, but don't.

Republicans study the financial pages of the newspaper. Democrats put them in the bottom of the bird cage.

Most of the stuff you see alongside the road has been thrown out of car windows by Democrats.

Republicans raise dahlias, Dalmatians, and eyebrows. Democrats raise Airedales, kids, and taxes.

Democrats eat the fish they catch. Republicans hang them on the wall.

Republican boys date Democratic girls. They plan to marry Republican girls but feel they're entitled to a little fun first.

Democrats make up plans and then do something else. Republicans follow the plans their grandfathers made.

Republicans sleep in twin beds—some even in separate rooms. That is why there are more Democrats.

The appeal of the candidates. Dwight D. Eisenhower [right] appealed to the crowd; "Ike" was a very popular president from 1953 to 1961. Ronald Reagan [left], another president who enjoyed considerable popularity, wades into a gathering of "hardhats" during his 1980 campaign. John F. Kennedy [middle] had the appeal of youth and vigor; he was the youngest person the country ever elected president.

tially more by the appeal of their candidates than have Democrats. Sometimes, as in 1972, this appeal has made a decisive difference; in that election, the net advantage to the Republican candidate was about 8.5 percent. In other elections, the net effect of candidate appeal has been relatively small. The net effect of Carter and Reagan was negligible in 1980, reflecting "the overall lack of enthusiasm for both nominees" (Asher, 1984: 163).

The Impact of Issues

"The issues" in presidential elections have changed. So, too, has the relative importance of the issues in election outcomes. In the 1940s, the main issues had to do with winning World War II. Then came labor problems and inflation. In the 1950s, the Korean War became a major political issue. In the early 60s, the major issues were race relations and civil rights. By the mid-60s, the Vietnam War had become the chief issue. After Vietnam, economic problems were the chief political issues; in the 1980s the main issues were unemployment and inflation.

At the same time, we have become more aware of national issues and problems. This is partly because education levels have climbed. We have become more sophisticated politically. This is suggested by unmistakable growth in the consistency of our political attitudes. Also, there is more ideological polarization, though the electorate is still not highly ideologi-

FIGURE 9–5   The effects of party, issues, and candidates on voting

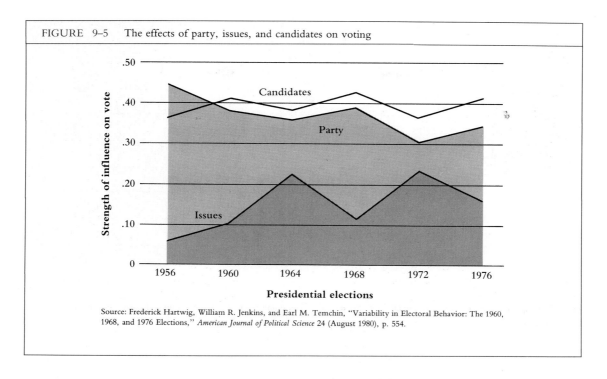

Source: Frederick Hartwig, William R. Jenkins, and Earl M. Temchin, "Variability in Electoral Behavior: The 1960, 1968, and 1976 Elections," *American Journal of Political Science* 24 (August 1980), p. 554.

cal. We now have "a more educated and cognitively competent public" than we had before the 1960s (Nie, Verba, and Petrocik, 1979: 148).

As a result of the greater impact of "the issues" in presidential politics, so-called **issue voting** has been growing. Issue voting involves how voters feel about issues and whether they vote for candidates whose positions on issues are the same as theirs. Figure 9–5 shows the changes in issue voting between 1956 and 1976. It indicates the correlations between voters' attitudes and their vote. Issue voting was fairly low in 1956 and 1960; it spurted upward in 1964, declined in 1968, shot back up in 1972, and declined somewhat in 1976.

In contrast, **party voting** (the relation between party membership and voting), the best guide to voting behavior, declined irregularly over the 1960s. Party voting did get a shot in the arm in the 1968 contest between Richard Nixon and Hubert Humphrey; and the 1976 race between Jimmy Carter and Gerald Ford heightened party voting somewhat. But party and issue voting are not incompatible. Evidence shows that partisans have become more issue oriented than they were in the 50s. This was most true in 1964 and 1968 (Pomper, 1975: 166–85). Party loyalty and issues worked together for about 26 percent of voters in the 1976 election; 17 percent were voting by issue position rather than by party; 30 percent were voting

FIGURE 9–6   Class voting in presidential elections

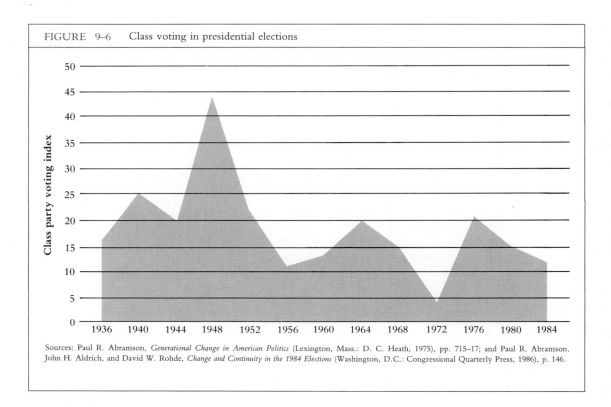

Sources: Paul R. Abramson, *Generational Change in American Politics* (Lexington, Mass.: D. C. Heath, 1975), pp. 715–17; and Paul R. Abramson, John H. Aldrich, and David W. Rohde, *Change and Continuity in the 1984 Elections* (Washington, D.C.: Congressional Quarterly Press, 1986), p. 146.

by party despite their feelings on issues (Nie, Verba, and Petrocik, 1979: 377).

The electorate is not made up of numskulls who cannot make rational choices based on important national issues. But the voter depends on the choices offered. Research shows a great potential for issue voting. Candidates can make it possible to choose on the basis of issues. If they show that they are clearly distinct from one another on issues, then many voters will choose on that basis. If, though, the choice is among candidates who differ little on issues, then voting will be more along party lines.

Class Voting

A striking difference between the voting behavior of Americans and Europeans is the lack of class voting here. **Class voting** means, for instance, that most working-class people vote for one party (in Europe, usually a socialist, labor, or communist party) and that most middle-class people vote for another party (usually conservative, center, or Christian Democratic). In our country, working-class people tend to vote Democratic and middle-class people tend to vote Republican. But class voting has never been strong here, and it has declined since the 40s. This is because we have weak social class identification and lack class consciousness. We also lack a major socialist or labor party, which may itself be due to the fluid character of our class structure.

The extent of class voting can be shown from the data for each presidential election. Subtract the percentage of nonmanual (white-collar, business, and professional) workers who vote Democratic from that of manual workers (skilled and unskilled workers) who vote Democratic. This "index of class voting" is shown for recent presidential elections in Figure 9–6.

Class voting was strongest in the 1948 Truman-Dewey contest. A huge majority of working-class people voted for Democrat Truman; a large majority of middle-class voters voted for Republican Dewey. But class voting has generally, though unevenly, declined since then. Solid working-class support for the Democrats has eroded, and they have more and more won middle-class votes. More than half of Truman's support in 1948 came from the working class, but working-class support for the Democrats steadily declined in later elections. By 1972, only a little over a third of Democratic voters were working class. On the other hand, only a fourth of those who voted Democratic in 1948 were middle class, but by 1956 four out of five Democratic votes came from the middle class. In 1968, middle-class Democratic votes equaled or exceeded those of working-class voters (Abramson, 1975: 23–25).

The nature and causes of personal voting choices are of great interest. But elections are collective decisions that affect the whole nation. These decisions give analysts a basis for finding patterns of electoral behavior for parties as a whole. At a more mundane level, they provide the personnel to run the government.

RENDERING THE ELECTORAL VERDICT

The Classification of Elections

Elections can be classified by using two criteria: Did the party with the largest number of members win or lose? Did the vote totals follow those of former elections, or did they show much change? By using these criteria, elections have been classified into four distinct types (see Figure 9–7). A **maintaining election** is one in which party loyalties are stable and the candidate of the majority party wins. The 1976 election of Carter is an example.

A **deviating election** is one in which the majority-party candidate loses. This occurred in 1952 and 1956, when a Republican, Eisenhower, was elected president despite the fact that a majority of Americans identified themselves as Democrats. In a deviating election, short-term forces overpower the long-term effects of party loyalty. A **converting election** is one in which basic changes take place in the distribution of party mem-

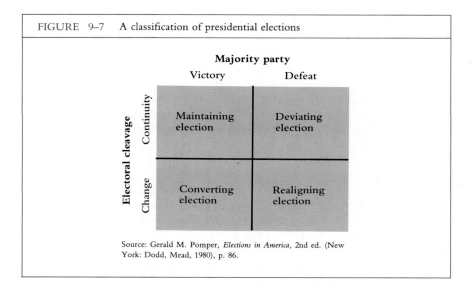

FIGURE 9–7   A classification of presidential elections

Majority party

Victory   Defeat

Electoral cleavage

Continuity

| Maintaining election | Deviating election |

Change

| Converting election | Realigning election |

Source: Gerald M. Pomper, *Elections in America,* 2nd ed. (New York: Dodd, Mead, 1980), p. 86.

bership, but the majority-party candidate wins. Finally, a **realigning election** is one in which the normal majority-party candidate loses due to changing party loyalties. Since World War II, the distribution of party membership has been stable, but deviating elections have been commonplace. This is shown by Eisenhower's election in the 1950s, Nixon's election in 1968 and 1972, and Reagan's elections in the 1980s.

The first party realignment took place in the early 1830s. It ended with the election of Martin Van Buren in 1836. The Democrats were then dominant until the Civil War. The election of Abraham Lincoln for the second time in 1864 was a realigning election. It ushered in a Republican dominance that lasted for 75 years. The election of 1896 showed the changing shape of the Republican coalition. That election was followed by Republican presidential victories in all but two elections up to the New Deal. The exceptions were the deviating elections of Woodrow Wilson, a Democrat, in 1912 and 1916. Finally, the election of 1928, though won by Republican Herbert Hoover, showed a basic shift to the Democratic party. That shift was fed by a growing economic depression, climaxing with the stock market collapse in 1929. Democrat Franklin Roosevelt's first victory in 1932 showed the rise of the so-called New Deal coalition of the Democratic party. This lasted intact until the early 1960s, and it still holds shape in many ways.

The 1964 election showed changes. The cause of those changes was the increasing numbers of people who said they were political independents. Political scientists have argued the meaning of the changes. Some believe that major and lasting shifts in electoral splits were under way. Some see the increase in the number of independents as meaning that voters are not aligned. This would portend basic future political changes (Burnham, 1970). The long-term forces affecting elections may change at a glacial pace. It is hard to see realignments while they are occurring, and thus, it is hard to interpret the long-run meaning of current developments. So analysts disagree in their interpretation of the changes that have taken place in elections since 1964. Each new election brings changed forecasts for future developments and alters the interpretation of past changes. Here, as with other kinds of analysis on a large, national scale, hindsight is the most scientific of methods!

Presidential Elections of the 1980s

The electoral fortunes of Republican and Democratic presidential candidates have waxed and waned in the last 40 years. But nationally, the 1980s were Republican years. In 1988, for the first time in 150 years a sitting vice president—George Bush—was elected president following two full terms served by a president of his own party. At the same time, the 1980s have produced divided party successes. While Republicans Ronald Reagan and George Bush were victorious presidential candidates, Democrats continued to be the dominant party for congressional and state offices. For part of the 1980s Republicans held a U.S. Senate majority. Otherwise, Democrats continued to win the lion's share of congressional, gubernatorial, and state legislative offices. One reason this occurred was that many voters, especially southerners, voted Republican for president and Democratic for congressional and state offices.

The 1980 election

Jimmy Carter was unknown to most Americans when he began to campaign for the 1976 Democratic nomination. Early in the race, the press referred to him as "Jimmy Who?" But his marathon campaign paid off. Carter was the overwhelming choice of the Democratic convention, and in the general election he won by a small margin against the incumbent, Gerald Ford. But his term in office was not very happy or successful. It was plagued by growing inflation and continuing unemployment. At the end, the Iranian hostage crisis arose. He came to be viewed by many as an ineffective president.

The Republican nomination in 1976 had been a close call for Gerald Ford. He was nominated by a narrow margin over Ronald Reagan, a former governor of California. Many Republicans felt that Reagan was the best candidate and could have won. But he would have to wait for another chance. The 1980 presidential campaign began in August 1979, when Republican Congressman Philip M. Crane of Illinois announced his candidacy. Six other Republicans followed: former Governor John Connally of Texas, former Ambassador George Bush of Texas, Senator Robert Dole of Kansas, Congressman John Anderson of Illinois, Senate Minority Leader Howard Baker of Tennessee, and former Governor Ronald Reagan of California. These candidates faced more primaries than had ever been held before. The race finally narrowed to Reagan versus Bush after Anderson lost to Reagan in Illinois. But Reagan's edge over Bush grew steadily. At the Republican convention in Detroit, Reagan won the nomination by a large margin. He chose his principal opponent, Bush as his running mate.

President Carter relied heavily on his incumbency to win the Democratic nomination. But his renomination was challenged by Governor Jerry Brown of California and, more seriously, by Senator Edward Kennedy of Massachusetts. Kennedy became the president's greatest threat. But in the midst of the primaries, Islamic revolutionaries seized the American Embassy in Teheran, the capital of Iran, and held the Americans there captive. The hostage crisis in Iran temporarily improved Carter's popularity, and his campaign efforts paid off. He easily won the early caucuses and primaries, and his wide victory in the Illinois primary in March virtually sealed his nomination. Kennedy did not withdraw from the race until the convention met. There, Carter was renominated by a 2-to-1 majority. Vice President Mondale was again chosen as his running mate.

After the Illinois primary, it became clear to Anderson that he could not win the Republican nomination. So on April 24, at Washington's National Press Club, he declared as an independent candidate. Later he named as his running mate Democrat Patrick J. Lucey, former governor of Wisconsin and ambassador to Mexico.

Although the candidates differed on issues, the campaign focused mainly on style. Carter charged that Reagan might lead the country into war. Reagan retorted to Carter's "scare" tactics. Much campaign energy was invested in the question of who would debate whom on television. The League of Women Voters wanted to sponsor three-way debates (Carter, Reagan, and Anderson). Carter refused. A Reagan versus Anderson debate was televised in September; some polls (notably the Harris survey) declared Anderson the winner. In October, a 90-minute Carter-Reagan debate was televised. It got a Nielsen audience rating of nearly 60 percent, well above that of the first Carter-Ford debate in 1976. The CBS News/*New York Times* poll showed that of those who watched, 44 percent thought that Reagan had won and 36 percent thought that Carter had won. The value of the two 1980 debates is debatable. Comedian Johnny Carson was moved to comment on the Carter-Reagan debate: "The debate was wonderful—it kind of took our minds off the issues for a while!"

The polls showed the on-and-off appeal of the candidates. Anderson's support generally declined. The Gallup polls suggested voter indecision between Carter and Reagan; they showed that the lead changed hands five times between April and the end of October. The precise results of various polls differed. All agreed on the eve of the election, though, that the outcome was "too close to call."

The verdict on November 4 was not close. Although Reagan received just over half of the popular votes, Carter won only 41 percent and Anderson won nearly 7 percent. But Reagan's bare majority of the popular vote won him a landslide majority in the electoral vote. The winner-take-all rule of the electoral college system enabled him to capture the electoral votes of 44 states, a total of 489 votes.

The 1976 election was a maintaining election, but in that election Carter won traditional Democratic votes only by narrow margins, except among blacks. The 1980 election was a deviating election. The Democratic party remained dominant (though not firmly so), but Republican Reagan won a majority of the popular vote. Partisan voting was somewhat restored in 1976, but voters widely abandoned party loyalty in 1980, when Republican gains were impressive in the growing South and Sunbelt states.

The 1984 election

If the 1980 election was, to some extent, a repudiation of the incumbent president, voters gave incumbent President Reagan a sweeping personal political victory in 1984. He garnered 59 percent of the popular vote, won a majority in every state except Minnesota and the District of Columbia, and enjoyed a landslide victory in the electoral college, with 525 votes.

Former Vice President Walter F. Mondale won the presidential nomination of the Democratic national convention, meeting in San Francisco in July, but only after a briskly contested preconvention fight. Seven other contenders vied for the Democratic nomination (discussed in more detail in Chapter 6). Initially, Senator John Glenn of Ohio seemed the most viable alternative to front-runner Walter Mondale. But Senator Gary Hart of Colorado turned out to be Mondale's principal nemesis after a stunning win in the New Hampshire primary held late in February. Throughout the weeks before the party convention, Mondale managed to maintain a lead in delegates chosen in caucuses or elected in primaries, but Hart won in a number of states, including California. When the convention assembled, Mondale won the nomination by a divided vote. Nearly 2,200 delegates voted for Mondale, and 1,200 voted for Hart. About 485 voted for Jesse Jackson, the Chicago-based civil rights activist, who attracted widespread support among blacks.

Divisiveness among the Democrats in their presidential choice was partly allayed by their unprecedented nomination of Representative Geraldine A. Ferraro of New York for vice president. She became the first woman vice-presidential nominee of a major American political party.

The serene Republican conclave in Dallas in August was a marked contrast to the contentious Democratic convention. Free of any controversy over their ticket for 1984, the Republicans enthusiastically nominated President Ronald Reagan and Vice President George Bush. In his acceptance speech, Reagan said that the American voters were about to be offered "the most clear-cut political choice in half a century." In accepting the Democratic party's nomination, Mondale had been more specific. Most notably, he promised to reduce the federal deficit by two thirds in his first term; more important, he pledged to raise federal taxes. In his acceptance speech, Mondale said, "Let's tell the truth. Mr. Reagan will raise taxes, and so will I. He won't tell you. I just did."

Although the campaign ranged across various domestic and foreign policy issues, Mondale devoted much more attention to these issues than Reagan did. Reagan's campaign stressed general economic well-being ("Are you better off than you were four years ago?") and condemned Mondale's promise that he would raise taxes to reduce the federal budget deficit. Though based on an accurate assessment of revenue needs, this promise played into Reagan's hands. Many voters responded to Reagan's counterpromise not to raise taxes. And many Democratic candidates found Mondale's promise to be an uncomfortable burden on their own campaigns. For instance, former Mississippi Governor William Winter, challenging the reelection of incumbent U.S. Senator Thad Cochran, said, "With that tax program, Mondale is like an 800-pound gorilla. You have to carry him around on your back because there's no place to put him down."

Three televised "debates" were held, two featuring the presidential candidates and one, the vice-presidential contenders. As in the past (see Chapter 8), these meetings were rigidly structured so that they were more like parallel press conferences than like true debates. Although none of the candidates made major errors, Reagan's lackluster performance in the first meeting briefly raised the hopes of Mondale supporters. The president rebounded in the second meeting, so the debates did little to alter the election's course overall. As usual, the press and the pundits focused more on style than on substance.

The polls played a highly visible role in charting the course of the campaign. Many opinion polls were in the field, and their estimates of the people's choices often varied wildly. While the polls seemed to indicate a close race just after the Mondale-Ferraro nomination in July, the outcome proved very different.

On election day, a record number of voters turned out to give Ronald Reagan an overwhelming victory. He got 59 percent of the popular vote, a boost from the 51 percent he had won in 1980. Mondale got only 41 percent, the same proportion that Jimmy Carter had won four years earlier. Reagan won lopsided majorities in every state but one. Mondale won his home state, Minnesota, by only about 15,000 votes out of the more than 2 million cast. Mondale did win 86 percent of the vote in the District of Columbia, so he gained its 3 electoral votes in addition to Minnesota's 10. With 59 percent of the popular vote, Reagan captured 98 percent of the electoral vote (see Figure 9–8).

The 1988 election

Rarely have incumbent vice presidents been successful in winning election as president. In 1836, Democratic vice president Martin Van Buren was able to defeat three Whig candidates for president (the leading candidate

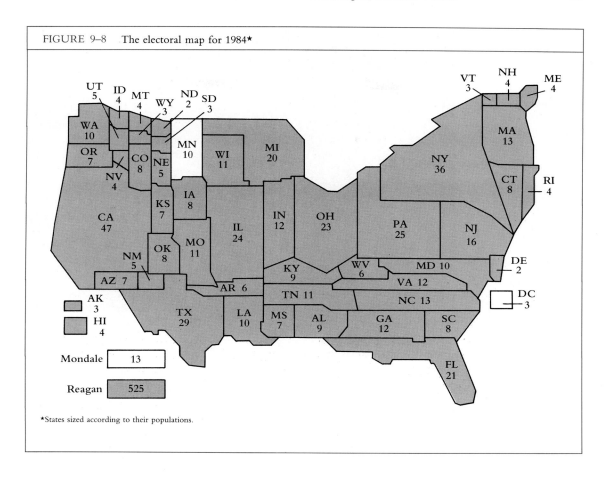

FIGURE 9–8   The electoral map for 1984★

*States sized according to their populations.

was William H. Harrison). Since that election more than a century and a half ago, no sitting vice president had won the White House until George Bush's victory in 1988.

The struggle to win a majority of the votes of the 4,162 delegates to the Democratic national convention was well under way in the last half of 1987. Seven candidates aggressively contended for the nomination: Congressman Richard A. Gephardt of Missouri; Senator Paul Simon of Illinois; Governor Michael S. Dukakis of Massachusetts; Rev. Jesse Jackson of Illinois; ex-Governor Bruce Babbitt of Arizona; Senator Gary Hart of Colorado; and Senator Albert Gore, Jr., of Tennessee. In the February Iowa caucuses, Gephardt took an early lead in the race; Dukakis garnered the most delegates in the New Hampshire primary. By "Super Tuesday"—the day, March 8, when primaries would be held in 21 states, including the entire South, Dukakis was the frontrunner, but Jackson continued to pile up delegate victories as well. Babbitt abandoned his presidential bid in February. By late April, Gephardt, Gore, Hart, and

Campaigning for the 1988 Democratic presidential nomination, Gov. Michael Dukakis talks with a group of people gathered at a Chicago coffee shop the day before the Illinois primary.

Simon had dropped out, and Dukakis's victory in the New York primary made him the clear leader for the Democratic nomination. The nomination was clinched for Dukakis when he swept primaries in California, Montana, New Jersey, and New Mexico on June 7. Then only one rival, Rev. Jackson, remained.

The Democratic national convention met at Atlanta's Omni Coliseum on July 18. There was an expectation of victory in the air, as delegates chanted "We will win" again and again. The party platform, hammered out in compromises between Dukakis and Jackson forces, was relatively brief and nonideological. Dukakis designated Senator Lloyd Bentsen of Texas as his vice presidential running mate. On July 21, the convention nominated Dukakis with 69 percent of the delegate votes. Jackson won important convention support, but he forcefully endorsed Dukakis's candidacy. Democrats left the convention more united than they had been for many years. One delegate said, "Everyone smells victory this year, and that makes all the difference."

Early skirmishes for the Republican presidential nomination featured Vice President George Bush, Senate Republican leader Robert Dole of Kansas, Rev. Pat Robertson of South Carolina, Congressman Jack F. Kemp of New York, ex-Governor Pierre S. du Pont IV of Delaware, and former General Alexander M. Haig, Jr. Robertson acquired some delegate support in the earliest caucuses, and Dole was the clear winner in the February Iowa caucuses. With no significant caucus or primary support, du Pont and Haig left the contest in mid-February. The March 8 Super Tuesday primaries, with fragmented results for the Democratic candidates, gave Bush a resounding win. He swept 16 of the 20 Super Tuesday states.

Vice President George Bush does some last-minute campaigning in Nashua, New Hampshire. Vice President Bush's victory in the New Hampshire primary was a turning point in his quest for the 1988 Republican presidential nomination.

Soon afterward, with only a fourth-place showing in South Carolina, Kemp withdrew. Robertson's candidacy was also a casualty of Super Tuesday. Then, at the end of March, Dole announced to fellow Republican senators in Washington that he was dropping out of the presidential race. Vice President Bush had clinched the nomination.

The 2,277 delegates to the Republican national convention assembled at the Superdome in New Orleans on August 15. Bush, whose nomination had been assured since Super Tuesday and his Illinois primary victory the next week, was nominated for president without dissent. Bush selected Senator Dan Quayle of Indiana as his vice presidential running mate. In his acceptance speech, Bush called for a "kinder and gentler nation," saying "I mean to win."

Until the Republican convention, Dukakis had led in the polls. But Bush's standing in the polls surged after the New Orleans conclave. Bush took the offensive right from the beginning, accusing Dukakis of opposing gun ownership and the Pledge of Allegiance, being soft on crime, and favoring a weakening of America's defenses. Dukakis, although endorsed by such large pro-Democratic organizations as the AFL–CIO and the National Education Association, did not take strong initiative early in the campaign to counter Bush's attacks.

The campaign featured three nationally televised debates, two between presidential candidates Bush and Dukakis, and one between vice presidential candidates Bentsen and Quayle. The first debate, held in Winston-Salem, North Carolina, on September 25, showed both candidates to be men of impressive experience and ability. Afterward, it was widely agreed that Dukakis deserved high marks for his substantive performance during

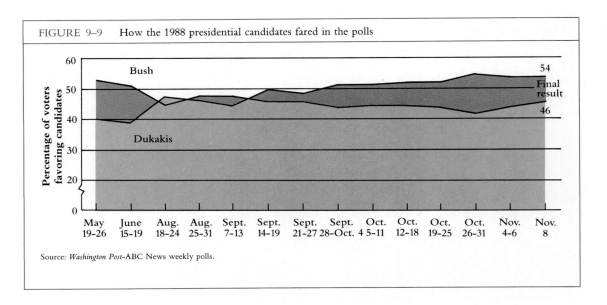

FIGURE 9–9   How the 1988 presidential candidates fared in the polls

Source: *Washington Post*-ABC News weekly polls.

the debate, but that Bush won on "likability." On October 5, the vice presidential candidates met to debate in Omaha. It was widely believed that Bentsen "won" the debate, the high point of which was when Bentsen declared that Quayle was "no Jack Kennedy."

The second Bush–Dukakis debate took place on October 13 on the campus of the University of California, Los Angeles. The media awarded the "victory" in this debate to Bush. After this second debate, criticism of Dukakis's campaign intensified, even on the part of some Democrats. Bush and campaigners in his behalf stepped up their mainly negative campaign. The polls continued to show Bush with a comfortable, though not a decisive lead. Nevertheless, Dukakis continued to campaign vigorously; at the end, he sought to take on the image of a fighter like Harry S Truman, who won the 1948 election despite all the predictions that Thomas E. Dewey, the Republican challenger, would win.

The polls proved correct. On election day, November 8, 54 percent of the voters chose George Bush for president, exactly the proportion accorded to him by the *Washington Post*–ABC poll (see Figure 9–9). Michael Dukakis did better than the polls suggested he might—he won 46 percent of the popular vote. But Bush won 426 electoral votes, while Dukakis won only 112. The Matthew effect of the electoral college system magnified Bush's popular vote majority—54 percent of the popular vote yielded him nearly 80 percent of the electoral vote (see Figure 9–10). Bush captured the electoral vote of all but 10 states and the District of Columbia. Dukakis won New York, Massachusetts, and Rhode Island in the East; he won the border state of West Virginia; he won the midwestern states of

FIGURE 9–10   The electoral map for 1988★

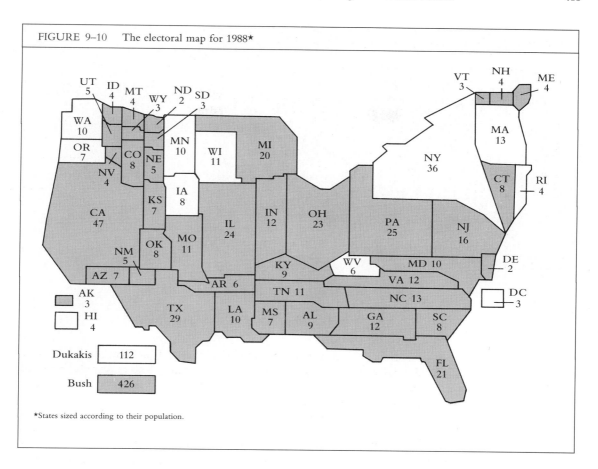

★States sized according to their population.

Minnesota, Iowa, and Wisconsin; he won the Pacific Northwest states of Washington and Oregon; and he won in Hawaii.

Who voted for Bush and for Dukakis? Bush won at least a bare majority of the popular vote in all regions of the country, though not in every state. The election outcome did see substantial disparities in the voting of men and women. While men supported Bush by a 57–41 percent margin, women divided about equally between Bush and Dukakis. And, in most of the states Dukakis carried, women were crucial to his successes; in Iowa, for example, where Duakakis won, 60 percent of women voters supported him compared to 49 percent of men. Young voters gave Bush a narrower margin than did their elders, and fewer voters between the ages of 18 and 29 voted for Bush than had supported Reagan in 1984. And fewer young voters went to the polls—voters under 30 accounted for only 20 percent of the electorate in 1988, compared to 24 percent in 1984. Dukakis was able to win back to the Democratic fold nearly half the Democrats who voted for Reagan in 1984, and he was supported by 86 percent

President George Bush celebrates his victory at the polls in the November 1988 presidential elections. The inauguration of every new president rekindles hope for a better world and brings a surge of public optimism and excitement.

of black voters. A bare majority of Catholics voted for Bush, but two thirds of Protestants and 81 percent of white fundamentalists or evangelical Christians voted for him. Dukakis won nearly two thirds of the Jewish vote.

Bush had won a hard-fought victory. He campaigned vigorously and effectively, and his campaign plans were well developed and well executed. Equally important, the times were on Bush's side—President Reagan's popularity was extraordinarily high, unemployment was dropping, the economy was in good shape, and the nation faced no excruciating international problem. Moreover, Dukakis's campaign was not very effectively shaped, and Dukakis did not prove to be a particularly inspiring campaigner to many voters whose support might have been won by a stronger Democratic campaign. At the same time, Dukakis's 46 percent of the popular vote was the highest for a Democratic presidential candidate in two decades, excepting Jimmy Carter's victory in 1976.

And it was a Democratic election year for offices other than president. Although the party of the winning presidential candidate usually can expect to gain congressional seats, in 1988 the Democrats actually gained three seats in the House of Representatives and one seat in the Senate. In

Part Three

THE GOVERNING INSTITUTIONS

The framers of the Constitution tried to create a *mixed government,* a government in which liberty would be balanced against the necessity of governing and power would be balanced within the constitutional system. They believed that liberty could be preserved only if governing power were divided between a national government and local states and between legislative, executive, and judicial branches of government. In *Federalist* No. 51, Alexander Hamilton developed these principles of division and balance in government, which he dubbed the theory of the *compound republic:* "In the compound republic of Amer-

ica, the power surrendered by the people is first divided between two distinct governments, and then the portion allotted to each subdivided among distinct and separate departments."

Today the compound republic is also complex. The legislative, executive, and judicial powers now lie in the hands of well-established institutions—organizationally intricate, stable, predictable, and deeply embedded in the American context. In Part Three, we unravel the complexity of these institutions, describing the work of Congress, the presidency, the bureaucracy, and the courts.

Chapter Ten

REPRESENTATION IN CONGRESS

*I*n California's 19th Congressional District, an expensive, close-fought election battle is raging. Just beyond the northern fringe of the Los Angeles metropolitan area and centered on the coastal cities of Santa Barbara and Ventura, the 19th is a political battleground in more ways than one. The pressures of growth are applauded in the northern and southern edges of the district but resisted by Santa Barbara voters whose costly homes overlook a phalanx of offshore oil rigs in the Santa Barbara channel. Home of Ronald Reagan's mountaintop ranch, the district has voted Republican in recent national contests but "has enough Democrats to keep it from being a safely Republican district" (Ehrenhalt, 1987: 148) and has sent Democrats to the state legislature in Sacramento.

One of these Democrats, State Senator Gary K. Hart (no relation of the Colorado presidential contender) challenged the district's veteran incumbent, Representative Robert J. Lagomarsino. For eight terms, Lagomarsino had built his career on attentive constituency service and a shrewd combination of conservative voting and active environmentalism. Hart challenged this record by charging that Lagomarsino had lagged in protecting the Santa Barbara channel and was far to the right of his constituency, especially in his support for Nicaragua's *contra* rebels. Both candidates were well known and well financed.

Three thousand miles to the east, the 100th Congress was lurching to a conclusion. The wearisome warfare between Congress, with its Democratic majority, and the Reagan administration, nearing its end, prolonged the legislative deliberations. A quiet but key player for the minority Republicans was Lagomarsino, secretary to the Republican Conference and senior member to two committees, Foreign Affairs and Interior and Insular Affairs. Lagomarsino's career in his district and his career on Capitol Hill have been intertwined: His past electoral successes have given him leverage in his committees and among his colleagues, while his policy stands and voting record have become an issue in his home base.

Robert J. Logomarsino, a veteran California Republican congressman, first won his seat in 1974 following a dozen years in the California Senate. After winning reelection easily in six subsequent campaigns, in 1988 he was seriously challenged by Gary Hart, a Democratic state senator.

The contest in California's 19th District illustrates the paradox of "the two Congresses" (Davidson and Oleszek, 1985). For the U.S. Congress has a dual character that is virtually unique among the world's national legislatures. It is at once a collection of 540 politicians elected from areas scattered across the map and a policy-making body that must resolve problems and write laws under which we live.

Congress's two-headed nature was fully intended by the writers of the Constitution. Defended by colonial assemblies in their clashes with the British Crown, our founders believed heartily in the primacy of representative bodies. They designed the House of Representatives as a body close to the people. With smaller constituencies than those of senators and shorter two-year terms of office, representatives would have (as James Madison put it in *Federalist* No. 52) "an immediate dependence on, and an intimate sympathy with, the people." The Senate was supposed to work at arm's length, its members chosen by states for six-year terms, but the people's voice was assured by the 17th Amendment (1913), a Progressive Era reform that provided for direct election. Today members of both House and Senate assign high priority to constituents' views and interests and spend much time and money cultivating goodwill at home.

Yet Congress is a *policy-making* as well as a *representative* body. It is no accident that the Constitution's very first article sets forth Congress's sweeping powers, including that of making all laws "necessary and proper" to carry out the enumerated powers. "In republican government, the legislative authority necessarily predominates," wrote Madison in *Federalist* No. 51. In parliamentary systems such as those in Europe, the assembly mainly debates and approves policies drafted by the government of the day—which is really a kind of executive committee of the majority party or coalition. Our Congress, in stark contrast, is a working body that writes, processes, and refines its own measures, relying primarily on "in-house" resources, before sending them to the president to be acted on.

This chapter and the next are devoted to the "two Congresses." In this chapter, we describe the individual men and women whose backgrounds and careers constitute the first Congress—Congress as an assembly of individual representatives. In Chapter 11, we explore the second Congress, the policy-making body that must somehow weave all of the local and regional concerns into laws affecting the entire nation and its place in the world.

According to American political theory, the legislative branch is uniquely the people's voice. "Here, sir, the people govern," observed Alexander Hamilton—who was himself suspicious of popular institutions. "This body," said a former member of Congress, "is a mirror in which America can see herself." The president is exalted and surrounded by retinues of aides and security guards; executive-branch agencies are often faceless, their workers countless and invisible; the courts work in magisterial isolation. But our traditions dictate that Congress remain open and accessible.

GETTING TO CONGRESS— AND STAYING

Who Are the Legislators?

The constitutional requirements for holding office are fairly broad: age (25 years of age for the House of Representatives, 30 for the Senate), U.S. citizenship (seven years for the House, nine for the Senate), and residency in the state.

The residency requirement is sometimes hard to apply, given the high mobility of Americans. Voters seem to prefer candidates with long-standing ties to the state or district. But well-known people are sometimes elected from places where they reside only in the loosest sense.

How representative?

In practice, the gateways to election are much narrower than the constitutional requirements. So not all Americans have an equal chance of serving.

As a whole, the members of Congress are an elite group. The average representative is about 50 years old, and the average senator is in the mid-50s—considerably older than the average voter, who is in his or her mid-30s. Members of Congress also tend to be Capitol Hill veterans. In the 1980s, the average representative had served a little more than 10 years, or 5.3 House terms, and the average senator had served about the same length of time—10.5 years, or 1.7 Senate terms. A new Congress convenes every two years (hence, the 100th Congress met during the Constitution's bicentennial year of 1987), following elections in which all of the

PRACTICE OF POLITICS

Minorities in Congress

Minorities are represented in the U.S. Congress—but they lag in both time and numbers. Time is required for minorities to gather the political momentum they need to capture a political area and to promote their candidates in legislative contests.

In the late 1980s, there were 23 black members (including 1 nonvoting delegate), all in the House of Representatives. Although this was the largest contingent of blacks ever to serve, it was only about 4 percent of the members of Congress, compared with the 13 percent of blacks in the total population. There were also 14 Hispanic members (including 3 delegates), 8 members of Asian/Pacific Island ancestry (including 2 delegates), and 1 native American.

About half of the blacks who served in Congress historically came to Washington during the Reconstruction Era following the Civil War. At that time, two blacks, both from Mississippi, served in the Senate. The last of the Reconstruction blacks retired from Congress in 1901.

Three decades passed before the first of the modern black members, Oscar De Priest of Illinois, was elected, in 1928. Only three more blacks were elected over the next 25 years. But by the 1960s, as concentrated black voting in urban areas increased, so did black representation in Congress. Today most black members come from districts with a

Following a stint in the Texas Senate, Barbara Jordan (D–Tex.) served with distinction in the U.S. House of Representatives from 1972 to 1978. She won acclaim for her performance in the televised House Judiciary Committee hearings concerning the impeachment of President Richard M. Nixon and as a keynoter at the 1976 Democratic National Convention.

majority of black or minority voters; few blacks are "crossover" candidates from predominantly white areas. Indeed, there has been pressure to choose blacks in such districts; longtime Representative Peter W. Rodino, Jr. (D–N.J.) was persuaded to retire in 1988 because, it was argued,

(Continued)

PRACTICE OF POLITICS

(Concluded)

his Newark district deserved black representation.

Coming from solid minority districts, black lawmakers tend to be returned to office indefinitely. Many of them reap the rewards of seniority by ascending to committee or subcommittee chairmanships. No fewer than seven blacks chaired standing or special House committees during the 100th Congress (1987–88). Two Hispanics chaired House committees.

The representation of minority groups usually lags behind their proportion of the general population. When minorities are concentrated (say, in an urban area), their cause is aided. Even so, several generations of struggle are often required before a minority group comes into its own politically. At first, the minority group will be represented by someone from the dominant racial or ethic group. Then, a transitional or "bridge" representative of the minority group will gain prominence and may even be elected. Finally, someone from the mainstream of the minority group will attain leadership and be elected as its representative to the legislature.

House seats and a third of the Senate seats are contested. Somewhere between 10 and 20 percent of the two chambers' membership turns over with each new Congress.

Educational and occupational levels also mark the lawmakers as an elite. By every measure, members of Congress are a highly educated group; in the mid-1980s, the Senate boasted five former Rhodes scholars. The professions dominate—especially law (nearly half of the members) but also business, teaching, journalism, and public service. In recent Congresses, only one or two members had blue-collar backgrounds.

The "log cabin–to–Capitol Hill" myth emphatically does not apply to today's legislators. Members of both chambers tend to come from middle- and upper-class families. A number are wealthy: an estimated one third of all senators are millionaires, a fact that no doubt helps them endure their $89,500 annual salaries.

Only a handful of blacks and Hispanics serve in Congress, though their numbers are growing slowly. The 100th Congress (1987–88) included 23 blacks (all in the House), most of whom came from heavily black districts and seven of whom chaired House committees. There were also 14 Hispanics (4 each from Texas and California), 2 of whom chaired committees.

Congress has been a mostly male institution; of the 535 members of the 100th Congress, only 25 were women; 2 of them served in the Senate.

PRACTICE OF POLITICS

Women In Congress

Not allowed to vote nationally until 1920, women have always been underrepresented in the halls of Congress. A little over a hundred women have served in Congress since that time.

Jeannette Rankin (R–Mont.), the first woman to serve in Congress, was one of the most remarkable figures in American history. Strong-willed and irascible, she served only two terms in the House (1917–19, 1941–42), just long enough to cast her vote against both World War I and World War II (in the latter case, she was the only dissenter).

Many of the early women lawmakers served after their husbands died in office—the so-called widow's mandate. Although some of these women merely served out the husband's term, a number stayed on to build sustained political careers in their own right. Virtually all of the women now serving in Congress have built their own political careers, and their numbers are steadily increasing. In the 100th Congress (1987–88), there were two women senators and 23 women representatives.

For a number of years after she bagan a career as a social worker in 1909, Jeannette Rankin campaigned for women's suffrage in California, Washington, and Montana. She also served as legislative secretary of the National American Women's Suffrage Association.

Indeed, only a hundred or so women have served in Congress since Jeannette Rankin (R–Mont.), the first woman to serve, was elected to the House in 1916. At first, many women were elected on the so-called widow's mandate, when they would take the place of husbands who died in office. Now, however, most women in Congress pursue their own political careers (Gertzog, 1984). Their growing influence on Capitol Hill was underscored in 1984, when Geraldine Ferraro (D–N.Y.) was chosen as the vice-presidential candidate of the Democratic party.

Thus, Congress is make up of people who do not strictly represent the population in terms of age, education, wealth, color, or sex. (The same applies to the courts and the management of executive agencies.)

Virtual representation

Must Congress be demographically representative? Not necessarily. Legislators can speak effectively for voters of different social rank or lifestyle. This is called *virtual representation*. Legislators from farming districts, for instance, can voice farmers' concerns even though they themselves have never plowed a field or milked a cow.

Speaking up for constituents is natural for legislators. They are in the business of cultivating public support. Before coming to Congress, most senators and representatives apprentice in state and local politics, most often in state legislatures. As transplanted locals, legislators reflect the values and attitudes of their home districts. If they lose touch with constituents' demands, they risk losing office.

Yet there is no substitute for having a grouping's own members serve in Congress. For example, the sensitivity of Congress to the needs of women and minorities has been heightened by the presence of women and minority members. And for voters of those groupings, having their own in office symbolizes a "coming of age." Such legislators become leaders for group members throughout the nation, not just in their own states or districts.

Congressional Elections

Congressional contests, especially House races, are given far less publicity than presidential elections. Yet the congressional election system (described in Chapter 9) is at least as important as the presidential election system, for it determines not only who controls a coequal branch of government but also direct representation for states and districts.

The Senate

Each state is represented equally in the U.S. Senate—two senators from each state. Because the states vary widely in population, the Senate is the one legislative body in the nation where the "one person, one vote" rule emphatically does not apply. Article V of the Constitution assures each state of equal Senate representation, regardless of population, and guarantees that no state will be deprived of its equal representation without its consent. No state is apt to give such consent, so for all practical purposes

Senate representation is an unamendable feature of the Constitution.

The founders stipulated that senators were to be designated by their respective state legislatures rather than by the voters, who chose members of the House of Representatives. Their idea was that the Senate would be a counterweight to the popular interests embodied in the larger House. This distinction was eroded when the 17th Amendment (1913) provided for direct popular election of senators.

As long as the states were relatively unpopulated and senators were selected indirectly, the Senate tended to be a collection of spokesmen for dominant state or regional interests—cotton, oil, tobacco, banking, and so forth. Today, however, a majority of the states boast highly varied economies, so that statewide electorates tend to be microcosms of the entire nation.

Although the six-year terms of senators seem long compared with the two-year House terms, senators are far less assured of reelection than representatives. The panoply of interests embodied in statewide constituencies tends to make statewide elections more competitive than elections in the smaller House districts. As a result, senatorial elections tend to be closer and incumbents more frequently defeated. Keenly aware of the possibility of defeat at the polls, senators travel home and cultivate their voters as assiduously as do their House counterparts.

The House of Representatives

Article I of the Constitution awards each state at least one member of the House regardless of population. Additional House members are apportioned among the states by population.

Following the federal census, congressional district boundary lines are redrawn, if necessary, to reflect population changes. For more than a century, the House was enlarged every decade to minimize the adverse effect of population shifts on state delegations. Since 1910, however, the House's size has stabilized at 435 (today it also includes 4 delegates and 1 resident commissioner). Thus, states gain or lose congressional seats with population movements. Today's shifts pit the older, industrial Northeast against the growing South and West—the Frostbelt against the Sunbelt. After the 1980 census Florida, California, and Texas gained House seats; New York, Illinois, Ohio, and Pennsylvania lost seats. Population projections suggest that the trend will continue (see Figure 10–1).

The "Incumbency Party" in Congress

The most important fact about House and Senate elections is that in most cases incumbents are running for reelection and usually prevail. "Congress is not controlled by the Democratic party or the Republican party," declared Fred Wertheimer, the president of Common Cause. "It is controlled by the incumbency party."

Figure 10–1 House of Representatives apportionment, 1980 and 2000

House Apportionment, 1980
(Representation in the House for the 98th–102nd Congresses)

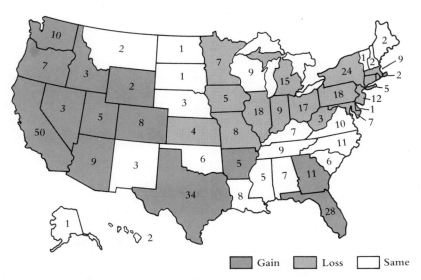

Projected House Apportionment, 2000
(Based on 1983 Population Estimates)

Source: Congressional Research Service.

TABLE 10-1   A Representative's typical day

Activity		Average time
In the House chamber		2:53 hours
In committee/subcommittee work		1:24 hours
Hearings	26 minutes	
Business	9 minutes	
Markups	42 minutes	
Other	5 minutes	
In his/her office		3:19 hours
With constituents	17 minutes	
With organized groups	9 minutes	
With others	20 minutes	
With staff aides	53 minutes	
With other representatives	5 minutes	
Answering mail	46 minutes	
Preparing legislation, speeches	12 minutes	
Reading	11 minutes	
On telephone	26 minutes	
In other Washington locations		2:02 hours
With constituents at Capitol	9 minutes	
At events	33 minutes	
With leadership	3 minutes	
With other representatives	11 minutes	
With informal groups	8 minutes	
In party meetings	5 minutes	
Personal time	28 minutes	
Other	25 minutes	
Other		1:40 hours
Total average representative's day		11:18 hours

Source: U.S. House of Representatives, Commission on Administrative Review, *Administrative Reorganization and Legislative Management* (95th Congress, 1st session, 1977, H. Doc. 95–232), pp. 18–19.

The "vanishing marginals"

House seats, for example, are among the least competitive offices in the American political system. Moreover, there is evidence that they have become less competitive over time. Political scientists (Mayhew, 1974) refer to the mystery of the "vanishing marginals"—that is, the declining number of truly competitive House districts, or **marginal districts,** (those won by, say, less than 55 percent of the vote). In any given election year, no more than 10 to 15 percent of all House seats are marginal in this sense.

Electoral turnover, too, is quite low. In 1986, no less than 98 percent of the incumbents running for reelection were returned to office. In 64 congressional districts, no candidate stepped forward to challenge the incumbent, who therefore ran unopposed. In the congressional elections held since 1976, an average of 60 House members have run without major-party opposition; about three quarters of these lucky officeholders have been Democrats. Sitting Senators usually win too, but their seats are more precarious: in 1986, for example, three fourths of the incumbents running for reelection were successful—a typical figure for the Senate.

Incumbent advantages

Differing explanations are advanced to explain the lack of competition for House seats. The nature of House districts is partly to blame. Few of these districts parallel any other geographic, community, or political dividing lines. Few towns or counties or natural areas (for example, watersheds or marketing regions) coincide exactly with congressional districts. Hence, there are no automatic forums or media outlets for candidates; nor is there normally a ready-made partisan organization.

Would-be candidates thus face the arduous job of piecing together a network of supporters and getting their names known in the district. To form a campaign organization, backers may have to be recruited from a multiplicity of local organizations. Buying TV time or newspaper space may be costly and wasteful: If a district is spread out, a number of outlets must be employed; if a district is only part of a metropolitan area, TV and newspaper exposure is expensive and wasteful, because it reaches many voters outside the district. To the extent that the district has been gerrymandered, competition is further dampened.

Incumbents, on the other hand, command powerful advantages over potential challengers—in resources, organization, and sheer visibility. They have staff help (including district offices), opportunities to help constituents with problems, free mailing privileges, and knowledge of national problems (Fiorina, 1977). Thus, there is some truth to the saying that old congressmen never die and hardly ever fade away.

The Job of the Legislator

Legislators differ widely in how they represent the people (see Table 10–1). Some are errand runners who spend most of their time keeping contact with their home bases and answering constituents' requests for help. Errand runners include freshmen legislators who are unsure of reelection, legislators from competitive or marginal districts, legislators whose districts are so close to the nation's capital that voters expect them to be back home each weekend, and senators near the end of their term who face a close reelection fight.

Other legislators channel their energies into legislative tasks. They let their staff aides handle back-home relations. Most legislators of this kind are from safe districts, have high seniority or leadership posts, or are so firmly entrenched that they have few reelection fears.

The voices of constituents sometimes come to members of Congress in unusual ways. This staffer in the office of U.S. senator John Warner (R–Va.) looks dismayed after Virginia shoe manufacturers flooded the office with demands that protectionist legislation for American workers be enacted. The demands were sent on pieces of leather in the shape of a shoe.

Whom to listen to?

Legislators also differ widely in their approach to lawmaking tasks. Their workload is so heavy that they cannot be fully informed on every matter. So they seek cues from many sources on how to vote. Some rely on their own knowledge or conscience; others follow instructions, either actual or implied, from their voters.

A pivotal distinction in a lawmaker's perception of representation was articulated by Edmund Burke, the 18th-century British philosopher and statesman, who held that legislators should voice the "general reason of the whole" rather than merely "local prejudices." Two dimensions are embedded in Burke's distinction. One turns on legislators' *styles* of representation: whether they accept instructions (the **delegate**), act on their own initiative (the **trustee**), or act on some combination of the two (the **politico**). The other dimension is the *focus* of representation: whether leg-

TABLE 10–2   Representational roles of House members

Role	Percentage
Trustee	28%
Politico	46
Delegate	23
Undetermined	3
Total	100%

Source: Roger H. Davidson, *The Role of the Congressman* (Indianapolis, Ind.: Bobbs-Merrill, 1969), p. 117.

islators think mainly in terms of the whole nation, their own constituencies, or some combination of the two.

In practice, legislators tailor their behavior to the situation (see Table 10–2). The critical distinction seems to be whether a member is electorally vulnerable or safe. The vulnerable member is closely tethered; the safe member is freer to be a statesman (Davidson, 1969). When push comes to shove, most legislators will slight their legislative duties to mend fences back home and keep their jobs. As one representative put it, "All members of Congress have a primary interest in being reelected. But some members have no other interest."

Skillful legislators learn to anticipate voter reactions and to spot the issues of highest concern. Legislators enjoy freedom of action to the extent that their voters are uninformed or unconcerned about the issues (Miller and Stokes, 1963). Elected officials would agree with the legislator who observed that although everything he did had a relationship to his district, the district was not his sole basis for choice.

Home styles

As important as legislators' stands on issues is how they project themselves in their home states or districts. Richard F. Fenno, Jr. (1978), calls this the legislators' **home styles.**

Home styles are made up of several factors. One factor is how legislators allocate resources. How do they use staff, office, or funds? How do they use their greatest resource—their own time? A study of 419 representatives found that the average member made 35 trips home (not counting recesses) and spent 138 days there (counting recesses). Nearly one third of these representatives returned to their districts every weekend (Parker, 1986).

A second factor in home style is the legislators' "presentation of self" in making face-to-face contacts with voters and in voicing issues and informing constituents. Does the incumbent project the image of a legislative craftsman, a national leader, a reformer, an errand runner, or a "good ol' boy (or gal)"? The repertoire of styles is virtually unlimited.

Each day, mail from constituents comes in to congressional offices. Here, a congressional staffer sorts one day's intake of constituent mail. Although some of this mail deals with major political issues or bills in Congress, most of it deals with such personal matters as difficulties in getting veterans' benefits or welfare benefits. Much of the mail asks the representative or senator to serve as an intermediary between constituents and government agencies.

Finally, legislators form certain themes to explain their work in Washington to the voters. They know far more about issues than the average person, so they can usually explain their behavior well enough to please all but the most demanding listeners. Not a few legislators bolster their home image by "running against Congress"—defending their own record while faulting the records of their House or Senate colleagues.

Constituency outreach

An important point of contact between legislators and the electorate is constituency service. This includes answering mail, solving constituents' problems, making speeches in the state or district, putting out newsletters or press releases, and meeting with voters.

Many of these are *casework* tasks—helping people cope with an ever-

TABLE 10–3   What is "constituency casework"?

Category of cases	Percent*
Inquiries about legislation	16
Requests for a government job	8
Help with Social Security	8
Hardship discharges from the military	7
Requests for government publications	7
Seeking appointments to military academies	4
Help with unemployment assistance benefits	4
Tax problems	2
Legal problems	1
Miscellaneous problems	49

*Figures total more than 100 percent because some respondents are included in more than one category.
Source: U.S. House of Representatives, Commission on Administrative Review, *Final Report* (95th Congress, 1st session, 1977, H. Doc. 95–272), vol. 2, p. 830.

more-complex government bureaucracy. (The leading types of casework are listed in Table 10–3.) Besides handling constituents' problems (for instance, investigating errors in Social Security or veterans' payments), legislators use casework to build support for reelection. In a 1976 study, 15 percent of all adults reported that they or a member of their family had asked for help from their representative. Of these adults, 7 out of 10 said that they were satisfied with the way their request had been handled (House Commission on Administrative Review, 1977).

The government subsidizes senators' and representatives' offices to help them keep in touch with their people (see accompanying box). These subsidies are sometimes derided as fringe benefits or perquisites. The House has an array of benefits; Senate subsidies vary with the state's population. The average House member is allowed a payroll of about $400,000 a year; Senate payrolls range from nearly $700,000 (for Delaware and Alaska) to more than $1.3 million (for New York and California).

As the accompanying box shows, the average representative receives perquisites valued at over $1.2 million for each two-year term, and the average senator's office operation requires more than that in a single year. Such resources are needed, but they also help stimulate support and firm up the legislator's reelection chances. In the hands of a skillful incumbent with an able staff, these resources give an edge that few challengers can beat. That edge is surely a factor in returning incumbents to office.

Members' offices

Legislators' workloads are now staggering. "It was a pretty nice job that a member of Congress had in those days," recalled former Representative Robert Ramspeck (D–Ga.), who came to Washington in 1911 as a staff

PRACTICE OF POLITICS

A Rough Idea of Congressional Allowances, 1988

There are two conclusions about allowances: (1) they have risen greatly in recent years, and (2) the exact figures are hard to obtain.

Following is a list of available figures for House and Senate allowances in 1988. In some cases, no dollar value is given because it is hard to determine the range of reimbursed costs—for example, in travel or telephone reimbursements. Most of the 1988 allowances can be transferred from one account to another.

	House	Senate
Salary	$89,500★	$89,500★
Washington office		$716,102–1,458,856†
Staff	$379,480	
Committee legislative assistants	‡	$243,543
Interns	$2,000	—
General office expenses	$67,000	$36,000–156,000†
Telephone/telegraph	15,000 long-distance minutes to district (min. $6,000)	§
Stationery	§	1.8 million–26.6 million pieces
Office space	2500 sq. ft.	4,800-8,000 sq. ft.
Furnishings	§	§
Equipment	Provided	Provided
District/state offices		
Rental	2,500 sq. ft.	4,800–8,000 sq. ft.
Furnishings/equipment	$35,000	$30,000–41,744
Mobile office	—	One
Communications		Provided by Senate Computer Center
Automated correspondence	§	
Audio/video reccordings;		
photography	§	§
Travel	Formula (min. $6,200; max. approx. $67,200)	§

★Salary established January 1, 1987; leaders' salaries are higher.

†Senators are allowed expenses based on a sliding scale linked to the state's population.

‡Provided for members of Appropriations, Budget, and Rules committees.

§Expenses are covered through the general office expenses line item. In most cases, supplies and equipment are charged at rates well below retail levels.

Source: Paul E. Duryer, "Salaries and Allowances: The Congress," CRS Issue Brief, (November 2, 1987).

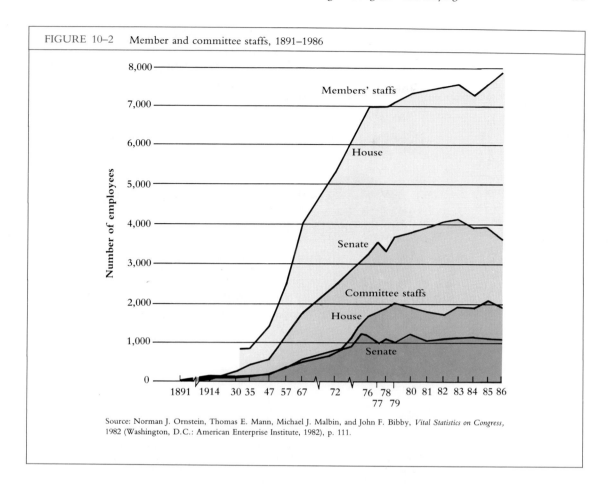

FIGURE 10–2   Member and committee staffs, 1891–1986

Source: Norman J. Ornstein, Thomas E. Mann, Michael J. Malbin, and John F. Bibby, *Vital Statistics on Congress,* 1982 (Washington, D.C.: American Enterprise Institute, 1982), p. 111.

aide. At that time, letters to legislators were confined mainly to the problems of rural mail routes, pensions for Spanish-American War veterans, free seed for farmers, and once in a while a legislative matter. One clerk was enough to handle the mail. Now constituencies are larger and more sophisticated in examining potential candidates, and the government has a bigger role in people's lives.

Behind the senators and representatives now stands a large bureaucracy (Figure 10–2). Legislators rely on staffs to handle the growing workload. Staffs communicate with local voters, help run committee and floor sessions, and even frame issues and clarify choices in policy debates.

There are four main categories of congressional staffs: personal staffs (some 12,000 people); committee staffs (about 3,000 people); housekeeping staffs at the Capitol; and supporting agencies—the Congressional Research Service, the General Accounting Office, the Office of Technology Assessment, and the Congressional Budget Office. The supporting agencies,

Members of Congress need help in performing the tasks that are expected of them. They rely on staffs of experts and assistants. In every congressional office, the leading staff person is the administrative assistant (AA). This veteran AA, Michael B. Levy, works for Sen. Lloyd Bentsen (D–Tex.). He heads the senator's Washington, D.C., staff of 33 people. Senator Bentsen also maintains three offices in Texas, where 21 other staff people implement his efforts.

which employ about 18,000 workers, serve many public and private needs in addition to those of Congress.

The first two categories—personal and committee staffs—have more than doubled in size since the early 1960s. Before World War I, senators outnumbered their paid personal staff members; by 1976, there were almost 3,300 such aides. At first, legislators were leery of voting for enough staff assistance, fearing the charge of wasteful spending. But this objection was overturned in the 1960s as legislators tried vainly to cope with the workload and compete with executive-branch expertise. Today senators' personal staffs range in size from 13 to 71, averaging about 36. Representatives' staffs average about 17.

Personal aides do many things. Constituent relations are their most time-consuming job. This includes handling casework, projects, requests for information, and correspondence and meeting with local voters and lobbyists. Personal aides also give press relations a high priority. Other staff aides handle a broad range of tasks that includes information gathering, legislative drafting, policy formation, and office management.

A legislator's good right arm is the **administrative assistant (AA).** He or she supervises the legislator's office and gives political and legislative advice. At best, an AA functions as the legislator's alter ego, negotiating with colleagues, voters, and lobbyists.

The legislative and research functions of a legislator's office are usually handled by one or more **legislative assistants (LAs)** or researchers. Their tasks include working with and representing the legislator's interests. Often they follow committee sessions that the legislator cannot attend. LAs research, draft, read, and analyze bills and other materials. They also write speeches, floor remarks, and articles.

Legislators can also call on the assistance of staff members of the committees to which they are assigned. The functions of these aides sometimes mingle with those of the personal staff.

Caseworkers handle questions on certain types of constituents' problems. For instance, they deal with Social Security or veterans' benefits. They are valued for their knowledge of federal programs and for their lists of phone numbers. They know which bureaucrats to call for quick answers.

Most personal staff aides work in crowded Capitol Hill offices. But more than a third of representatives' personal staffs and more than a fourth of senators' staffs are based in their home districts or states. Members of Congress have from one to six local offices in key locations at home. More and more casework and voter contacts are handled there.

Private domains

Personal staffs are guided by the legislators' ideologies, interests, personalities, institutional positions, and personal roles or styles in performing the duties of office. Legislators are masters of these little kingdoms. They (or their office managers) personally hire (and fire) every staff member. Although most staff members are well paid, they have no job rights and can be removed at any time.

Legislators insist that this system is dictated by the political nature of their office tasks and the need for loyal aides. But abuses occur; there have been frequent charges of discrimination and irregular assignments. In 1976, a Capitol Hill secretary, Elizabeth Ray, charged that she lacked clerical skills but had been hired to give sexual favors to Representative Wayne Hays (D–Ohio). The resulting uproar ended Hays's career in Con-

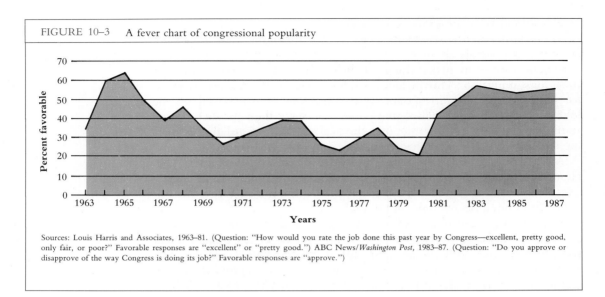

FIGURE 10–3   A fever chart of congressional popularity

Sources: Louis Harris and Associates, 1963–81. (Question: "How would you rate the job done this past year by Congress—excellent, pretty good, only fair, or poor?" Favorable responses are "excellent" or "pretty good.") ABC News/*Washington Post,* 1983–87. (Question: "Do you approve or disapprove of the way Congress is doing its job?" Favorable responses are "approve.")

gress and forced a wide-ranging study of House ethics and office procedures. Despite recurrent problems, however, no major changes have been
made in congressional staffing practices.

The Public Looks at Congress

Americans are of two minds about Congress. As an institution, it is an
enigma to most people. Its large size, puzzling procedures, and measured
pace all blur its image. Individual legislators, in contrast, are better understood and receive higher public approval.

Congress as policymaker

Most people think of Congress in public policy terms. They expect Congress, like the president, to solve problems and keep the ship of state on
an even keel. They also expect Congress to respond to (but not necessarily
follow) the president's initiatives (Parker, 1974).

Public approval of Congress rises and falls with economic conditions,
wars and crises, and feelings of optimism or cynicism—the same factors
that affect views of presidential performance (as we will see in Chapter
13). If people are unhappy, fearful, or cynical (as they were in the 1970s),
they hold Congress in low esteem; if people feel pleased about the state of
the nation, they tend to approve Congress's work (see Figure 10–3). An
irony of the Reagan era was that citizens reacted positively to vigorous
leadership in the White House but also raised their assessment of Congress, which often fiercely contested Reagan's policies.

Legislators as individuals

People have more detailed expectations for individual legislators than for Congress as a whole. If Congress is mysterious and distant, incumbent legislators are fairly well known in their states or districts. They are judged less on policy contributions than on service to their districts. How accessible are they? How well do they communicate with voters? Do they help in solving voters' problems? And do they have the ability to "bring home the bacon" in the form of federal contracts and grants? (Parker and Davidson, 1979)

Legislators and their staffs spend much time and effort fulfilling these expectations. This usually pays off. Voters repeatedly proclaim their representative to be "the best congressman in the whole country." Surveys consistently find that far more people rate their own representatives positively than give similar high marks to Congress as a whole.

The public's final verdict on its legislators is of course at the polls, and here the picture is quite positive. Incumbent representatives usually win reelection. Since World War II, on average 9 out of 10 House members running for reelection have been successful in any given election. Senate reelection is less of a sure thing: about three fourths of incumbent senators running for reelection are successful. As we have noted, the larger, more diverse statewide electorates are more prone to provide competition for incumbents than the smaller House districts. Not that voters need to unseat many lawmakers to get their message across: the failure of one or two incumbents at the polls is enough to make other incumbents take notice and adjust their behavior accordingly.

PARTIES AND LEADERS IN CONGRESS

Given the rampant individualism and the career interests of politicians, it may seem odd to talk about parties and leaders in Congress. Yet the political parties organize the two chambers, choose their leaders, and shape the legislative agenda. As we saw in Chapter 6, American political parties, while falling far short of ideological consistency or membership loyalty, are nonetheless powerful and stable institutions. This is equally true on Capitol Hill, where political parties and their leaders are the major centralizers of congressional power.

Partisan control hinges on the size of the parties' ranks in the two chambers. The majority party (having at least 51 senators or 218 representatives) organizes the respective houses. The party's size and unity determine how effective its control will be.

Anyone who doubts the congressional majority's power ought to ask Senate Democrats, who in 1981 lost their majority in that chamber for the first time in 26 years, or Senate Republicans, whose majority was snatched away from them after the 1986 elections. Suddenly their senior members no longer chaired the committees—set the agenda, called the meetings, or hired the majority staffs. Their floor leaders no longer scheduled the business or set the pace of debates. Their party no longer supplied the support personnel who keep the chamber running smoothly. About the only consolation for minority members is that they don't have to show up on time to preside over hearings or deliberations.

Recent political history has given the parties quite different roles in the two chambers. Democrats have since 1930 controlled the House for all but four years (1947–48, 1953–54), often with heavy majorities. Accordingly, Democrats have a tight grip on the House and its operations; the chamber's rules give the majority leeway to control the committee and floor agendas. The frustrated minority Republicans, with slim hopes of taking over in the foreseeable future, have often been reduced to the role of watchdogs and critics.

The Senate is a less partisan body. Party margins in the 1980s have been slender, and both parties have been in the majority at one time or another. Individual senators of either party command deference and influence; party members must often "cross the aisle" (deal with the other party's members) to forge winning coalitions behind measures.

Leadership in the House

The House of Representatives has a history of strong leadership. The chamber's chief officer is the Speaker of the House, who is cited in the Constitution and who combines the duties of presiding officer with those of a party leader. In the 19th century, the speakership soon evolved into the most visible and powerful post on Capitol Hill; forceful Speakers such as Henry Clay (1811–14, 1815–20, 1823–25), Thomas B. "Czar" Reed (1889–91, 1895–99), and Joseph G. "Uncle Joe" Cannon (1903–11) centralized power and whipped the House into line. Today's Speakers, by contrast, rely on persuasive skills, shrewd advisers, and a precise sense of timing to exert influence. Some, like Sam Rayburn (D–Tex.) (1940–46, 1949–52, 1955–61) and Thomas P. "Tip" O'Neill (D–Mass.) (1977–86), parlayed their powers into forceful control of the chamber.

Speakers manage House business. They control an array of formal powers that regulate the flow of legislation and keep the House running more smoothly than the fragmented, individualistic Senate. (1) Speakers refer bills to committees. They can refer bills jointly or in sequence to two or more committees, sometimes imposing deadlines for the committees to report. (2) Using their combination of skills and resources, Speakers influence standing committee assignments; they appoint members of select and conference committees. (3) Speakers coordinate the activities of the various committee and subcommittee chairmen. They take the lead in scheduling bills for floor consideration and help committee leaders sell the bills on the floor. (4) As the presiding officer, the Speaker has the power to recognize members on the floor (grant them the right to speak) and can vote to break ties.

Top row, left to right: Henry Clay (Ky.) first of the forceful Speakers of the House of Representatives (elected six times between 1811 and 1824); Thomas B. "Czar" Reed (R-Me.), served in the 1890s; Joseph G. "Uncle Joe" Cannon (R-Ill.), House Speaker from 1903 until 1911. Bottom row: Thomas P. "Tip" O'Neil (D-Mass.), 1977 to 1986, speaks under portrait of Sam Rayburn (D-Tex.), who presided most of the time from 1940 to 1961; and James C. "Jim" Wright (D-Tex.) elected in 1987 for the 100th Congress.

Speakers also have unwritten powers, depending on their personal qualities or bargaining skills. The legendary Rayburn, Speaker in the 1940s and 1950s, relied on parliamentary skills and a group of able lieutenants known as his "Board of Education." O'Neill, a big man with a shock of white hair and an Irish wit, was likable and fair-minded in dealing with fellow members. Though a seemingly unpromising TV personality, he adapted his style after 1981 to combat the Reagan administration through media appearances and pointed quotes, becoming the best-known modern Speaker. His successor, Jim Wright (D–Tex.), guided a lengthy agenda and embarked on daring policy gambits in his early years.

The Speaker is helped by the **majority floor leader**, who by tradition is next in line for the top position. The majority leader is the chief floor spokesman for the party, scheduling bills and marshaling the party's voting strength. The floor leader is assisted in turn by the chief majority **whip** and deputy whips (so called because their job is to whip the party's members into line). They notify members of pending business, poll them on their intentions, and try to bring members to the floor at the right moment to vote on key issues.

The minority leader (the opposition party's candidate for Speaker) and the minority whip perform similar tasks. But they have fewer rewards to dispense to their colleagues. Party leaders are judged on how they "count the House" (predict the outcome of votes), schedule key debates and votes for best effect, and gather majorities for key measures.

Leadership in the Senate

In the Senate, strong leadership has been the exception rather than the rule. Not until the turn of the present century did visible party leaders emerge, and even then they were no match for the powerful House Speakers (Rothman, 1966).

The presiding officer of the Senate is quite insignificant. The vice president, though the constitutional presiding officer, is not a member of the body. The **president pro tem** is an honorific office given to the senior majority-party senator. But most of the time, freshman senators take turns in the chair, leaning on the parliamentarians for advice.

Floor leaders and whips in the Senate have the same duties as their House counterparts, but they have much looser reins on their troops. Senate floor leaders have varying leadership styles. Lyndon Johnson's unique success as majority leader (1955–61) stemmed partly from his persuasive skills. He fostered a consensus atmosphere that encouraged senatorial courtesy, specialization of activities, and deference to senior members (Matthews, 1960). The unique character of the 1950s also aided Johnson: Party and seniority leaders were mostly conservative, and President Eisenhower did not press for much new legislation. Liberals chafed under Johnson's tight ruling clique; when they became dominant in the 1960s, they abandoned the hierarchical structure that Johnson had used (Huitt, 1961).

After Johnson left the Senate in 1961 to become vice president, the Senate changed radically. Membership turnover democratized the body. The power of the so-called inner club of favored senators was destroyed. Many earlier folkways, such as specialization and deference to seniority, were weakened or erased (Ornstein, Peabody, and Rohde, 1985). Committee assignments and staff resources were widely scattered. "We've had a dispersion of responsibility," explained Mike Mansfield (D–Mont.), who followed Johnson as majority leader (1961–76).

Majority leaders continue to shape the Senate in subtle but important ways. Mansfield's successor was Robert C. Byrd (D–W.Va.) (1977–80, 1987–88). Byrd wielded power through procedural mastery using unanimous consent agreements to influence floor schedules and debate. When the Republicans took over the Senate, Howard H. Baker, Jr. (R–Tenn.), became majority leader (1981–84) and capitalized on his party's consensus on economic matters. His successor, Robert Dole (R–Kans.) (1985–86) relied more on aggressive negotiating skills.

Republican congressional leaders meet the press outside the White House after conferring with President Ronald Reagan about the federal budget. From left to right: Robert Dole of Kansas, Senate minority leader; Robert Michel of Illinois, House minority leader; and Pete Domenici of New Mexico, ranking Republican member on the Senate Budget Committee. At the rear is Sen. Alan Simpson of Wyoming, assistant minority leader and Republican whip.

Still, Senate leaders are weaker than their House counterparts. The Senate's tradition of individualism and respect for the minority's rights means that any individual senator can delay or stop debate by objecting to procedural agreements or threatening to "speak at length" **(filibuster)** if an objectionable matter gets to the Senate floor. Party leaders are thus embroiled in perpetual negotiations with their colleagues to remove objections and clear the way for floor action.

Party Leaders at Work

Party leaders strive to bind together the scattered individuals and work groups of Congress. They orchestrate efforts to produce legislative results, in the form of budgets, laws, resolutions, confirmed nominations, ratified treaties, and the like.

Duties and powers

Randall Ripley (1967) specifies six major functions of party leaders (Known collectively as "the leadership"): (1) organizing the party, (2) scheduling business, (3) promoting members' attendance for important floor votes, (4) distributing and collecting information, (5) maintaining liaison with the president and his top advisers, and (6) persuading members to act in accord with party policies.

In attempting to shape legislative events, party leaders can draw on four types of resources (Ripley, 1967). First, they can use the chamber's rules for partisan ends. The leaders of the majority party, for instance, can hold off scheduling a controversial bill until enough votes for passage have been garnered. Second, they can influence many of the tangible rewards for individual members—the most important being committee assignments. Third, they can control many psychological rewards. Party leaders often shape the attitudes of chamber colleagues toward a member; isolation is the possible fate of one who is tagged as unreliable or a maverick. Finally, they can dominate internal communication channels within the chamber. Thus, they can monopolize vital information: knowledge of the upcoming schedule, the content of bills and proposed amendments, likely vote outcomes, and the president's wishes.

Party voting

Parties are the most stable and significant groups in Congress. Although party discipline is lax, party loyalty runs deep and is the leading determinant of voting in the two houses. Indeed, party-line voting in Congress was higher in the 1980s than at any time since the 1930s. Elected lawmakers, it seems, have become more reliably partisan than the voters they represent (see Chapter 6 on eroding party loyalties among the electorate).

Partisans in Congress tend to vote together because they represent similar constituencies. For Republicans, this means affluent suburban areas of business and professional people, older ethnic stocks, and rural areas of the Midwest and West; for Democrats, it means urban areas, much of the South, and concentrations of lower socioeconomic strata containing larger numbers of blue-collar workers, blacks, and Hispanics. Party mavericks—members whose voting records diverge from those of other party members—tend to come from districts that resemble those of the opposition. Such a maverick might be a liberal Republican from a northeastern city or a conservative Democrat from a midwestern farm region. Figure 10–4 shows the differences in voting between the two parties' senators, as reflected in ratings by business and labor groups.

According to one study (Froman and Ripley, 1965), six factors affect the success of party leadership. Victories are more likely when (1) leadership activity is high; (2) the issue is more procedural than substantive; (3) the visibility of the issue is low, thereby reducing pressures that

FIGURE 10–4   Voting of U.S. senators as ranked by business and labor, 1987

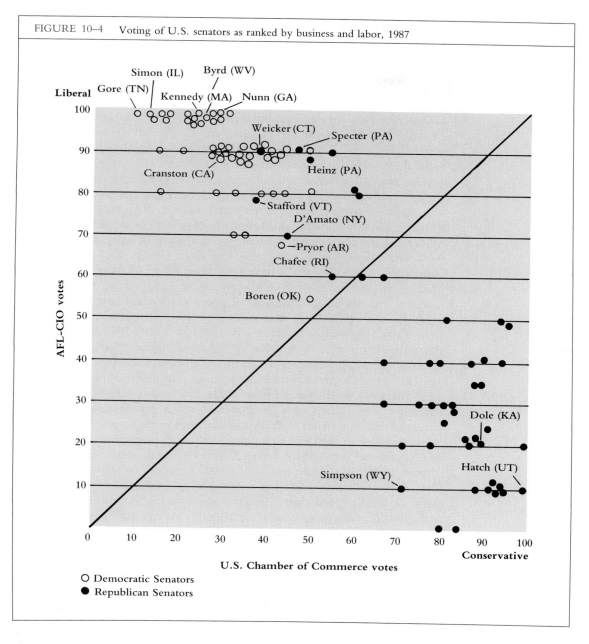

could counteract party loyalty; (4) the visibility of the action is low (for instance, party unity is usually easier to achieve on an unrecorded vote than on a roll call); (5) there is little pressure from constituencies; and (6) state delegations are not bargaining with party leaders over specific demands.

Party fragmentation

Many forces chip away at party lines. Regional differences can be especially potent. Traditionally, southern Democrats were less loyal to their party than were non-Southerners. Southern Democrats and Republican conservatives used to merge into a so-called **conservative coalition**—less active now than in the past. Still, in the early 1980s conservative House Democrats, sometimes called *boll weevils,* voted with the GOP to pass the "Reaganomics" package of tax cuts, military spending, and slashed domestic programs. Likewise, moderate northeastern Republicans deviate from the conservative mainstream of their party.

The apex of party voting in Congress came around the turn of the present century—a time of powerful party machines and party-line voting among the electorate. Between the 1930s and the 1970s congressional partisanship declined, in terms of both *party cleavage* (the frequency with which the parties oppose each other) and *party cohesion* (the degree to which members of each party stick together). During the New Deal era, lawmakers split along party lines on a wide range of issues—the Democrats tending to favor big government, social welfare programs, farm aid, and international involvement, all of which the Republicans tended to oppose. By the 1970s, these lines were blurred. "During the 1970s, majorities of the congressional parties were far more likely to agree with each other than they were to disagree" (Collie and Brady, 1985: 278). "Moreover, when party majorities opposed each other, each party lost, on the average, roughly one quarter of its membership to the opposing side."

In the 1980s party voting revived. In the House, conservatives dominated the Republican party as moderate and liberal Republicans (sometimes called *gypsy moths*) dwindled in numbers and influence. North-South issues declined in the Democratic party as race ceased to be a regional issue and Southerners moved toward their party's mainstream.

Still, parties must compete with other powerful influences on legislators. These influences include interest groups, state and regional delegations, committees and their clienteles, and informal voting blocs. In sum, party loyalty, though stubborn, is challenged on every side, and its impact is variable.

The Rise of Informal Caucus Groups

The parties are not the only groups linking lawmakers in the two chambers. Informal **caucus** groups or voting blocs have been a persistent and growing phenomenon. These are mainly bipartisan House groups, though some are strictly partisan and others draw members from both chambers.

Such groups are not exactly newcomers. During the 19th century, regional and issue-based factions were rife, in part because members from the same state or region often gathered at the same boarding houses during the brief legislative sessions (Young, 1966).

The modern-day model is the Democratic Study Group (DSG). This

The era of the caucus. In the 100th Congress, there were more than 100 caucuses on Capitol Hill. Here, five members of the Congressional Black Caucus, one of the most important caucuses, face reporters outside the Capitol. They are [left to right] Rep. William H. Gray III (D–Pa.), chairman of the House Budget Committee; Rep. Charles B. Rangel (D–N.Y.), chairman of the Select Committee on Narcotics Abuse and Control; Rep. Cardiss Collins (D–Ill.); Del. Walter E. Fauntroy (D–D.C.), chairman of the District of Columbia Subcommittee on Fiscal Affairs and Health; and Rep. Bennett Stewart (D–Ill.).

group formed in 1959 to promote the interest of liberal members. It was a minority bloc at first, but by the mid-1970s it had some 250 members, a majority of the House Democrats. It led many House reforms in the 1970s, such as assaults on the seniority system and dispersion of power. The DSG aided members with campaign funds and with weekly newsletters highlighting controversies contested on the House floor.

Since the 1970s, the number of informal caucus groups has soared; they now number more that 100 (Hammond, Stevens, and Mulhollan, 1983). There is a Black Caucus, a Women's Caucus, and a Hispanic Caucus. There are industry groups such as the Textile Caucus, the Steel Caucus, and the Tourism Caucus. And there are regional groups such as the Western State Coalition, the Rural Caucus, and the Northeast-Midwest Coalition (the so-called Frostbelt Caucus).

Some groups are party-based. Both parties have "class clubs," groups of members who enter the House in a given year. Other party groups follow the DSG's example in promoting ideological causes. The Republicans have an array of groups, ranging from the right wing's Conservative Opportunity Society to the moderates' "92 Group" (for victory in 1992).

State and regional delegations, not to mention state party caucuses, also meet. Their purpose is twofold. They focus attention on matters of mutual concern, and they help exchange information among members on various committees.

Informal caucus groups are as varied as Congress itself. Some are highly organized and well financed. They have staffs, whip systems, and newsletters. Others are mainly paper organizations—designed to let the folks back home know that their legislators are alert to a given issue. Whatever their status, such groups reflect the profusion of today's politics and are an alternative to party groups.

COMMITTEE AND SUB-COMMITTEE GOVERNMENT

Committees and subcommittees are the primary policy-making units in Congress. As Woodrow Wilson observed long ago (1980: 79), congressional government is committee government. "Congress in session is Congress on display, but Congress in committee is Congress at work."

From its very beginning, Congress turned to committees to draft and refine legislation. At first, ad hoc committees were designated to write bills once an issue had been thrashed out on the floor. By the third decade of the 19th century, a set of permanent (or standing) committees had been created to deal with recurrent topics and recommend legislation to the whole body. Today almost all legislation comes from or is refined by committees and their subcommittees.

By any standard, the House and Senate committee systems are complex: the Senate has 21 committees, and these in turn have 85 subcommittees; the House has 28 committees and 154 subcommittees. There are also four joint committees (with eight subcommittees)—not to mention many temporary panels, boards, and commissions. The 49 more or less permanent House and Senate committees are listed in Table 10–4.

Despite attempts to streamline, committee and even subcommittee autonomy is formidable. One scholar (Polsby, 1968: 556) concluded: "Committees nowadays have developed an independent sovereignty of their own, subject only to very infrequent reversals and modifications of their powers by House party leaders backed by large and insistent majorities."

Types of Committees

Standing committees

Of the several types of congressional committees, the most numerous and important are the **standing committees,** which have a fixed jurisdiction and can report legislation to the chamber dealing with that jurisdiction. These panels are regarded as permanent, lasting beyond any given two-year Congress. (Of course, each house may change or abolish a committee at any time, though this rarely occurs.) Standing committees handle most of the major policy categories—such as foreign policy, banking, taxes, public works, law enforcement, and general government affairs. In the 100th Congress, the Senate had 16 standing committees and the House had 22.

Most of the standing committees have subcommittees that consider specific parts of their jurisdiction. In the House, committees of 20 or more members must set up subcommittees.

The major distinction among standing committees is between *authorizing* and *fiscal* committees. Most of the standing committees are the former. They authorize, or draft, the substance of government policies, subject of course to the vote of the full chamber. The legislation they write empowers the government to do certain things, such as running training programs or prisons or diplomatic missions, but it does not empower the government to spend money for programs or to raise money for the Treasury. That is done through appropriations (spending) and revenue (taxing) bills.

To coordinate taxing and spending legislation, Congress has set up a complex budget process by which it sets guidelines regulating revenues and expenditures that are supposed to be followed by all of the committees. We will explain this process in Chapter 18. In brief, the three types of fiscal committees are *taxing* (Senate Finance, House Ways and Means), *spending* (Senate and House Appropriations), and *budgetary* (Senate and House Budget).

Temporary committees

In addition to standing committees, at any given time there may also be temporary committees formed to undertake a particular task, such as investigating the Iran-*contra* affair. Temporary committees are sometimes empowered to report legislation on a certain topic; more often, they just make recommendations.

Temporary committees have several forms. Some are designated **select committees,** appointed by the presiding officer; others are **special committees,** with members chosen through each party's normal committee assignment process. In practice, there is little difference between these two types of committees. The House Speaker can also appoint *ad hoc committees* made up of members of two or more standing committees that have jurisdiction over parts of a question. Only two such panels have been created—on energy policy and on the outer continental shelf. However, such committees could be a powerful tool in the Speaker's hands.

Joint committees

Formed by concurrent resolution or legislation, joint committees draw members from both the House and the Senate. Such committees are one way to coordinate a bicameral legislature. Today there are just four joint

TABLE 10-4 Committee and subcommittee seats, 100th Congress

Senate

Committee (year created)	Members	Dem-GOP ratio	Sub-units	Total seats
Agriculture, Nutrition, and Forestry (1825)	19	10–9	6	64
Appropriations (1867)	29	16–13	13	167
Armed Services (1816)	20	11–9	6	74
Banking, Housing, and Urban Affairs (1913)	20	11–9	4	54
Budget (1975)	24	13–11	—	24
Commerce, Science, and Transportation (1816)	20	11–9	8	78
Energy and Natural Resources (1816)	19	10–9	5	68
Environment and Public Works (1833)	16	9–7	5	61
Finance (1816)	20	11–9	7	79
Foreign Relations (1816)	19	10–9	7	68
Governmental Affairs (1921)	14	8–6	5	52
Judiciary (1816)	14	8–6	6	47
Labor and Human Resources (1869)	16	9–7	6	62

House

Committee (year created)	Members	Dem-GOP ratio	Sub-units	Total seats
Agriculture (1829)	43	26–17	8	160
Appropriations (1865)	57	35–22	13	191
Armed Services (1822)	52	31–21	9*	163
Banking (1865)	51	31–20	8	220
Budget (1975)	35	21–14	8	126
Energy and Commerce (1795)	42	25–17	6	140
Science, Space, and Technology (1958)	45	27–18	7	141
Merchant Marine (1887)	42	25–17	6	158
Interior (1805)	41	26–14	6	152
Public Works (1837)	52	30–20	6	192
Ways and Means (1802)	36	23–13	6	102
Foreign Affairs (1822)	43	25–18	8	137
Government Operations (1927)	41	24–17	7	103
District of Columbia (1808)	12	8–4	3	36
Post Office (1808)	22	14–8	7	59
Judiciary (1813)	35	21–14	7	111
Education and Labor (1867)	34	21–13	8	121

TABLE 10-4   (concluded)

Senate

Committee (year created)	Members	Dem-GOP ratio	Sub-units	Total seats
Rules and Administration (1947)	16	9–7	—	16
Small Business (1980)	19	10–9	6	52
Veterans Affairs (1970)	11	6–5	—	11
Special Aging	19	10–9	—	19
Select Ethics	6	3–3	—	6
Select Intelligence	15	8–7	—	15
Select Iran-*Contra*	15	9–6	—	15
Select Indian Affairs	9	5–3	—	8
Totals	359	(197–162)	84	1,040
Senators' Average	3.6	(55%–45%)	—	10.4

House

Committee (year created)	Members	Dem-GOP ratio	Sub-units	Total seats
⌠Rules (1880)	13	9–4	2	27
⌡House Administration (1789)	19	12–7	6	61
Small Business (1975)	44	27–17	6	115
Veterans Affairs (1825)	34	21–13	5	97
Select Aging	65	39–26	4	145
Standards of Conduct (1967)	12	6–6	—	12
Select Intelligence	17	11–6	3	41
Select Iran-*Contra*	11	6–5	—	11
Select Narcotics	25	15–10	—	25
Select Children, Youth, Families	30	18–12	3†	60
Select Hunger	26	16–10	2†	39†
Totals	979	593–384	144	2,950
Representatives' Average	2.2	61%–39%	—	7.0

*Task forces; no standing subcommittees.

†Includes one or more task forces or panels.

committees. Two of them—Printing and Library—handle housekeeping matters. A third, the Joint Committee on Taxation, is a holding company for a small but valued staff that advises taxing committees from the two chambers. The fourth, the Joint Economic Committee, is a forum for macroeconomic discussions and periodic reports. None of the joint committees has the power to report legislation directly to the two chambers. In the wake of scandals such as the Iran-*contra* imbroglio, some observers suggested that a new joint intelligence panel replace the House and Senate intelligence committees—to provide clearer congressional supervision and minimize the threat of security leaks. This course is unlikely: legislators jealously guard the prerogatives of their own chambers and tend to be suspicious of joint panels.

Conference committees

A more common joint body is the **conference committee,** an ad hoc panel formed to work out differences when a bill passes the two houses in different forms. Conferees (called managers) are picked by the presiding officer of each house, on the suggestion of the chairmen of the committees that handled the bill.

Conferees deal with the points of disagreement between the House and Senate versions of the bill. They are expected to uphold the positions of their own chambers. However, the conferees from each house vote as a bloc. To avoid deadlock, then, they must either compromise or "recede" from the position of their chambers.

Like all joint panels, conferences are avoided if at all possible. Actually, less than 1 out of 10 public laws is the product of a House-Senate conference. Most bills are approved by the second chamber without amendment or are sent back with amendments; occasionally a bill goes back and forth several times before it is approved by both chambers in identical form—as required to send the bill to the president. Conference bills tend to be controversial; sometimes members welcome conferences if they think that through them they can recover defeats suffered in their own chamber.

Committee Assignments and Careers

New senators and representatives must set up a beachhead in the nation's capital. This consists not only of their office staffs but also of their committee assignments and a package of issues or concerns that will define their service. Obviously, the committees to which they are assigned are crucial to their political fates.

All four congressional parties (that is, the House and Senate Democrats and Republicans) have bodies that make committee assignments: the Senate Democratic Steering Committee, the House Democratic Steering and Policy Committee, and the Republican committees on committees. All assignments are then ratified by the full party contingent. Democrats call this their caucus; Republicans call it their conference.

Legislators do not just wait for assignments to come their way. They submit their preferences, and if they are alert, they lobby party leaders and influential senior colleagues. There is constant pressure to raise the number of committee seats by adding committees or subcommittees and by increasing their size. Today the average senator serves on 11 committees and subcommittees and the average representative serves on 7.

Career goals

With all the work they have to do, why do lawmakers seek so many committee assignments? The answer is that they view assignments in terms of their career goals. Fenno (1973) lists at least three goals that committee service can further. First, some committees boost their members' reelection prospects. These include committees that deal with local or regional interests or with industries that make heavy PAC campaign contributions. The most notable such committees are those concerned with agriculture, banking, commerce and energy, merchant marine, transportation, public lands, and public works.

Second, committee membership enables legislators to shape policy. Some committees satisfy this need even though they lack direct election payoffs. Among these are committees dealing with the judiciary, education and human resources, foreign affairs, and similar broad policy topics.

Finally, some committees are valued because of their influence within the House and Senate. Members of these committees decide on matters of importance to their colleagues, if not always to the general public. This category includes some of the most prestigious committees: taxing (Senate Finance, House Ways and Means), spending (Appropriations), budget, and internal scheduling (House Rules).

The "pecking order"

Because some committees are more coveted than others, assignments create an informal pecking order. The House designates its committees as **exclusive committees,** semiexclusive committees, or nonexclusive committees. Members assigned to an exclusive committee do not normally serve on any other standing committee. (They may, however, serve on special or joint bodies.) The exclusive committees are Appropriations, Rules, and Ways and Means. The semiexclusive committees include most of the major authorizing panels. Members are usually limited to one such assignment, though they may also hold seats on nonexclusive committees. The nonexclusive committees include the housekeeping committees and those with narrow or less attractive jurisdictions.

When legislators transfer among committees, they drift toward the more prestigious ones (Bullock, 1973). In the House, the most attractive

Sen. Paul Sarbanes (D–Md.) and Sen. Richard Lugar (R–Ind.), members of the Senate Foreign Relations Committee, talk on Capitol Hill with a panel of North Atlantic Treaty Organization (NATO) representatives who have come to Washington to discuss the intermediate-range nuclear force (INF) treaty. The NATO representatives seated at the table are [left to right] John Cartwright, member of the British Parliament; Karsten Voigt, member of the West German Bundestag; Ton Frinking, member of the Netherlands parliament; and François Fillon, deputy of the French National Assembly.

committees are Armed Services, Foreign Affairs, and the three exclusive committees. The Senate's most attractive committees are Foreign Relations, Finance, Appropriations, and Armed Services.

A number of legislators, however, seek seats on minor committees because of their publicity value or the close link between these committees and their constituents' concerns. The committees on Small Business, Veterans' Affairs, and Merchant Marine and Fisheries are in this category. Some legislators value these assignments more than any other. One such committee, the 67-member House Select Committee on Aging, has become the largest of all. Although this committee lacks legislative jurisdiction, it is irresistible because of its powerful clientele (older people) and its colorful former chairman, octogenarian Claude Pepper (D–Fla.), who used the committee to publicize the cause of aging citizens.

Criteria for assignments

As far as possible, party leaders try to follow members' wishes in making assignments. They give special attention to new members and to members from competitive districts, who need a boost to be reelected. In filling seats on top committees, party leaders are pressured to honor regional or ideological factions within the party. Certain states or economic interests feel they have a right to be represented on the taxing and spending committees; if "their seat" is vacated, they press for a proper replacement.

Some committees, in contrast, are not very attractive; members must be persuaded to serve on them. One example is the House District of Columbia Committee. It has little to offer legislators from outside the Washington, D.C., area. The Senate, which had trouble staffing its District of Columbia Committee, transferred its work to the Governmental Affairs Committee in 1977.

Biased memberships

Many committees do not represent Congress as a whole. In general, committees attract legislators who are keenly interested in the subject matter with which the committees deal (Shepsle, 1978). This simple fact has vast consequences. Among other things, it helps lubricate the committee system. Highly motivated legislators are likely to take their committee work seriously; members who have been dragooned into service are not.

Self-selection also tilts the committees in certain policy directions. Liberals move toward committees dealing with education and human resources. Farm belt legislators are likely to want seats on the agriculture committees. The "resources" panels—House Interior, Senate Energy and Natural Resources—overrepresent the western states, which contain most of the public lands and national parks. In short, committees are often biased in favor of their major programs or clienteles.

The norm of specialization

Because members cannot possibly know the details of each piece of legislation, they often rely on "cues" from colleagues who serve on the relevant committee and are expert in the issue being considered. Thus, new senators and (especially) representatives are told to focus on committee work so that they will gain expertise and be listened to. In Congress as elsewhere, knowledge is a basis for influence.

The tendency toward specialization has diminished in the two chambers as a result of 1970s reforms that dispersed influence and made it easier for nonmembers of the relevant committee to exert leverage on an issue. Some members have gained policy prominence outside the committee system. Representative Jack Kemp (R–N.Y.), for example, was known as a tax expert and cosponsored the famous Kemp-Roth tax cut plan even though he never served on the Ways and Means Committee. Representative Henry Hyde (R–Ill.), though not on the Appropriations Committee, authored the controversial Hyde amendments forbidding the use of federal funds for abortions.

The degree of specialization varies in the two chambers. The larger House of Representatives still pays great deference to committee specialization; despite liberalized procedures since the 1970s, it is still difficult for a Kemp or a Hyde to exert policy leadership outside the committees of jurisdiction. Senators, in contrast, are obliged to be generalists. They have more committee assignments, take on a wider range of issues, and have procedural weapons to force committees to listen to their objections or deal with their amendments on the Senate floor. Hence, committee "turf" is more easily trespassed in the Senate than in the House.

The "Rule" of Seniority

Few features of Capitol Hill life have drawn as much comment as the **seniority system.** "Survival of the survivors" was the way a Ralph Nader study (Green, Fallows, and Zwick, 1972) once derided seniority.

Seniority is neither a formal rule nor a requirement. The rule can be stated simply: once assigned to a committee, members have a right to be reappointed and to advance by seniority (defined as continuous terms of service). The senior majority-party member is normally named chairman.

Pros and cons

Defenders of seniority point out that it has several advantages. It helps reduce conflict in Congress. It provides for automatic selection of committee leaders. It enhances the independence of Congress because it forces presidents to deal with committee leaders whose posts are almost untouchable. And it fosters professionalism because it discourages hopping from one committee to another.

Critics of seniority argue that it wastes the talents and energies of younger legislators by postponing their leadership duties: that it puts leadership in the hands of old and sometimes feeble members; and that it further insulates power within the two houses, making concerted party control over committee leaders very difficult.

Historically, the gravest charge against seniority was that it fostered biased policy making. By rewarding long service, seniority awards chairmanships (and ranking minority-party posts) to legislators with the safest seats—the regions under the parties' firmest control. During much of the Democrats' long era of control (from the 1930s into the early 1970s), this meant an overbalance of southern conservatives among committee leaders. Increases in the numbers of mainstream Democrats (that is, liberal non-Southerners) led to repeated confrontations with the "barons," or "old bulls," who sometimes ran their committees arbitrarily and treated newer members with contempt. (The Republicans, too, had generational disputes; but these were never as severe as those of the Democrats.)

Seniority today

Reforms adopted in the 1960s and 1970s chipped away at the prerogatives of seniority. First, committee rules now limit the chairperson's power and provide remedies for arbitrary behavior. Second, party caucuses now approve all committee assignments, including chairmanships. Several committee chairmen have actually been rejected by the Democratic Caucus and replaced by more junior members. In the 1980s, the House Armed Services Committee was chaired by Representative Les Aspin (D–Wis.), who stood seventh in seniority but was selected because the caucus deemed the former chairman too feeble and the next-ranking members too conservative. Third, subcommittees grew in number and autonomy, multiplying leadership posts and further limiting the chairmen's power. A few committees are little more than holding companies for their subcommittees—though the amount of decentralization varies from committee to committee (Smith and Deering, 1984: 125 ff.).

Within committees, seniority counts for less than it used to. Chairmanships, according to one observer (Ehrenhalt, 1981: 535), are "a title, awarded by seniority, that allows the bearer to parcel out committee funds and not much else." Strong chairmen, such as John Dingell (D–Mich.) of House Energy and Commerce or Dan Rostenkowski (D–Ill.) of House Ways and Means, dominate colleagues by force of personality or skill, not by age or tenure.

Committee leadership posts are now spread more broadly than ever before. In the 100th Congress (1987–88), Democratic senators held an average of two committee or subcommittee chairmanships; in the House, half of all democrats were committee or subcommittee chairmen. Committee leadership posts are well balanced among the parties' various regions and factions. Within committees, it is hard for chairmen to juggle subcommittee assignments, jurisdictions, or chairmanships to hoard power or influence a wide range of issues.

Committee democratization underscores the dispersion of authority in Congress. There are more leaders and more power centers the ever. This puts added pressure on party leaders. It poses the problem of how, or whether, Congress is going to get its members and committees together to produce timely, coherent policies.

Committee Politics

No two committees work in exactly the same way. Each committee has a unique external environment; and internally, each is a unique mix of members, ideologies, and styles.

Outside forces

Committees must respond to the procedures and moods of the larger chambers. Some committees, though, are more independent than others. Those dealing with technical subjects have great leeway. Their expertise is respected. Committees that handle hot issues can expect aggressive intervention from noncommittee colleagues.

Committees differ in the extent to which they must share their jurisdictions with other committees. Because jurisdictions frequently overlap, Senate and (especially) House committees are allowed to consider bills jointly or in sequence. (More will be said about this in Chapter 11.) Committees such as the Intelligence panels and the House Science, Space, and Technology Committee find the bulk of their workload shared with other panels. One way or another, they must cooperate to gain passage of the measures within their jurisdiction. Committees such as the Judiciary panels consider few bills in cooperation with other committees.

Some committees are arenas for intense interest-group struggles; others are almost ignored by lobbyists. The commerce panels (Senate Commerce, Science, and Transportation; House Energy and Commerce) are real battlegrounds for contending groups—including the energy, power, health, transportation, and telecommunication industries, not to mention consumer groups in these and other fields. In contrast, few groups pay much attention to the housekeeping committees (Senate Rules and Administration; House Administration).

Some committees deal with aggressive executive-branch agencies; others face weak or divided agencies, or none at all. For instance, foreign policy committees (Senate Foreign Relations, House Foreign Affairs) hear from few lobbyists but feel intense executive pressure. In a sense, the prime constituent of these committees is the State Department. The human resources committees face several departments (mainly Labor, Education, and Health and Human Services), which vie for program dollars.

Many committees or subcommittees boast firm alliances with executive agencies and relevant pressure groups, forming one leg of the triangular **subgovernments** discussed in Chapter 7. Such panels may become inside lobbyists for the policies with which they deal. They channel interest group demands to their colleagues and to the government agencies serving the interest groups. They view these agencies as their own special preserves, for which they supply funds, statutory authority, and continual guidance. Prime examples of such clientele committees are the House and Senate Veterans Affairs committees. These committees provide forums for the concerns of such groups as the American Legion, Veterans of Foreign Wars, and Vietnam Veterans. They relay these concerns to other lawmakers and admonish officials in the Veterans Administration to improve its services to veterans

Internal patterns

Responding to these outside factors, committees adopt their own patterns of behavior. Some have vigorous chairmen; others have fragmented leadership or hardly any at all. Some are highly partisan (for instance, the human resources committees) because they deal with bread-and-butter partisan issues. Others (such as the appropriations committees) have a consensus view of their mission that pulls in most, if not all, members.

Committees have distinct ways of fulfilling their missions. Fenno (1973) terms them *strategic premises*. These premises help the committees respond to their own members' goals, other House and Senate members' demands, and outside pressures.

In this chapter, we have described the first of the "two Congresses": the Congress that is a collection of individual politicians devoted to nurturing their careers. We have started with some obvious but fundamental facts about senators and representatives—namely, that they are elected by unique constituencies, that their careers depend on the continued support of those voters, and that such voter support depends less on their performance within Congress than on their success at marketing themselves at home.

Little wonder, then, that lawmakers spend the bulk of their time, not in making laws, but in image building, fund raising, and constituent outreach. Frequent trips back and forth from the home base are required not only of representatives but of senators as well; committee and floor schedules must be adjusted accordingly. Members' offices have been compared to small cottage industries devoted mainly to correspondence, newsletters, publicity, and constituent casework.

Even in lawmaking duties, members tend to behave as individual entrepreneurs rather than as part of a collective policy-making body. Members seek committee assignments that will further their careers—by providing constituency benefits, greater personal visibility, or lucrative PAC funds. Party leaders facilitate members' individual goals by distributing assignments widely, according to members' preferences if possible. Members climb the seniority ladders simply by getting reelected, not by intellectual or political contributions to lawmaking. Though responsible for organizing the two chambers to produce legislative results, party leaders have insufficient resources to set priorities or exert sanctions; they are forever deferring to individual members and committees, searching for consensus if possible.

Most of this would not surprise or worry the authors of the Constitution. They expected members of Congress to be bound closely to their constituents—senators to the states, representatives to the people. They designed the terms of office to reinforce constituency influence, not blunt it; Congress was not supposed to develop institutional interests apart from the interests of these constituencies (Malbin, 1987). So the founders would probably applaud the individualism, fragmentation, and localism now found on Capitol Hill. (However, they would doubtless consider the long careers of modern lawmakers a cause for concern.)

Legislators' activities revolve so tightly around their electoral careers

THE POLITICIANS' CONGRESS

that it has become fashionable for political scientists to talk as if this were all there is to Congress. "If a group of planners sat down and tried to design a pair of American national assemblies with the goal of serving members' electoral needs year in and year out, they would be hard pressed to improve on what exists," wrote Mayhew in a widely cited essay (1974: 81–82). Reelection success rates would seem proof of this contention.

Yet there is another aspect to our national legislature—a "second Congress," if you will. It is, as noted at the outset of this chapter, the Congress of collective policy-making, in which members' individual and parochial interests must be combined to pass policies governing the whole nation. These policies may be wise and coherent, or they may be foolish and contradictory. Constituency interests are rarely far from lawmakers' minds in making such policies; but they must also consider issues of fairness, consistency, and ease of implementation for the nation at large.

Congress as a policy-making body is more than simply the sum total of individual, career-seeking politicians. First, members of Congress cannot entirely control the policy agenda or the resources available to resolve public problems. This is especially obvious in periods of economic or social crisis or hardship. Second, Congress does not always serve members' electoral and career needs efficiently. Although incumbents are extremely successful at gaining reelection, Congress exacts high costs from members and their families—in time, personal health, inconvenience, and finances, among other things. Sometimes the pressures are so severe that members retire voluntarily to pursue other interests.

In other words, the "two Congresses" do not always harmonize. The representative and policy-making functions of our national legislature often move in opposite directions, exacting costs from both politicians and public policy. The second Congress, the policy-making body, is the subject of our next chapter.

CONCLUSIONS

In this chapter, we have considered the members of Congress as individual politicians with reelection and career interests.

1. The constitutional requirements for serving in Congress are few and simple (age, residency, and citizenship), but in practice Congress is an elite group of men and women. Overrepresented are males, whites, the professions, and upper socioeconomic strata.
2. Individual members of Congress spend a great deal of their time, money, and staff in ascertaining what their voters want and in publicizing themselves to those voters.
3. The electoral activities of modern senators and

representatives are typically rewarded with success at the polls. Incumbents are far more visible than their opponents, have more extensive resources, and often simply scare off potentially strong challengers.

4. The legislative duties of Congress embrace the entire gamut of the government's activities, ranging from taxing and spending powers to partnership in the making of foreign policy.
5. Party coalitions, though seemingly fragile, are persistent and powerful. Especially in the House, leaders have important formal powers, but in today's fragmented Congress informal powers are more likely to be employed.
6. Congressional government is committee gov-

ernment. Lawmakers view committee assignments as career assets that will aid them in reelection, influence, and policy leverage.

7. The committee system has become decentralized as a result of 1960s and 1970s reforms designed to curb the power of the senior committee "barons" and to enchance the influence of individual legislators. Alongside party and committee structures has grown a network of informal caucuses that links legislators with common regional, industry, ethnic, or philosophical goals.

FURTHER READING

DAVIDSON, ROGER H., and WALTER J. OLESZEK (1985) *Congress and Its Members.* 2nd ed. Washington, D.C.: Congressional Quarterly Press. An interpretive textbook on the notion of the "two Congresses"—the institution that makes policy versus the members who seek reelection.

FENNO, RICHARD F., JR. (1978) *Home Style: House Members in Their Districts.* Boston: Little, Brown. A pathbreaking exploration of House members' relationships with constituents in their home districts.

JACOBSON, GARY C. (1987) *The Politics of Congressional Elections.* 2nd ed. Boston: Little, Brown. Congressional electoral politics—nominations, campaigns, and voting patterns—explained by the leading student of the subject.

JOHANNES, JOHN R. (1984) *To Serve the People: Congress and Constituency Service.* Lincoln: University of Nebraska Press. Everything you would want to know about casework, the important constituent assistance performed by congressional offices.

MAYHEW, DAVID R. (1974) *Congress: The Electoral Connection.* New Haven Conn.: Yale University Press. This stimulating and important essay proceeds from the premise that Congress is a collectivity of reelection-driven politicians.

PARKER, GLENN R. (1986) *Homeward Bound: Explaining Changes in Congressional Behavior.* Pittsburgh, Pa.: University of Pittsburgh Press. A careful statistical study of the rise of constituency attentiveness among senators and representatives between 1947 and 1980.

Chapter Eleven

CONGRESS AT WORK

The silver and ebony mace, the symbol of congressional authority, has been placed on its green marble pedestal behind the rostrum of the House of Representatives. Quill pens, symbolic links with a more genteel past, have been sharpened in the Senate, where they are available to any member. At high noon on opening day, the Speaker in the House and the vice president in the Senate will smartly rap their gavels on the polished desks before them.

Thus begins a new session of Congress. The pace of the nation's capital, sometimes sluggish, quickens visibly when senators and representatives, the nominal bosses of the federal establishment, are back in town.

By the time Congress adjourns nearly a year later, the two houses will have spent some 1,200 hours in session, taken about 1,000 roll-call votes, and passed from 200 to 400 bills and resolutions and sent them to the president for signing. House and Senate floor debates will consume some 35,000 pages of the *Congressional Record,* a complete though not verbatim transcript of congressional proceedings. ✍

*F*or most of us, such activities *are* the U.S. Congress. These are the activities that the national media report, that commentators dissect in books and articles, and that American government classes explain in detail. Lawmaking on Capitol Hill is a detailed, fascinating process—unquestionably the most open and vivid example we have of policy-making in action. And it is unique: Insofar as Congress daily undertakes the detailed work of policy-making, it is virtually alone among the world's legislatures—most of which simply debate or ratify proposals presented by the government of the day.

In this chapter, we will detail lawmaking processes and procedures. These include not only passing laws and resolutions but also other policy-making forms—budgeting, confirming appointees, approving treaties, and overseeing the executive branch. We will stress the politics that underlies congressional procedures and the shifts in those procedures over time in response to changing conditions. Finally, we will consider the question of congressional power in relation to the presidency and the executive branch.

THE LEGISLATIVE WORK OF CONGRESS

Believing that legislative institutions should prevail, the Constitution's authors bestowed "all legislative powers" on Congress. Article I empowers Congress to pass laws on a variety of subjects, including coining money and regulating interstate commerce. The **power of the purse**—to draw funds from the public treasury and levy taxes to pay for the government's operations—is another cherished power that the Constitution has given to Congress. And if those powers are not enough to assure the prerogatives of the legislature, the Constitution permits Congress to "make all laws which shall be necessary and proper" for carrying out the enumerated powers—the so-called **elastic clause**.

The constitution also makes Congress an equal partner of the president in making foreign policy (see Chapter 20). The president negotiates treaties with foreign powers, but two thirds of the Senate must ratify treaties before they become the law of the land. The Senate also confirms the president's appointments of ambassadors, ministers, consuls, and foreign service officers. Through its power of the purse, Congress raises and equips armies and navies. And although the president is commander in chief of the military forces, only Congress can actually declare war.

The Power of the Rules

The House and Senate have each evolved distinct rules to govern their activities. This follows the constitutional provision that "each house may determine the rules of its proceedings" (Article I, Section 5).

Legislative rules are closely tied to ongoing political conflicts over policies. These rules are far from neutral. They promote certain types of strategies and discourage others. Rules are resources, and the members who master them hold an advantage over their colleagues.

The two houses have great freedom to act within their rules, so long as that action is backed by votes and support. If members are of one mind on an issue, for instance, they can suspend the rules or invoke unanimous consent (as long as nobody objects). In a few minutes, they can do what might otherwise take months. However, such consensus is not easily obtained. The rules persistently challenge backers of legislation to prove that they have votes and support. At the same time, there is little to prevent roadblocks from springing up at every turn, except the tacit agreement that congressional business must go on.

In this spirit, we offer a diagram of the steps in the legislative process (Figure 11–1). Any such diagram is bound to overgeneralize—to impose order on what is often a disorderly process. At every turn, steps may be bypassed, rules bent out of shape. Most bills are introduced and then referred to committees; but some are generated by the committees themselves, and others are introduced but not referred. Revenue bills are supposed to originate in the House; but on occasion, the spirit, if not the letter, of this constitutional mandate is violated. The point is clear: Rules and procedures on Capitol Hill are pliable, bending and stretching to the momentary needs of politics (Oleszek, 1988).

Bill Introduction

In a given Congress (lasting two years), 10,000 or more separate bills and resolutions (including many duplicates) are introduced by senators and representatives. This breaks down to an average of about 34 measures per senator and about 15 per representative. The comparable figures were far higher during the 1960s and 1970s, when economic prosperity and demands for new government programs swelled the number of legislative proposals.

Proposals for bills must be introduced (put in the "hopper") by a House or Senate member. Such a proposal may actually be drafted by anyone—legislators or their staffs, lawyers from a committee or subcommittee or the House or Senate Counsel's Office, a congressional support agency (such as the Congressional Research Service), a presidential staff member, an executive agency staff, or even a private lobbying group. Proposals of this kind cover any subject for which someone thinks "there oughta be a law."

Legislation comes in several forms. Bills are either **public** or **private**. A **public law** applies to whole classes of persons; a **private bill** helps or relieves specific people. To become laws, bills of either type must be passed in identical form by both houses and signed by the president. Joint resolutions are handled in the same way and have the force of law. Concurrent resolutions, though passed by both houses, merely express the

HOW SOMEBODY'S BRIGHT IDEA BECOMES A LAW

FIGURE 11–1   How a bill becomes law

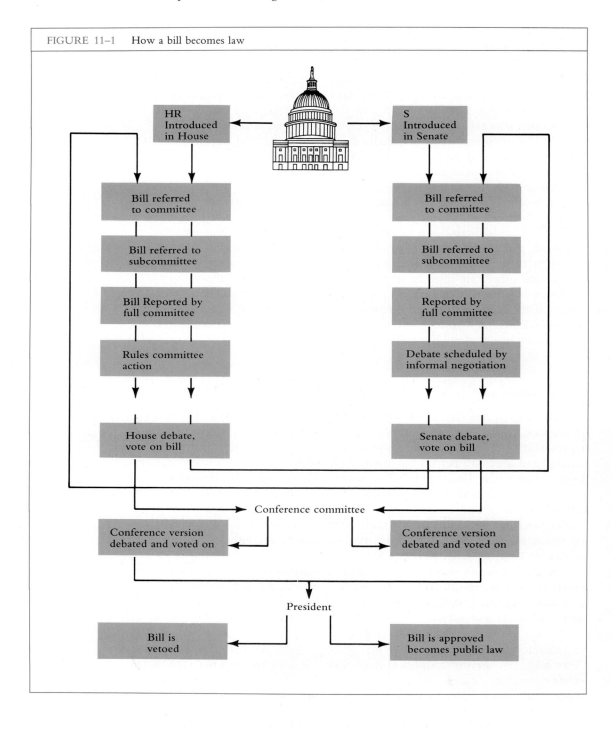

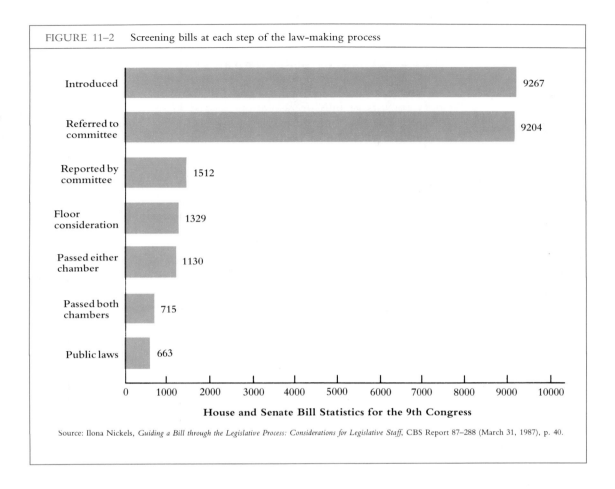

FIGURE 11–2   Screening bills at each step of the law-making process

House and Senate Bill Statistics for the 9th Congress

Source: Ilona Nickels, *Guiding a Bill through the Legislative Process: Considerations for Legislative Staff*, CBS Report 87–288 (March 31, 1987), p. 40.

opinion of Congress and are not signed by the president. Simple resolutions, introduced in either house, apply to that house only. When proposals are introduced, they are printed and assigned a number, such as S. 1, S. Res. 1, H.R. 1, or H. Res. 1.

Less than 5 percent of all the bills and resolutions introduced in Congress are sent to the president and signed into law. At each stage of the legislative process (see Figure 11–2), the number of measures is whittled down.

Jurisdictional jockeying

Once a bill has been introduced in each house, it is referred to the appropriate committee, based on the chamber's rules and precedents. Likewise, committee rules or precedents govern intracommittee assignment of bills to subcommittees.

Once a measure has been referred to a committee or subcommittee, it is not normally reassigned. But more and more, bills that embrace broad subjects are being considered by two or more committees. The record is held by a 1981 budget reconciliation bill, which went to 15 House committees. In recent congresses, on average, about a fourth of the workload of House committees and about a tenth of the workload of Senate committees consists of bills or resolutions shared in some way with one or more other panels. This occurs not only because so many modern laws are multifaceted but also because the two chambers (and especially the House) decided in the 1970s to give more members and committees a chance to shape legislation.

Overlaps and contested areas abound in committee jurisdictions. Legislators and their staffs therefore draft bills so that they will be referred to a favorable committee and kept away from an unfavorable committee. A legislator can also word a bill to enlarge the scope of his own committee. For instance, a law already handled by that committee may be amended, adding new responsibilities or subjects to the committee's jurisdiction.

Such flexibility provides multiple points of access to the legislative process. If one committee is hostile, another may be friendly. In clashes over prayer in the public schools, for instance, the House Judiciary Committee—dominated by opponents of school prayer—had no intention of reporting a proposed constitutional amendment on the subject. But the Education and Labor panel, which has jurisdiction over education, quickly processed and brought to the floor a bill giving religious groups "equal access" to school facilities. The bill, dubbed "son of school prayer," finally passed.

Committee Deliberation

The critical stage comes after a measure has been referred to a committee. A committee can process only a small portion of the proposals made and can favorably report (send to the floor) an even smaller proportion. Committees report from 10 to 15 percent of the measures referred to them. Committee chairmen may or may not refer a bill to a subcommittee (in the House, they are supposed to). And a committee may or may not actually consider a bill.

If a committee or subcommittee decides to act on a bill, it usually does so in four stages: staff research, committee hearings, markup sessions, and reporting.

Research

Committees and subcommittees have staffs that gather materials on the subject at hand and prepare briefs. At some point, the staff will draft a document that forms the basis for the committee's report on the subject. Good staff members become experts in their subject. They familiarize themselves with existing legislation, major unresolved issues, and current

A hearing of the Senate Committee on Foreign Relations. Secretary of State George Shultz testifies before the committee on issues involved in the intermediate-range nuclear force (INF) treaty negotiated with the Soviet Union.

thinking in the field. For committee investigations, the staff will review documents and take depositions from prospective witnesses.

Hearings

Formal hearings are the most common way in which committees gather information on a bill or a problem area. These hearings may last an hour or drag on for months. They may gain national attention or (more likely) play themselves out before tiny audiences in a hearing room. Committee hearings, which are normally published, form a key part of the public record on a given proposal or issue.

As a procedure designed to elicit information, congressional hearings would get low marks. Witnesses often read their testimony from prepared texts. Meanwhile, legislators leaf through the texts, sign mail, or review files. Attendance is haphazard; members come and go, often taking time to greet constituents or talk with aides. When a witness ends a statement, committee members comment or ask questions in turn, starting with the senior members.

Rarely is there a true interchange between legislators and the witness; generally, while a member is asking questions, his colleagues do not intrude. Witnesses have few defenses if legislators use the questioning as an opportunity to make a speech or engage in demagoguery. Usually, only one witness appears at a time. (Witnesses are often buttressed by assistants.) This affords few opportunities for a direct clash of ideas between witnesses of opposing views.

Gathering information is, however, but one aim of hearings. Hearings also focus public attention on a problem. They may record public or elite support for a given viewpoint, give interest-group representatives a chance to express their views, or test the political acceptability of a proposal.

For individual legislators, hearings serve as a platform to promote themselves or remind constituents that they are on the job. For society as a whole, hearings are sometimes exciting public melodramas in which evil forces are ferreted out and purged. Examples of such hearings include the periodic crime or lobby investigations and inquiries into scandals. Hearings may even be national confrontations, as were the Army-McCarthy hearings (1954), the Nixon impeachment hearings (1974), and the Iran-*contra* hearings (1987).

Hearings can affect the committee leaders' ultimate decision: whether to report, change, or drop the proposed legislation. Widespread support for the measure may surface; serious controversies or problems may appear; or the hearings may show that the measure's time has not yet come. On the other hand, hearings are not neutral, open-ended searches for information. Committee leaders often map out hearings, encourage witnesses to make specific points, lay the groundwork for what their committee intends to recommend, or lead their committee to the desired action.

Markups

Bills are adjusted and perfected in **markups**. These are meetings in which committee members debate the provisions of bills. Most markup sessions are open to the public; but faced with wrenching choices in cutting back programs, in the 1980s some committees began closing their doors so that lawmakers could negotiate in private, without lobbyists looking on. Markups are typically preceded by private bargaining, which is usually limited to committee and staff members. From time to time, though, outside experts—executive-branch lawyers, for instance—are called on for advice. Votes are taken on controversial matters.

At last, when all issues have been resolved, committee members vote on whether to report a measure to the full house. If a subcommittee handles a bill, it reports the bill to the full committee, which in turn votes whether to report the bill to the chamber.

Reporting

The report is the end product of a committee's successful deliberation on a bill or resolution. When considering a measure, a committee acts as an agent of the full chamber; if it contemplates further action, it must give the chamber a formal report. Most reports are positive—that is, they include a recommendation that the measure "do pass." Very rarely, the committee will report a measure or a nomination (in the Senate) with no recommendation, or even with a negative recommendation. This occurs when the committee, though divided or opposed to the action, nonetheless believes the chamber should have a chance to vote on it.

Reports may consist of a few sentences or hundreds of pages. Usually, they explain the committee's action and record how members voted. If the committee proposes amendments to the original bill, these are printed and explained. The hearing record may be summarized. In short, the committee report is intended to make the case for floor approval. Often included is language clarifying members' intentions about how the measure should be carried out by the executive and interpreted by the courts. Members dissenting from the committee's action may include their views in the report.

Bypassing the Committee

What if, as usually happens, a subcommittee or committee **pigeonholes** a measure—that is, fails to act on it? Almost always, this spells death for the measure, at least for the time being. Because so few measures enjoy majority support, committees that pigeonhole bills usually reflect the parent chamber's will. Even the bill's sponsors may be relieved when it dies in committee. To placate constituents or lobbies, legislators introduce many bills that do not express their own views. Sometimes committees take the heat for burying measures that their colleagues would rather not vote on.

Backers of a pigeonholed bill have several options. These include taking up the measure on the House or Senate floor by unanimous consent (requiring unanimity) or suspending the rules (requiring a two-thirds vote). As we will see, these procedures are commonly used to pass noncontroversial measures; but they are almost never invoked when the committee is opposed to a measure. Any committee that refuses to report a bill may be discharged of its duty. A **discharge** requires a motion, or petition, signed by a simple majority of the chamber's members, which is then voted on, according to the different procedures in each house.

These options are rarely invoked, for two reasons. First, committee specialization is honored in both chambers, though more so in the House than in the Senate. Members who challenge a committee's prerogatives can expect retaliation from the committee. Second, committees learn to predict the moods of the larger body. Committee leaders like to respond to their colleagues' demands; they pride themselves on reporting bills that command broad support in the House and Senate.

Rather than confronting a committee directly, a bill's sponsors might prevail by indirect tactics. They might rewrite the bill so that it can be referred to another committee. Or they might find a more receptive panel in the other house to advance the proposal and precipitate action. In the Senate, they might revive the measure as a floor amendment to another measure. (The Senate, unlike the House, permits *nongermane*, or unrelated, amendments to be proposed during floor deliberations.) Otherwise, the proponents of a thwarted measure must wait for another day and another battleground to win their cause—meanwhile building support through hearings, speeches, publicity, and lobbying.

From Committee to the Floor

Once a bill or resolution has been reported by a committee, it must get onto the House or Senate agenda. The same applies to presidential nominations reported by Senate committees.

The House

In the House, a bill reported from committee is placed on one of five *calendars*, or lists of pending business. These calendars, in rough order of importance, are *House* (authorization bills), *union* (revenue or spending bills), *private* (bills that deal with private matters and affect individuals), *consent* (uncontroversial bills that, however, a single member's objection may stop), and *discharge* (motions to discharge a committee from considering a bill).

Given the committees' function of screening out bills that lack broad support, it should come as no surprise that most measures that reach the House or Senate floor do in fact pass—many by lopsided margins. Nearly two thirds of the measures passed by the House in recent years followed expedited procedures reserved for noncontroversial issues: **unanimous consent** (taken from the consent calendar) and **suspension of the rules.** On certain days, measures can be brought up under unanimous consent if no one objects. In suspending the rules to pass a measure, a two-thirds vote is required; limited debate is allowed, but no amendments may be made.

Certain measures are privileged in the House. This means that they may be taken up directly after the committee reports them to the chamber. These include appropriation and revenue bills and a few other specific groups of measures.

For a controversial measure, however, the normal road to the House floor involves a "rule" drafted by the Committee on Rules to govern floor debate on the measure and approved by a majority vote of the chamber. Less than a tenth of all bills are handled in this way, but these include most of the hottest issues before Congress—budgets, taxes, trade, and major reauthorizations. When a rule is requested by a legislative committee, the Rules Committee must first decide whether to hold hearings; if it decides to do so, it may vote on whether to grant a rule. The rule specifies a time for debate and decrees whether amendments are in order or not

(open rules versus **closed rules)**. It also specifies whether **points of order** (procedural challenges) will be waived for certain parts of the bill. In recent years, such rules have become more detailed; nearly half of them limit amendments or waive points of order. Complex rules, as they are called, make it possible for the party leadership, working through the Rules Committee, to ease a bill's route to floor passage and to shape its final content.

The House grants extensive scheduling powers to its Rules Committee, which stands as the gatekeeper between the legislative committees and the House floor. But the committee can also withhold bills from floor action and bargain to include or delete given provisions. Therefore, the Rules Committee sometimes moves beyond its traffic cop role to that of final arbiter over the content of bills.

Control of the Rules Committee is crucial in the House. Strong 19th-century Speakers, such as "Czar" Reed and "Uncle Joe" Cannon, chaired the committee, using it as a lever for dictating schedules and committee assignments. In 1910, there was a revolt against Cannon's arbitrary powers. The Speaker was ousted from the Rules Committee; and committee assignments were delegated to the party caucuses. Between 1937 and 1967, conservatives dominated the Rules Committee, sometimes delaying or killing legislation desired by party leaders.

Today's Rules Committee is an arm of the majority-party leadership (Matsunaga and Chen, 1976). If the Speaker is a Democrat, he may nominate all Rules Committee Democrats, subject to caucus ratification. Thus the members of this key committee are adjuncts of the majority-party leadership, offering advice on floor strategy and providing the procedural tools to carry out that strategy. Of course, if enough members are unhappy with the leadership's strategy, they can vote to defeat the rule, thus barring the bill from the floor. But such defeats are fairly rare: party leaders usually make sure they have the votes they need before bringing out a rule from the Rules Committee.

The Senate

The Senate is more informal and relaxed than the House in these matters, but this does not mean that it is easy to bring measures to the floor. Senate bills are usually called up by unanimous consent. Because a single senator can object to this procedure, the majority and minority leaders consult to gain consent. Unanimous consent, of course, can be used to bring about any procedure; Senate floor leaders use it to control the pace and length of debate. It takes the form of complex **unanimous consent agreements** (often called *time agreements*), which may specify the amendments to be considered, set times for votes, and waive points of order. Getting interested senators to reach such agreements is a major task of floor leaders. Through such agreements, the Senate can sometimes control its debate as tightly as the House can.

Televising Senate floor debate. A technician stands next to one of six television cameras installed in the public galleries overlooking the Senate floor. Televised House and Senate proceedings are broadcast over C-SPAN.

Floor Debate

Floor debate is the most visible phase of lawmaking. A bill's supporters and opponents marshal their forces and contest the pros and cons. Amendments are introduced, debated, and voted on. For most legislation, the floor debate and votes on final passage are the only events that the media report. The floor debate can involve eloquence and high drama: momentous issues are joined and climactic votes taken.

Yet, as any visitor to Capitol Hill can tell you, routine House and Senate floor debates are a far cry from this colorful image. Attendance is often sparse. Members may not listen intently to the proceedings; they may wander about the chamber, consult with colleagues, or even read newspapers. Even when watched by the critical eye of the TV cameras, they all too often read from lengthy prepared texts.

Why are floor debates not true debates? The reason is that they cover ground already well plowed in committee hearings or markup sessions.

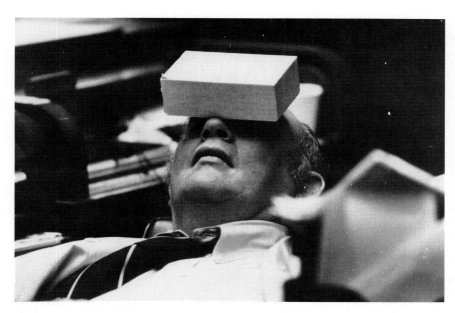

Filibustering in South Carolina. Filibusters are not confined to the U.S. Congress. Samuel Manning, a member of the South Carolina House of Representatives, uses a small box to cover his eyes as he rests during an all-night 1982 filibuster over a congressional reapportionment bill.

Members are not startled by the arguments; they have heard them before. Thus, floor debate is designed mainly to air key issues for colleagues and constituents and to set the stage for final votes.

Floor debate is controlled by the bill's managers—senior committee or subcommittee supporters. Opposition time is controlled by senior opponents from the relevant committee or subcommittee. Other members are allowed to speak or "revise and extend" their remarks to air their views. (That is, they may submit a written statement for the record.) Exchanges, called *colloquies*, are often staged among supporters of a position or between supporters and opponents—again to put their views on public record. If legislators or their staffs are unhappy with the wording of a specific argument, they can spruce it up before the *Congressional Record* goes to press. As in committee sessions, staff aides are on hand to prompt the bill's main sponsors and opponents with additional facts and arguments.

A **quorum**, consisting of a majority of members, is required to conduct business in either house. Quorums are not always physically present on the floor, but they are supposed to be available for votes. Members may ask for **quorum calls** if they want to delay the proceedings or merely to draw more members to the floor. When the House is considering a bill sent by the Rules Committee, it sits as a **Committee of the Whole** (that is, a committee consisting of all House members). This requires a quorum of only 100 members and thus allows more informal procedures.

In the smaller and more leisurely Senate, the rules of debate are simpler and more lenient. The Senate cherishes its privilege of free, unrestricted debate. When a small number of senators are unalterably opposed to a course of action, they may engage in an extended debate, called a **filibuster.** The object of a filibuster is to make a last-minute appeal to the public or merely to stall other business and wear out the opponents. The **cloture** rule can be used to shut off debate, with a vote of three fifths of the senators.

Senatorial courtesy demands that members be given ample time to pursue the subject at hand; repeated efforts to tighten the cloture rule have met with mixed success. At present, even if cloture is invoked, every senator in theory has up to an hour to speak on the measure being considered. In the past, filibusters were used to bring the Senate to a complete halt; recent filibusters, however, have been aimed at stopping certain bills while allowing other business to proceed. There is no question, however, that senators have been threatening and undertaking filibusters more often than ever before: there were more of them in the 1980s than in the prior 60 years of the cloture rule.

Congressional Voting

The most visible outcome of congressional deliberation is a law or resolution that the two chambers agree on. Every legislator has the right and duty to cast a vote.

Members of Congress cast votes on a staggering number of issues, both large and small. More than 500 votes are recorded in the House over two years; almost 700 are recorded in the Senate. These levels, though high, are far behind those of the 1960s and 1970s, which saw record numbers of measures processed by the two chambers.

Despite the large number of floor votes, the average senator or representative is recorded on 9 out of every 10 votes on the floor. Members protect their voting records in part because absenteeism may be raised as a campaign issue. If a member is not present to vote, he or she may be announced as "paired" with another member holding the opposite position.

Voting may be by voice, by division (standing), or by recorded vote. The House now records its votes electronically. Members insert ID cards into machines scattered throughout the chamber. Then, they push a button: yes, no, or present (abstain). The results are displayed on a giant illuminated tote board on the chamber's front wall. Voting in the House is thus simple and fast (about 15 minutes).

When votes are called, bells ring throughout rooms and hallways on either the House or Senate side of Capitol Hill. Members pour from their offices, committee rooms, or other haunts—including the gym, the swimming pool, and one of several eating places in the neighborhood—and make their way to the floor. After their votes have been recorded, they

Going to the House floor. Subways enable members of Congress to make a quick trip from their offices to the House or Senate chambers. This subway connects the Rayburn House Office Building and the Capitol.

wait long enough to find out the results, then drift away. For a brief moment, the chamber exudes the drama of the legislative process.

Interpreting votes

Legislators' votes on the House or Senate floor are not always easy to interpret. Votes are often taken on procedural matters that are somewhat independent of the issue at hand. Members may be unhappy with the way issues are posed, as when an amendment is badly drafted or a good bill is loaded down with objectionable features. Sometimes legislators straddle both sides of an issue to appeal to constituents. For instance, they may vote *against* the final passage of a bill but *for* a substitute version of that bill.

One must therefore be cautious in interpreting a legislator's vote on the floor. Nonetheless, nearly 100 lobbies—ranging from Common Cause to the American Bakers Association—issue voting indexes in which they rate legislators as "friendly" or "unfriendly." These indexes are not always balanced. The National Education Association, with 1.8 million members, is the nation's largest teachers' union. In 1980, it pegged its campaign support almost totally to the teachers' top legislative priority—the creation of a federal Department of Education (Hunt, 1980). One liberal who lost NEA support complained that "on every other issue, I've been on NEA's side, but they went nuts on this one." The National Rifle Association

(NRA) similarly targets legislators who display the slightest leanings toward gun control.

Determinants of voting

Taken as a whole, legislators' votes are remarkably consistent. Political scientists studying the voting patterns have identified a number of factors associated with members' floor votes. These factors include party, constituency, ideology, and presidential support or opposition.

The factor most strongly linked with votes is party affiliation. In a typical year, a third to a half of all floor votes could be called party votes. (So-called **party unity votes** occur when a majority of voting Democrats oppose a majority of voting Republicans.) The number of party votes grew in the 1980s after a long decline; the minority party wins about a third of such votes in a typical year.

Each legislator votes his or her party line about two thirds of the time. The Republicans tend to be more cohesive than the Democrats, who at times have been badly split. Partisan voting, as we have seen, is rooted in constituency differences: the Democrats tend to reflect urban, ethnic, and racial interests; the Republicans tend to reflect the views of the upper classes, whites, and people from small towns. These natural tendencies are strengthened by shared policy goals and membership in party groups.

Party loyalties are reinforced by partisan groups on Capitol Hill. New members turn to their parties for committee assignments. They meet with fellow Democrats or Republicans to exchange information and tips about issues to be voted on. Still, legislators realize that their votes must be explained to their voters, who are more influential than any party leader. "I'm goin' to dance with them that brung me," Representative Phil Gramm (Tex.) announced in 1981, referring to his conservative constituents when bolting the Democratic ranks to support President Reagan's budget plans. (Later, Gramm switched parties, became a Republican, was returned to office, and then successfully ran for the Senate.)

Legislators naturally reflect their constituents' views when they cast votes. For one thing, elected representatives usually share the opinions of "the folks back home." For another, the threat of defeat hangs over the heads of legislators who defy their constituents' wishes on key issues. Not many legislators are turned out of office for defying local sentiments, but there is a handful of such cases in every election. The example of that handful is more than enough to keep the rest of the legislators in line.

Members also hold ideological commitments that surface in their voting (Schneider, 1979). One ideological group is called the *conservative coalition*. This collection of Republicans and conservative Democrats emerged in the late 1930s in reaction to the New Deal. It enjoyed its greatest successes between 1939 and the 1950s, though it staged a brief comeback in the early 1980s (Manley, 1973).

Presidents also affect legislators' votes; political commentators are always keeping score of the president's wins and losses on Capitol Hill. The

Presidential support in congressional voting. President Ronald Reagan declares Sen. Phil Gramm (R–Tex.) champion and loyal presidential supporter. Senator Gramm, elected to the House as a Democrat in 1978, was expelled from his Democratic seat on the House Budget Committee after he revealed confidential party tactics in 1981 budget negotiations. He then switched parties and ran for the Senate as a Republican in 1984.

following conclusions can be drawn from examining the success rates of presidents:

1. All modern presidents have gained approval for a majority of the measures on which they took a position.
2. Partisan swings have an impact; when their party also controls Congress, presidents win three fourths or more of the votes on which they take a position.
3. Support for presidential positions is by no means assured; in fact, it tends to drop as the administration "ages."
4. Congressional support for presidents' positions has been extremely low since the 1960s, with the notable exception of Reagan in 1981.

5. Presidents have been taking clear-cut positions on a rising *number* of issues, but these positions have been winning a declining *percentage* of congressional votes.

Cue giving and cue taking

Legislators face a baffling number of votes on a wide range of issues. It is no wonder, then, that they rely heavily on the advice of others. Members engage in **cue-giving** and cue taking. Lawmakers take their cues on how to vote from better-informed colleagues, or cue givers—including party leaders, committee experts, the president or cabinet members, lobby representatives, and informal caucus groups.

Kingdon (1981) talked with representatives right after they cast votes. Based on these interviews, he devised a model of *cue taking* that predicted legislators' votes about 9 times out of 10. Much of the time, of course, legislators have no trouble in making up their minds. They often have firm convictions or have taken public stands on a given issue. This also happens when all of the influencing factors—for example, party leaders, interest groups, staffs, the White House, and constituency interests—point in the same direction.

Kingdon found that if members receive conflicting cues on an issue, they turn first to trusted fellow members; constituency pressures rank second; party leaders and interest groups are far less important than either of these influences. When members break from the stance indicated by a consensus of their cue givers, it is usually to follow their own conscience.

No model can capture every twist or turn of a senator's or representative's voting record. However, most legislators behave predictably on most votes. Such consistency not only simplifies their decisions; it also helps them explain their votes to other people.

From Bill to Law

After a measure passes one house, it is sent to the other house. Passage by one house does not ensure passage or even consideration by the second one. The measure is usually introduced separately, in identical or different form. Most measures may begin in either chamber. The Constitution specifies that the House originates revenue bills; by convention, the House also originates appropriations bills. In such fiscal matters, the Senate often plays the role of an appellate body, adjusting and sometimes liberalizing House-passed provisions.

The second chamber to approve a measure may request a conference committee to resolve differences between the House and Senate versions. If the originating chamber consents, conferees are picked to represent the views of the two houses. The conference report is resubmitted to the two chambers to be ratified. However, 9 times out of 10 conferences are not used: the second chamber simply passes the measure outright or sends it back to the first chamber with amendments.

Once a bill or a joint resolution has been duly passed by both houses, it is conveyed to the president. He must sign or veto the measure within 10 days. If he fails to sign it, it still becomes law—unless Congress adjourns and thus prevents the president from returning it.

The legislative output—bills and resolutions approved by both houses—reflects the nation's policy agenda, the political climate of the times, and congressional arrangements for structuring the workload (see Figure 11–3). In the 1980s, marked by a "fiscal squeeze" and only a few new policies or programs, the overall legislative output fell from the peak of the 1960s and 1970s. The average public law is today longer and more complex than the average public law of earlier years. Increasingly, major decisions about policy priorities are being "packaged" into huge, multifaceted measures: budget resolutions, continuing appropriations bills, omnibus authorizations, and major tax bills that may run to thousands of pages and embrace equal numbers of discrete policy decisions. In an era of program freezes and cutbacks, it is easier for lawmakers to explain their vote for a bundle of such decisions than to defend individual cuts. Finally, the 1980s have brought an explosion of **commemorative measures:** laws naming federal buildings; designating special days, weeks, or months; authorizing medals; or granting congressional charters (Davidson, 1986). Such measures have the virtues of being brief, uncontroversial, and best of all, virtually cost free.

The legislative process is long and mazelike, filled with hazards for a measure's sponsors. Many measures are proposed; few make their way to final passage. Measures can be halted at many points in the process. Therefore, the legislative process can be said to have a conservative impact on policy-making. Groups opposed to all or part of a measure have *defensive advantages.* They can amend or kill the measure at dozens of points in the legislative process. This is perhaps as it should be. Our national government would be vastly overloaded if everyone's "bright idea" were suddenly transformed into law.

A PAIR OF LEGISLATIVE CASE STUDIES

To explain how the maze of parliamentary rules and precedents works in concrete cases, we offer two examples. One is an imaginary bill, an uncontroversial commemorative resolution. The other is a real measure, the highly controversial reconciliation (or debt reduction) bill for fiscal year 1986. The abbreviated histories of these two measures show how varied lawmaking can be, depending on the level of conflict.

"National Textbook Authors' Appreciation Day"

Resolutions declaring commemorative days, weeks, or months are easily drafted and popular with legislators. They are usually in the form of joint resolutions, passed by both houses and signed by the president; they rarely stir up controversy, because they cost nothing beyond the $209 it takes to

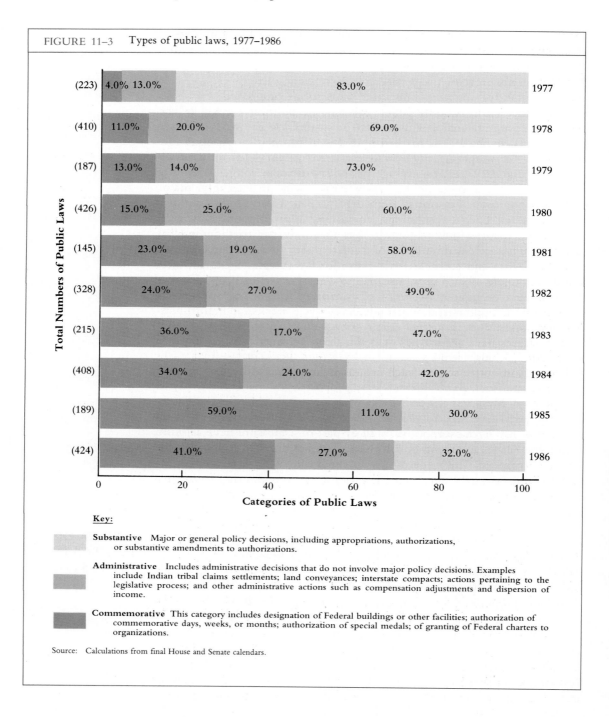

FIGURE 11–3   Types of public laws, 1977–1986

Total Numbers of Public Laws

(223)   4.0%   13.0%   83.0%   1977
(410)   11.0%   20.0%   69.0%   1978
(187)   13.0%   14.0%   73.0%   1979
(426)   15.0%   25.0%   60.0%   1980
(145)   23.0%   19.0%   58.0%   1981
(328)   24.0%   27.0%   49.0%   1982
(215)   36.0%   17.0%   47.0%   1983
(408)   34.0%   24.0%   42.0%   1984
(189)   59.0%   11.0%   30.0%   1985
(424)   41.0%   27.0%   32.0%   1986

0   20   40   60   80   100

Categories of Public Laws

Key:

Substantive   Major or general policy decisions, including appropriations, authorizations, or substantive amendments to authorizations.

Administrative   Includes administrative decisions that do not involve major policy decisions. Examples include Indian tribal claims settlements; land conveyances; interstate compacts; actions pertaining to the legislative process; and other administrative actions such as compensation adjustments and dispersion of income.

Commemorative   This category includes designation of Federal buildings or other facilities; authorization of commemorative days, weeks, or months; authorization of special medals; of granting of Federal charters to organizations.

Source: Calculations from final House and Senate calendars.

print a two-page resolution. In the 99th Congress (1985–1986), 307 of them were enacted, comprising nearly half of all the public laws over that two-year period (Richardson, 1987).

Our hypothetical commemorative declares April 1 as "National Textbook Authors' Appreciation Day"—a worthy and, one hopes, uncontroversial cause. After asking the Legislative Counsel's office to draft the brief resolution, the representative who is its chief sponsor circulates a "Dear Colleague" letter to all members of the House to solicit cosponsors. Numerous cosponsors will come forward: the average House member cosponsored no less than 123 commemorative resolutions in the 99th Congress.

Once cosponsors have been assembled, our representative will introduce the resolution by placing it in the "hopper" (a mahogany box on the clerk's desk in the House chamber). Acting for the Speaker, the **parliamentarian** automatically refers the measure to the Committee on Post Office and Civil Service, which in turn refers the measure to its Subcommittee on Census and Population. The subcommittee's staff reviews all proposed commemorations to ensure that they meet certain standards, such as national appeal and significance, and that they have obtained written cosponsorship or endorsement by a majority of members (at least 218). The subcommittee meets weekly to clear commemorative proposals for floor action, though it does not formally report them. In the Senate, the Judiciary Committee screens such proposals, requiring at least 50 cosponsors (including at least 20 Democrats and 20 Republicans).

Approval of the full House and Senate is as routine as the rest of the history of these measures. They are brought up under unanimous consent (described earlier) and are almost always approved. "Mr. Speaker," the committee representative says, "I ask unanimous consent that the Committee on Post Office and Civil Service be discharged from further consideration of H. Res. 100 and that the measure be passed." This motion is not debatable; so the observer in the gallery who blinks an eyelid may miss the proceedings. The measure's sponsors can, however, say a few words in its behalf by "reserving the right to object"—that is, by threatening to object to unanimous consent, speaking their piece, and then withdrawing the objection. The Senate majority and minority floor leaders usually do the honors in that chamber, often when no other senator (except the one who is presiding) is in the chamber.

A large number of routine bills and resolutions, as well as commemoratives, are handled in this quick, expeditious manner. These include procedural or administrative items, private bills, and many symbolic "sense of Congress" resolutions. Little member or staff time is consumed by such measures, though procedures ensure that members can object if they wish. Few do, for they hope that their own pet bills will be speeded in the same way. If members object, then more conventional, time-consuming procedures must be followed.

Reconciliation Act for Fiscal Year 1986

Procedures in effect since 1974 require that the House and Senate agree each year on a budget resolution setting overall revenue and spending targets for major categories of government activity. (The budget process is discussed in detail in Chapter 17.) Then, congressional committees consider alternative methods of meeting the targets, through a combination of spending cuts, revenue increases, and program changes. These provisions are incorporated into an omnibus **reconciliation bill,** in which existing laws and programs are made consistent with the agreed-upon budget numbers. In the 1980s, budget disputes were especially fierce, partly because of economic factors and partly because of disagreement between the White House and Congress over how budget deficits should be reduced.

The reconciliation bill for fiscal 1986 began its life in mid-1985, several months before the new fiscal year was to begin in October (Gettinger, 1986: 752–54). The House started with two bills: a package of spending cuts and revenue hikes reported by the Ways and Means Committee (H.R. 3128) and a collection of program changes recommended by authorizing committees and reported by the Budget Committee (H.R. 3500). These bills were passed in late October by partisan votes, the Republicans objecting to the spending levels. After the Senate Budget Committee reported its bill (S. 1730), which contained the recommendations of the Senate's authorizing committees, a month went by before the bill was taken up on the floor. Only after Senate leaders agreed to remove unrelated provisions limiting textile and shoe imports and handle them separately, did the bill pass by a 93–6 vote.

The House-Senate conference began, after more delays, on December 6, 1985—two months after the fiscal year had begun. It was one of the largest conferences in congressional history: more than 240 House and Senate conferees met in 31 subgroups. The conferees took two weeks to agree on terms, but only after Senator Bob Packwood (R–Ore.) persuaded them to add a manufacturers' tax that would pay for the "superfund" hazardous waste cleanup program.

The Senate adopted the conference report on December 19, the same day it was presented. But that was only the beginning of a three-month on-again, off-again process in which the conference report was bounced back and forth between the chambers nine times (see Figure 11–4). Parliamentarians could remember nothing like it. More than once, the measure was written off as dead. Before the process ended, Senator Packwood's superfund tax was stripped away (the House having rejected that appendage). To stave off a presidential veto, new amendments were added only after acrimonious negotiations with James C. Miller, director of the Office of Management and Budget.

When William H. Gray (D–Pa.), chairman of the House Budget Committee, brought up the measure for its final vote, on the evening of March

FIGURE 11–4   How the 1986 reconciliation bill became law

HOUSE

OCT. 24
House passed HR 3500, containing deficit-reduction proposals from most House committees.

OCT. 31
House passed HR 3128, containing deficit-reduction proposals from the Ways and Means Committee. (HR 3500 was later combined with HR 3128 for conference.)

SENATE

NOV. 14
Senate passed S 1730, containing deficit-reduction proposals from all Senate committees. The bill was renumbered HR 3128.

CONFERENCE

DEC. 19
More than 240 conferees, meeting in 31 groups over two weeks, reached agreement on HR 3128.

DEC. 19
House rejected the conference report, voting to strip off a conference provision establishing a new manufacturers' tax to pay for the "superfund" hazardous-waste cleanup program.

DEC. 19
House rejected the Senate proposal.

MARCH 6
House voted to strip off the superfund tax, but also offered compromises on health care and offshore oil revenues.

MARCH 18
House rejected the latest Senate proposal.

MARCH 20
House accepted March 14 Senate proposal, clearing the bill for the president.

DEC. 19
Senate adopted the conference report.

DEC. 19
Senate voted to reinstate the superfund tax.

DEC. 20
Senate voted again to keep the superfund tax.

MARCH 14
Senate agreed to delete the superfund tax, but at White House insistence also demanded elimination of welfare and offshore drilling provisions and further cuts in offshore oil revenues for states.

MARCH 18
Senate insisted on its March 14 proposal.

Source: *Congressional Quarterly Weekly Report*, April 5, 1986, p. 753.

20, 1986, he moved adoption of "the Senate amendment to the House amendment to the Senate amendment to the House amendment to the Senate amendment." A ripple of laughter greeted the motion; but everyone was relieved to be rid of the measure at last. No one was happier than the House and Senate reading clerks: the official text of H.R. 3128 ran to 310 pages of printed parchment, and a two-foot-high stack of documents had to be carried through Capitol corridors every time one of the chambers acted on it.

Although the 1986 reconciliation bill may be an extreme example, it shows how bewildering the legislative process can become when the stakes are high and the conflict is intense. Statistically, such controversial measures are relatively rare—not nearly as common as the uncontested commemorative resolutions we described above. But critical issues, especially in the fiscal jungle of the 1980s, reveal the legislative process in all of its complexity and contentiousness.

CONGRESSIONAL DECLINE AND RESURGENCE

Belittling Congress is an old American pastime. Lord Bryce, a 19th-century British observer, remarked that "Americans are especially fond of running down their congressmen." There is no public image of the executive and judicial branches that can compare with the cartoon character Senator Snort, the florid and incompetent windbag of George Lichty's "Grin and Bear It." Political wit, from Mark Twain and Will Rogers to Herblock and Johnny Carson, has always singled out Congress for special attention. Legislators themselves often foster the shabby public image of Congress by depicting themselves as gallant warriors contending against its evils: Such legislators "run *for* Congress by running *against* Congress' (Fenno, 1978: 168).

Serious critics, mainly scholars and journalists, fault Congress on a number of counts. In the prevalent textbook view, Congress is seen as combining disorder, corruption, and inertia. Average people, in opinion polls, seem to agree that these are defects of the legislative branch.

Despite its reputation for inertia, Congress has changed dramatically over the past generation. As we have noted, both chambers opened up their procedures in the 1960s and 1970s to permit more and more members to wield influence on policy-making. Our era is hard on legislatures the world over; Congress is subject to severe pressures. Some of these pressures come from the external environment. There have been changing public expectations, fast-moving events, and competing institutions. Such pressures challenge Congress to adapt by altering its practices or work habits. Other pressures come from internal developments, mainly membership turnover, factional shifts, and changing norms. For Congress to survive, it must relieve these pressures by adjusting its procedures and power structures. Congress has responded to both sets of pressures—how successfully remains to be seen.

Historically, Congress has been an equal partner in policy-making. The

The architecture of Capitol Hill. This helicopter view of Washington, D.C., looking east, reveals the heart of the nation's capital. This view includes the Capitol [big dome, center], the Russell, Dirksen, and Hart Senate office buildings (1, 2, and 3), the Senate office annex (4), the Supreme Court (5), two Library of Congress buildings (6, 7, and 8), the Cannon, Longworth and Rayburn House office buildings (9, 10, and 11), and a House office annex (12). Other numbered buildings are the Republican party's national headquarters (13) and the headquarters of the United Brotherhood of Carpenters and Joiners (14).

founders viewed the legislative branch as the keystone of democracy. They spelled out the powers of Congress in Article I of the Constitution. Except in times of crisis, Congress has aired and clarified the great issues of the day. After enduring a strong president, such as Jackson, Lincoln, or Wilson, it regained the initiative. At times, it all but eclipsed the presidency. In the late 19th century, Woodrow Wilson (1980: 31) saw Congress as "the predominant and controlling force, the center and source of all motive and of all regulatory power."

Few observers today would describe Congress in such expansive terms. "The decline of Congress" has been universally heralded—by friends as well as foes, by liberals as well as conservatives, by members of Congress as well as outsiders. Journalists have enjoyed taking members of Congress to task for their perquisites, their junkets, their occasional corruption, even their sexual exploits.

Yet, to paraphrase Mark Twain, reports of Congress's demise have been greatly exaggerated. True, the shaping experiences of this century—two world wars, the Great Depression, the extended Cold War, and the Vietnam War—have inflated the policy-making role of the president. Especially in foreign policy, Congress has yielded much of its constitutional power to "advise and consent." It has done so by deferring to the president's responsiveness to fast-moving world events. But the disillusionment that followed the Vietnam War, Watergate, and the Iran-*contra* affair led to a basic debate: How desirable is concentrated executive power? After Nixon's resignation, Congress showed renewed vigor in defending its prerogatives in foreign and domestic policy-making (Sundquist, 1981).

The Reagan years of the 1980s tested the Congress's resurgent powers. The conservative Reagan set the agenda by proposing higher defense spending, drastic tax cuts, and slashes in domestic aid programs. Although a bipartisan majority barely endorsed the "Reaganomics" scheme in 1981, support dwindled in succeeding years. (The opposition Democrats controlled the House and, after 1986, the Senate.) Battles between the two branches spanned the whole range of domestic and foreign policy issues: war powers, trade negotiations, civil rights, welfare policies, criminal justice, environmental protection, and deficit reduction.

Congressional traditions such as seniority have inspired generations of editorial writers and cartoonists. But these traditions have changed so much that they are almost unrecognizable. New organizations have brought a new generation of problems to Capitol Hill.

Congress will always be controversial. Unlike the president or the courts, it conducts its business largely in public. Its faults are out in the open for all to see. A presidential message may patch over quarrels among White House advisers or rivalries among agencies; a judicial ruling may cloak the uncertainties or biases of judges. People are therefore apt to conclude that the president speaks with one voice and that the courts manifest magisterial wisdom. No such illusions surround the actions of the legislative branch. Congress speaks with 540 voices. It reflects the variety and contradiction of American society itself.

If the president articulates people's hopes and aspirations, the houses of Congress reflect their interests. Public expectations, as we will see, place impossible demands on the chief executive; the babel of interests places equally impossible burdens on the legislative branch. No body of politicians can satisfy the demands of all major groups or interests, especially in an age of scarce resources. And no such body can represent those demands without making incoherent or even contradictory decisions. This is the dilemma of Congress as a representative institution.

CONCLUSIONS

In this chapter, we have examined the legislative work of Congress. Although individual lawmakers insert personal and parochial interests at every turn, they cannot control the content of the public agenda or the force of public demands on Congress as an institution. The 1960s and 1970s, buoyed by an expanding economy, brought a flood of new legislation. In contrast, the 1980s brought an era of policy contraction, in which legislators faced the unpleasant task of apportioning scarce resources among insistent interest groups.

1. The legislative duties of Congress embrace the whole range of the government's activities. The elaborate rules of the two houses not only promote orderly deliberation but also allow political preferences to be registered at many stages in the lawmaking process.

2. The procedures of the House are relatively rigid, designed to allow the majority to work its will. But the Senate is a more informal body, geared to protect the rights of individual senators. It makes many procedural arrangements by unanimous consent.

3. The legislative output of Congress reflects the public agenda, the political climate, and the internal arrangements that Congress uses to handle its workload. In the 1980s the measures enacted by Congress decreased in number, increased in size, and veered away from authorizing new federal programs or expenditures.

4. The procedures of Congress permit challenge and delay of proposed legislation at many stages, but they also allow expedited treatment of routine, noncontroversial measures.

5. A great deal is said about the "decline of Congress." But post-Vietnam, post-Watergate, and post–Iran-*contra* Congresses have displayed renewed independence and vigor.

FURTHER READING

DAVIDSON, ROGER H., and WALTER J. OLESZEK (1977) *Congress against Itself.* Bloomington, Ind.: Indiana University Press. A narrative account of how the House committee system operates and of efforts to change it in the "reform era" of the 1970s.

FENNO, RICHARD F., JR. (1978) *Congressmen in Committees*. Boston, Mass.: Little, Brown. A landmark comparative study of committees, focusing on internal dynamics and external forces.

KINGDON, JOHN W. (1981) *Congressmen's Voting Decisions*. New York: Harper and Row. One of the most sensible and instructive offering in the vast literature on congressional voting.

OLESZEK, WALTER J. (1988) *Congressional Procedures and the Policy Process*. 3rd edition. Washington, DC: CQ Press. The authoritative primer of congressional rules and procedures, written by the leading expert on the subject.

SMITH, STEPHEN S., and CHRISTOPHER J. DEERING (1984) *Committees in Congress* Washington, DC: CQ Press. An up-to-date survey of congressional committees in the post-reform era, from a comparative perspective.

Chapter Twelve

THE CONSTITUTIONAL PRESIDENCY

The ultimate paradox of the presidency, Thomas E. Cronin maintains, is that "it is always too powerful and yet it is always inadequate" (Cronin, 1980: 22). By some accounts, the office is weak and confined; by others it is dangerously out of control.

Consider the celebrated Iran-*contra* furor. In 1985 and 1986, lower-level White House staffers launched and carried out a highly secret foreign policy, apparently with President Reagan's blessing. The policy was an elaborate arms-for-hostages deal in which arms were shipped to Iran in exchange for the release by terrorists of American hostages and the payment of money, channeled through third parties, some of which eventually reached the *contra* forces fighting the Nicaraguan government in Central America. The vehicle for this policy was "the Enterprise," a shadowy network of private arms dealers and soldiers of fortune working under the aegis of White House operatives. Here is how Congress's Iran-*contra* investigating committee describes this singular operation:

> The Enterprise, functioning largely at [Lieutenant Colonel Oliver] North's direction, had its own airplanes, pilots, airfield, operatives, ship, secure communications devices, and secret Swiss bank accounts. For 16 months, it served as the secret arm of the [National Security Council] staff, carrying out with private and non-appropriated money, and without the accountability or restrictions imposed by law on the CIA, a covert *contra* aid program that Congress thought it had prohibited. (Select Committee, 1987)

After a small Lebanese newspaper blew the cover off this operation in late 1986, Iran-*contra* became the greatest scandal of the Reagan administration. Congress was outraged that the president had deceived it; the public was puzzled because the president had belied his own ideals—openness in his dealings and firmness toward terrorists. Although Reagan's personal popularity revived, his administration never fully recovered its credibility.

Did Iran-*contra* display the presidency's power, or did it reveal its weakness? The case for Iran-*contra* as a disturbing abuse of power is easily made. Having failed to convince Congress or the American public of the need to support the Nicaraguan *contra* "freedom fighters," the president engaged in an undercover policy that was hidden from scrutiny by Congress, the press, the public, and even his own chief advisers. This ill-conceived policy violated explicit provisions of law, implicit understandings with lawmakers, other countries' expectations about U.S. behavior, and the public's sense of propriety. More important, it showed contempt for other decision makers and impatience with democratic policy-making under our system of checks and balances.

But there is also an opposing view, held by the president and at least a few of his most zealous advisers: The so-called Reagan doctrine of aiding anticommunist "freedom fighters" throughout the world had been stalled for six years by congressional carping, bureaucratic infighting within the executive branch, and a confused and divided public. As for dealing with

Iranian terrorists in exchange for hostages, the harsh world of international intrigue sometimes demands actions that would win no popularity contests. To achieve results, the president had the duty, if not the authority, to take decisive albeit stealthy initiatives.

Whichever version we accept, the paradox of power and weakness has surrounded the American presidency ever since its invention in 1787. The office is vaguely defined, and its powers are limited and shared with others, mainly in Congress. Achieving decisive, coherent policies under such a system is often tortuous and time consuming. In spite of this, perhaps in part because of it, the presidency has expanded historically in importance and influence. With a huge military establishment and an extensive intelligence apparatus, the presidency can wield an awesome power in foreign affairs. The media and the public, moreover, have transformed chief executives into TV-age celebrities and prefer them to be strong and decisive.

The paradox of power and weakness in the presidency is the focus for this chapter. We outline the constitutional design for the office and discuss precedents and the techniques used by activist presidents. Then, we lay out the office's day-to-day duties: administration, politics, ceremony. We also examine the structure of the White House—what people work there and how they are organized. Knowing how the office works helps explain why the presidency, which is probably the most original invention of our Constitution, is also the most puzzling and elusive. In the next chapter, we will consider the "public presidency": not the office's decision-making powers but its ceremonial and symbolic meaning.

THE PRESIDENCY IN THE CONSTITUTION

In creating the presidency, the Constitution's drafters had to improvise. As advocates of parliamentary power, they had no intention of installing an all-powerful executive. No form of monarchy—not even a constitutionally limited one—was acceptable to them. Strong, legitimate legislative bodies were deeply implanted in New World soil—through the colonial (later state) legislatures, the Continental Congresses, and finally the Articles of Confederation.

Yet this very tradition of strong legislatures and weak executives was causing trouble. The Articles of Confederation failed to promote political or economic stability. Congress under the Articles could not provide for the common defense, conduct relations with foreign powers, or regulate commerce and coinage. James Madison declared that executives in the new

WORDS AND IDEAS

Alexander Hamilton on an Energetic Executive

Energy in the Executive is a leading character in the definition of good government. It is essential to the protection of the community against foreign attacks; it is not less essential to the steady administration of the laws; to the protection of property against those irregular and high-handed combinations which sometimes interrupt the ordinary course of justice; to the security of liberty against the enterprises and assaults of ambition, of faction, and of anarchy. . . .

The ingredients which constitute energy in the Executive are, first, unity; secondly, duration; thirdly, an adequate provision for its support; fourthly, competent powers. . . .

That unity is conducive to energy will not be disputed. Decision, activity, secrecy, and dispatch will generally characterize the proceedings of one man in a much more eminent degree than the proceedings of any greater number; and in proportion as the number is increased, these qualities will be diminished.

This unity may be destroyed in two ways: either by vesting the power in two or more magistrates of equal dignity and authority; or by vesting it ostensibly in one man, subject, in whole or in part, to the control and cooperation of others, in the capacity of counsellors to him.

Source: Alexander Hamilton, *The Federalist,* No. 70.

nation had become "ciphers," while legislatures were "omnipotent." He charged that constitutional limits were "readily overleaped by the legislature on the spur of an occasion." James Wilson, often called the father of the presidency, wanted an executive with "energy, dispatch, and responsibility." Alexander Hamilton, a champion of strong government, wrote that "energetic government" was the most prized goal of the Constitutional Convention (*The Federalist,* No. 70). Gouverneur Morris, leader of the Constitutional Convention's drafting committee, also favored a strong, independent executive.

The Constitutional Formula

These men—Madison, Wilson, Hamilton, and Morris—were among the brightest lights at the Constitutional Convention. They guided their colleagues to a series of fateful decisions that outlined the features of the modern presidency (Pritchett, 1982:118–21).

President Franklin Delano Roosevelt served longer than any other president. First elected in 1932, FDR determined in 1940 to break the two-term tradition set by President George Washington. Reelected for a third term, Roosevelt won yet another term, his fourth, in 1944. He died in April 1945.

An elected individual

The president is one person. Some of the delegates, fearing that a one-person executive too closely resembled a king, proposed a collegial executive or council to check executive power. These proposals were rejected.

Even more important, the president is elected independently, not picked by the legislature. Many ways of picking the president were suggested. Most of those who favored a strong executive preferred popular election. (Hamilton, as close to a monarchist as a colonial patriot could be, was an exception.) But the small-state delegates rejected this approach. Thus evolved an awkward compromise, the electoral college. That compromise proved to be a victory for popular government, for within a few years most of the states had passed laws providing that electors be picked by popular vote.

George Washington established a precedent for a two-term limit on presidential tenure by declining to run for a third term in 1796. The precedent held until Franklin D. Roosevelt successfully ran for a third term in 1940 and for a fourth term in 1944. As soon as the Republicans recaptured Congress after World War II, they pushed through a constitutional two-term limit, ratified in 1951 as the 22nd Amendment. Pronounced "not wholly wise" by Dwight Eisenhower, the amendment has been criticized by political scientists. It denies voters the right to reelect a popular president for a third term (as Republicans realized in the Eisenhower and Reagan years), and it makes an instant lame duck out of any second-term president.

A broad mandate

The president has broad, vaguely described powers. Article II of the Constitution, which deals with the presidency, is less than half as long as Article I, which describes Congress. It opens with the so-called vesting clause: "Executive power shall be vested in a president." Is this just a description of the office? Or is it a way of vastly expanding the Constitution's listed powers? No one knows for sure.

There is also the "take care clause," which directs the president to "take care that the laws be faithfully executed." This is probably a simple injunction to enforce laws passed by Congress, but presidents have sometimes used the clause to justify broad exercise of powers.

Shared policy leadership

The president exercises key powers along with Congress. These powers are legislating, administering laws, and conducting foreign affairs. Although there is said to be "separation of powers," what happens in practice is that *separate* institutions *jointly* exercise powers. As Madison observed, the Constitution creates not a system in which separate institutions perform separate functions, but a system in which separate institutions share functions, so that "these departments be so far connected and blended as to give to each a constitutional control over the others" (*The Federalist,* No. 48).

In lawmaking, for instance, the president plays a crucial part. He can convene one or both houses of Congress in special session. Although he cannot introduce legislation directly, he "shall from time to time give to the Congress information on the state of the Union and recommend to their consideration such measures as he shall judge necessary and expedient." The president must also sign or veto legislation within 10 days after Congress has passed it. To overrule a veto, a two-thirds vote is needed in each house. (Unlike some state governors, the president lacks the "item veto" and must accept or reject a bill *in toto*.) In the so-called pocket veto, the president can veto a bill without sending it back to Congress. But this occurs only if Congress adjourns and thus prevents the president from returning the legislation within the prescribed 10-day period.

The president must see that laws are carried out faithfully. The writers of the Constitution surely meant him to be the chief officer of the executive branch. They gave him the power to appoint "officers of the United States," with the advice and consent of the Senate. He selects judges, ambassadors, consuls, and other federal officers; congressional assent is not needed for lower-level appointees. He can demand written reports from department heads. (The Constitution nowhere speaks of a **cabinet.** It mentions only principal officers of the executive departments.)

On the precise structure of executive agencies, the Constitution is silent. Cabinet-level departments and other agencies are formed by statutes that specify the programs and policies of these agencies. In short, while the president is the chief administrative officer, Congress takes the lead in designing the executive branch's structure and detailing its tasks.

The president can also grant pardons and reprieves. This power is absolute, though the Justice Department publishes guidelines for applicants. Normally, the process receives little attention; few people are aware, for example, that President Reagan pardoned more than 300 men and women during his term of office. President Gerald Ford's pardon of former President Richard Nixon for his part in the Watergate affair, however, raised a storm of protest and enfeebled Ford's presidency.

Commander and chief diplomat

The Constitution grants the president expansive authority in diplomacy and national defense; but even here, it gives Congress a loud voice. Because diplomacy and national defense were traditionally royal prerogatives, the ruling monarchs resisted legislative involvement in these matters. Even champions of legislative rights and balanced constitutions, such as the philosophers Locke and Montesquieu, held that executives should have unchallenged authority to deal with foreign powers and cope with crises. The Constitution thus grants the president wide discretion in these areas. He appoints ambassadors and other envoys; he negotiates treaties; he is commander in chief of the armed forces.

Yet presidents must consult with Congress as they conduct foreign affairs and manage defense efforts. The Senate must approve ambassadors, envoys, and other major presidential appointees. Treaties must be ratified by two thirds of the Senate. Only Congress, which most directly represents the people, can declare war. (An early draft of the Constitution gave Congress the power to "make war." On second thought, the founders changed this to "declare war.") Through its cherished power of the purse, Congress can direct the flow of funds and equip the armed forces.

The presidency is the most innovative and daring invention in our political framework. It has been copied, but never duplicated, by nations that have adopted constitutions like ours.

Presidential succession

The Constitution wisely provides that the vice president will serve as president if the president dies, resigns, is removed or is unable to discharge the duties of office. This has ensured a smooth transition when presidents have died in office, four times at the hands of assassins.

A more vexing problem, presidential disability, is addressed to the 25th Amendment (ratified in 1967). The vice president becomes *acting* president

This collection of maps exemplifies three important problems in **governing America** for the next few decades. First, the problem of population mobility is depicted in Maps 1 through 4. These maps underscore the shifts in the American population, showing the general growth in the numbers of Americans living in the sunbelt states of the South and Southwest, the urbanization of the formerly rural South, the boom in the Hispanic population of the southwestern states, and, finally, the political consequences of these demographic changes in the redistribution of representation in the U.S. House of Representatives. Once mainly influenced by the urban-industrial states of the Northeast and Midwest, the future of American politics will much more lie in the hands of people living in the states of the southern rim—that crescent of states running from Virginia in the east to California in the west.

Second, Maps 5 through 26 illustrate the problem of electoral politics. In order to govern, parties and candidates must find ways to succeed at the polls. Maps 5 through 26 show the results of presidential elections from the turn of this century until 1984. Party fortunes have waxed and waned over the 22 elections during this period of time. The first three of these decades were part of a Republican era. From 1900 until 1932, Republicans captured the presidency, with the lone exception of Woodrow Wilson (who won both in 1912 and 1916). Franklin D. Roosevelt's landslide election in 1932 ushered in the New Deal era. Democrats captured the White House from 1932 until 1952; since Dwight D. Eisenhower's election in 1952, Republicans have won the presidency six times (1952, 1956, 1968,

1972, 1980, and 1984), and Democrats have been successful only three times (1960, 1964, and 1976).

Third, Maps 27 through 34 depict the relative position of the United States in the world. How does the U.S.A. compare with other countries in population growth, military spending, food production, manufacturing, or trade? America alone cannot solve problems of world overpopulation, hunger, war, poverty, energy, or threats to the environment. **Governing America** in the future will surely be guided in important ways by our position in relation to the rest of the world. Can we establish a more perfect union to meet the world challenges of the future?

TABLE OF CONTENTS

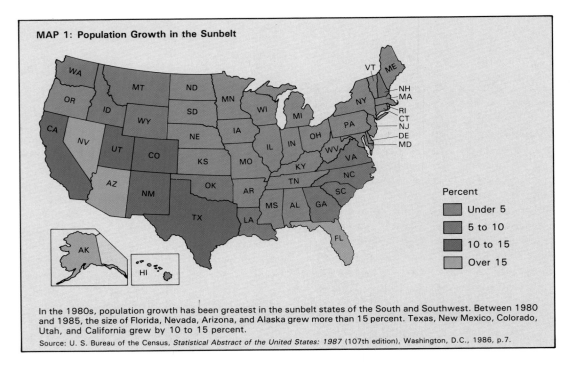

MAP 1: Population Growth in the Sunbelt

Percent
- Under 5
- 5 to 10
- 10 to 15
- Over 15

In the 1980s, population growth has been greatest in the sunbelt states of the South and Southwest. Between 1980 and 1985, the size of Florida, Nevada, Arizona, and Alaska grew more than 15 percent. Texas, New Mexico, Colorado, Utah, and California grew by 10 to 15 percent.

Source: U. S. Bureau of the Census, *Statistical Abstract of the United States: 1987* (107th edition), Washington, D.C., 1986, p.7.

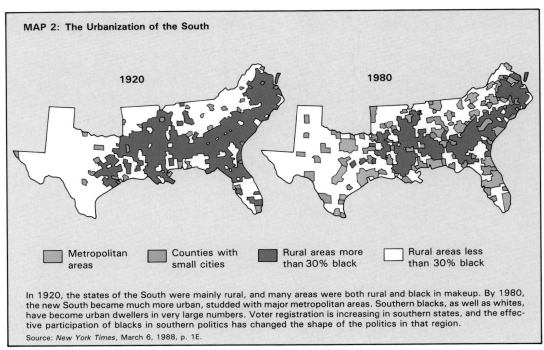

MAP 2: The Urbanization of the South

1920   1980

- Metropolitan areas
- Counties with small cities
- Rural areas more than 30% black
- Rural areas less than 30% black

In 1920, the states of the South were mainly rural, and many areas were both rural and black in makeup. By 1980, the new South became much more urban, studded with major metropolitan areas. Southern blacks, as well as whites, have become urban dwellers in very large numbers. Voter registration is increasing in southern states, and the effective participation of blacks in southern politics has changed the shape of the politics in that region.

Source: *New York Times*, March 6, 1988, p. 1E.

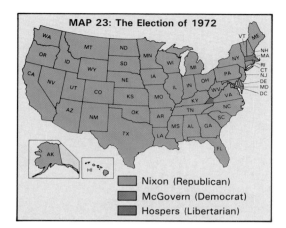

MAP 23: The Election of 1972

Nixon (Republican)
McGovern (Democrat)
Hospers (Libertarian)

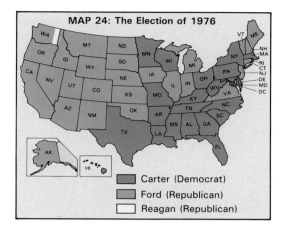

MAP 24: The Election of 1976

Carter (Democrat)
Ford (Republican)
Reagan (Republican)

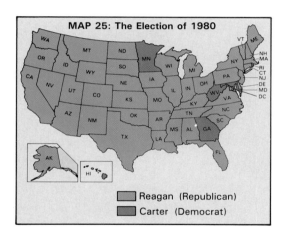

MAP 25: The Election of 1980

Reagan (Republican)
Carter (Democrat)

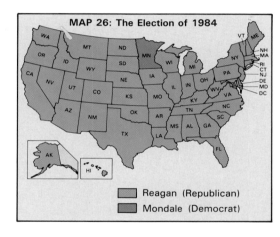

MAP 26: The Election of 1984

Reagan (Republican)
Mondale (Democrat)

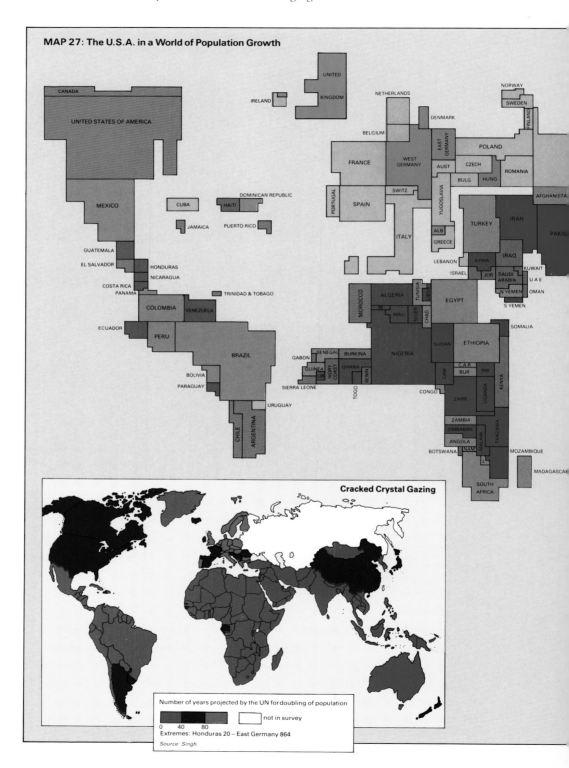

MAP 27: The U.S.A. in a World of Population Growth

Cracked Crystal Gazing

Number of years projected by the UN for doubling of population

0   40   80   not in survey

Extremes: Honduras 20 – East Germany 864

Source: Singh

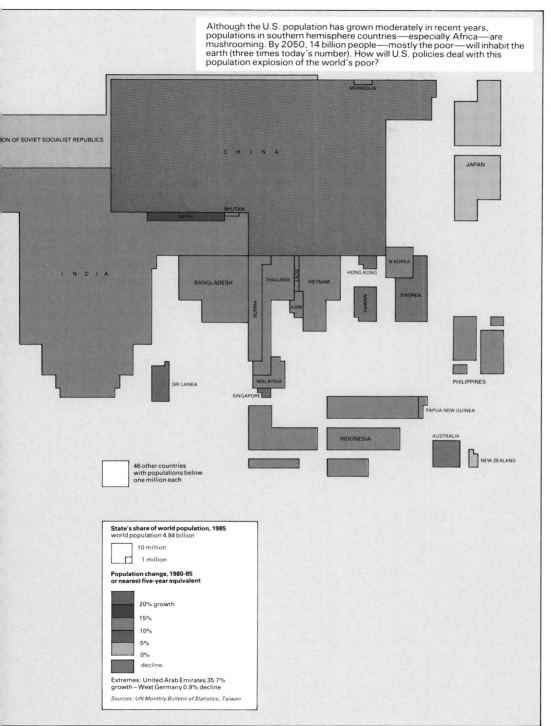

Although the U.S. population has grown moderately in recent years, populations in southern hemisphere countries—especially Africa—are mushrooming. By 2050, 14 billion people—mostly the poor—will inhabit the earth (three times today's number). How will U.S. policies deal with this population explosion of the world's poor?

MONGOLIA

ION OF SOVIET SOCIALIST REPUBLICS

C H I N A

JAPAN

BHUTAN

NEPAL

N KOREA

HONG KONG

I N D I A

BANGLADESH

THAILAND

LAOS

VIETNAM

S KOREA

BURMA

TAIWAN

KAM

SRI LANKA

MALAYSIA

SINGAPORE

PHILIPPINES

PAPUA NEW GUINEA

INDONESIA

AUSTRALIA

NEW ZEALAND

46 other countries
with populations below
one million each

State's share of world population, 1985
world population 4.84 billion

10 million

1 million

**Population change, 1980-85
or nearest five-year equivalent**

20% growth

15%

10%

5%

0%

decline

Extremes: United Arab Emirates 35.7%
growth – West Germany 0.9% decline

Sources: UN Monthly Bulletin of Statistics; Taiwan

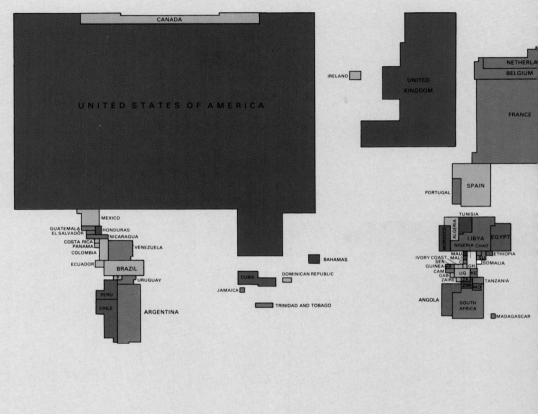

MAP 28: Military Spending by Superpowers and Small Powers

CANADA

IRELAND

UNITED KINGDOM

NETHERLA

BELGIUM

UNITED STATES OF AMERICA

FRANCE

PORTUGAL SPAIN

MEXICO

GUATEMALA
EL SALVADOR
HONDURAS
NICARAGUA
COSTA RICA
PANAMA
COLOMBIA
VENEZUELA

ECUADOR

BRAZIL

BAHAMAS

URUGUAY

PERU

CHILE

ARGENTINA

CUBA

DOMINICAN REPUBLIC

JAMAICA

TRINIDAD AND TOBAGO

TUNISIA
MOROCCO
ALGERIA
LIBYA
EGYPT
NIGERIA CHAD
IVORY COAST
MAU
MALI
SEN
G
GH
ETHIOPIA
GUINEA
SOMALIA
CAM
UG
KE
GAB
ZAIRE
ZIM
MO
TANZANIA

ANGOLA
SOUTH
AFRICA
MADAGASCAR

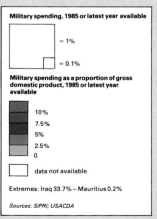

Military spending, 1985 or latest year available

☐ = 1%

▫ = 0.1%

Military spending as a proportion of gross domestic product, 1985 or latest year available

10%
7.5%
5%
2.5%
0

☐ data not available

Extremes: Iraq 33.7% – Mauritius 0.2%

Sources: SIPRI; USACDA

The United States and the U.S.S.R. dominate the world in the proportion of what their national governments allocate for military spending. In 1980, the U.S. spent some $520 billion on the military, and along with the U.S.S.R., accounts today for half of all the military spending in the world. How can American public policies both protect the national security of the United States and help limit military spending and foster arms control?

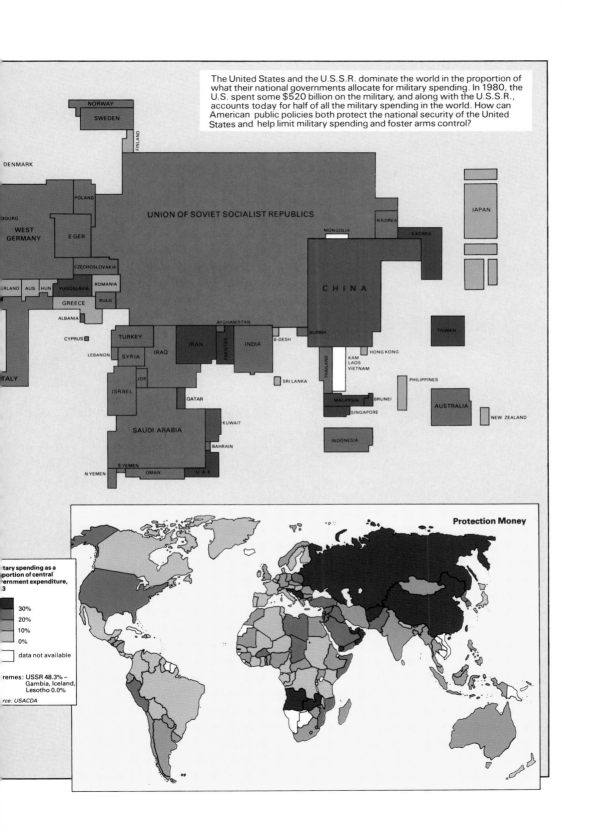

Protection Money

Military spending as a proportion of central government expenditure, 1983

- 30%
- 20%
- 10%
- 0%
- data not available

Extremes: USSR 48.3% – Gambia, Iceland, Lesotho 0.0%

Source: USACDA

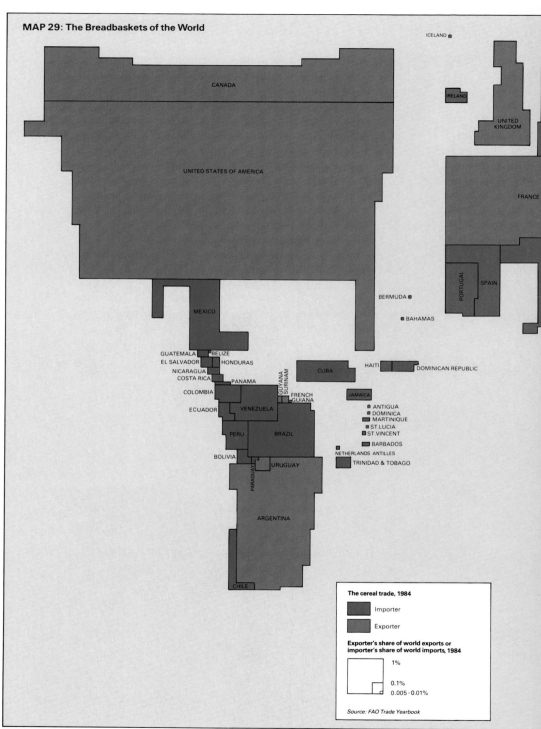

MAP 29: The Breadbaskets of the World

ICELAND

CANADA

IRELAND

UNITED STATES OF AMERICA

UNITED KINGDOM

FRANCE

BERMUDA

PORTUGAL | SPAIN

MEXICO

BAHAMAS

GUATEMALA | BELIZE
EL SALVADOR | HONDURAS
NICARAGUA
COSTA RICA | PANAMA
COLOMBIA
ECUADOR | VENEZUELA

GUYANA
SURINAM
FRENCH GUIANA

CUBA

HAITI | DOMINICAN REPUBLIC

JAMAICA

ANTIGUA
DOMINICA
MARTINIQUE
ST.LUCIA
ST.VINCENT
BARBADOS
NETHERLANDS ANTILLES
TRINIDAD & TOBAGO

PERU | BRAZIL

BOLIVIA

PARAGUAY | URUGUAY

ARGENTINA

CHILE

The cereal trade, 1984

Importer

Exporter

**Exporter's share of world exports or
importer's share of world imports, 1984**

1%

0.1%

0.005 - 0.01%

Source: FAO Trade Yearbook

in two situations: (1) the president informs Congress in writing that he cannot perform his duties; or (2) the vice president and a majority of the cabinet, or of some "other body" created by Congress, decide that the president cannot perform his duties. The president can reclaim the office at any time unless the vice president and a majority of the cabinet or other body contend that he has not recovered. In that event, Congress would decide the issue. The president would resume office *unless* a two-thirds vote of both houses backed the vice president. This procedure has not yet been tested. It arose from concern over the impact of serious presidential disabilities: Woodrow Wilson's stroke in 1919 disabled him for the rest of his term; Dwight Eisenhower was temporarily disabled by his 1955 heart attack.

When President Reagan was hospitalized with a gunshot wound after an assassination attempt in March 1981, the nation came close to using the disability procedure. Vice President George Bush, on a speaking tour when the incident occurred, rushed back to take charge informally. Meanwhile, senior White House staffers and a few cabinet members monitored events from the White House. But Reagan recovered quickly from surgery and the 25th Amendment's formal procedures were not invoked.

When, four years later, Reagan entered the hospital for removal of a tumor, he formally transferred his powers to Vice President Bush and then reclaimed them eight hours later, after undergoing surgery. Although the 25th Amendment was not invoked, it encouraged (though it did not require) such action. Reagan's handling of this situation is likely to set a precedent; however, experts on the question contend that future presidents should not hesitate to invoke the 25th Amendment and should develop written guidelines covering medical procedures that might be temporarily incapacitating.

If the vice presidency becomes vacant, the president nominates someone to fill it, subject to confirmation by a majority vote of both houses of Congress. This procedure, also specified in the 25th Amendment, has already been used twice. Vice President Spiro Agnew, indicted for taking bribes, resigned his post in October 1973. House Minority Leader Gerald R. Ford was picked by President Nixon to take Agnew's place and was confirmed by the Senate and House. Nearly a year later, Nixon himself resigned as a result of the Watergate scandal. As Nixon's successor, Ford in August 1974 picked former New York governor Nelson A. Rockefeller as vice president. Rockefeller was confirmed after long hearings in both chambers.

"Invitation to Struggle"

The Constitution provided for an independent and potentially strong chief executive. It did not clearly define the powers of the chief executive undoubtedly because the drafters were treading on new ground. They reserved Article I for the powers of Congress. That article detailed the basic scope of government as 18th-century intellectuals saw it.

Few precedents, in contrast, guided the drafting of Article II, which details the powers of the executive. This article is perhaps the most loosely drawn of all the constitutional provisions. In it, breathtaking powers are expressed in vague words. What is the "executive power" vested in the president? What does the "take care" clause mean? Just what are the president's powers as commander in chief?

At the same time, the article binds presidential powers to those of Congress and the courts. As constitutional scholar Edward S. Corwin once observed, the Constitution is an "invitation to struggle" among the arms of government (Corwin, 1957: 171). This has been most evident in relations between the president and Congress in spending, treaty, and war powers.

The precise nature and outcome of this struggle cannot be inferred from the Constitution itself. The founders left the resolution to history. To understand the makeup of today's presidency, we must study the office's development. The Constitution provided the springboard for today's strong presidency, but it only hints at the struggles that have actually taken place.

As we have seen, the Constitution is an imperfect blueprint for the presidential office as we know it. The Constitution's restrictions, its checks and balances, still apply, forcing presidents to bargain and cajole in order to exert leadership over the other branches. The founders, however, had no way of anticipating the historical growth of the office—caused by a burgeoning federal establishment, a mammoth military, a world leadership role, and a "public presidency" brought about by media technology.

Writing a job description for the modern presidency is not easy. One scholar, Thomas E. Cronin (1980: 154–84), approaches the challenge in a novel way. He groups the president's tasks into three broad, related policy areas, or **subpresidencies:** foreign affairs and national security, aggregate economics, and domestic policy.

Within each of these subpresidencies, the president performs at least seven types of roles. The result is the matrix of tasks shown in Figure 12–1. The president cannot do these jobs separately, but must weave them all into a daily schedule. This forces fateful and often uncomfortable choices in order to conserve time, energy, and political influence.

The Subpresidencies

Foreign affairs and national security

The president is the nation's chief agent in dealing with foreign powers. He is responsible for drafting foreign policy; as commander in chief, he is charged with ensuring the nation's security. These life-and-death matters are hard to delegate, so they generally take precedence. A study of State of the Union addresses found that national security matters occupy more presidential attention than any other topic (Kessel, 1975). Also, the emphasis presidents place on these matters tends to grow over time in a pattern related to the voting cycle. The focus on national security mounts during the first term, drops in the reelection year, and then during the second term rises to its highest level.

This focus on foreign and national security affairs arises from several factors. Presidents are assumed to have more leeway and better information in these areas than they have in domestic areas. Conversely, Congress and pressure groups are weaker in foreign policy than in domestic policy.

Presidents like to be know as "peacemakers," striving for "a generation of peace" as their legacy. Cronin calls this "running for the Nobel peace prize." Meeting with other heads of state to grapple with foreign policy seems more presidential than does bargaining with local politicians or haggling over federal reclamation projects. So modern presidents place their highest priority on foreign policy and national security objectives that need their personal involvement. Ronald Reagan was only the most recent president to turn to foreign policy goals as his domestic priorities met with mounting opposition; his administration ended with major arms accords with the Soviet Union, which he had earlier called "the evil empire."

FIGURE 12–1   A presidential job description

| | The "subpresidencies" | | |
Types of activity	Foreign policy and national security	Aggregate economics	Domestic policies and programs
Crisis management	Military crises; Cuban missiles, 1962; Iranian hostages, 1979–81; Grenada invasion, 1983	Coping with recessions (e.g., 1981)	Confronting air controller's strike, 1981
Symbolic leadership	Presidential state visit to Middle East or to China	Boosting confidence in the economy	Visiting disaster victims; greeting military or civilian heroes
Priority setting and program design	Balancing pro-Israel policies with need for Arab oil	Devising economic "game plan"; shaping budget proposals	Designing a new welfare program
Recruitment leadership	Selection of secretaries of state, defense; U.N. ambassador; arms negotiator	Selection of Secretary of Treasury, Office of Management and Budget director	Nomination of federal judges, members of regulatory commissions
Legislative and political coalition building	Selling Panama Canal Treaty, arms sales to two chambers	Lobbying for energy or anti-inflation legislative packages	Winning public support for deregulation, educational reforms
Program implementation and evaluation	Encouraging negotiations between Israel and Egypt	Implementing tax cut or fuel rationing	Improving quality of health care, welfare, retraining programs
Oversight of government routines	Overseeing U.S. bases abroad; maintaining foreign aid	Overseeing the Federal Reserve or the IRS	Overseeing National Science Foundation or Environmental Protection Agency

Higher priority ↑ Lower priority

Higher priority ← Lower priority

Source: Adapted from Thomas E. Cronin, *The State of the Presidency*, 2nd ed. Copyright © 1980 by Thomas E. Cronin. Reprinted by permission of the publisher, Little, Brown and Company, Inc.

Aggregate economics

The facts of economic boom-and-bust are brought home again and again to average people through their paychecks and their weekly bills for groceries, housing, and other needs. In addition, quantitative economic indicators abound; we can follow unemployment rates, consumer price indexes, the gross national product, trade deficits or surpluses, interest and mortgage rates, stock market averages, personal income levels, and many economic trends. Figures on these matters are widely aired. Public officials eagerly await and follow them. Politicians and interest-group leaders debating a president's successes or failures often cite them.

Presidents are seen as managers of the nation's overall economy—even when their actions can do little to affect it. They are expected to have "game plans" (such as "Reaganomics") aimed at fostering a healthy economy and at keeping inflation and unemployment in check. Presidents are blamed for economic downturns, though they are not always given credit when the economy rallies.

Presidents have many broad and narrow cures for economic ills. A key element in the economy is the federal budget. It sets priorities for economic activities, and it affects the availability of resources in the private sector. Tax proposals also encourage some kinds of economic activity and discourage others. The supply of money is regulated by the Federal Reserve Board. Members of "the Fed" are supposed to be independent of the administration; but forceful presidents try to reach agreements with the board about policy goals. Many other federal policies (for example, credit or securities controls) can be adjusted to speed up or slow down the economy.

Domestic policies

Carrying out domestic policies takes a large chunk of the federal government's personnel and budget. No one knows how many policies or programs the federal government really runs; one study stopped at 1,300—by no means the full number. These programs range from law enforcement and health care to maritime subsidies, farming research, and aid to the fine arts.

As chief executive, the president is responsible for overall management of the federal establishment—structure, top personnel, priorities, and day-to-day activities. On the whole, federal agencies and programs are well entrenched and resist bold restructuring. Periodically, however, presidents turn their attention to revamping the federal establishment: Johnson's "war on poverty," Nixon's brief flings with welfare reform and government decentralization, Carter's vow to streamline the federal structure, and Reagan's drive to halt domestic governmental programs are examples (Nathan, 1983). Yet domestic issues are often pushed out of the president's schedule by pressing security or economic matters.

Whenever presidents take a stand, they risk stepping on the toes of groups affected. No doubt, this explains why every president since Franklin Roosevelt has despaired at the state of federal organization and has found it easier to start new programs than to stop or redirect old ones. A White House aide was referring to domestic policy tangles when he said: "Everybody believes in democracy until he gets to the White House, and then you begin to believe in dictatorship because it's so hard to get things done. Every time you turn around, people just resist you, and even resist their own job" (Cronin, 1980: 223).

Crisis management. The Oval Office of the White House was the focal point for monitoring the Iranian crisis during the Carter Administration's final days in January 1981. Big crises engage top advisers; clockwise, from left, are CIA Director Stansfield Turner, two unidentified staff aides, White House advisers Hamilton Jordan and Jody Powell, Counsel Lloyd Cutler, President Jimmy Carter [sitting on desk, back to camera], Secretary of State Edmund Muskie, Treasury Secretary G. William Miller, National Security Adviser Zbigniew Brzezinski, Vice President Walter F. Mondale, and Attorney General Benjamin Civiletti.

In addressing one policy area, a president must weigh its impact on other areas. Almost everything that the federal government does, for example, affects foreign relations in some way; and foreign relations, in turn, affect the nation's overall economic health. Likewise, governmental programs, no matter how small in themselves, together set the government's fiscal role and ability to deal with foreign powers. In handling each of the three subpresidencies, a president has a set of roles, or types of involvement, from which to choose.

Types of Involvement

Crisis management
In times of danger, presidents have to direct the government's response and rally the public. Examples are the bombing of Pearl Harbor in 1941, the invasion of South Korea in 1951, the Soviet launch of *Sputnik* in 1957, the Soviet placement of missiles in Cuba in 1962, the ghetto riots in 1968, the fuel shortage in 1973, Iran's seizure of U.S. hostages in 1979, the Lebanon and Grenada interventions in 1983, and the space shuttle *Challenger* explosion in 1986.

A president has little control over the timing of crises. Yet when they happen, the president must thrust aside other duties to manage the government's response.

Public support for the president peaks during crises, when people are dismayed and fearful over unfolding events. So presidents and their advisers sometimes try to use a crisis—or, failing that, to stimulate a crisis atmosphere—to achieve longer-range goals. President Reagan's invasion of Grenada, for example, helped divert attention from troop withdrawals signaling the collapse of the administration's intervention in Lebanon. Dwindling support for President Johnson showed that he had failed to keep up a crisis atmosphere in connection with the Vietnam War. Despite short-lived crises such as the Gulf of Tonkin incident and the 1968 Tet offensive, the war dragged on. Expected victories did not occur; the nation at last tired of the whole thing.

President Carter was undone when he could not keep up a crisis-like urgency concerning the energy situation—which he called "the moral equivalent of war" (promptly dubbed MEOW). The crisis was real enough. But its development was gradual, not sudden; it would peak in the future, not immediately. Though Carter started several new energy programs, the public never quite accepted his call for conservation and self-denial. The Iranian hostage seizure, from November 1979 to January 1981, was another crisis that dogged Carter. At first, Carter's stock rose as people rallied against the Iranian terrorists. But as the months dragged on, the anger mixed with embarrassment over Carter's inability to end the situation.

Symbolic leadership

Presidents are supposed to honor the nation's traditions, stir hope and confidence, and foster a sense of national unity and purpose. "The presidency is a bully pulpit," said Theodore Roosevelt—who relished this role. Or, as Franklin Roosevelt put it, "the presidency is not merely an administrative office. That is the least of it. It is preeminently a place of moral leadership. . . . That is what the office is —a superb opportunity for reapplying, applying to new conditions, the simple rules of human conduct to which we always go back" (Corwin, 1957: 273).

Symbolic tasks transcend partisanship and stress unity over divisiveness. Therefore, they are prominently featured in presidential schedules. The symbolic role is displayed in patriotic festivals, ground-breaking or dedication ceremonies, funerals of famous people, and other ceremonies.

Presidents also use symbolism to focus public thinking on their goals and programs. Johnson turned off lights in the White House in 1964 to dramatize his austerity budget; Jimmy Carter marched in his own inaugural parade to stress his plain-folks style. Reagan showed an unerring sense of ceremony in public celebrations (such as the 1986 Statute of Liberty centennial) and in times of national grief (such as the memorials for the Marines killed in Beirut and for the *Challenger* crew.) As *Newsweek*

The president speaks to rally citizens to his cause. Today the president usually addresses the nation via television. In the early years of this century, President Theodore Roosevelt used speechmaking from a podium to dramatize his program of progressive legislation.

columnist Meg Greenfield (1986) observed, Reagan was a "genius at mobilizing public sentiments and acting out national rituals, legends and fantasies, the values that we insist motivate us as a people, whether they do or not."

Priority setting

Since the New Deal, presidents have been expected to present a small number of broad priorities, revealing the direction that they wish the nation to take.

Each year, the president has chances to give such priorities concrete form. On November 15, the president submits the current services budget. This projects the cost of keeping up current federal programs and spending levels through the next fiscal year. After Congress convenes in January, the president submits a budget message, with complete spending and revenue projections for the next five years. Through the rest of the budget process, until the new fiscal year begins on October 1, the president and his advisers help shape budget decisions. They testify and lobby with congressional budget and appropriations committees. The president even threatens to veto bills that depart from his goals. Once Congress has appropriated the money, the president can still affect priorities by deferring or stretching out spending (Fisher, 1975).

Another opportunity for priority setting is the annual State of the Union message. In this message, the president proposes new programs or revisions of present ones. Yearly reports on the economy and employment are also forums for priority setting. So are periodic speeches or reports on

*Man of the people.
President Jimmy Carter
and Rosalynn Carter
walked from the
inauguration at the
Capitol to the White
House. President Carter
did this to demonstrate his
informal, down-to-earth
style.*

special subjects. Speaking engagements are often used to air the president's priorities.

Reagan's presidency was a textbook example of priority setting, from his rewriting of the fiscal 1982 budget to incorporate "Reaganomics" to his fights for tax reform and for aid to anticommunist "freedom fighters" around the world. In an era when Congress and entrenched interests spurned discipline or control, Reagan dominated the airwaves and set the tone of debate on an issue-by-issue basis. Thus, even when pummeled by his opponents, he picked the issues and dominated the agenda.

Often presidents put their priorities in program packages—FDR's New Deal, Truman's Fair Deal, Kennedy's New Frontier, Johnson's Great Society, and Nixon's New American Revolution.

Recruitment leadership

One of the best ways that presidents can put their mark on the government is by appointing people to key federal posts. Priorities and programs will not go forward without competent, like-thinking people in cabinet and subcabinet spots. Through appointments to long-term judgeships or regulatory commissions, presidents can affect policy-making long after they leave office.

Recruitment peaks at the outset of a new presidency, when many jobs—about 3,000—must be filled in a brief time. As Cronin (1980: 164) points out: "Ironically, at the time when a president has the largest number of jobs to fill and enjoys the greatest drawing power, he has less time and information available to take advantage of his major prerogative than at any other point in his administration." Recruiting is normally frustrating and time consuming for all concerned. Reagan's initial recruitment effort was typical. It sputtered along for months while other activities, particularly budget redrafting, were in high gear.

Recruiting able people is no easy task. No president can know more than a small fraction of those who should be considered. Some of the president's friends—such as campaign aides and financial backers—may be unsuitable. Others may fall victim to bargaining among interested individuals and groups. To be successful, aspirants must have backers on Capitol Hill and within the president's electoral coalition; they must also surmount FBI investigation and scrutiny of their careers and financial dealings.

Appointees, for their part, are not always eager to work for the government. Some just do not want to move to Washington. Most face salary cuts if they join the federal payroll. Many, too, do not want to reveal their financial assets, forfeit their privacy, and have their outside activities restricted.

Many, therefore, decline to serve, and those who serve usually do so for a short time. Appointees in the executive branch stay for an average of 18 months. Most of these people arrive and leave almost unnoticed by the White House. Heclo (1977) calls presidential appointees "a government of strangers." Their varied paths to government and their brief service greatly reduce their impact on the departments and agencies that they direct on the president's behalf.

Of equal or greater impact are a president's appointments to the bench, both the Supreme Court and lower courts. Some presidents, such as FDR and Nixon, shaped the federal courts for a whole generation; Reagan appointed about half of the sitting lower-court judges. Although Carter made no Supreme Court appointments, he nonetheless influenced the judiciary through lower-court selections. Not all judges conform to expectations; one fourth of all Supreme Court justices consistently rule against the philosophy of the president who chose them (Scigliano, 1971).

The president's appointment power is not exercised alone, but with the **advice and consent** of the Senate. Wide berth is traditionally given presidents in picking cabinet and subcabinet aides. Not since Eisenhower has a cabinet nomination been withdrawn because the Senate was opposed; but several of Reagan's subcabinet designees were in effect rejected. One withdrew his name in the face of opposition; others were turned down by the Senate committee considering the nomination. More often, appointees are confirmed even in the face of doubts about their expertise or integrity.

With appointees to regulatory commissions or judgeships, Congress takes a livelier role. The Senate has rejected one fifth of all presidential Supreme Court nominees. Senators challenge nominees with pointed and sometimes embarrassing questions about sensitive legal-political issues such as civil rights, school prayer, and abortion. All of Reagan's Supreme

Former President Gerald Ford [left] and Senate Minority Leader Robert Dole (R–Kans.) [right] appear before the Senate Judiciary Committee to support President Reagan's appointment of Robert H. Bork [center] to the U.S. Supreme Court. After lengthy televised committee hearings, the Senate denied Bork's appointment.

Court choices were grilled by conservatives as well as liberals—conservatives, to assure themselves of the nominee's loyalty; liberals, to see whether they could find a fatal flaw.

Reagan's drive to reshape the courts slowed down after 1986, when Democrats won back the Senate. The next year, a controversial Supreme Court nominee, Robert H. Bork, was turned down by a Senate vote; another nominee, Benjamin Ginsburg, withdrew when controversial aspects of his background were revealed. On the third try, a centrist candidate, Anthony Kennedy, was confirmed. "No 'iffy' nominees are going to get through now," asserted a senior Democratic senator on the Judiciary Committee (Greenhouse, 1988). "The administration knows it has to send us·consensus candidates."

District court judges are normally subject to "senatorial courtesy," a tradition that requires consultation with the senators from the nominee's state before his or her name is formally submitted. Although the senators rarely weigh these candidates' intellectual qualities, they search the record for political blemishes (for example, insensitivity to minority rights).

For their own advisers, presidents have a freer hand. Few White House aides (one exception is the OMB director) require Senate confirmation. Presidents tend to prefer working with trusted, longtime associates. Kennedy had his "Irish mafia," skilled politicians (not all Irish) who had run his Massachusetts and national campaigns. Nixon had "the Prussians," a group of hard-bitten types who supervised the president's program and controlled access to him. Carter's Georgia advisers held positions close to their chief and were blamed by many for the White House's clumsiness in

Advising presidents. President Ronald Reagan talks to reporters after returning to the White House from Camp David, Maryland, as White House Chief of Staff Donald Regan [center] and National Security Adviser Robert C. McFarlane [left] look on.

dealing with Washington power centers. Reagan's White House was run by a few key advisers: a circle of three or four during the first administration; during the second, dominating single figures, Chiefs of Staff Donald T. Regan and Howard H. Baker, Jr.

Conformity versus diversity among advisors is a question that all presidents must resolve. Many, however, fail to face it squarely. Some, such as Johnson and Nixon, demand so much loyalty and conformity that dissenting ideas rarely reach them. Others, such as Roosevelt and Kennedy, welcome clashes of opinion and effectively meld diverse aides into a working team.

Recruiting leaders, then, is an important duty of a president. The types of people that presidents can attract, the kind of loyalty and esprit de corps that they can spark, say as much about their effectiveness as their programs or causes.

Coalition building

Another task for the president is building political and legislative coalitions to push his aims. Coalition building involves working with the legislative branch and party and interest-group leaders. Some presidents prefer to think of themselves as "above politics." They shy away from coalition building, which is so political. Yet coalition building is essential. Without it, the lofty phrases of the president's speeches will not bear fruit in legislation, programs, or policies.

Though as necessary as priority setting, coalition building is far more difficult and frustrating. It takes patience, compromise, and diplomacy. Of all the modern presidents, FDR was probably the best at it. He used the whole range of presidential resources to swing Congress, the Democratic party, the press, and the public behind his New Deal programs. Lyndon Johnson was probably the most adroit legislative tactician to serve in the White House. Ronald Reagan combined effective one-on-one persuasion with masterful use of the media to put pressure on lawmakers.

By contrast, Nixon often lagged in following through on his proposals: Complex reform plans for welfare policy and government reorganization were announced but soon dropped; staff follow-through on his New Federalism package was uneven. Carter was also faulted for inept follow-through and for failure to court congressional leaders in selling his programs.

Implementation

Presidents sometimes act as if their duties end once a legislative proposal has been accepted. But that is just the start. The law or program must be carried out by an agency willing and able to do the job; staff must be found to supervise the new program; procedures and regulations must be set; and once the wheels are turning, it should be (but often is not) monitored to see whether it is working as planned.

Implementation is a weak link in our government. Often laws have such vague or contradictory goals that is hard to know just what they are supposed to do. Federal agencies often have firm ideas about their missions and battle to protect their roles. Lobby groups and congressional subcommittees are always watching administrators, striving to bend programs to their purposes rather than to those of the president. Most domestic programs enforce rules or give out funds or services to state, local, or private groups. This makes it physically impossible or politically unfeasible for the president to keep up supervision. Evaluation—seeing whether programs really work—is a bureaucratic stepchild. It is rarely done and even more rarely heeded.

If presidents are unenthusiastic about the laws they are asked to "faithfully execute," they can act to hinder implementation. Appointing unsympathetic or even incompetent administrators is one tactic. Another is directing the Office of Management and Budget (OMB) to slow down agency spending or to veto agencies' proposed regulations. Inaction is also an option: for example, the sanctions on South Africa voted by Congress in 1985 were mostly ignored by Reagan administration officials.

Follow-through on programs is unglamorous and politically risky. Presidents are rarely inclined or have the time to pursue it. That is why political history usually focuses on how presidents influence the passage of legislation; it rarely mentions whether the legislation made any difference.

Oversight of governmental routines

The federal government is a machine of awesome size. It has hundreds of agencies and about 3 million civilian employees. In theory, the president manages this apparatus; in practice, there is little time to do this.

For the most part, presidents are not inclined to supervise government routines. This is unglamorous work, low in priority. The benefits are scattered and all but invisible. Every now and then, scandals involving federal employees demand presidential attention; but even here, a president will strive to steer clear of the impact of such scandals. This is another reason, no doubt, that presidents keep their hands off government routines.

Here, then, is one description of the presidency: three subpresidencies and seven forms of presidential involvement. They are listed roughly in order of importance, as seen by presidents themselves. Presidents tend to veer from domestic policies to macroeconomic and national security matters. They tend to neglect low-payoff implementation and routine management in favor of more glamorous and pressing activities in crisis management, symbolic leadership, or priority setting.

Some roles, such as dealing with international crises, are thrust on presidents. Like it or not, they must respond because the public expects them to. Other roles are left to their choosing. They can emphasize, delegate, or even ignore certain roles. Shrewd presidents allocate their limited time and influence to stress the priorities and programs that they wish to leave as legacies.

In allocating their energies, presidents show their own styles, interests, and political skills. Sometimes their choices are highly personal: FDR, a stamp collector, personally approved postage stamp designs; Kennedy, a former Navy officer, worried about naming new naval vessels. Carter delved into the finest details of policy proposals and, so it was rumored, supervised schedules at the White House tennis courts. At the other extreme, Reagan sketched only the broadest themes of his administration, evincing little interest in the substance, much less the detail, of policies.

The golden mean of presidential strategy, it would seem, lies in choosing when to take personal control of an issue or problem, and when to lay out general themes and let others handle the substance. Effective presidents must be able to follow either course. Purposeful presidents (and their aides) must carefully determine how, or whether, to become personally involved. Too many demands are made—too many people clamor for attention—for presidents to do otherwise.

THE WHITE HOUSE ESTABLISH-MENT

The White House bureaucracy is the most striking organizational feature of the modern presidency. It has grown by leaps and bounds since the 1930s, and today it has some 3,300 employees. (The figures are very unreliable, because employees are often detailed to the White House from other agencies.) The president's key advisers are in the Executive Office of the President, of which the White House Office is a part. Included in the EOP are several agencies that generally manage and coordinate functions for the executive branch.

The size of the president's staff invites criticism. Cronin (1980: 244) argues that the presidency has become

> a large complex bureaucracy itself, rapidly acquiring the many dubious characteristics of large bureaucracies in the process: layering, overspecialization, communication gaps, interoffice rivalries, inadequate coordination, and an impulse to become consumed with short-term, urgent operational concerns at the expense of thinking systematically about the consequences of varying sets of policies and priorities and about important long-range problems.

Various presidents have promised to pare down the White House payroll, but all have utilized large staffs whether credited to the White House or borrowed from other agencies.

The White House Office

The White House Office itself has some 350 people who report directly or indirectly to the president. Most of their job titles tell little about their functions. There are counsel to the president, counsellor to the president, assistant to the president, and special assistant to the president, as well as directors of various offices. It is not easy to generalize about the duties of these people, which reflect the personal style and political priorities of the president. (The location of key advisers, situated in the West Wing of the White House, is portrayed in Figure 12–2.) There are several distinct categories of staff functions, though.

Personal advisers

Chief aides on substantive and political matters coordinate and funnel information and advice flowing into the White House from many sources. Some of these aides are true experts, such as Henry Kissinger, Nixon's foreign policy specialist, or James Schlesinger, Carter's energy czar. Others are generalists, such as Kennedy's Theodore Sorensen, Johnson's Bill Moyers, Carter's Hamilton Jordan, and Reagan's James Baker.

Most presidents appoint chiefs of staff to exercise broad directorship over the White House and sometimes act as the president's alter ego. Sherman Adams, an efficient but crusty former New Hampshire governor, played this role for Eisenhower until scandal forced him to resign. Using the Eisenhower model, President Nixon chose H. R. "Bob" Haldeman as his first chief of staff. Haldeman was the leader of the so-called 'Prussians' who surrounded the president. They screened him from access by all but a select handful of trusted advisers. When Haldeman was fired for involvement in the Watergate cover-up, he was replaced by General Alexander Haig, who had the task of mapping out Nixon's retreat from office.

Ford and Carter resisted the chief-of-staff system; but it has since been reinstated as a way of managing the White House apparatus. After oper-

FIGURE 12–2   Who sits where in the White House West Wing

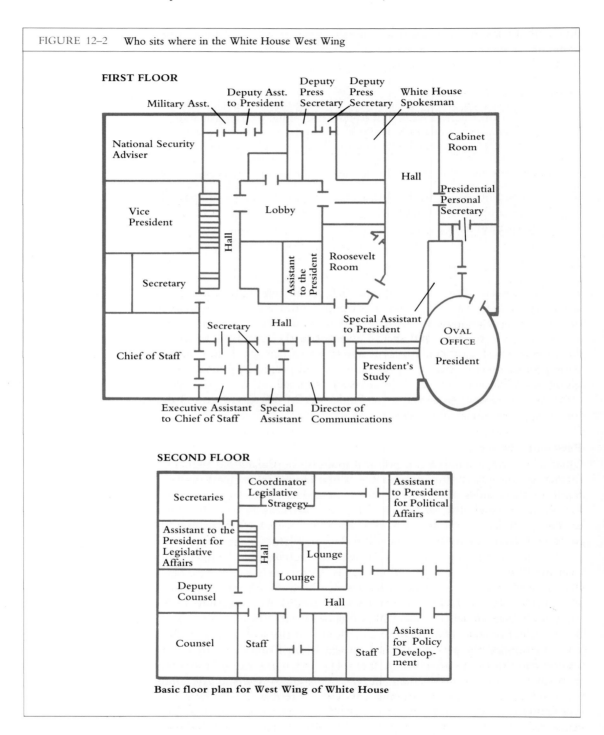

Basic floor plan for West Wing of White House

ating with a collective circle of aides during his first term, Reagan in his second term turned over his White House to dominant chiefs of staff, Donald T. Regan and Howard H. Baker, Jr.

National security aides

The National Security Council (NSC) dates from 1947. It is made up of the president, vice president, secretary of state, and secretary of defense. It advises the president on the national security implications of foreign, military, and domestic policies. Its small staff of professionals gives the president a counterweight to advice coming from the Defense and State Departments and the CIA. Henry Kissinger was NSC chief for Nixon; Zbigniew Brzezinski, for Carter. No less than six advisers served Reagan at one time or another.

The NSC staff gained power because presidents distrusted what they were being told by such old-line agencies as the Departments of State and Defense. But these agencies in turn questioned whether their expertise should be usurped by presidential staff. Conflicts between the NSC chief, called the national security adviser, and the secretary of state have repeatedly surfaced. Reagan's secretaries of state insisted on predominating over his national security advisers.

However, the presidents' national security advisers have played a growing policy-making role over their 40-odd years of existence. From facilitators or managers of national security processes, they have on occasion grown into powerful policymakers in their own right.

During the second Reagan administration, the NSC staff ran its own limited foreign policy apparatus in the so-called Iran-*contra* affair. This shadowy network of operatives, some in the government but most outside it, was run by NSC aide Lieutenant Colonel Oliver L. North, with the approval of the NSC chief, Rear Admiral John M. Poindexter. Later North, Poindexter, and two other members of the operation were indicted for, among other things, breaking laws and deceiving Congress. Before they were indicted, the blue-ribbon Tower Commission, appointed by President Reagan to examine the situation, had criticized the NSC for going beyond its mandate and actually running programs.

Domestic advice

During the Nixon years, a domestic counterpart to the NSC, the Domestic Council (now the Office of Policy Development), was set up by executive order (Kessel, 1975). Its membership comprises the "domestic cabinet" (heads of such departments as Treasury, Justice, Interior, Labor, Commerce, and Energy plus administrators of such agencies as the Veterans Administration and the Environmental Protection Agency); it has a professional staff like that of the NSC. Stuart Eizenstat, domestic adviser to President Carter, gained wide respect for his role in putting together presidential alternatives in domestic policies. The office was downgraded under Reagan, who gave lower priority to domestic policy formulation.

The National Security Council and the Office of Policy Development show the cabinet's tendency to fall into distinct components that cover foreign and domestic affairs. These councils are mainly coordinating agencies. They bring agency heads together to give and receive advice. If presidents distrust the advice they receive from agency heads, they can get alternative information and plans from White House staff aides to these councils.

Legal advice

The White House counsel's office has existed since FDR's time. Some counsels wielded great influence with their bosses, rendering not only legal advice but also policy formation, speechwriting, and political strategy. Since 1974 and the post-Watergate ethics laws, the Office of General Counsel (as it is now called) has come to the forefront in protecting the president and the official family from scandals or improprieties. In a scandal-ridden White House, the counsel's job is controversial and delicate.

Today's counsel, who heads what one termed a "great little law firm" of seven or so lawyers, handles a wide range of assignments for his client. The office reviews every speech the president delivers, every bill that is signed or vetoed, every official announcement, and every matter that might have legal bearing on the president (Kamen, 1984). Its duties have apparently become institutionalized, though its influence rests in part on the counsel's personal rapport with the president.

Press aides

Other White House staff fall into categories. The press staff manages the president's relationships with the White House press corps. It conducts press conferences, supervises press arrangements during presidential trips, and keeps in touch with the media. The press secretary, who heads this office, is one of the president's main advisers. The press secretary expects to be consulted on the consequences of major decisions and himself gives daily press briefings. A small staff within the press section monitors press coverage of the White House. They then write up a daily condensed version of major news stories and editorial comment for the president's morning reading.

Lobbying and public liaison

The congressional liaison staff manages day-to-day White House relations with Capitol Hill. The chief liaison officer (assistant to the president for legislative affairs) advises the president about possible Hill reactions to White House actions. This liaison aide is apt to hear first, and most strongly, about criticisms of White House actions. The staff usually consists of no more than 8 to 10 professionals. (Typically they have prior Hill experience.) They make day-to-day contacts with senators, representatives, and Hill staffers.

Other presidential aides keep in touch with various specialized "publics." Many groups plead to be represented on the White House staff; they look for an adviser who "has the ear of the president." The pleas are most insistent from groups that, unlike business, labor, or agriculture, lack a regular cabinet agency to look after their interests.

Some presidents have given in and designated staff people to link the White House to certain groups—governors and mayors, blacks, Hispanics, ethnics, women, scientists, and so forth. Carter and Reagan, however, opted for an omnibus approach: a White House office to conduct liaison with a variety of groups and orchestrate campaigns for key presidential programs. (Ann Wexler built this office for Carter; Elizabeth Dole and Faith Whittlesey continued under Reagan.)

Housekeeping functions

Housekeeping of various sorts must be done to keep the White House working. People are needed to arrange schedules for the president and his chief aides, to handle trips or visits, to answer mail, to plan White House dinners and social affairs. There is a French-trained chef, and there are even skilled calligraphers to hand-print invitations to state events. The First Lady has a social secretary as well as others who help answer mail and arrange her travel.

Our president is head of state as well as head of government. Therefore, the White House is more than a residence or a place of business; it is the closest thing we have to a royal palace or a national shrine. Thus, it is the setting for official visits and a glittering social life. State visitors stay in historic Blair House, across the street. A White House invitation is a prized possession for almost everyone, and a White House tour is a highlight of a trip to Washington. (Some guests go so far as to take "souvenirs," such as silverware.)

White House pomp and circumstance have been criticized, especially when President Nixon dressed White House guards in operetta-style uniforms and used trumpet fanfares and formal entrances and exits for noted visitors. Ford and Carter trimmed the pomposity, but Reagan restored some of the former glitter. Whatever the style, the White House remains a symbolic place and a setting for momentous meetings and conferences.

First Ladies, First Spouses

Presidential wives (and occasionally other female relatives) have evolved a distinctive set of roles. Although they aren't elected and have no formal duties, the spotlight inevitably shines on them, exposing them to praise or criticism. Since Edith Roosevelt (wife of Theodore), first ladies have been assigned a staff; Nancy Reagan had a staff of 18.

Sexual stereotypes being what they were, first ladies were originally seen only as helpmates and hostesses. Even these restricted roles drew crit-

Eleanor Roosevelt (1884–1962) was the first of the first ladies to play a major political role in her husband's administration. Here, she and President Franklin D. Roosevelt relax on the broad lawn of their estate at Hyde Park, New York, during a vacation. Eleanor Roosevelt's example of leadership was an important influence on the modern women's movement.

icisms: Martha Washington was criticized for the kinds of desserts she served and for the number of white horses that pulled her carriage.

Yet the tradition of activist first ladies soon took hold. Abigail Adams and Mary Lincoln, among others, took pleasure in political intrigues. Woodrow Wilson's first wife, Ellen, worked on behalf of the Slum Clearance Act of 1913; his second wife, Edith, was said to exercise great power during the 280 days that Wilson was incapacitated following a stroke suffered during a speaking tour to win support for the League of Nations. The most active first lady was Eleanor Roosevelt, who, to compensate for her husband's disability from polio, traveled the country to make appearances, give speeches, and observe conditions. After Franklin Roosevelt's death, her work on behalf of the United Nations and world understanding earned her the title "first lady of the world."

Today's first ladies are expected to have substantive concerns, not just to serve as hostesses. "If the president has a bully pulpit," Nancy Reagan observed (Gamarekian, 1988) "then the first lady has a white glove pulpit. It's more refined, more restricted, more ceremonial, but it's a pulpit all the same."

The activism of first ladies has been ensured by the era of two-career families; most spouses of presidential aspirants these days are people with independent careers of one kind or another. And when a woman is elected president, there will no doubt be a "first spouse" role to perform. Other nations have faced this question with female heads of government; the United States has simply been slow to come around.

The Executive Office of the President

The advisers already discussed are the front line of advisory and staff support for the president. They make up the White House Office. But a number of other agencies are a part of the Executive Office of the President. Although all such agencies report to the president, their value as advice givers or agents depends solely on how the president chooses to use them.

The Office of Management and Budget

Of these agencies, the OMB is surely the most important. It is the president's right hand in managing and monitoring the bureaucracy. OMB is a corps of professionals who analyze and screen budget requests from the departments and agencies; they work out procedures that promote economy, efficiency, and coordination, and they coordinate and clear agency advice on proposed bills. Although civil servants, OMB staff adopt a posture of loyalty to the president. They are the president's agents, expected to reflect and voice his priorities.

OMB's leverage is the yearly budgetary process. The office makes all executive agencies prepare budget requests, justify them under OMB scrutiny, and accede to OMB suggestions for shifts and cuts. OMB's suggestions are passed on to the president. He makes final decisions and resolves major issues, then submits the budget to Congress. (Congress has its own budget-making process, as we saw in Chapter 11.) If an agency wants to challenge an OMB recommendation, it may. But its chief officers must be willing to go straight to the president or one of his chief advisers to raise the issue. Needless to say, OMB is respected and feared by executive agencies and their managers.

In the Reagan administration, with its commitment to slowing growth in domestic spending, OMB became the cockpit for shaping the president's program. His first director, former Michigan Representative David A. Stockman, led the fight for budget cutbacks.

From its role with the budget, OMB has evolved other powers. It screens agency legislative requests—the so-called **central clearance** function. Thus, OMB puts the president's stamp on the legislative agendas of executive agencies. The Reagan-era OMB added the duties of coordinating federal regulations, information programs, and statistical indicators. Congressional leaders are extremely suspicious of OMB's coordinating role and have forced some curtailment of that OMB function.

The Council of Economic Advisers

Another key agency is the Council of Economic Advisers (CEA), formed by the Employment Act of 1946. It is supposed to watch the national economy, advise the president on economic growth, stability, and employment. The council's three members are appointed by the president with the advice and consent of the Senate. They are normally senior academic or business economists. The council's staff of economic analysts prepares studies and reports.

Council chairmen sometimes have a close relationship with the president, working as key advisers. Walter Heller, Kennedy's CEA chairman, spread the gospel of Keynesian economics, pushed a 1964 tax cut to spark the economy, and was widely credited as an architect of the mid-1960s economic expansion. Nixon's chairman, Paul McCracken, also served as a close presidential adviser. One of Reagan's CEA chairmen, Martin Feldstein, gained notoriety by warning against huge deficits when other counselors were trying to downplay them. Because the advice was unwanted, the White House considered doing away with the CEA, delayed naming Feldstein's successor, and generally downgraded the group's functions. At least for the time being, the president would seek economic advice elsewhere.

The Secret Service

While not technically a part of the president's official family, the Secret Service (under the Treasury Department) is a constant companion to everything the president or White House advisers do. Time was when presidents mingled freely with common people; that age ended with the assassination of President Kennedy in 1963. Subsequent "incidents" or threats have led to ever tighter security procedures.

Security is a major consideration in scheduling the president's travel or appearances outside the White House. Locations are carefully inspected; attendees at speeches or meetings are screened and searched. Sometimes, it is claimed, security checks become a device to rid the president's entourage of protesters. But in most respects, presidents and their advisers consider security a constraint: It limits the president's mobility, and it entails cumbersome and costly planning whenever the official family ventures beyond the White House confines.

The Vice Presidency

Historically, the vice presidency has been a frustrating, ill-defined job. Its first occupant, John Adams, complained that "my country has in its wisdom contrived for me the most insignificant office that ever the invention of man contrived or his imagination conceived." Throttlebottom, the vice president in George Gershwin's 1931 musical, *Of Thee I Sing,* had to join a White House tour to see the inside of the building. From all accounts, such vice presidents as Richard Nixon, Lyndon Johnson, and Hubert Humphrey found the job frustrating and humiliating.

Recent vice presidents—Walter Mondale and George Bush—have shown, however, that the job can have broader dimensions, (Light, 1984). Underpinning their success was a decision to pursue a policy of utmost loyalty to the president and to express dissent only in private, if at all.

Today's vice presidents play the following roles: (1) performing the constitutional duties of presiding over the Senate, voting in case of ties, and (rarely) trying to sell the president's program to senators; (2) assisting the president in administrative duties, sitting in on cabinet sessions, presiding in the president's absence, and coordinating interagency projects for the president; (3) serving as the president's emissary to foreign countries; and (4) being the president's troubleshooter in appearing before domestic audiences and, especially, in attacking the administration's political opponents.

One problem that the new vice presidency has not overcome is the difficulty of steering an independent course for a subsequent political career. Vice presidents who run to succeed their boss have to walk the tightrope between satisfying the outgoing president and striking an independent pose. Prior service as vice president proved hazardous for Nixon in 1960, Humphrey in 1968, and Mondale in 1984. Running in 1988, Vice President George Bush faced harsh questions about how he had advised the president in the Iran-*contra* affair. Although Bush declined to say what he told Reagan, it appeared that loyalty had led him to say little to oppose the policy.

The Cabinet

The cabinet, composed of department heads (and others of cabinet rank, like the UN ambassador), is a creature of history unknown to the Constitution. Most presidents convene their cabinets periodically, but few have used them to make decisions. Selected for varying reasons, cabinet members come to view themselves as champions of departmental interests rather than as collective decision makers.

Recent presidents, however, have entered office vowing to use the cabinet more effectively. Some have convened the cabinet regularly. Reagan formed six cabinet councils, each composed of several secretaries: commerce and trade, economic affairs, energy and natural resources, food and agriculture, human resources, and legal policy. These councils met frequently, sometimes with the president but always with White House staff support. They discussed working papers and tried to relate the president's overall policies to their respective domains.

President Reagan's cabinet. The president's cabinet includes the heads of the major departments and agencies of government. Like President Reagan, most presidents meet periodically with their cabinets, but the importance of the cabinet as a body has varied from president to president.

Coordinating agencies

Other White House agencies encourage concerted action on policies involving many departments and other agencies. As we have noted, it is often hard to persuade agencies to cooperate. Interagency committees and task forces abound. They often function like summit meetings of sovereign powers, with each agency's representative striving to guard its own turf. For this reason, presidents set up coordinating staffs. The theory is that a White House agency can exploit the president's prestige to "knock heads" and impel agencies to work together.

Certain policies have thus been coordinated through White House staff agencies at one time or another. These include environmental protection (Council on Environmental Quality, inflation (Council on Wage Price Stability), international economics (Council on International Economic Policy), and trade negotiations (Office of the Special Representative for Trade Negotiations).

Needless to say, a position on a White House organization chart does not always confer the clout required to get the job done. The president's personal intervention is often needed to persuade administrators that some agency autonomy must be given up in the interests of coherent policy-making.

During the last four decades, the presidency has turned into a large estab-lishment. The reasons for this "swelling of the presidency" are not far beneath the surface.

Gravitation to the White House

After FDR, presidents began to gather new functions, especially in crisis settings. They needed staff assistants who were instantly available and per-sonally loyal. Many came to believe that the president and his aides were best equipped to solve knotty problems and initiate urgent government efforts. Congress, too, tends to hold the president personally responsible for such matters. Therefore, it has authorized such White House agencies as the National Security Council, the Council of Economic Advisers, and the Council on Environmental Quality.

Successive presidents, Democratic or Republican, have grown restless with how established bureaucratic agencies perform. These agencies have become more cumbersome in resolving today's public problems. Many problems, such as international trade, inflation, and energy shortages, defy delegation to any one department. Writes Cronin (1980: 245):

> Occupants of the White House frequently distrust members of the perma-nent government. . . . Departmental bureaucracies are often viewed from the White House as independent, unresponsive, unfamiliar, and inaccessible. They are suspected again and again of placing their own, congressional, or special-interest priorities ahead of those communicated to them from the White House.

It is no surprise, then, that presidents surround themselves with their own people, whose loyalty and dedication keep the president's causes alive in the hostile world of special interests.

Flaws in the Presidential Bureaucracy

The swelling of the presidency is a mixed blessing. For one thing, presi-dential advisers tend to lack constituencies outside the White House. Un-less their single-minded loyalty to their boss is counterbalanced by wide experience in politics and government, they may give ill-informed advice.

Also, the advisory system is only as good as the people the president chooses. Some presidents, such as Roosevelt and Kennedy, relished the presence of first-class intellects bold enough to challenge the president's own ideas. Others, such as Nixon and Johnson, had fragile egos and were more comfortable surrounded by flatterers. This underscores the impor-tance of James David Barber's admonition that we ought to pay attention to the "presidential character" of aspirants to the office. The president's ability to deal with others, his ability to bear up under pressure, are qual-ities that can and ought to be assessed (Barber, 1977).

Finally, there are many chances for abuse in a swollen White House establishment. Much of its work is broad and only vaguely defined. Lines of power are rarely clear. This means that aides waste time jockeying for position and access to the president. It is too easy for such people to embark on their own projects to win their boss's attention and approval. They may trade on White House prestige and those magic words "The president wants. . . " The House "plumbers" group, of Watergate fame, was one such scheme. This mix of irresponsibility, lack of a constituency, and vague authority has led some (Hess, 1976) to urge that presidents downplay their own staff and give more duties to cabinet appointees.

Despite these drawbacks, the White House establishment is here to stay. It is another reflection of the modern, institutionalized presidency. It provides presidents with the staff support they need to do what citizens expect of them. It helps them communicate with the public, stay in touch with varied interest groups, and provide legislative leadership.

As we have seen, presidents prefer to surround themselves with loyal underlings. Presidential appointees in departments and agencies—even cabinet members—can be captured by agencies, their clienteles on Capitol Hill, and lobbyists. White House aides lack this base of operation. They are the president's own people, and their loyalty is both their strength and their weakness.

CONCLUSIONS

In this chapter, we have explored the paradoxes of the presidency—a job that, as Thomas Cronin says," is always too powerful and yet is is always inadequate" (1980: 22). We have underscored the contrasts between the image and the reality of the office—between its possibilities and its limitations.

1. Although champions of the rights of legislative bodies, the founders wrote a potentially powerful presidency into the Constitution. Having little to guide them, they sketched Article II of the Constitution in vague terms and left history to work the details.

2. The president's substantive duties may be grouped into three "subpresidencies": foreign affairs and national security, aggregate economic, and domestic policies.

3. In addressing these concerns, presidents engage in various types of involvement: crisis management, symbolic leadership, priority setting, recruitment of aides, coalition building, implementation, and oversight of government routines.

4. Organizationally, presidents are now aided by their own bureaucracy—the White House Office and the larger Executive Office of the President—composed of its own staff and staff borrowed from other civilian and military agencies.

5. Separate staffs for domestic and national security advice have grown powerful because presidents and their chief aides want sources of information separate from the regular departments. Although loyalty to the president frees these staffs from departmental biases, they run the risk of duplicating tasks and fostering resentment from the cabinet departments.

6. Impatience with the bureaucracy sometimes goads White House aides to dabble in the operation of government programs. This is almost always disastrous; the Iran-*contra* fiasco was only the worst example of this tendency.

7. The White House bureaucracy is essentially what the chief executive wants it to be. Although certain distinctive functions have merged (for example, press and legislative relations, legal counsel, and housekeeping), the lines of demar-

cation are vague and subject to presidential direction.

8. The vice presidency has emerged from nearly two centuries of obscurity to become an office of consequence. However, the premise of this office—loyalty to the president—hinders vice presidents seeking to run for the presidency and to establish their own identity in the process.

FURTHER READING

CAMPBELL, COLIN, S. J. (1986) *Managing the Presidency: Carter, Reagan, and the Search for Executive Harmony*. Pittsburgh, Pa.: University of Pittsburgh Press. An analysis of the machinery of the presidential office and of the relationship between the president and his advisers. The focus is on the Carter and Reagan administrations.

CRONIN, THOMAS E. (1980) *The State of the Presidency*. 2nd ed. Boston: Little, Brown. An ingenious interpretation of the promise and limits of the presidency, based in part on interviews with White House staff members, cabinet officials, and department advisers.

FISHER, LOUIS (1985) *Constitutional Conflicts between Congress and the President*. Princeton, N.J.: Princeton University Press. A provocative examination of legislative-executive relationships based on historical and political factors.

HESS, STEPHEN (1988) *Organizing the Presidency*. Rev. ed. Washington, D.C.: Brookings Institution. A critical examination of White House organizational arrangements from Franklin Roosevelt through Ronald Reagan.

NEUSTADT, RICHARD E. (1979) *Presidential Power: The Politics of Leadership from FDR to Carter*. New York: John Wiley & Sons. A classic exploration of the dilemmas faced by modern presidents in seeking to maximize their influence.

Chapter Thirteen

THE PUBLIC PRESIDENCY

$\mathcal{T}$he presidency has always been more than an office. It is also an individual, a personality, a public figure, at times a celebrity.

The founders, though lacking a model in history or theory for the office they wished to create, were nonetheless certain about the kind of *person* they wanted to occupy it. It was George Washington, presiding over their Philadelphia meetings in 1787, who provided a flesh-and-blood example of what the office ought to be. As the father of his country, Washington was a celebrity. When, after his election, he traveled from his home at Mount Vernon to New York, the first seat of government, his journey quickly turned into a triumphal procession, with crowds and celebrations at every stop.

Every modern president is automatically a celebrity—surrounded by aides and guards, hounded by the press, and besought by all kinds of interest groups and ambitious individuals. For many people here and around the world, the president *is* the U.S. government. So visible are presidents that they become the embodiment of citizens' hopes and aspirations, basking (at first, in any event) in the glory of the office. Just as surely, though, presidents are typically the targets of anger or blame when things go wrong. ✑

$\mathcal{T}$he presidential paradox addressed in this chapter is the contrast between the office and the public image of its occupant. Presidents are usually chosen, reported, and even judged on appearances that may have little to do with their mastery of the office or of the substantive problems that they face. Presidents are too lavishly praised and too readily blamed. Ronald Reagan was only the most recent president to experience this paradox of the office. Some of his predecessors—including Wilson, Hoover, Truman, Johnson, Nixon, and Carter—suffered deeply from the extremes of glory and defeat. Some of them were judged failures, leading commentators to conclude that, despite its extravagant trappings, the presidency is little more than a glorified clerkship. Other presidents achieved undeserved popular acclaim, a triumph of style over substance.

In this chapter, we examine all aspects of the "public presidency." We begin by describing public attitudes toward presidents and the factors that make them popular or unpopular. Then, we describe how presidents "go public" to sell their programs and mobilize support. In particular, presidents must lobby Congress and persuade it to follow White House leadership—not an easy task. We detail the president's legislative tools—some constitutional, others traditional. Finally, we discuss presidential efforts to shape and influence the federal bureaucracy, which stubbornly resists White House leadership.

THE "NATIONAL VOICE"

At the heart of the modern president's powers is visibility. He can capture public attention and mobilize approval and support. "In the presidential office as it has been constituted since Jackson's time," wrote the political commentator Henry Jones Ford (1967: 293), "American democracy has revived the oldest political institution of the race, the elective kingship. It is all there: the recognition of the notables, and the tumultuous choice of the freeman, only conformed to modern conditions."

Far more important than any constitutional powers is the president's ability to focus public attention on his initiatives and programs. As the only nationally elected figure (except the vice president), he is the constant object of media attention. He embodies the government as no one else does. In skillful hands, this is a unique resource for getting popular pressure behind his programs.

The unique visibility of presidents and the wide publicity given their words and deeds lie at the heart of the office's power. This popular link was glimpsed briefly in Andrew Jackson's time; it marked the presidencies of the two Roosevelts, Wilson, and Kennedy. "His is the only national voice in affairs," wrote Woodrow Wilson (1961: 68) in 1908, five years before entering the White House. "Let him once win the admiration and confidence of the country, and no other single force can withstand him, no combination of forces will easily overpower him." Overstated perhaps, but still a fair idea of what the modern presidency can do.

The Best-Known American

The president is the prime psychological symbol in politics. He is by far the "best-known American" (Greenstein, 1974). Almost everyone knows at least his name—something that can be said of no other politician. Not even the best-known celebrities, entertainers, and athletes (who may be known by as much as 90 percent of the people) can claim this.

As the best-known political figure, the president plays key roles in the political learning of children and young people. The president is the first political person they become aware of. By age nine, most children can name the current president. This reflects the importance of the presidency. Also, first-learned objects tend to condition perceptions of later-learned objects. In contrast to the president, other politicians may seem vague and mysterious, hard to understand. Many children, for instance, think that members of Congress are "the president's helpers," and such notions are by no means confined to the very young. A recent survey found that half of both 13- and 17-year-olds thought that the president could appoint members of Congress.

Researchers during the Eisenhower and Kennedy eras were impressed by the president's image as a benevolent leader. Children then held a rosy view of presidents; adults more often than not gave incumbent presidents high marks for performance. Ratings of presidential performance always ran higher than did those for Congress and other government bodies.

Popular images of the president eroded after the upheavals of the late 1960s and early 70s. For many, the Watergate scandal ended the myth of the presidency. Trust in the office—indeed, in all politics—slid. Throughout these adversities, however, citizens retained a glowing image of strong, successful presidents—such as FDR, Truman, Kennedy, and Eisenhower (who top the all-time popularity polls).

Public expectations for presidents therefore remain high. Despite a brief lapse following Vietnam and Watergate, the public expects above all that presidents appear strong and decisive and supports wider presidential authority. As Wayne (1982: 34) summarizes: "The presidency continues to be viewed as a large, multifaceted office, and the president as the wearer of many hats. . . . The ability to be forceful and decisive, to make good policy, and to inspire confidence are remembered as the qualities of previous presidents that would be most useful today."

A widespread belief that Ronald Reagan had these qualities probably contributed to his victory. His decisiveness in office triggered an unmistakable revival of confidence in political institutions—in the Republican party, in the presidency, even in the government itself.

In the wake of disillusionment with certain features of the Reagan administration, however, voters in 1988 shifted their expectations somewhat. While nearly half put a high priority on choosing "a strong leader and a take-charge person," the largest proportion (56 percent) wanted a president who was "honest with the people and played by the rules." Less

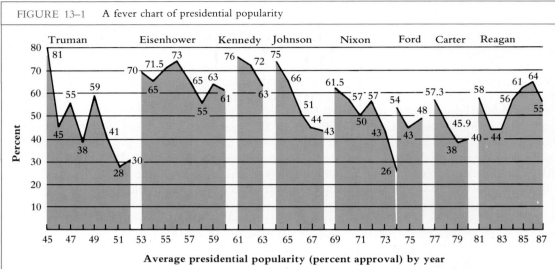

FIGURE 13–1   A fever chart of presidential popularity

The questions are: "How would you rate the job the [incumbent president] is doing—excellent, pretty good, only fair, or poor?" Favorable responses are "excellent" and "pretty good."

Source: American Institute of Public Opinion (Gallup poll).

important to citizens, interviewed by the Peter D. Hart organization, were such attributes as compassion, patriotism, and forward-thinking. As with so many of their political attitudes, citizens tend to fine-tune their expectations on the basis of recent experiences.

Public expectations are a resource for presidents; they are also a club to be wielded against presidents who fail to live up to them. Probably the public expects too much and blames too quickly. As Edwards (1983: 196–98) notes, citizens expect contradictory things of their chief executives: leadership and responsiveness, flexibility and firmness, statesmanship and political savvy, openness and control, empathy and distinctiveness. No doubt this is why a number of presidents have left office at various levels of disfavor; Johnson, Nixon, Ford, and Carter are examples. When a president is in tune with popular desires, people are eager to give him allegiance. When a president betrays the public's trust or fails to fulfill its expectations, frustration swiftly sets in. High expectations are not erased by disappointments.

Presidential Popularity Fever Chart

Whatever the public's view of the presidency, its assessment of individual presidents has varied widely. Since the 1930s, analysts have asked what

TABLE 13–1   Popularity ratings of presidents

President	Percent "favorable" ratings*		
	High	Low	Average
Roosevelt (1933–45)	84	54	68
Truman (1945–53)	87	23	43
Eisenhower (1953–61)	79	49	65
Kennedy (1961–63)	83	56	71
Johnson (1963–69)	80	35	56
Nixon (1969–74)	68	24	49
Ford (1974–77)	71	37	47
Carter (1977–81)	75	21	47
Reagan (1981–88)	68	35	50

*The percentages are of respondents who answered this question favorably: "Do you approve or disapprove of the way [name of incumbent] is handling his job as president?"

Source: American Institute of Public Opinion (Gallup poll).

sort of job people think the president is doing. Because major surveys ask this about once every two weeks, we now have an accurate "fever chart" of presidential performance from the Roosevelt era to the present. (See Figure 13–1 and Table 13–1.)

Throughout their terms, three presidents—FDR, Eisenhower, and Kennedy—had approval of the majority holding opinions. Other presidents had roller-coaster rides of highs and lows.

Honeymoon and morning after

Every modern president, no matter how popular, has started with a "honeymoon period" during which public expectation and approval are high. This is followed by a period of slipping support. As seen in Figure 13–1, the decline is sometimes slight, sometimes steep.

Recent presidents have suffered noticeable declines in support. Truman, upon FDR's death, was approved by 87 percent of the people. That was the highest approval score ever recorded. But at one point, he was approved by only 23 percent—about the lowest score yet. Johnson had highly favorable ratings in his first two years in office but later sank below 50 percent. Nixon was praised by 62 percent in January 1973—after the Vietnam peace was concluded. But his rating steadily declined over the next 18 months as the Watergate findings took their toll. Shortly before he resigned, it fell to 24 percent.

What affects the public's appraisal of a president's performance? Judging from the ebb and flow over the past 40 years, at least five factors seem to have an impact.

Underdog Harry S Truman, whose popularity as president sank even lower than Nixon's after Watergate, came from behind to defeat New York's Governor Thomas E. Dewey for president in 1948. This famous photograph shows President Truman holding up a copy of the Chicago Tribune *edition that erroneously declared Dewey the winner. The edition hit the streets before all of the votes were counted.*

Current events and conditions

Because presidents are the most visible and understandable part of the government, they are praised or blamed for whatever happens in the public arena. (Reagan-era opinions are presented in Figure 13–2.) "When the economy goes sour, or war drags on, or domestic violence erupts, the president is available to take the blame. Then when things go right, it seems the president must have had a hand in it" (Barber, 1977: 5).

Current events and changes do indeed make for short-term waves in a president's popularity. During Carter's term, for instance, brief but measurable downturns were recorded by pollsters after several events. In his first energy speech, Carter called on us to cut energy use, but many then doubted that there was an energy shortage. The Panama Canal treaty was widely resented as a "giveaway." Bert Lance, Carter's friend and his choice to head the Office of Management and Budget, resigned under fire. Whether or not the president is personally to blame, public opinion *makes* him responsible. From where the public sits, Kernell (1986: 173) notes, "fairness to presidents is less important than motivating them to deal with the country's problems."

Some think that the downward pull on presidents' popularity is caused by a **coalition of minorities** (Mueller, 1973). As presidents decide and act, they alienate staunch opponents of their actions. These people may be a minority, but if their views are strong enough, they will turn from the president's leadership. After more and more presidential decisions, the number of such groups grows. In Carter's case, such issues as energy and the Panama Canal pulled his ratings down.

Others hold that shifts in support are caused by a "fickle" segment of the public—the less partisan, less knowledgeable, and less involved in politics. They uncritically add to a new president's support at first. But they quickly turn away when things go wrong. "Unrealistic expectations are followed by an inexorable disillusionment" (Stimson, 1976: 9).

FIGURE 13-2   Reagan's Ups and Downs

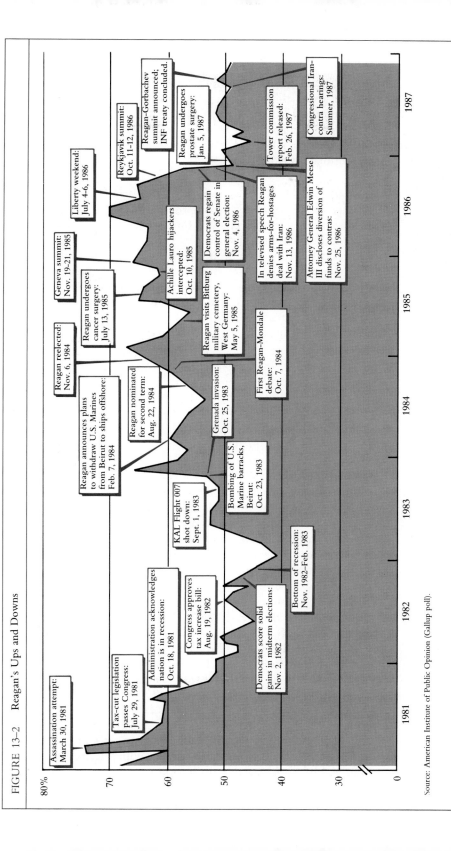

Source: American Institute of Public Opinion (Gallup poll).

Probably no one reason lies behind these shifts. Some of the shifts seem to stem from the coalition of minorities; others surely flow from the quirks of the least informed people. Whatever the precise causes, presidents clearly cannot help being linked in the public mind with social and political events and trends. Whatever the circumstances, people think that the president is closely involved.

Rally-round-the-flag

Another factor affecting presidential popularity is the rally-round-the-flag phenomenon, a crisis event that boosts the president's popularity. The crisis should be international, must involve the United States and especially the president, and must be dramatic and sharply focused. Numerous rallying points have occurred in the past 30 years. These include major crises (the Cuban missile crisis of 1962, the Iranian hostage crisis of 1979), military intervention (Grenada in 1983), major diplomatic developments (the Vietnam peace treaty of 1973, the Camp David accords of 1978), and dramatic technical breakthroughs (the Soviet launching of the *Sputnik* spacecraft in 1959).

A classic rallying of public opinion took place late in 1979, when militant terrorists captured 52 U.S. hostages at our embassy in Iran. In one month, Carter enjoyed the largest surge in a president's popularity in the four decades of the survey. But as the crisis dragged on, the anger and humiliation grew, popular support dwindled, and the president became the object of our frustrations.

Economic cycles

Another factor affecting public support of presidents is the *domestic economy*. The higher the unemployment or inflation rate, the lower a president's popularity is apt to be. Reagan's low point in popularity, for example, coincided with the bottoming-out of the 1982–83 recession. On the other hand, recovery does not seem to add to a president's popularity as much as a slump hurts it.

War

A *war* involving the United States also affects presidential ratings. But the effect varies with how the public views the war. A popular conflict such as World War II brings rally-round-the-flag support. By contrast, an unpopular contest, such as the Korean War (called "Truman's war") or the Vietnam War in its latter days, lowers ratings.

Scandal

Finally, a major scandal can speed the decline in a president's popularity, especially if the president himself is involved. The gradual but constant fall in Nixon's support in the months before he resigned in 1974 is a recent example.

Loss of the leader. President John F. Kennedy was assassinated in Dallas, Texas, on November 22, 1963. In a memorable scene, little John F. Kennedy, Jr., salutes as his father's coffin is placed on a caisson for removal from Washington, D.C., to Arlington National Cemetery. Other family members in the photograph are Caroline Kennedy [left front], Sen. Edward M. Kennedy (D–Mass.) [left], Jacqueline Kennedy [center], and Robert F. Kennedy [right], who was himself assassinated in Los Angeles on June 6, 1968, during his campaign for the Democratic presidential nomination.

The President as Symbol

The symbolism of the presidency is a constant feature of our life, despite the ebbs and flows of presidential popularity. Given the unique visibility of presidents, it is not surprising that they are often—perhaps too often—the object of adulation, hopes, fears, and frustrations. Beyond partisan or program support, they have a central place in public emotions.

This symbolic role is seen dramatically when a president dies or is very ill. News of Eisenhower's 1955 heart attack caused the stock market to drop to its lowest point since the 1929 crash. When Kennedy was killed in 1963, four out of every five people reacted as they would have reacted to the death of a loved one. In response to a national survey, 50 percent of those questioned said they wept, 43 percent said they lost their appetite, 48 percent said they could not sleep, and 68 percent said they were nervous and tense.

Kennedy was a young and vigorous man; but there was similar mass sorrow at the deaths of Warren G. Harding and Franklin D. Roosevelt. Such displays do not occur when an ex-president dies, and few people are affected the same way by the death of a favorite celebrity or athlete. So mourning seems to be a response to the loss of a leader, not just to the loss of a revered figure.

As national leaders, presidents stand for unity and security. They are at the helm of the ship of state. When they are suddenly gone, the ship seems adrift and the helm untended.

How Presidents "Go Public"

With unequaled public visibility and the powerful resource of public support, presidents inevitably "go public" to advance their policy objectives. Kernell (1986: 83) explains the strategy's appeal:

> Modern technology makes it possible. Outsiders in the White House find it attractive. And the many centrifugal forces at work in Washington frequently require it. The frequency with which presidents in the past half century have communicated directly with the American public shows that the more recent the president, the more often he goes public.

"A president must understand that he is expected to be the great national explainer," advise Grossman and Kumar (1981: 314–15). Thus, presidents and their advisers spend much time arousing public support for White House programs.

When presidents go public to sell their priorities, they can do so in various forms (Kernell, 1986: 85): "The most conspicuous is the formal, often ceremonial occasion, such as an inaugural address or a State of the Union message, when official duty places the president prominently before the nation. Going public may, however, involve no more than a pregnant aside to a news reporter."

Taking the public's pulse

Presidents and their advisers spend much time and effort trying to fathom the public mind, asking (as a Nixon aide put it), "Will it play in Peoria?" All presidents rely on scouts, trusted friends, or aides who travel the country and take the public's pulse. Franklin Roosevelt, paralyzed by polio, used his wife, Eleanor, and his alter ego, Harry Hopkins, to seek out the views of local leaders. Mrs. Roosevelt was a familiar sight around the country in the 1930s and 40s, acting as her husband's emissary. Some presidents take the public's pulse themselves. Promising to bring fresh breezes of populism to the nation's capital, Jimmy Carter set out on an ambitious program to meet with the people. He had White House phone-ins and visits with average people.

People rarely hold back in telling the president their views. A large staff keeps busy handling the flood of mail and phone calls received at the White House—as many as 50,000 letters and an average of 1,000 calls a day. Since 1960, White House mail has risen by 600 percent, largely because of expanded television coverage of the president.

WORDS AND IDEAS

Woodrow Wilson on the "Public Presidency"

His is the only national voice in affairs. Let him once win the admiration and confidence of the country, and no other single force can withstand him, no combination of forces will easily overpower him. His position takes the imagination of the country. He is the representative of no constituency, but of the whole people. When he speaks in his true character, he speaks for no special interest. If he rightly interprets the national thought and boldly insists upon it, he is irresistible; and the country never feels the zest for action so much as when its president is of such insight and caliber.

Source: Woodrow Wilson, *Constitutional Government in the United States* (New York: Columbia University Press, 1908), p. 68.

Woodrow Wilson (1856–1924). President from 1913 to 1921.

Public opinion polls give modern presidents precise measures of attitudes. Most presidents are avid poll watchers—at least when the polls are good. Lyndon Johnson used to carry flattering survey clippings in his wallet and whip them out to show White House visitors. As the Vietnam War dragged on and his ratings soured, his interest in the polls lagged. More recent presidents have had their own survey specialists to interpret findings and recommend steps to enhance presidential popularity with given groupings.

Care and feeding of the press

Press relations are an important segment of every president's White House operation. Reporters and commentators can help broadcast the president's message to the American people; conversely, they can probe and irritate when problems mount.

President Franklin D. Roosevelt confers with his trusted confidant and adviser Harry L. Hopkins. Hopkins served FDR as administrator of federal relief programs in the 1930s, as secretary of commerce, and as his personal emissary during World War II. For a time, Hopkins even lived in the White House.

The presidential images projected during the honeymoon period of a term are especially potent. Initial missteps by President Carter's inexperienced staff gained wide play in the press, fostering an image of ineffectiveness. Even when Carter's White House improved its performance, the earlier negative references persisted. Reporters touted President Reagan's strength as "the great communicator" on the basis of his seeming glibness and his early victories on Capitol Hill. Long after Reagan's popularity ratings sagged, along with his support levels in Congress, the press was cautious in criticizing him. In other words, the early-won reputations continued to hurt Carter and boost Reagan because these reputations were so frequently repeated in the media.

Shrewd presidential press aides do not wait for reporters to write the story; they try to create the story itself, or at least to control its "spin." Michael Deaver, Reagan's communications chief until he resigned in 1985, was a master at thinking up good, visual stories involving the president and geared to the nightly TV network news. As the cameras rolled, the reporters—primed with questions on major substantive issues—stood by helplessly. They vented their frustrations by shouting questions at the president as he walked away from the podium or climbed into his helicopter—thus seeming to confirm the view that reporters are rude and intrusive.

Presidential press conferences (described in detail in Chapter 8) can be

Presidential press conference. President Ronald Reagan meets with representatives of the news media in Washington, D.C. Reagan held less frequent yet more formal press conferences than those held by most of the other recent presidents. Under Reagan, reporters at a press conference were required to keep their seats and to raise their hands if they wished to be recognized.

an instrument of persuasion; but recent experience with them has disappointed all concerned. "Modern presidents," maintains one veteran reporter (Bonafede, 1987: 1067), "are using the press conference more to deflect criticism and soothe followers than to present ideas to reporters. The results seem to satisfy no one." Presidents are apt to schedule frequent press conferences when (1) they are personally comfortable with the format and (2) their administrations are enjoying relative success. Kennedy and Johnson held about two press conferences a month; Ford and Carter, one or more; and Nixon and Reagan, about one every two months.

One aspect of White House "news management" is to keep the press at arm's length when the president wants to avoid embarrassing questions. Thus at the height of the Iran-*contra* scandal in early 1987, White House aides clamped tighter-than-usual limits on Reagan's contacts with reporters, even barring them from taking pictures in the Oval Office.

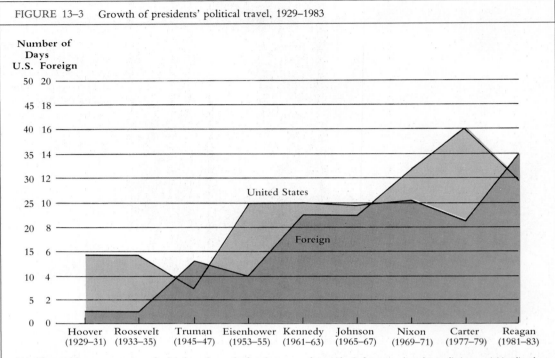

FIGURE 13–3   Growth of presidents' political travel, 1929–1983

Note: The trend lines represent days of political travel over the first three years of a president's first term—in order to eliminate activities directly focused on reelection. This is why Gerald Ford's 2½ years in office (1974–77) have been ignored.

Source: Samuel Kernell, *Going Public: New Strategies of Presidential Leadership* (Washington, D.C.: Congressional Quarterly Press, 1986), p. 97.

Speechmaking

Speeches and personal appearances are the centerpiece of the public presidency. Such events have been on the rise: Herbert Hoover delivered on average fewer than 10 major speeches a year and about the same number of minor speeches; Ronald Reagan gave about 70 major speeches in his first term (a third of them on TV) and almost as many minor ones (Kernell, 1986: 86). Personal appearances and days of political travel have also risen over the past 25 years (see Figure 13–3).

Presidents must effectively use the mass media if they are to prevail over others who are competing for the public's ear. In the preelectronic era, this meant a healthy set of vocal cords and a flair for colorful phrasemaking. Theodore Roosevelt's lively turns of speech, Woodrow Wilson's graceful and learned speeches, and Ronald Reagan's easygoing directness show the successful use of oratory.

Nowadays, presidents must adapt to the requirements of radio and TV. Franklin Roosevelt mastered radio; his 20 fireside chats and countless live

Radio mastery. A master of radio communication, President Franklin D. Roosevelt inspired citizens with his "fireside chats." Handicapped by polio and unable to stand or walk unaided, FDR had a good speaking voice, a sharp wit, and a flare for phrasemaking.

radio speeches helped sell his New Deal domestic programs and rally the nation during World War II. Kennedy and Reagan were to TV what FDR was to radio. Their good looks and casual speaking styles ideally suited the medium.

The White House employs speech writers, directors, and consultants to help presidents polish their media style. It is hard to imagine a president today facing the public without practice and coaching. Reagan used simple props to dramatize his economic messages. The president has a unique advantage in electronic communications. Not only does he get more automatic publicity than anyone else, but he can usually have free radio and TV time for the asking.

One of the most dramatic presidential appeals of modern times was President Reagan's speech before a joint congressional session in April 1981. His sweeping budget plan was being considered by Congress. He had just recovered from a would-be assassin's bullet. Public attention was riveted on him as he challenged Congress to approve his program. Reagan's performance harked back to Franklin Roosevelt's "100 days" of 1933 and to Lyndon Johnson's Great Society program of the mid-1960s.

Presidential travel

Local appearances and symbolic events are often more effective than set speeches. "Presidents can make the most of media coverage when they present their messages through activities that are likely to receive favorable coverage" (Grossman and Kumar, 1981: 314). The strategy is to portray

Master communicator. President Ronald Reagan delivers his weekly radio address from his California ranch.

the president as a newsmaker rather than just a speechmaker; the technique, at which Reagan's publicity chief Michael Deaver excelled, is to get the president on the nightly TV newscasts, conveying his messages in a variety of ways.

Travel and appearances are meticulously chosen to articulate the president's themes of the moment. Because presidents get more invitations than they can accept, they choose appearances for the most exposure and impact. (Even if they are not invited, they can simply show up and steal the spotlight.) Or they can simply schedule their speech in the White House's East Room and invite their own appointees and friendly legislators as the audience. Tours are planned to spotlight the president's objectives. In 1919, Woodrow Wilson was haunted by Senate opposition to the Treaty of Versailles. So he launched his desperate western tour to "lay my case before the people." After a tiring series of 40 speeches and many impromptu appearances, in an era without microphones, he collapsed. The victim of a crippling stroke, he never fully recovered.

Today's presidential forays have become logistic projects that have spawned full-time efforts at "presidential advance." In early 1986, for example, Reagan visited the island of Grenada for four hours and 20 minutes, an invasion that required more planning than the military operation three years earlier. An overnight stay was ruled out because there weren't enough hotel rooms (500 are needed for staff and press). The *Wall Street Journal* reported (Mayer, 1986: 1):

> Among the other items brought in just for the Reagan trip: two presidential limousines (a spare one just in case), three bomb-sniffing dogs, two surveillance/medical helicopters, a cavalcade of Secret Service vans, masses of satellite-communications equipment, the president's drinking water, and, if past trips are any guide, probably spare quantities of his type of blood. In fact, the Air Force's largest cargo plane, the C–5 (cost to operate: $12,769 an hour) has become such a regular sight lately that Americans here joke that "Grenada has shuttle service to Washington."

The Grenada trip, like many such trips, was undertaken for its media impact: pictures and a story line. Much of the advance work was aimed at getting good media coverage. The Reagan White House may have perfected its advance work to the level of high art, but all of the modern presidents and their advisers strive for the same results.

Other events

The day-to-day presidential schedule is crowded with brief scheduled events designed to exploit the "bully pulpit" and extend the chief executive's symbolic and persuasive reach. Some of these events are little more than handshakes and "photo opportunities"; others involve "dropping by" to convey words of greeting and encouragement at a meeting or conference. Or the president may actually meet with visitors to receive a report, exchange views, or present the White House viewpoint. Such events are choreographed by White House operatives.

In simpler times, things were different. In wartime Washington, Abraham Lincoln used to drop in unannounced to talk with government clerks, or even private citizens, at any hour of the day or night. Theodore Roosevelt and his family accepted New Year's greetings from thousands of citizens every year—anyone who visited the White House. Today, however, the first family is sealed off from such encounters by zealous staffs and nervous security officers.

With the president's time such a precious commodity, it was perhaps inevitable that someone would try to turn it into a fund-raising tool. When the White House was encouraging private donations to help the *contra* forces in Nicaragua, one private fund-raiser, Carl R. "Spitz" Channell, was said to have used White House access as bait to lure donors (Rempel, 1987: I, 16):

> They even went so far as to serve up the president himself. A handshake with Reagan could be arranged, for example, in exchange for private contributions of a few thousand dollars to the Nicaraguan rebels. Or, "one quiet minute" with the president could go for more than $200,000.

It is unclear how much money was actually raised through such tactics, or whether the president was aware of the precise details. What seems clear,

PRACTICE OF POLITICS

"The President, on cue"

Each working day the White House staff provided President Reagan with a schedule of events, supplemented with a background memo on each meeting and "suggested talking points." The memo listed the participants for each event and provided a "sequence of events," timed to the minute. ABC News White House correspondent Sam Donaldson obtained a copy of the president's script for Thursday, February 25, 1988. Here are some samples from that day's White House memos.

Source: *Washington Post,* February 29, 1988, p. A15.

THE WHITE HOUSE
WASHINGTON

February 24, 1988

DROP BY MEETING WITH CEO'S

DATE: February 25, 1988
TIME: 11:30 a.m. (20 minutes)
LOCATION: Cabinet Room
FROM: REBECCA G. RANGE

---

v. SEQUENCE OF EVENTS

11:30 a.m.   You enter Cabinet Room, are introduced by Senator Baker and deliver remarks. At the conclusion of your remarks you open the meeting to discussion.

11:47 a.m.   Rebecca Range will signal the end of the official portion of the meeting.

You move to the end of the Cabinet Room (under President Coolidge's picture) for handshake portraits with the participants.

11:50 a.m.   You depart.

PRACTICE OF POLITICS

(Concluded)

TALKING POINTS

-- Bob (Byrd), I appreciate you and your colleagues coming down today.

I know there has been a good deal of discussion in your hearings about the Treaty's implications for NATO.

On that point, I'm pleased you were able to make this trip together, and Bob, I want to thank you especially for undertaking this and for handling your discussions over there so effectively. And I'm really glad that you made it to Turkey. I want to hear about that part of your trip in particular.

(Senator Byrd and other Senators
report on their trip)

-- I want to thank all of you for your input and advice.

-- The next several weeks will be critical in terms of your ratification activities on the INF Treaty, and I will continue to work closely with you.

---

however, is that people outside, and perhaps inside, the White House were claiming to have exploited the presidential schedule in these ways.

It is often said that the president is the "chief legislator." This is not strictly true. Only House and Senate members may introduce legislation. Both chambers have committees that gather information, hold hearings, and bargain over the details of bills and resolutions—even before the entire membership votes on them. If the president is a legislator, he has powerful rivals.

Like other government powers, legislating is a blended power in which the president is a key party. If presidents cannot actually introduce bills, they can propose them; if they cannot physically take part in the legislative

THE PRESIDENT AND CONGRESS

process, their agents and allies can make their presence felt; if they cannot cast a vote on the House or Senate floor, they can affect the vote by using, or threatening to use, veto power.

The President's Legislative Powers

The president's legislative role is formally based on the opening clause of Article II, Section 3: "He [the President] shall from time to time give to the Congress information on the state of the Union, and recommend to their consideration such measures as he shall judge necessary and expedient."

Early presidents saw this as a routine, even odious, duty. Modern presidents see it as "*the* statement of legislative priorities" (Light, 1982: 160)—to focus the attention of Congress and the public on high-priority legislation. It was Woodrow Wilson who first went to Capitol Hill to deliver his State of the Union messages in person; ever since, his successors have done likewise (now in prime TV time) to push their programs. After his first year in office, with its hectic passage of New Deal legislation, FDR praised the cooperative spirit that had prevailed. "Out of these friendly contacts," he said in his annual address, "we are, fortunately, building a strong and permanent tie between the legislative and executive branches of the government. The letter of the Constitution wisely declared a separation, but the impulse of common purpose declares a union." Not all presidents view their relations with Congress in such benign terms; after 1937, FDR himself waged intermittent war over domestic policies. Yet the close ties of the legislative and executive branches are a main feature of national policy-making.

Presidents cannot dictate what Congress will or will not consider. But by pointing out legislative priorities, they help shape the congressional agenda. They can focus attention, publicize priorities, and mobilize public opinion. By doing this, they indicate what they see as the leading issues of the moment and what legislation the public is likely to expect. Thus, they supply Congress with something that its scattered and decentralized structure prevents it from providing for itself—an agenda. And though legislators often decry White House pressure, they complain just as loudly when presidents fail to convey their priorities.

Budget Making and Clearance

How do presidents reach their legislative priorities? These may arise from personal beliefs, campaign promises, or demands of influential backers (Table 13–2). In fact, there are always far more claimants for White House support than can be satisfied at any one time.

The formal mechanisms for sifting and choosing among the thousands of legislative proposals are **budgeting** and **central clearance.** These functions are performed by the president's management arm, the Office of

TABLE 13–2   Sources of ideas for the president's agenda

Source	Percentage of respondents mentioning
External sources	
Congress	52%
Events and crisis	51
Executive branch	46
Public opinion	27
Party	11
Interest groups	7
Media	4
Internal sources	
Campaign and platform	20
President	17
Staff	16
Task forces	6

Note: The respondents (past and present White House aides) were asked the following question: Generally speaking, what would you say were the most important sources of ideas for the domestic agenda? The number of respondents was 118.

Source: Paul C. Light, *The President's Agenda* (Baltimore: Johns Hopkins University Press, 1982), p. 86.

Management and Budget (OMB). The director of OMB is a leading spokesperson for the president's legislative preferences, especially where spending levels are involved.

Along with budget requests, federal departments and agencies submit to OMB their proposals for new laws or revisions of old laws. OMB's analysts then comment on the proposals. Consulting with White House staff members, OMB selects those that fit the president's goals. The final say remains with the president, who accepts or rejects initiatives urged by the cabinet, staff aides, legislators, or lobbyists.

Selling the President's Program

Except when giving certain speeches, presidents are not normally seen on Capitol Hill pushing their legislative program. They do not, for instance, testify before committees. (In 1977, though, congressional committees went to the White House to receive President Carter's "testimony" on his energy package.)

The brunt of the selling job rests with cabinet and agency officials. Usually flanked by aides, they sit again and again before Hill committees to argue for the president's stands, even those with which they differ in private. Almost every day, several top administration officials are on Capitol Hill meeting with some committee or subcommittee. Key officials are in special demand as witnesses. Their statements and responses are watched closely for clues as to what the president will accept or reject in legislation.

At a later stage, when bills are being worked over ("marked up") in committee sessions, administration experts are usually consulted. Sometimes they sit in the meeting room to advise and guide. The relationship between congressional committees and administration experts varies markedly; it depends on how close the president's objectives are to those of the committee leaders. If a committee sympathizes with the president's proposal, the ties are likely to be close and cordial. If the committee's goals are at odds with the president's, the relationship will be cool or combative; the president's spokespersons will be kept at a safe distance from committee deliberations.

To push their aims, presidents command the largest corps of lobbyists in the nation's capital; they are legislative liaison officers from the White House and various agencies. The White House Congressional Liaison Office manages the president's day-to-day relations with senators and representatives. It follows the progress of bills in which the president is interested. All of the departments and agencies, too, boast legislative liaison staffs that follow legislation dealing with their organization and answer congressional requests. These staffs are expected to adhere to the White House viewpoint; their prime loyalty, though, is to their organization, not to the president.

White House liaison staffers keep in touch with Capitol Hill developments. They deal especially with congressional leaders. They coordinate the activities of administration spokespersons and alert the president when personal intervention is needed.

Conversely, liaison staffers should impress on the president and his aides the importance of getting along with Congress. They must warn of the political repercussions of certain actions. A president may need to close a military base in a key congressional leader's district; the liaison officer must tell the president what will happen if he does so. Presidents and their advisers easily become restless over the balky ways of Congress. Its failure to give quick allegiance to the president's proposals is often vexing. This restlessness must be tempered by political realism. One of President Nixon's liaison chiefs started wearing a button with the slogan "I Like Congress" to remind other staffers of congressional sensibilities. From all accounts, the gimmick was not very successful.

Dispensing Favors

Presidents can give out countless favors, big and little, to woo congressional support. The most effective favors raise the standing or ambitions of a senator or representative. A presidential appearance in the home base of the legislator is usually a plus. Alert administrators allow legislators, especially those of the president's party, to announce new federal projects in their state or district. The idea is to help legislators foster the view that they have the president's ear.

Patronage, though less important than it once was, can still cement relations with influential legislators. Staff jobs or seats on government advisory committees can be used to reward a legislator's protégés or key backers. In 1986, to gain confirmation of a controversial judicial nomination, the Reagan White House bargained with judgeships in at least two other states, winning the votes of the senators from those states.

Lesser perquisites are also used. The pens that the president uses to sign bills into law are passed out to the bill's supporters, along with signed pictures of the ceremony. These mementos have prized places on congressional office walls. So do autographed pictures of the president and his family. (When Carter sent out unsigned pictures, there was grumbling in congressional cloakrooms—after all, didn't every post office have such a photo?) Access to the White House, for serious policy talks or a gala dinner, is always flattering. When Senator J. William Fulbright's (D–Ark.) Senate Foreign Relations Committee became a forum for anti–Vietnam War views in the 1960s, Fulbright vanished from White House guest lists, even when by protocol he should have been invited.

The Veto Power

The president's final weapon in lawmaking is the **veto.** The president must sign or veto a bill within 10 days after it has been sent to him. (Bills and joint resolutions go to the president for signature; simple resolutions, as statements of congressional views, do not.) A two-thirds vote in both houses is needed to override a veto—a formidable majority for congressional leaders to muster.

Veto threats

The veto is the nuclear deterrent in the president's arsenal. If Congress does not override the veto, it must drop the bill or draft a new bill more in line with the president's views.

Like the atom bomb, the veto has been more useful as a threat than in practice. "Make my day!": With that warning, Congress was put on notice that bills calling for new federal spending would be gleefully turned aside by Reagan. Most of the time, the threat does the job: not only do lawmakers fear the president's publicity engines, but they normally prefer to have a bill passed rather than vetoed, even if they must yield certain points.

Exceptions to this rule occur when the White House and Congress are controlled by opposing parties or when an election is just around the corner. Congressional leaders are not above sending the president a bill that they know he will reject. If it is vetoed, they can take the issue to the country, picturing the president as heartless or unresponsive. Presidents

TABLE 13–3   Presidential Vetoes, 1789–1987

	Regular vetoes	Pocket vetoes	Total vetoes	Vetoes over-ridden
Washington	2	—	2	—
John Adams	—	—	—	—
Jefferson	—	—	—	—
Madison	5	2	7	—
Monroe	1	—	1	—
John Quincy Adams	—	—	—	—
Jackson	5	7	12	—
Van Buren	—	1	1	—
William Harrison	—	—	—	—
Tyler	6	4	10	1
Polk	2	1	3	—
Taylor	—	—	—	—
Fillmore	—	—	—	—
Pierce	9	—	9	5
Buchanan	4	3	7	—
Lincoln	2	5	7	—
Andrew Johnson	21	8	29	15
Grant	45	48	93	4
Hayes	12	1	13	1
Garfield	—	—	—	—
Arthur	4	8	12	1
Cleveland	304	110	414	2
Benjamin Harrison	19	25	44	1
Cleveland	42	128	170	5
McKinley	6	36	42	—
Theodore Roosevelt	42	40	82	1
Taft	30	9	39	1
Wilson	33	11	44	6
Harding	5	1	6	—
Coolidge	20	30	50	4
Hoover	21	16	37	3
Franklin Roosevelt	372	263	635	9
Truman	180	70	250	12
Eisenhower	73	108	181	2
Kennedy	12	9	21	—
Lyndon Johnson	16	14	30	—
Nixon	26	17	43	7
Ford	48	18	66	12
Carter	13	18	31	2
Reagan	35	27	62	8
Total	1,415	1,038	2,453	102

Source: Gary Galemore, Congressional Research Service.

can, of course, also take their case to the people, saying that they are holding the line against an irresponsible Congress. (Figures on presidential vetoes are presented in Table 13–3.)

Pocket vetoes

If the president fails either to sign or to return a bill within 10 days, it becomes law anyway—*unless* Congress by adjourning has kept him from returning the bill for further action. This is the so-called **pocket veto,** a tempting device because it lets the president kill a bill without an obvious veto. The pocket veto means that Congress must start the bill all over again; it forecloses an early vote to override the veto.

Presidents sometimes try to use pocket vetoes when Congress has recessed for only a brief time. Nixon's frequent use of pocket vetoes was one part of his war against Congresses controlled by the Democrats. In December 1970, he pocket vetoed the Family Practice of Medicine Act (P.L. 91–696), which had passed the House, 412–3, and the Senate, 64–1. Thus, he was seeking to evade an almost certain override of his veto. The bill's chief sponsor, Senator Edward Kennedy (D–Mass.), took the case to court. Both district and appeals courts struck down the president's interpretation of the pocket veto. The case did not reach the Supreme Court. The lower courts' decisions (buttressed by a later memorandum from the attorney general) seemed to establish the pocket veto as limited to the final adjournment of Congress, when further action is precluded. However, the issue surfaced again when President Reagan pocket vetoed an El Salvador aid bill during the 1983 congressional session. Challenged by a bipartisan group of leaders in both chambers, the president's broad reading of the pocket veto provision was again rejected by a U.S. court of appeals panel.

Applying Grass-Roots Pressure

In the end, the president's most potent legislative weapon is his standing in the country. If he is riding high in the polls, his natural competitors— senators, representatives, bureaucrats, and lobbyists—will think twice before crossing him. But if he is being knocked about by public criticism, others sense that they can openly defy him.

When the popular Eisenhower was in the White House, Democratic leaders (who controlled Congress all but two of those years) hesitated to attack him directly. They preferred a posture of "responsible" opposition. In contrast, the Democratic 93rd Congress (1973–74) mustered the courage to fight Nixon on various fronts once it saw that he had been undermined by the Watergate scandal. Legislators who had been shy about opposing Nixon suddenly found the voice to speak out.

The popular Eisenhower and the post-1973 Nixon are extreme examples; but people in Washington read the president's popularity all the time. They take his public rating into account when deciding whether, and how often, to bow to his wishes.

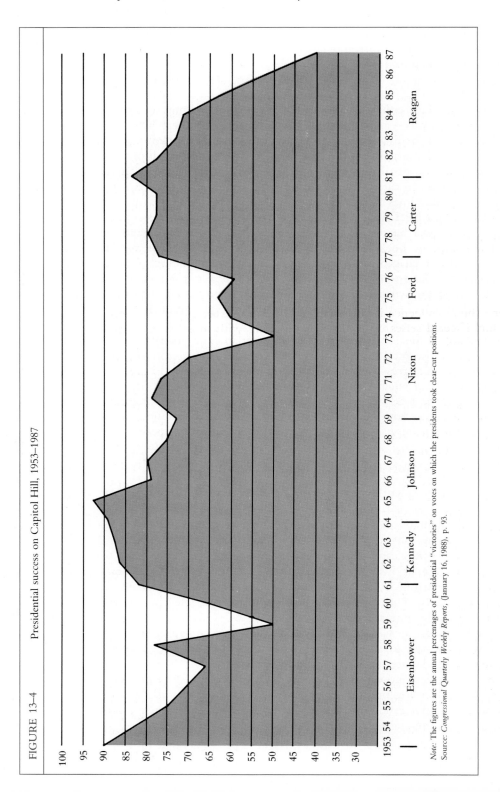

FIGURE 13–4   Presidential success on Capitol Hill, 1953–1987

Note: The figures are the annual percentages of presidential "victories" on votes on which the presidents took clear-cut positions.
Source: *Congressional Quarterly Weekly Reports,* (January 16, 1988), p. 93.

The President versus Congress?

Which is more powerful, Congress or the president? Has power shifted toward Congress or toward the president? Journalists forever chalk up the president's "wins" and "defeats" on this or that measure; some publications print "box scores" showing the president's success in coaxing bills through Congress.

An overview of the success of presidents on Capitol Hill is given in Figure 13–4. The figure shows congressional approval of the issues on which presidents took a clear-cut stand. All of the modern presidents gained congressional approval of at least half the measures on which they took a stand. The most successful were Eisenhower, Johnson, Kennedy, and Reagan early in his term. But presidents have to struggle for Capitol Hill support. In turn, this support tends to decline in the later years of the president's tenure. Partisan swings affect presidents' success rates. So does the temper of the times; the 1970s in particular brought low support from Capitol Hill.

The relative power of the president and Congress is an elusive question. For one thing, influence itself is hard to measure, especially in the complex, multifaceted series of events that go along with most policy enactments. Second, what is most "influential" in the legislative process? Is it the initiation of an idea, the final passage, or some other phase of the process? Third, whoever reaps credit for legislation depends heavily on the media. Here, presidents have a marked advantage over Congress.

Presidents automatically command public attention when they propose legislation. Yet their proposals may be no more than hasty borrowings from ideas that have been floating around Capitol Hill for years.

Still, several conclusions can be drawn concerning the power of the two branches. First, the *absolute* power of *both* branches has risen historically. The reason is that federal government itself has grown. In the 1700s, government was small and remote from the daily lives of most Americans. Today, government intrudes into almost all aspects of our lives. You can see this in the growing congressional and presidential workload. Both the president and Congress, then, have shared in the fact that government has been a "growth industry."

Second, most commentators agree that the president has gained power in relation to Congress over the long haul. For most of the 1800s, and even into this century, leaders on Capitol Hill outshone presidents. In the post–Civil War years, the presidency was very weak; Woodrow Wilson referred to our system at that time as "congressional government." Today the president has more resources than ever to affect legislation and mobilize public opinion.

Finally, the president and Congress have varying degrees of influence in different policy fields. In some fields, the president has almost free rein; in others, he is well advised to defer to legislative coalitions. Foreign policy and national security have been traditional sectors of presidential lead-

State of the Union. Modern presidents lay out agendas in annual speeches to Congress, televised at prime time. The president (shown here are Presidents Reagan, Kennedy, Johnson, Nixon, Ford, and Carter) speaks from the rostrum of the House of Representatives, in whose chamber House and Senate members meet in a joint session. Behind the president sit the vice president and the Speaker of the House (shown here are Vice President George Bush and Speaker Jim Wright, Vice President Lyndon Johnson and Speaker John McCormack, Vice President Hubert Humphrey, Vice President Nelson Rockefeller, Vice President Walter Mondale and Speaker Tip O'Neill).

ership. In contrast, Congress has kept a tight grip on measures that aid geographic and interest-based segments of the public—for example, tax codes, tariffs and trade restrictions, grant-in-aid programs, contracting and procurement, and all types of public works projects (including the placement of military bases).

The president heads the world's largest organization—the U.S. government. It has about 3 million civilian employees and 2 million in the military. From the piles of papers deposited in presidential libraries, it can be seen that the administrative side of the presidency has been burgeoning. At the Franklin Delano Roosevelt Library in Hyde Park, New York, 5 million pages document a 12-year presidency that included the Great Depression, the New Deal, and World War II. At the Jimmy Carter Library in Atlanta, Georgia, there are no less than 25 million pages spanning four years.

As we have seen, most presidents have little time or desire to intrude in day-to-day administrative affairs. But they recognize that the vast federal setup must implement their goals and carry their programs and services to average citizens. An alert, responsive federal structure can react quickly to changing events and enhance the effect of programs. A sluggish or uncoordinated follow-up can blunt the impact of programs.

As chief executive, the president is formally responsible for government conduct and effectiveness. He appoints secretaries of the various departments (cabinet members) and heads of key agencies, members of regulatory commissions, and ambassadors—about 4,000 appointments in all.

These officials are supposed to act as the president's emissaries. They are expected to carry the idea of political control throughout the government. But in practice, presidential appointees are pulled in opposite directions, their loyalty to the White House challenged by their agency and its constituencies.

The White House versus Agency Loyalties

Agencies cherish their own traditions and rights. More important, they have their own allies on Capitol Hill and among interest groups. These forces shape agency viewpoints and goals as much or more than the president does. The president and his aides are certain to be gone in four or eight years, but these people will stay. Who, then, is the agency going to listen to?

Thus, cabinet officers and other key officials are sometimes harassed men and women. They are appointed by the president and serve at his pleasure. At the same time, they cannot last long without support or at least assent from the civil servants in their agency, the congressional leaders who support and fund it, and the lobby groups that are affected by its activities. Secretaries of labor, for instance, must keep effective lines open to key labor leaders, especially in the AFL–CIO and major independent unions. That is why most labor secretaries have been people with close ties to the labor movement.

Once in a while an agency's constituents may force an appointee to resign. Reagan's first secretary of the interior, James G. Watt, spurned the traditional role of mediating among his department's battling clienteles— environmentalists and public lands users (cattle, timber, mineral, and energy interests). Support from these groups eroded; and after a string of public indiscretions, Watt was left with few allies and had to resign in October 1983.

The President and the Subgovernments

Despite constitutional authority and the power to appoint, presidents confront networks of entrenched interests that neither they nor their deputies can untangle.

For one thing, not one but many federal agencies have a stake in the outcome of most policies. Thus, time and effort are needed to lay the metes and bounds of each agency's duties. This is often done by convening interagency task forces.

Committees on Capitol Hill are also touchy about changes that might lessen their influence. Shifting the Forest Service from the Department of Agriculture to the Department of the Interior, for example, would no doubt please the House Interior and the Senate Energy and Natural Resources committees, which handle interior matters. But it would meet with strong opposition from the two agriculture committees.

Behind both executive agencies and congressional committees are lobby groups with a direct stake in keeping or changing policies. Faced with the veto power of these subgovernments, many presidents have despaired of achieving major shifts in program content or priorities.

Therefore, it is no surprise that every president since FDR, liberal and conservative alike, has railed against the complex, confused, uncontrollable federal setup. "To change anything in the na-a-a-vy," said Roosevelt, an old navy man himself, "is like trying to punch a feather bed. You punch it at one end, and then you punch it at the other, and the whole thing's back where you started. You punch it with your right and you punch it with your left until you are finally exhausted, and then you find the damn bed just as it was before you started punching" (Neustadt, 1976: 110).

The Reorganizational Imperative

Almost all of the modern presidents have struggled to remold the federal structure. They have had varying degrees of success. Harry Truman went so far as to call on the Democrats' archfoe, Herbert Hoover, to head a major reorganization effort; Dwight Eisenhower did the same thing a few years later. Lyndon Johnson proposed merging the Commerce and Labor departments, but he quickly dropped the plan when business and labor groups spoke up.

In 1971, Richard Nixon unveiled a sweeping reorganization scheme that would have formed four superdepartments, with all other agencies relegated to a lower status. Two years later, Nixon devised a cunning plan to tighten the reins on departments and agencies. He infiltrated their staffs with loyal White House staffers, forcing the agencies to report through four supercabinet members who were loyal Nixon advisers. The plan was dropped when the Nixon administration became paralyzed by Watergate (Nathan, 1983).

Nixon's successors have had no more success. Candidate Jimmy Carter promised sweeping reforms in government organization; President Carter moved more cautiously. His reorganization effort stalled, and he ended up creating two new departments—Energy and Education. Reagan vowed to downgrade those departments but soon gave up the effort; in fact, he wound up creating yet another one, the Department of Veterans Affairs.

Understandably, presidents tend to see themselves as powerless Gullivers in the land of Lilliput. They feel hemmed in by government stubbornness and by alliances of interest groups and congressional committees. But they have at least one tactic to bypass the subgovernments and assure responsive, loyal help. They can enlarge the White House staff and expand its duties. This is a technique that modern presidents have been unable to resist.

PRESIDENTIAL POWER: TOO MUCH OR TOO LITTLE?

After Vietnam and Watergate, it became popular to put down the "imperial presidency." Checks on presidential power from Congress, the courts, and public opinion were emphasized. As Arthur M. Schlesinger, Jr., wrote, "The pivotal institution of the American government, the presidency, has got out of control and badly needs new definition and restraint" (1973: x). George Reedy, former press secretary for Lyndon Johnson, pointed to the pomp and pageantry that had come to surround the institution. "By the 20th century," he wrote (1970: 22), "the presidency had taken on all the regalia of monarchy except robes, a scepter, and a crown."

If the trappings of power are impressive, the reality of that power is elusive. Presidents themselves are impressed, not by their power, but by the strong forces that work to limit and negate it. In his last months in office, Harry Truman spoke wryly of his successor, Eisenhower. "He'll sit here," he would say, tapping the desk for emphasis, "and he'll say, 'Do this! Do that!'—*and nothing will happen!* Poor Ike—it won't be a bit like the army. He'll find it very frustrating" (Neustadt, 1976: 77). In a TV interview in December 1962, Kennedy confessed that Congress looked much stronger from the White House than from a senator's office.

President Richard M. Nixon gives a victory sign as he boards a presidential helicopter after his resignation in August 1974. Nixon felt that the presidency lacked power and that hostile forces sought to thwart his programs and ambitions. The burglary at the Watergate resulted from a combination of paranoia and ambition among his supporters. Nixon was the first president ever to resign from office.

Presidents of both parties and varied persuasions have been dismayed and frustrated by the limits of their influence. Nixon was obsessed with this problem. He thought that he had received a mandate from the people, yet he saw himself as thwarted on every hand by hostile forces. To subvert those forces, Nixon devised a variety of strategies. These included taking apart federal programs, drafting reorganization plans, infiltrating agencies with White House staffers, and spying to ensure a landslide victory in 1972. It would go too far to say that Watergate grew out of a weak, frustrated presidency, not an imperial one. At least, we can say that both the people and the president expect far more than the presidency can ever fulfill.

The public mood since Vietnam and Watergate has fluctuated wildly. At first, there was massive reaction against presidential leadership, accompanied by widespread cynicism about government. Other political actors—including Congress and the media—rediscovered their will to resist presidential moves. Ford and Carter thus conducted their presidencies on weak strategic ground. Yet their incapacity to cope with such challenges as inflation and foreign crises brought counterdemands for strengthened leadership. Commentators lamented presidential inability to "form a government"; some even resurrected old proposals to bind Congress to presidential initiatives through changes borrowed from parliamentary systems. Despite the promises of Nixon's successors to rid the presidency of royalty and myth, public and press attention remained riveted on the office.

Reagan's stunning success in selling his program on Capitol Hill in 1981 showed that strong leadership rested more on circumstances and skills than on institutional arrangements. Reagan continued to be seen as a strong leader, even when his policies and programs were resisted or thwarted. These events were only the latest in the recurrent ebb and flow of executive powers. They confirmed again Edward S. Corwin's portrayal of the Constitution as an "invitation to struggle" over power.

For their part, presidents have every reason to foster the cult of the presidency. They rightly sense that public attention and support are their strongest resources for putting their imprint on public policy. Other institutions—Congress, the press, the bureaucracy, and the courts—have vital roles to play, but they lack the president's capacity to capture the public imagination. And they are ill equipped to provide coherent or coordinated leadership.

The American public, for its part, wants to believe in presidential leadership. Its high hopes as each new administration begins are continuing evidence of that desire. And with the right person in the White House, the public may fulfill its hopes.

CONCLUSIONS

In this chapter, we have completed our examination of the presidency by going beyond the formal, constitutional office and examining its public aspect. We have underscored the contrasts between the image and the reality of the office—between its promises and its limitations.

1. Much of the modern presidency's influence flows, not from its constitutional and statutory powers, but from its unique visibility and its ability to "go public"—to focus public attention and mobilize public support.

2. Public support for presidents peaks after their initial election and generally falls off thereafter—as decisions are reached and segments of the public alienated. This general trend can be halted by crises (rally-round-the-flag) or favorable economic conditions. It is accelerated by adverse economic conditions, wars or other conflicts that drag on inconclusively, and scandals involving the administration.

3. Presidents seem to fulfill a deep psychological function, revealed most dramatically when they die or become gravely ill.

4. In transcending their constitutional constraints to mobilize public support, presidents and their staffs devote concerted attention to probing public opinion, dealing with the press corps, writing and delivering speeches, arranging the president's travel and visitor schedule—in general, shaping the news or controlling how news events are interpreted.

5. In shaping national policy, presidents must cope with Congress—a large body of leaders elected from constituencies that are not national in scope. Presidents have many resources for leading Congress. These include agenda setting,

central clearance, legislative liaison, dispensing of favors, and veto powers. In the end, the most potent weapon of presidents is grass-roots support.

6. The federal bureaucracy is the other great institutional challenge to the presidency. In theory, presidents head the bureaucracy. In fact, they struggle simply to avoid being overwhelmed by it.

FURTHER READING

GROSSMAN, MICHAEL B., and MARTHA J. KUMAR (1981) *Portraying the President: The White House and the News Media.* An interesting and heavily documented study of the inner workings of the relationship between the White House and the press.

KERNELL, SAMUEL *Going Public: New Strategies of Presidential Leadership.* Washington, D.C.: Congressional Quarterly Press. An examination of the strategy of "going public" to overcome constitutional restraints on presidential power. The more recent the chief executive, the more active is his public strategy; but this makes it harder for presidents to bargain with other elite actors.

LOWI, THEODORE (1985) *The Personal Presidency: Power Invested, Promise Unfulfilled.* Ithaca, N.Y.: Cornell University Press. The rise of the "plebiscitary" presidency leads inevitably to wild claims and acute disappointment. Lowi's prescriptions are provocative: stronger parties, a multiparty system, cabinet government, and enhanced congressional powers.

ROCKMAN, BERT A. (1984) *The Leadership Question: The Presidency and the American System.* New York: Praeger. A sensitive and perceptive inquiry into the "ultimate dilemma" of the presidency: How can leadership be exerted in a system of numerous institutional constraints?

INSIDE BUREAUCRACY

$\mathcal{T}$he president and Congress set broad goals for the nation to achieve. Are these goals reached automatically? Do citizens work toward them without further government action? The answer to both questions is an emphatic no.

In fact, modern government requires many additional employees to achieve its purposes. Most of these employees are what we call *bureaucrats*—individuals who make their careers in governmental organizations that have a variety of social purposes and specific tasks. Although the bureaucrats and their organizations (bureaucracies) are not elected, they have an enormous day-to-day impact on citizens. A modern democratic society faces three basic challenges related to bureaucracy: (1) to keep the scope and organization of bureaucracy in line with basic decisions about what government should *and* should not do; (2) to motivate the bureaucrats to work efficiently and, at the same time, be responsive to the nation's elected leaders; and (3) to make sure that the bureaucrats proceed in ways congruent with basic democratic values. ∽

*G*overnments exist both to provide services and to keep order. To engage in both tasks, governments need to be organized. The units in which government employees work have many different specific names; generically we can think of them as **agencies.** Like other large organizations (corporations, unions, churches, colleges), governments have specific subunits.

The agencies responsible for the government's day-to-day functioning are collectively known as the **bureaucracy.** Individual agencies are often called **bureaucracies.** Individual agency employee are often known as **bureaucrats.** We intend these terms to convey neither a positive nor a negative image. Bureaucracy in general and individual bureaucracies and bureaucrats can perform well or badly. The labels themselves are neutral descriptors. As you read this chapter, remember that government agencies are bureaucracies and that agency employees are bureaucrats.

Government agencies have a number of common traits, regardless of their specific tasks. Each agency has a clear boundary. It has a name, and it is charged with administering specific programs. Employees belong to a single agency. There are clear rules for hiring and promoting employees. Each agency, at least in theory, relates the objectives of specific programs to broader goals or, as bureaucratic jargon often puts it, "missions." Each agency divides its labor among different subunits of employees. The subunits and the individual employees in them relate to one another in a hierarchical fashion: "Chains of command" are related to subunit tasks and to the rank of individual employees. There are superiors and subordinates. Individuals are supposed to know to whom they report, to whom they are equal, and who they supervise.

In dealing with clients, each agency employs procedures that are supposed to be automatic and impersonal. These procedures stress written communications, preservation of communications in files, and clear rules to govern both employee and client behavior.

In this chapter, we will analyze the federal bureaucracy, stressing recent developments. Some state and local bureaucrats also carry out federal purposes, usually with federally provided funds. Although formally employed by state, city, or county, these bureaucrats are sometimes paid with federal money. State and local bureaucrats outnumber federal bureaucrats. If public school teachers are included, about one in every five American workers is a government employee of some type.

In the sections that follow, we examine the nature of bureaucracy, the politics of bureaucracy, the question of degree of control or autonomy, and bureaucratic performance and survival.

WHAT IS BUREAU-CRACY?

Large problems require large organizations. In government, those organizations are agencies (bureaucracies). Throughout our history, the agenda of government has grown. New agencies have been created to address new or expanded items on that agenda. When the new government began its labors in 1789, the bureaucratic establishment was small. It has grown steadily since then. Bureaucracy is, in every sense, a fourth branch of government paralleling Congress, the president, and the courts. Bureaucracy is part of the executive branch, but it is also separate from the executive branch in important ways. Congress and the courts, like the president, have some controls over bureaucracy. The American federal bureaucracy is not out of control, as some politicians allege from time to time, but it does possess a great deal of independence and autonomous strength.

Bureaucracies: Organizations that Get Things Done

Bureaucracies abound in the lives of Americans—and in the lives of the people of any other modern country. Some bureaucracies are governmental; many are private. Government bureaucracies make rules that have the force of law behind them. People can evade these rules or challenge them; most of the time, they obey them. Bureaucracies disburse funds, run programs, provide services, and enforce laws. We often speak of an action of the federal government; most of the time, one or more bureaucracies are essential to achieve that action.

All U.S. citizens interact with government bureaucracies. They pay federal income tax to the Internal Revenue Service. Their cars have air pollution devices required by regulations of the Environmental Protection Agency. Regulations from the Food and Drug Administration determine whether they can buy specific medicines or foods with specific additives.

As a citizen, you interact with the same federal bureaucracies with which other citizens interact. As a student, you are also familiar with a variety of campus bureaucractic organizations: the registrar, bursar, academic departments, campus police, and student aid offices.

Bureaucracies must be primarily concerned with getting things done if they are to achieve what other government organs and the citizenry expect of them. However, bureaucrats—like the members of any kind of organization—are also concerned about the welfare of the organization itself. Therefore, not all bureaucratic energy goes into making programs work. Some of it is spent on nurturing the health and longevity of the bureaucracy itself.

The Development of Government Bureaucracy

The Constitution provides for bureaucracy indirectly. The framers surely knew that government needed to create various offices to carry out the purposes assigned to it by the Constitution; they almost as surely had no idea of how large government bureaucracy would become. Articles I and II of the Constitution mention executive departments and department heads. They also allocate a number of substantive tasks to the federal government. These tasks imply the necessity of creating and developing agencies. Congress could "establish Post Offices and post Roads." This required a bureaucratic agency. Congress could "coin Money." This also required a bureaucratic agency. Congress could "raise and support Armies" and "provide and maintain a Navy." Military bureaucracies were inevitable if Congress chose to use these powers.

The Constitution also specifically empowers Congress to give the president, department heads, or courts power to appoint various officials—the individuals that ultimately head bureaucracies.

In short, the Constitution gives Congress the power to create and delegate powers to agencies to implement programs that Congress approves. Sometimes the president is barely involved, if at all, in such delegations. The scope of bureaucratic activities is so great that judicial and presidential restraints on those activities can be used only selectively. Congress has more potential for controlling bureaucracy, but it often lacks the incentive to do so.

In Chapter 2, we sketched the growth of bureaucracy during the 200-year history of the independent United States. Bureaucracy has proliferated, as have programs. But there is no reason to portray the United States as peculiarly dominated by bureaucracy. All modern, industrial societies have lots of bureaucrats. However, U.S. bureaucrats have one unique feature: They are very active in building and participating in their own coalitions and networks of allies dedicated to specific policy goals. Bureaucrats in the other developed Western nations tend to be more neutral in terms of policy. (See Aberbach, Putnam, and Rockman, 1981.)

Throughout our history, agencies have been formed for one of four broad social purposes:

1. To provide necessary and desirable services that cannot be provided outside the government. These services include national defense, diplomacy, mail, and housekeeping for the government itself.

2. To promote and help fund specific economic sectors, such as farmers, labor unions, and parts of private business.

3. To regulate the conditions under which different kinds of private activity can or cannot take place.

4. To redistribute part of society's income and other benefits to the less fortunate.

In 1789, Congress created small bureaucracies that were involved only in general services. The War Department dealt with defense. The State Department dealt with diplomacy. The Treasury and Justice departments handled the government's financial and legal business. Soon after our existence as an independent nation began, Congress added two more bureaucracies in the general services area: the Post Office and the Navy Department.

In the mid-1800s, Congress created several new major bureaucracies, especially the Departments of Agriculture and the Interior. These departments administered subsidies for such private activities as building rail-roads and settling the West and supervised the construction of internal improvements, such as roads. At the same time, the Treasury began protecting our growing domestic industry by administering tariffs on imported goods from foreign nations.

Beginning in the late 19th century, as the problems of society changed and as political coalitions responded to those changes, Congress created regulatory agencies, primarily to regulate private business. During the last hundred years, the government has undertaken four major waves of regulatory activity. Each of these waves resulted in new bureaucracies that became permanent (Wilson, 1975).

The first wave came between 1887 and 1890. It produced the Interstate Commerce Act (to regulate railroads) and the Sherman Antitrust Act (to regulate trusts formed to achieve monopolies). The second wave came between 1906 and 1915. It produced the Pure Food and Drug Act, the Meat Inspection Act, the Federal Trade Commission Act (to prevent unfair business practices such as deceptive advertising), and the Clayton Act (to strengthen antitrust law).

The third wave came in the 1930s. It produced the Food, Drug, and Cosmetic Act; the Public Utility Holding Company Act (to prevent the concentration of economic power in public utilities); the Securities Exchange Act (to regulate the stock market); the Natural Gas Act; and the National Labor Relations Act (to prevent unfair labor practices by business). The fourth wave, aimed at protecting consumers and the environment, began in the late 1960s. It produced the Water Quality Act, the Clean Air Act, the Truth in Lending Act, the National Traffic and Motor Vehicle Safety Act, amendments to drug control laws, and the Motor Vehicle Pollution Control Act. Rhetoric favoring deregulation and some attempts at deregulation became prominent in the late 1970s and into the 1980s. New regulatory efforts ceased.

During the 1930s, the government also responded to the vast social problems both caused and revealed by the Great Depression. It created programs and agencies that were charged with redistributing income and wealth to the less fortunate. Agencies now housed in the Department of Health and Human Services, Education, Housing and Urban Development, Labor, and Justice were formed at that time. In the 1960s, the government reinvigorated its efforts against poverty and also launched efforts against racial discrimination. In doing so, it created the Office of Economic Opportunity (now defunct), the Commission on Civil Rights (the scene of a continuing political struggle between the Reagan administration and civil rights groups), and the Equal Employment Opportunity Commission (which underwent a major change in philosophy during the Reagan administration).

Congress watched over agencies with great care throughout the 1800s, and so they did not then develop much independent political weight. But later, as agencies grew in size and number, their independent political

All presidents create groups particularly suited to their personal styles of managing. Here, in 1981, President Reagan meets with an organization of his own creation, the National Security Planning Group. Secretary of Defense Caspar Weinberger is to the left of President Reagan, and Secretary of State George Shultz is in the right-hand corner.

weight increased considerably. At the same time, Congress gave them more power and paid less attention to their use of it. When government increased its scope in the 1930s, Congress increased the leeway it gave bureaucracy. It delegated power in a vague way, which greatly increased the independence of bureaucratic influence, an independence that persists (Lowi, 1979).

The Scope and Shape of Bureaucracy

Congress and presidents create, reorganize, and—occasionally—eliminate pieces of the bureaucracy. But bureaucracies also develop lives of their own, with their own momentum, their own inertia, and their own bases of political and public support.

The federal bureaucracy is vast and complex. In 1988, there were almost 3 million civilian federal employees. Only one in eight of them worked in the metropolitan Washington D.C., area. Most of the rest were spread throughout the United States. A few worked overseas. State and local governments employed more than 13 million individuals. Table 14-1 shows the distribution by functional area of federal government employees and state and local government employees in 1984. Three fifths of federal employees worked in the areas of national defense and international relations and the postal service. Over half of all state and local employees worked in the area of education.

Figure 14-1 provides a further look at what federal bureaucrats do. One

TABLE 14–1   Civilian government employment by function, 1984

	Distribution of employees	
Function	Federal government	State and local governments
National defense and international relations	36%	0%
Postal service	24	0
Education	1	52
Highways	★	4
Health and hospitals	9	10
Public welfare, police, fire, sanitation, parks and recreation	3	14
Natural resources	8	1
Financial administration	4	2
All other	15	16
Total	100%	99†
Total number of employees	2,942,000	13,494,000

★Less than 0.5 percent.
†Does not add to 100 because of rounding.
Source: *Statistical Abstract of the United States, 1986* (Washington, D.C.: U.S. Bureau of the Census, 1986), p. 294.

fourth of them deliver the mail. Over one third of them help provide national security. At the small end of the scale, 3 percent are involved in administering justice. Bureaucrats are individual human beings, not machines. They have specific jobs. White-collar jobs are held by four out of five bureaucrats: accountants, attorneys, secretaries, engineers, medical technicians, nurses, computer specialists, clerks. Blue-collar jobs are held by one out of five bureaucrats: warehouse and custodial workers, food service workers, plumbers, electricians, carpenters. What these individuals are assigned to do and how well they do it helps determine the impact that the government has both on society and on individual citizens.

About two out of every five federal civilian employees are women, and about one out of every four is a member of a minority. However, relatively few women or members of minorities are in the most important jobs. Most of those jobs are still filled by white males. And even high-ranking women and members of minorities are less likely to have supervisory or managerial authority than their white male colleagues at the same rank (Lewis, 1986).

Individual departments and agencies vary considerable in size. In 1987, the Department of Defense employed almost 1.1 million civilians and the Postal Service employed over 800,000. Other large employing units were the Veterans Administration (243,000), the Department of the Treasury (146,000), the Department of Health and Human Services (131,000), and

FIGURE 14–1   Distribution of the federal civilian work force by activity, 1986 (3 million full-time equivalent workers)

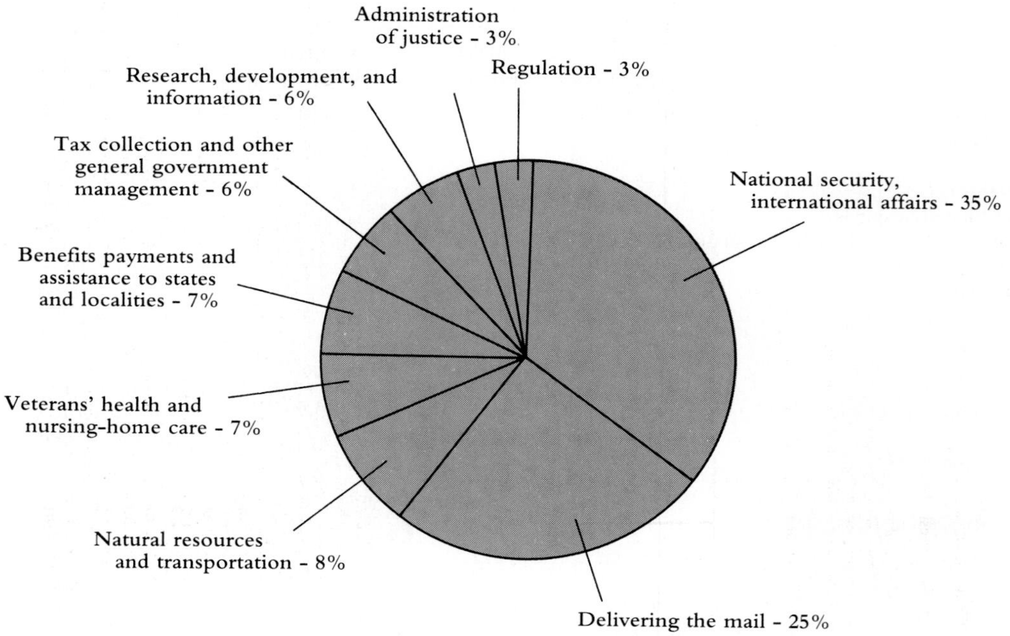

Administration
of justice – 3%

Regulation – 3%

Research, development, and
information – 6%

Tax collection and other
general government
management – 6%

National security,
international affairs – 35%

Benefits payments and
assistance to states
and localities – 7%

Veterans' health and
nursing-home care – 7%

Natural resources
and transportation – 8%

Delivering the mail – 25%

Source: Congressional Budget Office from budget documents prepared by the Office of Management and Budget.

the Department of Agriculture (107,000). Small departments included Labor (18,000), Energy (17,000), Housing and Urban Development (12,000), and Education (5,000).

Figure 14-2 reproduces an "organization chart" of the entire executive branch from *The United States Government Manual,* a yearly volume that describes government agencies in some detail. This figure will give you a feel for the very large number of agencies that are, technically, responsible to the president as part of the executive branch.

Figure 14–3 will help you understand the complexity within a single department—in this case, Health and Human Services. The figure presents a simplified view of the major organizational unit in the Department. Any single issue might be dealt with by many of these units. The principal substantive office would report to the highest level of the department, which in turn might submit the recommendation to various staff offices for review of matters involving civil rights, personnel administration, relations with Congress, and legal issues. At the same time, many or all of the regional office might get involved by stating their own views and

FIGURE 14–2   Organization of the federal executive branch

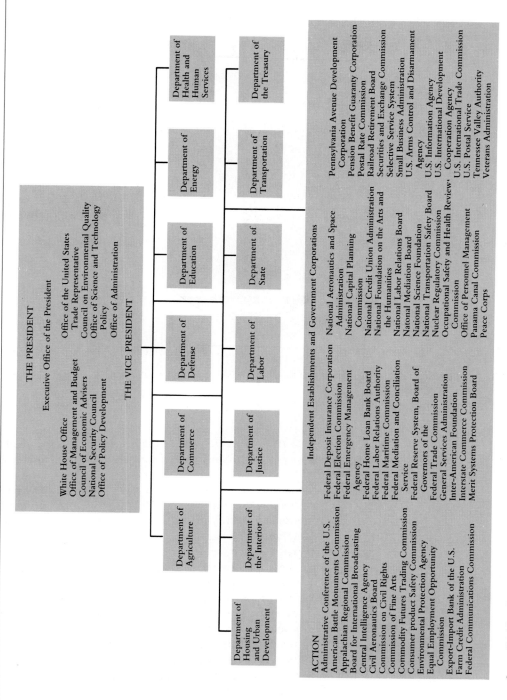

THE PRESIDENT

Executive Office of the President

White House Office
Office of Management and Budget
Council of Economic Advisers
National Security Council
Office of Policy Development

Office of the United States
Trade Representative
Council on Environmental Quality
Office of Science and Technology
Policy
Office of Administration

THE VICE PRESIDENT

Department of Housing and Urban Development

Department of Agriculture

Department of the Interior

Department of Commerce

Department of Justice

Department of Defense

Department of Labor

Department of Education

Department of State

Department of Energy

Department of Transportation

Department of Health and Human Services

Department of the Treasury

Independent Establishments and Government Corporations

ACTION
Administrative Conference of the U.S.
American Battle Monuments Commission
Appalachian Regional Commission
Board for International Broadcasting
Central Intelligence Agency
Civil Aeronautics Board
Commission on Civil Rights
Commission of Fine Arts
Commodity Futures Trading Commission
Consumer product Safety Commission
Environmental Protection Agency
Equal Employment Opportunity
Commission
Export–Import Bank of the U.S.
Farm Credit Administration
Federal Communications Commission

Federal Deposit Insurance Corporation
Federal Election Commission
Federal Emergency Management
Agency
Federal Home Loan Bank Board
Federal Labor Relations Authority
Federal Maritime Commission
Federal Mediation and Conciliation
Service
Federal Reserve System, Board of
Governors of the
Federal Trade Commission
General Services Administration
Inter-American Foundation
Interstate Commerce Commission
Merit Systems Protection Board

National Aeronautics and Space
Administration
National Capital Planning
Commission
National Credit Union Administration
National Foundation on the Arts and
the Humanities
National Labor Relations Board
National Mediation Board
National Science Foundation
National Transportation Safety Board
Nuclear Regulatory Commission
Occupational Safety and Health Review
Commission
Office of Personnel Management
Panama Canal Commission
Peace Corps

Pennsylvania Avenue Development
Corporation
Pension Benefit Guaranty Corporation
Postal Rate Commission
Railroad Retirement Board
Securities and Exchange Commission
Selective Service System
Small Business Administration
U.S. Arms Control and Disarmament
Agency
U.S. Information Agency
U.S. International Development
Cooperation Agency
U.S. International Trade Commission
U.S. Postal Service
Tennessee Valley Authority
Veterans Administration

Source: *United States Government Manual*, 1985–86 (Washington, D.C.: Office of the Federal Register, 1985), p. 827.

FIGURE 14-3   Organization of the Department of Health and Human Services

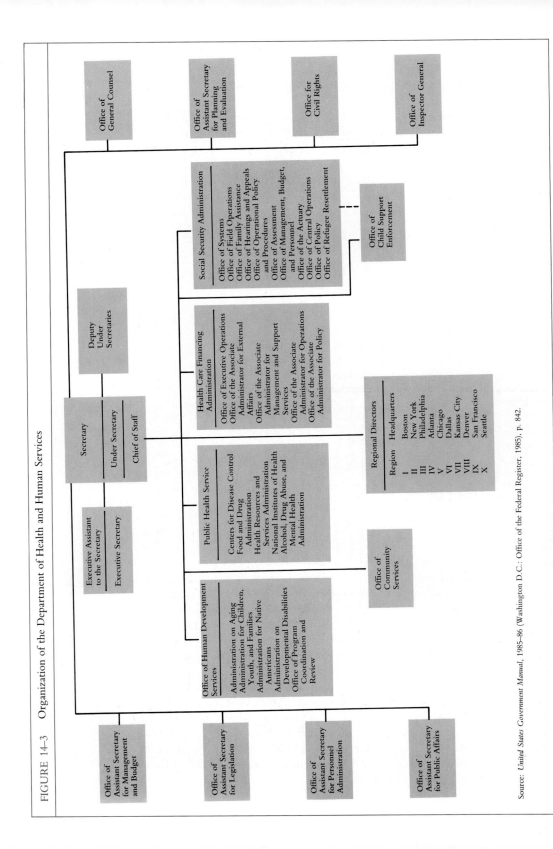

Source: *United States Government Manual*, 1985–86 (Washington D.C.: Office of the Federal Register, 1985), p. 842.

preferences. Bureaucracy is not simple. Decision making takes time and many layers of approval.

Each unit on the organization chart in Figure 14–3 has a rich and complicated life of its own. Some of these units do work that attracts considerable public attention. The Centers for Disease Control (CDC), for example, is in the forefront of efforts to identify and combat communicable diseases. In the last few years, it has been at the center of federal activity aimed at containing the spread of AIDS (acquired immune deficiency syndrome). The CDC people who conduct this work are bureaucrats. They work for a single part of the Public Health Service that was first established in 1973. CDC now has nine major operating components and a base budget of more than half a billion dollars. It employs about 3,300 people.

The decisions that led to the complex organizational structures portrayed in Figures 14–2 and 14–3 were made over time. Both organization charts represent the outcome of many debates and struggles. Organization charts may seem dry to the reader, but they are the end product of fierce political struggles. One longtime inside observer of such debates summarized the situation well (Seidman and Gilmour, 1986: 15).

> Organizational arrangements are not neutral. We do not organize in a vacuum. Organization is one way of expressing national commitment, influencing program direction, and ordering priorities. Organizational arrangements tend to give some interests and perspectives more effective access to those with decision-making authority, whether they be in the Congress or in the executive branch.

There has been nothing inevitable about the particular organizational developments in the executive branch. Congress and various parts of the executive branch, including individual agencies themselves, have made conscious decisions over the years to create new agencies, to transfer duties or units between agencies, and—occasionally—to terminate agencies. Individuals in charge of specific agencies constantly make detailed decisions about the arrangement of units and functions.

Some organizational decisions create a home for a new or largely new activity. Congress established the National Aeronautics and Space Administration (NASA) in 1958 to respond to the launching of the satellite *Sputnik* by the Soviet Union. This marked the start of our serious space effort. The formation of the Office of Economic Opportunity, in 1964, marked the start of the war on poverty. This agency housed many programs, both new and existing, in the social welfare field.

Some organizational decisions are made to give extra emphasis to programs already under way. For example, supporters of vigorous federal efforts to control air pollution were displeased with the performance of a series of agencies responsible for the programs in this area. As a variety of politicians and interest groups demanded more effective air pollution control, Congress moved this activity from agency to agency until it found one that performed acceptably (Jones, 1975).

A decade of activity by the National Aeronautics and Space Administration was successfully climaxed when U.S. astronauts walked on the moon in 1969. In this photograph, taken by Apollo 11 *commander Neil A. Armstrong, astronaut Edwin E. "Buzz" Aldrin, Jr., lunar module pilot of the* Apollo 11, *is shown walking on the moon.*

In 1963, when Congress established the first federal enforcement power with regard to air pollution, the Public Health Service in the Department of Health, Education, and Welfare was the agency charged with carrying out the law. The Public Health Service opposed the law and dragged its feet in enforcing it. Congress then assigned responsibility for air pollution control to other agencies. Finally, it created the Environmental Protection Agency and included air pollution control among its duties.

In late 1987, fittingly on Veterans Day, President Reagan proposed that the Veterans Administration (a large independent agency created in 1930) be elevated to departmental status. Doing this would put the head of the agency in the president's cabinet. Members of Congress—all of whom have large numbers of veterans and their families in their states and districts—would find it very difficult to reject this proposal if it were forced to a vote. Reagan's gesture to the veterans seemed to be in conflict with his administration's efforts to control what it viewed as the spread of bureaucracy. Moreover, his proposal was disapproved by experts on organization both inside and outside the government. These experts were virtually unanimous in concluding that it made no sense administratively or managerially. But political considerations led to congressional and presidential approval of cabinet status for the VA in October 1988.

Federal departments are often formed to cluster similar governmental activities and give them more prominence. This holds true for the departments of Agriculture (1862); Labor (1913); Commerce (1913); Defense (1949); Health, Education, and Welfare (1953); Housing and Urban Development (1965); Transportation (1966); Energy (1977); and Education (1979). In his 1980 campaign for the presidency, Ronald Reagan pledged to dismantle the Departments of Energy and Education to symbolize his emphasis on eliminating what he considered needless and inefficient federal bureaucratic activites. As president, however, he was unable to deliver on these promises, and by 1984, he had suspended his efforts to fulfill them.

Some organizational decisions diminish the importance of an activity. Presidents Nixon and Ford, who opposed the idea of a war on poverty, eliminated the Office of Economic Opportunity, the most visible symbol of President Johnson's antipoverty program. A small residue of antipoverty programs were adminstered by the Community Services Administration, a small marginal agency, until 1981, when it too closed its doors with the approval of Congress.

When the president, Congress, and high-ranking executive branch officials undertake agency reorganization, they usually argue that their proposals will promote efficiency, improve the quality of services, and save money.

The president has a special role to play in reorganizing agencies, though he usually must have congressional approval or at least the absence of congressional disapproval. Between 1939 and 1973, under an often renewed statute, the president had broad powers to propose reorganization in the executive branch, but Congress kept the power to veto those changes. During this period, the president proposed 74 changes; Congress vetoed 9 of them. The reorganization statute lapsed for a few years in the 1970s, but then it was reestablished in 1977 at the request of President Carter.

Presidential candidates often announce broad plans for making the bureaucracy more efficient and cheaper. But after being elected, they usually make only a small dent in the bureaucracy because they find that the reality of bureaucracy is much more complex than they had realized. In his 1976 campaign, Jimmy Carter pledged to cut the federal bureaucracy from an alleged 1,900 agencies to 200. In fact, he eliminated only a few advisory committees. He stopped making such efforts in 1979, when his aides told him that he had no chance of success.

Ronald Reagan had a greater impact on the bureaucracy. He got Congress to approve reduced budgets and staffing levels for agencies whose tasks did not much interest his administration and to approve increased budgets and staffing levels for agencies whose tasks were central to his administration's vision of what government should do. However, he did not redeem his pledge to trim the size of the federal bureaucracy; in fact, federal civilian employment was 5 percent greater in early 1986 than it had been in early 1981. The Department of Education work force shrank by 37 percent, and the Departments of Energy, Labor, and Housing and Urban Development lost close to a quarter of their employee positions. But civilian employment in the Departments of Defense and Justice increased by about 15 percent. These figures clearly reflect Reagan's aversion to social programs and his attraction to "law and order," both domestically and internationally.

THE POLITICS OF BUREAU- CRACY

Agencies and the individuals in them are heavily involved in politics. They bargain about program goals, responsibilities, and the size and distribution of funds. They participate both in creating policies and in implementing the programs that have been designed to carry out enacted policies. Bureaucracies do not passively administer the laws for which they are responsible. They help shape the laws in the first instance, and they have considerable discretion on how to interpret the laws as they administer them. Bureaucrats engage in the same general policy debates as are engaged in by the elected officials of the government: the president and the members of the House and Senate (Meier, 1979).

Our top bureaucrats and their agencies compete directly with one another for their share of such resources as money, responsibilities, and staff positions (Neustadt, 1973). The most successful bureaucrats have developed the political skills needed to compete successfully. Because bureaucrats and agencies must compete for resources, they develop supporting coalitions of constituents. These constituents include individuals, interest groups, Congress as a whole and in parts (subcommittees), and parts of the executive branch (such as the president, the White House, and the Office of Management and Budget). In a general sense, consituencies for bureaucracies are all of those who see themselves as affected—in any way—by the policies and acts of bureaus. The bureaucrat wants to build supportive constituencies. Activists in these constituencies want bureaucracies that favor their interests.

Dealing with Congress

Congress and the bureaucracy interact constantly. Ideas for laws come from both, and both must participate in working out details. The bureaucracy is primarily responsible for implementing programs, and Congress is in a position to oversee bureaucratic performance.

Congressional oversight of bureaucracy

Bureaucrats are given great latitude in administering programs that affect the lives of many citizens. Congress retains an interest in seeing how the bureaucracy carries out its responsibilities under the law. **Oversight** is the term applied to congressional activities designed to yield information about bureaucratic behavior. Such information is supposed to lead to congressional decisions about how to make programs better and bureaus more efficient and responsive.

Congress has often affirmed its formal commitment to oversight. The Legislative Reorganization Act of 1946 enjoined all congressional committees to exercise "continuous watchfulness" over the administrative units within their jurisdiction. The 1970 Reorganization Act was more specific: "Each standing committee shall review and study, on a continuing basis, the application, administration, and execution of those laws, or parts of laws, the subject matter of which is within the jurisdiction of that committee." The power of oversight was underscored in 1974 by House committee reforms and the Budget and Impoundment Control Act. Senate committee reforms in 1977 added the concept of "comprehensive policy oversight." This gave committees a mandate to look at broad questions even if they extended into other committees' jurisdictions. Congressional committees wield strong weapons, both statutory and informal, in carrying out oversight mandates. These weapons include legislative vetoes, statutory requirements, congressional investigations, and congressional power over personnel appointments.

Legislative vetoes　During the Hoover administration, Congress started writing legislative provisions that enabled it to veto specific actions by parts of the executive branch. Congress could thus stop proposed bureaucratic action by vote, sometimes by only one house or even by only one committee in one house, without presidential approval. Congress has included a **legislative veto** provision in several hundred laws. In mid-1983, the U.S. Supreme Court ruled that legislative veto provisions violated the constitutional separation of powers. The exact meaning and impact of this decision, however, were not immediately clear. In fact, both Congress and the executive branch continued to observe legislative veto provisions already in place. Congress also amended some of these provisions to meet specific objections made by the Court. Most important, Congress included legislative veto provision in new statutes, and these provisions were observed by the executive branch. In short, the Court's decision does not seem to have affected the use of the legislative veto as a congressional tool for oversight (Fisher, 1985).

Statutory requirements　Congress stays alert to trends in programs by requiring departments and agencies, and even the president, to submit information or reports on many matters. The Constitution, of course, authorizes the president to report periodically on the state of the union, and other presidential reports are mandated by law. For example, a yearly economic report is required under the 1946 Employment Act.

Department and agency heads traditionally file annual reports. These are now supplemented by special reports. Many laws require administrators to look at a specific problem and report back to Congress, usually within a set period. Recommendations, too, are often mandated.

If Congress objects to an administrative action, it can, in effect, over-

Climactic hearings. During the 1954 Army-McCarthy hearings, Senator Joseph McCarthy (R–Wis.) lectures about communist conspirators in the military. His adversary, Joseph Welch, the Army's special counsel, looks skeptical.

turn the action or prevent the action from being carried out. Congress may do this in one of several ways: (1) by enacting a single-purpose provision that overturns a specific rule, (2) by changing program authority to remove an agency's jurisdiction over the matter in question, (3) by placing limits on an agency through authorization or appropriation measures, (4) by requiring interagency consultation, and (5) by requiring congressional notification before an action has been taken (Kaiser, 1980).

Congressional investigations Congress has the power to gather information that will help it discharge its duties. "A legislative body," wrote Telford Taylor (1955: 21-22) during the stormy McCarthy era, " is endowed with the investigative power *in order to obtain information,* so that its legislative functions may be discharged on an enlightened rather than a benighted basis."

Executive activities are examined during Capitol Hill appearances by department or agency heads. Hardly a day passes when key administration officials do not appear before House and Senate committees. The question-and-answer format used lets legislators follow up inquires and is a flexible type of oversight.

The first congressional inquiry was held in 1792. It concerned General St. Clair's disastrous expedition against the Wabash Indians. During the Civil War, President Lincoln's actions were scrutinized by the Joint Committee on the Conduct of the War. After Lincoln's death, another joint committee led Congress's takeover of reconstruction plans. In World War II, the Senate's Special Committee to Investigate the National Defense Program was chaired by a little-known Missouri senator named Harry Truman. It served as a model for legislative oversight. The committee provided responsible watchfulness; it aired charges of graft and corruption and saved the government billions of dollars. In 1954, there were the dramatic Army-McCarthy hearings. They were ostensibly convened to probe

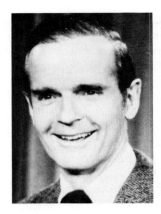

OFFICE OF
SENATOR WILLIAM PROXMIRE
WISCONSIN

FOR RELEASE AFTER 6:30 PM SUNDAY, MAY 14, 1984 FOR MONDAY AMs

Senator William Proxmire (D-Wis.) instead of a Golden Fleece award for May gave a Merit Award to Brigadier General David B. Hoff of the Wisconsin Air Guard "for solving a safety hazard on A-10 aircraft in three months with $1,100 of his own money when all the experts said it would cost tens of thousands of dollars and take two years."

Proxmire is a Member of the Defense Appropriations Subcommittee. Monthly he awards a "Golden Fleece" for the most wasteful, ridiculous or ironic use of the taxpayers' money. From time to time, in place of the "Fleece" he gives a Merit Award signifying an extraordinary contribution by an individual or government agency.

"Brigadier General David _____ he 18th Tactical Fighter

A senator versus the bureaucracy. In a monthly press release, Sen. William Proxmire (D–Wis.) usually lambasted an agency with a Golden Fleece Award for wasteful spending of the taxpayers' money. Only occasionally did he give a Merit Award to a frugal bureaucrat. Many bureaucrats welcomed his retirement after the 1988 session of Congress.

Senator Joseph McCarthy's (R–Wis.) farfetched charge that the U.S. Army was "soft on communism." The televised hearings helped expose McCarthy's shallowness and cut short his stormy career. Congressional investigations of administration misdeeds in connection with the Watergate break-in in 1974 and the Iran-*contra* scandal in 1987 were equally dramatic.

Congress is a political body, a fact reflected in its inquiries. Members of Congress are quick to seize the benefits from inquiries about executive wrongdoing or inefficiency: public acclaim for uncovering scandals, partisan advantage for exposing malfeasance by the opposition party, political advantages for voicing the unhappiness of interest groups over how certain programs are run, even the personal self-advertisement from being in the spotlight. Congressional investigations are political as well as informational tools.

Another trait of congressional investigations is that they tend to focus on specific charges or events. They rarely look at questions of philosophy or grand design. Critics sometimes complain that Congress should be like a corporate board of directors. They argue that it ought to restrict itself to broad policy questions, leaving detailed questions of program operation to administrators.

Yet legislators rarely adhere to administrative theory. Again, the explanation is political: Specific instances of wrongdoing or inefficiency are likely to attract the media; broader questions are not. Overseeing through publicity is exemplified by the "Golden Fleece" awards bestowed by Senator William Proxmire (D–Wis.). Proxmire presented one of these awards each month to an agency that he thought had spent money carelessly. One month he castigated the Law Enforcement Assistance Administration (LEAA) for a study of why prisoners escape; another month he criticized the National Park Service for studying misbehavior on public tennis courts. The agencies' anguished explanations always received less attention than Senator Proxmire's charges.

Congressional power over appointments   Another oversight tool is Congress's influence in approving and removing executive-branch officers. The Senate has constitutional power to advise on and consent to many presidential appointments. Usually, the Senate approves appointees. Though few are rejected, others are simply left unconfirmed. Some are eventually withdrawn by the president, who then submits new names. A nomination that faces defeat is normally withdrawn to spare the nominee and the president embarrassment.

There is more involved in screening appointees than just checking qualifications. The Senate has a political stake in confirming executive nominees (Moe, 1975). Confirmation is an adjunct to legislative oversight of executive agencies. An official who has gone through the confirmation ordeal presumably becomes more sensitive to future legislative requests.

Senators also tend to take a proprietary interest in agencies and programs handled by their committees. They prefer administrators who are easy to deal with. They look for people mindful of the committees's prerogatives and sympathetic to the political support groups with which both the agency and the committee must bargain.

The extent of Senate aggressiveness depends on the office for which a nominee is considered. Normally, the Senate allows the president wide discretion in picking cabinet members; the theory is that he is entitled to his own advisors. Heads of independent agencies and commissions are scrutinized more closely. The theory here is that they serve not only the president but Congress and the public as well.

In extreme cases, Congress can remove officials by *impeachment*. The president, vice president, and all civil officers of the United States can be impeached for "treason, bribery, or other high crimes and misdemeanors." Under Article I of the Constitution, the House "shall have the sole power of impeachment" and the Senate "shall have the sole power to try all impeachments." If the House votes to impeach an official, it tries the case before the Senate; a two-thirds vote is needed to convict.

The House of Representatives has impeached only 13 persons in our entire national history. The first case, which involved a U.S. senator, was an inappropriate use of impeachment since either chamber can simply expel members if it chooses. Of the other 12 impeachments, 10 involved federal judges, one involved President Andrew Johnson, and one involved a cabinet member. The Senate convicted only 4 of the 12, all of whom were judges. When President Nixon resigned in 1974, he faced what looked like certain impeachment by the House.

Congress can also use punitive measures against individual officeholders to display unhappiness with their policy decisions. An example of such a measure is described in the accompanying box.

How effective is oversight?   The record of Congress in overseeing the executive branch is generally conceded to be spotty at best, abysmal at

---

THE PRACTICE OF POLITICS

Ready, Aim, You're Fired: Chairman Whitten Bags Bureaucrat

By some lights, George S. Dunlop just might have the best job in town: status and a fancy title, office with a view, $77,500 annual salary, budget of $416,000 . . . and very little to do.

Dunlop doesn't like it a bit, actually, but he is in the unhappy position of having been caught square in the sights of the fiscal elephant gun that Representative Jamie L. Whitten (D–Miss.) occasionally fires at the Agriculture Department.

Whitten fired again last month and Dunlop took the hit. The chairman of the House Appropriations Committee abolished Dunlop's job as assistant secretary for natural resources and environment.

Whitten was angry and fed up at the almost constant haggling between congress and the administration over soil conservation budgets. Whitten and Congress have insisted that the Agriculture Department spend appropriated money; the White House keeps trying to cut the conservation account.

And since Whitten obviously could not abolish the presidency, whence come the orders to withhold funds, or the secretary of agriculture, he went for the next best target: George Dunlop, overseer of the Soil Conservation Service (SCS) and the U.S. Forest Service.

At Whitten's behest, the House voted to eliminate Dunlop's assistant secretaryship and ordered that he keep his hands off the conservation programs. But the Senate, where Dunlop has friends from his days as staff director of the Agriculture Committee, took no action.

When House and Senate appropriations conferees met last month to work out differences in the two farm spending bills, they stayed split over this and several other issues for days and Whitten would not relent.

As the stalemate dragged on, Whitten finally agreed to a "compromise." There would be no more assistant secretary for natural resources and environment. But Congress would create a new assistant secretary for special services to which Secretary Richard E. Lyng could appoint Dunlop.

Supervision of the SCS and the Forest Service was transferred to Lyng; Dunlop was barred from dealing in a supervisory way with either agency, but his new slot would carry the $416,000 appropriation his previous activities got.

Source: Ward Sinclair, "Ready, Aim, You're Fired," *Washington Post,* January 1, 1988.

worst. Certainly, few congressional committees fulfill the 1946 Reorganization Act's injunction; they rarely exercise "continuous watchfulness" over federal agencies under their purview. A leading student of the subject concludes, "There is a large gap between the oversight the law calls for and the oversight actually performed" (Ogul, 1976:5).

Most critics speak as if oversight must be continuous and comprehensive. They speak as if the unblinking eye of Congress should watch all government activities at all times. But the government's vast size and scattered activities make such a goal impossible to achieve. The best we can hope for is frequent spot checks of executive activities. They should be conducted often and without warning so that fear of congressional review is always there.

Oversight does not often get the attention of legislators. Like most people, members of Congress tend to see legislating mainly as passing laws. They view the process as closed when the president signs a bill. Exposing defects in the legislation might yield some publicity. But it also carries the risk of making legislators unpopular with the bill's sponsors, administrators, and beneficiaries. Oversight is most likely when legislators are willing to incur these political risks. It may take place, for example, when they strongly oppose the bill that has been enacted or when they support the bill but feel that administrators are thwarting its purposes.

Mutual support

Bureaucrats need to build support in Congress, mostly with the subcommittees responsible for their bureaus. This does not mean that the bureaucrats will not do their job. But it may mean that many decisions are shaped at least in part by their desire to please their congressional allies. Statements by bureaucrats such as the following (Fenno, 1966: 308–9) show the strength of that desire:

> Sometimes you wonder just who you are working for. . . . Sometimes I'll go over to the committee and talk about something with them. The first time I went, they told me it was confidential. And I said "When I came through that door, I started working for the committee. Whatever goes on in here just didn't happen as far as I'm concerned when I leave here." And I tell them that every time. Sometimes, I'm over here and the secretary or someone will try to worm it out of me what's going on. But they know I won't tell them. . . . I've gone out and tried to develop contacts with congressmen, because that's the way the game is played. . . . Some people higher up in the department object to our having any informal contacts with congressmen, but we'll just have to get around that, I guess.

Many circumstances require interaction: budgeting; agency organization and reorganization; the creation, alteration and termination of agencies; personnel matters; evaluation of program performance; and decisions about where projects should be located. On all of these decisions, the members of Congress (usually in a subcommittee) and the bureau (represented by a few top officials) have a stake in reaching agreements that benefit both.

Budget decisions are most vital from the agency point of view. Agencies need good relations both with subcommittees that provide funds and with outside support groups that ensure budgetary success (Fenno, 1966). An agency with strong support from outside interest groups gets large increases in its budget. The rapport that the agency builds with the subcommittee is critical in determining how much of any year's request the committee will get. Agencies in good standing with their subcommittee will get most of their requests. Those on shakier ground will risk heavier cuts in their requests.

Mutual antagonism

A recent example will illustrate what can happen when an agency crosses the wishes of Congress. For nearly 6½ decades, the Federal Trade Commission (FTC) kept a low profile in choosing cases to prosecute. Choosing such cases was one of its main tasks and also its most politically sensitive task (Katzmann, 1980). But in 1977, President Carter appointed an aggressive chairman who led the FTC into a more visible proconsumer and antibusiness (especially big business) position. Businesspeople reacted immediately by lobbying Congress to restrain the FTC.

Congress signaled the FTC to become less aggressive. It refused to renew the agency's authorizing legislation, which meant that the FTC could not get regular funding through appropriations. The congressional attack peaked in the spring of 1980, when Congress passed a new authorization law that gave it a formal role in overseeing the FTC's actions. Most important, Congress could veto any FTC rules that did not need presidential agreement. The restrictions would have been even more severe if President Carter had not intervened and persuaded some of the anti-FTC forces in Congress to back down. In the turmoil, the FTC actually closed down for lack of money for three days in May and June 1980. This was another symbolic reprimand from Congress.

The FTC continued to experience problems with Congress into the Reagan years. In 1982, Congress exercised a legislative veto to disapprove an FTC rule that required used-car dealers to disclose defects in the vehicles they sold. The rule had taken 10 years to develop. In 1982 and 1983, Congress failed to produce authorizing legislation for the agency, largely because some regulated businesses continued to complain. In 1984 and 1985, the hostility diminished, largely because the FTC became much less aggressive in acting on complaints about the practices of some businesses.

Dealing with the President

The president is, of course, only one person. The mind boggles at the thought of one person controlling 3 million civilian and many hundreds of thousands of military bureaucrats. In fact, presidents can use their control only selectively and sporadically. They do not intervene in most routine matters.

End of the Cuban missile crisis. After the Bay of Pigs fiasco, the Soviet Union attempted to install missiles in Cuba. The U.S. military ignored a presidential directive to remove U.S. missiles from Turkey and made it more difficult for the president to get the Soviet Union to remove its missiles from Cuba. Nevertheless, the president's efforts succeeded. Here, a Soviet ship leaves Cuba with a cargo of missiles in November 1962.

Even in important matters, a president may find that the bureaucracy is not following his policies. In 1962, our country and the Soviet Union were negotiating about Soviet missiles in Cuba. The Soviet Union alleged that our missiles in Turkey were just as close to Soviet borders as their missiles in Cuba were to ours. President Kennedy said he had ordered removal of the U.S. missiles in Turkey sometime before. But the military bureaucrats had not carried out his order, apparently because they disagreed with him. This case is especially dramatic because the president is commander in chief and this was a military matter. Bureaucrats in less visible and sensitive areas have even more leeway to interpret presidential orders.

Presidents may make statements about the impact they are going to have on the whole bureaucracy. But they really have to pick the few policy areas that they think are most important and try to make sure that the bureaucracy follows their will in those areas. President Nixon felt that the bureaucracy was sabotaging his policies, so he developed an elaborate four-part strategy for reducing his dependence on Congress and increasing his control over the bureaucracy. His strategy failed only when his presidency collapsed because of Watergate (Nathan, 1983).

President Reagan made a more focused assault on the bureaucracy than had his predecessors. He was determined to make at least some key agencies—such as those dealing with environmental matters, civil rights, consumer protection, and social programs—responsive to his policy preferences. He used all of his powers and those of his appointees to cut back the number of these agencies' employees and the amount of money they requested and received from Congress and to prevent them from vigor-

Controversial administrators. Both James Watt, as secretary of the interior, and Anne Gorsuch Burford, as head of the Environmental Protection Agency, were aggressive but controversial in pushing Reagan administration policies. Both had dedicated supporters and persistent opponents, and both left government after a few years.

ously pursuing goals that he found distasteful. In addition to exercising his normal budgetary powers, Reagan took great care in making appointments to these agencies, in reassigning senior civil servants from one agency to another (a new power that Congress gave the president in a 1978 statute), in reducing the number of employees where such reductions did not require congressional approval, and in effecting administrative reorganizations inside individual agencies (Nathan, 1983; Newland, 1983).

Reagan's assault on specific agencies terrified many career bureaucrats. Morale plummeted at many agencies. In April 1982, the *Washington Post* printed the results of a survey of over 500 federal workers in six agencies. Only 25 percent of those surveyed rated morale in their agency as excellent or good; the rest rated it as not so good or poor. Seventy percent found their work less satisfying than they had found it two years earlier. Fifty-five percent were concerned that they would lose their jobs.

Controversy broke out over the policies and appointments in the agencies that had changed the most. James Watt, secretary of the interior, and Anne Gorsuch Burford, head of the Environmental Protection Agency (EPA), were attacked for seeking to make their agencies more probusiness—more eager to sell federally owned natural resources to private interests in the case of Interior and less eager to clamp down on polluters in the case of EPA. Some of Reagan's most controversial appointees—Watt, Burford, and Secretary of Labor Raymond Donovan—left under fire, but their successors, though less controversial, continued to pursue most of their policies. Overall, the Reagan administration showed considerable skill and tenacity in bending the bureaucracy to its will.

A careful study of the cutbacks in five domestic agencies during the first Reagan term discovered that the administration got a great deal of what it wanted, even when it had been opposed by Congress (Rubin, 1985). Agencies with strong interest-group support could avoid some cutbacks and policy redirection. Most agencies, however, changed significantly in the face of persistent and determined efforts by Reagan appointees to reduce their size and to reorient their policies.

Some of any president's personal impact on the bureaucracy comes through his power of appointment, though relatively few positions are filled in this way. A president currently makes about 1,700 policy-level appointments to the executive branch. About 450 of these appointees—the field staff of the Justice Department, ambassadors, members of the U.S. delegation to the United Nations, and members of State Department boards and commissions—do not serve in core positions.

Through the Civil Service Reform Act of 1978, Reagan had a lever that his predecessors had lacked. That act created a new Senior Executive Service (SES) of about 7,000 of the highest civil servants in government. Eligible people who chose to join it got a chance for higher pay and cash bonuses. The president also got new authority to transfer these people. Reagan used that authority to promote his policies. Previously, the president had had some impact on senior civil servants, especially political independents, (Cole and Caputo, 1979), but the SES increased the impact.

The president cannot possibly appoint only people he knows and trusts. Many appointments will be suggested by those he trusts or owes some political debt. In fact, the president never meets many of his appointees.

Presidents sometimes have problems counting on their own appointees to carry out administration policies faithfully. These appointees are often, in many ways, "strangers" in Washington (Heclo, 1977). They are new to the city and do not stay very long. Of necessity, they are put in situations where lack of experience and high turnover stand out. This is in contrast to the experience and relatively low turnover of other people in key policy roles: career bureaucrats, congressional staff, and member of Congress (Ripley and Franklin, 1987).

In addition, even direct presidential appointees have their own policy preferences. They often respond to individuals with whom they deal daily. They may strongly disagree with presidential wishes. Under Jimmy Carter, for instance, HEW Secretary Joseph Califano developed a national health insurance plan (never enacted) that was quite different from the president's preference. Some Reagan appointees have defended programs and agencies that the president did not support. Terrel Bell, secretary of the Department of Education, appointed to a supposedly doomed agency, became a reasonably effective supporter of its continued existence.

Dealing with the Office of Management and Budget

For the last five decades, the greatest help that presidents have received in trying to affect the bureaucracy has come from the Office of Management and Budget (OMB). OMB performs four major functions in dealing with federal agencies. It approves the legislative proposals that agencies make to Congress, prepares budget requests for future years, manages spending in the current year, and oversees agency management. Also, OMB personnel work with agency personnel to gather and exchange information. No matter who was president, OMB has been consistently important in money matters. Its importance in legislative clearance and management has varied (Berman, 1979).

Presidents have altered the way in which OMB functions as an institution. Both Nixon and Ford made OMB more hierarchical and politicized (Heclo, 1975). Under Carter OMB was also politically visible. He involved it in volatile issues and made political appointments to its top positions. Carter's first appointee to the directorship, Bert Lance, became controversial because of his former banking practices and was forced to resign in mid-1977. Reagan also made a highly visible appointment as his first OMB director—a young Republican congressman named David Stockman, who brought an aggressive style to OMB. Stockman was a powerful and controversial figure in the years following Reagan's inauguration. Another strong director, James C. Miller, III, replaced Stockman in 1985.

Although OMB is a professional organization, it has room for much presidential input. Since the Bureau of the Budget was created, in 1921, each president has used it differently in dealing with agencies, Congress, and the public. This has been most true since it was transferred to the Executive Office in 1939.

The agencies responsible for individual programs and OMB often disagree. But there have also been instances of close and cooperative relations. When there are arguments and bad feelings, agencies may have enough political support to compromise with OMB or completely avoid a negative OMB decision. For instance, agencies may appeal to the White House, or they may appeal to Congress for changes in laws. In general, the potential for OMB control of agencies diminished with the Budget and Impoundment Control Act in 1974. This act reduced the president's power to refuse to spend money that Congress had assigned for specific purposes. It also required Senate confirmation of the director and deputy director of OMB.

The Reagan administration strengthened OMB's hand by giving it new powers to clear all rules and regulations coming from any federal agency. These rules and regulations determine the precise meaning of laws. The administration wanted to control such determinations instead of allowing individual program agencies to exercise considerable autonomy.

Dealing with Clients

Clients are people or organized groups that deal with bureaucracy and benefit from its activities. Individual clients are often portrayed as hostile to and victimized by "faceless bureaucracy." But some clients have good experiences with bureaucracy and some have bad experiences. Most individuals have a generally positive view of the bureaucracies with which they have had personal dealings (Katz et al., 1975). This positive view is especially pronounced among individuals who have received specific services from a bureaucracy. Understandably, people have a less positive view of their interactions with bureaucracies that have taxed them or have limited or regulated their behavior. Skillful bureaucrats can develop supportive constituencies of individuals who have been served by a specific bureaucracy.

Although individual clients are politically important to agencies, client groups are even more important. The ideal relationship for both bureaucrats and the groups with which they interact is one of mutual support based on common interests.

A number of factors foster cooperation and policy accord between an agency and its client groups. First, people in many parts of the government alternate between a job with an agency and a job with a group, company, or association that does business with that agency. In the late 1970s, for example, a report from Common Cause (a "public interest" lobby) showed that about half of the appointees to regulatory commissions came from regulated companies or from law firms that worked for such companies. On leaving office, about half of the personnel of regulatory commissions went to work for these companies or law firms. Such connections build strong policy agreement and political ties between an agency and its client groups.

Second, an agency can help create external groups to support it. This usually results in long-run basic policy agreements. Sometimes it is hard to tell which body is more important—the agency or the spin-off group. For instance, the Department of Agriculture fostered the American Farm Bureau Federation. The Department of Labor aided the growth of labor unions, which often have special access to parts of the department. The Department of Labor also helped finance an interest group—the Interstate Conference of Employment Security Agencies. This group lobbied the department to create policies, opposed by some top department officials, for state employment agencies. The officials were almost helpless when they faced the united opposition of the bureaucrats in their own department and the group whose staff they funded.

Third, most agencies create and use advisory committees that draw important members from client groups. These committees help make sure that agency policy does not vary from what the clients want (Brown, 1972; Petracca, 1986).

Fourth, programs and agencies that disburse funds and other benefits are much more apt to agree with clients than to regulate them. Both the agencies and the clients want the greatest flow of benefits. This provides jobs and influence for the agencies and benefits for their clients. The Army Corps of Engineers, for example, has close relationships with groups that benefit from its water projects (Drew, 1970). Member of Congress would

THE PRACTICE OF POLITICS

Will the Real Bureaucracy Stand Up, Please?

Betty Jones, a mother of four young children, has received public aid for seven years. She is now in the county welfare office in Los Angeles proving for the 14th time in those seven years that she is eligible to continue getting help. She has been in the office for five hours waiting for her turn. The office does not take appointments. The surroundings are dingy. She had no one to care for her two preschool children, and so they are with her. The children are cross, hungry, and tired. They had to catch the bus at 7 A.M., transfer twice, and ride for an hour to get to the office at 8 A.M., when it opened.

Now it is 1 P.M. The pace has slowed for the last two hours as those in charge went to lunch. Those dealing with the clients are clearly on edge today; they have many cases to review and are shorthanded. Two of their usual staff of 10 are ill; a ruling of a distant Washington, D.C., agency called the Office of Management and Budget has "frozen" two slots. Betty doesn't know whom she will see; whoever it is won't know her or remember her anyway. Most of the workers seem to dislike her, though she doesn't know why.

Betty is worried about getting home in time to greet her first- and second-grade children when they return from school. She has to leave in an hour to make it. But will she miss her chance to be interviewed? Will she have to waste another day on a pointless trip to answer the same questions and fill out the same form?

Bill Smith is a cattleman in Wyoming. He has 10,000 head of cattle and needs access to federal land for some of them. It is time to renew his grazing permit. He also must ask for a change in his permit that will allow him to add 500 head to the 2,000 already grazing on public land.

A few months ago, the advisory committee, of which he is a member, made a suggestion to the Department of the Interior, which controls the land: Allow one owner to graze up to 2,500 cattle on public land. So Bill should have no trouble getting the change. The fees charged by the government have not changed in six years and are quite low.

This afternoon, Bill has to go to the bank and the hardware store at the county seat. He also expects to drop by the office of the Interior Department. In 15 minutes, he can complete the simple form that will both grant him the added herd and extend his permit for another year. He and Al Greene, the government agent who has run the office for 10 years, are old friends; Bill is looking forward to chatting with Al while taking care of his business.

Which is the real bureaucracy— Betty's or Bill's? In fact, they both are. Bureaucracy can provide services efficiently and smoothly; it can also complicate people's lives for no apparent reason.

like to bolster these relationships because they also get political credit for individual projects. Neither Presidents Carter nor Reagan achieved more than partial success in restraining costly and questionable water development projects, though both worked hard to do so (Ripley and Franklin, 1987: 100–101, 111–13).

Fifth, groups can exert influence over agencies by working closely with Congress. Groups closely tied to specific congressional subcommittees can influence congressional funding decisions and other programmatic decisions that affect individual agencies in the bureaucracy.

Relations between Bureaucratic Units

Bureaucratic units must work with each other from time to time. Their jurisdictions may overlap, and their programs may reach the same clients. Members of different units may be put on interagency committees to promote cooperation. In general, the units are wary of each other and real cooperation is rare. Normally, the behavior of such units ranges between uneasy truce and open hostility. Each unit is mainly concerned with its own budget, personnel, programs, clients, aims, rules, space—in short, its own "turf." No forced coordination or cooperation works well.

The following instance is typical. In 1975, the State Department was working with Canada on a water diversion project in North Dakota that would affect a drainage basin extending into Canada. The Canadian bargainers opposed the project as a pollution threat in violation of a 1909 treaty between the two countries. The State Department bargainers were told by the Interior Department, which would handle the project, that no alternatives were available that would lessen the pollution problem. Therefore, the State Department had to bargain on the basis of a plan that the Canadians opposed.

In fact, the Interior Department did have alternatives that would have met some of the Canadian's objections. But an assistant secretary of interior had written a memo ordering that these alternatives be withheld from the State Department, the Canadians, and "local interests" in North Dakota and Minnesota. This deliberate withholding of information made the task of one agency (the State Department) harder and helped another agency (the Interior Department) to build a project in its own way.

AMERICAN FEDERAL BUREAU- CRACY: AU- TONOMOUS OR CON- TROLLED?

American bureaucracy can be described by two sets of conflicting adjectives. On the one hand, it often behaves as if it were *autonomous*. But it can also seem to be *controlled*, because it is strongly influenced by outside forces. It can be described as *conservative* when it strongly defends and promotes existing policies. Yet it sometimes advocates and implements important *progressive* policies.

Federal bureaucracies have two major sources of power: technical knowledge and skill *and* political influence (Rourke, 1976; Meier, 1979).

Knowledge and skill promote autonomy. The need to maintain political influence promotes partial control, though such influence may also make any individual bureaucracy appear autonomous to an outsider not important to that bureaucracy's political future.

Federal agencies usually have more substantive expertise than any other actor in the policy process (such as the president, Congress, or an interest group). That expertise allows bureaucrats to advise others authoritatively on what policies to adopt. It serves to give bureaucrats considerable leeway to make detailed decisions about programs.

Government bureaus and their key employees can also rally political support for their jurisdiction, policy, agency size, and budget claims. Those who want to change the policies of an agency face a tough job if that agency is well run and entrenched. Not only is the weight of knowledge likely to lie with the agency; the agency is also likely to be in a strong political position. People and groups pushing an alternative view almost always have to rely on building countercoalitions. They may seek support from people and groups in the legislative branch, the private sector, and other parts of the bureaucracy. They may look to the White House or to dissidents in the agency itself. But the design of the federal bureaucracy works against overturning the strong substantive preferences of an agency. Opponents of those preferences have less knowledge of the facts than the agency does.

The autonomy of bureaucracy also stems from its size and fragmented nature and from the civil service system. Size and fragmentation make the physical aspects of control—whether by the president, OMB, Congress, or the public—very difficult. The civil service system has grown dramatically since 1883. It protects most government employees from being fired for political reasons. It also gives them a regular career ladder.

But bureaucratic autonomy is not used to reach a single set of goals. Bureaucrats differ on what is right in any given instance. They can and do argue, and their arguments help create a lively ongoing debate over points of policy. This debate can lead to open rebellion, despite the formal rules of hierarchical decision making. During the Nixon years, for instance, staff members in both HEW and the Justice Department made effective protests against agency officials who were delaying the implementation of civil rights policies.

Bureaucrats tend to be relatively liberal on policy matters. They are likely to disagree with very conservative policies. However, there is no evidence that the attitudes of bureaucrats differ from the predominant attitudes of the general population about basic institutional structures or the form of the national economy (Rothman and Lichter, 1983). And only some bureaucrats are strongly interested in policy matters; others focus mostly on matters of interest to their profession (for example, chemist, lawyer, doctor, engineer); still others focus simply on their own careers (Downs, 1967; Wilensky, 1967).

Bureaucracies also admit outside influence into their inner workings, partly because of the movement of personnel. Some people from outside the career service enter policy-level jobs. People who stay outside the career service may serve as influential part-time consultants. A few people come and go as appointees. Clients and legislators and their staffs also work closely with bureaucracies.

Much of the time, bureaucracy has a conservative impact on policy. Bureaucrats tend to set up routines that make supporting what exists easier than adopting strikingly new policies. Some of what exists, though, may not have a conservative effect. Congress may legislate innovative programs for the bureaucracy to run, and the bureaucracy itself sometimes creates programs that are seen as quite innovative and progressive:

> Farmers in the last century and more recently trade unionists and the urban poor have looked to executive agencies for the redress of their grievances against more powerful segments of society, and the services of these organizations have provided the means by which the welfare and status of these disadvantaged groups have been greatly improved. In Europe . . . such groups more commonly have identified bureaucracy as part of the political system that must be overcome if public policy is to be changed in ways that are advantageous for them. (Rourke, 1976: 154)

Is bureaucracy controlled, or does it just work its will with few checks? The least effective controls come from the public, which has little leverage. Some controls can be exercised by Congress, the president and the institutional presidency, and the courts.

In some ways, Congress can best effect coordinated control. But, in fact, the political interests of members tend to prevent this (Fiorina, 1977, 1979). When there is no effective control of this sort, members can increase their individual impact on single agencies and programs. Often this effort can help them with the electorate back in their states or districts.

Within the executive branch, we noted limits on the president and OMB in coordinating control. Some such control is possible by the top ranks of the bureaucracy. But people in these ranks may be ignored by the civil servants with whom they must work (Heclo, 1977).

In short, there are no consistently reliable sources of coordinated and central control within the government itself. But each of the sources of control can have some effect under specific conditions and at different times.

The public has only blunt weapons to control bureaucracy. And it usually has little interest in doing so. Bureaucrats themselves, though wary of citizen participation in policy matters, are not wholly against it. Middle-level bureaucrats are not completely reliable supporters of democratic norms and ideals. They are, however, more democratically inclined than is the general public (Wynia, 1974).

Inside an agency, the chief and top-level staff have many ways of gaining control over the bureaucracy. But these can be overcome by the resistance of subordinates. In many cases, Congress has deliberately kept the top leadership of federal departments weak in terms of staff and authority, preserving a special, direct relationship with the smaller units of these departments.

Determined heads of agencies can push their organizations, but only with unrelenting work. The Department of the Interior is a good example of an agency that went in two very different directions under back-to-back secretaries. Neither of them was able to get all he wanted. The first was Cecil Andrus, secretary of the interior during the Carter administration and governor of Idaho before that. Andrus endorsed a variety of pro-conservation policies and got some movement from the department. But near the end of his tenure as secretary, he made the limits of his power over his own bureaucracy clear:

> When I was governor, I could implement a decision quickly. I could even implement a poor decision. . . . Here you can't even implement a good decision in timely fashion.
>
> It's like playing 100 games of chess, and you're one person playing against the other hundred, and you have to run around to make all your moves. It's competitive and fascinating, but tiring.
>
> There are so many competing interests on every issue. You end up compromising with Congress to get bills passed and compromising with your own bureaucrats and those in the other government agencies to make them work. By the time you get a good idea implemented, it doesn't really resemble its parents. (*Washington Post,* October 9, 1980; *New York Times,* November 18, 1980)

Andrus' successor, Reagan's appointee James Watt, was secretary of the interior from 1981 until his resignation in late 1983. Watt pursued very different policies. He tried very hard to move the department to a pro-development stance, and he diminished the department's conservation and environmental efforts. Like Andrus, he had some success. But, as one of his assistant secretaries testified, he also faced limits: "Everyone assumes that Watt wakes up every morning, scratches his bald head, and says, 'Let's go out and rape the coast of California today.' But it just doesn't happen that way. There are rules and laws we have to live with"(Mosher, 1983: 1230).

Even aggressive secretaries face problems. If laws specify the details of programs, those details cannot be changed, no matter what the secretary wants. Moreover, some laws give the final authority not to the secretary but to a lower-ranking bureaucrat who may not even be a presidential appointee.

Changing Bureaucracy

A tally of the federal organizations created in 1923 that survived until 1973 discloses a very high survival rate (Kaufman, 1976). Great social changes caused by the depression, World War II, and the social unrest of the 1960s took place during these 50 years. Yet 148 of the 175 federal agencies existing in 1923 survived (about 85 percent), and 109 of these agencies (about

BUREAU-CRATIC SURVIVAL AND PERFOR-MANCE

62 percent) barely changed their status. They were still in the same federal department; they were at about the same spot in the hierarchy. Moreover, the activities of the 27 abolished agencies did not end—they were moved to other units.

Even agencies with minor functions develop backers. Members of Congress and interest groups make them very hard to kill. For example, after Congress once again gave blessing to his funding, the chairman of the American Battlefields Monuments Commission, which has had very little to do for decades, said, seemingly with a straight face, "You see, the people who criticize us don't really know us. And all we have to do to get them to understand is to give them the facts" (*Washington Post,* February 4, 1977).

Even units charged by presidents with cleaning up the bureaucracy have a hard time finding targets that they think can be sunk. In mid-1979, for instance, OMB came up with only three after more than a year of looking: the Annual Assay Commission, set up in 1792 and still performing functions that had been obsolete for more than 10 years; the U.S. Marine Corps Memorial Commission, which had done nothing for more than 20 years; and the Low Emission Vehicle Certification Board, which had done nothing for 3 years—there were no vehicles (presumably electric) to certify for government purchase.

But agencies do change. Their goals change, their budgets change, and their personnel change. Some survive even after finishing their original tasks, because they get involved in new ones. NASA had a severe funding and personnel decline after reaching its first goal—putting a man on the moon. But it succeeded in getting new tasks. Its next major task—the space shuttle—was so costly that its fortunes in terms of budget and employees revived strongly. The Challenger disaster in January 1986 and the subsequent report underscoring NASA's incompetence put the agency's future in serious doubt once again.

Changes in national administration can also have some impact, though agencies are skilled at fending off presidents. At a gross level, Ronald Reagan has been unsuccessful at eliminating the Department of Education, the Department of Energy, the Economic Development Administration in the Department of Commerce, Amtrak, and the Small Business Administration. However, he has been successful in making sizable personnel and program cuts in the Departments of Education, Housing and Urban Development, and Labor and in the Environmental Protection Agency.

Performance

How well does bureaucracy perform? The question is simply put. The answer is complicated because "performance" has several layers of meaning.

In an abstract sense, bureaucracies have both strengths and weaknesses. An agency that is working well can

Proceed in an orderly and predictable way to process its work, including work resulting from contacts with citizens.

Work impartially and fairly, treating all people alike.

Keep a staff of qualified professionals.

Keep a staff whose hiring and advancement depend on merit (if a civil service system is in place and working).

Keep good records and files that can be used to track down the facts in any specific dealings with a client.

Many problems can plague bureaucracies and the people they are supposed to serve. A malfunctioning bureaucracy can

Be rigid in applying rules so that it "goes by the book" and cannot cope with exceptional cases.

Treat clients impersonally, rudely, and without respect.

Be slow in processing its work.

Create meaningless paperwork.

Be subject to hidden political forces so that it caters to some clients at the expense of others.

Be unresponsive to the central leadership of high-ranking officials, including the president.

Be staffed by workers who are so worried about job security that they cannot produce adequate services.

Honesty is one concrete aspect of performance. Corruption—bribes, theft, and using official positions to make money—does occur. These forms of corruption occurred on a large scale in the General Services Administration in the 1970s. But it is rare. There are also more subtle forms of corruption. An official may favor a private interest even though he or she does not stand to gain in a direct sense.

The most important questions about performance are difficult to answer. There are at least three major sets of such questions (Fried, 1976):

1. Whose values and what values are pursued? Does an agency seek goals of the people and groups that it is responsible to? Is it responsive to those people and groups?

2. With what success are the values pursued? Is the agency effective in reaching its goals?

3. What procedures does the agency use in seeking its goals? Does it respect individual and group rights as it seeks its goals?

All of these questions bear on the vital issue of government legitimacy. Public attitudes toward any one agency or toward the whole bureaucracy are shaped by how these questions are answered. If most people think that most agencies are pursuing proper values fairly and with some success, then those agencies will be considered legitimate. On the other hand, there may be a widespread view that agencies are seriously deficient on one or more standards. Then, the legitimacy of the agencies (and of government in general, since bureaucracy is such a large part of it) is in some danger.

CONCLUSIONS

Our main concern has been to introduce you to the complexities of federal bureaucracy in the United States. Bureaucracy is at the heart of day-to-day governmental activities. It deserves serious attention from every citizen.

The challenges of governing related to bureaucracy, identified on the opening page of this chapter, are necessarily woven throughout any assessment of the bureaucracy—whether by scholar, journalist, student, or average citizen. These challenges are never met in a definitive and permanent way. They are a continuing part of the nation's dynamic political life. Bureaucracy neither automatically passes nor automatically fails the tests of (1) appropriate scope, (2) efficient performance, and (3) democratic performance. In this chapter, we have sought to give you, as a student, enough knowledge about bureaucracy to reach your own judgments on these vital matters.

A few specific conclusions summarize the material presented in this chapter:

1. Bureaucracy is inevitable in a modern nation. But its size and organization represent many choices: How many services will the federal government provide? What is the nature of the delivery system used to transfer these services to clients? And what is the relative political weight of client groups?

2. Federal agencies do not just carry out policies made by elected officials. They help shape the policies that they carry out. And in the implementation process, agencies have leeway to give their own meaning to those policies.

3. The federal bureaucracy is vast. It is best understood if viewed as a collection of separate fiefdoms, not as an integrated whole. Each agency is involved in a different network of political contacts. Agency leaders try to cultivate support with a large number of these contacts.

4. Skillful bureaucrats can help their agencies toward their most important goals. But they must also take account of the goals of Congress, the president and his appointees, and client groups.

5. Bureaucratic agencies rarely die. Therefore, people and groups that need good performance from such agencies should try to push them in desired directions. They should not nurse the unrealistic hope that they can eliminate the agencies. This advice applies equally to presidents and average citizens.

FURTHER READING

FRIED, ROBERT C. (1976) *Performance in American Bureaucracy.* Boston: Little, Brown. A thoughtful examination of how well the U.S. bureaucracy does its job.

GOODSELL, CHARLES T. (1985) *The Case for Bureaucracy: A Public Administration Polemic.* Chatham, N.J.: Chatham House Publishers. A well-reasoned defense of the performance of American bureaucracy.

HECLO, HUGH (1977) *A Government of Strangers.* Washington, D.C.: Brookings Institution. An examination of the relationships between political appointees and career bureaucrats.

KAUFMAN, HERBERT (1981) *The Administrative Behavior of Federal Bureau Chiefs.* Washington, D.C.: Brookings Institution. A close analysis of what these key bureaucrats can and cannot do.

MEIER, KENNETH J. (1979) *Politics and the Bureaucracy: Policymaking in the Fourth Branch of Government.* North Scituate, Mass.: Duxbury Press. A short, basic text that analyzes U.S. bureaucractic behavior.

Chapter Fifteen

COURTS, JUDGES, AND JUSTICE

The U.S. Supreme Court in 1988. Seated from left are Thurgood Marshall, William Brennan, William Rehnquist, Byron White, and Harry Blackmun. Standing from left are Antonin Scalia, John Paul Stevens, Sandra Day O'Connor, and Anthony Kennedy. Kennedy, O'Connor, and Scalia were appointed Associate Justices, and Rehnquist was elevated to Chief Justice, by President Reagan.

The following statement, which appeared in the *Washington Post*, March 5, 1980, was made by Joseph L. Rauh, Jr., law clerk to two Supreme Court justices in the 1930s, in reference to a 1979 book on Supreme Court decision making based largely on interviews with the law clerks of Supreme Court justices.

> It has taken this long-ago Supreme Court law clerk a good while to reach this point, but it seems to me . . . that Bob Woodward and Scott Armstrong rendered a very real public service in *The Brethren* by detailing an unmistakable picture of the Supreme Court as a political rather than a legal institution. . . . Precisely because the important issues that come before the court are broad matters of public morality and political statesmanship rather than narrow questions of law, it was inevitable that the justices and their law clerks would turn out as activists fighting for their own views on public questions, just as do their legislative counterparts.

Surely, Rauh, who went on to become a distinguished lawyer and a well-known political activist, could not have been talking about the U.S. Supreme Court. Is that court not composed of nine old jurists in modified choir robes who behave gravely, intellectually, and in accordance only with the words of the Constitution, previous cases, and the logic of the law? Do not U.S. courts, especially the Supreme Court, simply make "just" decisions? Do they not avoid political disputes that occupy lesser mortals, such as presidents, members of Congress, and bureaucrats?

In fact, Rauh was right on target: The Supreme Court and the entire court system are part of the government. They are involved in politics. They make decisions about matters vital to individuals, groups, social classes, and governmental institutions. Like legislatures, executives, and bureaucracies, courts make policy. The policies they make, like those made by other organs of government, result from complex interactions among individuals whose views of what constitutes good public policy are often different. ✑

---

*T*he Preamble to the Constitution asserts that one of the broad purposes of creating that document is to "establish Justice." In any society, courts and judges presumably play a large role in the quest for justice. What role do they play in the United States? How are they integrated into the total political system?

Courts dispense justice through decisions in individual cases. By virtue of that fact alone, they are part of the nation's governing apparatus. But American courts also make policy since, like the other organs of government, they make and interpret law daily. Thus, U.S. courts are both political and judicial. This twofold nature of our courts presents society with three major challenges: (1) to keep judicial business flowing smoothly and in timely fashion; (2) to strike a healthy balance between allowing courts to shape public opinion and maintaining public pressure on courts to make rulings not radically at odds with what the public finds acceptable; and (3) to redefine the proper scope of court decision making constantly, so that social purposes are well served without overreaching the competence of judges, all of whom are unelected at the federal level.

In this chapter, we will first look at how courts fit into the scheme of democratic government. We will consider the ways in which courts both differ from and resemble other governing institutions. Second, we will examine the organization of the U.S. court system, introducing the idea of jurisdiction and describing how courts conduct their business. Third, we will focus on the political aspects of federal courts. Fourth, we will explore the sources of the courts' policy-making power, the restraints on judicial power, and the general substantive scope of court action. (Chapter 19 provides a more detailed examination of civil rights and liberties, an area vital to all citizens, on which the Supreme Court has an enormous impact.) Finally, we will pursue the question of how active courts should be in forming policy.

Why Do We Need Courts?

In many ways, all law is public policy. Law is a central means for allocating resources and codifying values, and politics in general also allocates resources and codifies values. Thus, legal decisions inevitably intertwine themselves with political decisions.

Constitutions—both federal and state—and laws at all levels of government are not self-explanatory in all their details. Judges in all types of courts must interpret constitutional and statutory provisions constantly when applying them to specific cases. These interpretations not only decide individual cases but, when aggregated into lines of legal precedent, also help decide broader questions of public policy.

Courts, like legislatures, executives, and bureaucracies, are concerned with distributing the benefits and protections of government. They are all concerned with regulating private activity and resolving social conflict. There are, however, important differences between judicial and nonjudicial policies (Jacob, 1984). The most obvious difference lies in who is responsible for making decisions. Judges and, in effect, the lawyers appearing before them and arguing cases are responsible for policies coming from the judiciary. Other policies are made by varying combinations of legislators, executives, bureaucrats, and representatives of the private sector. There is no tidy division of labor between judicial and nonjudicial decision makers. Both deal with some of the same substantive areas.

Courts and the Law

All of the political institutions in a democratic society help resolve conflict. U.S. courts perform this task in two ways that set them apart from other governing institutions. First, these courts deal only with cases in which two parties have a specific disagreement that requires adjudication. There must be a concrete question involving an injury that one party is alleged to have committed against the other. The parties in a lawsuit may be individuals, classes of people, groups, corporations, or governments (including both agencies and individual officials). The alleged injury may involve criminal behavior or a civil matter, such as property, contracts, or domestic relations. Either party may bring its grievance (suit) against the other party in accordance with established procedures, laws, and court jurisdiction (which court can hear which cases). The court focuses on the specific disagreement that is at issue in the specific case.

Second, U.S. courts primarily hear cases in which an injury is alleged to have already occurred. In some instances, courts will intervene to prevent future or continuing injury by issuing injunctions and restraining orders. But they will not consider cases in which two friendly parties create a legal controversy to get a court ruling on some questions of mutual concern. Except for a few state courts in limited classes of cases, U.S.

courts will not comply with public officials' requests for advisory opinions on the constitutionality of statutes.

The American Judiciary Compared with the Judiciaries of Other Nations

In all nations, including the United States, courts are important in hearing and deciding disputes between a variety of parties on many issues. In all nations, including the United States, a large number of public and private bodies other than courts help resolve disputes (Sarat and Grossman, 1975). In general, however, U.S. courts have a much more important part in the governing process than do the courts in other democracies. What courts can hear and decide is broader in scope in the United States than in other democracies. Specifically, U.S. courts have powers to restrain the behavior of other governmental units and even to mandate action by those units that courts in other democracies do not have.

Our courts are important in part because individual rights and liberties are such a vital part of our political tradition. In addition, the federal nature of our government helps create questions that are subject to judicial action. However, the courts in other nations that place a considerable stress on individual rights and have a federal system are not nearly as important and active as ours (Goldman and Jahnige, 1985). Even more important in explaining the importance of U.S. courts are the willingness of governments and, especially, individuals to bring matters to court *and* the general reverence of government officials and individuals for courts and their decisions. The general American tendency to define individual rights broadly—a tendency that has existed at least as far back as the 18th century—underscores the importance of our courts.

ORGANIZATION OF THE U.S. COURT SYSTEM

The United States has a large and complex court system. The federal courts are part of that system; and the Supreme Court is only one of the federal courts. The structure of the major federal courts is shown in Figure 15–1.

The most important federal courts include the Supreme Court in Washington and 12 courts of appeals and 90 district courts spread throughout the nation. Courts of appeals and district courts hear cases from specific geographic areas. The Supreme Court has just nine justices. The courts of appeals have a total of 168 permanent judgeships with between 6 and 28 judges in each court. The number of judges assigned to a court of appeals depends on its workload.

Every state has at least one district court, and the most populous states have up to four. Each district court has between 1 and 27 judgeships, depending on its workload, with a total of 556 district judgeships in the 50 states and the District of Columbia. Some senior judges—those over retirement age—carry partial workloads to help keep the business of the

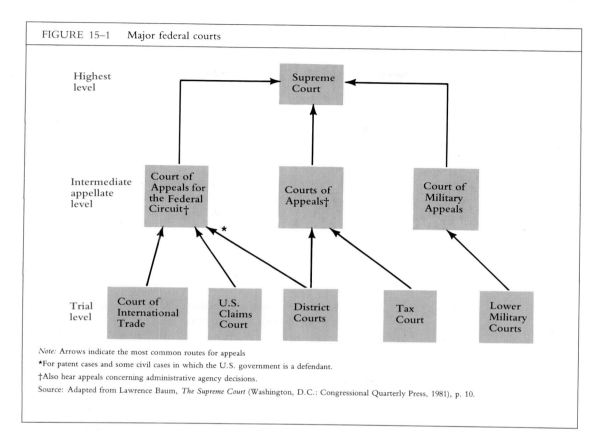

FIGURE 15–1   Major federal courts

Note: Arrows indicate the most common routes for appeals

*For patent cases and some civil cases in which the U.S. government is a defendant.

†Also hear appeals concerning administrative agency decisions.

Source: Adapted from Lawrence Baum, *The Supreme Court* (Washington, D.C.: Congressional Quarterly Press, 1981), p. 10.

courts moving. One Supreme Court justice is assigned to supervise certain activities in each of the 12 circuits of the system.

A few additional federal courts deal with cases from the District of Columbia and the U.S. territories, such as Guam and the Virgin Islands. These courts function in much the same way as the state courts. Each of the specialized courts shown in Figure 15–1 works in the subject area indicated by its title.

Original Jurisdiction and Appellate Jurisdiction

Both the federal and state court systems have a variety of **trial courts** and one or more levels of **appellate courts.** Trial courts have original jurisdiction and hear cases for the first time. The trial may take place before a judge and jury or before judge alone. Appellate courts hear appeals from the losing party in a trial court.

In the federal court system, district courts are the primary trial courts. Courts of appeals are purely appellate. Except in cases involving foreign diplomats or in conflicts between two states of the United States—both quite rare—the U.S. Supreme Court is strictly an appellate court.

In the states, there are two types of trial court: general jurisdiction (different states use different names), which hear all kinds of cases, and limited jurisdiction (usually county or municipal courts). Most of the states have two levels of appellate courts, the top level being the state supreme court.

The formally defined jurisdiction of the federal courts is broad, though the Supreme Court has been seeking to limit access to the federal court system in recent years. All cases involving the Constitution, statutes passed by Congress, treaties involving the United States, and admiralty or maritime matters can automatically be brought before the federal courts. It does not matter who the parties are. A case can also be brought before the federal courts if it involves any of the following parties: (1) the United States, (2) two or more states, (3) a state and one or more citizens of another state, (4) citizens of different states in disputes involving more than $10,000 (an amount that can be changed by statute), (5) a state or citizens of a state and foreign nations or citizens, and (6) foreign diplomats.

Federal courts address a wide variety of subjects. Congress has passed laws in a vast array of areas; this opens those areas to the scrutiny of the federal courts. Congress can remove appellate jurisdiction from the Supreme Court (it has done so only once). It cannot, however, remove jurisdiction from the federal court system as a whole. That jurisdiction is specified in the Constitution. Nor can Congress alter the kinds of cases that can be originally brought before the Supreme Court. These are also specified in the Constitution.

Hierarchy and the Flow of Judicial Business

Each of the states has a court system that only occasionally comes into contact with the federal courts. Each of the states has its own judicial hierarchy and rules. Only when cases involving federal laws or the U.S. Constitution come up in state courts can those cases ultimately be reviewed by the U.S. Supreme Court.

As we saw earlier, the federal district courts have original jurisdiction. Only some cases from the Interstate Commerce Commission come to them on appeal. District court cases are usually heard by a single judge. All jury trials in the federal court system are held in district courts, though not all district court cases involve jury trials. The federal courts of appeals get their cases from three sources: district courts, the Tax Court, and the independent regulatory commissions. The majority come from district courts, where the losing party has the right of appeal to a court of appeals. Most cases in the courts of appeals are decided by three judges.

The Supreme Court gets its cases from four sources: state supreme courts in the instances mentioned earlier, the Court of Appeals for the Federal Circuit (a court created in 1982 to hear appeals in cases involving patents, trademarks, international trade, and claims against the federal government), the district courts in some cases, and the courts of appeals. Most of the cases come from state supreme courts and federal courts of appeals. The Supreme Court has a number of procedures for deciding what cases it will hear. The most visible and most influential judicial pronouncements on public policy—those from the Supreme Court—are made on subjects chosen at the Court's discretion.

Lawyers have some effect on what questions the Supreme Court will consider. They may elect not to appeal certain cases if they think they will get a negative result. For instance, beginning in the mid-1970s, lawyers saw that the Supreme Court was becoming more hostile to broadening the scope of individual rights. They therefore chose to keep certain issues away from the Court, and instead sought to keep cases in state supreme courts or simply accepted a loss rather than risk an unfavorable, precedent-setting decision by the Supreme Court.

The losers in court suits—even if they lose in the Supreme Court—have other avenues of appeal, mainly Congress and the state legislatures. For example, a number of Supreme Court decisions limited the impact of the federal Freedom of Information Act. The act was supposed to make more information on the internal workings of the federal government available to the public. Those pushing for maximum availability induced Congress to make the law more explicit. In effect, a successful appeal to Congress overthrew the Supreme Court decisions.

Because it can take many years and a great deal of effort and expense for a case to reach the Supreme Court, the cases that get there tend to represent persistent legal problems or powerful social concerns, or both. Yet the parties concerned—and the public—may not be satisfied with the Court's final decision. The decision may settle only the immediate dispute, and broader implications of the decision may be vague or unclear. The Court may change its mind in whole or in part in later decisions. Interpretations of the decision may vary among various lower federal courts and state courts.

State courts in particular have considerable latitude in areas that also come to the U.S. Supreme Court. In the area of constitutional rights, for instance, state courts may conclude that state constitutions set stricter standards than the federal Constitution. In recent years, a number of state supreme courts have followed this course of action as a number of national Supreme Court decisions have restricted earlier, broader definitions of individual rights.

Increasing Workload

The federal courts face a large and growing workload. The Supreme Court *docket* (list of cases awaiting attention) grew fourfold from the late 1930s to the 1970s. It stabilized during the 1970s and then increased a bit in the early 1980s. In the 1985 term (1985–86 on the calendar), a total of

5,158 cases were on the Supreme Court docket. The Supreme Court has almost total discretion over which cases it accepts. This authority, granted by statute in 1925, allows the Court to keep its caseload manageable. In the 1985 term, for example, the Court heard oral argument on only 171 cases. Most of the other cases in which Supreme Court review was sought were denied a hearing, dismissed, or withdrawn. In 161 cases, the Court's decision included written, signed opinions in which reasoning behind the decisions was stated. Such cases include both concurring and dissenting opinions. No signed opinions were provided in the other 10 cases.

District courts and courts of appeals must hear all cases brought to them that are properly within their jurisdictions. Their workload has increased dramatically. Between 1960 and 1985, the number of cases in courts of appeals increased from fewer than 4,000 a year to over 33,000. In that same period, the number of civil cases filed in district courts increased from few than 60,000 a year to over 270,000. The criminal case workload of the district courts increased from 27,000 in 1960 to over 41,000 by 1975. In 1985, it was about 38,500.

Much of the increase in civil cases has stemmed from laws in the social welfare and civil rights fields that create questions requiring interpretation by federal courts and also create new opportunities for **class action suits** (suits brought on behalf of a whole class of people rather than just a single person) (Ball, 1980). The Civil Rights acts of 1960 and 1964, the Freedom of Information Act of 1966, the Federal Coal Mine Health and Safety Act of 1969, the Occupational Safety and Health Act of 1970, the National Environmental Policy Act of 1970, the Truth-in-Lending Act of 1970, the Equal Employment Opportunity Act of 1972, and the Consumer Products Safety Act of 1972 all helped increase the number of cases coming to the federal court system.

More than 16,000 people work in the federal court system. In addition to judges, there are staff members for the judges (clerks, secretaries), probation officers, bankruptcy referees, U.S. magistrates, court criers, court reporters, nurses, interpreters, and custodians. The most important staff members are the law clerks who help judges in all of the federal courts and in major state courts deal with the mound of business before them. These law clerks are temporary workers, the best graduates of good law schools, who serve for a year or two before starting their own careers. They have some influence on some cases, but they tend to exaggerate their own importance (Woodward and Armstrong, 1979).

COURTS AND POLITICS

Since courts are important makers and interpreters of public policy, it follows that they are enmeshed in the political life of the nation. Some individual judges and justices also remain active and visible public figure outside their courtrooms. Supreme Court Justices William Douglas, Warren Burger, and William Rehnquist, for example, made numerous public speeches in recent decades. When Louis Brandeis was on the Supreme

The pursuit of policy goals. Supreme Court Justice Louis Brandeis helped finance the activities of Harvard Law School professor Felix Frankfurter in the 1920s and 1930s. Frankfurter later also became a member of the Supreme Court.

Court (1916–39), he financed the activities of Felix Frankfurter, then a law professor at Harvard and later a Supreme Court justice himself, in behalf of policy goals important to Brandeis (Murphy, 1982). A number of Supreme Court justices have advised presidents privately even while on bench.

The federal courts are involved in politics in many ways. Choosing federal judges is a highly political process. Both the party identification and the geographic origin of judges affect their decisions. The Supreme Court displays a special kind of politics that is related to small-group decision making. The federal courts are involved in highly political relations with Congress, the executive branch, and interest groups. Even the structure of the federal courts is, in part, political, a point we will discuss later in the chapter.

The Selection of Federal Judges

The president appoints federal judges to lifetime terms. Only nonconfirmation by Congress can prevent those appointments. Only congressional impeachment (used a handful of times in our entire national history) can force a federal judge from his or her position. The power to shape the federal judiciary through appointments is one of the most important powers of the president.

What kinds of people do presidents appoint to federal courts? Between 1789 and 1988, 104 individuals have sat on the U.S. Supreme Court. All but one of them have been male, and all but one of them have been white. Most of them have been Protestants, have come from upper social strata, and have had a great deal of prior experience in politics and public office.

A black Supreme Court justice. President Lyndon Johnson and the first black Supreme Court justice, Thurgood Marshall, just after Marshall took the oath of office in August 1965. Marshall's family is at the left of the picture.

Other federal judges often come from lower social strata than do Supreme Court justices. But they are still drawn from the more privileged parts of society, and they also tend to have had a lot of political experience and prominence. Most federal district judges are natives of the state in which they sit, and most judges of the courts of appeals are natives of the region for which they are responsible. All of the recent presidents have appointed people to federal judgeships who have served as judges or prosecutors (or both) and who have also been activists in their own political party (Goldman, 1983, 1985, 1987).

Supreme Court justices

Supreme Court appointments always attract attention. This is because observers and informed citizens—as well as government officials—know that these appointments help shape the general philosophy of the Court, which in turn influences its specific decision.

Some Supreme Court appointments attract special attention because they are unusual in some way. Examples in this century include the first Jewish justice (Louis Brandeis, appointed by President Woodrow Wilson in 1916), the first black justice (Thurgood Marshall, appointed by President Lyndon Johnson in 1967), and the first woman justice (Sandra Day O'Connor, appointed by President Ronald Reagan in 1981).

When a president is trying to alter the ideological complexion of the Supreme Court, his appointments also attract special attention. This was true of the appointments made by President Franklin Roosevelt in the late

A woman justice. President Ronald Reagan ended the all-male membership of the Supreme Court with his 1981 appointment of Sandra Day O'Connor. She is shown here with Reagan and Chief Justice Warren Burger after taking her oath of office.

1930s and early 1940s. It was also true of the appointments made by Ronald Reagan. Reagan wanted a more conservative Supreme Court (and federal judiciary in general) than the one he inherited. In picking Justice O'Connor in 1981, he made a start. His next appointments did not come until mid-1986, when he named Associate Justice William Rehnquist, a staunch conservative, to succeed the retiring Warren Burger as chief justice (Burger was also a conservative but had not been terribly effective in winning over other members of the Court) and Antonin Scalia to replace Rehnquist as an associate justice. Scalia, a well-known and articulate conservative, had served for several years on the federal Court of Appeals for the District of Columbia. In 1986–87, the Court did not change its collective views dramatically. Rehnquist's positions continued to be predictable and very conservative; Scalia's positions were less predictable. The liberal and moderate members of the Court, however, were all advanced in years, and Reagan clearly hoped to be able to reshape the Supreme Court further before he left office in early 1989.

Reagan had another chance to change the complexion of the Court when Justice Lewis Powell announced his immediate retirement in June 1987. This time, however, Reagan had a great deal of difficulty in nominating an acceptable candidate. He first nominated Robert Bork, a controversial court of appeals judge and a former law professor. Bork had long outspokenly advocated very conservative views. The Senate Judiciary Committee held lengthy confirmation hearings at which Bork and a number of his supporters and opponents testified. At the same time, both the pro-Bork and anti-Bork forces engaged in mass-media campaigns designed to get important segments of public opinion to express themselves to their senators. The committee voted narrowly against confirming Bork

President Reagan moves the Court in a conservative direction. In 1986, Reagan introduces William Rehnquist and Antonin Scalia, his nominees for the positions of chief justice and associate justice, and their wives. Rehnquist and Scalia were confirmed in September 1986.

but sent the nomination to the full Senate for debate and a vote. On October 23, 1987, after acrimonious debate, 58 senators (52 Democrats and 6 Republicans) voted against confirmation and 42 senators (40 Republicans and 2 Democrats) voted for confirmation. The Bork nomination was dead. Bork resigned from the court of appeals several months later.

The Administration quickly nominated another law professor, Douglas Ginsburg, to the vacancy. That nomination self-destructed in days when it was revealed that Ginsburg had smoked marijuana on a few occasions some years earlier even while he was already a professor at the Harvard Law School. Before the Senate began processing the nomination, it was withdrawn.

Finally, the administration succeeded in its third try, when it nominated Anthony Kennedy, a respected conservative court of appeals judge. Kennedy did not espouse Bork's controversial and aggressive views. The Sen-

A controversial nominee. Robert Bork, nominated as a Supreme Court justice by President Reagan, was rejected by the Senate in 1987 after a fierce battle over his nomination. Some of Bork's judicial decisions and views were considered too conservative by many Senate liberals and moderates.

ate Judiciary Committee unanimously recommended confirmation, and the full Senate quickly followed its lead by vote of 97 to 0 on February 3, 1988. Kennedy joined the Court soon thereafter.

In general, presidents seek people for the Supreme Court who agree with them ideologically and belong to the same political party. Presidents cannot always predict ideological agreement, however, because the business of the Court is so different from the business of the president and because of the force of legal precedent in helping shape specific Supreme Court decisions. Discussion among the nine justices is also important in helping shape their views. Most presidents have been embarrassed or angered by the decisions of their appointees on at least some occasions.

Still, presidents can change the general tenor of Supreme Court decisions over time. After Franklin Roosevelt appointed a number of justices, the Court's views on civil liberties and on the government's power to regulate the economy changed significantly. The Court then sanctioned government regulation that it had prevented before and became more active in protecting individual liberties such as free speech. President Nixon's appointments helped produce a Court that was more reluctant to define constitutionally protected liberties broadly. President Reagan hoped that a Court led by Chief Justice Rehnquist would become even more conservative.

The Senate must confirm the President's choices for Supreme Court seats by a majority vote, as is true for all presidential judicial nominations. Presidents consult with leading members of Congress, party leaders, trusted friends, and even sitting justices in deciding whom to nominate for Supreme Court vacancies. Presidents also take a very personal interest in their choices because the Supreme Court wields such great power over public policy.

As we have seen in the discussion of the Bork nomination, the Senate does not confirm Supreme Court nominations routinely and automati-

A short-lived nominee to the Supreme Court. In late 1987, media coverage of his admission to smoking marijuana while a law professor at Harvard caused Douglas Ginsburg to withdraw his name before the confirmation process could begin.

cally. Nixon's nominations of Clement Haynsworth in 1969 and G. Harrold Carswell in 1970 were rejected. During our history, the Senate has turned down 12 Supreme Court nominees. Another 16 nominations failed because either the president withdrew the nomination or the Senate postponed action or failed to act on it.

The Senate's successful opposition to 28 appointments demonstrates that it has not been a rubber stamp for the president. Rejections have occurred for various reasons (Abraham, 1985; Scigliano, 1971). In some cases, the Senate opposed not the nominee but the president making the nomination. In other cases, the nominee was involved with a highly debatable public issue or had expressed strong partisan views and so was too controversial. The Senate has also used opposition to a nominee to express its dislike of current Court decisions. And some nominees have been turned down because their qualifications or ability appeared to be too low.

Other federal judges

The appointment of federal judges for district courts and courts of appeals is more complicated than the appointment of Supreme Court justices both because those judges are more numerous and less visible and because politicians, especially members of Congress, urge their personal choices on the president. Again, the Senate must confirm presidential nominees. A number of people become involved in negotiating the choice of such judges with the president's representative, usually the attorney general. Incumbent federal judges (including Supreme Court members) have influence. Various political party leaders in addition to senators often make their views public. The Standing Committee on the Federal Judiciary of the American Bar Association (ABA) makes suggestions, and the candidates themselves usually take part.

President Eisenhower told his attorney general to give the ABA committee veto power over candidates. Yet he chose a few whom the ABA had rated "not qualified." The ABA has at times pressed for automatic

TABLE 15–1   Presidential appointments of women, blacks, and Hispanics to courts of appeals and district courts, 1963–1986

President	Total number of appointments	Women		Blacks		Hispanics	
		Number	Percent	Number	Percent	Number	Percent
Johnson, 1963–69	162	3	2%	7	4%	3	2%
Nixon, 1969–74	224	1	*	6	3	2	1
Ford, 1974–77	64	1	2	3	5	1	2
Carter, 1977–81	258	40	16	37	14	16	6
Reagan, 1981–86	287	24	8	5	2	12	4

*Less than 0.5 percent.
Sources: Calculated from data in Sheldon Goldman, "Reagan's Judicial Appointments at Mid-Term: Shaping the Bench in His Own Image," *Judicature* 66 (March 1983): 334–47; and Goldman, "Reagan's Second Term Judicial Appointments: The Battle at Midway," *Judicature* 70 (April–May 1987): 324–39.

veto power. But the political realities of the appointment traditions and the importance of the jobs have worked against that. Presidents do heed ABA recommendations, however.

In general, if a senator of the president's party opposes a nominee for a federal judgeship in his or her state, the Senate will reject that choice. This practice is called **senatorial courtesy.** The practice does not mean that senators can name the winning candidate for an opening, but it does mean that they can usually prevent an appointment.

Political and ideological controversy can break out over nominations to federal judgeships. In early 1986, for example, the Senate Judiciary Committee rejected one Reagan nominee, Jefferson B. Sessions III, largely because a majority of the committee found him to be insensitive to racial issues. This was only the second time in 48 years that the committee had rejected such a nomination. At about the same time, the committee reported another Reagan nominee, Daniel Manion, to the floor without recommendation. After intense maneuvering on the Senate floor, Manion's nomination was narrowly approved.

As they do with the Supreme Court nominations, presidents and their advisers try to pick people for federal judgeships whose views are like their own. But presidents must also pay a variety of political debts and make a number of calculations in making appointments. For example, President Kennedy appointed a number of southern segregationists to federal judgeships to build southern support in Congress for legislative initiatives outside the civil rights area.

Until very recently, few women, blacks, or Hispanics served as judges in the federal judiciary. President Carter had a number of new judgeships to fill and made a determined effort to increase the representation of these groups. Table 15–1 contains information on the number and percentage of appointments to courts of appeals and district courts that went to women, blacks, and Hispanics under the last five presidents. Carter was the most active in appointing individuals from all three categories. Reagan was the least interested in finding black nominees.

The most reliable predictor of who will get appointed to openings on the federal bench is party affiliation. Presidents give few of these prized positions to members of the other party. With the exception of Gerald Ford, all of the presidents beginning with Franklin Roosevelt in 1933 made more than 90 percent of their appointments to district court and appeals court vacancies from their own party. Ronald Reagan made 95 percent of his appointments to seats on district courts and appeals courts from his own party.

Ronald Reagan's impact on the federal judiciary will be great and long-lasting. He increased and made more formal the White House role in the selection of judicial nominees (Goldman, 1985). By the end of his second term, he had named more than half of all the federal district court and appeals court judges.

The Impact of Party and Public Opinion

Party affiliation is important not only in the appointment of judges but also in influencing the kinds of decisions that those judges make (Goldman, 1975; Nagel, 1961; Richardson and Vines, 1970; Carp and Rowland, 1983). Democratic judges are generally more liberal than Republican judges, especially on economic issues. In the 1950s and 1960s the decisions of Democratic judges were particularly supportive of organized labor.

After 1968, the differences between Democratic and Republican judges on civil liberties questions became more pronounced (Rowland and Carp, 1980). Democratic judges were likely to favor the defendant in criminal cases; to favor minorities, aliens, or women in class action suits on discrimination; and to favor individuals rather than governments in cases involving freedom of speech or religion.

Public opinion, both local and national, also affects the decisions of federal courts (Barnum, 1985). Consider the civil rights cases brought in southern federal courts in the 1950s and early 1960s. At that time, blacks were more likely to win in areas with a small black population and were more likely to lose in areas with a large black population. This pattern repeated the general southern politics of the day: The most intense attempts to prolong white domination occurred in areas where the black population was large (Richardson and Vines, 1970: 95–100). In later years, as southern politics in general became more moderate, this relationship grew much weaker (Giles and Walker, 1975).

Changing national public opinion about the Vietnam War was paralleled by the changing behavior of federal district judges in sentencing convicted draft evaders (Cook, 1977, 1979; Kritzer, 1979). As public opposition to the war grew, these judges became more and more likely to give lighter sentences—sentences as mild as probation.

Politics within the Supreme Court

When more than one judge must decide a case, the internal politics of negotiation helps explain the decision. Nowhere is this truer than on the Supreme Court. The nine justices are keenly aware of one another's views. As Walter Murphy, a leading scholar of the Court, has said so well, "The Supreme Court operates not only by principled persuasion but also by negotiation, even bargaining. That statement is undoubtedly true now, as it was in the beginning and perhaps ever shall be" (*Washington Post,* December 16,1979). The accompanying box gives the views of one recent justice on how bargaining occurs. When he made the comments he was a sitting member of the Court.

The justices must agree (though not unanimously), first, which cases to hear; second, who wins and who loses in each case; and, third, what legal reasoning should be used in support of each decision. Choosing which cases to hear entails important political considerations. The justices may delay making a decision in a substantive area until a case comes along that they agree presents the issues clearly. Or justices who favor changing a previous court ruling may oppose hearing a case that presents the same issues until they are sure they can win.

Negotiation plays a large role in arriving at decisions on who wins and who loses. Because the justices reach their decisions in private, it is difficult to pinpoint who persuaded whom to vote in a particular way, but intense persuasive activity undoubtedly takes place. The chief justice can be especially influential in shaping Court decisions (Rohde and Spaeth, 1976). On highly controversial issues, the chief justice may think it important that the Court decision be unanimous. He may stall and maneuver until everyone agrees, even if this means delaying a ruling for a considerable time. Chief Justice Earl Warren followed this strategy to ensure the unanimity of the 1954 decision in *Brown* v. *Board of Education,* which declared state-enforced school segregation unconstitutional. Realizing how important and how potentially divisive this decision would be in society, he thought that the Court should present the country with a unanimous decision and a single opinion.

Negotiation over the nature of the Court's opinions, which formally lay out the reasoning behind a decision, is particularly important. The chief justice can exert influence to shape these opinions to suit his own policy preferences (Slotnick, 1979). He has the undoubted power to assign the writing of majority opinions when he is in the majority, and Warren Burger even made such assignments when he was in the minority. Justices who disagree with the majority often write dissenting opinions. Justices who agree with the outcome but base their judgment on different reason-

WORDS AND IDEAS

What Really Goes on at the Supreme Court

The Court is a place where justices, and their small staffs, work extremely long hours; where the work is sometimes tedious, though always intellectually demanding; where we take our responsibility with the utmost seriousness; and where there is little or no time for socializing. . . .

We rarely discuss cases with each other before going to conference. After a tentative vote has been taken, the drafting of opinions is assigned to the individual justices. When a justice is satisfied with his draft, he circulates it to the other chambers. Comments usually are made by exchanges of memoranda, although we feel free to visit justices and discuss differences. There is less of this than one would like, primarily because of our heavy caseload and the logistical difficulties of talking individually to eight other justices.

The process that I have described actually may take months after a case is argued. The preparation of an opinion often requires painstaking research, drafting, and revising, and additional efforts to resolve differences among justices to the extent this is feasible.

It is this unstructured and informal process—the making of the decision itself, from the first conference until it is handed down in open Court—that simply cannot take place in public. . . .

The nine justices often are portrayed as fighting and feuding with each other.

This is a wholly inaccurate picture of the relationships at the Court. At the personal level there is genuine cordiality. No justice will deny this. We lunch together frequently, visit in each other's homes, celebrate birthdays, and enjoy kidding each other during our long and demanding conferences. . . .

We do indeed have strong professional differences about many of our cases. These are exposed for the public to see. Unlike, for example, the executive branch, we record fully our disagreements in dissenting opinions. Frequently the language of a dissent is not a model of temperate discourse. We fight hard for our professional views. But, contrary to what one may read, these differences reflect no lack of respect for the members of the Court with whom we disagree. In the course of a given term, I find myself more than once in sharp disagreement with every other justice.

It is fortunate that our system, unlike that in many other countries, invites and respects the function of dissenting opinions. The very process of dissent assures a rigorous testing of the majority view within the Court itself, and reduces the chance of arbitrary decision making. Moreover, as "Court-watchers" know, the forceful dissent of today may attract a majority vote in some future year.

Source: Lewis F. Powell, Jr., remarks delivered at the Southwestern Legal Foundation, May 1, 1980, in *Views from the Bench*, ed. Mark W. Cannon and David M. O'Brien (Chatham, N.J.: Chatham House Publishers, 1985), pp. 71–73.

ing may write concurring opinions. But only majority opinions have the force of law.

Political Pressure from outside the Court System

Federal judges can afford to be independent in many important ways. Except for rare cases of personal misbehavior, they have lifetime appointments. But they are not completely isolated from society and from the other institutions with which they must interact. Social trends will eventually be reflected in their decisions. The evidence on sentences for draft evaders, noted above, supports this view.

As we have seen, Congress helps determine the makeup of the federal bench through its involvement in judicial appointments. Congress also determines the number of federal judges, the number of federal courts, and the structure of appellate jurisdiction. It has often added new judgeships to create new jobs for party loyalists as well as to facilitate the processing of a growing judicial workload. Congress can also limit court jurisdiction or the impact of specific decisions by statute. We will return to these areas of congressional influence when we address general limits to judicial power in a later section.

The executive branch has one major political access route to the federal courts other than its appointment power. This involves the relationship between the federal courts and government lawyers. U.S. attorneys—the government prosecutors in each federal judicial district—and their aides deal closely with the lower federal courts. The degree of this closeness varies greatly from judge to judge. Some judges identify so closely with the office of the U.S. attorney that they want it to succeed in its prosecutions. They offer advice on cases to prosecute, strategies to adopt, and other details of the prosecutors' role. Such identification is aided by the fact that both attorneys and judges are usually party activists; moreover, many of the attorneys aspire to a judgeship later in their career (Goldman and Jahnige, 1985; Eisenstein, 1978).

The *solicitor general* (the chief advocate for the Justice Department in court cases) works closely with the Supreme Court. He generally uses restraint in petitioning the Court for hearings, thereby increasing his chances for favorable treatment when he does petition. Overly aggressive solicitor generals can diminish administration influence.

Interest groups try to influence federal court decisions by having their legal staffs work on specific test cases. The cases in which the Supreme Court outlawed racial segregation in public schools were sponsored by lawyers for the National Association for the Advancement of Colored People (NAACP).

Interest groups give judges information and arguments in two other ways. First, in a pending case, an interest group may file a brief as **amicus curiae,** a friend of the court. This is a written argument on some or all of the points in the case. Even though the group filing such a brief is not

A fifth-grade public school teacher and his students pose for a class picture. The racial balance in public schools changed as a direct result of a 1954 Supreme Court decision (Brown v. Board of Education) outlawing school segregation.

directly party to the case, judges read and absorb some of the information that the brief contains. In the *Bakke* case (1978), which dealt with reverse discrimination, about 60 *amicus curiae* briefs were filed. Conservative interest groups have used this technique increasingly in recent years (O'Connor and Epstein, 1983). The existence of *amicus curiae* briefs increases the chances that the Court will agree to hear a case (Caldeira and Wright, 1987). Second, interest groups generate and help place articles favorable to their points of view in periodicals that judges read, such as law reviews.

FEDERAL COURT POLICY-MAKING

Federal courts are important policymakers. In addressing this fact, we first summarize the general sources of judicial power in the United States. Second, we note that, like all U.S. governing institutions, courts are limited in what they can do. Third, we sketch the history of the Supreme Court in terms of its general power and of its activity level in important policy realms. Finally, we consider the general scope of action of the entire federal court system.

Sources of Judicial Power

Much general power comes to the federal court system because of its great popular prestige. People—including government officials—respect federal judges at all levels and are usually willing to comply with their decisions. The most visible and dramatic power held by the federal judiciary is the power of judicial review—that is, the power to declare actions by other officials and units of government (including the president, Congress, federal bureaucracies, and state and local officials and agencies) to be unconstitutional. In addition, federal courts can not only prevent governmental actions but they can also require specific actions, particularly through class action suits. Supreme Court justices enhance their use of judicial power and maximize the impact of their decisions by selecting the cases they hear with great care.

Limits on Judicial Power

Like the rest of American governmental power, judicial power is immersed in the elaborate checks and balances system devised by the founders and expanded by subsequent political practice.

Inherent limitations

The range of issues addressed by nonjudicially generated policies is almost unlimited. Courts, however, deliberately avoid some issues, especially (since 1937) broad economic policy and foreign relations. Many judicially originated policies are visible mainly to those directly involved and to the legal community. Nonjudicial policies are likely to be more visible to more people more quickly. Judges necessarily restrict their immediate impact to the parties in a case; they achieve a broader impact by implication or by the use of precedent in subsequent cases.

Congressional limits

In addition to its role in the appointment of judges and justices, Congress has five means of influencing judicial decisions. Those means requiring statutory action, of course, also involve the president.

First, Congress can try to reverse decisions by statute. Sometimes the Supreme Court will, in effect, say that it would welcome a new statute clarifying congressional intent. Congress may also pass legislation directly opposed to the will of the judiciary.

Second, Congress can show its displeasure with federal court decisions by refusing to increase the pay or benefits classes of judges. Congress cannot, however, decrease the compensation of judges already in office.

Third, Congress can alter the structure of the federal judiciary. The Constitution gives Congress power to create the federal judiciary. According to the Constitution, there must be a Supreme Court. But other than that, Congress has had a free hand in shaping the federal judiciary. Even the number of Supreme Court justices can be changed by legislation. But, the failure of an attempt in 1937 to increase the Court's size from 9 to 15 makes it seem likely that this will not happen.

Several features of federal court structure are subject to statutory change: the number of judges, the number and jurisdiction of courts, the location of courts, and the geographic makeup of appellate circuits. All of these features have sparked political debate at one time or another. A recent instance in which court structure became a live political issue occurred in the 1960s. Southern conservatives in Congress tried to redraw appellate court boundaries to put a greater number of southern states into a conservative (that is segregationist) circuit. Integrationists in Congress blocked this move (Richardson and Vines, 1970: 17–18). Dividing the circuit covering the Deep South was again considered in the late 1970s. There was some controversy, but the issue was resolved with relative ease and Congress made the division.

Fourth, Congress can propose constitutional amendments that would reverse unpalatable Court decisions. Three fourths of the state legislatures must ultimately approve the proposed amendments. Irate members of Congress often threaten to initiate constitutional amendments (for example, in reaction to decisions banning prayer in public schools or striking down state laws that make abortion illegal on constitutional grounds). But actual attempts at amendment are rare, and only a few such attempts ultimately result in constitutional amendments. The 11th Amendment (adopted in 1795) clarified federal jurisdiction over suits against states. This came after a Court ruling on a matter disturbing to the states. The 13th, 14th, and 15th amendments were adopted after the Civil War. They were needed to reverse the Court's statement in the *Dred Scott* case (1857) that blacks were not citizens. The 16th Amendment (adopted in 1913) allowed a federal income tax. This came after the Court had ruled such a tax unconstitutional. The 26th Amendment (adopted in 1971) lowered the voting age to 18 for all elections. This followed a Court ruling that Congress could lower the age for federal elections but not for state and local elections.

Fifth, Congress can change the appellate jurisdiction of the Supreme Court by statute. This has happened only once, though the potential remains. After the Civil War, Congress prevented the Supreme Court from considering some Reconstruction laws by removing them from appellate jurisdiction. In the 1960s, some conservatives in Congress were so upset by Supreme Court decisions expanding the constitutional rights of accused criminals that they tried, without success, to limit the Supreme Court's jurisdiction in some criminal matters coming from state courts. Additional efforts—also unsuccessful—have been made by conservatives in Congress to limit Supreme Court jurisdiction over school desegregation and school prayer.

Presidential limits

As noted, the president plays a role in all of the congressional limits that require statutory action. His power over appointments is, of course, a critical limit on future decisions of the judiciary. In addition, the executive branch must implement court rulings in some major areas of court action. Courts can only issue guidelines and make pronouncements. The president and the agencies of the executive branch have the tools for turning these pronouncements into reality. Presidents usually defer to court opinions, though the vigor with which they order executive-branch implementation has varied enormously. Early in the 19th century, President Andrew Jackson had this to say about a Supreme Court decision that he did not like: "John Marshall [the chief justice, who wrote the opinion in this case] has made his decision; now let him enforce it." Subsequent presidents have been less outspoken than Jackson, but the executive branch still has the power to limit the impact of court decisions.

Noncompliance with court decisions

Individuals usually comply with court decisions. Once they have exhausted all possible appeals, they usually go to prison if sentenced or pay their fine if fined. However, when courts speak to other governmental institutions—other courts, police departments, agencies, Congress, the president—compliance is more variable. This variability stems from a number of causes. The decisions may be unclear; court decisions are usually no clearer than other statements of policy, such as statutes or presidential speeches. Other institutions may interpret the decisions in ways other than the court thought it intended. Such differing interpretations may be genuine, or they may stem from a desire to evade a ruling. In short, there is nothing self-enforcing about court decisions, including those of the Supreme Court.

Moreover, court decisions do not necessarily have an immediate impact. In recent years, for example, broad Supreme Court rulings in many vital areas have been implemented slowly and in differing ways, and sometimes not at all (Wasby, 1976). These rulings include the 1954 ruling declaring racial segregation in public schools unconstitutional, the 1973 ruling that women have a right to abortion (Bond and Johnson, 1982), ruling that prayers in public schools are unconstitutional (Muir, 1968), and rulings regarding the details of police procedures in handling accused criminals (Milner, 1971).

The decisions of lower federal courts result in even more noncompliant behavior then do those of the Supreme Court. In recent years, for example, the Social Security Administration has denied benefits to many individuals even though cases involving individuals in similar circumstances resulted in federal district court decisions that these individuals were eligible for benefits. The bureaucratic agency would not generalize from the rulings of the district courts, which upset federal judges.

The Growth of Supreme Court Power and Activism

The Constitution sets up the federal judiciary in very few words. With two short paragraphs in Article III, the framers created a Supreme Court, left the creation of other federal courts to Congress, and defined the jurisdiction of the federal courts. In 1789, the first year of the new government, Congress quickly fleshed out the federal courts through the Judiciary Act.

The system of checks and balances created in Philadelphia left the courts in an ambiguous position, particularly with regard to interpreting acts of Congress. The courts were also in the middle of the debate between federal and state power.

Many of the framers felt that the courts had the power to interpret acts of Congress. They also felt that the courts should be able to declare laws unconstitutional because the Constitution was supreme over all statutes. In *The Federalist,* Alexander Hamilton argued that the Supreme Court would, in fact, have the power to review congressional statutes and declare them unconstitutional. However, not everyone agreed with him.

In the famous case of *Marbury* v. *Madison* (1803), discussed in detail in Chapter 2, Supreme Court itself addressed this issue. Writing for a unanimous Court, Chief Justice John Marshall declared that the Supreme Court did, indeed, have the power to review acts of Congress. This declaration applied specifically to a law in which Congress had expanded the Supreme Court's original jurisdiction beyond that contained in the Constitution. The Court ruled that Congress had erred in giving it jurisdiction that properly belonged with the district courts. In doing so, it boldly articulated the principle of **judicial review**—the right of the Supreme Court to declare acts of Congress unconstitutional and therefore null and void.

After *Marbury,* the Court was shy about using this explicitly claimed power. It did not again declare a congressional act unconstitutional until 1857. In that year, in the *Dred Scott* decision, the Court held that the Missouri Compromise, which distinguished between slave states and free states, was unconstitutional. The Court declared that blacks were not citizens. By the autumn of 1985, the Supreme Court had made 134 declarations that all or part of a federal statute was unconstitutional (Abraham, 1986). A few of these declarations concerned major statutes: the Missouri Compromise of 1820, the first federal income tax, federal child labor laws, the first federal attempt to set minimum wages, and much of the early New Deal legislation in the economic realm. But most of the statutes affected by Court declarations of unconstitutionality were of minor importance.

The Supreme Court's findings of unconstitutional federal statutes have not been evenly spaced. Until 1864, only two such findings had been made. Between 1864 and 1936, the Court made 71 such findings. In the 1920s and early 1930s, the court became particularly aggressive in limiting the federal government's power in the economic realm. Beginning in 1937, however, it abandoned its attempts to stop the growth of the federal government's economic power. Between 1937 and 1953, it became almost as shy about declaring federal statutes unconstitutional as it had been before the Civil War. After 1953, however, it gradually became more aggressive. From 1954 through 1958, it found federal laws unconstitutional in four cases. From 1960 through 1969, the Court headed by Chief Justice

Earl Warren made 21 more findings of unconstitutionality with regard to federal statutes. From 1969 through the fall of 1985, the Court led by Chief Justice Warren Burger made 33 such findings. The post-1954 findings of unconstitutionality have been primarily in the realm of individual rights.

The Supreme Court applied the power of judicial review not only to national statutes but also to state laws and local ordinances. It has declared about 1,100 such laws and ordinances unconstitutional (Baum, 1985).

Prior to the Civil War, the Court boldly upheld the supremacy of the national government in relation to state governments. In the landmark case of *McCulloch* v. *Maryland* (1819) the Court, again speaking through John Marshall, made two vital rulings. It upheld a broad interpretation of the national government's power to legislate, and it declared that state laws infringing on that power were unconstitutional. These rulings are still the judicial underpinning of the American conception of federalism; an underpinning made secure once the Civil War had ensured the nation's continued existence.

The Scope of Action

In general, a government is one of the parties in cases that help shape the nature of public policy. The federal courts make rulings in a number of major substantive areas. We will characterize some of these areas briefly to illustrate the breadth of judicial action, and we will provide a few examples of the practical consequences.

Most important, the federal courts constantly deal with cases concerning competing claims about liberties, rights, and the meaning of equality. Chapter 19 is devoted to this vital topic.

Although the federal courts have not sought to restrain the economic power of the federal government since 1937, they continue to be involved in cases concerning economic matters—labor-management relations, antitrust, environmental regulation, and the regulation of stocks, bonds, and other securities. Government regulatory activity usually generates such cases.

The basic principles of *McCulloch* have not been challenged in subsequent rulings, but the federal courts still have to resolve disputes about the specific meaning of American federalism. In February 1985, for example, the Supreme Court, by a 5-to-4 vote, reversed a 1976 ruling in a decision that was widely regarded as strengthening federal power at the expense of state and local governments. The decision held that federal minimum wage and maximum hours standards cover the employees of publicly owned mass-transit systems. The decision restored all state and local employees to coverage by the federal Fair Labor Standards Act, from which they had been exempted in a 1976 case. The decision aroused the ire of many state and local officials.

THE PRACTICE OF POLITICS

Courts and Social Policy: A Sampler

In just the past few years, courts have struck down laws requiring a period of in-state residence as a condition of eligibility for welfare. They have invalidated presumptions of child support arising from the presence in the home of a "substitute father." Federal district courts have laid down elaborate standards for food handling, hospital operations, recreation facilities, inmate employment and education, sanitation, and laundry, painting, lighting, plumbing, and renovation in some prisons; they have ordered other prisons closed. Courts have established equally comprehensive programs of care and treatment for the mentally ill confined in hospitals. They have ordered the equalization of school expenditures on teachers' salaries, established hearing procedures for public school discipline cases, decided that bilingual education must be provided for Mex-

ican-American children, and suspended the use by school boards of the National Teacher Examination and of comparable tests for school supervisors. They have eliminated a high school diploma as a requirement for a fireman's job. They have enjoined the construction of roads and bridges on environmental grounds and suspended performance requirements for automobile tires and air bags. They have told the Farmers Home Administration to restore a disaster loan program, the Forest Service to stop the clearcutting of timber, and the Corps of Engineers to maintain the nation's nonnavigable waterways. They have been, to put it mildly, very busy, laboring in unfamiliar territory.

Source: Donald L. Horowitz, *The Courts and Social Policy* (Washington, D.C.: Brookings Institution, 1977), pp. 4–5.

Federal courts occasionally interpret the powers of the president. In 1952, the Supreme Court declared that President Truman's seizure of the nation's steel mills was unconstitutional. Truman had seized the mills because they were closed by a strike when the armed forces, then fighting in Korea, badly needed products containing steel. Truman acquiesced in the decision and returned the mills to company management. In 1974, the Supreme Court ruled unanimously that President Nixon could not withhold the Watergate tapes from the courts. Nixon also acquiesced.

In July 1986, a major Supreme Court ruling interpreted the Constitution's separation of powers principle. The Court decided, by a 7-to-2 vote, that a key provision of the Gramm-Rudman Act unconstitutionally allowed the comptroller general to decide on and enforce automatic budget

A Concorde lands at New York City's Kennedy Airport in 1977. Shortly after this landing, a federal judge ruled that the New York Port Authority could ban these supersonic aircraft from taking off and landing. Because of the noise generated by the Concordes, that ban has remained in effect at New York airports.

cuts if the president and Congress could not produce the annual deficit levels permitted by Gramm–Rudman. The Court reasoned that the comptroller general was "subservient to Congress" and thus could not be given major powers of execution, which the Constitution reserves to the president and the executive branch. As a result of this decision, Congress and the president again bore the final responsibility for determining how to reduce the deficit.

Federal judges have considerable latitude in selecting the substantive areas in which they will be most active. In the 1970s and 1980s, the federal courts in general became aggressive in a number of areas of social policy (Glazer, 1975; Horowitz, 1977). The accompanying box offers one overview. The activism of some federal district judges was particularly evident. A few examples will indicate the kinds of areas in which rulings by federal district judges have been important:

In overseeing the details of school desegregation in Boston, a federal judge issued more than 400 rulings between 1974 and 1983.

A federal judge ruled that the New York Port Authority had no power to ban Concorde supersonic jet aircraft from landing in New York City airports.

A federal judge ordered the grounding of DC–10 aircraft after a fatal crash in Chicago in 1979.

A federal judge delayed the implementation of many strip-mining regulations developed by the Interior Department's Office of Surface Mining after the passage of the federal strip-mining law in 1977.

A federal judge in 1987 held that the Veterans Administration (a federal agency) was guilty of "reckless and callous disregard of its obligations" in administering its compensation and pension programs; she appointed a special master to enforce her judgments against the agency.

HOW ACTIVE SHOULD COURTS BE?

What is the proper place of the policy activities of unelected judges in a representative democracy? Should they be active in making policy statements, or should they defer to the decisions of elected officials?

Activism versus Restraint

The relative merits of **judicial activism** versus **judicial restraint** have been debated throughout our history. Those supporting activism attribute special responsibilities to courts, especially in the area of individual rights, and think that courts can properly extend their judgments beyond the letter of the Constitution or the letter of statutes. Those supporting restraint oppose what they view as "judge-made law" and think that courts should not go beyond narrow interpretations of the Constitution or statutes.

Supporters of judicial activism are likely to believe that highly educated, experienced jurists should check the follies and shortsightedness of elected representatives, who are often more interested in gathering votes than in protecting constitutional rights. They regard jurists as the primary defenders of minority rights against unwise majority decisions, a broad concern of the nation's founders. Supporters of judicial activism are also likely to support specific judicial decisions that they think would have no chance of adoption in popular assemblies—for example, decisions safeguarding the rights of accused criminals, legalizing abortion, or banning school prayer.

Charles Black (1970), a well known Yale University law professor, puts these points quite well:

Democracy is not simple. Our government is not based on the principle that today's majority forthwith gets all it wants. . . .

To the judicial process, as to other processes in government, are committed the conservation and furtherance of democratic values. The judge's task is to identify those values in the constitutional plan, and to work them into life in the cases that reach him. Tact and wise restraint ought to temper any power, but courage and the acceptance of responsibility have their place too. . . .

The judicial power is one of the accredited means by which our nation seeks its goals, including the prime goal, indispensable to political as to personal health, of self-limitation. Intellectual freedom, freedom from irrational discrimination, immunity from unfair administration of law—these (and others similar) are constitutional interests which the Court can protect on ample doctrinal grounds. They often cannot win protection in rough-and-tumble politics. The Supreme Court is more and more finding that its highest institutional role is the guarding of such interests.

Supporters of judicial restraint argue that courts are elitist, nondemocratic parts of the governing apparatus and therefore should defer to elected officials—legislatures and executives—and that the views of voters—embodied in the decisions of elected officials—should not be frustrated by courts. These individuals are also likely to disapprove of a number of specific judicial decisions that they view as resulting from lack of restraint.

William Rehnquist (1976) now Chief Justice of the United States, stated the essence of the argument for judicial restraint in a 1976 law review article:

Under the familiar principle of judicial review, the courts in construing the Constitution are, of course, authorized to invalidate laws that have been enacted by Congress or by a state legislature but that those courts find to violate some provision of the Constitution. Nevertheless, those who have pondered the matter have always recognized that the ideal of judicial review has basically antidemocratic and antimajoritarian facets that require some justification in this nation, which prides itself on being a self-governing representative democracy. . . .

Judges . . . are a small group of fortunately situated people with a roving commission to second-guess Congress, state legislatures, and state and federal administrative officers concerning what is best for the country . . . . If there is going to be a council of revision, it ought to have at least some connection with popular feeling. Its members either ought to stand for re-election on occasion, or their terms should expire and they should be allowed to continue serving only if reappointed by a popularly elected chief executive and confirmed by a popularly elected Senate.

It is misleading to equate liberal political views with activist judges and conservative political views with restrained judges. Both very conservative judges and very liberal judges are capable of inventing reasons, concepts, and, in effect, law to reach the conclusions they favor (Shapiro, 1978). Moreover, liberal judges, like conservative judges, are quite capable of shying away from sweeping, activist pronouncements.

In our nation, controversial issues are rarely settled finally and definitively. Judicial pronouncements, as well as pronouncements by legislatures, executives, and bureaucracies, are subject to challenge and amendment. Judicial power, though significant, is also limited. Judges are not the only unelected wielders of power. Presidential appointees, career civil servants, career military officers, and staff members in Congress also wield considerable power without being elected. Courts are subject to restraint by others—both elected and unelected. Courts also restrain others—both elected and unelected. In short, there are many facets to the debate over the proper role of judges and "judge-made law" in the United States. Consequently, such simple observations as the fact that that federal judges, unlike presidents and members of Congress, are not elected should not lead to conclusions about the proper level of judicial activism or restraint. In addition, it should be borne in mind that proclamations of the virtues of either activism or restraint may be reactions to specific decisions that the observer finds undesirable or distasteful.

Public Attitudes

Do ordinary citizens care whether judges are active or restrained? What views do they have on specific judicial decisions? On courts and judges in general?

A poll commissioned in mid-1986 by the *New York Times* and CBS (the results are reported in the *New York Times,* July 13, 1986) showed that at that time Americans were about evenly divided on whether the Supreme Court was, in general, "too liberal or too conservative in its decisions": 34 percent said that it was too liberal, and 38 percent said that it was too conservative. In 1973, 35 percent felt that the Court was too liberal and 26 percent felt that it was too conservative. Between 1973 and 1986, the Court, had, in fact, become more conservative. The shift in public opinion suggests that at least some people felt that it had become too conservative.

When compared with data from earlier Gallup polls, the data of the 1986 poll also reveal changes in the public's overall rating of Supreme Court performance:

Year (data source)	Percent saying excellent or good	Percent saying fair or poor
1963 (Gallup poll)	43	41
1973 (Gallup poll)	37	51
1986 (*New York Times*–CBS poll)	46	48

These changes are probably tied to changes in general preferences for liberal or conservative policies. In 1973, following the Warren years, the Court seemed quite liberal even though the general political preferences of the public were becoming more conservative.

Two prisoners in the New Mexico State Prison relax as other inmates look on. In a number of decisions, the Supreme Court has expanded the rights of the accused and of prisoners. Decisions of this kind generally gained public favor.

Public opinion about Supreme Court decisions protecting the constitutional rights of accused criminals became gradually more favorable over the years (perhaps in part because the Burger and Rehnquist courts restricted those rights somewhat more than the Warren Court). In 1986, 34 percent of those polled felt that the Court had gone "too far in protecting the rights of people accused of crimes" and 51 percent believed that the Court "has generally done what is necessary to see that the accused are treated fairly."

Opposition to the Supreme Court's 1973 decision preventing states from making abortions illegal also moderated. Gallup polls in 1974 and 1981 found public opinion to be about evenly divided between supporters and opponents of the decision. A Gallup poll in 1983 and the *Times*-CBS poll in 1986 found somewhat more support for the decision (50 percent in favor and 43 percent opposed in 1983; 49 percent in favor and 43 percent opposed in 1986).

Courts probably do not respond to short-term changes in public opinion. Over time, however, strong changes in public opinion are likely to be reflected in the opinions of federal judges and justices. The electoral and appointment processes are the primary mechanisms for transmitting such changes to the courts. Judges are insulated from public opinion, but only partially and only for a limited time. Presidents will appoint and the Senate will confirm judges and justices who will reflect changing public values and beliefs.

Over time, too, as shown by data on public opinion about decisions on the rights of accused criminals, abortion, and civil rights, public opinion tends to become more favorable to court rulings, especially those of the Supreme Court. Courts are not only influenced by public opinion; they also help create public opinion. As with the nation's other governing institutions, there is a subtle interplay between the actions of courts and the beliefs of the public.

When questioned by pollsters, members of the public express opinions—often negative—about the Supreme Court and its decisions. However, polls also offer good evidence that the public does not know a great deal about the functioning of the federal courts or the nature of their decisions (Hearst Corporation, 1983). Because there is a strong tradition of respect for the judiciary and its policy role, general support for the courts as institutions remains strong despite negative reactions to specific decisions. The people who dislike specific decisions do not generally conclude that the courts' powers should be altered.

Evidence of the public's high regard for the judiciary is provided, for example, by a Roper poll conducted in mid-1981. This poll reported that the public perceived federal judges as more likely to act in the public interest than any other public officials or leaders of major private sectors and professions. The American people trust judges. They show little interest in philosophical debates over judicial activism and restraint but a great deal of interest in a few major judicial decision areas. Over time, they generally come to accept what the judges decide. Or if they continue to oppose particular decisions, the political process of limiting courts and judicial power results in moderated or even changed decisions. In short, the dynamic interaction among judicial decisions, judges, elected officials, and public opinion contains powerful self-correcting features.

A Question of Balance

The federal courts deal with many highly controversial social issues, such as abortion, race relations, criminal justice, the use of busing to achieve racial balance in schools, obscenity, affirmative action, the death penalty, the boundaries of legislative districts, and overcrowding in prisons. Judges differ both in their policy views on such issues and in their views about how much activism or restraint they should exercise in dealing with these issues. Public opinion is also divided on specific issues and on the proper role of the courts in our political life.

Do the courts—especially the Supreme Court—lead or follow other institutions and public opinion in the kinds of policies they make? As with most important questions about our government, the answer is complicated. Some claim that the Supreme Court is just part of a ruling national policy alliance—never far behind or far ahead of the general drift of public opinion (Dahl, 1957; McCloskey, 1960). Others claim that the courts have more independent and innovative input into public policy (Casper, 1976). For the 1960s and 70s, the latter view seems reasonable. But this does not mean that the former view is inaccurate for our history as a whole. Perhaps a middle-of-the-road judgment is most accurate. The courts can sometimes push national policy and opinion in a few substantive areas. But in most areas, they are pushed and limited by the same forces and context that push and limit the government as a whole.

Some forces, such as the weight of precedent and long tenure for justices, favor slow change in the content of decisions. Yet the Supreme Court does make major changes in its policy stances. The Warren Court of the 1950s and 60s became known as a pioneer both in racial integration and in constitutional rights for criminal suspects. But, typically, it was replaced by the more conservative Burger Court. In the 1980s, the Supreme Court began making selected changes in the liberal doctrines of the past but did not move as quickly and uniformly to the right as some had predicted, hoped, or feared.

CONCLUSIONS

By now, it should be unmistakably clear that the federal courts, especially the Supreme Court, are broad-gauged governing and political institutions as well as narrow legal institutions dispensing justice to individuals involved in lawsuits. The three challenges mentioned at the beginning of the chapter are faced constantly by the court system and by the political system and the public in general. Seeing that the courts' business flows smoothly and on time is the easiest of these challenges to meet, since changes in procedures and jurisdictions and increases in judicial personnel can usually be made in response to perceived needs. However, the challenges regarding the balance between public opinion and court decisions and the proper scope of judicial action in the governing arena present political questions to which there are no definitive answers. Courts both generate broad political debate and are the subject of such debate. In a democratic society in which courts are important, that situation is both inevitable and healthy.

The overview of courts presented in this chapter leads to several general conclusions:

1. Courts resolve numerous specific conflicts by using a variety of routine procedures and well-established doctrines based on precedents accumulated over many years. Some of these conflicts, however, lead to broader judicial statements that have major political importance for the entire society.

2. There are many courts in the United States. All of them are capable of generating decisions whose importance goes well beyond the scope of an individual case. The Supreme Court is consistently the most important court in making decisions with broad importance.

3. Negotiation and bargaining characterize the behavior of judges and other persons involved in the federal court system. Judges negotiate with one another in reaching decisions. Both individually and collectively, judges also engage in various forms of negotiation and bargaining with the president, bureaucrats, legislators, and interest groups.

4. Courts make decisions about a vast range of socially important policies. In so doing, they both shape those policies and contribute to ongoing public debate about them.

5. Over time, courts are responsive to broad changes in public opinion. The content of court decisions changes to reflect shifts in public opinion and the views of successful political coalitions. The weight of precedent in legal decisions slows change but does not prevent it.

6. Courts and individual judges engage in varying degrees of activism or restraint. The philosophical debate over the proper degree of activism is intermingled with personal opinions about the wisdom of specific decisions. The debate between those with differing views about activism and restraint has been and will remain a permanent feature of the American political landscape.

FURTHER READING

ABRAHAM, HENRY J. (1986) *The Judicial Process*. 5th ed. New York: Oxford University Press. An examination of decision making in U.S. courts, especially the Supreme Court, with comparative materials on courts in Great Britain, the Soviet Union, and France.

BAUM, LAWRENCE (1985) *The Supreme Court*. 2nd ed. Washington, D.C.: Congressional Quarterly Press. An assessment of the policy-making function of the Supreme Court.

GOLDMAN, SHELDON, and THOMAS P. JAHNIGE (1985) *The Federal Courts as a Political System*. 3rd ed. New York: Harper & Row. An in-depth examination of the federal courts, including district courts and courts of appeals.

WOODWARD, BOB, and SCOTT ARMSTRONG (1979) *The Brethren: Inside the Supreme Court*. New York: Simon & Schuster. An "inside" look at decision making in the Supreme Court, 1969–76.

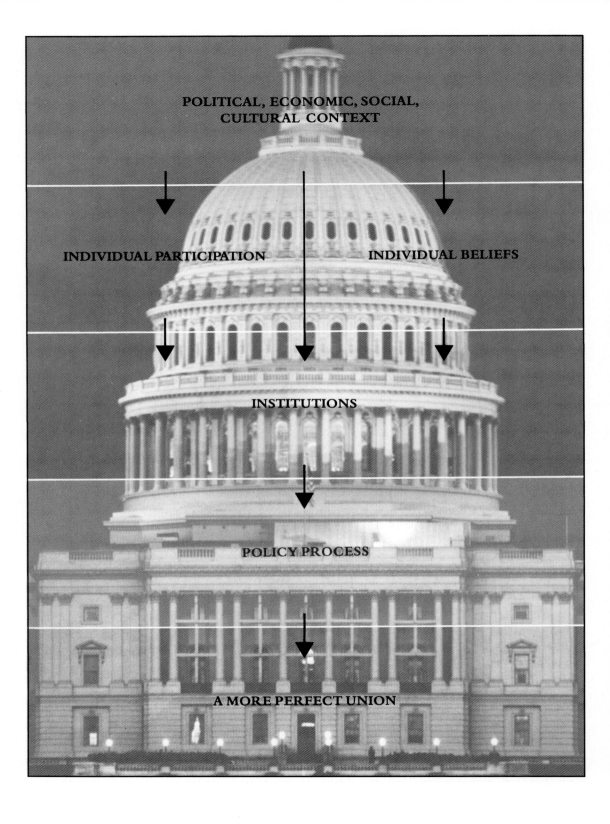

GOVERNING PROCESSES AND PUBLIC POLICIES

*T*hose who forged the Constitution were interested in much more than merely the creation of new governing institutions based on solid constitutional principles. They wanted government to exercise powers to make public policies and implement them. One reason why the new government survived was that its governing processes worked effectively to forge policies and put them into effect.

In Part Four, we elaborate a basic model of the national public policy process. The model provides a framework for analyzing public policies wherever they are made. Using this basic model, we conduct an analysis of policymaking and implementation in three crucial realms of the governing process—economic and fiscal policies, civil rights and liberties,

and foreign and defense policies. That analysis exemplifies how governing in America actually works.

A student who understands the context of American politics, how individuals and groups are politically mobilized, the structure of the major governing institutions, and the processes by which public policies are made, will appreciate that governing over 220 million men and women is a massive experiment. Part of that experiment's success lies in protecting democracy and freedom; part lies in putting effective public policies to work. We Americans must constantly take stock of how the experiment is working. Are we moving toward a more perfect union?

MAKING PUBLIC POLICIES

The content of public policies is complicated, and so is the process by which those policies are made. How can a citizen make sense out of what is going on? Is every development unique, or are there patterns that can enable an intelligent observer to make sense out of various government activities that create policy?

Governments are ultimately responsible for policies and programs that are supposed to enhance the well-being of citizens. In the United States, as the federal government takes the lead in making and implementing such policies and programs, it must deal with complicated topics in a complex cultural, political, and institutional context. The principal challenges facing the policy-making apparatus are (1) to identify public problems on which governmental action can be helpful, (2) to deal with those problems in a timely fashion and in ways that avoid paralysis in the process, and (3) to keep a politically and culturally diverse population generally supportive of the main thrusts of governmental endeavor, both domestic and foreign.

*T*he previous six chapters introduced the major institutions of the federal government. Before that, we dealt with important contextual features of American politics and government, with the role of the individual in politics, and with the mobilization of individuals to magnify their impact on politics. Now we will begin our examination of how these parts fit together to make policy.

Involved in the policy process are national legislative, executive, bureaucratic, and judicial institutions; parallel institutions in the states and localities; and interest groups at those three territorial levels. Democratic politics is an open politics. Openness means that few issues are "settled" permanently. It means that those whose views do not prevail in clashes over policy have an unlimited right to try again. Messiness and uncertainty result from the application of open politics to contests over policy. However, democracy is sustained by that messiness and uncertainty. But even in the midst of apparent disorder, regularities can be discerned in the policy process. This chapter portrays some of the major regularities in relation to the steps in the policy process, to the actors that take part in policy-making, and to types of policy.

After having provided a general introduction to policy-making in this chapter, we proceed in Chapter 17 to look at the politics and some of the substance of domestic policies in general. Chapter 20 does the same for foreign and defense policy. In Chapters 18 and 19 we examine two substantive policy areas of particular importance to the American people: first, economic policy, and second, liberties, rights, and equality. Chapter 21 examines the policy impact of government and governmental responsiveness to public needs.

STEPS IN THE POLICY PROCESS

Policy is the government's official statements about its goals and planned actions. To have any potential for impact, policy must be carried out through concrete actions, usually in the form of programs. Most national policies are contained in laws duly passed by Congress and signed by the president. Some policies may result from presidential, bureaucratic, or judicial activity without formal statutory action by Congress.

There are three main stages in forming and carrying out policies. First, the government must decide what problems or areas to look at. This is **agenda setting.**

Second, the government must say what it will do. It adopts some goals and methods as legitimate, it rejects other goals and methods. This is policy and program formation and legitimation.

Third, the government must take concrete actions to reach its goals. This is program implementation.

Every implemented policy has some **impact** on society. What differences do policies actually make? Are they resulting in intended outcomes?

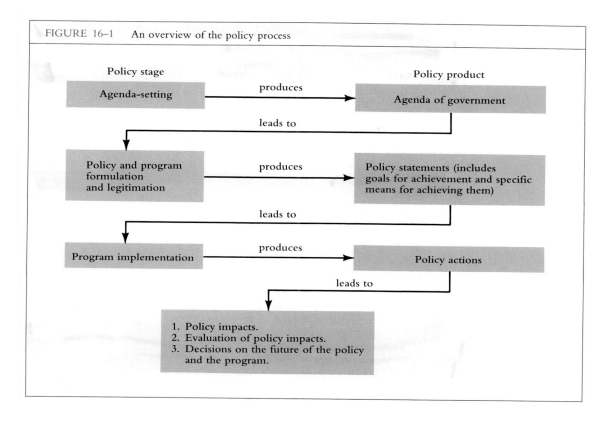

FIGURE 16–1   An overview of the policy process

Must they be modified or even scrapped? Policymakers address these questions by evaluating programs after they have been in effect.

This capsule view of the policy process is shown in Figure 16–1.

Setting the Agenda

The policy agenda consists of all the topics on which the government focuses at any given time. No single document or speech contains the national government's agenda. That agenda is not in the president's State of the Union message nor in the president's vest pocket. It is a composite of all the items that Congress, the president and the institutional presidency, and high-ranking bureaucrats are considering. Some additional items are on the agenda primarily because federal courts are paying attention to them. The agenda is very large, and it is always in flux. Agenda priorities are hard to pinpoint. And, of course, at any given time, different people have different priorities. The budget is perhaps the best single reflection of the entire agenda because it allocates dollars to specific governmental activities. Comparing budget changes over time gives some clues to changing agenda priorities.

How does an item get on the agenda? And how does it stay there long enough to be acted on? First, the item must interest enough people to be visible. An item that concerns only a handful of people is not likely to stay on the agenda. Many people are worried about cancer; therefore, the quest for cancer cures easily stays on the governmental agenda. Allergies are rarely life-threatening, and they are worrisome mainly to the people who suffer from them; therefore, medical responses to allergies are much harder to get or keep on the governmental agenda.

Second, a potential agenda item cannot seem to threaten most of the population. Civil rights for black Americans were kept off the agenda for a long time because many white people thought that any move toward racial equality threatened their own place in society. Individuals were hesitant to bring civil rights suits to courts. Few attorneys would take civil rights cases even when willing plaintiffs could be found. Most members of Congress and most presidents had little interest in pursuing civil rights questions until the last few decades. When civil rights questions got back onto the governmental agenda, it was because some whites joined black leaders in counteracting the fears and prejudices of other whites.

Third, in mobilizing support for putting an item on the agenda, it is necessary to get the attention and commitment of some people who occupy high positions in government or the private sector. Such people might include the president, some members of the House and Senate, or leaders of major corporations, unions, or interest groups.

The exact origins of changes in the governmental agenda are hard to pinpoint (Cobb and Elder, 1983). Actors both in and out of government are likely to be important. There are many routes to winning a place on the agenda. Some problems gain attention because of the writings of scholars and more popular authors. In the early 1960s, poverty was rediscovered as a problem worthy of attention. In part, this was because of works written by Robert Lampman, an academic economist, and Michael Harrington, a political activist and author.

A careful study of agenda setting in Washington (Kingdon, 1984) found three major sources of agenda items: the problems themselves, specific policy proposals, and a political context that made pushing an agenda item fruitful. When these three sources flowed in the same direction, the likelihood of getting a place and a high priority for a specific item was greatest. This study used the image of an open "window" for getting an item on the agenda. Windows were opened when a complex set of conditions allowed such openings. But they could close quickly. Those who favor putting a specific item on the agenda need to move rapidly and at the right time to take advantage of open windows.

Some problems are noticed because skillful lawyers bring them to the courts and force a decision that sparks later action. For instance, lawyers for the National Association for the Advancement of Colored People

AIDS—a new health problem on the agenda. The deadly disease AIDS (acquired immune deficiency syndrome) was thrust on the agenda of government in the mid-1980s. In New York City, physicians demonstrate for gay rights and national funding for AIDS research and treatment.

pressed the cases that led to the 1954 decision in which the Supreme Court declared segregated public schools unconstitutional. That decision helped set a major agenda item for the entire government for succeeding decades.

Some problems gain attention because of sudden, widespread publicity. When the Soviet Union launched *Sputnik* in 1957, it immediately dramatized the lagging U.S. space program and the underlying deficiencies in scientific and mathematical education. When the Arab nations dramatically raised the price of oil in 1973 and again in 1979, U.S. energy policy was immediately put on the agenda. In the 1980s, massive federal budget deficits and massive trade deficits received full media coverage, putting those items near the top of the governmental agenda. Publicity helped put the plight of homeless people on the federal agenda in the mid-1980s. At about the same time, AIDS, a well-reported medical problem, was catapulted onto the governmental agenda.

Some problems are eventually placed on the agenda because of the persistent efforts of individual government officials. In two instances, for ex-

Paul H. Douglas (1892–1976), a Democratic U.S. senator for Illinois from 1949 to 1967, was one of the staunchest Senate liberals of the 1950s and 1960s. He championed welfare legislation and aid for economically depressed areas.

ample, a lone senator waged a long campaign, finally successful, to put a major item on the federal agenda. Senator George Norris (R–Neb.) worked for decades to have the government address the problems of the Tennessee River basin; his efforts resulted in the creation of the Tennessee Valley Authority in 1933. And Senator Paul Douglas (D–Ill.) worked for nearly a decade to get the federal government to deal systematically with the problems of economically depressed regions; as a result, the Area Redevelopment Administration was created in 1961. In 1986, the state of Ohio provided an amusing and instructive example of how an important official can get a matter on the governmental agenda quickly. Insurance companies had become increasingly reluctant to write certain kinds of liability insurance, despite pressure from the state legislature. Nothing happened to break the impasse until the speaker of the Ohio House of Representatives, a powerful individual, became riled when Fourth of July fireworks displays were canceled in his district because of the unavailability of affordable liability insurance for the sponsoring municipalities. The speaker immediately told two House committee chairpersons to have their committees report bills solving the problem. At the end of the summer, he then called the full House into a special one-day session to pass such a bill. In this case, one powerful officeholder was able to move an item to the top of the agenda quickly.

At the agenda-setting stage, broad goals may be adopted by many actors. Sometimes a generally accepted goal emerges—for example, that the deficit should be reduced. Sometimes a number of goals that conflict with one another may be adopted. Often an item is added to the agenda without the adoption of clear goals or even without a clear definition of the problem (Nelson, 1984).

Formulating and Legitimating Policies

When an item has been placed on the governmental agenda, various persons and groups formulate policy alternatives for addressing that item. Legitimation is the ratification of one alternative or, more likely, a compromise among several alternatives. Other alternatives are largely or wholly rejected. The processes of formulation and legitimation are intertwined: some alternatives are legitimated almost as soon as they are formulated; others are not.

In a single field, numerous alternatives may be formulated and even legitimated in a short period of time. Take, for example, the tangled history of energy policy since 1972. Congress, interest groups, presidents and their advisers, and various parts of the bureaucracy all groped to solve the problem. Over a few years, many alternatives were proposed: deregulate natural gas; regulate natural gas more; break up oil companies; subsidize oil companies to increase exploration efforts; penalize manufacturers for making inefficient cars; penalize car owners through taxes on gas guzzlers; suspend air pollution control laws to allow the burning of coal; subsidize research on removing pollutants from coal. Some of these alternatives got temporary legitimation but were rejected later.

During formulation and legitimation, these things take place: policymakers collect, analyze, and distribute information; they develop alternatives; coalitions form to advocate various alternatives; and a decision is made.

At some point in this process, only a few alternatives with any chance of adoption are left. The supporters of those alternatives make their cases where they think they will have the most influence. In the mid-1980s, for example, as Congress grappled with the problem of reducing the federal deficit, Senator Phil Gramm (R–Tex.) and his supporters developed an alternative under which an automatic formula would produce deficit reduction if Congress failed to do so. He and his supporters worked incessantly in Congress to get this alternative legitimated. Also in the 1980s, as the United States faced a huge and growing trade deficit, supporters of various alternatives for reducing that deficit worked hard in Congress, with relevant interest groups (trade associations, unions, and individual corporations), and with the public in general to promote the merits of those alternatives. Some favored open protection in the form of high tariffs; others favored the imposition of tariffs on foreign nations that were judged to be exploiting their labor force; still others favored mostly free trade.

Finally, a decision is made. For example, Congress adopted the Gramm-Rudman-Hollings Act in late 1985 to attack the deficit problem. Some decisions are purely symbolic. A good example is the Communist Control Act, passed by Congress in 1954. Liberal Democrats sponsored the act to protect themselves from charges of being "soft on communism." They hoped that no president would use it. The act was so badly designed that it was unworkable and probably unconstitutional as well.

A final policy statement that has received legitimation will include a general goal, such as "eliminate poverty" or "reduce the federal deficit." It will also contain specific means to achieve that goal: create community action programs to help fight poverty; create automatic spending reduction procedures to help reduce the deficit. At the national level, policy statements are most often made in statutes. But they may also be made in speeches or executive orders, statements by bureaucrats, agency regulations in the *Federal Register,* and court decisions. Some policy statements are highly visible; others are not. A major statute is easily identified; a regulation buried in the *Federal Register* is hardly noticed.

Numerous actors help formulate and legitimate decisions. Formally, such decisions are most often made by Congress and the executive branch. But different parts of those institutions become involved (the entire Congress, specific committees and subcommittees, individual members of Congress, the president, presidential advisers, cabinet members, specific bureaucratic agencies, and individual bureaucrats), as do organizations and individuals in the judiciary and outside government altogether.

Implementing Programs

Once a policy statement has been made, the organization or organizations assigned to carry it out must see to the myriad details of implementation. **Implementation** is the set of actions by which public and private actors try to achieve the goals contained in policy statements (Van Meter and Van Horn, 1975). The federal government declared war on poverty in 1964, but if concrete actions had not been taken to improve the economic conditions of the poor, nothing much would have happened. In 1985, the Gramm-Rudman-Hollings Act declared that the government would balance its budget by 1991. But unless Congress, the president, and the Congressional Budget Office all played the parts that this statute assigned them, implementation along the desired lines would not occur.

Implementing actions include allocating funds, assigning personnel, developing and issuing regulations, enforcing those regulations, collecting and distributing information, writing and signing contracts, and setting up organizational subunits, such as field offices, coordinating committees, and task forces. For example, under the Job Training Partnership Act (the current federal program for employing and training individuals disadvantaged in the labor market), the Department of Labor has to allocate funds both to local Service Delivery Areas (usually cities and counties) through state government and to some federally run programs. It also has to continually update regulations, based on the statute, on what people are eligible for what services and on what activities represent proper expenditures. Both the Department of Labor and state governments must enforce those regulations. They and the local Service Delivery Areas must publicize the programs and seek out eligible applicants for the training provided. Service Delivery Area staff must screen applicants for eligibility and assign accepted applicants to specific programs. Contracts must be signed with training institutions: public schools, private for-profit training institutes, and nonprofit community-based organizations. In each Service Delivery Area, a Private Industry Council must be created and staffed. That council must also adhere to the regulations. All of this is only a partial catalog of the activities that must be undertaken to implement a single program.

The same steps that are taken in formulating and legitimating policy are taken again in making implementation decisions. Actors in the process collect, analyze, and distribute information; they develop alternatives and choose among them; they advocate specific implementation options; and finally, they choose one option. Under the Job Training Partnership Act, local implementers ponder the merits of training in welding versus the merits of training in licensed practical nursing and the merits of using the public schools as the training agent versus the merits of using the local Urban League; advocates of different programs and delivery agents make their choices; and finally, the staff and the Private Industry Council make the decision.

Evaluating Policy Outcomes

What differences do government actions make? All policies are assumed to have planned results. But they are also apt to have unforeseen results. The impact of a program is determined in part by the reaction of the people who are intended to benefit from it. Splendid health clinics may be built, for example. If people choose to use them, the desired results of better health will occur, and therefore better attendance at school and better productivity at work. If no one uses them, however, they can have no impact. This might happen because the clinics are too far from bus routes or because the intended users distrust public programs and agencies in general.

Governmental and nongovernmental organizations evaluate policies and programs in many ways, both formal and informal. They can evaluate many aspects: design, implementation, impact, and so on. An evaluation of the Job Training Partnership Act, for example, would seek to find out whether the program was properly designed to reach its intended beneficiaries, whether appropriately qualified people conducted the training, and

Many Cooks; How's the Broth?

On a single day in 1989, all of the following took place:

The president and the secretary of labor met. The latter urged the president to support expanded subsidies to private businesses for worker training. At the same time, the secretary urged increasing the percentage of workers who did not have to be disadvantaged in the traditional sense of the term to be eligible for training.

In the Washington headquarters of the Department of Labor (presumably run by the secretary of labor), a few civil servants met and began planning for next year's training programs at the same level and with the same regulations as this year's programs.

In the Denver, Dallas, and Atlanta regional offices of the Department of Labor, prohibitions against stipends during training were being waived for local Service Delivery Areas requesting waivers. In the New York, Boston, and Seattle regional offices, such requests were being denied.

Meetings were going on in 17 different state bureaucracies about what regulations to draft and what reports to require from local Service Delivery Areas. By the end of the day, 17 different patterns of answers had begun to emerge.

In Service Delivery Areas all over the country, there was confusion among professional staff about what they could and could not do and to whom, what, and when they had to report about what they did do.

The staff of the representative who chairs the Employment Opportunities Subcommittee of the House Committee on Education and Labor was preparing a bill that would add a major new component to the federal employment and training law. This component would be run directly by the federal government and would be targeted exclusively at the poor.

The staff of the senator who chairs the Employment and Productivity Subcommittee of the Committee on Labor and Human Resources was preparing an amendment to the existing statute that would wipe out all eligibility requirements for trainees. Anyone chosen by local businesses would be eligible.

Staff members of the National Association of Counties were preparing draft legislation that would return to local units some aspects of the program now under state control. They called staff members in the United States Conference of Mayors and the National League of Cities to get support.

The staff of the National Governors Association was preparing a draft that would further strengthen the role of the states in training programs.

The staff of the National Alliance of Business was discussing ways of giving more control over local decision making in training programs to local businesspeople organized in the Private Industry Councils mandated by federal law.

What's going on here? Who's in charge of what? Is the policy process always so confused and complex? Everyone seems to be running in different directions. How do these people get together?

whether those who received the training obtained employment, held on to that employment, and were paid a better wage than they earned before receiving the training.

Actors and Relationships

The core of our national governmental policy process is located in Congress and the executive branch. These public institutions and actors are often supplemented by nongovernmental institutions and actors, especially interest groups. The relationships are not simple.

Congress and the executive branch can be best understood in terms of their key components. Both the House and the Senate have party leaders, committee and subcommittee leaders (often chairpersons), and rank-and-file members. The executive branch consists of the president personally; the institutional presidency, which includes the Executive Office of the President and high-ranking presidential appointees, such as the departmental secretaries who sit in the cabinet; and the civil servants in the numerous bureaucratic agencies that make up the operating level of the executive branch. Each of these six components of the central Washington policy-making institutions interacts with all of the other components; but these interactions differ in importance. Figure 16–2 indicates the interactions most important to the formulation and legitimation of national policy. Implementation is mainly the province of the executive branch. Chapter 17 contains more detailed analyses of the most important relationships in the formulation/legitimation and implementation of different types of policy.

Figure 16–2 indicates that the two most important relationships within the executive branch are the relationship of the president with the institutional presidency and the relationship of the institutional presidency with the civil servants in specific agencies. The president cannot be in direct touch with more than a handful of civil servants because his numerous commitments simply leave no time for extensive contacts. The institutional presidency is responsible for informing the agencies about presidential preferences and for bringing agency preferences to the attention of the president.

Within Congress, all three components relate directly to one another. Committee and subcommittee leaders act as intermediaries between party leaders and rank-and-file members, but party leaders also maintain direct relations with rank-and-file members. The committee and subcommittee leaders are generally the most important individuals in determining what matters Congress will act on. The party leaders make many of the strategic and tactical decisions about how best to get full House and Senate approval for the work of committees and subcommittees.

There are three especially important relationships between the executive branch and Congress. First, the president and the party leaders meet frequently, generally on strategic and tactical matters. Second, actors in the

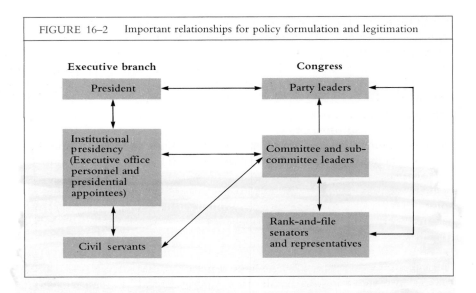

FIGURE 16–2   Important relationships for policy formulation and legitimation

Executive branch

Congress

President

Party leaders

Institutional presidency (Executive office personnel and presidential appointees)

Committee and sub-committee leaders

Civil servants

Rank-and-file senators and representatives

institutional presidency meet with committee and subcommittee leaders, chiefly on substantive questions. Third, high-ranking civil servants (and military officers in the Department of Defense) meet often with committee and subcommittee leaders on substantive matters.

The different institutional actors have different weights in the various steps that lead to the formulation and legitimation of policy. Collecting, analyzing, and distributing information are dominated by the bureaucracy. Alternatives are usually developed and chosen through bargaining among the bureaucracy, Congress, and the president, with smaller input from interest groups. In advocacy, the president and his advisers and appointees can have the most influence, but their limited resources force them to focus on just a few issues. Congress has much influence in advocacy; the bureaucracy and interest groups have less influence. The president and Congress dominate final decisions on policy statements.

Subgovernments

Policies and programs are created and implemented by groups of actors and institutions that have to work with one another. Typically, those with the most at stake in a specific decision are the most important in making it. The label "subgovernment," a notion we introduced at the end of Chapter 7, is often used to characterize these groups of most heavily involved actors (Cater, 1964). A **subgovernment** is a small cluster of people who make most of the routine decisions in a policy area. These people come from key parts, often subcommittees, of Congress and congressional staff, from the executive branch (bureaus responsible for specific programs), and from the private sector (most often industries or producer-oriented interest groups). Subgovernments work without much publicity or attention from outsiders. The press, the president, and the party leaders in Congress often ignore or are unaware of their work. They are very important in some kinds of policies (these will be identified at the end of the chapter) and far less important in other kinds.

There is a constant flow of people between positions in different parts of a subgovernment. Congressional staff members and interest-group lobbyists may go to work for an executive-branch agency with which they have been working. Congressional staff members and civil and military officials in the executive branch move into jobs in interest groups and producer-oriented associations with which they have been working. Small wonder that subgovernments have been called "incest groups" (Lewis, 1977) and "iron triangles."

Most officials think that it is completely legitimate to blur the lines between the governmental and nongovernmental members of subgovernments. In their view, this enables those most affected by policies to be in constant contact with officials during policy formulation, legitimation, and implementation (Lowi, 1979).

Subgovernments decide the details of policy in those areas in which they are most potent. Their principal advantage is expertise in the details of a specific policy or program. Their principal disadvantage is that they use public resources for the benefit of the interests to which they are most attached without weighing the merits of these claims of those interests against the merits of the claims of competing interests. The accompanying box describes a classic case of subgovernments in action. In this account, Theodore Lowi, a political scientist, uses the words *system* and *triangle* to refer to subgovernments.

National, State, and Local Implementation

Federal, state, and local bureaucrats interact constantly as they seek to implement programs, many of which are joint ventures. Members of Congress oversee the implementation of these ventures in ways designed to produce desired distributions of federal benefits that will please interest groups and constituents and thus be helpful in reelection efforts. Members of Congress often pay lip service to the "principles" of federalism, but they are actually concerned with claiming credit at the local level for national actions beneficial to their states or districts. Members of Congress are oriented toward pleasing local interests. To claim effectiveness, they must be seen as helpful in providing tangible benefits to their own states and localities.

The key to understanding the impact of federalism on policy implementation is an examination of federal grants-in-aid to states and localities.

THE PRACTICE OF POLITICS

How the Farmers Get What They Want

The politics within each system is built upon a triangular trading pattern involving the central agency, a congressional committee or subcommittee, and the local district farmer committees (usually federated in some national or regional organization). Each side of the triangle complements and supports the other two.

The Extension Service, for example, is one side of the triangle completed by the long-tenure "farm bureau" members of the agriculture committees in Congress and, at the local level, the American Farm Bureau Federation with its local committees. Further group support is provided by two intimately related groups, the Association of Land Grant Colleges and Universities and the National Association of County Agricultural Agents.

Another such triangle unites the Soil Conservation Service, the agriculture subcommittee of the House Appropriations Committee, and the local districts organized in the energetic National Association of Soil Conservation Districts. Further support comes from the Soil Conservation Society of America (mainly professionals) and the former Friends of the Land, now the Izaak Walton League of America.

Probably the most complex of the systems embraces the parity program. It connects the Agricultural Stabilization and Conservation Service with the eight (formerly ten) commodity subcommittees of the House Agriculture Committee and the dozens of separately organized groups representing the various commodities. (Examples: National Cotton Council, American Wool Growers Association, American Cranberry Growers Association.) These groups and congressmen draw support from the local price-support committees wherever a particular commodity is grown. . . .

These systems have a vigorous capacity to maintain themselves and to resist encroachment. They have such institutional legitimacy that they have become practically insulated from the three central sources of democratic political responsibility. Thus, within the executive branch, they are autonomous. Secretaries of agriculture have tried and failed to consolidate or even to coordinate related programs. Within Congress, they are sufficiently powerful to be able to exercise an effective veto or create a stalemate. And they are almost totally removed from the view, not to mention the control, of the general public.

Source: Theodore J. Lowi, "How the Farmers Get What They Want." *Reporter,* May 21, 1964, p. 36.

Crumbling streets and highways. Which partner—nation, state, or locality—has how much responsibility for repairing Fifth Avenue in New York City [left] or Interstate 70 in western Pennsylvania [right]? The answer is complicated.

We examine the grant system in the following section, which is followed by a brief examination of President Reagan's "New Federalism" proposals.

Federal grants to states and localities

After World War II, the federal government greatly expanded the system of grants to states and localities. Until the late 1970s, there were increases in the amount of money spent on that system, the percentage of the gross national product for which it accounted, the percentage of state and local expenditures for which it accounted, and the number of its individual programs. The system had shrunk a bit by the late 1980s, but it still remained very large and it seemed unlikely to shrink more. Spending on grants to states and localities had stabilized at about 9 percent of all federal outlays and about 14 percent of all federal domestic outlays.

Most of the grants to both states and localities were **categorical grants** targeted at specific purposes. Only a small proportion were **block grants** in which the recipients had lots of discretion about how to use the money within a broad substantive area. In 1972 a program of general revenue sharing was begun that gave state and local governments great latitude in deciding how to spend the money. The states were dropped from the program in 1980, and the entire program died in 1986.

Federal regulators are numerous and important in the categorical grant programs. They are only slightly less numerous in the block grant programs. The federal presence is very much in evidence as these programs operate.

Members of Congress try to maximize the share of the grant programs that is awarded to their own constituencies. Naturally, not all constituencies can get an above-average share; consequently, there is considerable politicking in Congress over the creation of these programs and especially over the formulas for allocating federal money to them.

A recent review of American federalism (Reagan and Sanzone, 1981: 157) reached the conclusion that "federal financial aid has created a nationally dominated system of shared power and shared functions." When Congress directs that decisions be left to state and local officials, it often does this to pass along tricky and potentially damaging political choices to those officials and thus spare itself the embarrassment of having to make such choices (Derthick, 1970: 196).

In many cases, Congress participates directly in multiplying the number of federal regulations to which state and local officials are subject as they administer programs funded wholly or in part by the federal government. In other cases, Congress delegates the regulatory power to federal bureaucrats, who then proliferate the network of controls under which state and local officials must perform (Dodd, 1981; Kettl, 1983; and Stewart, 1982).

In this system, Congress has the best of both worlds. It can help control decisions when a majority of its members calculate that they have more to gain than to lose politically if this is done. Otherwise, it can use its lawmaking power and its less formal influence over bureaucratic behavior to delegate sticky decisions to state and local officials so that they wind up running the risks. When it does this, there is no diminution of the credit that members of Congress can claim for providing the benefits in the first place.

As federal aid grew rapidly in size and importance in the 1950s and 1960s, major administrative problems developed. There were too many administrative requirements. The federal government did not react to changes in state and local priorities. Washington offices of federal agencies did not let field offices make decisions. There were too many programs in the same area. Regulations were often complex and confusing.

Despite some attempts to create cooperation between the federal government and the states and localities, problems remained in the 1980s (Kettl, 1983; Walker, 1981). States and localities still had a hard time getting information from the federal government on grants. The government released money in an irregular way. Thus, states and localities had problems in planning their expenditures. Federal administrative processes were still complex. Federal programs still overlapped, and there were still redundant programs.

Administrative problems were far less prevalent in programs that primarily subsidized existing private activities than in programs that attempted to focus on the poorer classes in society (Peterson, 1984b). The units involved in implementing the programs could function more smoothly when they were allocating "goodies" than when they were making hard choices about who benefited and who did not.

How much and what kind of federal aid comes either through state or local governments or straight to local citizens? This is seemingly a simple

...and after years of unsuccessful child rearing, we're going to return this kid to its rightful parents!

Cutting welfare down to size. The administration of President Ronald Reagan sought to cut back on welfare programs, to cut the growth rate of entitlement programs, and to return programs to the states and localities.

question. But it is extremely hard to answer because of the vast array of programs and the various arrangements for spending.

Federal, state, and local purposes—as carried out through programs using public funds—are inextricably mixed. They cannot help but affect one another.

In the 1970s, states and localities depended on the federal government for about one fourth of all their spending. In the 1980s, that proportion shrank to about one fifth. States and localities—mostly the latter—became agents to carry out federal programs, mainly in the social services. But they did not have direct access to the tax base that supported those programs, and they did not have complete control over the means for carrying them out. Congress and the federal bureaucracy controlled the purse strings and set the conditions for carrying out programs, yet people depended on nonfederal bureaucrats to run the programs. This led some city officials to conclude that they were not really responsible for the poor but only agents for programs that the "feds" mandated. As Mayor Margaret Hance of Phoenix said: "The poor are a federal, not a local, responsibility. If Washington cannot afford these programs, we certainly can't. Local people do not feel that welfare programs should be financed by local taxes" (*New York Times,* December 21,1980). Since President Reagan was able to deliver on his promises to cut federal programs for the poor, those individuals had an increasingly tough time finding any level of government that would sustain programs for them.

In Chapter 3, we presented general data on the size of the grant system and allocation of grant money to various purposes. What is often not re-

Federal Aid in Arlington County, Virginia

Arlington got $24.2 million in federal funds in fiscal 1983, ended last June 30, representing 12 percent of the county's total expenditures of $206 million. The federal inflow was $6 million less than the year before—partly because of the Reagan cutbacks—but close to what the county collected in fiscal 1980 and 1981.

A big chunk of the funds last year—around $11.3 million—went for means-tested programs in which the county acts as a conduit for federal help to the poor and near poor. Arlington does have its needy, with 7.2 percent of the population below the official poverty level in the 1980 census. Among the various programs means-tested were Indochinese refugee assistance ($2,876,600), rent subsidies from the Department of Housing and Urban Development ($2,049,267), and low-level jobs and job training under the Comprehensive Employment and Training Act ($1,403,974).

Most of the remaining $12.9 million that Arlington received last year, however, benefited people who on average have distinctly above-average incomes. A big chunk of the money was general revenue sharing, which Washington disburses to almost every county and city—$4.6 billion this year. Arlington got $2,617,463 in fiscal 1983. It all went to the fire department—an odd use for federal funds, it might seem, but Arlington was well within its rights. . . .

Education also gets generous federal help. Arlington's schools—19 elementary, four intermediate, and three high schools—received $4,140,466 last year from the Department of Education under 22 programs. One of the largest programs was impact aid, which cost the U.S. Treasury $512,869. Impact aid is meant to compensate localities for the cost of educating the offspring of military personnel, who presumably do not support the schools through taxes. Every administration since Eisenhower's has tried to eliminate the program, only to run into implacable congressional resistance. Military personnel who live off post do pay real estate taxes, so their children certainly should be excluded from the head count that determines the amount paid. Even when soldiers do not pay property taxes, a military base confers considerable economic benefits on a community.

Last year the Department of Education's grants to Arlington schools supported programs that ranged from vocational education ($850,827) to bilingual education ($102,936) to adult basic education ($77,180) to "expository writing" ($32,528) to a special program for "gifted and talented" children ($49,083). This year the school authorities spent $34,000 in discretionary federal money to buy 20 microcomputers for elementary schools.

Source: Irwin Ross, "One County's Pipeline to the Treasury." *Fortune,* February 20, 1984, pp. 50–52. © 1984 Time Inc. All rights reserved.

alized, however, is how pervasive federal grants are at the local level. The accompanying boxes discuss the various ways in which a county close to Washington, D.C. (Arlington County, Virginia), and a county between Los Angeles and San Francisco that happens to house President Reagan's ranch (Santa Barbara County, California) have come to rely on federal aid, ways probably not widely known to their citizens.

Reagan's New Federalism

Early in his presidency, Ronald Reagan made a series of proposals involving the nature of American federalism. These proposals were aimed at making major changes in the grant-in-aid system by reducing the number of programs and cutting spending. They also sought to return many powers to the state governments from the federal government in such areas as welfare. Reagan had three principal goals in attacking the centralized federal grant system that had developed rapidly in the 1960s and 1970s. First, he wanted to reduce spending on existing programs. Second, he wanted to reduce the number of categorical programs by creating new block grants that lumped existing programs into broader functional categories. Third, he wanted to stop the creation of new programs.

The Reagan administration succeeded in achieving only its third goal. Congress did not even attempt to create new programs; it was much too busy trying to preserve as much of the grant system that it had created over the previous decades as possible.

Spending on grant programs was reduced somewhat during the Reagan years. The Carter administration, with congressional approval, had begun to rein in such spending. In terms of constant 1978 dollars, total federal aid to states and localities decreased from $77.9 billion in 1978 to 73.1 billion in 1981 (the last Carter budget) to $64.1 billion in 1982 (the effects of the Reagan cuts) and then was back up to $66 billion in 1984 (after Congress dug in its heels). There was a cut of 6 percent during Carter's administration, and the net impact of the Reagan years from 1981 through 1984 was a further cut of 9 percent.

Reagan's block grant proposals had only modest success. Even in 1981 (the peak year for Reagan's impact on domestic programs), only nine block grants were enacted (all in the Omnibus Reconciliation Act). Two of them involved only single categorical programs. Total spending in 1982 for the consolidated programs was just over $6 billion out of a total of over $88 billion for all grant-in-aid programs. A handful of additional minor categorical programs were consolidated after 1981, but most of the proposals for additional block grants went nowhere.

Congress rejected a Reagan proposal for fundamental redistribution of responsibilities from the federal government to state governments. Reagan's major proposals in 1982 failed completely. His proposal that the federal government assume responsibility for Medicaid in exchange for giving responsibility for welfare and food stamps to the states also fell on deaf congressional ears.

PRACTICE OF POLITICS

Federal Aid in Santa Barbara County, California

GOLETA, Calif.—The president of the United States lives near this coastal town that hugs the edge of the Santa Ynez Mountains. While no one has ever seen dollar bills flutter down from his passing helicopter, Ronald Reagan's government has been dispensing checks here, even as he chops wood and plots budget cuts up at his ranch.

Goleta, a Santa Barbara suburb of fast-food stops, think tanks, and avocado groves, supports 66,075 residents who share much of their famous neighbor's distaste for waste, taxes, and overregulation.

But as the federal government brings about $1 billion to them and the other 240,000 residents of Santa Barbara County each year, they and their president are finding the federal largess so woven into their daily lives that they seem willing to accept the taxes and triplicate forms that go with it. . . .

Defense installations in Santa Barbara County received $965,224,000 in fiscal 1982, most of it going to Vandenburg Air Force Base. For fiscal 1984, the county government got $9,185,124 in welfare under aid to families with dependent children,

Construction at Vandenberg Air Force Base. This never-used facility, built in the late 1960s to realize the U.S. Air Force's dream of an orbiting space station, is being resurrected as a launch and landing facility for the National Aeronautics and Space Administration (NASA) space shuttle program. Vandenberg Air Force Base, located in Santa Barbara County, California, benefited from Federal aid dollars in fiscal 1982.

(Continued)

PRACTICE OF POLITICS

(Concluded)

$1,767,032 for welfare administration, $683,377 for food stamps, and $475,000 for airport work. And county assistant administrative officer David Elbaum said the sheriff has been guaranteed at least $210,000 over several years for the trouble of providing extra protection for President Reagan.

The county will receive $3,220,932 in federal revenue sharing this fiscal year, 30 percent of which has been alloted to a bewildering array of local public service groups. The Blue Jacket Teen Age Club got $500,

Afro-American Community Services $5,200, the Goleta Valley Girls' Club Inc. $5,000, and the Lompoc Rape Crisis Center $8,800.

Gary Gleason, general manager of the Santa Barbara transit district, is . . . willing to accept the demands of federal regulation in exchange for $560,000 in operating funds—about 16 percent of his budget and $2,220,000 in capital funds to help him buy 20 new buses.

Source: Jay Mathews, "Federal Largess Is Blooming in Reagan Back Yard." *Washington Post,* February 2, 1984.

In short, Reagan's efforts to change the nature of the national–state–local relationship had only a few successes. Congress—supported by important interest groups and the bureaucracies at all three territorial levels who ran the programs already in place—preserved the essence of the grant system. Congress also successfully prevented wholesale shifts in responsibilities from the federal and local governments to the states (Beam, 1984; Chubb, 1985; Ceaser, 1984; Nathan and Doolittle, 1984a, 1984b; and Peterson, 1984a). Reagan's achievement, from the administration's point of view, was to stop further large-scale growth of the federal grant system and to stop the creation of new grant programs.

Cooperation, Conflict, Bargaining, and Slow Change in Policy

We have now seen that the policy process in the United States involves many steps and many actors. It is also an open process, which means that conflict can occur easily. Cooperation can also occur. Bargaining both among actors and institutions and across the three territorial levels of government in our federal system is essential in many cases for policy to be made in the first place or for change to be made in existing policy. Inevitably, in such a complicated situation, policy change is slow in most instances.

It is difficult to reach coordinated decisions rapidly in the American setting. When such complexity prevails, action is never automatic and inaction is the most natural outcome. But since various individuals and institutions much prefer action to inaction, they have a strong incentive for cooperating with one another rather than pushing conflict without letup. Or if differing views about the most desirable policy make cooperation difficult, then they see the necessity of bargaining with one another and arriving at mutually acceptable compromises. Bargaining within Congress, within the executive branch, between Congress and the executive branch, and among national, state, and local governments are all hallmarks of policy-making in the United States. Policy usually gets made in fits and starts and slowly. Some critics contend that this system is inefficient and irrational. But these drawbacks may well be the price of an open political system.

Congress and the executive branch share powers. National, state, and local governments share powers. These basic facts help shape the character of American policy-making. Not only do Congress and the executive branch engage in endless bargaining; the units of the federal system do so too, particularly with regard to the grant programs that we have sketched above (Van Horn, 1979; Williams, 1980; Nathan and Dommel, 1978; Ingram, 1977). When there is direct confrontation, the national government generally prevails over the state and local governments. Members of Congress and the national bureaucracy have a natural interest in keeping states and localities dependent on them so that they can claim credit for programs beneficial to congressional constituents and bureaucratic clients. But the states and localities retain enough power to be able to bargain on some matters.

A political system in which compromise and bargains are needed to make decisions promotes slow policy change. Those who take part in such a system do not want to upset these bargains by raising basic issues again and again. The initial bargains are generally supported and reaffirmed over time. This means that the basic shape of most policies and programs stays the same for a long time.

The way policymakers think also promotes slow policy change. When they approach a problem, they usually do not think it through from scratch. They prefer to make some changes in existing programs and policies rather than design new ones. They are wary of new approaches. A problem never faced before or a crisis may be analyzed from scratch, but such cases are exceptional.

Another reason for slow change is that people cannot see all sides of a problem or amass all of the relevant data (Lindblom, 1959). Because of this, problems are only partly analyzed and alternatives usually do not stray very far from policy as it stands.

TYPES OF POLICIES

When the government makes policy decisions, many institutions and individuals have a great deal at stake. Based on what the interested parties want to win and what they might lose, policies can be categorized into various types. These types of policies structure distinctive kinds of political relationships, which we will explore in Chapters 17 and 20. Seven basic policy types—four in the domestic arena and three involving foreign and defense policy—account for most of the concrete instances of policy.

Domestic Policies

Domestic policies are meant to affect what happens within the nation. There are four types of domestic policies: distributive, competitive regulatory, protective regulatory, and redistributive. In each of these types, distinctive political patterns of interaction occur among influential policymakers during formulation/legitimation and implementation. For example, subgovernments are dominant in policy-making that fits into the distributive and competitive regulatory domestic policies and the structural foreign and defense policies described below. The more controversial types of domestic policy—protective regulatory and redistributive—allow a larger role for Congress as a whole, for the president and the institutional presidency, and for interest groups. The president and Congress as a whole also play a major role in strategic foreign and defense policy. The president dominates crisis foreign and defense policy.

Distributive policies provide subsidies for private actions by individuals, groups, and corporations. The government desires these actions. A subsidy is a payment meant to induce desired private activities. In theory, these private activities would not be undertaken without government subsidy. Everyone appears to win as a result of distributive policies. Subsidizing one private action (the growing of specific crops, for example) does not prevent simultaneous subsidy programs for other private actions (the buying of homes or the construction of ships, for example). Many policies involve subsidies that are not apparent at first glance. Examples of distributive domestic policies include

Land grants for railroad companies and homesteaders in the 1800s to induce developing and settling the West.

The building of the interstate highway system.

Direct cash payments to purchase certain farm products (feed grains, wheat, rice, dairy products, soybeans, honey, cotton, oils, tobacco, peanuts, sugar, wool, mohair). Price supports for the same products. Direct loans for farm improvements—for animal and equipment purchase, soil and water conservation, or insurance. Tax subsidy (through deductions) for farming. Insurance against crop failure.

Grants for scientific research.

Grants for airport construction and improvement, hospital construction, sewage systems, and mass transit.

Grants of patents to companies and inventors to promote invention.

Development of water resources (dam building, diversion) by the Army Corps of Engineers, the Bureau of Reclamation, and the Soil Conservation Service.

Bumper wheat crop. This farmer combines wheat on his farm near Chester, Montana. Distributive agricultural policies support the price at which the farmer sells this wheat.

Tax deductions for interest on home loans and local property taxes to promote home ownership.

Special benefits for veterans.

Low-cost permits for grazing on public lands.

Revenue sharing with states and local governments.

Subsidies for merchant marine construction and operation.

Competitive regulatory policies limit the number of people or groups that can supply or deliver certain goods and services. Some potential deliverers that want the business win; some lose. Some decisions allocate scarce resources that cannot be divided, such as TV channels and radio frequencies. Some decisions limit competition in the supply of goods and services. Only certain deliverers can supply them; others are excluded. Some decisions regulate the quality of services delivered by setting standards of performance. For example, a license for a TV channel may be given in exchange for agreement to abide by specific regulations on the content of programming. If those standards are not met, a new deliverer

Mass transit in Washington, D.C. The national capital's Metro is one of the most modern subway systems in the world. It was built, and continues to operate, with the aid of large Federal subsidies.

may be chosen. This type of policy is a hybrid. It subsidizes the winning competitors, but it also tries to regulate the delivery in the public interest. Examples of competitive regulatory policies are

Granting and reviewing licenses to run TV and radio stations.
Authorizing certain airlines to operate certain routes.
Authorizing certain trucking companies to haul named products over set routes.

In recent years, national policy has decreased competitive regulation by reducing the federal role with regard to airlines, railroads, truck lines, and even some aspects of communications.

Protective regulatory policies protect the public by setting conditions for various private activities. They ban conditions thought to be harmful (air pollution, false advertising). They require conditions thought to be helpful (publishing interest rates on loans). Examples include

The rule that requires banks, stores, and other grantors of credit to disclose their true interest rates.
The certification of commercial airplanes and the licensing of pilots.

The licensing of drugs before they can be sold.

The setting of rates for airlines, truck lines, railroads, barge lines, and pipelines.

Bans on unfair business and labor practices and on business combinations that restrain competition.

Penalties on the owners and makers of cars that emit more than a set level of pollutants.

Minimum wage and maximum hour limits for workers in some industries.

Limits on strip mining and rules for restoring the land after mining.

The control of private power rates through competing, publicly produced power.

Wage and price controls.

Bans on harmful food additives.

Ad campaigns about the dangers of smoking.

High taxes to reduce the use of scarce resources such as oil.

The Reagan administration has pushed for substantial deregulation in the protective regulatory area, but it has had very limited success in changing statutes. The administration, however, has relaxed the enforcement of many protective regulations.

Redistributive policies distribute wealth, property rights, or some other value among distinct groups (such as social classes or racial groups) in society. The policies are called *redistributive* because they transfer some value to one group *at the expense of* another group. Some relatively wealthy people view themselves as losers in a tax revision that increases taxes on their wealth and income in order to increase programs for the poor. Some Anglos see themselves as losers in programs designed to give special help to minorities.

Redistribution can, in fact, take from the poor or minorities and give added advantages to the wealthy or Anglos. However, those engaged in debate over public policies rarely regard such policies as redistributive. The political focus is on programs intended to benefit the disadvantaged in society. Examples include:

Progressive personal income tax rates—richer people pay a higher percentage of their incomes.

Income maintenance through a negative income tax or tax credits that give money to some poor people who pay no taxes.

The prohibition of racial discrimination in housing, public accommodations, and education.

Affirmative action in the hiring of women and minorities by federal contractors.

Employment and training programs that are mainly for the poor.

Food stamps for the poor.

Special legal services for the poor.

Government-sponsored health insurance for the elderly.

Foreign and Defense Policies

Foreign and defense policies are intended to affect the behavior of other nations and also provide security for the United States and its allies. (They will be discussed in greater detail in Chapter 20.) There are three types of such policies: structural, strategic, and crisis. In each of these types, distinctive political patterns of interaction occur during the decision-making process.

Structural policies procure, locate, and organize military personnel and materiel. Since the government competes with no one in this field, defense is totally subsidized. But exactly how that subsidy is allocated varies greatly. Examples of structural defense policies are

Defense procurement decisions, some of which involve competition among manufacturers.

The placement, size, and closing of military bases and other facilities in the United States.

Decisions on new weapons systems (types of aircraft, ships, tanks).

The size of reserve military forces.

Programs that send surplus farm products overseas.

Strategic policies set our basic national military and foreign-policy stance. Examples include

The basic mix of military forces: the ratio of offensive to defensive weapons; the ratio of ground-based missiles to submarine-based missiles to manned bombers; the ratio of combat troops to support troops.

Foreign trade: the creation of import tariffs and quotas, for example.

Sales of arms to foreign nations. Should we arm Israel? Should we arm Saudi Arabia? How much? At what price? With what types of weapons?

Foreign aid: the amount and use of both economic and military aid; the ratio of military aid to Israel and the Arab nations; the use of aid to reward or punish other nations for their policies.

The number and location of U.S. troops overseas.

The extent of U.S. involvement, if any, in specific military-political situations overseas: Vietnam, Cambodia, Laos, Angola, Zaire, Rhodesia, El Salvador, Iran, Lebanon, Nicaragua.

Levels of immigration into the United States.

Crisis policies are short-run responses to immediate problems that are perceived as serious, have burst on the agenda with little or no warning, and demand immediate action. Examples are the U.S. response to

Japan's attack on Pearl Harbor in 1941.

France's collapse in Southeast Asia in 1954.

The attack by Britain and France on the Suez Canal in 1956.

The Soviet Union's placement of missiles in Cuba in 1962.

North Korea's seizure of a U.S. naval ship in 1968.

Cambodia's seizure of a U.S. merchant ship in 1975.

Iran's seizure of hostages in 1979.

The Soviet Union's invasion of Afghanistan in 1979.

The Soviet Union's threat to invade Poland in late 1980 and early 1981.

Israel's invasion of Lebanon in 1982.

The deteriorating military situation in Lebanon in 1984.

The Popularity of Distributive Policies

The importance of subgovernments, the premium put on bargaining, and the general complexity of policy-making in the United States work together to produce a situation in which defining policies as distributive is the line of least resistance. Everyone can win, and therefore everyone can gain politically. In an era of ballooning deficits, however, the tension between taking this line and curbing those deficits is great. Both courses of action cannot be pursued at once. Deficits cannot shrink if policy is constructed so that everyone gains.

Over time, policies and programs may change character and move from one category to another. In domestic policy, most movement of this kind is toward distribution. In foreign and defense policy, a similar movement from strategic policy to structural policy is seen because structural policy is defined in the familiar terms of who gains domestically. Structural decisions are easier to make than strategic decisions.

The Model Cities program of the mid-1960s provides a good example of movement of a domestic policy. This program started with a redistributive goal, offering more services to those in the poorest parts of inner cities. But it quickly became partly distributive by offering subsidies to local governments. And it was partly regulatory, since it focused on managing relations between Washington agencies and local governments and among the Washington agencies that delivered the service.

Special revenue-sharing or block grant programs were begun in the areas of employment and training in 1973 and in community development in 1974. They also illustrate the movement of programs from redistributive to distributive. Before the special revenue-sharing programs began, categorical employment and community development programs were aimed at the poorest people. Many employment and training programs were aimed at specific segments of the poorest groups: youths, older workers, and minorities. Community development projects were aimed at the parts of cities and towns where the poorest people lived. In the newer programs, some eligibility restrictions were dropped or loosened. There was a broader group of potential clients. But Congress gave the programs the same amount of money or somewhat less. How the money was parceled out to states and localities quickly became the focus of debate. Policymakers were mainly concerned with distribution to government bodies. Redistribution to social classes did not interest them. For both programs, much of the debate at the local level was over what groups got the contracts for local service delivery, not over what services would be delivered or who would get them.

The most common shift in domestic programs has been toward distribution. The politics of subsidy decisions is easier than the politics of redistribution. This is because direct head-to-head confrontations are rare. And, most of the time, all of the parties seem to come out winners. When there is a shortage or scarcity, redistribution is more likely. But policymakers who consider redistribution to the disadvantaged normally court political controversy.

CONCLUSIONS

This chapter has introduced the topic of policy-making in general. It is through an examination of policy-making that we see the contextual factors of American politics, politically active individuals, and governmental institutions interacting with one another. The following five chapters will explore the most important aspects of policy-making and several critical substantive areas in more detail.

The challenges of governing sketched in the first paragraph of this chapter recur constantly in all aspects of policy-making. This chapter helps us understand why these problems are so central. It is not easy—either intellectually or politically—to agree on what problems require government action. People disagree about the general scope of le-

gitimate government action, about what government action should do in concrete situations, and about how helpful or harmful government action can be. Another constant challenge is avoiding the paralysis that can be induced by a system featuring multiple governmental and nongovernmental policy-making institutions, multiple geographic layers of government, and elaborate procedures by which these institutions and layers must interact. By definition, it is enormously difficult to get continuing agreement that the federal government is acting wisely. The key to meeting these challenges is bargaining and compromise. Only through processes that encourage bargaining and allow compromise can the challenges be met even in part and even temporarily. Permanent solutions to these challenges are impossible and, in fact, undesirable in a democratic system of government.

The overview of policy-making in this chapter is summarized in several general conclusions:

1. The federal government is enormously complex. Yet there are identifiable general stages to policy-making. First, policymakers set agendas. Second, they formulate and legitimate policies. Third, they implement those policies.

2. Many actors, both individuals and institutions, are important in determining policy outcomes in an open political system such as that of the United States. Subgovernments are often important in determining policy, but they do not dominate all policy areas.

3. The federal nature of our governing system adds another enormously complicating and fragmenting dimension to policy-making in the United States. In many programs, achieving national goals requires not only action by the federal government but also action by state and local governments. The federal influence is stronger than state and local influences in many policy areas, despite President Reagan's attempts to alter the balance of influence in favor of the states. But federal influence is not dominance.

4. Built into the American political system are great incentives for individuals and institutions to reach compromises on the substance of policy through bargaining.

5. Policy is generally stable. It is difficult, though not impossible, to make major policy changes.

6. Seven distinct policy types produce distinctive patterns of interaction among the various institutions of government and the private sector. These are the distributive, competitive regulatory, protective regulatory, and redistributive domestic policy types, and the structural, strategic, and crisis foreign and defense policy types.

FURTHER READING

JONES, CHARLES O.   (1984)   *An Introduction to the Study of Public Policy.* 3rd ed. Monterey, Calif.: Brooks/Cole Publishing. A short but thorough and thoughtful treatment of the flow and analysis of public policies.

KINGDON, JOHN W.   (1984)   *Agendas, Alternatives, and Public Policies.* Boston: Little, Brown. A careful and interesting examination of agenda setting in Washington.

LOWI, THEODORE J.   (1979)   *The End of Liberalism.* 2nd ed. New York: W.W. Norton. An interesting argument that the dominance of pluralism in American policy-making has resulted in policy with no integrity.

O'TOOLE, LAURENCE J., JR., ed.   (1985) *American Intergovernmental Relations: Foundations, Perspectives, and Issues.* Washington: Congressional Quarterly Press. A large book of short readings on American intergovernmental relations that explore historical and theoretical perspectives; political fiscal, and administrative aspects; and a sampling of contemporary issues.

Chapter Seventeen

SHAPING DOMESTIC POLICIES

No matter how well developed and refined governmental processes are, they do not produce policies automatically. Even when the U.S. government addresses public problems that can seemingly be "solved" or at least "attacked" with minimal reference to other nations or to world events, the substantive results of the normal processes of government are not highly predictable. And even when policies and programs are created, what actually happens during their implementation may dramatically alter what can be expected by both those who created the policies and programs and those who were supposed to benefit from them.

As the government shapes domestic policies during both formulation/legitimation and implementation, the political system faces a number of challenges. Foremost among these challenges are (1) making sure that channels of access and communication between the rulers and the ruled are numerous and unclogged as policy is made; (2) balancing the need for and the benefits of coalition building, which is at the heart of democractic politics, against the need to produce sensible policy products; and (3) implementing programs so as to be true to their discernible purposes and to facilitate the desired results.

*C*hapter 16 introduced policy-making in the United States in broad strokes. It defined the steps or stages of the policy process, and it identified and discussed four types of domestic policy and three types of foreign and defense policy. This chapter deals broadly with domestic policy in general—a sweeping category that contains a vast array of substantive areas. In Chapters 18, 19, and 20, we explore three exceptionally important policy areas in more detail: economic policies, spending, and taxing (Chapter 18); liberties, rights, and equality (Chapter 19); and foreign and defense policies (Chapter 20).

In the present chapter, we focus on two important stages of the policy process: (1) the making of domestic policy (formulation and legitimation) and (2) its implementation. To illustrate our general discussion, we use examples involving actual policies of recent years. Inevitably, our examples only dip into the reservoir of policies in which the national government has been involved.

In the first part of this chapter, we deal with two major aspects of the formulation and legitimation of domestic policy (we collapse those terms into the more general term *policy-making*). One aspect is the access to decision making of various individuals, groups, and institutions as policy is formulated and legitimated. The other aspect is coalition building and compromise in the formulation and legitimation of domestic policy. Recall that formulation is the development of alternative goals and of methods by which government can reach them. Legitimation is the selection of one set of goals and methods over its competitors—the set selected is made legitimate.

In the second part of the chapter, we deal with implementation. Here, we define implementation, examine patterns of influence in the implementation of domestic programs, and illustrate implemention by presenting several concrete cases.

FORMULATION AND LEGITIMATION OF DOMESTIC POLICY

Access To Decision Making In The Shaping Of Policies

Who makes policy decisions? The answer has much to do with the substance of the decisions made. Many actions in politics are based on self-interest. Individuals with access to the processes, institutions, and people through which decisions are made are apt to use that access to push for policies promoting their own interests.

Both policy formulation and legitimation are competitive. This means that there is no single elite that makes all of the policy decisions. The system is porous. Many people and groups can gain access to important processes and thus develop influence over the outcome. However, some people and groups have more access and influence than others.

Not everyone can gain access to decision processes. There are several reasons for this situation. One is that formal rules govern some of the main aspects of decision making. Some people have routine access to official bodies. By definition, a member of Congress has potential influence

Organized groups get access. Organized farm workers picket in Chicago as a means of getting access to policy-making.

over decisions that require the passage of a statute. A private individual in Seattle with great interest in the statute but no official position has very little potential for influencing such decisions. Simply because of the office he holds, the president of the United States has more access to decision making than does a taxpayer in Des Moines. But the citizens of Seattle and Des Moines can still have some influence over decision processes. They can vote for members of Congress. They can join and support interest groups that lobby on issues. They can write to the president and members of Congress.

Another reason why different people have different levels of access to and influence in decision making is that they are not equally knowledgeable about the processes, issues, and timetables involved in specific decisions. A lot of policy formulation and legitimation activities are invisible except to the individuals most directly affected. Other individuals who have an interest in a specific decision may be denied access and influence because they do not know how or when it is being made. Individuals who belong to an organized group are likely to be better informed because the group collects and distributes information about decision making.

Still another reason for unequal levels of access and influence is that some groups have more resources than others. Groups with a good deal of money can mount major lobbying campaigns. Groups with only a little money cannot afford to do so. Large groups can organize drives to register voters and to influence officials and policies by changing the nature of the

FIGURE 17–1   Channels of access from the public to officials

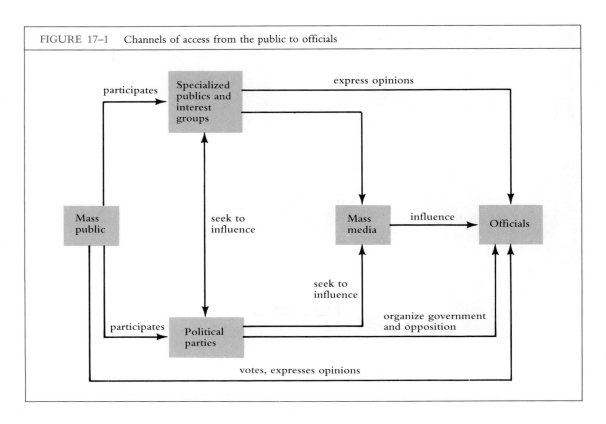

electorate. Smaller groups lack the resources needed to undertake such efforts.

Access and **influence** are different. People or groups with access have a chance to engage in some phases of policy formulation and legitimation, though they may not like the final results. People or groups with influence will see at least some of their preferences become part of an approved policy. Access, though necessary for influence, does not guarantee it.

Channels of access

Channels of access between people inside and outside the government run in two directions—from the public to officials and from officials back to the public. Figures 17–1 and 17–2 diagram the major channels.

Several major features of the figures should be underscored. First, there are many potential channels in both directions. They may not always be used, but they are available. Second, people and groups in society try to influence one another as well as officials. If they can form coalitions with common views before seeking to influence officials, they are likely to have more success. Third, no one group or cluster of groups in society monopolizes access. Fourth, since channels run in both directions, groups and

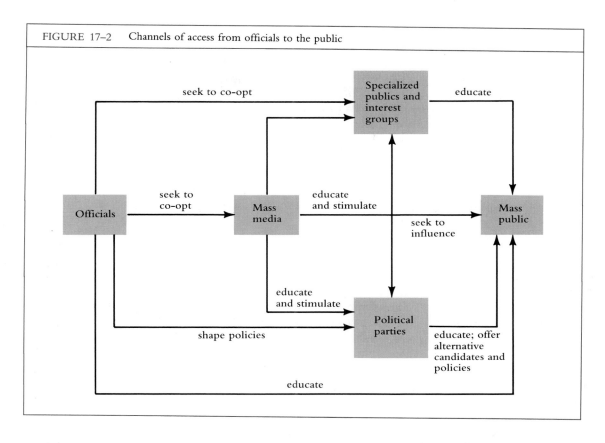

FIGURE 17–2   Channels of access from officials to the public

institutions in society have access to officials and the potential for influencing them and vice versa. Officials do not merely absorb pressures, and
they do not call all of the shots.

Another way to view access is to think about its potential with regard
to the specific actions undertaken during formulation and legitimation.
Which institutions and actors are likely to dominate which actions? What
differences will these patterns of dominance be likely to make? Here it is
useful to think of formulation and legitimation as each comprising four
clusters of activities: (1) collecting, analyzing, and distributing information; (2) developing alternatives; (3) advocating specific alternatives and
opposing others; and (4) reaching formal decisions about which alternative
to ratify, if any.

Federal bureaucracies do most of the collecting, analyzing, and distributing of information, since they have far more resources for undertaking
these activities than do the other major actors (Congress, the president,
and interest groups). Those actors can only provide some marginal data
and try to influence the kinds of information obtained. Because information gathering and processing come first in both formulation and legiti-

mation activities, they help shape subsequent choices. Though the bureaucracy's degree of access to decision processes diminishes at later stages, its impact continues to be felt because of its importance at this first stage.

The next two stages—developing alternatives and advocating positions on them—are highly competitive. During the development of alternatives, Congress, the president, and the bureaucracy all have a great deal of access to decision making. Interest groups have less access, but they can have some importance.

The most competitive stage of all is the one in which alternatives are advocated; at this stage, all of the major actors have a great deal of access. The president can become the most visible advocate on a few important issues. Reagan, for example, mobilized his resources for this purpose with regard to taxing and spending policy in 1981 and with regard to aid for the Nicaraguan *contras* throughout his presidency. But Congress, the bureaucracy, and interest groups also have resources that they can use to support or oppose the president's preferences.

When formal decisions are made, the dominant participants are Congress and the president. Major policies usually require formal legislation, and Congress and the president are, of course, central in the legislative process. However, what has happened during the first three stages limits the results of the decision stage. The alternatives have been narrowed. Although Congress and the president do not merely ratify foregone conclusions, their options are limited. The compromises, agreements, and bargains that have already been struck, usually over a long period of time, shape much of what emerges from this final stage.

Patterns of influence in shaping domestic policy

Different clusters of actors and institutions have more or less access to and influence on policy development, depending on what policies are at stake. (Ripley and Franklin, 1987; Lowi, 1964). In Chapter 16, we defined and discussed four types of domestic policies—distributive, competitive regulatory, protective regulatory, and redistributive. Figure 17–3 summarizes the most important relationships for determining these types of policies. For both distributive and competitive regulatory policy-making, subgovernments dominate. The president and the central bureaucracy have much less influence. Congress as a whole also has very little influence, and it typically supports the decisions of subcommittees. Subgovernments treat these areas of policy as their private preserve, and for the most part they are left alone.

The top layers of the executive branch and Congress play a more important role in protective regulatory policies. Congress and these top layers bargain with each other and with those parts of the private sector that are to be regulated. But agencies and subcommittees can and do get involved.

In redistributive policy decisions, the most important bargaining takes place among the top level of the executive branch, Congress, and peak

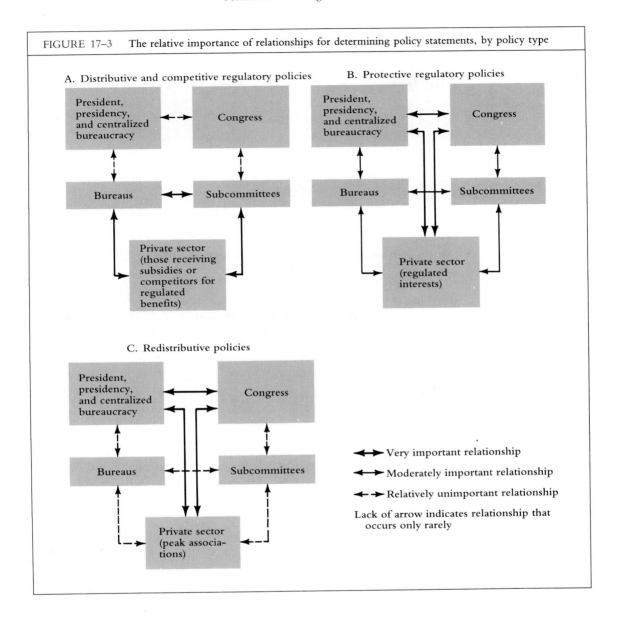

FIGURE 17–3   The relative importance of relationships for determining policy statements, by policy type

A. Distributive and competitive regulatory policies

President, presidency, and centralized bureaucracy ←→ Congress

Bureaus ←→ Subcommittees

Private sector (those receiving subsidies or competitors for regulated benefits)

B. Protective regulatory policies

President, presidency, and centralized bureaucracy ←→ Congress

Bureaus ←→ Subcommittees

Private sector (regulated interests)

C. Redistributive policies

President, presidency, and centralized bureaucracy ←→ Congress

Bureaus ←→ Subcommittees

Private sector (peak associations)

←→ Very important relationship
←→ Moderately important relationship
←→ Relatively unimportant relationship
Lack of arrow indicates relationship that occurs only rarely

associations in the private sector. (*Peak associations* are conglomerates of other groups. Examples include the U.S. Chamber of Commerce and the AFL-CIO.) Bureaus and subcommittees are much less involved in the final decision than they are in the other areas, but sometimes congressional committees break deadlocks and suggest compromises. Bureaus rarely get involved in the final compromise process, but may help shape some of the debate and its outcome. This is true because they are so important in col-

James Earl "Jimmy" Carter (1924–   ). Soon after his election as president in 1976, Jimmy Carter sought to make major changes in national policies involving water development. He sought to cut 32 water projects from the federal budget but failed to consult with members of Congress from the states affected. As a result, this effort met with an angry congressional response.

lecting, analyzing, and distributing the information used by all of those involved in the decision making.

Examples of access and influence

Water policy   Early in 1977, President Jimmy Carter said that he wanted to spend less for water development projects and took steps to cut a number of these projects from the budget for fiscal year 1978. Water development projects are among the purest examples of distributive policies, policies in which any president has minimal influence. Yet Carter thought that the president should be more important in making decisions about such projects. He tried to make them a matter of national priority and arrive at a more rational use of public resources.

The policy formulation phase of the debate began on February 21, when the president named 19 projects that he wanted to cut from his budget. Later he added more projects to his "hit list," and the total grew to 32. On April 18, the president ended this phase of the debate by announcing the outcome of his review of the 32 projects.

That final outcome was instructive. The president suggested that funding for 18 of the 32 projects be stopped. (He left the door open, though, to restoring 3 of the 18.) For the other 14 projects, funding for 5 would be reduced and funding for 9 would stay the same. The projects that were kept in whole or in part were mostly the largest projects, the ones with the most active political support, and those closest to being finished.

Also instructive is the harvest of ill will that Carter reaped by trying to intrude in a matter not normally in the presidential province. Some of his supporters in Congress were angry over his approach and over his failure to consult with them. The Senate majority leader, Robert C. Byrd (D – W. Va.), described a Senate vote opposing the president as "a clear signal to the White House that this Congress expects to be consulted [on] matters which come within the responsibility of the legislative branch." He also called the president's handling of the water project review "a serious aberration" (*Washington Post,* March 12, 1977).

In an exchange on the Senate floor, Warren G. Magnuson (D–Wash.) and J. Bennett Johnston, Jr. (D–La.), captured the essence of distributive policy formulation: Everyone with something at stake supports everyone else so that all can gain what they want.

> **Mr. Magnuson:** I could go on for quite a while about this so-called move that is going on downtown on the water projects.
>
> **Mr. Johnston:** Nobody is going to be doing anything but trying to restore their water projects. I can tell the Senate that I am not. We can let the rest of this jobs bill go. We are going to drop everything to try to get these water projects on-stream again. I do not doubt that we are going to win the fight.
>
> **Mr. Magnuson:** In the long run, we will win it. We can override the president's veto in the long run.
>
> **Mr. Johnston:** That is right.
>
> **Mr. Magnuson:** But it stops everything. . . . Can the senator from Louisiana imagine a senator from Washington going to his state and holding a hearing on the benefits or demerits of Grand Coulee Dam?
>
> [*Laughter*]
>
> They would hang me from a tree if I were to hold a hearing on it, after this has been established for years.
>
> This is absolutely incredible. I know about the projects that the senator from Louisiana has there. This is the lifeblood of the economy in some of those areas.
>
> It is the best thing we can do. There are other things we can do, but it is the best single thing we can do to revive our economy, to keep these projects moving, because we are going to have something of value to show for it when they are done.

A maverick member of Congress loses. Appropriately disguised for the occasion, Rep. Silvio Conte (R–Mass.) appeared at a 1983 news conference to protest a "pork barrel" water projects bill. Said Conte: "The congressmen have their nostrils right in the trough, and they're slurping it up for their districts at the expense of all the taxpayers." The bill passed on a voice vote.

President Reagan was much less disposed than President Carter to attack water development projects directly. However, the Reagan administration pursued some of Carter's initiatives, particularly by urging that funding for projects should come not only from the federal government but also from the localities that would benefit from them. But the Reagan administration's commitment was not consistent in practice. In 1984, deferring to election-year political necessity, it funded a dam safety bill completely from the federal Treasury rather than get western Republican congressional candidates in hot water by insisting on cost sharing. And in a 1985 supplemental appropriations bill, it supported funding for 45 new water projects, 21 of which had no cost-sharing provisions.

The pork barrel instincts of most members of Congress (which typify policy-making in the distributive arena) remained strong during the Reagan years with regard to water projects. Reagan did, however, make some headway in the area of cost sharing, both because his staff was more flexible and skillful than Carter's in dealing with Congress on water issues and because mounting concern about federal deficits made for closer scrutiny of any federal spending.

The great underlying strength of the water project subgovernment was demonstrated by its tussles with the Carter and Reagan administrations. In this realm, presidential access to and influence over decision making is limited. Skillful and persistent presidents can make dents in the distributive arena, but only with extraordinary efforts.

Energy policy   In April 1977, President Carter proposed a large package of energy legislation that dealt comprehensively with all forms of energy. The package contained a long and complex set of measures that were in part distributive (offering subsidies to the producers of certain kinds of energy), in part competitive regulatory (setting up mechanisms for choosing which producers would provide certain forms of energy), and in part protective regulatory (regulating certain forms of production for the common good).

Carter developed his proposals with help from only his closest advisers. Once he made the package public, many other people and groups took part in the formulation process. Despite the secrecy surrounding the administration's deliberations, lobbyists were able to reach individuals in the administration who were important in the early decision making.

Before Carter announced his package publicly, oil industry lobbyists got technical decisions made in their favor that would give them hundreds of millions of dollars more in revenues over the next few years. The *Washington Post* said in late April that the "oil companies and industry trade associations such as the American Petroleum Institute have had an intense lobbying effort under way. It began before Carter's inauguration, and reached saturation level in recent weeks. One aide to presidential energy adviser James R. Schlesinger said, 'We've been under carpet bombing by lobbyists of every stripe.' "

The lobbyists influenced important technical details. For example, Carter was first going to propose that to be exempt from price controls, oil would have to come from new wells drilled at least 5 miles from an old well. This would prevent new wells from tapping into the same oil pool as an old well just to get the oil exempted from price control. Over the last weekend before the proposals were made public, the distance was reduced to 2.5 miles. In explaining how the oil industry got to the proposal drafters, one high oil official said, "Somebody tapped somebody on the shoulder."

A list was made by the *Washington Post* (April 23, 1977) of those in the "energy establishment"—the key parties in the lobbying actions set off by the president's April 1977 proposals. The list included

Five major environmental and/or consumer groups.

Seven major oil companies.

Five major oil, gas, and coal associations.

Six law firms representing the oil industry (and one firm listed as "antiestablishment").

Eight lobbyists for oil and gas companies and associations.

Four senators and five representatives in critical spots in the Senate and House, such as the chairmen of the Senate Finance Committee, the House Ways and Means Committee, and the Senate and House Interior committees.

Eight key figures in the administration in addition to the president

New sources of energy. One of many energy alternatives is solar power, pictured here in California. Despite President Carter's efforts, no coherent energy policy was adopted in the United States. The oil lobby was behind the defeat of his 1977 energy proposals.

(such people as the chairman of the Council of Economic Advisers, the energy adviser, the secretary of the Treasury, the head of the Office of Management and Budget, and the secretary of the interior). Thirteen member nations of the Organization of Petroleum Exporting Countries (OPEC).

Under intense and diverse lobbying, Carter's comprehensive package disintegrated. A few specific pieces of energy legislation were enacted, but the United States failed to adopt an overall policy on the production and consumption of energy.

President Reagan was convinced that the market forces affecting the supply and use of energy should be unfettered by government action. He proposed no new protective regulatory measures and sought to dismantle some of the measures in place. His major proposal with regard to energy policy was to deregulate natural gas completely and quickly. He also wanted to demolish the newly created Department of Energy. He achieved neither of these goals. Reagan's vision of unifying energy policy by allowing maximum freedom for market forces was also unattainable. Diverse points of view continued to prevail in specific areas. The political system continued to produce disjointed and sometimes contradictory energy policies and programs. Many competing interests, agencies, and points of view continued to influence the realm of energy policy.

Employment and training policy   Since the early 1960s, the federal government has created a number of programs for training and retraining unemployed or underemployed workers. Throughout the 1960s, 1970s, and 1980's, a great many groups and individuals had access to and influence over the shape of federal employment and training policy. The configuration of the actors in formulation and legitimation changed over time, however. In effect, changes in the structure of the programs in place and changes in the perceptions of the government officials responsible for making the policy dictated that different actors would have different amounts of clout at different times.

The general thrust of employment and training policy from the early 1960s until 1982 was to increase the number of programs and also to increase the number of the participants who helped shape their details (Baumer and Van Horn, 1984; Franklin and Ripley, 1984). In the 1960s, the federal programs were "categorical"—that is, they were aimed at fairly narrowly defined groups of beneficiaries and the contracts for program delivery were written directly between the national Department of Labor and local delivery agencies, such as school systems, employment service offices, and various community-based agencies. The contractors quickly became powerful interest groups that helped perpetuate programs in forms that increased the amount of program money flowing in their direction.

The Comprehensive Employment and Training Act (CETA), enacted in 1973, gave new powers to city and county governments by funneling most of the program money through them. CETA also specified a greater role for organized labor and private business. These actors were added to the mix of local public organizations (schools, employment service offices) and nonprofit organizations (for example, community action agencies and Urban League affiliates) that were already important in this policy area. And, as with any program, the federal bureaucrats themselves were also important actors who had their own interests. The states were given only a bit of influence in CETA. The general operating principle behind both congressional and Department of Labor behavior with regard to CETA was to structure roles for all interests and to create a program that could offer something for almost everyone.

The pattern in which diverse interests contended for CETA money was changed when the Reagan administration pushed hard for ending CETA, a goal it achieved in 1982. The administration wanted no federal employment and training program, though it finally supported a successor to CETA generated by a few members of Congress with strong support from lobbies for business and the states. This successor—the Job Training Partnership Act (JTPA)—gave much more power to the private business sector and the state governments than CETA had given them. It also reduced the roles of the federal government and local governments (cities and counties). The same actors contended for influence under JTPA as had contended for influence under CETA, but now the structure rigged the outcomes so that the states and private businesses were most likely to benefit and so that some of the interests and groups that had been particularly potent under CETA had much less access to and influence over programmatic decisions.

In short, the employment and training policy area offers a good glimpse into the interaction between statutes and the influence exercised by those who seek to influence program choices.

Coalition Building and Compromise

Consider the following. The president has announced that he strongly favors a new national health insurance program to be funded out of general tax revenues. Benefits would be available to all, but extra help would go to the poor in the form of routine medical and dental checkups. The chairman of the House Ways and Means Committee, which will handle the bill, supports the idea except for the extra help for the poor. The chairman of the Senate Finance Committee, which will also handle the bill, is opposed to funding the scheme out of general tax revenues. Instead, he favors a special flat payroll assessment that would tax all wage earners equally on the first $10,000 of their income. The American Medical Association is opposed to the whole idea. The organization representing the largest health insurance companies says that it will support the president *only* if the statute guarantees the private insurance industry all of the insurance business at profitable rates. Other groups and people have also taken a variety of positions on the details of the program.

How does anything concrete ever emerge from such a situation? Is so much disagreement fatal to the creation of a new program?

There may or may not be action. A new policy may or may not be approved. The key to success is twofold. **Coalitions** supporting and opposing the proposal must be built, and *compromises* must occur so that one coalition is strong enough to prevail. Without coalitions—clusters of people and groups that can agree at least for a while on a desirable outcome—few policy initiatives would ever succeed. And compromises are what builds coalitions and holds them together. Additional compromises allow a sizable coalition to become large enough to win.

Throughout policy formulation and legitimation, coalitions have to be built and rebuilt. They are rarely permanent. During the formulation phase, coalitions need not contain a majority. They must, however, be large enough to persuade others that their proposal should be considered for final approval. During legitimation, majorities must be fashioned not just once, but many times, to keep a solution moving toward formal adoption. In Congress alone, majorities are needed in subcommittees and then in full committees in both the House and Senate; they are needed on the floor not just for final passage, but also for major amendments and

Presidents get involved in coalition building. Proesident John F. Kennedy [left] in the White House and President Lyndon B. Johnson [right] on Air Force One use the telephone to help build coalitions for their proposed policies.

major procedural motions. Majorities are again needed in each of the delegations from both the House and Senate that meet as the conference committee and again in both the full House and Senate to pass the conference report.

One technique often used to build a winning coalition is to exempt certain groups from the negative effects of a proposed policy (Leman, 1979). This lessens or eliminates their reasons for opposition. When minerals other than coal were exempted, a winning coalition was built for a strip mine bill in 1977. Tobacco was exempted from the jurisdiction of the Food and Drug Administration. This was done to neutralize the strong political opposition of the tobacco industry to the creation and existence of that agency. Many bills include a *hold harmless* clause when they cut benefits or change programs. "Hold harmless" means that those who currently benefit will keep getting their aid, or at least a high percentage of it, no matter what a new law might say in general. In 1973, part of the price for passing the Comprehensive Employment and Training Act (CETA) was to guarantee all localities at least 90 percent of the employment and training funds that they got in the last pre-CETA year, no matter what the new funding formula gave them. Likewise, there was a seven-year hold harmless clause (with declining percentages) attached to the Community Development Block Grant Act of 1974. That act consolidated a number of categorical aid programs for cities such as sewer and water grants and public facilities grants.

Constant coalition building has at least four results for the development of policy. First, it takes a long time to approve a policy. Second, compromise is a must to form and reform coalitions and majorities and to hold them together. Third, given the time span and the many compromises that are made, policies often change a great deal during formulation and legitimation. Backers may wind up with a product quite different from what they originally wanted. Fourth, since it is so difficult to get action, it is usually easier not to act than to act.

Five examples of major policies follow to illustrate these points. Analysis of minor policies confirms the same points (see Redman, 1973; Reid, 1980).

The development of federal aid formulas

The devising of formulas for the distribution of federal aid is one of the easiest areas in which to show compromise and coalition building. Senator Abraham Ribicoff (D–Conn.) summed up the essence of the process in the Senate. In speaking about the formula for giving out about $4 billion for public works jobs, he said, "Day in and day out on this floor all of us get these sheets of paper [with various proposed formulas], and everybody fiddles around with a formula to find out . . . whether it will give a dollar more to 26 states, and then you become a winner—and then the national interest is forgotten." Senator Howard Metzenbaum (D–Ohio) addressed the tension between national interest and local interest during the same debate: "Sure I want to be a broad United States Senator, with national concerns, but charity begins at home" (*New York Times,* March 20, 1977).

The details of formulas for distributing federal aid are usually complex. But such technical details have a lot to do with what areas get how much money and, in the end, with how much money and services are available for which people and which sections of the country. Seemingly trivial details in formulas can have major impacts on the distribution of funds. For example, when the formula for general revenue sharing was devised, relative need was measured in part by adequacy of housing and the more needy local areas got more money than the less needy. However, lack of plumbing was a factor in determining whether housing was inadequate, but lack of adequate heating was not. Since lack of plumbing was more prevalent in the South and lack of adequate heating was more prevalent in the Northeast, this meant that southern governments got more money in the allocation and governments in the Northeast got less.

When the aid formula for distributing federal money to local school districts through the Elementary and Secondary Education Act of 1965 was devised, welfare payments were counted as income in determining local need. This cut the proportion of the population counted as being below the official poverty line in a number of northeastern cities. It also cut those cities' share of federal aid to public schools. When Congress made decisions on both this formula and the one discussed in the previous paragraph, members from the Northeast were not trying to help poor Southerners at the expense of their own constituents. They had simply been unable to fashion a coalition that could prevent the adoption of formulas that did not work in their favor. In both instances, they favored having a program over having no program. The price they had to pay for having a program was to acquiesce to the majority coalition's desires on these details of the aid formulas.

When CETA was passed in 1973, it replaced a large number of categorical programs in the employment and training field. The formula used to disburse funds under the program shifted resources from the South to the West and North, and away from central cities toward the suburbs (Mirengoff and Rindler, 1976). This happened mostly because of the weight given to unemployment and poverty in the formula and because a formula was used at all. In the bargaining that led to the formula for CETA, the coalition of suburban interests was stronger than the coalition for the central cities. Likewise, the southern interests were outnumbered. So the urban and southern interests were shortchanged. These interests had to accept unfavorable compromises to have a program at all.

The formula for distributing general revenue-sharing money is also very complex. It, too, resulted from a geographic compromise during policy formulation and approval. A major study (Nathan, Manvel, and Calkins, 1975: 18) sums up how the formula came about:

> The greatest challenge to the revenue-sharing conference committee lay in reconciling the complicated and quite different House and Senate versions of the distributional formulas for state-by-state allocations. The House version favored high-population, industrialized states, the Senate version, low-income, rural states. The Solomon-like compromise that was reached retained both formulas and allowed each state's allocation to be determined according to the formula most favorable to it. The Senate formula was retained for intrastate distribution.

It is hardly by chance that the House formula favored populous states (the House is based on population). Nor is the more rural Senate formula a surprise (all of the states have two Senate seats, regardless of population). In this case, the two coalitions were equally strong—one was dominant in the House and the other in the Senate. So the compromise gave both coalitions most of what they wanted.

The 1985 farm bill

For many years, agricultural interests carved out a domain in which they got most of what they wanted from federal policy. The Reagan administration wanted to change this situation. A great deal of coalition building and compromise resulted in a major new farm bill—the Food Security Act of 1985. Its provisions reflected the strength of interest that had dominated federal agricultural policy for the previous decades. But the persistence of the administration in challenging those interests also resulted in compromises that represented genuine change.

Beginning with the Agricultural Adjustment Act of 1933, the federal government became an active partner in a wide variety of decisions made by farmers. Governmental intervention came in the form of price-support

New farm legislation. In December 1985, President Ronald Reagan signed a new farm bill at a White House ceremony. Looking on are [from left to right] Sen. Robert Dole (R–Kans.), Senate majority leader; Rep. Virginia Smith (R–Neb.); Vice President George Bush; and Rep. Tom Coleman (R–Mo.). The new farm bill retained the long-standing structure of price supports and payments to farmers, but the former would be gradually reduced. The bill also included measures to reduce the overproduction of some farm products.

loans, acreage and production controls, target price levels, marketing orders, support of storage facilities, an abundance of tax breaks, support of agricultural research and development, and support for low-interest loans.

By the 1980s, economic and political factors were making life more complex for the beneficiaries of the system that had been built—layer on layer—for half a century. These factors included

1. Escalating international competition that resulted in declining U.S. agricultural exports and increased imports.
2. Overproduction that created surpluses and lower prices.
3. Rapidly increasing farm debt that resulted in a large number of farm foreclosures and bankruptcies.
4. Rapidly increasing federal expenditures on farm subsidies.
5. The general problems of mammoth federal deficits and a huge and growing trade deficit.
6. The presence of the Reagan administration and its different perspectives on many aspects of agricultural policy.

In 1981, the new Reagan administration tried and failed to cut price-support loans and target price levels. In 1985, fresh from its 1984 election triumph, it again tried to alter farm policy. It presented a package whose adoption would have dramatically changed the U.S. government's role in agriculture. The proposed law would have quickly removed a variety of subsidies and exposed American agriculture to more market forces, including international competition. The traditional supporters of the large existing package of federal help for farmers opposed these changes and favored continuing existing programs of price supports and income supplements. They also wanted to devise new aid programs for farmers in financial trouble.

Vast numbers of lobbyists, as well as members of Congress and various parts of the executive branch, participated in the debate over farm policy in 1985. Farm groups such as the American Farm Bureau Federation and the National Farmers Organization and groups representing specific commodities (all longtime actors in the shaping of agricultural policy) were joined by environmental, consumer, and business groups (the last represented, for example, dealers in fertilizers, farm equipment, and food). These competing forces registered a great diversity of opinion. As usual with comprehensive farm bills, debate over sweeping policy principles was downplayed in favor of a series of discussions and compromises over a number of specific provisions.

Spokespersons for all of these contending interests met in various configurations and various settings to hammer out the final bill toward the end of 1985. Neither the Senate bill nor the House bill came close to the administration's original proposals. The House bill was fairly close to what already existed. President Reagan signed the final compromise into law on Christmas Eve.

The final bill represented some change from the existing law, but it retained the existing structure of price supports and income payments to farmers. The administration was pleased that the level of price-support loans would be reduced modestly over the bill's five-year life, that the level of governmental activity in support of exports would be increased, and that compulsory reduction in corn and wheat acreage and voluntary buyout of dairy herds would help reduce agricultural overproduction. Overall, the traditional farm interests had done well. Just how well was quickly revealed when the U.S. Department of Agriculture announced that the cost of the new program for its first year alone would probably be close to double the original estimate ($35 billion compared to the $17.5 billion that had been predicted).

Federal regulation of strip mining

Congress took 10 years to decide on federal regulation of strip mining. The process stretched from 1968 to mid-1977. In 1968, the Senate began by holding hearings on the first specific bill on the subject. In 1971, President Nixon proposed a bill, and in 1972 the House passed a bill, but the Senate did not act. In 1973, the Senate passed a bill. In 1974, the House passed a bill and went to conference with the Senate on its 1973 bill. After long talks, Congress passed a bill. But President Ford pocket vetoed it, thus stopping an attempt to override the veto. By mid-March 1975, Congress again presented a bill to the president, who again vetoed it. The attempt to override the veto was delayed until July because of dwindling support in the House. When the attempt came, it failed by three votes.

In late 1975, attempts were made in the House Interior Committee to revive the bill. They failed, largely because another successful Ford veto was anticipated. In 1976, the Rules Committee twice prevented bills from reaching the House floor.

In 1977, an important actor changed: Jimmy Carter replaced Gerald Ford in the White House. The coalition in favor of strip-mining regulation had been patiently built for 10 years. Now it could pass a bill that would get the president's approval. But the rules of the game in 1977 were the same as always: Compromise was still a must to keep a winning coalition in place. What follows is a glimpse of the coalitions on both sides and the compromises made in 1974 and 1977.

In 1974, the basic controversy was whether there should be a federal law on strip mining at all and, if so, how strong it should be. Coal producers and most electric companies, which are major coal users, wanted no bill at all. They claimed that coal companies would willingly reclaim strip-mined land and that state laws were sufficient to produce that result. Their argument stressed two points. First, federal controls would reduce output, thereby reducing the chances of cutting national dependence on foreign oil for energy. Second, controls would raise the price of coal, which would also work against its use.

Those favoring the bill were led by environmentalists outside Congress and a few leading Democrats in Congress, especially Representative Morris Udall of Arizona. They argued that, without strict regulation, strip mining would ravage the country, that the companies would leave new areas looking like the depressed parts of Appalachia. They also argued that the states lacked the power or the will to regulate strip mining effectively and they disputed the claim that regulation would impair coal production.

In 1974, a large number of organized groups had access to decision making in the House Interior Committee, in its subcommittee dealing with the bill, and in the conference committee. These included environmental groups; coal, steel, and electric companies; the U.S. Chamber of Commerce; and the United Mine Workers union (UMW). Many executive-branch agencies also lobbied hard for some provisions.

The coalitions on both sides were broad-based but unstable. The legislation was complex; many of its features could be considered separately. Some coalition members had only one narrow interest to protect. And as long as they got their way on that one interest, they would stay with their coalition. The UMW was most concerned with an amendment to tax strip-mined coal more than deep-mined coal. The former was mined mostly in the West, where the UMW was weak. The latter was mined mostly in the East, where it was strong. Some Pennsylvania interests supported the bill mainly because they wanted to ensure an exemption for anthracite coal, which is found only in Pennsylvania.

Executive-branch agencies were badly divided over the bill. Despite the White House's well-known position, officials and agencies disagreed both in public and in private. When the bill finally came to President Ford, his two top energy officials gave him conflicting advice on whether to sign or veto the bill. He chose to veto it.

By 1977, the proponents had a supportive president eager to sign a bill, but they had lost some strength in Congress. They had to engage in yet more compromise to keep a winning coalition together.

The first compromise made by backers of the bill was to limit it almost exclusively to coal mining. Earlier bills had covered, for example, copper. But the chance of a strong negative coalition being formed by a number of the interests targeted for regulation led to the focus on coal.

As in 1974, issues were not settled quietly and finally in subcommittee and committee. Rather, decisions made there were reexamined, debated, and extensively changed on both the House and Senate floors. And some issues remained to be resolved in the conference committee.

In general terms, the House committee produced a moderately strong bill in late April. That bill was strengthened even more on the House floor and passed a week later. In the Senate, the outcome was different. The committee produced a moderately strong bill in early May, but a few weeks later the bill was weakened greatly on the Senate floor. The net result exempted owners of small mines from some provisions and weakened some environmental provisions.

The conference committee bill, reported in July, was somewhere between the two versions. Mining interests gained several concessions. Both houses passed the bill, and the president signed it in early August. The United States now had a strip-mining law with some real restrictions. But enough concessions had been made to the coal mining companies to prevent them from building a coalition able to kill the bill altogether.

Medicare

Government-sponsored health insurance has been on the national agenda in a serious way since 1935 (Marmor, 1973). Federally supported health insurance for a part of the American population was provided in the 1965 law that set up Medicare. This program provides medical insurance for the elderly, using the apparatus of the social security system for funding. Since 1965, there has been a continuing debate about extending federally supported health insurance to the entire population. No additional programs have come close to being passed, however. The accompanying chronology gives some idea of how long Medicare itself took to develop.

The main feature of the debate over Medicare was the persistence of two diametrically opposed coalitions. One of these coalitions viewed any government activity in the realm of health insurance as an unacceptable invasion of the private enterprise system in the fields of health insurance and health care. The other viewed government health insurance as a social welfare program that any humane government in a wealthy nation should provide for its citizens. The two coalitions used the same arguments year after year. Opponents of national health insurance had access to many levers in Congress that allowed them to stop action.

In the late 1950s, the focus of the debate shifted from national health insurance for the whole population—which was going nowhere—to national health insurance for the elderly. Those opposed to such a measure used the same arguments that they had used against general health insurance. But the concentration on the elderly gave the proponents of national health insurance new appeals. Public opinion polls showed that the public favored national health insurance for the elderly long before Medicare passed.

The election of 1964 provided the right political conditions for the success of Medicare: a landslide victory for Lyndon Johnson as president and strong majorities of Democrats in both houses of Congress. Johnson and many congressional Democrats were committed to the proposed health insurance program. Even under those favorable conditions, it took six months of final bargaining in early 1965 to arrive at the compromises that allowed both the House and Senate to pass the same bill.

Federal aid to education

After World War II, debate over federal aid to education was complex and tangled (Bendiner, 1964; Eidenberg and Morey, 1969; Munger and Fenno, 1962; Sundquist, 1968). Right after the war, the federal government began to increase its special-purpose aid to education at all levels. But a logjam formed on the question of broad general aid—especially to elementary and secondary schools. An ideological dispute over the proper role of the federal government in an area traditionally under local control became intense. The logjam was broken only by shifting the form and aim of general-purpose aid. Aid-to-education measures seen as helping many special segments of the population or defined geographic areas were much easier to pass than broad, general-purpose measures seen as shifting aid from one racial or religious group to another. The final breakthrough on a form of general-purpose aid came in 1965. It was possible only because the focus was shifted from race and religion to poverty and because subsidy features were stressed. The compromise was based on changing the definition of the benefits to be provided.

Through all the debates, House and Senate members and a few key people at both the White House and the Department of Health, Education, and Welfare (HEW) were important. They framed initiatives, attempted compromises, and shifted the debate until the most controversial questions were muted. Generally, those involved were subcommittee chairmen, ranking House and Senate members, and HEW officials at the assistant secretary level or above. But because of the broad involvement of many groups and interests, agreement at this level was never enough to generate policy decisions. Large organizations such as the National Education As-

The Development of Medicare, 1935–1965

1935 The Roosevelt administration explores compulsory national health insurance as part of the Social Security Act, but no legislation is recommended to Congress.

1943 Three Democratic senators cosponsor a bill to broaden the Social Security Act. It would include compulsory national health insurance paid for with a payroll tax. No legislative action results.

1945 In his health message, President Truman proposes a medical insurance plan for persons of all ages. It would be paid for through a social security tax.

1949 The Truman proposal is considered and hotly contested in congressional hearings. No legislative action results.

1954 President Eisenhower opposes the concept of national health insurance as "socialized medicine." He suggests an alternative: reimburse private insurance companies for heavy losses on private health insurance claims. No action is taken on this proposal.

1957 Representative Forand introduces the "Forand bill." It provides hospital care for needy elderly social security beneficiaries, to be financed through increased social security taxes. No action is taken by Congress. Heavy AFL–CIO lobbying, though, generates public interest.

1960 The Forand bill is defeated by the House Ways and Means Committee (17–8). Chairman Mills opposes the bill.

1960 As a substitute for the Forand bill, Congress enacts the Kerr-Mills bill. It is designed to encourage the states to help older, needy persons (those not poor enough to qualify for Old Age Assistance but too poor to pay their medical bills).

1960 Health care is an issue in the presidential campaign; Kennedy vows support.

1961–64 President Kennedy's version of the Forand bill is submitted each year in the House and Senate, but the House Ways and Means Committee defeats it.

1962 The Senate defeats an amendment to a public welfare bill that includes the Kennedy proposal (52–48).

1964 The Senate passes (49–44) a medicare plan similar to Kennedy's proposal. It is in the form of an amendment to the Social Security Act. The plan dies when House conferees (from the Ways and Means Committee) refuse to allow its inclusion.

January 1965 The 1964 elections bring many new Democrats to Congress. The makeup of the Ways and Means Committee is changed to give it a majority of medicare supporters.

January 1965 President Johnson makes medical care his number one legislative priority.

July 1965 The medicare bill is signed into law after passage in both houses by generous margins.

Source: Adapted from material in *Congressional Quarterly Almanac*, 1965, pp. 236–47.

Schools get federal grants-in-aid. Grant programs of the national government have poured billions of dollars into local public school systems.

sociation, civil rights groups, and Catholic and Protestant groups also got involved. And the highest levels of the executive branch—usually including the president—got involved too.

General aid to school districts failed for more than 20 years because of hostility toward federal control of a traditionally local function. After 1954, some also felt that aid would be used as a lever to force public school integration. There was also the issue of whether private, especially Roman Catholic, schools would get aid. Combinations of these three issues again and again killed general aid in Congress. The proaid coalition in the Senate was formed early, and the Senate passed bills in 1948, 1949, 1960, and 1961. But in the House, the antiaid coalition kept control either of the whole House or at least of the Education and Labor Committee or the Rules Committee from 1943 through 1964. The full House killed bills on the floor in 1956, 1957, and 1961. In 1960, the Rules Committee killed a bill that had passed both houses but required a conference committee. It prevented action in a number of other years. The Education and Labor Committee membership was very hostile to federal aid from 1943 through 1955.

The logjam was broken in 1965. Liberal Democrats made sweeping gains in the House in the 1964 election as a result of President Johnson's landslide. But even more important, the effort to achieve general-purpose aid was replaced by a special-purpose approach. Both backers and opponents of general-purpose aid decided at last that some aid was better than none. The different sides in the fight over the status of religious schools compromised; they allowed those schools to share in some of the aid given to public schools. Since the successful program was aimed at poor children, not at school systems as such, it looked like special-purpose aid. A number of special-purpose programs had passed since the end of World War II and the new program, though far larger than any before, followed those precedents. Thus, the proaid coalition was finally able to enact at least part of the education program it wanted. The various titles of the new legislation included aid for equipment, classrooms, staff, and construction; aid for library resources; matching aid for supplemental education centers; aid for education research; and aid for state departments of education.

WHAT IS IMPLEMENTATION?

Implementation is what governments do and cause to be done after statements of policy intent have been made at the end of the formulation and legitimation process. As shown in Figure 17–4, implementation activities are preceded by formulation and legitimation activities, which result in statements of policy intent and in specific designs of programs.

Many factors affect and help shape the nature of implementation. These include the kinds and levels of communications among the individuals and agencies responsible for implementation; the kinds of enforcement activities undertaken to ensure that goals are met; the types of agencies responsible for implementation; and a variety of political, economic, and social conditions. Implementation activities lead to program performance, which helps shape the impact of governmental programs.

Core Implementation Activities

There are four kinds of government actions in implementation (see Jones, 1984: chap. 8). The first is *acquisition.* Responsible agencies amass the needed resources, including personnel, equipment, land, raw materials, and—above all—money. The second is *interpretation.* The agencies put the language of statutes into concrete directives and regulations. The third is *organization.* Bureaucratic subunits and routines are created. The fourth is *application.* Agencies provide services, payments, limits on activity, or whatever else has been agreed on as their tangible product.

Let's use a concrete case to illustrate. In 1977, Congress created a Young Adult Conservation Corps (YACC). The purpose of this program was to create work for jobless youths on conservation projects. The program was also supposed to provide training and other support services so that alumni of the corps would be better able to compete for jobs in the real labor market. Day-to-day operations were directed by the Departments of Agriculture and the Interior under the general guidance of the Department of Labor.

To begin the program, these three departments had to *acquire* staff. This meant transferring some people and hiring others. They also acquired sites for YACC camps, equipment (shovels, axes, Jeeps, food, furniture), raw materials (seedling trees, fertilizer), and dollars to pay for all this.

The departments had to *interpret* the law by making regulations that

FIGURE 17–4   The flow of policy activities

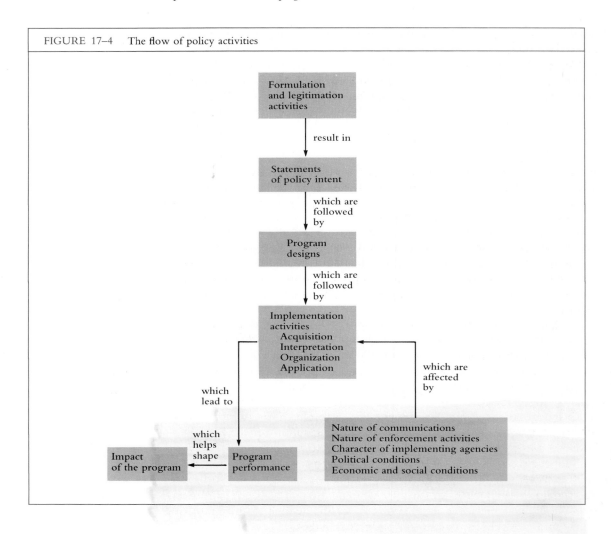

were published in the *Federal Register*. These regulations were issued in draft, and any interested parties could review and comment on them for a month or two. A final version was published after the departments agreed on what changes, if any, to make on the basis of the comments received. The regulations covered such items as eligibility standards and how to determine them, allowable expenses, accounting methods, records needed on both fiscal and nonfiscal matters, and required reports.

The departments had to *organize*. Each of the departments assigned internal responsibilities and developed forms for processing paperwork. Also, because of the joint nature of the venture, interdepartmental committees were formed to oversee the entire program and reach agreement on various issues.

Finally, the departments were ready to *apply* their programs to the target population. They enrolled participants, put them to work, paid them, and helped them get permanent jobs when their time in the YACC was over.

The Context of Implementation

Formulation and legitimation are intertwined with implementation. Policy continues to be refined—in effect, made—during implementation. This means that the details of implementation change constantly. The politics of coalition building, negotiation, and compromise characterizes implementation just as it characterizes formulation and legitimation. This means that the goals at which implementation aims and the details of implementation are subject to constant change. Some agencies achieve stable routines that lead to relatively calm implementation of their programs. Other agencies have to implement programs in a constantly changing political context.

Implementation helps determine the impact of government programs. Implementation decisions determine in part which persons or groups get what concrete benefits.

Implementation of some programs requires the voluntary participation of people or groups outside government. The intended beneficiaries may have to apply for benefits, enroll in a program, prove that they qualify, or show up to use a specific facility. For example, if an agency builds, equips, and staffs a job counseling center, but people from the neighborhood do not use it, then meaningful implementation cannot take place.

Budgetary decisions are one of the most important types of implementation actions. Budgetary actions in both the executive branch and Congress are accompanied by further refinements of policy. Budgetary decisions provide money, the basic resource without which no program can be mounted. Decision making on budgets is elaborate and time consuming, and during its course many disputes take place over both general policy and specific spending levels.

Implementation goals are often murky, and they usually change during implementation. They are also likely to be diffuse and implicit. Goals become clear—or are even invented—during the implementation process itself.

Whether or not goals are clearly stated, the implementation process may change the actual goals being pursued. One such change involved the Model Cities program in the late 1960s. The program was supposed to focus federal funds on the poorest parts of cities so as to attack problems in a unified way. But the program, in practice, became mainly an experiment in smoothing administrative processes between federal and city agencies and among diverse federal agencies. The goal of helping people in the inner city was replaced by the goal of helping bureaucratic agencies try out various modes of coordination.

Another goal change involved Title II of the Comprehensive Employment and Training Act of 1973. Its aim was to provide public service jobs with local government units for the chronically unemployed. When a major economic recession developed in late 1974 and 1975, that aim was quickly changed. The focus shifted to people who were just unemployed for the time being, even if they were not poor, uneducated, or members of a racial or ethnic minority.

A structural feature of bureaucracies helps explain some of the seemingly inevitable slippage between program intent as stated in a statute and program intent as revealed by the details of implementation. The individuals and groups that are the primary shaping agents in creating statutes are different from the people responsible for day-to-day implementation. The people in the White House, the executive branch, Congress, and major national interest groups who set broad program goals during formulation and legitimation are not the people who decide what goals are pursued—and how they are pursued—during implementation. The individuals responsible for the details of daily administration rarely take part in broad policy decisions. They are therefore often confronted with broad and perhaps confusing statements of general policy and identification of goals that they neither understand nor agree with.

Policy and program designers rarely assess the abilities of agencies to carry out programs. The requirements for successful implementation may simply exceed the capabilities of the responsible agencies. An agency that is suddenly given a task, for example, may not have a staff that is large enough or appropriately trained to perform that task.

Bureaucracies have a great deal of discretion in how they choose to implement a law and in what parts of the law they choose to implement. Sometimes such choices are based on the policy preferences of a bureau chief working with allies in Congress and the private sector. During the Reagan years, some agencies reflected the policy preferences of the administration, which differed substantially from the intent of Congress when statutes were created. This general point is underscored in the accompanying box, which discusses regulatory enforcement during the first year and a half of the Reagan administration.

The same lack of regulatory enforcement discussed in the box also characterized implementation of most civil rights laws during the Reagan Administration (Ripley and Franklin, 1986: 198-202). A slowdown in civil rights enforcement activities was evident in many federal agencies: the Civil Rights Division in the Department of Justice, the Office of Civil Rights in the Department of Education, the Office of Federal Contract Compliance Programs in the Department of Labor, the Equal Opportunity Employment Commission, the U.S. Civil Rights Commission, and

PRACTICE OF POLITICS

The Reagan Bureaucracy Slows Regulatory Enforcement

In 18 months the Environmental Protection Agency has reduced the number of cases referred for enforcement action by more than 70 percent. Inspections for clean air violations fell by 65 percent. Since January 1981, the enforcement division has been reorganized four times, and three enforcement chiefs have been fired (two appointed *and* fired by Gorsuch). According to internal memoranda, the enforcement section is faced with the loss of 43 percent of its field staff.

At the Occupational Safety and Health Administration, created to protect workers, Auchter quickly eliminated unannounced inspections for 80 percent of manufacturing firms. The number of violations cited fell 49 percent, inspections declined 10 percent, follow-up inspections dropped 55 percent, and fines imposed for violations fell 77 percent. Heavy fines—over $10,000—plummeted 90 percent. Auchter has proposed to forgive penalties for violations that are later corrected, thus removing one incentive to correct hazards before they are discovered by inspectors.

At the Food and Drug Administration, charged with protecting us from dangerous and mislabeled foods, drugs, cosmetics, medical devices, and man-made radiation, citations over 18 months dropped 88 percent and seizures of dangerous products fell 65 percent.

In 1980, the National Highway Traffic Safety Administration, enforcer of auto safety, initiated 118 engineering analyses of possible defects. Last year 19 analyses were begun.

The enforcement staff of the Consumer Product Safety Commission—responsible for protecting the public from hidden hazards in toys, appliances, power equipment, household chemicals, and hundreds of other products—has been reduced 46 percent since the Reagan administration took office. Recalls have been cut 60 percent.

The Interior Department's Office of Surface Mining (OSM) is supposed to regulate coal mining and enforce land reclamation requirements. In six eastern states, the number of inspections fell 38 percent between 1980 and 1982, while violations charged fell 62 percent. In six western states where OSM oversees state-administered programs, OSM was required by law to conduct 162 inspections, but it conducted only 40 and charged only three violations.

Source: Jonathan Lash, "Don't Like a Law. Don't Enforce It," *Washington Post*, October 10, 1982.

specific units in the Departments of Housing and Urban Development, the Treasury, and Health and Human Services.

Actors in Implementation

Many people and groups are involved in policy implementation. The primary responsibility for implementation falls on bureaucrats, but other people, both inside and outside the government, also participate. Legislators get involved when formulation and legitimation questions merge into implementation questions. Congressional intervention is particularly likely when implementation concerns decisions affecting the territorial distribution of federal resources, such as decisions on the size and location of military bases in the United States. The courts get involved by either requiring or prohibiting specific actions in response to lawsuits. Private citizens and groups get involved by pushing requests for benefits or by seeking to influence the language of regulations so as to benefit themselves.

The fact that the United States is a federal system with large bureaucracies at different territorial levels adds more complexity and more actors to domestic policy implementation (Van Horn and Van Meter, 1976). State and local officials can affect implementation profoundly. National groups in Washington (for example, the U.S. Conference of Mayors, the National Governors Association, and the National Association of Counties) represent various state and local officials. Such groups often lobby the bureaucracy to affect the details of implementation.

At any one time, there are apt to be several modes and levels of state and local participation in the implementation of a federally enacted domestic program. For example, state and local officials can have an impact on U.S. Department of Agriculture implementation decisions in three different modes (Talbot and Hadwiger, 1968). In one set of programs, such as those of the Commodity Exchange Authority, the Consumer and Marketing Service, and the Agricultural Research Service, state and local influence is primarily sporadic and informal. These programs are run directly by the U.S. Department of Agriculture and the decentralization that occurs in them is decentralization to federal field offices, not to state and local units. In a second set of programs, such as those of the Federal Extension Service, the Cooperative State Research Service, and state experiment stations, the national government exercises general supervision but leaves most of the administrative decisions to the state and local levels of government. Substantial funds and most of the personnel decisions are under the control of those levels. A third set of programs such as those of the Agricultural Stabilization and Conservation Service, the Rural Electrification Administration, the Soil Conservation Service, and the Farmers Home Administration, lies between the first two sets. There is more national supervision than in the second set but more state and local participation than in the first set.

The fact that most federal agencies are decentralized can lead to prob-

TABLE 17–1   Participants in policy implementation

Executive officials and organizations	Legislative officials and organizations	Bureaucratic officials and organizations	Nongovernmental individuals and organizations	Judicial officials and organizations
Federal level:				
President Executive Office of the President staff	Congress Congressional staff and support agencies	Department and agency heads Staff—civil servants (in Washington, in field offices)	Corporations, labor unions, interest groups, advisory bodies, media (all with national focus and impact)	Federal judges (three levels) Law clerks Marshals Masters, experts Federal attorneys
State level:				
Governor Governor's staff	State legislature Staff and support agencies for legislatures	Department and agency heads Staff—civil servants (in state capital, in field offices)	Same as above (with state focus and impact)	State judges Law clerks Miscellaneous state judicial officials
Local level:				
Mayor, county commissioners, etc. Staff	City councils, etc. Staff	Department and agency heads Staff—civil servants (in central office, in field offices)	Same as above (with local focus and impact)	Local judges Law clerks Miscellaneous local judicial officials

lems in implementation. Most domestic agencies have some sort of field structure and delegate different tasks to their field units. Often the gap between the policy layer and the operations layer falls along geographic lines. The entire policy layer is in Washington. The workers in the field offices are all in the operations layer. Such a situation reinforces the potential for slips between policy intent and service delivery.

Table 17–1 summarizes the array of individuals and agencies at the three territorial levels of government that implement national programs.

Patterns of Influence in the Implementation of Domestic Programs

Typically, different subsets of actors are most heavily involved in implementing different types of policies (Ripley and Franklin, 1986). Figure 17–5 summarizes the patterns of involvement and influence in the four types of domestic policy discussed in Chapter 16. Note that the diagrams in Figure 17–5 take into account the four principal layers of bureaucracy involved in implementation: the federal bureaucracy in Washington, federal field offices, state bureaucracies, and local bureaucracies.

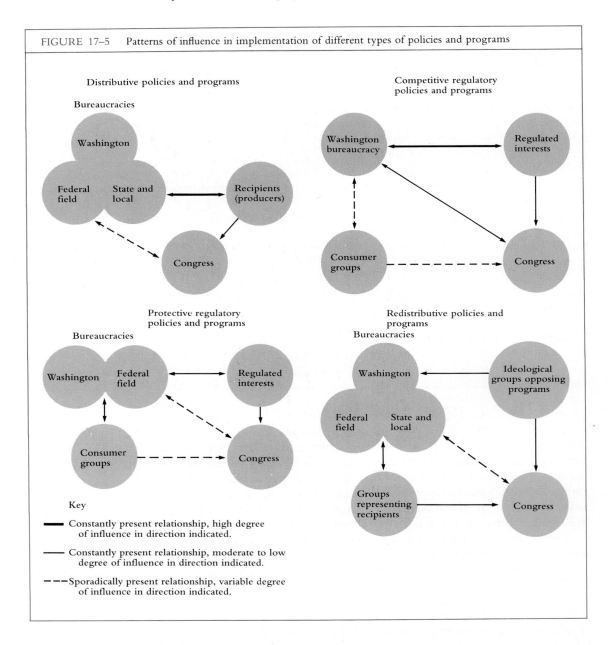

FIGURE 17–5   Patterns of influence in implementation of different types of policies and programs

Distributive policies and programs

In the implementation of distributive programs, the main actors come from various layers of federal, state, and local bureaucracies; the beneficiaries of the programs (chiefly producer interests); and Congress. The recipients and the bureaucracies are closely linked; influence flows both ways when detailed decisions are made about implementation. The recipients also have some influence on Congress regarding such decisions. And Congress and the federal part of the bureaucracy interact on occasion, each influencing the other.

Competitive regulatory policies and programs

Competitive regulatory implementation has four main actors—the Washington federal bureaucracy, the regulated interests, Congress, and, sometimes, consumer groups (representing consumers who are recipients). The main two-way relationship with a lot of mutual influence is between the bureaucrats and the regulated interests. This does not imply that the regulated interests always dominate the regulators. It does imply that the regulators and the regulated develop mutually defined interests, though they may continue to disagree on some matters. One relationship of secondary importance is between the regulated interests and Congress; the regulated interests exert some influence over Congress. Another is between Congress and the bureaucracy. Consumer groups are only sporadically active. They have limited influence on Congress and a limited relationship with the bureaucracy.

Protective regulatory policies and programs

There are four main actors in protective regulatory implementation. They are the federal bureaucracy both in Washington and in the field, the regulated interests, Congress, and consumer groups. Here, the most important relationships are within the bureaucratic cluster. There is an important two-way relationship between the bureaucrats and the regulated interests, but that relationship may be hostile much of the time.

The regulated interests also have much influence with Congress. In turn, Congress carries on a sporadic two-way relationship with the bureaucrats. Consumer groups have a fairly strong two-way relationship with the bureaucrats, and they can influence Congress from time to time. The regulated interests and consumer groups are at odds most of the time. Both have ties to Congress and the bureaucracy, which they use to promote their differing views. The three nonbureaucratic forces disagree with and push the bureaucrats from different directions at once. This puts the bureaucrats in a stressful situation, but also gives them some freedom to choose among different options.

Redistributive policies and programs

In implementing redistributive policies and programs, the chief actors are bureaucracies—federal agencies in both Washington and the field and many state and local agencies. Other actors are the recipients and those representing them, people ideologically opposed to the programs, and Congress. The bureaucrats, especially at the local level, have wide leeway to make decisions. There are no cozy, mutually beneficial, two-way relationships. But the recipients, *if organized,* can have a fairly strong two-way relationship with the bureaucrats. Those who are opposed on ideological grounds, *if organized,* can pressure the bureaucracies to restrict the program. Or they can pressure for change by moving the program toward distributive rather than redistributive ends. They can also put the same kind of pressure on Congress. Groups representing beneficiaries also have access to Congress, however, and thus compete for congressional attention and favor. Congress, in turn intervenes in redistributive bureaucratic implementation activity, but only occasionally.

Government in Action: Cases of Implementation

We think it important that you have a good sense of the reality of implementation politics, so in the closing pages of this chapter we present some examples of policy implementation. We have chosen cases that illustrate implementation in different policy areas. We have also chosen cases that show varying degrees of success or failure. Success in implementation simply means that things are going about as planned; it does not necessarily mean that the policy is desirable. Likewise, failure means that a lot of things are going wrong during the implementation process; the policy itself may be good or bad.

Many implementation problems show up in these cases; they involve such internal matters as fuzzy goals and poor management. They also show poor coordination between layers of government, unpredicted reactions from private sector actors, and insufficient political support at all levels.

Maritime industry subsidies: smooth implementation of a distributive program

There are many specific subsidy programs for the merchant shipping and maritime industries (Lawrence, 1965; Jantscher, 1975). The principal ones are

An operating subsidy that offsets the higher operating costs of American shipping lines compared to foreign lines.

A construction subsidy to shipyards so that they can reduce their prices and make their products more competitive with foreign-built ships.

Cabotage laws requiring ocean commerce between U.S. points to be carried in ships built and registered in the United States. These provisions add to the cost of shipping. The added costs are paid by consumers in the form of higher prices.

Tax subsidies that provide what amount to interest-free loans to shipowners to buy ships and equipment from U.S. manufacturers.

Requirements for using U.S. rather than foreign ships for certain kinds of overseas shipments.

This package of subsidies has been in place for decades and has changed little, except for additions. Political support for the basic laws wards off

Regulating strip mining. In 1977, Congress passed legislation creating the Office of Surface Mining (OSM) and regulating the surface mining of coal. However, a number of factors have made implementation of the regulations uneven at best.

any attempt at change. Under these conditions, implementation is free of controversy and almost automatic. A number of interests—shipowners, shipbuilders, maritime unions, relevant bureaucrats, and relevant House and Senate members—dominate the creation and continuation of the laws. These interests also work together easily to make sure that the aid is distributed swiftly and without hitches. Some of the subsidy provisions are self-executing. Tax write-offs only need to be used by accountants for the affected companies. But when a government agency must act, controversy rarely occurs.

Strip-mining regulation: troubled implementation of a protective regulatory program

Earlier in this chapter, we summarized the story of how the federal law regulating surface (strip) mining of coal was enacted. That law provides a good example of how slow and unstable implementation can be in the protective regulatory arena. In its short life since the passage of the law, in 1977, the Office of Surface Mining (OSM) in the Department of the Interior—the agency charged with implementing the law—has undergone major changes in the way it has performed its tasks. Court decisions have played an important part in helping shape its actions.

The agency sought to be aggressive from 1977 to 1981, but it was often foiled. It became much more passive after 1981, but not completely dormant. Differences in the intentions of the Carter and Reagan administrations explain some of the changes in OSM, but other factors were also at work.

1. The hostility between opposing groups generated in the controversy-filled debates over creating the law carried over into the implementation process. Even though the final bill was the result of compromise, those opposed to the bill sought to weaken implementation.

2. Changing public opinion lessened the zeal for vigorous implementation. When the bill was passed, the national environmental movement was riding high. Shortly thereafter, as the economy slumped, the need to develop more American energy sources and to reverse unemployment trends in industry became more evident. As a result, there was a decline in the public's enthusiasm for promoting a clean environment.

3. The fact that OSM was a brand-new agency created problems. Any new agency struggles to establish routines and to get employees to accept and internalize them. These tasks are, of course, made more difficult when the agency's primary program is mired in controversy and when the signals sent by the bureaucratic superior (successive secretaries of the interior in this case) change quickly and dramatically.

4. A wide variety of individuals and agencies were involved in implementing the technically complex provisions of the strip-mining law. At the federal level, those involved included bureaucrats and political appointees in the Department of the Interior (including the office of the secretary, the solicitor general's office, and OSM), judges in the federal court system (where numerous lawsuits were filed), lawyers in the Department of Justice, and various congressional committees engaged in oversight. At the state and local levels, those involved included state bureaucrats and governors' staffs, coal companies, utilities dependent on coal, and a diverse set of citizen and environmental groups.

By late autumn 1984, both the federal courts and a key oversight committee in the House of Representatives had blasted OSM for failing to enforce the law adequately. At that time, the secretary of the interior admitted that the implementation record had been dismal and vowed improvement (for more detail see, Ripley and Franklin, 1986: 156–63; Menzel, 1983).

Federal aid to education: a mix of distribution and redistribution

In 1965, President Johnson and Congress broke a 20-year logjam over a number of sticky issues, and a very large federal aid to education bill became law. The bill had five major programs in five separate titles, summarized earlier in the chapter.

The following discussion focuses on implementation of Title I, whose central purpose was to aid disadvantaged students, from its inception in 1965 through 1972 (Murphy, 1971, 1973; Bailey and Mosher, 1968). During that time, the annual cost of that single title grew from $1 billion to $1.6 billion. Two very complex formulas were used to distribute the money. The first determined how much money would go to each county in the country. The second determined how the money would be divided among school districts within each county. Title I tried to give more money to the schools with the poorest and most disadvantaged children. The money was for specific projects aimed at compensatory education. The states were to approve projects by applying federal standards. The school districts, though, got their money automatically as a matter of right through the two formulas. The U.S. Office of Education (USOE) was supposed to accept or reject local assurances that the law would be followed in spending the money. It was also supposed to offer guidance in administering the program at state and local levels.

From 1965 to 1970, the program did not work as planned. The money was allocated according to the formula, but little effort was made to see that it was spent as provided in the law. Audits of abuses, for example, were delayed or not carried out. In many ways, the program was treated simply as general aid to elementary and secondary education. Local school districts had virtual autonomy in deciding how the money should be spent. Some school districts may have made a real effort to focus on the most disadvantaged, but that was almost a matter of chance. In 1970 and 1971, a few concerned people caused a flurry of activity. But that activity subsided.

What explains these disappointing outcomes?

The people who had helped produce what they assumed to be a reform of the educational system were not the people responsible for implementing the reform. There was virtually no overlap between the two groups. The reformers had come from Congress, the high levels of the executive branch, and a few leading interest groups. The implementers were housed in the USOE, an old and small bureaucracy that was greatly expanded to handle the new chores. Those mainly responsible for implementation were longtime civil servants with well-defined and long-held views about how to proceed—views often hostile to the reformers' goals.

The USOE was badly understaffed, very small, and almost a century old. It had never done anything innovative. Suddenly, it was called on to carry out a huge, innovative program and to do it very rapidly. The agency made some valiant efforts, but these efforts were plagued by its long-standing limitations. Likewise, the state education agencies, which also had a critical role in implementation, were for the most part ill prepared for programmatic activity requiring innovation or a high degree of competence.

The program's goals were murky, the inevitable result of fashioning a winning coalition to pass the bill. Some in that coalition really wanted to help the disadvantaged. Others were mainly interested in obtaining more money for public secondary and elementary schools in their states or districts.

The basic distribution of administrative powers in the program created problems. Much power was simply given to state education agencies and local school districts. But even the power kept by the USOE was not used in any direct or forceful way. For example, the office was authorized to accept or reject assurances submitted by each state that the law would be followed. Rejection of a state's assurances meant that funds would be withheld. The USOE always accepted the assurances without assessing their meaning or sincerity. The authority to withhold money is usually politically unworkable. Any such action would bring instant protests from members of Congress, local governments, and national interest groups for state and local governments.

The Office of Education was also given the power to develop basic criteria for state and local governments. Again, in form, the final sanction of withholding funds was possible. But even during passage of the law, a loud minority in Congress made it clear that they would object to USOE efforts to use this power. In fact, the USOE never tried very hard anyway.

The norm of home rule in public education was strongly entrenched. Many implementers constantly fought focusing on the poor and disadvantaged. Both the USOE and the state agencies deferred in word and deed to the local school districts. They were reluctant to monitor, criticize, or enforce. Good relations among professional educators required that none hassle the others and that local autonomy be respected.

Finally, there was no strong, sustained pressure from reformers that Title I programs focus explicitly on the poor. Such pressure might have kept the USOE and state and local groups moving toward that goal, even if slowly. An outburst of complaints in 1970 and 1971 had some impact, but that impact was temporary.

Few would argue that implementing Title I of the Elementary and Secondary Education Act has done no good. Local school systems have obtained funds that they would not have gotten otherwise. But whether the program was used to help poor children is a different question. For the first seven years, the answer seems to be no.

Implementation of desegregation in housing and schools: redistribution and race

Public housing in Chicago: the triumph of local power (1963–1971)   In Chicago's public housing program in the early 1950s, local priorities overshadowed federal priorities on almost all issues. The federal agency— which later became the Department of Housing and Urban Development

Housing segregation. Racial groups are still segregated in much public housing. In Boston, these tenants are working on the grounds of the Bromley low-income housing project.

(HUD)—was mainly a funnel for money to help the city do what it liked in the housing field. This was especially true in the area of race. The city used federal money to increase or continue segregation in housing for blacks.

The decade of the 1960s was one of civil rights ferment and some important national policy statements. A 1962 executive order and civil rights statutes in 1964 and 1968 made it illegal for a local public housing agency using federal funds to practice racial discrimination.

How did these provisions affect public housing programs at the local level—specifically in Chicago? Basically, they did not (Lazin, 1973). Throughout the 60s, Chicago used its federally funded program to promote racial segregation through decisions about who could live where in public housing. Blacks and whites were kept apart. Chicago may have been atypical. The national political clout of its mayor, Richard Daley, was greater than that of any other local official in the country. But, in fact, many problems promoted the outcome and probably would have promoted it no matter who the mayor was. The basic patterns of local control over a federal program continued and were strengthened by federal actions. It would be a mistake to think that the federal government struggled valiantly to uphold the law only to be thwarted by a crafty, determined, and politically savvy local government. In fact, the feds and the locals worked together to promote racially segregated housing despite formal, legally binding statements to the contrary by the president and Congress.

The authority under which HUD could have pursued racial desegregation in housing was itself murky. The executive order and the two civil rights statutes referred to above did not really define such key terms as *racial discrimination* and *affirmative action*. Neither did the HUD regulations. In fact, the HUD regulations were unclear and often did not make discrimination illegal.

Both nationally and locally, HUD operated under norms that stressed deference to local wishes. It bargained with local officials, and it worked for good relations with local officials to get local support for its other programs and for its existence in general. HUD did not question local assurances that the city was doing all it could to get rid of racial discrimination and segregation in housing, even when such assurances were obviously untrue. Few took a view different from the official city position in dealing with HUD. The one persistent local legal challenge to the Chicago Housing Authority actions paid off modestly only in 1984 through a decision by a federal judge.

The federally supported public housing program probably helped provide better housing for some poor people in Chicago and elsewhere. But despite national policy, the program did not help reduce segregation in housing in general. In Chicago, the program was used to increase such segregation.

Desegregation in schools: southern success and northern problems In 1964, Congress passed the Civil Rights Act. Among other things, this act prohibited racial discrimination in any program getting federal money. Local public schools were a natural target for federal actions since they all received federal aid. At first, implementation came from the office of the commissioner of education in the Department of Health, Education, and Welfare (HEW). In 1967, an Office for Civil Rights (OCR) was created in HEW (Rabkin, 1980; Bullock, 1980). One of its prime concerns has been segregation in public schools.

The OCR record has been mixed. OCR moved well and successfully in dealing with racial segregation in public schools in the South, but in dealing with the same problem elsewhere, its record has not been impressive. In the South, OCR appeared to move with determination. In the North, it engaged in weak and spotty enforcement despite broad verbal claims. The two different results of OCR can be linked to some systematic differences in implementation in the South and elsewhere.

First, in the South, the target was quite clear and progress was easy to measure. All-black and all-white schools needed to be changed. Segregation was clearly the result of years of state law and so could be easily shown as violating the 1964 Civil Rights Act. In the North, though, segregation was not the result of state laws. Illegal segregation had to be proved in each case. Therefore, fieldwork and investigation consumed a lot of time and energy.

Second, the mandate for OCR in the South was clear. The law was broad, but OCR and its legislative and bureaucratic leaders were willing and anxious to focus on the southern schools. In cases elsewhere, however, both Congress and bureaucrats ceased being helpful. OCR was left to flounder.

Third, in the southern case, Congress and several presidents supported OCR's efforts. But elsewhere, their support was uneven. No one was consistently supportive. Some high legislative and bureaucratic officials supported some efforts, were bitterly critical of others, and were simply not interested in many.

In addition, hitting the southern target was easy. OCR could rely on its Washington staff to do most of the work. This meant that instructions to OCR bureaucrats could be followed easily and only a small number of people would be involved. Elsewhere, OCR had to create and rely on a large field staff for enforcement. This increased internal coordination problems.

OCR was also clearly committed—in both word and deed—to southern desegregation. Its commitment elsewhere was much less apparent.

Finally, in the South, the local forces opposed to desegregation were weak and isolated by the late 1960s and 70s. Elsewhere, the local forces opposed to desegregation were more numerous and much stronger. They also had a lot of political clout at the national level.

CONCLUSIONS

This chapter focused on the making and implementing of domestic policy. It explored patterns of formulation, legitimation, and implementation in general and underscored the most important aspects of those general patterns through the use of specific examples of policies being made and implemented.

The challenges of governing outlined at the beginning of this chapter recur constantly. In principle, the channels of access between rulers and ruled are present. But those channels are sometimes clogged. Incessant coalition-building activity is vital to democratic politics. However, the need for such activity protracts the time between perception of a problem and government response. Implementation is neither automatic nor easy. It is subject to a variety of political pressures. That fact enhances our open politics, but it may also produce frustrating distortions in the conversion of policy statements into policy actions

There is a tentative and unsettled quality to public policy in the United States. The early stages of arriving at a policy often take a long time. Even if approval is not achieved for a lengthy period, formulation continues as coalitions form, dissolve, and form again. When a policy is approved, there are almost immediate pressures from some quarters to change it. Congress often considers amendments to major bills within a year after passage and often adopts major changes within a year or two. Some seek to have an approved policy implemented without change. Others seek to kill the programs designed to implement the policy. Implementation itself is open to pressures from competing interests. Implementation decisions alter important aspects of domestic policy without formal legislation.

The analysis of the formulation/legitimation and implementation of domestic policies contained in this chapter can be summarized by a few general statements:

1. Access to decision-making processes is the prerequisite for influencing decisions. Those with more access shape more policy to their liking than do those with less access.

2. Access channels are partially open in the United States. This creates meaningful competition over the nature of public policy in many areas.

3. There are regular patterns in terms of who is most important in making different kinds of policy decisions. Entrenched interests with the most at stake are hard to displace.

4. Shaping public policy requires building coalitions. Those who fashion what turns out to be the winning coalition must make many compromises. Program goals become unclear in this process.

5. Implementation is likely to be smoother in distributive policy areas than in other areas. All involved stand to gain something tangible. Therefore, each has an incentive to reach the specified goals without delay.

6. Implementation is likely to be most difficult when redistribution is at stake. In such cases, some groups see themselves as losers if implementation is smooth. They have great incentives to seek allies who will help them slow or subvert implementation.

7. Implementation is unlikely to be problem-free, but the problems can be identified and solved. The political patterns underlying some problems are strong and persistent, but they do not inevitably produce program failure, as some critics of government assert. Rather, they produce pitfalls and dangers. Dedicated implementers need to know about these and try to avoid them as best they can. Miracles cannot be expected from government units. Their implementation activities are complex and require both will and some luck to bring everything together as planned.

FURTHER READING

REDMAN, ERIC (1973) *The Dance of Legislation*. New York: Simon & Schuster. An interesting story of how a bill becomes a law, in this case the Emergency Health Personnel Act of 1970.

REID, T.R. (1980) *Congressional Odyssey: The Saga of a Senate Bill*. San Francisco: W.H. Freeman. Another good bill-becomes-a-law book, this one focused on a waterway-user-charge bill that passed in 1978.

RIPLEY, RANDALL B., and GRACE A. FRANKLIN (1986) *Policy Implementation and Bureaucracy*. 2nd ed. Chicago: Dorsey Press. An analysis of the implementation of different types of domestic policies and programs in the United States.

RIPLEY, RANDALL B., and GRACE A. FRANKLIN (1987) *Congress, the Bureaucracy, and Public Policy*. 4th ed. Chicago: Dorsey Press. A basic analysis of the relationships among Congress, the bureaucracy, the presidency, and organized interest groups in the shaping of federal laws.

SUNDQUIST, JAMES L. (1968) *Politics and Policy*. Washington, D.C.: Brookings Institution. A classic analysis of federal policy-making in the 1950s and 1960s.

ECONOMIC POLICIES, SPENDING, AND TAXING

$\mathscr{H}$elping create economic prosperity has always been a central aim of the government of the United States. What would be the best ways to render that help? To which social classes should help be given? What specific economic policies, including key spending and taxing policies, would be most likely to further this aim? Such matters have been at the heart of political debate throughout our national history.

In our country, rulers and ruled alike accept Alexander Hamilton's view that there is an intimate intermingling of economic and political concerns. Hamilton expressed that view in *The Federalist,* No.12:

> The prosperity of commerce is now perceived and acknowledged by all enlightened statesmen to be the most useful as well as the most productive source of national wealth, and has accordingly become a primary object of their political cares. By multiplying the means of gratification, by promoting the introduction and circulation of the precious metals, those darling objects of human avarice and enterprise, it serves to vivify and invigorate the channels of industry, and to make them flow with greater activity and copiousness. The assiduous merchant, the laborious husbandman, the active mechanic, and the industrious manufacturer—all orders of men, look forward with eager expectation and growing alacrity to this pleasing reward of their toils.

The vast array of the national government's economic actions has important consequences both for individuals and for society at large. Consensus on the best course is rare; basic disagreement rooted in differing political beliefs is normal. The national government faces four perpetual major challenges in the economic sphere:

How, within the limits set by broad national beliefs about the proper role of government in the economy, to allow the national government to have the most favorable impact on the performance of the U.S. economy.

How to arrive at the most productive balance between private economic activity and government intervention.

How to promote agreements among important policy-making organs of the executive and legislative branches that are both positive in impact and acceptable politically.

How to keep the policies agreed on in place long enough for them to have the desired impacts. ✑

When government officials ponder their role in the U.S. economy, they face a confusing and often paradoxical set of circumstances. Both they and the population in general want economic prosperity. Voters hold them responsible for the state of the economy. But they are also faced with strong and widespread beliefs that the government's role in the economy should be limited, and they must also confront both domestic and international market forces that limit the impact of the measures they take. Finally, even when the limits imposed by market forces and beliefs about the appropriate governmental economic role are taken into account, there is neither political nor professional agreement on what governmental measures will produce what economic effects. Moreover, the solutions to perceived economic problems are not merely matters for technical debate. They are also the constant subjects of heated political debate.

This chapter explores the important world of governmental economic policies. We will discuss some of the main institutions, processes, and policy options. As with all policy issues in the United States, the "solutions" reached when disagreements occur are temporary compromises.

First, we examine a few aspects of governmental responsibility for economic well-being in the United States. Second, we discuss governmental influence in six major types of economic policy as well as economic indicators and what they mean. Third, we focus on major features of government spending. Fourth, we do the same for government taxing. Finally, we probe the meaning of deficits, a particularly visible issue in the 1980s.

THE NATURE OF GOVERN-MENTAL RE-SPON-SIBILITY FOR ECONOMIC WELL-BEING

Questions about the economy and government's role in it are central to political debate. What is the most efficient organization for the economy? What is the fairest way to distribute wealth? How involved should the government be in directing the economy? Citizens in the Western democracies have, in principle, arrived at four broad answers to these questions. Some have supported a classic free market capitalist stance: People should work out their own economic relations and choices with a minimum of government activity. Others have supported a modified capitalist position: In many situations the market works all right, but in other situations it produces unacceptable inequalities and distortions that must be rectified by government action. Still others have opted for a democratic socialist perspective: The economy requires considerable public ownership and governmental intervention, but significant portions of economic activity should be left to private decision making. Finally, some (a minority in all of the Western nations) have adopted a communist economic perspective: All the means of production should be collectively owned, and there should be very little unplanned private economic activity.

In the United States, the democratic socialist and communist positions on government involvement in the economy have appealed to few people. Our political debate—unlike that in the other Western democracies—has focused almost exclusively on variants of the classic capitalist and modified capitalist positions. Our political "conservatives" favor as few restrictions on the free market as possible. Our political "liberals" are willing to accept government action to compensate for what they view as distortions of unfettered capitalism. The spectrum of views about the economy with any chance of succeeding politically is shorter in the United States than in any other Western democracy.

The Clash of Economic Theories in U.S. Politics

Within the confines of "conservative" to "liberal" views in the U.S. context, there are ongoing debates about economic policies. These policies have major political ramifications. In public debate over economic policies, economic theory and political ideology become entangled. Support of economic theory often stems from a political conviction rather than from scientific effort to understand the economic world. Economists are elevated to sainthood or spurned as demons, depending largely on what politicians make of their ideas.

At present and for the last several decades, four broad economic theories have had considerable political appeal. The labels for the theories are *Keynesianism, incomes policy, monetarism,* and *supply-side economics.*

Keynesianism

The essence of the theory called **Keynesianism**, developed by the British economist John Maynard Keynes (1883–1946), is that the government must intervene to help adjust the level of demand for goods and services. When demand is too low, the rate of unemployment increases and the economy slows down. Under these conditions, government must stimulate demand by reducing taxes and increasing spending. When demand is too high, prices increase rapidly and an unacceptably high rate of inflation results. Under these conditions, government must inhibit demand by removing money from the economy through increased taxes and reductions in spending. For large portions of the time between 1933 and 1981, the federal government relied on some form of Keynesian theory in making a number of economic decisions.

Incomes policy

Some economists and politicians contend that indirect governmental interventions to control prices and wages are inadequate. Instead, they advocate an ***incomes policy***, or direct controls on prices and wages. Such a policy becomes particularly attractive in inflationary times. During World War II, when full employment, high wages, and scarce goods could have produced rampant inflation, the government imposed controls on prices and wages. Inflation again became a problem in the 1970s—resulting in part from a major tax cut in the early 1960s combined with dramatically

The British economist John Maynard Keynes (1883–1946) influenced the economic thinking of two generations of Americans. Keynesian economics calls for using the fiscal and monetary powers of government to guide a capitalist economy. Keynes's most influential book, published in 1936, was The General Theory of Employment, Interest and Money.

increased government spending for the Vietnam War. The Nixon administration experimented with limited wage controls to combat this inflation. In general, however, the federal government has been shy about pursuing an incomes policy.

Monetarism

Pure **monetarism** is most often associated with the economist Milton Friedman. The essence of this theory is that if the government simply keeps the money supply growing at the same rate as the growth of productivity the unhampered operations of the market will produce the most efficient use of economic resources. In this view, any governmental intervention beyond manipulating the money supply is likely to produce undesirable economic distortions. The Reagan administration put considerable faith in monetarism. In most administrations, the chairman of the Federal Reserve Board believes in monetarism because that theory stresses the importance of the Federal Reserve System.

Supply-side economics

The essence of **supply-side economics** is quite simple: Taxes should be cut dramatically and kept low to encourage a steady flow of private investment, which will support the continuous growth of the economy. The key to stimulating private enterprise and productivity is to support the producers (the "supply side" of the economy) by lowering taxes and thus giving them more capital to invest and more incentive to produce. Once taxes have been cut, government is supposed to intervene little, if at all, in the economy. When the Reagan administration came into office, it was committed to supply-side theory. The theory was used to justify the major tax cut that passed Congress in 1981. That piece of legislation, however, did not stimulate the expected torrent of investment. Pure supply-siders claimed that the expected benefits were not forthcoming because the tax cut was too small. Congress felt otherwise, and in 1982, in another major tax law, it reversed a number of the supply-side features of the 1981 tax law and raised taxes.

Political Accountability for Economic Conditions

Although the federal government can affect the state of the economy only in limited ways, American voters hold their elected officials responsible for economic conditions. Economic concerns at the personal level are salient to many voters much of the time. Such concerns surface at elections. Politicians are well aware that good economic times usually favor incumbents running for reelection and that bad economic times can spell trouble for such incumbents. Politicians are also aware that voters expect their public officials to talk about and offer solutions to perceived problems. Thus, it is not surprising that President Reagan dealt primarily with economic matters in 15 of the 37 press conferences that he held between early 1981 and mid-1986.

Political scientists have conducted a number of careful studies of the relationship among economic conditions, voting patterns, and government actions to stimulate desirable economic conditions near election time (Kiewiet, 1983; Tufte, 1978). These studies demonstrate that citizens' concerns about economic issues influence their political actions. Voters think about such issues in both personal and national terms, though they often blur the two dimensions. The conclusions they reach help them decide how to vote. Voters pay more attention to economic issues when voting for president than when voting for members of the House or Senate. When they make their decisions, they take into account both past economic performance and the future economic performance that is likely to result from the election of specific candidates and political parties. Voters who feel that economic conditions are good are likely to vote for incumbents seeking reelection.

Close to election time, officeholders seek to strengthen their prospects

A Consolidated Rail Corporation (Conrail) freight train pulls its way up the "Horseshoe Curve" near Altoona, Pennsylvania. Conrail was originally a government corporation, formed by the U.S. government to maintain service when it took over the private train companies in the Northeast. Once Conrail became a moneymaking endeavor, the government sold it. Today it is a private corporation.

for reelection by taking measures intended to improve economic conditions. Such measures include increases in transfer payments to individuals (for example, increases in Social Security benefits), changes in the tax code, and special programs for individual economic sectors, such as agriculture or declining industries.

GOVERN-MENTAL INFLUENCE OVER THE ECONOMY

Two broad factors limit governmental influence over economic activity in the United States. First, there are certain economic activities in which the government rarely engages, because citizens and officeholders alike do not ordinarily regard these as legitimate government activities. In general, to take one important area, the government chooses not to acquire business ventures unless they are failing and the products or services they provide are deemed vital to the nation. For example, the government formed and owned the Consolidated Rail Corporation (Conrail) only after much of the privately held railroad network in the Northeast went bankrupt. Shippers needed rail service, so the government, reluctantly, stepped in. As soon as Conrail became profitable, the government sold it to private investors.

Because of the government's relatively limited ownership role, decision makers in the private sector determine most American economic developments. The government helps set some of the rules by which they must abide, but it is often a minor actor in the making of major economic decisions with national ramifications.

Second, even in those instances in which the government chooses to intervene in economic matters, its influence may be limited by external forces beyond its control. There is a difference between governmental involvement and governmental influence. Being involved does not equal being influential. Analysts at the Urban Institute provide a good example of how external forces can overwhelm the efforts of even an active government:

> On October 29, 1980, candidate Ronald Reagan posed his now famous question: ". . . ask yourself are you better off than you were four years ago." The question was good politics but bad economics for it assumed economic events during 1977–80 flowed from President Carter's policies.
>
> The facts are less heroic. Economic progress depends on a president's policies, but it also depends on influences outside the President's control: the economy he inherits, rainfall in the Midwest, movements in the price of oil, state and local government decisions, and so on. These influences, moreover, have lives of their own, so that economic periods do not neatly coincide with presidential administrations.
>
> The years 1981–84 are a case in point. Politically, they represent President Reagan's first term in office. Economically, they represent the second through fifth years of a period that began with the 1979 fall of the Shah of Iran and a major round of OPEC price increases for oil. The history of this economic period—rapid inflation, deep recession, recovery and no net growth in family incomes—parallels the events that followed the first major OPEC price increases in 1973–74.
>
> During this period President Reagan's policies have been important in determining the balance between deeper recession and higher inflation. His policies have also served to increase income inequality. But even with respect to inequality the president's policies have been less important than inflation and other forces beyond any single person's control. (Levy and Michel, 1983)

With these general limits in mind, what can we say about the actual degree of governmental influence over the economy? What governmental policies can reasonably be expected to have some impact on the economy and, therefore, on the relative well-being of American citizens?

The most important policy tools for government intervention in the U.S. economy are *fiscal policy* and *monetary policy*. The most important other policy tools of this kind are *trade policy*, *industrial policy*, *energy policy*, and *environmental policy*. We will discuss each of these policy tools in turn, and then we will discuss briefly the major indicators of economic performance that are used within government circles and in society generally.

In 1982, despite cold, wind, and rain, dozens of unemployed workers assembled in front of the New York offices of the Association of Builders and Carpenters. They were among the 2,000 job-seekers who applied for the 400-odd apprentice jobs offered by the association. A "healthy" unemployment rate of around 6 percent meant little to these job-seekers.

Fiscal Policy

Fiscal policy uses taxes and government spending to influence the economy. Taxing and spending decisions also ultimately determine how much money the government must borrow if it spends more than it raises through taxes. The annual borrowing required by the government is called the *deficit*.

Within their aggregate decisions about spending, revenues, and borrowing, decision makers have to make a large number of debatable, important, and sensitive choices. Which individuals, economic sectors, regions, and social classes will receive what benefits from spending? Who has to pay how much in taxes? How large will the deficit be, and what consequences will it have for whom? Such questions occupy a great deal of attention on the part of the president, other major institutions of the executive branch, and Congress.

Before the Great Depression of the 1930s, the government paid little attention to fiscal policy. Indeed, it viewed itself as peripheral to the basic economic functioning of the nation. There was no single budget process in the executive branch until 1921, when a rudimentary budget process was created there. Congress did not succeed in creating a centralized budget process for itself until 1974. Similarly, before the 1930s, neither the executive branch nor the legislative branch considered tax policy as a co-ordinated package. Instead, both branches considered taxes one at a time.

The first joint executive-legislative statement of faith in the federal government's power to affect the entire economy was the Employment Act of 1946 (Bailey, 1950). In that statute, the government, in effect, proclaimed its responsibility for the general well-being of the economy and assumed that it had the tools and influence needed to produce that well-being. Full employment was taken to mean a very low rate of unemployment (perhaps 2 or 3 percent). Rapid growth of the economy without inflation was presumed to be natural in the United States. The economy was generally strong in the 1950s and 1960s, though there were worrisome recessions in the 1950s. Except for such temporary setbacks, economic growth seemed to be the foreordained happy fate of the American economy. Successive governments of both parties took credit for that growth, though their specific economic policies differed. In the 1970s and 1980s, as economic growth slowed and both inflation and more severe recessions became problems, the government ran up against the limits of what its fiscal policies could achieve. It also began to accept a higher rate of unemployment as "full employment." By the 1980s, 6 percent unemployment was taken to signify a generally healthy economy.

Monetary Policy

Monetary policy uses the supply of money and interest rates (the cost of borrowing money) to influence the economy. Governmental influence on money and credit stems primarily from actions of the Federal Reserve Board and the accompanying system of Federal Reserve banks, created in 1913. Congress and the president do not directly make such policy. However, they do not let the "Fed" operate in a political vacuum. Its activities are highly volatile politically and have significant influence economically (Huitt, 1963; Woolley, 1984; Kettl, 1986).

The chairman of the Federal Reserve Board—Paul Volcker from 1979 to 1987 and Alan Greenspan since 1987—is accorded great attention by people interested in financial markets and in the state of the economy generally. The president appoints the chairman every four years.

The Fed was created in part to remove federal banking activities from the pressures of day-to-day politics. The Federal Reserve Board oversees the activities of 12 member banks, dispersed throughout the country, in their dealings with commercial banks. Each of the 12 banks has a president. Five of those presidents sit with the seven governors of the entire system, who are appointed for 14-year terms by the U.S. president, to form the Federal Open Market Committee. That committee meets in se-

In 1987, President Reagan appointed the economist Alan Greenspan (1926–   ) as chairman of the Board of Governors of the Federal Reserve System. Greenspan had served previously as chairman of the Council of Economic Advisers under President Gerald R. Ford. His appointment meant that President Reagan had named all the members of the Federal Reserve System, the first president to have done so since Franklin D. Roosevelt.

cret and makes decisions about buying and selling government securities (the "paper" through which the government borrows money by promising to repay the principal borrowed and a specified rate of interest) on the open market. The Fed also decides what percentage of deposits (reserves) banks are required to keep on hand in cash. It also sets the interest rate (the "discount rate") that it charges commercial banks to borrow money from it. These controls over the government securities market, reserve levels, and federal interest rates give the Fed powerful tools for implementing monetary policy.

The Fed is more insulated from political pressures than most of the other organs of government in the United States. However, both Congress and the executive branch, especially the president, can bring pressure to bear on the Fed to adopt specific policies that they prefer for economic and political reasons.

Ultimately, what is at stake in monetary policy is the size of the supply of money in all forms (currency, checking accounts, traveler's checks, savings by individuals and institutions) and the relative ease with which money can be borrowed. The amount of money in circulation affects the stability of prices and the level of interest rates. In general, as more money becomes available, interest rates drop and prices increase. Debtors favor this situation because they want to borrow money at low rates and to repay in money that is worth less than the money they borrowed. Creditors—those who lend money—generally favor a more restricted money supply, which keeps interest rates higher and prices more stable.

The job of the Fed is complicated by the impact of international events over which it has no direct control. If the value of the dollar is falling, for example, the Fed may increase interest rates in an effort to stop that fall. Foreign traders in currency, however, may not react in the expected way. The heads of the seven major noncommunist industrial nations (the United States, Germany, Japan, Great Britain, France, Italy, and Canada) meet regularly to hold economic summit meetings where they discuss interrelated economic policies. The U.S. president and his chief economic counselors take positions for the United States at these meetings, but, of course, the other countries may reject those positions.

Trade Policy

For the first century or more of American independence, our trade policy was also our revenue policy because at that time a very large share (over 90 percent) of the national government's revenue came from tariffs, the charges collected on imported goods. Tariffs also protected American businesses from foreign competition. Tariffs still serve a protective purpose, though the revenues they provide are now a tiny portion of total governmental revenues.

Agricultural interests historically opposed tariffs because free trade made it easier for them to export food and other crops and helped keep down the price of the imported manufactured goods they needed. Manufacturing interests tended to favor protection. The Republican party was closely allied with the manufacturing interests that grew rapidly after the Civil War and became identified with the cause of high tariffs in the late 19th century. The Democratic party of that era was strong in the agricultural areas of the South and West and espoused the cause of free trade. Throughout the 19th century and until the enactment of the Reciprocal Trade Agreements Act of 1934, congressional consideration of a comprehensive tariff bill was an occasion for major political maneuvering and deal making in which all kinds of specific interests received benefits.

After 1934, the executive branch became dominant in trade policy. Beginning with Franklin Roosevelt in the 1930s, presidents developed broad national trade policies. Congress had generally created separate policies for every possible import and had also created different tariff rates for goods coming from different foreign countries. Political debate over trade continued, but more stable policy was possible since the executive branch was less susceptible to interest-group pressure than Congress had been (Bauer, Pool, and Dexter, 1963).

In the 1980s, as American industries such as steel, automobiles, and textiles lost large portions of the American market to foreign producers,

Imports from Korea. In 1986, the first 2,300 Hyundai Excels for sale in the eastern United States roll off a ship to the applause of the Korean company's officials. American auto manufacturers and their employees faced stiff overseas competition.

demands for more protection were heard. In general, the Reagan administration championed free trade. The most ardent proponents of protection were members of Congress, often Democrats. The battles over trade policy of the 1980s were waged not just over how free trade should be but also over the proper authority of Congress and the executive branch in trade matters.

Industrial Policy

In the late 1970s and early 1980s, a flurry of political activity (and related arguments among economists) surrounded what was called *industrial policy*. Some people wanted the federal government to develop a package of actions identifying and supporting healthy industries in which the United States could compete successfully internationally. These people also wanted the government to phase out its support for economic sectors and activities in which the United States was not competitive internationally. Some of them felt that the international economic success of the Japanese had resulted from such policies. They argued that the United States should follow the Japanese example (Reich, 1983). There were also those who questioned this explanation of Japan's success, the desirability of the proposed policies, and the view that the United States had no industrial policies already in place (Lawrence, 1984; Schultze, 1983).

The debate over industrial policy vanished from the public agenda as quickly as it had come onto it. But industrial policy exists in fact, whether or not it bears that label. The health of specific U.S. industries is affected by current government policies that offer a mix of subsidies, tax incentives and disincentives, and trade restrictions. The short-lived and relatively unproductive attention that industrial policy, as something supposedly new, received in the early 1980s underscores two significant facts. First, in a society in which private economic activity is viewed as primary, public policies that overtly direct industry decisions are not likely to gain much support. Second, considerable numbers of people believe that government policies can create prosperity in specific industries in the face of both national and international market forces. Such beliefs are wrong, but they can still be important politically.

Energy Policy

When President Jimmy Carter came to office in 1977, he proclaimed that the development of national policies to produce self-sufficiency in energy was "the moral equivalent of war." Policies dealing with energy—what kind to support, what kind to discourage, what patterns of use to seek—are important. But after a brief flurry of activity following the two oil "price shocks" administered by the Organization of Petroleum Exporting Countries in 1973 and 1979, the problem of developing a coherent national energy policy excited little attention among the public or the politicians. Individual policies involving taxes, spending for various subsidies, and tariffs collectively had some impact on energy production and consumption. But the federal government developed no consistent way of coordinating these policies.

Environmental Policy

The federal government has instituted various specific policies on environmental pollution—primarily policies on air, water, and soil pollution. There is a continuing debate over the impact that these policies have on the quality of the environment and over the negative impact that some of them may have on economic development, unemployment, and energy self-sufficiency. For example, restrictions on the use of high-sulfur coal to limit air pollution might cause unemployment in the coal industry and might also require extra oil imports. On the other hand, relaxation of these restrictions might result in the increased acidity of rainfall, with its devastating effects on scenic beauty and on animal and plant life. Such increases might also damage our relations with Canada since rain whose acidity stems from American factories falls in Canada. The government has made little effort to develop a coherent set of policies in the environmental area.

Indicators of Economic Performance

Knowing how the economy is doing is useful to policy-makers in deciding what actions the government might take. Such knowledge is also useful in enabling citizens to evaluate the effectiveness of the economic policies of the government in power.

Although professional economists use a large number of indicators to examine the economy in detail, a few general economic indicators are particularly visible to policymakers in the executive branch, members of Congress, and the general public. These indicators receive coverage in the mass media and so are easily accessible to everyone. Inevitably, the economic indicators that are widely known and consulted become involved in political debate. The most important **economic indicators** are:

1. Employment and unemployment. The unemployment rate in the civilian labor force is the most well known economic indicator of all. The government releases a new figure monthly to wide media attention. This is immediately available to anyone who pays attention to the news as reported on television or radio or in newspapers or magazines.

2. Prices and wages. Both wholesale and retail price levels can be measured in a variety of ways. The consumer price index is widely used as the single best measure of changing prices. Those prices usually go up. Rapid price increases lead to political and economic worries about inflation. Wage gains are compared to price increases to calculate how much "real wages" (based on their purchasing power) are changing.

3. Growth. The most commonly used indicator of growth in the total economy is the change in the gross national product (GNP)—the value of all the goods and services that the economy produces. GNP was over $4 trillion in 1987. For the economy to be truly growing, the percentage change in GNP must be higher than the percentage change in prices.

4. Investment. Investment is provision for future economic growth through providing capital to businesses. Examples of investment include purchases of bonds or of stock offerings in new businesses. There is no generally accepted best measure of total investment, though the most commonly used measure is all investment except for investment in personal residences.

5. Interest rates. There are numerous interest rates in the economy that involve many different lenders and many different borrowers. Frequently used measures include the "prime rate" (the rate that banks charge when they lend money to their largest corporate customers); the rates on home mortgages; the rate paid by the U.S. government for short-term Treasury bills, one of its major devices for borrowing; and an index of the rates paid by corporations to purchasers of the bonds they issue.

6. Balance of trade and related international indicators. The difference between the value of imports and the value of exports is called the balance of trade. The United States has been running a large deficit for several years, which is used politically by those supporting trade protection. An

"Buy American." The bumper sticker of this Ford pickup is one citizen's response to the balance-of-trade deficit and loss of employment to foreign companies.

important related indicator is the balance of payments, which includes, in addition to trade, transfers of money between nations, such as foreign aid, tourist expenditures, and currency transfers. Another important indicator is the relative value of the U.S. dollar against other major industrial currencies, especially those of Japan and West Germany. Finally, a calculation is made on who holds all debts, both public and private. If foreign governments, corporations, and individuals owe more to U.S. governments, corporations, and individuals than vice versa, then the United States is a creditor nation. If the opposite is true, then the United States is a debtor nation. As our economy was developing in the 19th century, we were a debtor nation—that is, we were a good outlet for the investment of surplus capital from other countries. After World War II, we were the world's largest creditor nation for a number of decades. In the last few years, we have again become a debtor nation, and currently we are the largest debtor nation in the world. Some argue that this is a dangerous position for us to be in. Others, pointing to our 19th-century experience, argue that it makes little difference.

7. *Federal budget deficit.* The annual amount by which the spending of the federal government exceeds its revenue is called the deficit. A surplus results in the unlikely event that revenue exceeds spending. (We will probe the meaning of the deficit later in the chapter.) The deficit became very visible politically in the 1980s. In addition to looking at the deficit, some observers look at the size of the total national debt (that is, all money borrowed by the federal government over the years that it must still repay) and at both the deficit and the national debt in relation to GNP.

In political debate, none of the indicators in the above seven categories has a fixed and unambiguous meaning. Even economists don't agree on the precise meaning of these indicators; politicians agree even less. Two politicians with different sets of beliefs will come to quite different conclusions about the policy implications of the same set of statistics. Both officeholders and the general public have reached a consensus that high unemployment, high rates of inflation, a large negative balance of trade, and a large deficit are bad. There is no consensus, however, on how best to reverse these situations.

SPENDING: INSTITUTIONS, PROCESSES, AND POLICIES

Numerous institutions become involved in federal spending decisions. Their interactions are complicated. The programs and reputations of bureaucratic agencies are at stake; the ability of members of the House and Senate to deliver goodies to their constituents is at stake; the reputation of the president, his closest advisers, and the central presidential institutions and their ability to direct the overall course of government priorities are at stake. Since the stakes are high, it is not surprising that the politics of spending is intense.

Some of the complexities and oddities of the "budget process" are nicely caught in a 1986 book by six distinguished economists from the Brookings Institution:

> The process by which the U.S. government arrives at a budget is complicated and arcane, and it is hard to find anyone who likes it. . . . Surprisingly, despite all the talk about the budget and the budget process, no budget for the U.S. government is ever enacted as [a single document]. . . . Because of the separation of powers, the history of budget making in the U.S. government is two separate histories: that of executive branch efforts to evolve a procedure for crafting the president's budget proposals and that of congressional efforts to make spending and taxing decisions in a more orderly way. (Aaron and others, 1986: 111,113)

Before turning to a discussion of the executive branch in budget-making decisions and then to a discussion of Congress, it is useful to introduce a schematic overview of the principal stages, participants, and timetable of the overall budget process—a process that requires constant interaction between the executive branch and Congress and also invites the constant intervention of hundreds of interest groups. Figure 18–1 presents such an overview.

The Executive Branch

The two principal agencies that help the president and his staff engage in an orderly and continuous review of agency requests for funding are the Office of Management and Budget (OMB) and, to a much lesser extent and at a more general level, the Council of Economic Advisers. OMB was created as the Bureau of the Budget in 1921 and retained that name

FIGURE 18–1   The national budget cycle

Stages	Executive Formulation		Legislative Approval	Execution	
Stages	Requests ⟶	Central review and submittal ⟶	Authorization, appropriation, and budget resolution ⟶	Obligation and outlay ⟶	Audit
Main Participants	Agencies	President and OMB	Congress: Budget, authorizing, and appropriations committees	Agencies and OMB	GAO
Timing		12–18 months (agencies), 9 months (President) before the start of the fiscal year	Jan. to Sept. 30 (9 months before and up to the start of the fiscal year)	Oct. 1 to Sept. 30 (the 12 months of the fiscal year)	Oct. 1– (up to 12 months after the fiscal year)

Source: Lance T. LeLoup, *Budgetary Politics,* 4th ed. (Brunswick, Ohio: King's Court, 1988), p. 10.

until 1970. It was moved from the Department of the Treasury to the Executive Office of the President in 1939. It has a professional staff that appraises and amalgamates agency requests and then presents them to the president's advisers and eventually to the president. Agencies can appeal OMB's decisions to the president. This executive-branch process, which takes many months, results in the annual **Budget of the United States Government,** a multivolume document published in the winter of each year along with the president's annual budget message summarizing his requests. The title of the document is misleading. It is not the final budget—as the Brookings scholars noted, no such single document exists. It is, in fact, the president's detailed spending proposals for the following fiscal year, which runs from October 1 through September 30.

The role of the Council of Economic Advisers, created by the Employment Act of 1946, is to forecast economic developments, provide advice that helps in the formulation of national fiscal policy, and prepare the annual *Economic Report of the President.* Unlike OMB, the council does not bear day-to-day responsibility for formulating and overseeing the details of budget preparation and execution.

A lot of budgeting in the executive branch is, in effect, a struggle between the desire of the president and OMB to centralize decisions and the desire of the agencies to decentralize decisions. The agencies want decentralization because it enables them to be responsive to their congressional and interest-group allies.

Budget figures show broad general trends. But within those trends and on a year-to year basis, there is a constant battle between various agencies and their supporters for their share of the budget pie. Agencies develop strategies for building support both from interest groups and other clients and from congressional subcommittees. A large part of their budget may come automatically because it is "uncontrollable" unless major statutory changes are made. But that fact is forgotten because the visible struggle is over what is controllable and can be changed (Wildavsky, 1988).

Agencies try to build support from key figures in and out of government because such support has an impact on their budgetary success. In general, assertive agencies do better than passive ones. The agencies that ask for more will get more.

The complex interaction of agencies and congressional appropriations subcommittees helps determine the yearly budget figure. Subcommittee members review agency policy and program implementation. They make decisions about dollars. They also make decisions about what regulations to issue, where to place facilities, and what people to put in key positions.

The Reagan administration has constantly tried to reduce the budgetary autonomy of the agencies and to create more centralized, "top-down" budgeting under the control of OMB (Heclo, 1984; LeLoup, 1988; Schick, 1984).

Congress

Raising and spending money lies at the heart of the prerogatives of Congress. The "power of the purse" was the lever by which European parliaments increased their power over kings for centuries. The Constitution's authors were well aware of this history. Thus, they gave Congress full power of the purse, including both power over government spending and taxing.

The power of Congress over government spending is sweeping. According to Article I, Section 9 of the Constitution, "No money shall be drawn from the Treasury, but in consequence of appropriations made by law."

The funding process

This constitutional mandate is carried out through yearly appropriations bills voted by the House and Senate. By tradition, the House acts first. Executive budgets are considered in detail by the House and Senate appropriations committees—more specifically, by their subcommittees. Each of these committees has 13 subcommittees. Each year, the subcommittees examine agency requests. Agency heads justify those requests during hearings at which they answer questions about operations and programs. Based on these hearings, the subcommittees report bills, which are usually accepted both by the full committees and by the House and Senate. Three times in its history, including late 1986 and late 1987, Congress has been unable to pass separate appropriation bills and has, instead, passed one giant bill. The bill agreed to just before Christmas 1987 contained budget authority of more than $600 billion. It was 2,100 pages long.

The subcommittees of the two chambers behave somewhat differently. House subcommittees have ingrained habits of budget trimming. Senate subcommittees often play the role of appeals courts. They hear agency complaints about House cuts and often restore some of the cuts. The final figures worked out between the House and Senate usually fall between the levels recommended by their respective subcommittees.

Funding as oversight

The yearly appropriations process provides an effective way of overseeing executive agencies. Because the process is repeated annually, legislators become familiar with agencies and programs. And because funding is the lifeblood of any agency, the bureaucrats are very attentive to the criticisms or suggestions of their appropriations subcommittees.

Appropriations subcommittees usually focus on the details of agency budgets and programs, leaving larger problems and priorities somewhat blurred. These subcommittees work only on agencies and programs within their jurisdiction and they take last year's spending level as the starting point for their decisions. There is little chance to weigh competing priorities and funding options. The congressional budget process created in 1974, discussed below, was set up in part to remedy this shortcoming.

Congress appropriates funds only for programs already authorized by law. Historically, program authorizations were open-ended, that is, without a specific ending date attached. They were renewed only when Congress got around to rethinking or changing the programs. In recent decades, Congress has written more and more authorizations with fixed expiration dates. These are often for only a few years or even for a single year. Thus, agencies must return to Congress not only for funding but for basic legislation as well. In seeking control of executive activities, Congress has made the executive branch ask for renewal of authority more often. This has multiplied the opportunities for oversight. It has also increased the number of votes in Congress that must be taken on identical or similar questions year after year and even within the same year.

A number of authorizations have pushed growing portions of federal spending outside the yearly appropriations process. These funds are expended, not through appropriations, but automatically in accord with eligibility requirements (entitlements), through trust funds, or through long-term contracts.

The Budget Act of 1974

Before 1974, there was no single congressional budget process. The Budget and Impoundment Control Act of 1974 was a landmark innovation. It sprang from two roots: internal conflict among congressional committees and tensions between Capitol Hill and the White House.

External pressures on Congress were the chief impetus for the new process. In his first term, President Nixon impounded (that is, refused to spend) unprecedented amounts of funds. In early 1973, he began to mount an intensive "battle of the budget," threatening more impoundments if the Democratic Congress tried to spend more than he wanted. He charged that Congress was fiscally irresponsible. Senators and representatives were hard-pressed to defend their prerogatives. A more responsible budgetary process was one answer to Nixon's challenge.

Another impetus for change lay in fights between authorizing and appropriations committees. Authorizing committees generated intense pressure for funding the programs under their purview. To make sure that their pet programs continued, these committees sometimes created ways of spending not subject to the regular appropriations process, so-called backdoor spending. Authorizing committees also made short-term authorizations (often annual) with dollar amounts attached. They then helped bring pressure for "full funding" of the programs they sponsored.

Warfare resulted. The authorizing committees often accused the appropriations committees of ignoring expert judgment and providing meager funding. The appropriating committees, for their part, built the image of the Dutch boy with his finger in the dike, holding back the greed of the authorizing committees.

The Budget Act of 1974 set up procedures for Congress to determine national budget priorities and review presidential impoundments. It created House and Senate Budget Committees; the Congressional Budget Office, a full-time professional staff devoted to budget analysis; a complex set of new budgetary procedures; a timetable for budgetary actions; a change in the dates of the fiscal year; requirements for standardized budget terminology and information in the president's budget; and new provisions for controlling presidential impoundments.

According to the timetable in the 1974 act, all standing committees are supposed to submit reports to the House and Senate Budget Committees early in the process. These reports are used to form the first concurrent budget resolution for the fiscal year beginning October 1. They include the committees' views and estimates on matters within their jurisdiction. This is meant to force the authorizing committees to take a hard look at spending. They must also assign priorities to present or potential programs in their jurisdictions.

From the authorizing committees' reports, the House and Senate Budget Committees prepare the first concurrent resolution. It states the spending targets for each major budget category, of which there are now 17. Adopting such targets has forced the House and Senate to make tough choices. The targets limit the leeway of authorizing appropriating committees. Budget targets and ceilings impinge on committee policy-making authority by setting outer spending limits.

At the same time as the above activities are taking place, the appropriations subcommittees are working their way through the president's budget, which is usually presented in late January. By the end of summer, Congress is supposed to act on appropriations bills. Then, the budget committees draw up a second concurrent resolution that sets ceilings and reconciles the earlier targets with the later appropriations actions of Congress. The government fiscal year begins on October 1; soon after that, the congressional process begins again for the following year.

The congressional budget process is not self-enforcing; it is marked by delays and loose ends. Budget estimates go out of date quickly. By the 1980s, the timetable actually followed had strayed from the one specified by the act. Simultaneously, the reconciliation procedure came to the forefront.

Under the original act, reconciliation occurred at the end of the budget process to bring spending in line with the binding targets of the second budget resolution. After 1980, this was pushed forward several months. The resulting two-stage process works this way. During the first stage, Congress adopts a first budget resolution giving each authorizing committee a dollar figure and a deadline to report legislation for achieving the savings. During the second stage, the budget panels combine committee recommendations into an omnibus reconciliation measure. The 1981 reconciliation package, embracing some $140 billion in savings over a three-year period, overshadowed other budget steps and even the entire appropriations process.

In an era that stresses the limits of government activity, the congressional budget process is a powerful tool. In 1981, President Reagan selected the budget process, not a package of new legislation, as the forum for his initial program. Aided by Budget Director David A. Stockman and key allies on Capitol Hill, the president used the budget mechanism as a lever to change government policy.

Since these procedures started, the House and Senate Budget Committees have played a key role in organizing decisions on spending and revenue (Schick, 1980). Generally, the budget committees have avoided setting line-item (specific) funding limits. But the committees or their leaders sometimes oppose bills reported by other committees to hold the line on spending targets. The budget committees also have the power to recommend revenue levels.

Gramm-Rudman: The Attempt to Reduce Deficits

In late 1985 Congress, in desperation, passed the Gramm-Rudman-Hollings bill. (Senator Hollings' name is dropped from most references to this bill, and Senators Gramm and Rudman usually get all of the credit or blame for it.) The essence of the publicized part of the bill was to force Congress and the president to arrive at spending (and, by extension, taxing) decisions that would steadily reduce the size of the annual deficit until it reached zero by 1991. Some programs were protected from cuts, however. The procedures were fairly elaborate, and they involved many insti-

The Balanced Budget and Emergency Deficit Control Act of 1985, called the Gramm-Rudman-Hollings Act after its Senate cosponsors, set a maximum federal deficit amount for the fiscal years between 1986 and 1991, progressively reducing the deficit. The leading sponsor of this legislation was Sen. Phil Gramm (R–Tex.). The other sponsors were Sen. Warren Rudman (R–N.H.) and Sen. Ernest F. "Fritz" Hollings (D–S.C.).

tutions. In principle, those institutions were given a chance to arrive at decisions within the deficit target for each year. If they failed, an automatic procedure for cutting spending was invoked.

In mid-1986, the Supreme Court ruled that Gramm-Rudman contained a violation of the Constitution's separation of powers provisions. The specific sticking point for the Court was the role played by the General Accounting Office, because the head of the agency—the comptroller general—can be removed by Congress, though he never has been. Congress had anticipated such a decision and had fallback provisions in the original statute. In September 1987, it passed a new version of Gramm-Rudman that changed the provision found unconstitutional by the Supreme Court. The new version also relaxed the deficit targets enacted in 1985 and changed the goal of a balanced budget to 1993, two years later than the date set in the 1985 statute. Skepticism about the effectiveness of the new version was widespread throughout Congress and the executive branch, and among nongovernmental observers who followed economic policy matters. Even many congressional supporters of the bill said that they considered the new law more important as a symbol than as a real attack on the deficit problem.

A less-publicized feature of Gramm-Rudman than its deficit provisions—perhaps a more important feature in the long run—is its changes in the congressional budget process itself. The broadest general change is the accelerated timetable for the budget process. Table 18–1 compares the most important deadlines contained in the 1974 act with the same dead-

TABLE 18–1   Congressional budget deadlines, 1974 and 1985

Required action	1974 act	1985 act
President submits his budget	15th day after Congress convenes	1st Monday after January 3
House and Senate committees submit views and estimates to Budget committees	March 15	February 25
Congressional Budget Office (CBO) submits report to Budget committees	April 1	February 15
Budget committees report first concurrent resolution to their houses	April 15	April 1
Congress adopts first concurrent resolution	May 15	April 15
Congress completes action on reconciliation legislation	September 15	June 15
Fiscal year begins	October 1	October 1

lines in the 1985 act. Of course, Congress may miss any or all of the deadlines; there is no penalty for doing so. But there is a strong incentive for members to meet deadlines with high public visibility. Otherwise, they are made to look foolish in the mass media, which seizes on missed deadlines as a symbol of congressional incompetence or worse.

The new budget process also tightens House and Senate procedures for considering budget and funding measures. In the House, there is a June 30 deadline for passage of all 13 regular appropriation bills. The House is not supposed to adjourn for the Fourth of July recess unless it has passed the reconciliation measure and all of these bills.

In the Senate, the Budget Committee's central role in the budget process is underscored. As in the House, changes in floor procedure strengthen the hand of the Budget Committee in superintending the process and resisting attempts to gain exemptions.

The 1985 act continues the attempt of Congress to reverse the dispersion of power that marked congressional budget decision making in the 1960s and early 1970s.

Budget Patterns

Without money, government can do nothing. Decisions about what agencies and programs get how much are important. Money does not solve problems by itself, but implementation of attempts to solve problems cannot start without it.

TABLE 18–2   Budget outlays of the U.S. government, 1930–1990

Fiscal year	Current dollar outlays ($ billions)
1930	3.3
1940	9.5
1950	42.6
1960	92.2
1970	195.7
1980	590.9
1985	946.3
1990 (est.)	1,093.8

Source: *Budget of the United States Government, Fiscal Year 1987* (Washington, D.C.: U.S. Government Printing Office, 1986), p. 6e–45.

Budgeting is the heart of modern government. It sets priorities and it provides limits for government action. It is a tangible expression of where government hopes to have an impact. Politically, it provides a highly visible focus for competition among varying interests both in and out of government.

The size of the budget has grown with the size of government. In 1792, the entire federal government spent only $5 million. In the war year of 1917, the federal government spent over $1 billion for the first time. In 1990, it is expected to spend well over $1 trillion. Table 18–2 summarizes the size of federal budget outlays in current dollars from 1930 through a projection for 1990. If inflation is taken into account, government spending has grown at a slower rate than appears to be the case at first glance. For example, when government spending in 1985 is compared with government spending in 1960 in current dollars, it appears to have gone up more than tenfold. However, a constant dollar comparison of government spending for those years reveals that the increase was less than threefold.

It is unreasonable to assume that the budget starts from zero each year. Rough estimates of portions of the annual budget that are "relatively uncontrollable" hover around three fourths of all expenditures. Naturally, major statutory changes can increase the controllability of some items thought to be "relatively uncontrollable," but such changes are rare and difficult to achieve.

A meaningful way of considering overall **budget controllability** is to divide the budget into four broad categories: national defense, **entitlement programs** and other mandatory spending, nondefense discretionary spending, and interest that the government must pay to service its debt (LeLoup, 1986: 51–61). In 1985, 27 percent of budget outlays went to national defense, 45 percent to entitlements and other mandatory spending, 18 percent to discretionary spending for nondefense items, and the

TABLE 18–3   Federal budget outlays by general purpose (selected years, 1960–1987)

| | *Percentage of total federal outlays* | | | | |
Year	*National defense*	*Payments to individuals*	*Net interest*	*Aid to state and local governments*	*Other*
1960	49	26	7	8	10
1970	40	32	7	12	9
1980	24	47	9	16	4
1987 (proposed)	28	41	15	10	6

Source: *Statistical Abstract of the United States. 1982–83* (Washington, D.C.: U.S. Government Printing Office, 1982). p.247, for 1960, 1970, 1980; and *Budget of the United States Government, Fiscal Year 1987* (Washington, D.C.: U.S. Government Printing Office, 1986), p. M–2, for 1987.

remaining 10 percent to interest. The interest spending is mandatory since it is built into the government securities that are sold to raise money. In effect, much of defense spending is also mandatory: payroll, payments to retirees, and basic force maintenance cannot vary much. Even much procurement is on fixed multiyear schedules written into contracts with manufacturers. Thus, only a modest portion of defense spending and much of the discretionary spending for nondefense items bear the brunt of political debate over spending decisions and stand to suffer most of the cuts made, even though together they represent only about one fourth of all spending.

In 1985, $436 billion was included in the category comprising "entitlements and other mandatory spending." The two largest programs by far were Social Security ($185 billion) and Medicare ($69 billion), which accounted for 58 percent of all the spending in this category. The spending in this category is projected to be $577 billion by 1990, of which $254 billion will be for Social Security and $119 billion will be for Medicare. These two items are expected to account for 65 percent of all the spending in their category.

Another way to gauge overall growth of the federal budget is to look at federal outlays (spending) as a percentage of the gross national product. This percentage gives a rough indication of whether the government is becoming a larger or smaller factor in the economy. It grew from 10 percent in 1940, to 16 percent in 1950, to 18 percent in 1955. It remained in the 18–22 percent range from the mid-1950s until the early 1980s. Then, it began to grow again, reaching about 25 percent in 1985.

Changes in spending patterns reflect changing priorities. Table 18–3 breaks down four budgets between 1960 and 1987 into four major categories of spending. Until Reagan's presidency, the percentage of GNP spent on national defense was falling, though the number of dollars spent for this purpose was increasing. The percentage spent for payments to

Senior citizens march for Medicare. Members of the Senior Citizens Forum support passage of federal medicare legislation in this 1964 parade down the boardwalk in Atlantic City, New Jersey. Medicare is funded by federal taxes.

individuals was rising. The Reagan administration reversed both trends. As the federal deficit ballooned during the Reagan administration, the net interest percentage rose substantially. But the Reagan administration reduced the percentage of spending on aid to state and local governments, which had grown over the preceding two decades.

TAXING: INSTITUTIONS, PROCESSES, AND POLICIES

Like spending, taxation is so important that major figures in both Congress and the executive branch are constantly and heavily involved in negotiations over tax policy. The president and his closest advisers—the Office of Management and Budget, the Department of the Treasury, and the Council of Economic Advisers—all ponder tax matters. In Congress, the Joint Committee on Taxation, the Budget Committees, and especially the House Ways and Means Committee and the Senate Finance Committee are intimately involved in tax policy.

In Congress, the House of Representatives is awarded the constitutional privilege of originating tax legislation. This lends special significance to the House Ways and Means Committee (Manley, 1970). That committee also has jurisdiction over other important related matters: debt, tariffs, other trade regulations, Social Security, Medicare, and Welfare. The Finance Committee is the Senate counterpart of the House Ways and Means Committee. Occasionally it will take the lead on tax matters.

Despite the great attention paid to taxation, tax policies are only sporadically coordinated with overall economic policies and conditions. As a partial remedy for this state of affairs, revenue issues were integrated into the new congressional budget process created in 1974. The House and Senate Budget Committees, using Congressional Budget Office reports, introduce resolutions covering the overall size and shape of both revenue and spending laws. The Ways and Means Committee and the Finance Committee are not thrilled with this challenge to their power. Feuding between them and the Budget Committees has often broken out.

The expression "tax policy" implies a comprehensive scheme to distribute the tax load. In fact, there is no such scheme. All levels of government make decisions about taxes without coordinating them (Pechman, 1987). The tax system is like a crazy quilt. Even the major federal tax act of 1986, despite some simplifications, did not reduce the complexity or the contradictory nature of different provisions of the federal tax code. And, of course, it had no direct impact on the taxes levied by state and local governments.

Who Pays?

You have, no doubt, looked at a paycheck and wondered why you get only $140 for a week's work when the boss has told you you are being paid $200 a week. Withheld income taxes are probably a large part of the reason for the missing $60. Federal income tax is withheld. In many states, a state income tax is withheld. And a city or other local income tax may also be withheld. A sizable amount will probably also be withheld to pay for Social Security.

But the taxes apparent on a paystub are only part of what an individual pays in taxes. Individuals also pay state and local sales taxes, local property taxes (directly if you own property, indirectly if you rent), and a variety of less visible taxes, such as the federal taxes on telephone bills, airplane tickets, cigarettes, and gasoline.

When all of the taxes paid by individuals are taken into account, it is found that almost everyone pays about the same proportion of his or her income in taxes, regardless of amount of income. That proportion hovers at around 25 percent (Pechman, 1985: 48; for somewhat different estimates, see Moon and Sawhill, 1984).

The federal personal income tax is moderately progressive. That is, people with higher incomes pay a higher percentage of their income in taxes. A significant reduction in the progressive features of the federal personal income tax was made in 1981. Tax experts predicted that the impact of the 1986 income tax revision would not change the modest degree of progressivity during the period from 1981 to 1986.

State and local personal income taxes are mildly progressive in some jurisdictions and proportional in others. Sales taxes, property taxes, and federal Social Security payroll taxes are generally regressive. Those with higher incomes pay a lower percentage of their income in these taxes.

The total impact of just the two principal federal taxes—personal income tax and the Social Security payroll tax—is close to proportional. In 1982, families of four with the median income for such families paid 25 percent of their income in these two taxes, those with twice the median income (the relatively well off) paid only 26 percent, and those with half of the median income (the relatively poor) paid 20 percent. This represented substantial change—both in amounts and in relative percentages—from 1955, when families of four with the median income paid 9 percent, those with twice the median income paid 12 percent, and those with half of the median income paid 4 percent. In 1982, everyone was being taxed more heavily, but the differences in rates of taxation for people earning different amounts were smaller.

Where Does the Federal Government Get Its Money?

The federal government gets some money by borrowing through such means as the sale of bonds and Treasury certificates. In 1985, borrowing represented one dollar out of every five needed by the federal government.

Most of the federal government's money comes from taxes. There are four major categories:

1. Personal income taxes.
2. Social insurance taxes and contributions. These include Social Security and Railroad Retirement taxes, unemployment taxes and deposits from employers, contributions by federal employees to their retirement system, and payments for extra medical insurance under the Medicare program.
3. Corporate income taxes.
4. Other taxes. These include excise taxes on a variety of products, services, and activities (such as taxes on airport and airway use, telephone bills, and gasoline and other fuels), estate taxes, gift taxes, and tariffs on foreign imports.

In the last few decades, the government has reduced its reliance on taxation of corporate income, though the 1986 tax act increased the proportion of total revenues that corporations would pay. Corporations can sell unused tax benefits to each other. At the same time, the government has increased its reliance on social insurance taxes. Individual income taxes have remained the largest source of federal revenue. Figure 18–2 shows the mix of federal tax receipts over the last several decades.

Federal tax laws are complex. They have many loopholes that let peo-

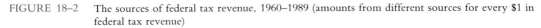

FIGURE 18–2   The sources of federal tax revenue, 1960–1989 (amounts from different sources for every $1 in federal tax revenue)

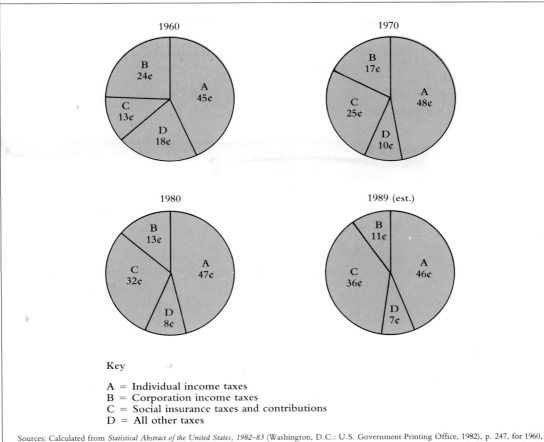

Key

A = Individual income taxes
B = Corporation income taxes
C = Social insurance taxes and contributions
D = All other taxes

Sources: Calculated from *Statistical Abstract of the United States, 1982–83* (Washington, D.C.: U.S. Government Printing Office, 1982), p. 247, for 1960, 1970, and 1980; and *Budget of the United States Government, Fiscal Year 1987* (Washington, D.C.: U.S. Government Printing Office, 1986). p. 4–3, for 1989 estimate.

ple and corporations legally avoid certain taxes. Although the 1986 Tax Act closed many loopholes, a number remained.

The government uses the tax code as well as more direct methods to subsidize a great deal of personal and corporate behavior that it wishes to encourage. One measure of such subsidization is **tax expenditures,** which represent revenue that the government forgoes by exempting certain income from taxation or allowing certain deductions and credits. Such tax expenditures total hundreds of billions of dollars annually. The budget for 1988 estimated such revenue losses in more than a hundred categories.

Major losses of tax revenue for 1988 included over $7 billion from individuals because they could deduct local property taxes on owner-occupied dwellings, almost $15 billion because they could deduct other nonbusiness state and local taxes (primarily state and local income taxes), over $20 billion because they could deduct interest on home mortgages, over $43 billion because they paid no taxes on contributions to employer mortgage plans, and over $12 billion because many Social Security benefits were not taxed. Over $23 billion was lost from corporate income tax because of provisions allowing for the accelerated depreciation of machinery and equipment.

THE MEANING OF DEFICITS

Since Ronald Reagan became president, the country has engaged in what might best be called **deficit** mania. The Reagan policies of greatly reduced taxes, greatly expanded defense spending, and reduced domestic spending produced dramatically increased deficits. This has led to impassioned public rhetoric about the disastrous consequences of deficits and about the necessity—not just the desirability—of reducing them. Despite the rhetoric, however, the focus on budgets in general in the Reagan years and the increased concern with deficits has not altered the basic decision-making patterns on budgetary matters. The actors and the interests are the same (Smith, 1985). Even a process as potentially unsettling as the Gramm-Rudman Act does not change the basic pattern, which is one of ultimate congressional deference to the president on aggregate budgetary matters, including spending, taxing, and deficits. Since World War II, according to one observer,

> the most stable force has been the control of the fiscal agenda by the institutionalized presidency. Throughout the postwar period Congress has operated within a budget framework initially specified by the president, who (with the help of the OMB, the Treasury, and the Council of Economic Advisers) is best able to construct an overall national fiscal policy. However much Congress may modify the details of [national fiscal] policy, it seems to have accepted the executive's prerogative to define the budget's general contours. (Peterson, 1985: 379)

The deficit and the total amount of federal debt have both been subjects of political controversy throughout our history (Ornstein, 1985). Heated political debate was generated by the mammoth deficits (and, to a lesser extent, the corresponding increasing size of the total federal debt) produced during the Reagan Administration.

How large is the deficit? How large is the national debt (which, roughly speaking, is the accumulated deficits minus what has been repaid)? Table 18–4 summarizes the size of the annual deficit both in current dollars and as a percentage of the gross national product every third year from 1970 through 1985. The deficit dipped in the middle of this period but grew both in absolute and percentage terms at the beginning and end. Table 18–5 summarizes the size of the gross federal debt both in current dollars

TABLE 18–4   Annual federal deficits as a percentage of gross national product, 1970–1985

Fiscal year	GNP ($billions)	Deficit ($billions)	Deficit as a percentage of GNP
1970	990.5	2.8	0.3
1973	1,285.5	14.9	1.2
1976	1,699.6	73.7	4.3
1979	2,452.2	40.2	1.6
1982	3,141.5	127.9	4.1
1985	3,936.8	212.3	5.4

Source: *Budget of the United States Government, Fiscal Year 1987* (Washington, D.C.: U.S. Government Printing Office, 1986), p.6e–42.

and as a percentage of GNP every fifth year from 1955 through 1990. The gross federal debt grew steadily in absolute terms, though as a percentage of GNP it reached a low point in the 1970s and then began to rise again.

Economists disagree about the specific consequences of deficits (Cagan, 1985). Most, however, believe that prolonged large deficits will have a number of negative results (Aaron and others, 1986). The late Walter Heller, an economics professor and chairman of the Council of Economic Advisers under Presidents Kennedy and Johnson, described what he called a "chain of deficit damages" (*Wall Street Journal,* October 26, 1984; see also Bell and Thurow, 1986). The major problem, according to Heller, is

TABLE 18–5   Gross federal debt as a percentage of gross national product, 1955–1990

Fiscal year	GNP ($ billions)	Gross federal debt ($ billions)	Gross federal debt as a percentage of GNP
1955	387.6	274.5	58.5
1960	507.7	290.9	46.7
1965	673.6	323.2	38.8
1970	990.5	382.6	28.8
1975	1,523.5	544.1	26.1
1980	2,667.6	914.3	26.8
1985	3,936.8	1,827.5	38.4
1990 (est.)	5,623.4	2,976.7	36.5

Source: Special Analyses, *Budget of the United States Government, Fiscal Year 1987* (Washington, D.C.: U.S. Government Printing Office, 1986), p. E 9.

that large deficits keep interest rates high because the government's borrowing needs compete with the borrowing needs of business, consumers, and home builders. High interest rates in turn help produce (1) an overvalued dollar in international exchange, (2) larger trade deficits because of the reduced price competitiveness of U.S. exporters and the greater price competitiveness of foreign exporters to the United States, and (3) special problems for Third World nations that have borrowed large sums of money repayable in dollars. Large deficits, in Heller's view, would also impair future productivity because they increased the difficulty of borrowing to make private investments. Heller also thought that such deficits would worsen the future U.S. position in international finance and trade, result in soaring interest charges on the government's debts (which would preclude more productive uses for government spending), and make the government unwilling to engage in Keynesian pump priming in combating future recessions.

A minority view is stated by another economics professor, who contends that "the deficit is an inherently arbitrary accounting construct that provides no real guide to fiscal policy" (Kotlikoff, 1986: 53; see also Eisner, 1986). For Kotlikoff, the fundamental problem of the economy is a "long-term decline in saving which may well be the result of the unreported but enormous economic deficits associated with Social Security and other unfunded federal government retirement programs in the last three decades" (p. 65). In his view, the deficit as traditionally measured has "little or no relationship to the issue of fundamental concern." But he recognizes that, politically, the traditional numbers have produced "national hysteria."

Regardless of which economic views prove most nearly correct, deficits have undoubtedly been one of the primary topics of political debate during the 1980s. The rhetoric, however, has produced little concrete action to reduce deficits. Congress seems content with a Gramm-Rudman Act rendered toothless by the Supreme Court and replaced by a symbol of dubious value. Rhetoric thrives. Meaningful action is in short supply.

CONCLUSIONS

In the United States, economic policy questions are political questions. This means that the challenges identified at the beginning of this chapter have produced no permanent political consensus. There is continuous disagreement over what economic policies are best. We have sought to identify some of the major policy options in several important areas. The organs of government produce economic policies. These policies change continually, often rapidly.

A few general conclusions summarize our exploration of the turbulent arena where politics and economics meet:

1. Politics and economics are constantly intertwined in the processes of government, the selection of policies, and the electoral process.

2. Government economic policy can have important effects, but those effects are severely limited both by the great economic power in private hands within the United States and by interna-

tional events and the economic decisions of other nations.

3. There are competing theories about the best way to exercise governmental influence on the economy. There are disagreements among both politicians and economists on the validity of those theories and on the consequences of acting in accord with any of them.

4. Despite limited governmental influence on economic well-being, voters tend to hold the incumbent president and members of his party broadly responsible for economic conditions, both personal and national.

5. The major types of economic policy are fiscal policy (which includes both spending and taxing) and monetary policy. Other policy areas that have significant economic impacts are trade, industrial development, energy, and the environment.

6. Economists, politicians, the media, and the public use many economic indicators to monitor the state of the economy. These indicators are subject to interpretation and even manipulation for purposes of political advantage.

7. Many institutions and individuals in both the executive branch and Congress deal with aspects of U.S. economic policies. Private interests have ample opportunities to seek and exercise influence over such policies. This multitude of institutions, individuals, and interests often produces poorly articulated, internally inconsistent economic policies.

8. In recent years, the annual federal deficit has become a major item of political and economic controversy. Concern over the deficit led Congress, in late 1985, to pass a mandatory plan for moving to a zero deficit by 1991—the Gramm-Rudman act. A Supreme Court decision declared part of the act unconstitutional, and Congress enacted a replacement that may have only limited effect.

FURTHER READING

BUDGET OF THE U.S. GOVERNMENT. This yearly document, published, usually in February, by the U.S. Government Printing Office in Washington, is both a political statement by the incumbent administration and a valuable collection of information about government agencies and programs and the overall importance of government in society.

KIEWIET, D. RODERICK (1983) *Macroeconomics and Micropolitics: The Electoral Effects of Economic Issues.* Chicago: University of Chicago Press. An exploration of the mix of national and personal economic perspectives that help people decide how to vote.

LeLOUP, LANCE T. (1988) *Budgetary Politics.* 4th ed. Brunswick, Ohio: King's Court. A thorough examination of budgeting institutions, processes, and results.

PECHMAN, JOSEPH A. (1987) *Federal Tax Policy.* 5th ed. Washington, D.C.: Brookings Institution. A careful analysis of the nature and impact of federal tax laws.

TUFTE, EDWARD R. (1978) *Political Control of the Economy.* Princeton, N.J.: Princeton University Press. An argument that many national economic decisions in both the United States and other capitalist democracies are made for the purpose of electoral gain.

LIBERTIES, RIGHTS, AND EQUALITY

What liberties do American citizens enjoy? What do we mean by equality? How fast do the meanings of liberties, rights, and equality change? In what direction? Whose values and interests are best served by the changes?

The essence of a free society lies in its ability to define and protect liberties, rights, and equality for individuals. Inevitably, the specific meanings of liberties, rights, and equality are subject to lively political and legal debate. Three major challenges face a free society in arriving at definitions of liberties, rights, and equality and putting those definitions into practice: (1) to define liberties and rights in ways that characterize a free society and a free people and yet do not prevent the maintenance of public order, (2) to make the government the protector of agreed-on liberties and rights rather than a force hostile to them, and (3) to use the political process to debate continuously the meaning of equality in ways that result in agreement on the aspects of equality that should be pursued as national goals and on the government's role in promoting those aspects. ✍

*G*uaranteed personal freedom is the distinctive mark of the United States and a handful of other nations. Most of the world's people are governed by systems that provide relatively little freedom. Although we Americans take our freedom for granted, it does not exist automatically. It is guaranteed by the actions of vigilant political activists, judges, members of Congress, presidents, executive-branch officials, and an aggressive press; it is supported by norms that are transmitted from generation to generation. Our freedom can also be threatened by the actions of both private citizens and public officials. The nature of freedom is constantly debated. Both rights and liberties are aspects of freedom, and equality is related to freedom in complicated ways.

In creating the government of the United States, the framers of the Constitution sought "justice" and "the blessings of liberty." In previous chapters, we examined how basic American beliefs relate to the changing meanings of both liberty and justice and how various liberties waxed and waned as our political culture developed. We also examined the workings of our government's basic institutions. Specific decisions of these institutions help shape the operational meaning of liberties, rights, and equality.

In this chapter, we will examine some of the most important contemporary aspects of liberties, rights, and equality. Much of our focus will be on the work of the federal courts, especially the Supreme Court. At any given time, Supreme Court decisions give the most concrete meaning to liberties, rights, and equality. Those decisions are also the focal point of ongoing political activity. Major Supreme Court decisions are front-page news all over the country. As Chapter 15 made clear, courts are part of our nation's governing apparatus. Nowhere is this fact more important than in the operational definitions of liberties, rights, and equality afforded by Supreme Court decisions.

In some nations, courts function without much public attention. Not so in the United States. The plaza in front of the Supreme Court has even been the location of political demonstrations, such as those conducted by "prolife" groups on the anniversary of the Court's decision creating a right to abortion. Because of the importance of Court decisions to the life of the nation, nominations to membership on the Court are often hotly contested. When President Reagan nominated Robert Bork to the Court in the summer of 1987, politicians and commentators of all political hues realized that this nomination could have important repercussions for years in such areas as abortion and affirmative action.

The status of liberties, rights, and equality cannot be understood without knowing something about the Supreme Court's decisions. This chapter does not focus exclusively on those decisions, nor does it examine all of the Court decisions that affect liberties, rights, and equality. Yet those decisions are the closest thing to a codification of our specific rights and liberties that we as a nation possess.

In the sections that follow, we will look first at the general setting for liberties and rights. Second, we will examine the current meaning of a number of specific liberties and rights. Third, we will examine aspects of equality. Finally, we will offer a summary comment on the relation of freedom to public opinion and the Federal Courts.

The Meaning of Liberties and Rights

The terms *rights* and *liberties* are used a great deal in political debate in the United States. A **liberty** is an act that cannot be limited by government. **Right** is a stronger term. It is a claim, backed by law and government action, to certain protections, guarantees, or benefits. Government is not only barred from interfering with rights; ideally, it is also obliged to take positive action to obtain them for individuals and to prevent their limitation. Free speech, for example, is both a liberty and a right. It is a liberty because government cannot interfere with a person's expression of opinions or beliefs. But it is also a right because the government must act to prevent interference with such expression.

Abortion provides another example of the practical effects of treating something as a liberty as contrasted with treating it as a right. Backers of abortion argued that women should have the liberty to control their own bodies. When they extended the argument and claimed that the liberty should also be a right, fierce political debate ensued.

Throughout our political history, liberties and rights have been treated interchangeably in political debate. There is a theoretical difference between them, described above, but trying to sort out liberties from rights in a rigorous classification would be a confusing exercise. It would also be an exercise that is not undertaken in the political process by which liberties and rights get defined. The Bill of Rights itself deals largely with liberties, and these first 10 amendments to the Constitution were added shortly after its ratification because it was considered deficient in protecting both liberties and rights. The rest of this chapter, therefore, looks at liberties and rights together. It also looks at those explicitly contained in the Constitution, including the Bill of Rights, and those contained implicitly in the Constitution.

Liberties and rights have always been treated as special in the United States. The Declaration of Independence speaks of "Unalienable Rights," one of which is "Liberty." The protection of liberties and rights is central to the existence of a democratic society. But those liberties and rights are neither absolute nor unchanging. They are both broadened and narrowed in the give-and-take of political debate and decision making.

Before we examine specific liberties and rights it is useful to see why conflicts can arise over them. We will do this by looking at a few examples.

In the late 1970s, the American Nazi party wanted to hold a parade in Skokie, Illinois, a Chicago suburb with a large Jewish population. The residents of Skokie, many of whom had survived the Nazi attempt to exterminate Jews during World War II, opposed granting the party a pa-

Rights for all. The First Amendment to the Constitution protects all Americans, regardless of their ideology or message, from interference with free speech and from arbitrary exercise of power.

rade permit. The American Nazi party and its lawyers, joined by the American Civil Liberties Union, sought the permit. The lawyers argued that free speech means allowing even the vilest points of view to be expressed. They regarded the parade as a symbolic act equivalent to speech. The courts sided with this view and upheld the right of the American Nazi party to a parade permit.

A dimension of obscenity provides a second example of the controversy that competing claims related to free speech can generate. Local governments and citizens may try to prevent "adult" bookstores and movie theaters from locating near residential areas because they threaten the morals of children. The store and theater owners argue that their activities and businesses are protected by First Amendment guarantees of free speech and, by extension, free expression. There is a benefit in banning smut-pushers from the neighborhood, but that benefit must be balanced against the value of the right of free expression. Rights, in theory, are not subject to balances or limitations supported by the will of the majority. In practice, however, courts do balance them and approve some limitations.

In many cases, of course, the moral arguments, and even the constitutional arguments, are just window dressing for other interests, often economic. Pornographers are not likely to be civil libertarians; they are probably out to make quick bucks. Segregationists bitterly opposed the expansion of rights for blacks in a host of ways. They often used "moral" claims based on how they interpreted freedom of association. (That is, they wanted to associate only with whites in certain activities.) In actuality, however, the claims of the segregationists were often based on a mixture of economic motives and strong fear and hatred. They feared, in the end, economic competition from an upwardly mobile black community.

Controversy over pornography. Adult bookstores selling pornographic materials are often picketed by opponents, as here in Chicago. The courts have imposed some limitations on such materials.

And they simply disliked blacks, at least those blacks who claimed to be equal.

It is wise to be skeptical of moral assertions. One should not swallow whole the moral platitudes issued by either side in a controversy over rights and liberties. Neither side wants to compromise its view of its own "rights and liberties." In fact, in the normal way of doing political business in our nation, compromise is usually the solution to controversies. As in other areas, one day's compromise becomes the next day's controversy. Argument quickly breaks out that may well lead to yet another compromise. This does not mean, of course, that there is anything inevitable about the expansion of rights and liberties. Rights and liberties can also be diminished, and sometimes they are. Contending forces push in many directions and have varying strengths at different times. And government, inevitably a participant and sometimes a referee in such controversies, will itself take different positions at different times.

Does Government Defend Freedom?

All parts of the federal government are involved in defining rights and liberties in the abstract and, more important, in practice. They can deprive us of our rights and liberties; they can expand them; or they can bargain and negotiate compromises.

Ideally, of course, the government should protect rights and liberties, and some of the time it does. But the government can also violate rights and liberties. It has used the Federal Bureau of Investigation (FBI), the Internal Revenue Service (IRS), and other agencies to spy on American citizens. This has been done in blatantly illegal and highly offensive ways from the post–World War II period up until the last few years. (We make

Internment of Japanese-Americans during World War II. People of Japanese ancestry arrive at an inland relocation camp in 1942 after being removed from the West Coast. The U.S. Supreme Court found the relocation program constitutional in 1944.

the happy assumption that such activities have stopped, but that assumption may be inaccurate.) This spying was ordered by presidents, carried out by bureaucrats, and probably known about and approved by some members of Congress.

The government also interned 110,000 people of Japanese ancestry (two thirds of them U.S. citizens) in what amounted to concentration camps for most of World War II. The people in these camps were, in effect, prisoners. They lost all of their civil liberties as well as their property and livelihood. Here, there was nothing secret. The internment was ordered by President Franklin Roosevelt and carried out by many federal and state authorities. It was approved by the vast majority of Congress in legislation that gave the president power to take such action. And it was finally sanctioned by the courts in decisions on suits brought by those affected. The government's claims that some people of Japanese ancestry might aid the war effort of Japan against the United States were powerful enough to convince even Supreme Court justices noted for their devotion to civil liberties. Hugo Black, usually a friend of civil liberties in his 34 years on the Supreme Court (1937–71), delivered the Court's opinion in the case of *Korematsu* v. *United States* (1944). (Korematsu was an American citizen convicted for failure to leave a restricted area as ordered.)

> It is said that we are dealing here with the case of imprisonment of a citizen in a concentration camp solely because of his ancestry, without evidence or inquiry concerning his loyalty and good disposition towards the United States. . . . Regardless of the true nature of the assembly and relocation centers—and we deem it unjustifiable to call them concentration camps with all the ugly connotations that term implies—we are dealing specifically with nothing but an exclusion order. To cast this case into outlines of racial prejudice, without reference to the real military dangers which were presented, merely confuses the issue. . . . Congress, reposing its confidence in this time of war in our military leaders—as inevitably it must—determined that they should have the power to do just this [that is, exclude people of Japanese ancestry and concentrate them away from the West Coast].

Robert Jackson, one of the justices who dissented, pointed out that *only* people of Japanese ancestry were removed to camps. German and Italian aliens were not removed, nor were Americans of German and Italian ancestry, nor were citizens who had been convicted of treason but were out on parole. West Coast whites eagerly bought the property of Japanese-Americans who had been removed to camps at ridiculously low prices.

This highly visible violation of civil liberties continues to have repercussions. About half of those who were interned are still alive today; many of them were children during World War II. Through class action lawsuits, they have sought monetary restitution for the wrong done them. Two of the individuals whose cases reached the Supreme Court in the 1940s and who at that time were convicted for resisting internment had their convictions overturned in federal district courts more than 40 years later: Fred Korematsu in 1984 and Gordon Hirabayashi in 1986.

The federal government has also violated civil liberties on other occasions. Congress passed the Alien and Sedition Acts in the 1790s. These acts provided penalties for persons overly critical of the government. During the "red scare" after World War I, the attorney general of the United States swiftly deported suspected subversive persons without legal process. From time to time, the federal government has, for political reasons, restricted the travel of Americans abroad. Travel to Castro's Cuba, for example, was restricted until 1977. After a period of unrestricted travel from 1977 to 1982, the Reagan administration again imposed limits on travel. In 1984, the Supreme Court upheld those limits.

States and localities have an even spottier record in relation to rights and liberties than that of the federal government. State law in the South kept blacks "in their place" for many decades. Units of local government are often involved in censorship activities.

Government action is not the only threat to liberties and rights. Private individuals and groups attack one another's rights. There is no ambiguity about who is wrong in some instances of such attacks—for example, instances in which racist groups deprive blacks of their civil rights (as was done in numerous lynchings over many decades). Other instances do involve ambiguities. For example, two competing arguments can be made about the attempts of feminists to close theaters showing pornographic movies. Many of us believe that such movies are disgusting and reinforce dangerous stereotypes of women as sexual playthings, often violently abused. On the other hand, the precedent of letting any group prevent some other group from engaging in free expression is very disturbing. Suppose the members of a right-wing evangelical church demand the closing of theaters that show movies with explicit sexual themes? What if they forcibly prevent patrons from entering such a theater? Or suppose the same people enter a library or school textbook warehouse and destroy books that they find offensive—books espousing the theory of evolution, for example. Your own values would help you identify "good" and "bad" persons in such confrontations. But ultimate "right" and "wrong" in the sense of protecting a free society are harder to pinpoint.

The ideal role of the federal government in relation to rights and liberties can be defined as refraining from actions that infringe on them, preventing state and local governments from infringing on them, conferring and supporting specific rights and liberties by positive action, and protecting people against the actions of others that infringe on their rights and liberties.

Neither the executive branch nor the legislative branch has acted consistently in line with this ideal role, however. Throughout our history, the judicial branch—the federal courts in general and, above all, the Supreme Court—has served as a special friend of liberties and rights. The court's record has not been spotless. Nor are the meanings of liberties and rights self-evident. But courts have the undoubted power to declare statutes or other acts by any other government officials and agencies unconstitutional. Those government officials and agencies obey such decisions. This gives the courts enormous power in society in defining liberties and rights and in requiring both governmental and private behavior consistent with those definitions. That power, coupled with the authoritative status of the Supreme Court's pronouncements about the meaning of rights and liberties, gives the Supreme Court a uniquely important role in the policy areas examined in this chapter. It should not be forgotten, however, that other parts of the government, as well as parts of the private society, are also involved in producing operational definitions of rights, liberties, and equality. Liberties, rights, and equality are parts of public policy, and they should be viewed as such. They are subject to change and conflict; they are both defined and guaranteed through the governing process. The reliance on the Supreme Court for definition and guarantees is unusually heavy, but as Chapter 15 sought to make clear, the courts themselves are an integral part of the governing process.

In this section, we will examine aspects of four of the major liberties and rights important in the United States: freedom of expression, freedom of religion, guarantees that accused criminals will get fair trials and be treated within the bounds of the Constitution if convicted, and the emerging right to privacy.

LIBERTIES AND RIGHTS: THE MEANING OF A FREE SOCIETY

Freedom of Expression

The ability to express oneself freely about all matters, especially political matters, is perhaps the most important prerequisite for a free society. The First Amendment to the Constitution, adopted in 1791, says that "Congress shall make no law . . . abridging the freedom of speech, or of the press; or the right of the people peaceably to assemble, and to petitition the Government for a redress of grievances." What has the First Amendment's prohibition against limits on freedom of expression come to mean in practice? In this section, we will look first at the general meaning of free speech. Second, we will examine obscenity as a special class of speech whose status under the First Amendment is often hotly debated. Third, we will look at the operational meaning of freedom of the press.

Free speech

The First Amendment has been construed to limit or prohibit government action against almost any kind of expression: public speeches, private conversation, printed materials of all kinds, and radio and television broadcasts. "Free speech" has been applied to include picketing and demonstrating, wearing armbands and buttons, placing slogans on car license plates, and engaging in artistic presentations and entertainment of all kinds. It has also been applied to the creation and maintenance of political organizations, questions involving loyalty oaths and other programs aimed at subversion, and the right to travel abroad freely. Court decisions have also excluded a few kinds of speech from the protection of the First Amendment. We will examine obscenity, a major category in which some exclusion can occur.

Over the years, court decisions have applied many portions of the Bill of Rights, including the First Amendment, to state and local governments as well as the federal government. This has been done by gradually incorporating the guarantees against federal government action contained in the Bill of Rights into the 14th Amendment, which was adopted after the Civil War and was aimed explicitly at preventing certain kinds of state activity. The critical phrase in the 14th Amendment used for this **incorporation** is that no state shall "deprive any person of life, liberty, or property without due process of law." The Supreme Court extended 1st Amendment guarantees against government encroachment to state and local governments in a 1925 decision.

The Supreme Court must determine precisely what free speech means. It has never adopted the position that no forms of speech can be suppressed by government action. Therefore, it has had to develop doctrine that distinguishes between constitutional and unconstitutional suppressions of speech. It started the process of developing such doctrine in a 1919 decision that speech could be restricted if it created "a clear and present danger" that might result in "substantive evils that Congress has a right to prevent," such as the forcible overthrow of the government. In 1927, it elaborated on this central notion: "In order to support a finding of clear and present danger it must be shown either that immediate serious violence was to be expected or was advocated, or that past conduct furnished reason to believe that such advocacy was then contemplated." In short, the Court looked for a link between speech and action that could be banned. Merely supporting ideas was not enough to restrict speech; there had to be a great likelihood that illegal or violent action would follow.

The doctrine of clear and present danger has had to be interpreted case by case. Over time, the Court added a second doctrine: Society's interests in guarding free speech had to be "balanced" against society's interests in preventing unwanted or illegal action. That doctrine was used, for instance, in a 1972 case. In that case, the Court ruled that a newspaper reporter could not refuse to appear before a grand jury investigating crime because the reporter wanted to protect confidential sources vital to news gathering. The Court stated that the social interest in investigating crime was greater than the social interest in guarding the reporter's sources.

In assessing limits on speech in the name of ensuring "national security" or preventing "subversion," the Court has restrained the government in some of its attempts to impose such limits. But it has not made all such limits unconstitutional. It upheld federal statutes banning membership in the Communist party, forbidding support for overthrow of the government by force and violence, and requiring the Communist party to file membership lists. At the same time, it imposed limits making it either very hard or impossible to enforce those statutes.

The Supreme Court has also upheld federal security programs. But it has required fairly strict safeguards during implementation. It has not directly overturned statutes designed to prevent "subversives" from traveling abroad by denying them a U.S. passport; instead, it has interpreted such statutes so as to make them largely unenforceable.

The Court has also shied away from direct confrontation with Congress over inquiries into subversive activities. Here again, though, it has set some limits on what congressional committees can do.

In dealing with state statutes, inquiries, and loyalty and security programs aimed at subversion, the Supreme Court has not only imposed procedural requirements but has also felt freer to rule some of these statutes and activities unconstitutional than it has in the case of congressional actions.

In another area—criticism of public officials—the Supreme Court has effectively developed the doctrine that people are almost immune from libel or slander prosecution for anything they say or write about public officials.

Obscenity

Should obscene speech be protected as free speech? That question has been hotly debated both in society in general and in the courts. In its decisions, the Supreme Court has wavered between allowing restrictions and ruling them unconstitutional. The Court first addressed the issue in 1957. In the *Roth* case, the justices agreed that obscene materials were not protected by the First Amendment. They defined "obscene material" as that "which deals with sex in a manner appealing to prurient interest." If the average person, applying contemporary community standards, found that the main theme of the material taken as a whole appealed to prurient interests, then the material was not constitutionally protected. This standard was open to many different interpretations. The Court, though, was generally reluctant to use it to support censorship until the mid-1960s.

In 1966, the Supreme Court further confused its own doctrine. It became more restrictive in two ways. It made the motives of those selling allegedly obscene material a factor, and it ruled that material designed to appeal to the prurient interests of sexual deviants was not constitutionally protected. It became more liberal, though, by ruling that if the allegedly obscene material had *any* redeeming social value, then the Constitution protected it.

In 1973, the Supreme Court chose a conservative path on obscenity. But it still left confusion about what its decisions would mean in future cases. In the case of *Miller* v. *California,* the Court defined "hard-core pornography," which was not constitutionally protected, by asking three questions:

1. Would the average person, applying contemporary standards, find that the work, taken as a whole, appeals to prurient interests?
2. Does the work, taken as a whole, lack serious literary, artistic, political, or scientific value?
3. Does the work depict or describe, in a patently offensive way, sexual conduct specifically defined by the applicable state law?

The Court explicitly endorsed the idea that different states and localities could apply different standards: "It is neither realistic nor constitutionally sound to read the First Amendment as requiring that the people of Maine or Mississippi accept public depiction of conduct found tolerable in Las Vegas or New York City. . . . People in different states vary in their tastes and attitudes, and this diversity is not to be strangled by the absolutism of imposed uniformity."

The Court's opinion gave examples of material that might be repressed: "patently offensive representations or descriptions of ultimate sexual acts, normal or perverted, actual or simulated, or patently offensive representations or descriptions of masturbation, excretory functions, and lewd exhibition of the genitals."

Recent examples of speech excluded from First Amendment protection involved pornography involving children (in a 1982 case) and prohibition of "vulgar and offensive" language by public school officials (in a 1986 case).

Obscenity represents a gray area in the realm of speech. Even if the Supreme Court reached perfect doctrinal clarity—which it probably will be unable to do because of the balancing required between free speech and society's claims to regulate offensive behavior—other organs of government (state legislatures, city councils, mayors), lawyers, and interest groups (the American Civil Liberties Union, for example) would continue to debate the standards for determining what is protected and what is excluded from constitutional protection. When the Attorney General's Commission on Pornography reported in July 1986, it was given a great deal of coverage by the mass media. Various groups issued statements praising or condemning its work.

Free press

In protecting the press from censorship, the Supreme Court has generally reacted negatively to what the justices see as *prior restraint,* which is prohibition of publication altogether. In 1971, the *New York Times* and the *Washington Post* secured copies of the so-called *Pentagon Papers,* which contained secret information on the war in Vietnam. They were given to the two newspapers by dissident government officials to help bring the Vietnam War to an end. The federal government tried to block publication, claiming that publication would compromise national security. The Court ruled in favor of the newspapers, which were allowed to publish the material. But the doctrine under which the decision was made was less than clear. All nine justices wrote their own opinions. Six of them agreed with the overall position of the newspapers; three agreed with the government. But the justices in the majority disagreed on many points of doctrine. Most of them noted that in some circumstances they might approve prior restraint.

Three recent decisions offer good examples of how the Court has reversed itself in the process of stressing different meanings of the free press clause of the First Amendment. In the case of *Gannett* v. *De Pasquale* (1979), the Court ruled that representatives of the press had no right to attend a pretrial hearing on evidence. If the judge and the lawyers for both sides agreed to it, such exclusion was allowed. The case was decided 5 to 4, but no single opinion was signed by all five justices in the majority. There were several majority opinions, all of which used somewhat different reasoning.

There was a general outcry in the press against this ruling. A large number of trial court judges began to close trials after the Court ruling in

Gannett. Chief Justice Warren Burger gave an interview in which he stressed his own view: this ruling did not apply to trials themselves. Justice Lewis Powell made public comments in the same vein. He had voted with the majority in the *Gannett* case, but he said that the press might have an independent First Amendment right to attend trials.

In 1980, the Court ruled in the case of *Richmond Newspapers, Inc.* v. *Virginia*. This time, it held that the press had a First Amendment right to attend trials. Chief Justice Burger, speaking for the Court, said, "We hold that the right to attend criminal trials is implicit in the guarantees of the First Amendment." Justice John Paul Stevens, in a concurring opinion, said that he thought the Court had created a new right under the First Amendment. It was a right not just to make information public (upheld in the *Pentagon Papers* case) but also to collect it. Some newspaper columnists were quick to underscore this claim. But a more sober judgment was given in another concurring opinion by Justice Potter Stewart: "This does not mean that the First Amendment right of members of the public and representatives of the press to attend civil and criminal trials is absolute. Just as a legislature may impose reasonable time, place, and manner restrictions upon the exercise of First Amendment freedoms, so may a trial judge impose reasonable limitations upon the unrestricted occupation of a courtroom by representatives of the press and members of the public."

The third decision was reached in 1986. In this case, the Supreme Court ruled that both the press and the public had a First Amendment right to attend pretrial hearings in most criminal cases. The right was not made absolute under all conditions. But Chief Justice Burger, who wrote the majority opinion, followed up on his post-1980 comments and expanded the right by, in effect, overruling the 1979 *Gannett* case.

In January 1988, the Supreme Court ruled, by a vote of 5 to 3, that the First Amendment did not protect "school-sponsored publications, theatrical productions, and other expressive activities." The case stemmed from the actions of a high school principal in a St. Louis suburb who censored articles on divorce and teenage pregnancy that were to appear in the school newspaper. The majority of the Court held that the publication of such newspapers was "affirmatively promoted" by the school and part of the curriculum. Therefore, it concluded that school administrators could exercise control, including prepublication censorship, over them. Justice William Brennan, writing in dissent, said that the principal "violated the First Amendment's prohibitions against censorship of any student expression that neither disrupts classwork nor invades the rights of others, and against any censorship that is not narrowly tailored to serve its purpose."

Freedom of Religion

The First Amendment says that "Congress shall make no law respecting an establishment of religion, or prohibiting the free exercise thereof." As with the guarantees of speech, press, assembly, and petition, the provi-

WORDS AND IDEAS

A High School Newspaper Editor Reacts to a Supreme Court Decision, 1988

It's time to add a new word to the First Amendment to the U.S. Constitution: *except*. In the past, this word could have been in the Constitution to describe the situation of blacks and women. After last Wednesday's 5–3 Supreme Court ruling in the *Hazelwood* v. *Kuhlmeier* case, the word *except* needs to be included to illustrate that the Constitution no longer applies to anyone still in school.

The Supreme Court decided the principal of Missouri's Hazelwood East High School did not violate the students' First Amendment rights of freedom of the press when he censored two pages of the school newspaper, *Spectrum,* dealing with teenage pregnancy and effects of divorce on children.

"A school need not tolerate student speech that is inconsistent with its basic educational mission, even though the government could not censor similar speech outside the school," Justice Byron R. White wrote, concerning the decision.

Dissenting judges said the court condoned "thought control" and "brutal censorship," saying, "Such unthinking contempt for individual rights is intolerable."

As the 5–3 decision indicates, the constitutional questions are complex. I am not a lawyer. However, I am a student, and I'm becoming a little suspicious that the mission of American schools may no longer be to prepare students to live in a democracy. The Supreme Court's decision in this case certainly doesn't reinforce this goal.

I realize principals must be politicians, but they must be educators

(Continued)

sions on religion have been interpreted to apply to all levels of government. Note that there are two provisions: governments cannot "establish" religions (that is, they cannot give state aid to favor religion in general or any specific religion over others); and they cannot restrict the free exercise of religion. The intent of the framers was to keep government neutral on matters of religion.

In practice, the deceptively simple language of the **establishment clause** can have many interpretations. It has been interpreted to approve and to disapprove various forms of public aid to religious schools. When the Supreme Court has approved such aid in the form of free busing, textbooks, and public health measures for students at religious schools, it has argued that these children as individuals are the objects of the programs. They, not the religious institutions, benefit. In 1983, the Court approved a Min-

---

WORDS AND IDEAS

(Concluded)

first. Even if a principal now has a legal right to arbitrarily censor a school newspaper, he should never try to do it, unless the material is libelous, is in bad taste, or contains a personal attack. These are the same guidelines for every prestigious newspaper. Censorship for any other reason negates everything students learn about democracy in school.

Unfortunately, the principal may be tempted to censor something in a school newspaper to avoid tarnishing the reputation of the school, or having people breathing down his or her neck. This is what happened in Hazelwood.

I am a journalism student. We are taught responsible journalism and the guidelines for writing and printing stories. We are also taught to look for stories that will interest and affect our readers.

Teenage pregnancy and the effects of divorce on children directly affect students. After all, some students want to read about things other than the homecoming dance and the chess club. Issues of the world *do* affect high school students, and *do* belong in a school newspaper.

Telling students they can't address controversial subjects in their newspaper—their forum—is hypocritical, and sets a dangerous precedent for other students' rights, such as free speech in the classroom.

The Supreme Court decision has helped to make everything students learn in school meaningless.

The next time I'm in U.S. history and government class, and my teacher starts talking about the United States Constitution, I will start doodling. Why should I pay attention if it doesn't apply to me?

Note: The above article was written by Ryan Donmoyer, editor of *Phoenix Feathers*, the high school student newspaper in Worthington, Ohio. It appeared in the *Upper Arlington [Ohio] News*, January 20, 1988. Reprinted courtesy of Suburban News Publications.

---

nesota statute that allowed parents of students in both public and private schools, including church schools, to deduct some costs of education from their state income tax returns.

Some states have sought to require the teaching of "creationism"—essentially the view of creation presented in the biblical book of Genesis—along with evolution. A federal district judge ruled in 1982 that an Arkansas law to that effect was unconstitutionally promoting religion. In 1987, the Supreme Court made a similar decision in a case coming from Louisiana. The majority of the Court found that Louisiana was seeking to advance a religious viewpoint, a state act that violated the establishment clause.

In March 1984, the Supreme Court ruled that the city of Pawtucket, Rhode Island, could fund a public nativity scene at Christmas without

SUPREME COURT OF THE UNITED STATES

No. 82–1256

DENNIS LYNCH, ETC., ET AL., PETITIONERS *v.*
DANIEL DONNELLY ET AL.

ON WRIT OF CERTIORARI TO THE UNITED STATES COURT OF
APPEALS FOR THE FIRST CIRCUIT

[March 5, 1984]

THE CHIEF JUSTICE delivered the opinion of the Court.

We granted certiorari to decide whether the Establishment Clause of the First Amendment prohibits a municipality from including a crèche, or Nativity scene, in its annual Christmas display.

I

Each year, in cooperation with the downtown retail merchants' association, the City of Pawtucket, Rhode Island, erects a Christmas display as part of its observance of the Christmas holiday. . . . situated in a park . . .

Constitutional Nativity scene. This Pawtucket, Rhode Island, Christmas display of the Nativity was declared constitutional by a majority of the U.S. Supreme Court. Shown here is the first page of the Court's majority opinion in the case.

violating the establishment clause. Chief Justice Burger, writing for the majority, said that such a scene did not endorse a specific religion—it "engenders a friendly community spirit of good will in keeping with the season."

Justice Brennan, joined by three other justices, dissented vigorously, in part:

> Contrary to the Court's suggestion, the creche is far from a mere representation of a "particular historic religious event." It is, instead, best understood as a mystical re-creation of an event that lies at the heart of Christian faith. To suggest, as the Court does, that such a symbol is merely "traditional" and therefore no different from Santa's house or reindeer is not only offensive to those for whom the creche has profound significance, but insulting to those who insist for religious or personal reasons that the story of Christ is in no sense a part of "history" nor an unavoidable element of our national "heritage."

A 1980 case involved New York State reimbursement to private schools, including religious ones, for certain educational tasks. The Court upheld the state program. Justice Byron White wrote the majority opinion, and he was unusually candid about the fuzzy nature of the issues:

> This is not to say that this case, any more than past cases, will furnish a litmus-paper test to distinguish permissible from impermissible aid to religiously oriented schools. But Establishment Clause cases are not easy; they stir deep feelings; and we are divided among ourselves, perhaps reflecting the different views on this subject of the people of this country. What is

Prayer in public schools. Despite U.S. Supreme Court rulings against prayer in public schools, these children in a Boston public school are being led in prayer. A child who chooses not to pray remains seated at her desk.

certain is that our decisions have tended to avoid categorical imperatives and absolutist approaches at either end of the range of possible outcomes. This course sacrifices clarity and predictability for flexibility.

In 1985 and 1986, the Court drew sharper lines between religious practices and government accommodation to religion, limiting the degree of the latter. In a 1986 decision, the Court ruled that the U.S. military could constitutionally forbid its members from wearing a yarmulke (a skullcap that orthodox Jewish men wear as a symbol of reverence) while indoors on duty. In the 1985 decision, the Court ruled that public schools could not send teachers into parochial school classrooms to provide special education. This decision was followed by a directive from the U.S. Department of Education that required changes in tutoring programs for about 180,000 children in parochial schools across the country. In another 1985 decision, the Court declared unconstitutional a Connecticut law giving employees the right not to work on whatever day they designated as their Sabbath. The Court specifically said that the Connecticut law violated the establishment clause of the First Amendment: The state had gone too far in bending to religious views.

The Supreme Court has ruled that religious observances and instruction may not take place on public school property but that students may be released from school to attend such observances and receive such instruction elsewhere. In 1962, the Court ruled that public prayers and Bible reading in public schools were an unconstitutional breach of the wall dividing church and state. Since that ruling there has been continuous controversy between groups in society holding different views on this matter.

Proprayer forces have continued to fashion new methods for allowing nonmandatory religious observance in public schools.

In 1985, the Supreme Court invalidated a 1981 Alabama statute that permitted a one-minute period for silent prayer in the public schools. Justice John Paul Stevens, in the majority opinion for the Court, found that the purpose of the Alabama statute was religious and therefore a violation of the establishment clause of the First Amendment. Stevens quoted from an earlier case: "If there is any fixed star in our constitutional constellation, it is that no official, high or petty, can prescribe what shall be orthodox in politics, nationalism, religion, or other matters of opinion or force citizens to confess by word or act their faith therein." He added: "The State of Alabama, no less than the Congress of the United States, must respect that basic truth."

Crime and Punishment

The Bill of Rights details the rights of people accused of crimes. The framers spelled out a number of guarantees. These guarantees had developed in English law and were embedded in the Constitution. The Fourth Amendment prohibits "unreasonable searches and seizures." The Fifth Amendment prohibits trying a person twice for the same crime (double jeopardy) and protects people accused of crimes against self-incrimination. The 6th Amendment guarantees jury trial and representation by an attorney. The 8th Amendment prohibits "cruel and unusual punishments." Over the years, the Supreme Court has also ruled that under the **due process** clause of the 14th Amendment these guarantees apply equally to the states.

The Warren Court was active in defining and extending the rights of suspects and people accused of crimes. The Burger Court modified a number of the Warren Court's rulings in a more conservative direction. But it did not retreat completely to the pre-Warren doctrines. The best known of the Warren Court's decisions was made in *Miranda* v. *Arizona* in 1966. The Court had ruled earlier that improperly seized material could not be used as evidence in state criminal trials. In this case, the Court disallowed confessions gained without proper protections:

> The prosecution may not use statements . . . stemming from custodial interrogation of the defendant unless it demonstrates the use of procedural safeguards effective to secure the privilege against self-incrimination . . . . Prior to any questioning, the person must be warned that he has a right to remain silent, that any statement he does make may be used as evidence against him, and that he has a right to the presence of an attorney, either retained or appointed. . . . If . . . he indicates in any manner and at any stage of the process that he wishes to consult with an attorney before speaking, there can be no questioning. Likewise, if the individual is alone and indicates in any manner that he does not wish to be interrogated, the police may not question him.

After the initial ruling in 1966, the Court gradually began to put limits on the meaning of what at first glance seemed like sweeping statements. The accompanying box notes some of the major adjustments that have been made—most of them restrictive but a few expanding the rights granted in *Miranda*. The Reagan administration, through Attorney General Edwin Meese, has made known its preference that the Court simply overturn the *Miranda* decision as the best way to emphasize "law and order" and cease "coddling criminals."

In general, since a 1961 Supreme Court decision, evidence obtained by illegal searches and seizures cannot be admitted as evidence in court. Therefore, the police would be wasting their time if they collected evidence illegally. However, such evidence can be used if the police can show that it would have come to light had legal means been used. The Court has also held that evidence obtained under a search warrant later found to be defective could be admitted in court if the police, at the time, were acting in good faith in relying on the warrant.

The Court has also been concerned with the rights of prisoners. It has decided cases involving censorship of prisoners' mail, the access of prisoners to legal materials and assistance, and protection of prisoners when they are charged with violation of prison rules. In all of these cases, it has strengthened prisoners' rights. It has not, though, always gone as far as advocates for prisoners wished. In 1984, for example, the Court held that the 4th Amendment's prohibition against unreasonable searches and seizures did not apply to prison cells.

Cases dealing with crime and police behavior are always sensitive political issues. They also stir passionate feelings on the part of judges. For example, the Supreme Court ruled in 1979 that it was not unconstitutional to put two people detained before trial in a cell designed for one. Justice Thurgood Marshall dissented, along with three colleagues. After the ruling, he took the unusual step of criticizing his colleagues in public. He accused the majority of showing no sensitivity for defendants too poor to afford bail. He said that they preferred "instead to provide us with such enduring legal homilies as, 'There is no one man, one cell principle lurking in the due process clause.' " He added, "For a prisoner in jail, that ain't funny" (*New York Times,* May 28, 1979).

In 1972, the Supreme Court struck down the death penalty *as then applied* as "cruel and unusual punishment" and therefore prohibited by the Eighth Amendment. But a majority of the justices were unwilling to say that the death penalty was unconstitutional in all cases. The Court struck down the mandatory death penalty and its application to rape. But it has allowed executions if the states provide for consideration of aggravating and mitigating circumstances and for thorough appeals in each case. In 1987, the Court decided that the death penalty could be applied even if it were assessed more heavily against one race than against others. The Court also decided that accomplices to murder could be executed. The

HISTORICAL PERSPECTIVES

Major *Miranda* Decisions, 1966–1986

June 13, 1966 U.S. Supreme Court rules 5 to 4 in *Arizona* v. *Miranda* that a confession cannot be used as evidence in a criminal case unless a suspect in police custody is warned of the right to remain silent and to have counsel present during questioning. The case involved Ernest Miranda of Phoenix, who was convicted, with the help of a confession, of kidnapping and rape.

February 24, 1971 Ending its absolute prohibition against using evidence obtained before a suspect is advised of *Miranda* rights, the Supreme Court votes in *Harris* v. *New York* that such statements can be used to impeach a defendant's credibility if he takes the stand in his own behalf.

June 10, 1974 In *Michigan* v. *Tucker,* the Court rules that leads developed from a confession given without a *Miranda* warning can be used as evidence. The evidence was obtained before the *Miranda* rules went into effect.

May 11, 1980 In a case emphasizing the difficulty in defining "police interrogation," the Court says statements made by a police officer to a suspect in a paddy wagon did not constitute "interrogation" and therefore no *Miranda* warning was required. The officer's statements, that children might be wounded by a gun the suspect was believed to have hidden nearby, prompted the suspect to lead police to the weapon, which helped convict him.

May 18, 1981 In *Edwards* v. *Arizona,* the Court holds that when a suspect requests consultation with an attorney, police must end questioning and may not resume unless the suspect initiates it.

June 12, 1984 The Court makes a major modification, voting that in cases where the public safety is endangered, police may question a suspect before warning him of his rights.

March 4, 1985 The Court votes in *Elstad* v. *Oregon* that if a suspect confesses before police warn him of his rights, and confesses again after being warned of his rights, the second confession may be admitted as evidence in a criminal trial.

March 10, 1986 The Court decides that *Miranda* warnings are not constitutional rights in and of themselves but only serve to aid in the insurance of constitutional rights.

Source: *Washington Post,* June 13, 1986.

The abortion controversy. Citizens opposing abortions and citizens supporting a right to abortion have demonstrated in most American cities. In Washington, D.C., antiabortion activists demonstrate [left] and Rep. Patricia Schroeder (D–Colo.) addresses a pro-choice rally [right].

Court has backed away from any implication that the Eighth Amendment might prohibit the death penalty altogether.

The Right to Privacy

The Constitution does not directly mention a right to privacy, but some judges have inferred such a right from language in the Constitution. The Supreme Court first proclaimed a right of privacy in 1965. Since then, courts have spelled out their interpretations of the right (Grossman and Wells, 1980: 1315–25). One of the most controversial applications was made in 1973, when the Court ruled, in the case of *Roe* v. *Wade,* that the Constitution prevents the states from making most abortions illegal or from seriously restricting facilities for performing abortions. Since that time, abortion has been a frequent subject of court decisions and of legislative action, in both Congress and many states. Almost all politicians have taken a position on the issue, even if they would have preferred to avoid it. Some politicians have eagerly championed or rejected the right to abortion; others have taken a moderate position. But the nature of the issue and the emotional commitments of both sides in the controversy allow little room for moderate positions. President Reagan has been an outspoken foe of abortion and the *Roe* decision.

Since 1973, the abortion issue has constantly been on the national political agenda. The accompanying box recounts the highlights of the issue's development.

Much of the specific controversy over the abortion issue has focused on public funding for abortions, which helps increase abortion rates among poor women (Hansen, 1980). In June 1980, the Supreme Court ruled that poor women had no constitutional right to public funding for abortions.

HISTORICAL PERSPECTIVES

The Development of the Abortion Issue, 1973–1986

January 22, 1973 The Supreme Court (in *Roe* v. *Wade*) rules that abortion must be legal nationwide and that facilities for abortion cannot be restricted.

July 1, 1976 The Supreme Court rules that husbands cannot veto abortions by their wives and that parents cannot veto abortions by their unmarried daughters.

September 30, 1976 Congress passes the Hyde Amendment. It severely restricts the use of federal Medicaid money for abortions.

October 22, 1976 A federal district judge (John Dooling) rules that the Hyde Amendment is unconstitutional.

June 20, 1977 The Supreme Court rules that states have no legal obligation to pay for "nontherapeutic" abortions. The Court does not define that term, though.

June 29, 1977 The Supreme Court tells Judge Dooling to restudy his decision in light of the June 20 decision. The congressional spending restriction resumes in August.

July 2, 1979 The Supreme Court opens the door for states to require either parental consent *or* an alternative procedure (such as consent of a judge) in abortions for unmarried minor females.

January 15, 1980 After many months of elaborate proceedings, Judge Dooling again declares the Hyde Amendment unconstitutional.

June 30, 1980 The Supreme Court reverses Judge Dooling's decision. It holds the Hyde Amendment constitutional. In so doing, it says that neither the federal government nor the states are obliged to pay for any abortions, even those that are medically necessary.

June 15, 1983 The Supreme Court, by a vote of 6 to 3, reaffirms its 1973 decision.

June 28, 1983 The Senate, by a vote of 49 to 50, defeats a proposed constitutional amendment stating that "the right to an abortion is not secured by this constitution." (Passage of the amendment would have required a two-thirds favorable vote.)

June 11, 1986 In striking down a Pennsylvania statute restricting abortion, the Supreme Court, again affirms its 1973 decision.

Source: Adapted from the *New York Times,* July 1, 1980, for events through 1980. © by *The New York Times Company.* Reprinted by permission. Updated by authors.

It upheld Congress's ban on the federal funding of most abortions through the Hyde Amendment. In a companion case, it also found constitutional a state ban on public funding. The members of the Court disagreed strongly and explicitly over the constitutional and social meaning of these rulings. In part, they focused on the standing of indigent (poor) women—those unable to have an abortion unless it was publicly funded. Excerpts from Justice Potter Stewart's opinion for the majority of the Court and from the separate dissenting opinions of Justices Harry Blackmun and William Brennan are quoted in the accompanying box.

Although unwilling to require public funding of abortions, the Court held to its 1973 view in *Roe* that units of government could not prevent abortion. In a 1983 case, the Court specifically reaffirmed "that the right of privacy, grounded in the concept of personal liberty guaranteed by the Constitution, encompasses a woman's right to decide whether to terminate her pregnancy." In 1986, the Court struck down a Pennsylvania statute restricting abortion. A majority of the Court grounded this decision in *Roe's* interpretation of the meaning of liberty embodied in the Constitution. Justice Harry Blackmun wrote for the majority that "few decisions are more personal or intimate, more properly private or more basic to individual dignity and autonomy than a woman's decision . . . whether to end her pregnancy. A woman's right to make that choice freely is fundamental. Any other result, in our view, would protect inadequately a central part of the sphere of liberty that our law guarantees equally to all."

Despite these Court reaffirmations of *Roe,* the abortion issue remains on the political agenda. The 1986 decision was made by only a five-to-four vote. In an appearance of the solicitor general before the Court, the Reagan administration specifically asked it to overturn *Roe.*

In 1986, the Supreme Court addressed another area of privacy—sexual relations. In a five-to-four decision, it upheld a Georgia law that made sodomy (oral or anal sex, either homosexual or heterosexual) a felony. The specific case involved two homosexual males. The majority opinion (written by Justice Byron White) held that the Constitution contains "no fundamental right to engage in homosexual sodomy" and that a long history of prohibitions against such acts cannot be interfered with by the courts on constitutional grounds. The vigorous dissent, written by Justice Harry Blackmun, argued on the basis of the fundamental constitutional right to privacy in personal and intimate matters such as sexual expression. As Blackmun put it, "We protect these rights not because they contribute, in some direct and material way, to the general public welfare, but because they form so central a part of an individual life."

The battle over the existence and meaning of a constitutionally protected right to privacy will continue. Almost surely, courts will consider legislation requiring mandatory testing for possible drug abuse and testing for the presence of the AIDS virus. When that happens, they will again have to weigh the rights of society against the individual's rights to privacy.

PRACTICE OF POLITICS

The Clash of Judicial Opinion: Public Funding of Abortions

Justice Potter Stewart for the majority:

> Although government may not place obstacles in the path of a woman's exercise of her freedom of choice, it need not remove those not of its own creation. Indigency falls in the latter category. The financial constraints that restrict an indigent woman's ability to enjoy the full range of constitutionally protected freedom of choice are the product not of governmental restrictions on access to abortions but rather of her indigency.
>
> Although the liberty protected by the due process clause affords protection against unwarranted government interference with freedom of choice in the context of certain personal decisions, it does not confer an entitlement to such funds as may be necessary to realize all the advantages of that freedom. To hold otherwise would mark a drastic change in our understanding of the Constitution.

Justice Harry Blackmun, dissenting:

> There is condescension in the Court's holding "that she may go elsewhere for her abortion"; the Government punitively impresses upon a needy minority its own concepts of the socially desirable, the publicly acceptable, and the morally sound. There truly is another world "out there," the existence of which the Court, I suspect, either chooses to ignore or fears to recognize.

Justice William Brennan, dissenting:

> The Hyde Amendment is a transparent attempt by the Legislative Branch to impose the political majority's judgment of the morally acceptable and socially desirable preference on a sensitive and intimate decision that the Constitution entrusts to the individual. Worse yet, the Hyde Amendment does not foist that majoritarian viewpoint with equal measure upon everyone in our Nation, rich and poor alike; rather, it imposes that viewpoint only upon that segment of our society which, because of its position of political powerlessness, is least able to defend its privacy rights from the encroachments of state-mandated morality.

Source: Opinions delivered in the case of *Harris* v. *McRae* (1980).

EQUALITY: THE MEANING OF A JUST SOCIETY

What is equality? What aspects of equality are attainable with governmental aid? What aspects should be pursued? Does equality clash with some liberties? How can a society simultaneously pursue important liberties and some aspects of equality? All of these questions have been debated in the abstract for thousands of years. In a nation with the ideals of the United States, they receive practical treatment in the political process, including its judicial portion.

The Constitution contains language at least implying that individuals should be treated equally (Grossman and Wells, 1980: 409–15). The 14th Amendment, adopted after the Civil War, was intended to protect the newly freed blacks from legal discrimination. It provides that no state can "deny to any person within its jurisdiction the equal protection of the laws." Since the phrase **"equal protection of the laws"** has no fixed meaning, it has become the focus of many political and legal controversies. As **equal protection** is defined in concrete instances, the practical meaning of equality in the United States emerges. Political debate over the meaning of equality is constant and widespread. Does it mean equal "opportunity" or equal "outcomes"? How is equality affected by a specific tax proposal or a specific form of public school funding? How can equal political rights be guaranteed for all Americans? How far should the government go in requiring private society to afford equal treatment to all people? Such questions, put in the form of concrete policy choices, have been hotly debated throughout our history and will continue to be hotly debated. Supreme Court decisions define the current meaning of equality in many specific areas, but those decisions themselves change over time. Free societies never stop debating the meaning of a concept as fundamental as equality.

The constitutional basis for judicial interpretations of equality lies in the equal protection clause of the 14th Amendment. The courts have long held that neither the federal government nor governmentally sanctioned or enforced private action can result in denial of equal protection.

The following pages explore a few specific aspects of equality. First, we examine the status of racial and ethnic equality. Second, we look at gender equality. Third, we look briefly at gay rights. Fourth, we touch on elements of political and economic equality.

Racial and Ethnic Equality

Our society has always made racial and ethnic distinctions in practice and imposed inequalities based on race or ethnic origin. Racial and ethnic minorities in our society have been and remain subject to debilitating and shameful discrimination. They have all sought redress and engaged in a mix of political and legal efforts to remove discrimination. Their struggle for equality has been long and painful. They have made advances, but often slowly. Some oppressed minorities, especially black Americans, have relied heavily on lawsuits involving constitutional claims.

In general, the Supreme Court has been suspicious of any law or regulation that classifies people by race. It examines such classifications with extra care to make sure that they are not unconstitutional. Classifications not based on race—such as those setting up income tax brackets—are examined much more cursorily. However, the Court does not always use the doctrine of "strict scrutiny" to invalidate government action based on a racial classification. Recall that the Court gave a clean bill of constitutional health to the decision under which 110,000 persons of Japanese ancestry were interned during World War II. That decision was based solely on a racial classification.

The Supreme Court has been a vital political actor in the area of racial equality. It helped generate the governmental and public agendas under which racial discrimination in public education, other public facilities, and voting was challenged. It upheld as constitutionally legitimate broad federal statutes banning discrimination in housing, employment, education, public facilities, and voting.

Black Americans

Since emerging from slavery at the end of the Civil War, black Americans—our largest racial minority—have had a long struggle to achieve various aspects of equality (part of this story is told very well in Kluger, 1976). Their cause has been a major feature in our domestic politics for decades. Here, we will look briefly at desegregation in public education, attacks on other areas of racial discrimination, and affirmative action as applied to blacks.

Desegregation in public education   The supreme Court's role in promoting equal treatment for black Americans was made dramatically clear in its 1954 decision in *Brown* v. *Board of Education*. That decision reversed an 1896 precedent approving separate but equal public facilities for blacks and whites. The *Brown* case applied specifically to public education. The Court held that separateness (segregation) in education in and of itself caused inequality.

For some years, most of the southern school systems—which had most of the country's legally segregated schools— did little or nothing to comply with the *Brown* ruling. Instead, many of them deliberately evaded and stalled school desegregation. By 1964, only 2 percent of black children in southern schools attended class with whites.

In that year, Congress passed an important civil rights act after a struggle between highly visible and resourceful interest groups and public officials on both sides of the issue (see Sundquist, 1968: chap. 6). President Lyndon Johnson was both the symbolic leader and a very forceful participant in the drive for this legislation.

Among its many provisions, the Civil Rights Act of 1964 included Title VI: "No person in the United States shall, on the basis of race, color, or national origin, be excluded from participation in, denied the benefits of, or be subjected to discrimination under, any program or activity receiving federal financial assistance." Public schools received such assistance. The federal government now had an explicit weapon in pursuing the Court's decision of 10 years earlier; it could withdraw financial support.

For the first few years, major enforcement of Title VI in education came from the commissioner's office in the Office of Education (in the Department of Health, Education, and Welfare.) In 1967, though, an Of-

Linda Brown Smith (right) is shown here with her children. Her father, Oliver Brown, started the class action suit, Brown v. The Board of Education of Topeka, Kansas. *This case led to the 1954 U.S. Supreme Court decision that black children should be able to attend the same schools as white children, thereby declaring segregation in public schools unconstitutional.*

fice for Civil Rights (OCR) was formed in HEW (see Rabkin, 1980; and Bullock, 1980). Both the commissioner and OCR wrote broad regulations to apply Title VI prohibitions against racial discrimination in southern public schools. Then, they moved swiftly to carry out those regulations. Efforts were supported or at least not hampered by Congress and the president. Federal judges at all levels also took part in the drive against segregation in the South. They struck down as unconstitutional various local schemes designed to delay or avoid true integration. In many cases, federal judges drafted and approved the details of local desegregation plans. Despite the hostility of local school systems, the weapon of cutting off federal funds was too strong to resist in most cases. In some cases, that weapon was supplemented by additional pressures (Rodgers and Bullock, 1976).

The results of Title VI as implemented in southern systems are impressive. In 1964, more than 98 percent of black public school students attended all-black schools. This figure had dropped to 68 percent by 1968, and to less than 9 percent by 1972.

When the Office of Civil Rights and the federal courts turned their attention to segregation in northern school systems, they faced a much tougher battle. Here, there had never been laws requiring segregation, but housing patterns had produced schools largely segregated by race. What did the Constitution and good public policy require in these cases? Political opposition to desegregation—from both local governments and public opinion—was often very strong. The debate often focused on the busing of children, both black and white, to schools outside their neighborhoods so as to achieve desegregation despite housing patterns. In 1971, the Supreme Court first approved busing as a constitutionally acceptable method for achieving desegregation. In 1982, it held that the people of Washington State could not prevent busing to achieve racial balance, which they had attempted to do through a statewide initiative and referendum. At the same time, however, the Court held that the city of Los Angeles could, again through a referendum of its citizens, retreat from a probusing policy that exceeded constitutional standards of nondiscrimination. The new policy in Los Angeles still met the federal standard. Busing remains politically controversial.

Demographic trends have worked against true racial integration in large northern cities. Many whites have sent their children to predominantly white private or parochial schools; other whites have fled the cities to live in white suburbs; and birthrates for both blacks and Hispanics have been high. Therefore, the number of white children in northern school systems has been decreasing. Unless courts approve or, more to the point, mandate busing schemes that cross municipal lines to encompass whole counties or metropolitan areas, legal action to achieve integration seems doomed to fail (see Orfield, 1978). In 1974 in a Detroit case, the Supreme Court rejected such a plan—unless it could be shown that suburban school districts had also discriminated against minorities. The Court has refused to disturb some cross-district busing plans in other cities. It has held, in short, that although the Constitution prohibits racial discrimination, it does not require racial integration.

In 1983, the Supreme Court displayed its continuing concern that government action not sanction racial discrimination in education. It ruled that the Internal Revenue Service properly denied tax-exempt status to Bob Jones University in South Carolina and to Goldsboro Christian Schools in North Carolina because they practiced discrimination.

Other areas of discrimination   After the *Brown* decision, the Supreme Court ruled that discrimination based on race in a number of public facilities other than schools, such as swimming pools, beaches, and golf courses, was also unconstitutional. As early as 1915, the Court began to rule against various attempts in southern states to keep blacks from voting. Congress passed a weak statute in this area in 1957. In 1965, however, with strong leadership from President Johnson, it passed the Voting Rights Act, which quickly ended discrimination against black voters.

In 1964 and 1968, Congress passed major legislation banning racial discrimination in public accommodations, employment, and housing. The Supreme Court declared these statutes constitutional when they were tested in specific cases.

Bakke becomes a doctor. Allan Bakke graduated from medical school in 1982. He was admitted to medical school after a 1978 Supreme Court ruling (Regents of the University of California v. Allan Bakke) that he had been discriminated against in favor of less qualified minority candidates for admission.

Affirmative action   The policy of affirmative action became widely used and very controversial in the 1970s and 1980s. Specific provisions in laws and regulations required special efforts to hire and retain individuals thought to be disadvantaged in the labor market by a history of discrimination. These individuals included blacks, other ethnic and racial minorities, and women. Here, we focus on affirmative action as applied to blacks. Those opposed to affirmative action often labeled it "reverse discrimination" because, in their view, it discriminated against white males.

In a series of important cases from 1978 through 1987, the Supreme Court gave concrete meaning to affirmative action for blacks.

In 1978, it decided the *Bakke* case. It made two rulings. One ruling was that Allan Bakke had been illegally barred from the medical school of the University of California at Davis because that school had explicitly set aside for minorities some of its slots for students. At the same time, a majority of the justices ruled that the Constitution permits some attention to race and past discrimination in developing affirmative action programs in higher education.

Allan Bakke is now a doctor. But the *Bakke* ruling did not generate dramatic change in affirmative action programs. Those who design such programs avoid explicit quotas for minorities, though federal judges approve even quotas in some situations.

In 1979, a year after the *Bakke* case, the Supreme Court decided the case of *United Steelworkers of America* v. *Weber*. It upheld a voluntary affirmative action program, sponsored jointly by a union and a company, that a white worker challenged. Its ruling was based on an interpretation of that part of the Civil Rights Act of 1964 forbidding racial discrimination. The majority concluded that the act did not ban this particular voluntary plan, but the court did not set guidelines for future plans. Again, it stated that each plan would have to be tested separately. This plan was designed "to eliminate a manifest racial imbalance," was temporary, and, in the Court's view, would not hurt white workers. Therefore, it was not prohibited.

In 1980, the Supreme Court again legitimated consideration of race in efforts to right past wrongs. The Court ruled that Congress did not violate the Constitution when it passed a bill setting aside 10 percent of 1977 Public Works Employment Act funds for minority businesses. The majority said that "the Congress has not sought to give select minority groups a preferred standing in the construction industry, but has embarked on a remedial program to place them on a more equitable footing with respect to public contracting opportunities."

In June 1984, in a decision warmly applauded by the Reagan administration, the Court ruled that seniority outweighed affirmative action in determining the order in which layoffs must occur. Since affirmative action programs mean that many of the minorities (and women) hired are likely to be the newest employees, this decision opened the way to some reestablishment of mostly white (and mostly male) groups of employees in some occupations and locations. The decision itself involved the fire department in Memphis.

In 1986, the Court decided three important affirmative action cases. The first decision involved a plan by the Jackson, Michigan, school board to give preference to minorities in laying off teachers. There were five separate opinions, and no more than three members of the Court joined in any single opinion. The white schoolteachers won in that the specific plan was held to deny them equal protection of the law. This part of the ruling followed the precedent of the Memphis firefighters case. The Court said, however, that plans giving preference to minorities were not in principle unconstitutional but had to be very precisely constructed so as to remedy past discrimination.

Six weeks later, the Court, to the dismay of the Reagan administration (which consistently opposed affirmative action plans and even challenged them in court), ruled in two cases that affirmative action plans were constitutional even if they benefited individuals who had not been held back because of discrimination. One of these cases, involving the city of Cleveland and minority firefighters, upheld an agreement mandating promotions for minorities in a ratio tied to white promotions. The other case, involving a local of the sheet metal workers' union in New York City, upheld a federal court order that set a target of close to 30 percent for the hiring of minorities.

Justice William Brennan wrote both opinions. In the Cleveland case, he wrote: 'It is . . . clear that the voluntary actions available to employers and unions seeking to eradicate race discrimination may include reasonable race-conscious relief that benefits individuals who were not actual victims of discrimination." In the New York City case, he wrote:

First, the District Court considered the efficacy of alternative remedies [to hiring targets], and concluded that, in light of petitioners' [the Union's] long record of resistance to official efforts to end their discriminatory practices, stronger measures were necessary. The court devised the temporary membership goal and the Fund [a fine paid by the union to be used in increasing minority membership] as tools for remedying past discrimination. More importantly, the District Court's orders will have only a marginal impact on the interests of white workers. We concluded that the District Court's orders do not violate the equal protection safeguards of the Constitution.

In 1987, the Court narrowly upheld another affirmative action plan devised by a federal district court judge. This judge had required the state of Alabama to promote one qualified black state trooper for every qualified white state trooper that it promoted. The Reagan administration opposed the plan, but the Court's majority rejected the administration's reasoning and decided that their remedy for past discrimination was constitutionally valid.

Other ethnic minorities

The courts have made few constitutional decisions involving three other large racial or ethnic minorities—Hispanics, native Americans, and Asian Americans. In one of those decisions, the Supreme Court upheld the Bureau of Indian Affairs in giving Indians preference in hiring for its own jobs. It based the ruling on a congressional statute that it found constitutional.

Blacks have made heavy use of the courts and lawsuits in their quest for equal treatment. These other minorities have been much less inclined to do so. Leaders of all three groups are politically active, however, in seeking equality (see Garcia and de la Garza, 1977; and Kickingbird and Kickingbird, 1977).

The courts have been active in cases involving the rights and benefits of Indians under old treaties with the United States, but such cases do not concern equality under the Constitution. In 1982, the Supreme Court ruled that children who are illegal aliens have a constitutionally protected right to free public education. The specific case involved Mexican children in Texas.

There have long been many Americans of Chinese and Japanese descent. In recent years, a large number of Filipinos and Vietnamese have also come to this country. Discrimination against Chinese was tested in some Supreme Court cases in the late 19th century. The Court ruled at that time against blatantly discriminatory state or local action. But much discrimination never reached the courts and remained intact for a long time. A great deal of discrimination against Asian Americans remains; it is probably most intense for the newest immigrants. Some of these groups are only starting to organize politically. Lawsuits thus far have not been central to their strategies for gaining equal treatment. Even political activity has been limited to a small number of areas on the West Coast. Many

HISTORICAL PERSPECTIVE

Proequality Sex Discrimination Decisions in the Supreme Court

1977 The provision that widowers had to show they had been dependent on their spouses before being allowed to collect Social Security benefits was struck down; widows did not have to prove the same dependence.

1977 The legal provision that women could exclude three more lower earnings years than men in calculating Social Security benefits was upheld. It was seen as a permissible remedy to offset some of the effects of past discrimination in employment.

1978 A Los Angeles rule that female employees make a larger contribution to pension plans because they live longer than men was struck down. It was seen as an impermissible discrimination.

1979 An Alabama law providing that husbands, but not wives, could be required to pay alimony was struck down. It was based on stereotypes about the earning power of the sexes.

1979 A Missouri law granting women automatic exemption from jury duty on request was struck down. It was based on invalid assumptions about the relation of women to family needs.

1979 A New York law allowing an unwed mother, but not an unwed father, to block adoption of an illegitimate child was struck down.

1980 A Missouri law requiring a widower to prove financial dependence on his wife to collect benefits from her work-related death but not requiring such proof from a widow was struck down.

1982 A state university in Mississippi policy of admitting only

(Continued)

of the older families of Asian ancestry are well integrated. The newer immigrants are not yet citizens and are not well organized politically.

Gender Equality

Equality between the two genders is an aspect of equality that has been at the center of the political agenda for the last few decades. An aspect of equality that has also been debated in recent years is that of equality for people regardless of their sexual preference—often characterized as "gay rights." The following sections introduce issues involving both women's rights and gay rights.

Women have developed considerable political skill in their pursuit of equal treatment and the rights due them. The proposed Equal Rights Amendment, which failed to win the number of states needed for adop-

---

HISTORICAL PERSPECTIVE

(Concluded)

women to its nursing school was struck down in part because it perpetuated stereotypes about what occupations are appropriate for women.

1983 The Pregnancy Discrimination Act of 1978, an Amendment to the Civil Rights Act of 1964, was interpreted by the Court to require that employer health insurance plans cover pregnancy costs for workers' spouses.

1983 The Court interpreted federal law against sex discrimination to prohibit pension plans paying unequal retirement benefits to men and women because women tend to live longer. (However, the Court refused to order back payments, a ruling that disappointed advocates of equal treatment for women.)

1984 The Court ruled unanimously that Title VII of the 1964 Civil Rights Act prohibits discrimination among their employees by law firms on the basis of sex, race, religion, or national origin. The case involved a woman lawyer who had been denied a partnership at a prestigious Atlanta law firm.

1986 The Court decided unanimously that private businesses could be held liable for sexual harassment by supervisors. Title VII of the 1964 Civil Rights Act "affords employees the right to work in an environment free from discriminatory intimidation, ridicule, and insult."

1987 The Court held unanimously that states could force all-male organizations to admit women.

1987 The Court ruled that employers could develop affirmative action promotion plans giving preference to women over men.

---

tion, was a focal point of debate in the 1970s and the early 1980s. The amendment, as proposed to the states by Congress in 1972, simply stated: "Equality of rights under the law shall not be denied or abridged by the United States or by a State on account of sex."

Those seeking equal treatment for women have been quite active in the legal arena. On a number of occasions, courts, including the Supreme Court, have paid attention to the content of women's rights. However, many of the court decisions on this matter have relied, not on interpretations of the Constitution's equal protection clause, but on the interpretation of statutes. Courts have been less inclined to be skeptical about distinctions based on gender than about distinctions based on race (Ducat and Chase, 1983: 871).

The Supreme Court has made decisions that have both pleased and disappointed advocates of women's rights (Goldstein, 1979, 1981). The ac-

HISTORICAL PERSPECTIVE

Antiequality Sex Discrimination Decisions in the Supreme Court

1974 California law set up disability insurance for disabled private employees not covered by workers' compensation; the law's exclusion of coverage for normal pregnancy was upheld as a rational state decision.

1975 Federal laws providing for a guarantee of longer service for women than men in the U.S. Navy despite nonpromotion were upheld.

1976 Private employers with plans for compensating employees temporarily unemployed because of disability are not required to include pregnancy as one of the disabilities covered.

1979 A Georgia law letting the mother of an illegitimate child sue for the wrongful death of the child but banning such a suit by the father of such a child if he has not made the child legitimate was upheld.

1979 A provision of the Social Security Act denying "mother's insurance benefits" to mothers of illegitimate children who never married the wage-earner father was upheld.

1981 A California law punishing men but not women for "statutory rape" was upheld on the ground that a state legislature could take notice of the special problems of women.

1981 A congressional statute establishing draft registration for men only was upheld.

1984 The 1972 federal law barring sex discrimination in schools and colleges receiving federal aid was interpreted narrowly so that only individual programs within a school or college proved to be discriminatory would be denied federal money. Previously, aid to the entire institution was at stake.

companying boxes summarize a number of complicated cases in this area, which are divided into those viewed as "antiequality" and those viewed as "proequality." A 1987 case coming from a county transportation agency in California was the first in which the Supreme Court ruled on affirmative action with regard to women. All of its previous affirmative action rulings had involved blacks. In the 1987 case, a woman's promotion to the position of road dispatcher in connection with the agency's affirmative action plan was challenged. The court upheld the constitutionality of the plan.

Women's rights will continue to be debated through general political and legal processes. This area often provokes highly emotional responses on both sides.

Homosexuals demonstrate in Washington, D.C. The U.S. Supreme Court has yet to rule on equal rights for homosexuals.

Gay Rights

Discrimination against women is often a matter of practice, not law. Discrimination against homosexuals is often a matter of both practice and law. Nationwide media attention has been given to a number of local controversies over the merits of proposed laws prohibiting discrimination against homosexuals.

Thus far, the Supreme Court has not ruled on the meaning of "equal protection of the laws" with regard to homosexuals. The one Supreme Court case bearing directly on homosexuals—on the Georgia statute prohibiting sodomy, discussed earlier—was decided on the basis of the meaning of privacy, not the meaning of equality. State and local courts have not been consistent in either striking down or upholding state law or local ordinances affecting gay rights. Thus, the nature of equality for homosexuals varies from location to location.

The Importance of Political and Economic Equality

Racial and ethnic minorities, women, and homosexuals are all identifiable groups. The specific meaning of political and economic equality for each of these groups has been at issue in numberless debates and confrontations. At a broader level, society must also deal with questions about the meaning of political and economic equality, not just for groups that have historically been discriminated against, but for individuals who are not neatly or obviously members of an easily identifiable group—for example, all individuals identifying with a particular political party in the case of drawing legislative district lines or all poor people in the case of funding for public schools. Policy decisions on the broad meaning of political and economic equality are constantly being made. Such decisions involve the entire policy apparatus summarized in Chapter 16.

The Supreme Court has been involved in some aspects of equality broadly defined. It has felt more comfortable dealing with political equality than with economic equality.

Beginning in the early 1960s, the Supreme Court has ruled that the boundaries of legislative districts for both houses of state legislatures and for the U.S. House of Representatives must be drawn so that the populations of the districts are equal. This is the "one person, one vote" principle. Rulings of this kind are intended to help guarantee equal representation for all individuals. Put another way, the Court has sought to guarantee that state legislatures do not construct districts so as to favor one set of interests over others. Before the Court began making these rulings, many states legislated district lines favoring rural areas over urban areas for their own legislatures and for the U.S. House.

Throughout the 1960s, court decisions became stricter with regard to the amount of variance allowed. Court rulings pushed for a standard as close to literal equality in numbers as possible. The lower federal courts were deeply involved in redistricting.

The Burger Court of the early 1970s loosened the standards somewhat. The Court still held to the general principle of equality, but it was willing to tolerate more deviation, at least for state legislative districting. It often ruled that states could respect subdivision boundaries (such as county lines or New England town lines) for legislative districts. For state districts, the Court seemed willing to accept deviations of up to 10 percent between the most and least populous district. The Court also carefully looked at deviations of up to 20 percent; however, automatic approval of such deviations was not expected. For congressional seats, the Court stuck to a policy of strict numerical equality. This was reaffirmed in a 1983 case in which the Court held that New Jersey congressional districts would have to be drawn again, even though there was only a tiny numerical difference between the largest district (527,472) and the smallest district (523,798).

In mid-1986, the Supreme Court entered an area of legislative districting that it had previously avoided—the drawing of district lines to favor a specific political party, commonly called **gerrymandering.** The Court said that gerrymandering could be unconstitutional even if districts met the "one person, one vote" standards. The majority said that such claims of unconstitutionality would be sustained "only when the electoral system is arranged in a manner that will consistently degrade a voter's or a group of voters' influence on the political process as a whole." The three dissenters favored the long-standing view of the Court—reversed in this case—that "partisan gerrymandering claims of major political parties raise a nonjusticiable political question that the judiciary should leave to the legislative branch as the framers of the Constitution unquestionably intended. The losing party . . . in every reapportionment will now be invited to fight the battle anew in federal court." The specific Indiana redistricting challenged in this case was not overturned.

For a brief period in the 1960s, the Supreme Court, then dominated by liberals, flirted with the idea that economic inequality in some of its aspects violated the Constitution's equal protection clause. That flirtation ended rather quickly, however. Virtually all of the decisions about economic equality are made in the political process involving the other organs of the government. Debates over taxes and redistribution of wealth are among the longest and most heated as these organs decide on the merits of competing claims.

Debate over the treatment and distribution of wealth, over how much equality to legislate, and over how much inequality to leave intact, has often been central to our politics. Such debate surfaced in the 1930s and again in the 1960s. At other times, this issue has been out of the limelight. For a long time, the Supreme Court was willing to let states legislate against the poor in many ways, often indirect (Grossman and Wells, 1980: 649–56). Only in the 1960s did the Court even make sure that poor people got proper legal representation when charged with crimes. At that time, the Court also began to examine welfare systems, which were challenged in various cases. It looked at conditions attached to the receipt of welfare, eligibility for welfare, due process considerations, and limits on the amount of welfare grants. On the last point, the Warren Court seemed headed for requiring equality to the extent of setting a subsistence level for everyone. The Burger Court continued to oversee eligibility standards, but basically it gave the states a free hand in setting benefits where federal law allowed them that prerogative.

The case of *San Antonio School District* v. *Rodriguez* in 1973 sounded the death knell for efforts to deal with economic questions under the equal protection clause. This case challenged the method that Texas used to fund school districts, which resulted in the allocation of very unequal resources to rich and poor districts. The Court held that such unequal funding was not unconstitutional. In the majority opinion for the Court, Justice Lewis Powell concluded that the Texas method of funding schools (which was similar to that of most states) "is not the product of purposeful discrimination against any group or class." Justice Potter Stewart concurred in the decision and was exceptionally candid in admitting that a perceived injustice could not be cured by the Court's interpretation of the Constitution:

> The method of financing public schools in Texas, as in almost every other state, has resulted in a system of public education that can fairly be described as chaotic and unjust. It does not follow, however, . . . that this system violates the Constitution of the United States. . . . Unlike other provisions of the Constitution, the Equal Protection Clause confers no substantive rights and creates no substantive liberties.

Justice Thurgood Marshall was eloquent in dissent:

> In my judgment, the right of every American to an equal start in life, so far as the provision of a state service as important as education is concerned, is far too vital to permit state discrimination. . . . Nor can I accept the notion that it is sufficient to remit these appellees to the vagaries of the political process. . . . I, for one, am unsatisfied with the hope of an ultimate "political" solution sometime in the indefinite future while, in the meantime, countless children unjustifiably receive inferior educations.

The majority of the Court, however, decided, in effect, that questions of economic equality and inequality would have to be left to "the vagaries of the political process."

FREEDOM, PUBLIC OPINION, AND COURTS

The content of liberties and rights changes as the relative strength of political coalitions with competing views about them changes. The United States is one of the freest societies in the world (Gastil, 1982; Taylor and Hudson, 1972). It does not do a poor job with regard to liberties and rights. However, we have no reason to be smug or self-satisfied. Our record is not unblemished.

The status of our liberties and rights is related to public opinion about them. In Chapter 4, we made two important points about public opinion in relation to free expression and racial equality. First, the American people support liberties and rights more in the abstract than in concrete situations. Second, the American people in recent decades have become more supportive of liberties and rights and of equality for minorities.

However, fluctuations in such attitudes still occur. Negative attitudes among the public could create situations in which specific liberties and rights might be threatened. Ultimately, the context of public opinion both pushes and limits what courts and other government agencies do about liberties and rights.

A major recent study of American beliefs about civil liberties (McClosky and Brill, 1983: 437–38) concluded with a succinct statement that seems absolutely true:

> Civil liberties are fragile and susceptible to the political climate of the time. Hard-won civil rights and liberties are not eternally safeguarded, but are highly vulnerable to assaults by strategically placed individuals and groups who find certain rights or liberties morally offensive, dangerous to safety and stability, and devitalizing to the political order. Such assaults become especially threatening when the civil liberties under attack do not enjoy widespread popular support. This . . . is often the case, a result in great part of the failure of large segments of the population to have effectively internalized the libertarian norms to which the American political culture, from the beginning, has been dedicated.

This chapter has dealt extensively with the courts in the areas of liberties, rights, and some aspects of equality because the courts play an especially important role in guarding liberties and rights and defining some kinds of equality. But the courts cannot do this job alone. Because of the way federal judges and justices are chosen, the federal courts inevitably follow dominant political opinion to some extent. And despite the importance of courts in the area of liberties and rights, they are still weaker than the other organs of government. A persuasive statement of the ultimate frailty of the courts was made by Shirley Hufstedler, who served as a federal court of appeals judge. She favored a federal judiciary that would be aggressive in its protection of liberties, but she stressed the limits of the federal judiciary:

> The decision-making process is individualized and personal. Federal judges have no bureaucracies to tap and, with trivial exceptions, no experts to help them who are not supplied by the litigants as witnesses. The average personal staff of a federal judge is one secretary and two law clerks. Supreme Court justices have two secretaries and as many as four law clerks. Since the chief justice of the United States and the chief judges of the lower courts have additional administrative duties, they are given slightly larger personal staffs. . . .
>
> Americans have expectations about what courts can do that cannot be fulfilled. Courts are primarily deciders, not supervisors or social problem solvers. Judges know, for instance, that when they decide that a school system must be integrated, they are not "solving" racial hatreds; when judges grant divorces, they are not "solving" matrimonial problems. Evils do not vanish with the wave of a court decree. (*Washington Post,* January 1, 1978.)

CONCLUSIONS

This chapter has concentrated on the nature of liberties, rights, and equality in the United States. The Supreme Court is a legal and, more important, a political focal point for debates over the concrete meanings of liberties, rights, and equality. It plays the same roles with regard to debates over prohibited and required government actions in relation to liberties, rights, and equality. Institutions and individuals outside the judicial system also engage in these vital debates.

The challenges identified at the beginning of the chapter are not the kind that are "solved." They are posed continually. This chapter has assessed the current state of the response to these challenges.

Our discussion of liberties, rights, and equality can be summarized in a few broad conclusions:

1. The status of liberties, rights, and equality is absolutely critical in a society that aspires to be open, free, and democratic.

2. Liberties, rights, and equality change their meaning in relation to changing circumstances and as the result of political controversy.

3. Ideally, the federal government should be a particular friend to and a guarantor of liberties and rights. But sometimes it isn't.

4. Federal courts, especially the Supreme Court, play a special role in protecting liberties and rights. But their aggressiveness in this role varies and, ultimately, they cannot do the job alone.

FURTHER READING

BULLOCK, CHARLES S., III, and CHARLES M. LAMB, eds. (1984) *Implementation of Civil Rights Policy*. Monterey, Calif.: Brooks/Cole Publishing. Examines the conditions associated with progress toward equality in implementation in specific areas of civil rights: housing, voting, education, and employment.

KLUGER, RICHARD (1976) *Simple Justice: The History of* Brown *v.* Board of Education *and Black America's Struggle for Equality*. New York: Alfred A. Knopf. A detailed history of civil rights for blacks in the United States, with a special focus on the long legal proceedings that led to *Brown* v. *Board of Education* in 1954.

LEWIS, ANTHONY (1964) *Gideon's Trumpet*. New York: Random House. A case study of the Supreme Court's major decision that the Constitution requires the provision of free legal counsel to indigents accused of felonies in state courts.

PRITCHETT, C. HERMAN (1984) *Constitutional Civil Liberties*. An analysis of the content of American civil liberties as interpreted by the Supreme Court.

Chapter Twenty

FOREIGN AND DEFENSE POLICIES

$\mathscr{W}$e all inhabit a "global village," according to communications scholar Marshall McLuhan—a tight world society in which we are intensely involved in what happens in every corner of the planet. As citizens of a premier world power, we are veritable busybodies in this global village.

As a case in point, consider the upheaval in the Philippines that in 1986 resulted in the overthrow of the Ferdinand Marcos regime and the installation of reformist Corazon Aquino. The entire drama was played out in media splendor before our eyes. It was on a television program ("This Week with David Brinkley") late in 1985 that columnist and ABC commentator George Will grilled dictator Marcos by satellite and literally baited him into scheduling an election. This was no doubt the first foreign election in history caused by a U.S. television network.

In subsequent weeks, the Philippine election drama was played out on television and in the press. The candidates gave speeches and interviews—aimed at U.S. audiences as well as Filipinos. The press coverage was intense, and images of Philippine citizens guarding polling places to protect their ballots evoked great sympathy. Senators sent to monitor the Philippine election were stunned when they returned home and found so many of their constituents expressing concern over the outcome. As one Senate aide said of the media blitz: "They covered it almost like it was an American primary out in the hinterlands" (Roberts, 1986; Shales, 1986).

The end came dramatically on February 24, in a desperate phone call that Marcos made to the White House. Speaking with Senator Paul Laxalt (R–Nev.), President Reagan's close ally (for diplomatic reasons, Reagan did not speak to Marcos directly), Marcos finally asked: "Should I step down?" Replied Laxalt, "I think you should cut, and cut cleanly. I think the time has come." The United States had finally withdrawn its support of the Marcos government.

Since World War II, Americans have become increasingly aware that there are few corners of the world without significance to their nation's interests. "Afghanistanism" used to be a newspaper term of derision for stories or editorials dealing with remote and boring subjects; yet the Soviet invasion of Afghanistan, a major news story in 1979, clouded U.S.–Soviet relations for nearly a decade. More recently, Americans have been drawn into the politics of South Africa, Ethiopia, Libya, Nicaragua, and Chile, not to mention Angola and Sri Lanka. As a superpower, the United States cannot afford the luxury of neutrality or nonalignment: its policies, even when marked by neglect or ineptitude, affect other nations' ties with their neighbors and sometimes their internal affairs. $\mathscr{S}$

*F*oreign and defense policy-making and implementation are the subjects of this chapter. We will discuss the nation's foreign policy and security goals, and the resources needed to pursue them. We will emphasize the political backdrop for such policies. We hope to dispel the notion that foreign policy is something apart, far removed from the rest of American policy. The chief policymakers—the president and Congress—are described. So are the bureaucracies that play powerful roles in shaping the policies they implement—especially the State and Defense departments and the intelligence agencies.

WHAT IS FOREIGN POLICY?

Foreign policy is the sum total of the decisions and actions that guide a nation's dealings with other nations. The chief factors in foreign policy are *national goals* and *national resources* used to achieve them. Statecraft is the art of putting the two together. Every nation, regardless of size or strength, must balance its goals against its resources.

Setting Goals in Foreign Policy

Competing goals

The chief goal of foreign policy is to nurture the nation's core interests; but what are those interests? The safety of the nation's territory would probably rank at the top of the list, although the United States has not faced an invasion since the War of 1812. Protecting the safety of our citizens, property, and business or cultural interests would also rank high. Although it may seem that Americans are singled out for punishment by others (terrorists, for instance), in fact our core interests have been relatively well served in today's world. In most areas of the world, our policies are aimed at protecting these interests. These policies normally command broad consensus among decision makers.

Beyond nurturing of our interests, however, foreign policy goals become far more controversial. We want world peace, but we also want to resist the spread of communism. We want good, stable relations with other nations, but we also want other nations to respect their citizens' rights and follow democratic practices. We want to check the international arms race, but at the same time we want a strong defense that is second to none. We like to sit down and talk with Soviet leaders, but we are profoundly suspicious of them (Ladd, 1986). And so it goes.

Any foreign policy issue can offer many competing goals—some unattainable, others mutually exclusive. From our very first decades as a nation, "great debates" have erupted among policymakers over foreign policy objectives: for example, ties to Old World powers such as England and France during our nation's early years, high versus low tariff levels, American expansionism abroad, and military involvement in foreign wars.

In the Philippines case, Americans disapproved of the Marcos regime's repressive tactics. But what was the cost of intervening in the internal politics of a nation 8,000 miles away? And what was the impact on U.S. military bases in that country? This conflict among policy goals is all too familiar as we confront human rights issues around the world: in Eastern Europe, in Nicaragua, in Chile, or in South Africa.

Changing conditions

Foreign policy objectives are hard to pin down also because they cannot be applied equally to every situation that crops up. People sometimes talk as if they expect foreign policy to be consistent. But conditions vary, so that strict consistency is rarely feasible. The stance we take toward human rights violations in South Africa may not be right for Korea or Chile, for example.

Changing times, too, demand frequent reassessment. According to the old saying, generals tend to prepare for fighting the previous war; diplomats, too, tend to define problems in terms of prior crises.

The lesson of World War II seemed to be that the United States could not afford isolationism, that we should answer threats to liberty wherever

Legacy of Vietnam. This double exposure juxtaposes the Vietnam Veterans' Memorial in Washington, D.C., and the statue of three servicemen nearby. The memorial lists the names of the more than 50,000 Americans who were killed in the Vietnam War.

Demonstrators flee police in South Africa. Fifteen people were killed when police charged a march in Cape Town intended to bring about the liberation of political prisoner Nelson Mandela. The leader of the African National Congress, the major South African black organization, Mandela has been in prison for more than 25 years.

they occur. "Appeasement" was frowned on; leaders sought to avoid the fate of British Prime Minister Neville Chamberlain, who compromised with Hitler in a vain quest for "peace in our time."

During the 1950s and 60s, this "lesson" steered us into such conflicts as the Korean and Vietnam wars. But conditions in Asia were far different from what they had been in Europe. It was one thing to side with Britain or France against the Nazis; it was quite another to intrude in less developed countries with strong nationalistic social movements and little tradition of democratic government. At home, it was one thing to wage all-out war; pursuing limited political wars at less than full capacity was a different story.

The lesson of Vietnam, paid for with 56,000 American lives and untold billions of dollars, taught caution in foreign involvement. But is this a reliable guide for other crises involving other issues? When new problems arise—as in Lebanon or El Salvador—policymakers must decide whether past experience can be applied to them.

Means and ends

Even if foreign policy goals are agreed upon, it is not always clear what action to take. The human rights emphasis of the Carter era is an example. It struck a responsive chord with those dedicated to the principles of the Declaration of Independence. What tactics, though, are most apt to enhance the rights of other nations' citizens? Criticisms of human rights violations may influence world opinion, but they may also harden the targeted nation's actions toward dissidents.

The debate over sanctions against South Africa's white-dominated regime, however acrimonious, is primarily a dispute over means. Politicians in this country are virtually unanimous in condemning that regime and calling for an end to its policy of *apartheid*. What is less clear is what course of action would be most likely to bring about change. Would boycotts and sanctions force concessions, or would they threaten the economic well-being of South African blacks as well as whites? Would international pressures stimulate reform, or would they help bring about a bloody civil war? Despite the pronouncements of some leaders, the answers to these questions are neither simple nor self-evident.

In sum, it is no easier to identify our foreign policy goals than to define our policy on housing or abortions. Foreign policy goals, like those of domestic policy, are many and often in conflict. Those goals shift with circumstances, and they must be applied with care and flexibility.

Resources for World Power

A nation attains policy goals by allocating *resources*. These include economic strength, natural resources, educational and technological sophistication, and military right. Like goals, resources vary. The notion of resources is kin to the concept of *power,* applied here to sovereign states rather than to individuals or groups. Broadly defined, power is a nation's ability to influence other nations in directions that favor its interests.

Power is an elusive concept. People often equate it with military force. But military resources are not always relevant to the solution of foreign policy problems. Abundant natural, human, or economic resources are just as vital in the international sweepstakes. Nations also draw strength from the legitimacy or stability of their political regimes and from the loyalty of their people. Power, in other words, is many-sided, changing, and relative to the problem at hand.

Geopolitics

The U.S. course in the world arena is decisively shaped by its resources. One of those resources is geographic position. Advocates of **geopolitics** (a form of geographic determinism) hold that this factor, more than any other, decides a nation's fate in world affairs. Geography, argued Nicholas Spykman (1942: 41), "is the most fundamental factor in the foreign policy of states because it is the most permanent."

Geographic position has dictated much of our foreign policy throughout our history. Separated from Europe and Asia by broad oceans, America has been virtually free from military incursions. (In 1814 the British sacked the Capitol, and in 1941 the Japanese bombed—but did not invade—Pearl Harbor in Hawaii, then a U.S. territory.) Long unprotected boundaries to the north and south were a threat when unfriendly powers ruled adjoining land. But even this threat was removed over time. Border security meant that our country could develop free from the threat of outside aggression.

This seeming remoteness fueled an isolationist philosophy—aloofness from other nation's affairs. In his 1796 Farewell Address, George Washington warned against "entangling alliances" with other nations. Every year on his birthday, the address is recited in both chambers of Congress. However, his isolationist spirit became obsolete with the advent of global economic ties, not to mention intercontinental missiles and nuclear weapons.

By any count, America is blessed by geography. It commands a continental domain with abundant natural resources to aid its rise to world leadership. It is the world's leading or near-leading producer of most minerals; despite its energy deficit, it produces 65 percent of the world's natural gas, a fourth of its crude petroleum, and a fifth of its coal. It is the world's premier manufacturing nation, leading in most classes of manufactured goods. It is also the world's greatest agricultural producer—even though having, of all the world's nations, the smallest proportion of farm workers. The country's commanding position flows largely from self-sufficiency in many classes of raw materials and manufactured goods.

Economic development

It has become more and more obvious that a nation's power—including its capacity to wage war—is built on its economic base. By almost every sign, our economic resources are vast and resilient. The gross national product (GNP) is nearly $5 trillion. Even when growth and productivity lag, our country compares well with other major industrial nations.

Our educational and technological capacity are paramount resources. The productivity of our labor force of more than 100 million is high because of training and automated equipment. Research laboratories contribute basic knowledge; they also offer many inventions and technological refinements to raise productivity and living standards.

A striking example of the potential of science, technology, industry, and organization was the U.S. space thrust. When in 1961 President Kennedy voiced the goal of a moon landing, it seemed remote. But eight years and $24 billion later, Apollo 11 astronauts achieved that goal.

The power generated from our economic machinery is awesome. We rely on tax rates no higher than those of comparable industrial countries (and lower than some), yet our country supports many domestic social programs and global aid. Since World War II, it has spent some $150 billion in foreign economic, military, and technical aid. Its military arsenal can kill every person on earth many times over. It has even borne the brunt of major military efforts without destroying its domestic economy: the Korean War was waged with 14 percent of the GNP; the Vietnam War at its height involved only 8 percent of the GNP.

The Limits of Power

Still there are severe limits to what the resources of even the world's strongest nation can achieve. American power is awesome but not infinite.

Interdependencies

Many problems flow from economic interdependence. Like other developed nations, our country relies on abundant, cheap raw materials for a sophisticated economy and comfortable living standards. It has vast natural resources to support its economy, but there are crucial gaps.

Less developed nations with critical raw materials—like oil—can force concessions from developed countries. They can resort to the time-honored practices of controlling supplies and prices. Whether this can tilt the world's balance of power, only time will tell. Many of the very poorest nations lack valuable raw materials to use in bargaining.

The other side to interdependence is that industrial nations need outlets for their goods and services. Between 1965 and 1982, U.S. exports doubled as a percentage of GNP. Despite vast internal markets, American firms are looking outward and concerning themselves with trade barriers and the ability of other nations to buy goods.

Policies beyond price

Some policy goals are unattainable at any price, or are so costly that no nation would rationally use the resources they require. The Vietnam War was a lesson in the limits of power. True, it was not an all-out effort. Sensing that the public would not support such an effort, Presidents Johnson and Nixon took pains to contain the war and to hide its true cost from the average person. Yet by all the usual standards, the effort was massive; at its height, it involved 800,000 American troops.

The ultimate challenge of Vietnam was not military, however. Senator J. William Fulbright (D-Ark.), one of the war's bitterest foes, questioned (1966: 15) whether even the United States could "go into a small, alien, undeveloped Asian nation and create stability where there is chaos, the will to fight where there is defeatism, democracy where there is no tradition of it, and honest government where corruption is a way of life." Wanting to halt the advance of international communism, the United States helped an ill-supported, corrupt regime stave off a popular movement. Supporters of that movement drew strength from the cause of national liberation and military aid from communist allies. It was, in short, a civil war that outside military help could affect but not decide. Our armed forces could defoliate the country, but they could not create a viable regime where none existed.

This lesson in the limits of power should come as no surprise to those with knowledge of history. Two hundred years earlier, Great Britain, then the world's strongest power, lost 13 colonies under like circumstances. The colonies were shaken by civil strife, and the eventual outcome was by

In the 1960s, Senator J. William Fulbright (D–Ark.), chairman of the Senate Foreign Relations Committee, called for an end to American participation in the Vietnam War.

no means certain. Had Parliament chosen to throw more military resources into the fray, it might have tilted the victory to the loyalists. But Parliament was divided; it would not strip its defenses in other parts of the world. Even if England had won militarily, would that have ensured loyalty and peace in the colonies? Probably not. Certain objectives, in short, are so costly that they are beyond the practical reach of even the most richly endowed nation.

TYPES OF FOREIGN AND DEFENSE POLICIES

Bearing in mind the dilemma of balancing goals and resources, it helps to think of several types of foreign and defense policies. (A similar breakdown of domestic policy is given in Chapter 17.) These are **crisis policies,** reactions to direct challenges to the nation's security or core interests; **strategic policies,** advancing the nation's interests by military force or otherwise; and **structural policies,** involving economic interests or deployment of resources or personnel.

Crisis Policies

Self-preservation is not the only goal of foreign or military policy; but when it is directly threatened, other goals must be cast aside. One definition of an international crisis is a sudden challenge to the nation's safety and security. Examples range from the Japanese attack on Pearl Harbor in 1941 to the attack on the marines in Lebanon in 1983.

Crises engage policymakers at the highest levels. They include the president, the secretaries of state and defense, the National Security Council, and the Joint Chiefs of Staff. During a crisis, policymakers keep a tight rein on information flowing upward from line officers. Indeed, crisis management is so important (see Chapter 12) that President Reagan insisted on a White House team led by Vice President Bush for that function.

Public and media attention rivet on crises. People tend to support whatever course the decision makers choose. Patriotism runs high, as people hasten to "rally 'round the flag" (Mueller, 1973: 208–13).

Most foreign and defense policy-making is aimed at deterring crisis; it tries to prevent direct challenges to the nation. Yet, with public attention and support at their highest levels, crisis politics gives officials unique chances for leadership. Thus, leaders sometimes promote a crisis atmosphere in the hope of mobilizing public support. President Carter sought vainly to raise public consciousness on the energy crisis by calling it "the moral equivalent of war." His failure to maintain a crisis atmosphere during the prolonged Iranian hostage affair helped cause his loss of support.

Strategic Policies

Strategic policies embrace most of what are thought of as foreign policy questions. Decision makers must plan strategies toward other nations while guarding interests at home. Examples include the basic mix of military forces and weapons systems; arms sales to foreign powers; trade inducements or limits; economic, military, and technical aid to less developed nations; major treaties with other nations; and participation in such global bodies as the UN and world banking agencies.

Strategic policies engage not only top-level executive decision makers but also committees of Congress and middle-level executives. The State Department is an agency for strategic decision making, as is the office of the secretary of defense. The individual uniformed services may also become involved.

Strategic policies engage ideological, racial, ethnic, and economic interests. At times, they command widespread public and media attention. The Panama Canal Treaty debate of 1978, the sale of AWACS planes to Saudi Arabia in 1981, the start of arms talks with the Soviet Union in 1985, and the controversy over South African sanctions in 1986 are all examples of strategic policy issues. Increasingly, such issues involve structural (distributive) politics; interest groups compete for strategic policies that will benefit them—for example, arms sales and grain sales.

Structural Policies

Foreign and military programs call for vast resources—millions of employees and billions of dollars each year. Deploying these resources is structural policy-making. Structural policies include weapons systems and procurement, location of military installations, weapons and surplus food sales to foreign countries, and trade restrictions to protect domestic industries.

Structural policy-making is about the same for foreign and defense issues as for domestic issues. Indeed, it is usually treated as domestic politics, often indistinguishable from distributive policy making. Structural decisions engage a wide span of political groups. Defense contracts and installations, for instance, are hotly sought by business firms, labor unions, and local communities and by their political representatives in Washington.

PRESIDENTIAL LEADERSHIP AND FOREIGN POLICY

Those making foreign policy face an environment that both limits and helps their actions. They cannot ignore public opinion (or inattention), the media, interest groups, or electoral politics. But these forces, no matter how strong, cannot manage our relations with other nations. That is the task of the president, Congress, and the bureaucracy.

Constitutional Powers

In foreign and military affairs, the president has the burden of leadership. His constitutional powers, though shared with Congress, are impressive. He appoints ambassadors and other U.S. emissaries; he receives representatives of other nations; he negotiates treaties and other agreements.

Diplomat in chief

The president is expected to manage day-to-day relations with foreign governments, consistent with laws and treaties. The Constitution (Article II, Section 2) provides that the president "shall have power, by and with the advice and consent of the Senate, to make treaties, provided two thirds of the senators present concur."

Over time, treaties have been a vital part of our relations with foreign powers. When made and duly ratified, they are the law of the land. But, as we will see, not all treaties negotiated and signed by the president are acceptable to the Senate. Moreover, treaties are not self-executing: often laws must be passed or funds provided to carry out their terms.

Today presidents use **executive agreements** to reach accords of the type typically reserved for treaties. Such agreements have no formal status

The president as chief diplomat. In November 1985 President Ronald Reagan attended a Brussels, Belgium, meeting of the North Atlantic Council, an agency of the North Atlantic Treaty Organization (NATO). He met with a number of European leaders. Among them were British Prime Minister Margaret Thatcher, shown here sharing a laugh with the president.

in the Constitution. But they have been used six times as often as treaties, and by every president since George Washington. Those agreements have become the standard method for dealing with foreign powers. During our first half century, 60 treaties and 27 executive agreements were signed. As of January 1, 1983, there were 966 treaties and 6,571 executive agreements in force.

Treaties are still reserved for our most important obligations to foreign powers and multilateral agencies. Debates over Senate ratification often turn into town meetings on the course of American foreign policy. Examples include the Treaty of Versailles (1919; rejected); the United Nations Charter (1945); the antiballistic missile (ABM) treaty of 1972; and the intermediate nuclear forces (INF) treaty of 1987.

The president's dominance in the conduct of diplomacy, including formal negotiations with other nations, has led some observers to conclude, erroneously, that foreign affairs are the exclusive domain of the president. This view surfaced during the 1987 congressional hearings on the Iran-*contra* affair, when some witnesses portrayed congressional involvement as an illegitimate interference with executive prerogatives.

Two historical sources are cited by advocates of presidential supremacy in foreign affairs. One is this statement made by John Marshall in 1800 (before he became chief justice): "The president is the sole organ of the nation in its external relations, and its sole representative with foreign nations." But Marshall did not claim that the president could make foreign policy single-handedly; he merely noted that the president executes policy arrived at jointly. The other source is Justice George Sutherland's 1936

HISTORICAL PERSPECTIVES

Going to War in the 1980s

At 2:27 on a Sunday morning in Augusta, Georgia, President Reagan's phone rang. National Security Adviser Robert C. McFarlane told the president that an explosion had ripped through a building housing U.S. Marines in Beirut, Lebanon. About 45 marines were thought to have died (the eventual figure was 240).

The phone call capped the fateful weekend of October 21–23, 1983. Originally, the president had gone to the Augusta National Golf Club to relax and reassure his host, Secretary of State George P. Shultz, that he had the president's ear and was in charge of foreign policy. The trip also proved a useful "cover" for planning a military venture under consideration: invasion of the Caribbean island of Grenada to dislodge a leftist coup.

That weekend, the president got little rest and played little golf. The first afternoon, a gunman smashed onto the course and demanded to speak to the president, who was on the 16th fairway; two hours later, the man surrendered, after holding several people hostage in the pro shop. Secretive huddles were held on the Grenada situation. Then came the phone call about the Beirut disaster. The presidential party decided to return to Washington—not only for the symbolic message that the president was in charge but also as a continuing cover for the Grenadan planning.

Four hours after the phone call, the presidential helicopter landed on the White House south lawn in a pouring rain. Standing with Mrs. Reagan, Shultz, and McFarlane, the president called the Beirut bombers "bestial" (Williams, 1983). Over the next three days, Reagan consulted on steps to protect the marines in Lebanon, issued statements, gave final approval to the Grenadan invasion, and met privately with congressional leaders. On Tuesday morning, he announced the invasion to the nation; two days later, he delivered a stirring prime-time speech on the twin crises.

These events dramatically showed both the reach and limits of our foreign policy. As a major world power, the United States is sooner or later affected by nearly everything that happens around the world. For strategic reasons, we have been involved for decades in the Middle East, among other things aiding the fragile regime of Lebanese President Amin Gemayel and even joining a multinational "peacekeeping" force. Long-standing Caribbean concerns were aroused by the possibility that the island airport on Grenada could be used to ship arms and troops to destabilizing forces in other Central American countries.

Yet U.S. forces anywhere are targets of criticism—and terrorist strikes. Within a few months, the United States and its peacekeeping

(Continued)

HISTORICAL PESPECTIVES

(Concluded)

allies had quit Beirut, leaving Lebanon to an uncertain fate. The Grenadan exercise, while a military success, was strictly small potatoes; and in any event, U.S. troops soon left Grenada because the mission was completed.

The Lebanon and Grenada situations—though both classic international crises allowing wide presidential discretion—also showed the thin line separating foreign and domestic affairs. American lives were at stake: not only troops but embassy personnel and civilians (including 1,000 medical students in Grenada). And though leading Democratic presidential contenders briefly halted their campaign schedules during the crisis, it wasn't long before the president's handling of foreign policy, especially the Lebanon disaster, became prime topics of the 1984 presidential campaign.

A navy corpsman holds the hand of a dead marine as rescue and search operations are underway at the marine headquarters in Beirut.

---

opinion in *U.S.* v. *Curtiss Wright Export Corporation* that legislation dealing with foreign affairs "must often accord to the president a degree of discretion and freedom from statutory restriction which would not be admissible were domestic affairs alone involved." Because the case dealt with a president's implementation of a congressional enactment, Justice Sutherland's expansive language was beside the point, and it does not support a claim of exclusive presidential domain in foreign affairs. The most that can be said, as Justice Robert Jackson later noted (in *Youngstown* v. *Sawyer,* 1952), is that "the president might act in external affairs without congressional authority, but not that he might act contrary to an Act of Congress."

War powers

As with other sovereign powers, the president and Congress share so-called **war powers.** Congress has the exclusive authority to "declare war" (Article I, Section 8); the president is commander in chief of the military

(Article II, Section 2). With virtually every armed intervention in our history, these clauses have generated "lively disagreement among the president, Congress, and the Supreme Court, and between the central government and the states" (Hyman, 1986).

The United States has formally declared war five times: the War of 1812 (1812–14), the Mexican War (1846–48), the Spanish-American War (1898), World War I (1917–18), and World War II (1941–45). In only one of these cases did Congress actually delve into the merits of waging war, and that was in 1812, when the vote was rather close. In every other case, Congress overwhelmingly supported going to war, though the declarations themselves merely acknowledged that a state of war already existed. (In two cases—the Mexican and Spanish-American conflicts—it later regretted its action.)

The power to declare war is unreliable. Although our country has declared war five times, it has used military force on foreign soil nearly 200 times. Most of these actions were authorized by presidents on the pretext of protecting life or property abroad.

In the post–World War II era, our country was bound by a network of treaties and agreements pledging mutual assistance if signatory nations were attacked. Thus, President Johnson was told by his advisers that no declaration of war was required in Vietnam. They said that he already had ample powers under the 1964 Gulf of Tonkin Resolution, the now-defunct Southeast Asia Treaty Organization (SEATO) treaty, and his "inherent powers."

On numerous occasions since World War II, presidents have cloaked foreign intervention under the rationale of protecting American lives and property abroad. These included Lebanon in 1958, the Dominican Republic in 1965, the Cambodian "incursion" of 1970, the South Vietnamese invasion of Laos in 1971, the *Mayagüez* incident of 1975, the Iranian rescue mission of 1980, and Lebanon and Grenada in 1983. The Korean (1950–53) and Vietnam (1965–73) wars were justified on the grounds of treaty obligations and "inherent powers" derived from the broad notion of executive authority.

Backlash over the Vietnam War spawned the War Powers Resolution (P.L. 93–148), which became law in 1973 over President Nixon's veto. Under it, the president must (1) consult with Congress before introducing U.S. troops into hostilities, (2) report any commitment of forces to Congress within 48 hours, and (3) terminate the use of forces within 60 days if Congress does not declare war, extend the period by law, or is unable to meet. (The president may extend the period to 90 days, if necessary.)

The War Powers Resolution has proved an awkward compromise. While it may have deterred some actions, it has not kept presidents from intervening in emergencies. By the end of 1987, presidents had reported to Congress on a dozen occasions that troops were deployed. In several other cases, the military action was brief and no report was filed. In still other cases, the executive branch claimed that reports were not required because U.S. personnel were not entering into hostilities or imminent hostilities. Thus, the Reagan administration failed to meet the congressional reporting requirement when it sent military advisers to El Salvador in 1981 and when it provided protection for oil tankers in the Persian Gulf in 1987.

In some cases, members of Congress sat on the sidelines, only later questioning the actions. Other cases were debated at length. When President Reagan committed forces to the Lebanon peacekeeping mission, he initially declined to adhere precisely to the resolution. He feared that the timetable set in motion by the resolution would limit his flexibility and might encourage hostile factions to delay coming to the bargaining table. The impasse was resolved when Congress, led by House Speaker Thomas P. O'Neill, passed a resolution authorizing deployment of troops for 18 months (extending beyond the 1984 elections). When the Lebanon mission later collapsed, both the White House and congressional leaders sought to place the blame elsewhere. In the El Salvador and Persian Gulf deployments, members of Congress opposed to the president's actions challenged them in court on the grounds that they violated the Constitution and the War Powers Resolution. The suits were rejected as the judges in essence invoked the "political questions" doctrine: If Congress wished to invoke the resolution to monitor the president's actions, it should do so directly. But in neither instance were the votes available to discipline the president, so the impasse stood.

With each new crisis, the War Powers Resolution will be attacked or defended, depending on the view held of the proposed intervention. Presidents will continue to seek flexibility and to resist congressional "meddling" with their powers as commander in chief. Members of Congress will insist on being consulted and will strive to control the use of troops abroad. If the venture succeeds, members of Congress will applaud the president's courage; if the venture fails, scapegoats will be sought.

The War Powers Resolution, it seems, has not satisfied anyone. Presidents have resisted or ignored it, and members of Congress have been unwilling to enforce it. On the other hand, no one knows what presidential forays it may have discouraged. (Some observers suspect that President Reagan might have waged war against the Sandinista government of Nicaragua had the existence of the War Powers Resolution not deterred him.) In any event, by 1988 it was apparent to everyone that changes were needed and efforts to reformulate the enactment had begun.

Expanding powers

The president's foreign policy prerogatives have been enhanced by historical precedent and court interpretations. To free 52 U.S. citizens held hostage in Iran, President Carter in 1981 waived all pending legal claims by U.S. citizens against that country. Although the action was highly controversial, Carter was upheld. In a 1984 ruling (*Regan* v. *Wald*), the Supreme Court, by a 5-to-4 vote, even upheld a questionable executive order forbidding most Americans to spend money on travel to Cuba. "It did so," remarked commentator Anthony Lewis (1984), "by taking a worshipful view of executive power—by virtually assuming that anything the executive branch does under the label 'foreign policy' is lawful." When Reagan imposed an economic boycott against Libya in early 1986, he told U.S. citizens to leave that country promptly or face fines and imprisonment.

Presidents do not have unlimited leeway; even in global crises, they cannot circumvent procedures established by Congress (*Youngstown Sheet and Tube Co.* v. *Sawyer*, 1952). But in the crunch, judges are extremely hesitant to limit presidents.

Presidential Advisers

Presidential primacy in foreign affairs rests in part on the fact that the president can call upon various expert advisers in formulating policies. The quality of the president's advisory system is nowhere more important than in foreign and defense matters.

The secretary of state

Over time, the president's prime foreign policy adviser has been the secretary of state—the senior cabinet official and, in earlier times, a presidential contender in his own right.

This post has drawn some of the nation's most distinguished public servants. A few were at least as noteworthy as the presidents who appointed them; some forged policies of lasting importance. John Quincy Adams (1817–25) was the true author of the Monroe Doctrine, which proclaimed opposition to foreign intervention in the Americas. George C. Marshall (1947–49), the grand military strategist of World War II, advised President Truman and drew up postwar policies of global alliances and aid to war-torn and less developed countries.

Contemporary secretaries of state may or may not be major foreign policy architects; they may or may not be close personal advisers of the president. Two who were both were John Foster Dulles (1953–59) and Henry Kissinger (1973–77). Their power flowed not from their cabinet post but from their unique relationship with the president.

The National Security Council

A potential instrument for White House coordination is the National Security Council (NSC), created by the National Security Act of 1947. The function of the NSC is to advise the president on "domestic, foreign, and military policies relating to the national security."

Each president has used the NSC differently. Eisenhower used it repeatedly. But it fell into disuse after 1961, though Kennedy and Johnson

Two secretaries of state who dominated foreign policy were John Foster Dulles (1953–59) and Henry Kissinger (1973–77). Dulles [left] personified the Cold War policies of containing communism and challenging Soviet power in the international arena. Kissinger, [right], shown talking to Israeli Prime Minister Golda Meir, personified post–Cold War pragmatism and an orientation toward closer relations with such communist powers as the USSR and China.

used it on occasion to ratify decisions reached through informal negotiations.

In 1969, Nixon reestablished the NSC as "the principal forum for presidential consideration of foreign policy issues." When Kissinger was national security adviser, NSC committees and aides began to multiply once more, as they had under Eisenhower. The basic NSC structure remained in place under later presidents. Its size and importance vary with the presidents' personal style and their relations with such key advisers as the secretaries of state and defense and the director of central intelligence. As a general rule, weaknesses of any of those officials will enhance the president's reliance on the NSC and its head, the national security adviser.

White House versus State Department

This ebb and flow has led to inevitable tensions between the NSC and agencies outside the White House, mainly the State Department. NSC staff directors such as Henry Kissinger (until he went to the State Department) under Nixon and Zbigniew Brzezinski under Carter (1977–81) tended to outshine the secretaries of state, downgrading the State Department's influence.

Reagan and his initial foreign policy advisers declared their intention of restoring the secretary of state as the administration's principal foreign policy voice. Strong figures—Alexander Haig and then George Shultz—were at the helm at State, while the NSC had no less than six successive directors, three of them from the military and none of them major policymakers in their own right.

Institutional rivalries nonetheless dogged the Reagan administration. Haig resigned when he decided that the president was not giving him the support he desired in disputes with the NSC and the Defense Department.

Diplomacy face-to-face. Secretary of State George Shultz often met with Soviet Foreign Minister Eduard A. Shevardnadze. Here, in 1986, they sit opposite each other during an afternoon session at the State Department in Washington, D.C.

Shultz built a strong record but was barred from the decision loop in the biggest foreign policy fiasco of the Reagan period—the so called **Iran-contra affair.** A group of conservative interventionists scattered about various foreign policy agencies had concocted from some of the president's statements what they called "the Reagan doctrine": namely, that the United States should be prepared to intervene on behalf of anticommunist "freedom fighters" throughout the world—in Central America, Africa, and even Eastern Europe. Reflecting the natural caution of the diplomatic and defense bureaucracies, Shultz (along with Defense Secretary Caspar Weinberger) opposed the scheme of trading arms to Iranian "moderates" in exchange for funds that would be channeled to the Nicaraguan *contra* rebels fighting the procommunist Sandinista regime. Meeting resistance from the Departments of State and Defense, a group of NSC zealots led by Lt. Col. Oliver L. North constructed a secret, private apparatus, dubbed "the Enterprise," to get the job done. (The events are described more fully in Chapter 12.) Once the scheme was exposed and widely denounced, the reputations of Shultz and others who had counseled against it were enhanced.

The Imperial Presidency

Constitutional powers aside, presidents draw facts and advice from diverse executive agents, making the foreign policy role the main source for the growth of what has been called "the imperial presidency" (Schlesinger, 1973). Many think that presidents should play the dominant role in foreign policy. In this view, presidents, unlike legislative bodies, offer "energy, speed, and dispatch" in dealing with foreign development.

The Vietnam War challenged the doctrine of presidential control of foreign affairs. It pointed out the dangers of one-sided executive decision making: biased information, rigidity, intragroup conformity, and blind loyalty to prior commitments. It cast doubt on the sufficiency of presidential leadership, and it stiffened the will of Congress to make itself heard.

As the Vietnam era recedes from view, critics wonder whether the presidency has been too tightly restrained by new congressional controls. Certainly all presidents since Nixon have thought this. Congress typically lacks the organization or the consensus to act decisively in foreign affairs, but the Constitution gives Congress many of the trump cards. If Congress has the will, it can halt a president in his tracks; even if it is divided, it can insert itself into the foreign policy process and frustrate the president's wishes.

No matter how forceful a president's foreign policy initiatives, they must have the support of Congress. All foreign policy programs entail congressional participation at some stage.

Congressional involvement in foreign policy is flowing, not ebbing. The lines between foreign and domestic policy are growing more and more obscure. Major foreign policies now carry large dollar amounts for trade, aid, or military help. These bring into play Congress's cherished power of the purse. Since the 1970s, there have been strong reassertions of initiative in Congress, especially when major national commitments have been at stake.

CONGRESS AND FOREIGN POLICY

Constitutional Powers

The Constitution makes Congress a full-fledged partner in arriving at foreign policy decisions. The president is expected to manage day-to-day foreign relations, but Congress can shape those relations in ways both large and small.

Treaty ratification

Although initiated by the president, treaties are made "by and with the advice and consent of the Senate." The Senate's consent is signified by the concurrence of two thirds of the senators present and voting. The treaty power of the Senate, not shared with the House, lends it special prestige and tradition in this area.

The Senate's active role in ratification was shown during its 1988 debate on the intermediate nuclear force (INF) treaty that President Reagan and Soviet Premier Mikhail Gorbachev had signed the previous fall. Selected senators served as "observers" during the Geneva, Switzerland, negotiations leading to the treaty. Some senators' questions about procedures for verifying the reduction in missiles sent U.S. and Soviet diplomats back to the bargaining table to work out details. Other senators, stung by what they regarded as the Reagan administration's unwarranted "reinterpretation" of an earlier treaty (the 1972 ABM treaty), sought precise agreement on the meaning of key provisions. Senate committee and floor debate on the INF treaty extended over several months—the longest such debate since the Senate considered the Treaty of Versailles in 1919. In the end, the treaty was ratified overwhelmingly.

Congress may or may not be taken into the president's confidence as treaties and executive agreements are reached. To avoid Woodrow Wilson's humiliation when the Senate rejected the Versailles Treaty, modern chief executives usually inform key senators during the negotiation process.

The Senate may accept or reject a treaty. However, it rarely rejects treaties outright. (It has turned down only 19 treaties since 1789). More often, the Senate attaches reservations to a treaty, amends it, or simply postpones action. This can render the treaty inoperative or force the president to renegotiate all or part of it. One study (Crabb, 1983: 104) found that between 1789 and 1963 the Senate had approved without change 944 treaties, or 69 percent of those submitted to it.

The hurdle of obtaining a two-thirds Senate vote has led some to suggest that the Constitution be amended to require, say, a simple Senate majority. The tendency of presidents to resort to executive agreements, which do not require ratification, has been another result. However, lawmakers have been suspicious of this practice. From time to time, a constitutional amendment requiring Senate ratification of executive agreements has been pushed. Since the Vietnam War, the Senate Foreign Relations Committee has shown increased vigor in reviewing such agreements.

The power of the purse

Until World War II, our foreign operations required little money. This changed radically after the war. At that time, we became a major provider of economic, military, and technical aid. We also contributed to international and regional development banks and to various types of loan programs.

The yearly debate over such aid allows Congress to influence foreign policy, for better or worse. Congress can place "strings" on foreign aid; it can restrict or prohibit funds for countries that do not conform with certain conditions. Presidents and aides usually deplore these strings as limiting their dealings with other countries.

In the final analysis, no major foreign or military enterprise can be sustained unless Congress provides the money. Presidents may be able to conduct an operation for a time using existing funds and supplies, as Johnson did at first in Vietnam. But sooner or later, the issue of funding must be confronted. Our role in South Vietnam finally ended when Congress refused to provide emergency aid funds. Many of the Reagan administration's clashes with Congress took the form of fights over funding—for example, aid to the *contra* rebels in Nicaragua, to the Savimbi forces in Angola, and for Jordanian arms deals.

Foreign and defense policies increasingly require economic resources. This has served to heighten Congress's leverage. It has also equalized the role of the House in comparison with the Senate, because of the historic taxing and funding role of the House.

Other congressional powers

Another senatorial prerogative (Article II, Section 2) is confirming presidential appointments of ambassadors, ministers, and consuls; appointments and promotions in the Foreign Service; and appointments to high-level posts. The Senate Foreign Relations Committee now studies thousands of appointments, mostly of Foreign Service officers. Confirmation proceedings are often used to air views on the president's foreign policy rather than to probe the candidate's fitness. If the appointee is too controversial or too extreme for the committee, there can be trouble. In 1981, a storm of controversy arose over the human rights views of Ernest Lefever, a Reagan State Department choice; finally, Lefever withdrew his name.

Congress holds other high cards in the foreign policy game. It has power over interstate and foreign commerce, a critical function in these days of worldwide trading. By exercising its normal legislative powers it can shape foreign policy. Statutes and joint resolutions (such as the Gulf of Tonkin Resolution during the Vietnam War) help define foreign policy; they empower or limit executive policymakers. Congressional committees oversee foreign policy activities, sometimes through investigations but more often through routine hearings and informal consultations. When considering critical actions, therefore, presidents often confide in congressional leaders.

Who Speaks for Congress?

A subject as widespread as foreign affairs causes a huge jurisdictional tangle among Capitol Hill committees. Foreign policy issues are considered by 17 of the 22 standing committees in the House and by 14 of the 16 standing committees in the Senate. (see Table 20–1). In each chamber, foreign affairs, armed services, and appropriations committees bear the major foreign policy duties.

The Senate Foreign Relations Committee has a distinguished history because it considers treaties and nominations of foreign policy officials. Normally, it sees itself as a partner and adviser to the president. During the height of dispute on the Vietnam War, in the late 1960s and early 1970s, the committee, led by Senator J. William Fulbright (D–Ark.), was a forum for antiwar debate. Since then, it has resumed a more supportive role. Despite the committee's prestige, its subject matter is sometimes hazardous for its members: Not a few members, Fulbright included, have been

TABLE 20–1 Congressional committees dealing with international matters

Senate	House of Representatives
Agriculture, Nutrition, and Forestry Sale, donation of feed Agriculture imports, exports	***Agriculture*** Same as Senate Agriculture, Nutrition, and Forestry
Appropriations Funding for foreign operations, including State, Defense, AID (foreign aid), USIA, international organizations	***Appropriations*** Same as Senate Appropriations
Armed Services The common defense, including foreign military operations and assistance	***Armed Services*** Same as Senate Armed Services
Banking, Housing, and Urban Affairs International monetary and banking affairs Export controls Export and foreign trade promotion	***Banking, Currency, and Housing*** International monetary and banking affairs International development, trade
Budget Overall budget levels for defense and international affairs	***Budget*** Same as Senate Budget
Commerce, Science, and Transportation Interstate, foreign commerce Trade promotion, foreign investment Ocean policy	***Education and Labor*** Foreign labor
Energy and Natural Resources Mineral extraction from the oceans Territorial possessions of the United States, including trusteeships	***Energy and Commerce*** Interstate, foreign commerce Tourism
Environment and Public Works Ocean dumping Air pollution	***Foreign Affairs*** Foreign policy of the United States generally Foreign agency authorizations
Finance Foreign trade, including tariffs and customs Reciprocal trade agreements Nontariff restrictions Taxation of foreign sales and earnings from foreign investments	***Government Operations*** Same as Senate Governmental Affairs
	Interior and Insular Affairs Territorial possessions
Foreign Relations Foreign policy of the United States generally treaties Presidential nominations of ambassadors and other officers of United States Foreign agency authorizations	***Judiciary*** Same as Senate Judiciary
	Merchant Marine and Fisheries Oceans Oceanography Fishing and fisheries Merchant marine Shipping regulations International maritime conventions Navigation Panama Canal
	Public Works and Transportation International aviation

TABLE 20–1 *(Concluded)*

Senate	House of Representatives
Governmental Affairs	***Science, Technology, and Space***
Organization of the government, including foreign policy agencies	International scientific cooperation
Nuclear export policy organization and management	Space exploration
	Technological transfer
Judiciary	***Select Intelligence***
Immigration and naturalization	Same as Senate Select Intelligence
State and territorial boundaries	
Protection of trade and commerce against unlawful restraints	***Select Narcotics Abuse and Control***
	International drug traffic
Labor and Human Resources	***Small Business***
World labor standards	Same as Senate Small Business
Regulation of foreign laborers	
Labor performance of U.S. firms overseas	***Veterans Affairs***
	Same as Senate Veterans Affairs
Select Intelligence	
Authorization, oversight of foreign intelligence agencies (CIA, NSA, military intelligence)	***Ways and Means***
Covert operations	Same as Senate Finance
Small Business	
Impact of international forces on U.S. small businesses	
Veterans Affairs	
Foreign battlefield cemeteries	

Source: Senate, House rules.

defeated for reelection, partly because their work was portrayed as conflicting with local concerns.

For most of its history, the House Foreign Affairs Committee worked in the shadow of its Senate counterpart. This changed after World War II, when foreign aid programs thrust the House—with its unique powers of the purse—into virtual parity with the Senate (Carroll, 1966: 20). Today the House committee ranges nearly as widely as the Senate committee. It tends, however, to attract members who are more liberal and internationalist in outlook than the chamber as a whole—with the result that its reports often generate fierce debate on the House floor.

The Senate and House Armed Services committees straddle the national security arena. They annually authorize Pentagon spending for research, development, and procurement of weapons systems; construction of military facilities; and civilian and uniformed personnel.

Pointers on the U.S. defense budget. Budget Director James Miller III urges the Senate Budget Committee to support President Reagan's 1988 trillion-dollar budget. The chart shows that the funding available for defense purposes increased considerably during the early 1980s.

Members of the Armed Services committees are less interested in global strategy than in structural matters—force levels, military installations, and defense contracts (Huntington, 1961). Thus, military policy is in many ways an extension of constituency politics.

The two committees have tended to attract members favorable to military spending and home-district installations. One junior member branded the House committee as "the Pentagon's lobby on the Hill." But the committees recently reflected Capitol Hill skepticism over the magnitude of Reagan administration defense spending in the mid-1980s; they are fond of Pentagon "whistle-blowers" and critics of waste; and in 1986 they spurred plans for reorganizing the Pentagon.

Other congressional panels get into the act. Because defense spending is the largest controllable segment of the yearly federal budget, appropriations committees and subcommittees exert detailed control over foreign and defense policies. Senate and House oversight committees review intelligence activities. Tariffs and other trade regulations are the province of the taxing committees (House Ways and Means, Senate Finance). Banking committees handle international financial and monetary policies. President Reagan's request for $100 million in aid for the Nicaraguan *contras* was voted on by four committees (Appropriations, Armed Services, Foreign Affairs, Select Intelligence) before it reached the House floor.

The profusion of congressional power centers leads chief executives to contend that they don't know whom to consult when crises arise and that leaks of sensitive information are likely with so many players. In fact, however, chief executives are free to consult with as few or as many lawmakers as they like—in some cases with only the joint party leaders, in others with chairmen of the relevant committees (Armed Services, Foreign Affairs/Relations, Select Intelligence).

The Ebb and Flow of Power

If the Constitution invites the president and Congress to struggle over control of policy, nowhere is that fight more overt than in foreign affairs. Relations between the two branches have been volatile since World War II.

The Cold War era

The closing years of World War II and the first postwar years (1943–50) were a period of *accommodation:* "Close cooperation was initiated between high-level executive officials and the committee and party leaders of Congress" (Bax, 1977). This made for a consistent postwar policy: It permitted speedy approval of unprecedented American treaty and aid pledges; it kept foreign policy out of partisan politics. This was the era of bipartisanship. Two Capitol Hill statesmen, Senators Arthur H. Vandenberg (R–Mich.) and Tom Connally (D–Tex.), chaired the Senate Foreign Relations Committee during that time.

During the next years, a period of *antagonism* (1950–53), partisan squabbling broke out over the "loss" of China to the Communists, the Korean War, and Truman's dismissal of World War II hero General Douglas MacArthur.

With Eisenhower's election (1953), a period of *acquiescence* set in. A national consensus favored the policy of containment—keeping communism within its existing borders. Congress got into the habit of ratifying the president's plans; it cut marginal amounts from program budgets but generally supported presidential initiatives. This period lasted beyond Eisenhower's terms and into the 1960s. The high-water mark occurred in 1964, when Johnson persuaded Congress to approve the Gulf of Tonkin Resolution, a vague grant of authority to act in Southeast Asia. The next year, Johnson began escalating the Vietnam effort without further consultation with Congress.

Controversy over Vietnam brought a period of *ambiguity* (1967–70), with questioning and uneasiness. Nixon's invasion of Cambodia in 1970, done without consulting Congress, launched a period of *acrimony* (1970–76), marked by disputes over Vietnam and almost every other phase of foreign policy.

The post-Vietnam era

In 1975, American participation in the Vietnam War was halted by action of Congress. Since then, Congress has shown little desire to follow blindly wherever the president leads. I.M. Destler (1981: 167) described the 1970s changes:

Grenada oversight. In 1983, U.S. troops invaded the island of Grenada in order to end military rule there and to expel Cuban military advisers. Here, Rep. Louis Stokes (D–Ohio) shares C rations with a soldier during a congressional fact-finding tour of Grenada.

The congressional revolution against presidential foreign policy dominance began as a revolt against the people, ideas, and institutions held responsible for the Vietnam War debacle. In terms of its objectives, this revolution was highly successful. Congress reined in the president and constrained the use of military and paramilitary power. It also elevated policy goals the executive had neglected such as human rights and nuclear nonproliferation.

This congressional activism survived the Reagan era, which witnessed a level of foreign intervention that had not been seen since the period before the Vietnam War. Reagan launched the Grenada invasion in 1983 and a military strike at Libya in 1986—acts authorized swiftly and without the prior consultation envisioned in the 1973 War Powers Resolution. The struggle continued over such Reagan initiatives as MX missiles, "Star Wars" research (the Strategic Defense Initiative), aid to anticommunist "freedom fighters," and Middle East arms sales. For its part, Congress pulled the president toward arms control talks, human rights activism (especially in South Africa), and trade protection for certain domestic industries.

After the Iran-*contra* affair

Reagan's foreign policy influence was already on the wane when the Iran-*contra* scheme surfaced late in 1986. The scandal undermined the president's image of firmness in dealing with terrorists and in managing his own administration. It also eroded the sense of trust and deference that members of Congress tend to harbor toward the president, even of the opposite party.

The Reagan administration's command of foreign policy weakened still further in the wake of the Iran-*contra* affair. The need to shore up public confidence propelled the president to conclude wide-ranging arms reduction agreements with the Soviet Union, which he had once condemned as "the evil empire." Aid to the Nicaraguan *contras* was virtually abandoned, and indeed Democratic Speaker Jim Wright (Tex.) moved into the vacuum and assumed leadership on the issue. Congress assumed an aggressive posture on a wide range of foreign policy issues.

When pressed by circumstances, presidents tend to act as they see fit, holding Congress at arm's length and trusting that success will stifle its criticism. On the other side, Congress is unwilling to yield its renewed powers. Thus, the delicate balance of power continues.

Makers of foreign policy are not totally free to set the nation's course with other nations. The basic goals and resources, as we outlined, are the raw materials from which foreign policy is fashioned. Policymakers are also held back by factors from the political arena: public attitudes and opinions, media coverage, interest-group actions, and electoral politics.

THE POLITICAL BACKDROP

Public Opinion and Foreign Policy

International relations are not solely the province of professional diplomats. Regardless of government forms, diplomacy takes place in a context of public tolerance or disapproval. People will not commit resources or make sacrifices unless they understand overall goals. Policies gain added support if they are seen as right and legitimate. Proclaiming the reasons for forming a new nation, the Declaration of Independence was written "with a decent respect to opinions of mankind"; today public opinion plays an even greater role in global politics.

Volatile views

However important as a foundation for the conduct of policy, the public's views on foreign affairs tend to be poorly formed, lacking depth, and hence highly volatile.

"The majority of Americans," according to a respected study (Katz et al., 1954: 35), "are not interested in foreign affairs as such, as they appear to take an interest only in those problems clearly affecting their own interests." Recent studies verify that citizens show more interest in local or national events than in events in other countries or even U.S. relations with those countries. The top foreign policy goals, as seen by citizens, are those that strike at the home front: protecting American workers' jobs, keeping up the dollar's value, and maintaining energy supplies. Lagging somewhat behind are such goals as worldwide arms control, containing communism, combating world hunger, and defending our allies (Reilly, 1983: 8–13).

A general feeling exists that we should "keep the country out of war" while at the same time "maintaining a strong defense posture." Although a majority of Americans support the country's active involvement in world affairs, the commitment to internationalism has eroded since the post–World War II period (Reilly, 1983: 11–14).

To the extent that people view foreign events, they tend to do so simplistically. Lacking historical background, they tend to see events as episodic, as separate and unrelated happenings. They think that events are caused by good or evil individuals—a Stalin or a Churchill, a Kissinger or an Ayatollah Khomeini. They see the nation's vital interest as resting with the countries most visible to them: Japan, Canada, Great Britain, Saudi Arabia, West Germany, Israel, and Mexico (Reilly, 1983: 16–17).

At the level of specifics, most people have scant understanding of the techniques, methods, or issues of foreign policy. After several years of elite debate over policy toward the Sandinista regime in Nicaragua and in the midst of a fierce Capitol Hill debate over aiding the *contras,* surveys revealed that people were unsure what the issues were or which side they were on. Only 38 percent knew which side the Reagan administration backed.

Because of inattention and scanty information, Americans' foreign policy views are subject to changes in mood (Almond, 1960). Even during global crises, private and domestic affairs—for example, jobs, inflation, and crime—have a strong pull on public attention and loyalty. Mass publics lack personal experience or stable beliefs to anchor their commitments and are therefore susceptible to guidance from the president or other visible foreign policy leaders. Many people seem disposed to follow American policy wherever it may lead: "My country, right or wrong."

Foreign policy elites

Mass opinion may be unstable, but the views of informed elites, attentive publics, are given disproportionate weight by decision makers (Almond, 1960). The White House and the State Department cannot ignore mass opinion. Yet, on a daily basis, they deal mainly with foreign policy elites.

Elites are roughly defined as the people who inform themselves about world developments. They regularly read the *New York Times* or some major metropolitan journal; they belong to such organizations as the Council on Foreign Relations (a New York–based group with numerous local chapters) or the League of Women Voters; they travel abroad or attend conferences on global questions; they have business or professional stakes in worldwide developments; they perceive a wider range of pressing international issues than does the general public, and they are far more committed to internationalism. Most important, they express their views in letters or statements to newspapers, journals, Congress, and other key groups.

At the heart of foreign policy elites is a fairly well-defined bipartisan group of businesspeople, lawyers, and scholars who are centered in, but not limited to, the international trading centers of the Northeast and the West Coast. A majority of high-level diplomats and makers of foreign policy—and nearly every secretary of state since World War II, regardless of party—have come from this group.

As with so many phases of American life, foreign policy elites have become broader and more diverse. Diplomats are no longer picked from the upper social stratum or a few selective schools. Persons from centrist, establishment groups such as the Council on Foreign Relations are being matched by representatives of "think tanks" (scholarly research organizations) from the left and right wings and of grass-roots groups like the nuclear freeze movement. As the Council's president recently conceded, "It's no longer the case where you can get everybody important in foreign policy together in one room in New York" (Bernstein, 1982: 29).

Foreign Affairs in the Mass Media

Communications media help shape foreign policy views. However, most newspapers, journals, and electronic media give less time or space to foreign developments than to news closer to home. They assume that readers or viewers prefer it that way.

Moreover, foreign stories are very costly to gather and relay. Consequently, despite advances in recent years, most news outfits are understaffed in foreign capitals. (The *New York Times* is by far the most ambitious: it has 34 reporters in 27 foreign bureaus and a foreign desk of 26 people, and it spends more than $10 million a year gathering foreign news.) Most newspapers, if they try at all, simply dispatch a few ill-prepared reporters on this assumption: "Send them in with a parachute and you can do some stories your second day there and as you go on, they'll get better" (Shaw, 1986: 14). Vast areas of the world are untouched by even such coverage.

Television, on which a majority of people rely for news, is especially thin in covering foreign affairs. A common complaint of critics is that "television news only does stories about foreign countries when there's a war or some other violent crisis going on" (Bedell, 1982). Thus, TV coverage of military clashes, terrorist actions, and ceremonial events overshadows its treatment of complex underlying factors.

As a result, reporting tends to be episodic—focusing on specific events and paying little attention to long-range trends or developments (Cohen, 1965). Anyone who follows international affairs through the mass media gains a strobe-light view of the world—people and events are seen in a jerky, uncoordinated way. The Ethiopian famine, for example, seemed to happen overnight. After the TV networks procured a poignant BBC–TV tape on the subject, suddenly TV cameras were everywhere in that nation. When the networks discovered South African violence, they displayed it prominently on nightly newscasts. The film coverage ceased when the South African government banned the cameras. Although clashes continued between the South African government and the country's majority black population, they rarely appeared on the world's TV screens. It was as if a switch had been turned on and then turned off just as quickly.

Lacking adequate resources for covering foreign news, the media normally rely on official news sources—the president, the secretaries of state and defense, and other government sources. The "official line" thus forms the basis for most media stories on foreign and military matters. Reporting also relies on *stereotypes* to help public understanding. These simplified views of reality sometimes distort the truth. Some less developed nations, for instance, think that Western media convey negative images of their countries, so they have imposed strict limits on news coverage of their affairs.

Interest-Group Involvement

The powerful groups that dominate domestic policy-making have become increasingly vocal in foreign affairs. That is because the bread-and-butter issues motivating their members are now ensnared by world economic, social, and political developments. Thus, structural issues—in trade, finance, arms sales, weapons procurement—involve business, labor, and professional lobbies much as do domestic areas. In crisis or strategy issues, however, fewer groups speak out.

Structural issues

Interest groups are more alert to structural (distributive) aspects of foreign relations. When global affairs impinge on their jobs or profits, they are vocal and determined. In industries hard pressed by foreign competition—shoes, textiles, steel, electronics, and automobiles—business and labor band together to lobby for quotas or other restrictions. "Tougher" stands against foreign trade restriction and so-called unfair foreign competition are urged by labor unions and firms in such industries, backed up by politicians from hard-hit regions.

In contrast, multinational or leading-edge firms such as IBM are eager to sell their goods and services overseas and favor lower trade barriers. Since the 1960s, such firms have pressed the nation to adopt a policy of reducing trade restrictions (Bauer, Pool, and Dexter, 1963). Today the president's trade representative and other officials expend much effort in opening foreign markets for American investment and sales.

Major defense and aerospace contracting firms favor higher defense spending and are active advocates for the weapons systems that they build. Unions in such firms usually agree with management, because jobs are at stake.

Another source of income for firms of this kind is international arms sales (called *transfers*). These are often more lucrative than sales to the government. Hence, industry has a lively interest in arms sales, often financed by U.S. aid or loans (Sampson, 1977). U.S. firms are also vigorous lobbyists in foreign capitals, using a variety of tactics, including bribery, to sell their wares.

Ethnic and racial politics

Ethnic groups are another potent force in foreign policy. The United States is a nation of immigrants, with citizens from almost every nation it deals with. And this has a policy impact. For example, groups representing areas in Eastern Europe—Poles, Czechs, Slovenians, and others—observe patriotic days and support publicity efforts, such as Captive Nations Week, that oppose Soviet domination of these areas. President Ford remarked in the second TV debate of the 1976 campaign that Eastern Europe was not under Soviet rule; ethnic groups with ties to those countries were among the first to protest. Greek interests, led by friendly members of Congress, succeeded for a time in cutting off foreign aid to Turkey because of Turkey's incursion in Cyprus.

America's support of Israel since its creation in 1948 flows from many factors. A major factor is the presence of active Jewish communities in large cities in such key states as New York, Illinois, and California. Politicians in these areas understand Jewish support for Israel; New York mayors have been known to snub Arab visitors. One of the most successful lobbies in the nation's capital is the American Israel Political Action Committee (AIPAC), which has cultivated politicians of both parties to garner aid and other benefits for Israel.

Ethnic and racial groups exert influence insofar as they can mobilize domestic support for their interests abroad. "The 'secret weapon' of ethnic interest groups," wrote former Senator Charles McC. Mathias, Jr. (R–Md.) (1981: 996), "is . . . the ability to galvanize for specific objectives in the strong emotional bonds of large numbers of Americans to their cultural or ancestral homes."

Strategic issues

Many groups focus on specific policies, but only a small number of groups pay attention to the larger issues of global or military strategy. Some organizations study problems and issue reports. Examples are the Council on Foreign Relations and the League of Women Voters. Scholarly specialists keep track of issues within their frame of reference and are sometimes called on to advise the government. In the 1970s, a group called the Trilateral Commission was created. Sponsored by New York business interests and with members from Europe, Japan, and the United States (hence the name), it is a forum for policy papers and talks on foreign policy affecting economically developed nations.

A number of citizens' groups have taken up the causes of disarmament and human rights. The nuclear freeze movement helped to promote arms limitation talks and limit defense spending. Church groups with worldwide ties through missionaries and coreligionists have been active in such issues as South African apartheid, Central American refugees, and Middle East-

Beleaguered president. Lyndon Johnson's successes in the early years of his presidency were undone by the growing unpopularity of American involvement in the Vietnam War. President Johnson is shown working in the Oval Office of the White House.

ern affairs. Needless to say, groups are to be found on both sides of these controversies. Though interest groups are entering foreign policy arenas in ever-increasing numbers, most of them focus on particular aspects of foreign policy rather than its global dimensions.

Electoral Politics and Foreign Policy

Foreign policy issues often affect election outcomes. Eisenhower's 1952 campaign was helped by dislike of the Korean War and Truman's "appeasement" of communism. A military man, Eisenhower promised, "I shall go to Korea" to inspect the situation. He inspired confidence and acted quickly to end the war. Campaigning for the presidency in 1960, Kennedy charged that the Republican White House had lagged behind the Russians in weapons, causing a dangerous "missile gap," and promised to "get America moving again."

Eight years later, the Democrats lost out largely because of the Vietnam War; this split the Democratic party, forced Johnson to retire, and helped elect Kennedy's former opponent, Nixon. Carter's failure to end the Iranian hostage crisis helped cause his falling public ratings and his 1980 defeat.

Beyond the intrusion of international events, presidential elections can be affected by foreign policy issues as tactical factors. First, foreign policy stands can mobilize activists—for example, in such "litmus-test" issues as Nicaragua, support for Israel, or arms control. Second, presidential candidates' qualities are measured against international challenges. While presidential contenders typically arise out of domestic politics, once they are nominated they are assessed in terms of their presumed experience, toughness, and judgment. Finally, presidential campaigns tend to reinforce widely held stereotypes of the two political parties. Republicans are seen as strong on national defense and tough in dealing with the Soviets. Democrats are seen as more successful in trade issues and keeping defense spending under control. Whether true or not, these themes are staples of presidential rhetoric.

Bipartisanship

Bipartisanship in foreign policy has always had its advocates; occasionally it has come close to being official policy. According to the canon of **bipartisanship,** "politics stops at the water's edge." To ensure unity in dealing with foreign powers, it is argued, leaders of both parties should support the president's initiatives and should not question major foreign policy tenets in political campaigns. Needless to say, incumbent presidents and their advisers are among the most enthusiastic fans of bipartisanship.

Bipartisanship flourished in the post–World War II years; Truman consulted such GOP stalwarts as Senator Arthur H. Vandenberg (R.–Mich.) on the United Nations and on such postwar aid programs as the Marshall Plan and Point Four. Bipartisanship broke down in the 1950–53 period. Blamed for this were the Korean War, reverses in China, and propaganda by the GOP's right wing, mainly Senator Joseph R. McCarthy (R–Wis.). After Eisenhower's 1952 election, bipartisanship was again the order of the day. Democratic leaders such as Senator Walter F. George (D–Ga.) played Vandenberg's role of "loyal opposition" during the Eisenhower era.

Bipartisanship was one of the Vietnam War's many casualties. The war escalated while its purposes or outcomes were still obscure. Bitter debates broke out between the two parties and within Johnson's own party. People asked whether post–World War II bipartisanship had not blurred controversy and kept dissenting views from being aired.

In fact, bipartisanship has through the years been the exception, not the rule. In almost every generation, there have been bitter foreign policy debates. These have involved war and peace, tariffs, relations with major powers, neutrality versus intervention, and many other issues. Except for World War II, all of our declared wars (plus undeclared ones such as the Civil War, Korea, and Vietnam) have been as bitterly fought in political arenas as on the battlefields.

Military hardware. Defense spending is used to maintain military bases and to buy such equipment as these F–15 fighter aircraft. Defense contracts for military hardware, built in factories around the nation, tend to be politically attractive locally. These aircraft are flying by Mount Ranier in echelon formation.

Local issues

In local campaigns, broad-scale strategic issues intrude only on occasion. Yet structural issues often come up. These involve government spending, location of facilities or personnel, or ethnic or racial problems. In these instances, foreign and defense policies blend with domestic policies.

In ethnic or racial enclaves, politicians learn to stress the hopes of local groups. At public functions in ethnic neighborhoods, New York City candidates are seen eating dollops of Polish, Greek, Middle Eastern, and other ethnic specialities. They down such traditional dishes as knishes and blintzes, tamales, ham hocks and chitlins, pizza and ices. More important, they voice the international concerns of ethnic and racial groups.

Elective officials whose districts have defense plants or major contractors boost measures that will assure jobs and prosperity. The late L. Mendel Rivers (D–S.C.), chairman of the House Armed Services Committee, whose hometown included the Charleston Navy Yard among other defense facilities, used to campaign on the slogan "Rivers Delivers!"

Not all projects are welcomed with open arms. Installations with adverse environmental, esthetic, or security effects are increasingly scrutinized and resisted by local communities. The phenomenon is called NIMBY—"Not in my back yard!" The major drawback of the MX missile, in fact, was an awkward basing mode that no communities wanted near them; finally, it was decided to adapt existing missile silos to accommodate the MX—a questionable compromise.

Day-to-day foreign policy emissaries are neither in the White House nor on Capitol Hill. They are in the "permanent government," agencies with ongoing missions for implementing policy. With blurred lines between foreign and domestic policy, almost every federal agency gets into the act sooner or later. The chief foreign policy actors are found in the White House, the Department of State, the Department of Defense, and the intelligence community.

THE FOREIGN POLICY BUREAU-CRACIES

We can learn from watching the push and pull of the various foreign policy bureaucracies, each with different traditions, missions, and information sources (Allison, 1971). Some analysts believe that bureaucratic rivalry is all there is to executive-branch foreign policy, that there is no single, identifiable foreign policy for the country (Allison and Halperin, 1972). Yet the bureaucracies work in an atmosphere affected, if not controlled, by the president, Congress, and public opinion, however vague these publics' preferences may be on specific foreign policy problems.

The Department of State

The nation's foreign office is the Department of State. Its yearly budget ($2.5 billion) and size (fewer than 24,000 employees) rank it among the smaller cabinet departments. Yet it oversees relations with more than 150 independent nations and more than 50 international organizations. Couriers hand-carry documents some 10 million miles a year among its almost 300 diplomatic outposts overseas. Its command post is on the seventh floor of its huge Washington headquarters. From there, the secretary and aides scan incoming cables, communicate with embassies abroad, and monitor crises as they unfold.

How State is organized

The department is organized both by geography and by function. Basic operations are handled by five regional bureaus: African Affairs, European Affairs, East Asian and Pacific Affairs, Inter-American Affairs, and Near Eastern and South Asian Affairs. (A separate bureau works with international organizations.) Within each of the bureaus, country desks keep contact with each of the nations in its region.

The chain of command for a country such as India starts with the ambassador and the country team in our embassy in the capital, New Delhi.

State Department head-quarters in the "Foggy Bottom" neighborhood of Washington, D.C.

From there, it moves to Washington, where it goes first to the "Indian desk," then to the assistant secretary, then to the secretary, and finally to the president.

Superimposed upon this traditional organization is a trend toward functional bureaus and offices that cut across geographic lines. These include Educational and Cultural Affairs, Economic and Business Affairs, Politico-Military Affairs, Security and Consular Affairs, Protocol, and Congressional Relations. The Policy Planning Staff provides overall strategic and policy advice.

The Foreign Service

The heart of the State Department's staff is the diplomatic corps—about 4,000 foreign service officers (FSOs) who serve traditional diplomatic functions. Created in 1924, the Foreign Service was for many years a small, elite corps of high-status people. FSOs were integrated with allied civil service workers in 1954, and in 1980 the career system was speeded up to broaden representation. The new system may have further democratized Foreign Service, but not without a loss of morale and, many would say, specialized skills.

Embassies

Ambassadors are the president's representatives to foreign governments. Two thirds of all ambassadors are FSOs; the rest are private citizens or wealthy campaign contributors who can afford the high cost of diplomatic life in foreign capitals. President Reagan courted criticism from foreign

PRACTICE OF POLITICS

A Visit to the State Department: How We Keep Watch on the Turks

For every country, the State Department has a desk officer who is tied to various bureaucratic sources of information. The desk officer for Turkey is located in the department's office for Southeast Europe, which includes Greece, Turkey, and Cyprus. He is charged with knowing everything that is going on in Turkey and explaining it all to anyone who asks.

This desk officer talks to members of Congress and their staffs who want to know the latest news about Turkey. Through them, he keeps track of views on Capitol Hill. He gives bankers a "risk assessment" for Turkey when they call (which is often), getting in return information on Turkey's financial standing. He is constantly in touch with officials at the Turkish Embassy, listening to their complaints and learning about their policies.

The desk officer speaks Turkish fluently and reads Turkish newspapers, keeps up with media coverage of Turkey, attends social events, and reads all of the cables from the U.S. Embassy in Ankara, Turkey's capital. He also keeps up with scholarly writings on Turkey. Every week, he contributes to his office's memorandum on developments in southeast Europe.

At the other end of the desk officer's cables is the U.S. ambassador in Ankara. Although U.S. ambassadors do little independent policy-making, relying instead on directives from Washington, they have two advantages that flow from the superpower status of the United States: they usually have quick access to top government officials in their host country, and they are in constant touch with Washington via the department's sophisticated cable and satellite communications network.

Source: Adapted from Joanne Omang, "Expert Eyes Keep Watch on the Turks," *Washington Post*, July 7, 1983, pp. A1, A16.

policy professionals because 41 percent of his chief-of-mission appointments came from outside the State Department.

Since foreign policy spills over into domestic affairs, many agencies keep counselors or aides in foreign countries, often attached to the mission. Military are normally assigned to the mission to monitor developments and conduct relations with allies; labor and agricultural attachés promote U.S. exports and exchange information; and so on. Forty-four of our government agencies have aides in the U.S. Embassy in London. At one point, 700 civilians were attached to the embassy in New Delhi; only 100 of these worked for the State Department.

Intelligence officers, masked by innocuous titles, collect information and cultivate contacts in the host country. Most of their activities are harmless; others, such as espionage and covert operations, constitute a different brand of foreign policy. While ambassadors voice our stated policies, covert activities at variance with these policies may emanate from their own embassies without their knowledge.

A department without constituency

The State Department is a constant target for critics from all sides. They snipe at State's bureaucratic complexity, convoluted procedures, slow responses, and excessive caution. Successive presidents have despaired of getting prompt, decisive action from the State Department. "Damn it, Bundy, I get more done in one day in the White House than they do in six months at the State Department," Kennedy once said. "They never have any ideas over there . . . never come up with anything new." (Schlesinger, 1965: 406).

At the heart of the problem is lack of a strong domestic constituency. Unlike other federal departments, State has not forged strong ties with major domestic interest groups.

Clienteles are really the host goverments with which State deals abroad. Because State is absorbed in the daily challenges of comprehending and coping with these governments, its officers tend to view U.S. policy in terms of its impact or reaction abroad. A key part of a diplomat's job is conveying to superiors the likely impact of proposed policies. "Because of its traditional role in diplomacy, the State Department has come to be regarded as spokesman more for foreign viewpoints than the national interests" (Irish and Frank, 1975: 231).

Giving other nations' viewpoints will not win thanks from policymakers who want quick answers and fret about domestic interest groups and public opinion. This does not mean that the State Department is disloyal—a frequent charge during the McCarthy era of the early 1950s. Rather, it recognizes that it has a shaky political base, a fate it shares with foreign offices the world over.

Other Agencies

Several independent agencies handle key parts of our foreign policy, guided by the president and the secretary of state.

Foreign aid

The International Development Cooperation Agency, an umbrella agency, is responsible for development aid to other nations. Its major component, the Agency for International Development (AID), gives out nonmilitary assistance—economic, technological, agricultural, and humanitarian—to foreign countries. Another component is the Overseas Private Investment

Corporation (OPIC). This helps Americans make profitable investments in about 80 developing countries.

The Peace Corps, created by President Kennedy in 1961, dispatches motivated, trained volunteers to help developing nations. Its 5,200 volunteers work in 62 countries—in teaching, farming, medicine, community development, and technical jobs. Originally a separate agency, the Peace Corps is now part of ACTION, an umbrella agency for both overseas and domestic volunteer programs. Earlier Peace Corps workers were often enthusiastic and idealistic youths. Today the Peace Corps workers are more apt to be mature technicians.

Foreign aid of any kind is politically suspect, for it is often seen as a "giveaway" that benefits foreigners at the expense of our own citizens. Especially in times of high domestic unemployment or budgetary stringency, foreign aid is vulnerable to cutbacks. Presidents and their advisers, whatever their political persuasion, tend to support foreign aid because it serves foreign policy goals. Reagan, for example, though suspicious of domestic aid, supported expanded foreign aid throughout the 1980s; members of Congress, stung by cuts of their favorite domestic programs, severely cut back his proposals.

Propaganda

The U.S. Information Agency (USIA) promotes U.S. policies by distributing information. On the one hand, it informs the rest of the world about our country; on the other, it manages cultural exchanges between the United States and other countries. USIA cannot give out information at home, but it has considerable autonomy; under it, the government's information apparatus has been centralized for the first time.

USIA has branches with libraries and information centers in more than 100 countries. It produces and distributes motion pictures and other materials. Its Voice of America broadcast network beams entertainment, news, and features in 36 languages throughout the world. Its job is to portray American society and policy to its listeners. Its editorial commentaries are no longer subject to prior censorship, but they are reviewed by USIA after transmission. USIA often seeks guidance from the State Department in explaining foreign policies.

Two other radio networks inform people in other countries of developments not likely to be reported by their own press. Radio Free Europe broadcasts in six languages to five East European countries. Radio Liberty broadcasts to the Soviet Union in 16 languages. Based in Munich, these networks were launched in the early 1950s by the Central Intelligence Agency; they were divorced from it in 1971. Commentaries must follow guidelines and should avoid agitation or propaganda. They are closely monitored by officials, including a watchdog Board of International Broadcasting.

As a government propaganda outlet, USIA walks a tightrope. Although it cannot thwart government policy, it must give balanced reporting to retain credibility with audiences. The content of broadcast and other communications media is a source of lively controversy. Policymakers want to use these media to spread official policies; journalists see them as avenues of information and resent controls. A trend toward more independent programming was halted in the early 1980s by the Reagan administration, whose controversial USIA director, Charles Z. Wick, emphasized pro–United States and anti-Soviet themes.

Foreign trade

Promoting international trade carries such a high priority that the U.S. trade representative is a cabinet-level post with the rank of ambassador and a staff located in the Executive Office of the the President. The trade representative, who reports directly to the president, directs all U.S. trade negotiations and formulates overall U.S. trade policy.

The U.S. International Trade Commission is a six-person body charged with making investigations and hearing complaints about practices under customs, tariffs, and trade laws. In recent years, the commission and its staff of some 400 have been deluged with complaints from U.S. firms (now about 200 a year) about unfair competition from foreign goods—for example, that the goods are subsidized by a foreign government or are "dumped" on the U.S. market at bargain prices. If the commission finds such practices, the president may take steps to protect the domestic industry: import duties may be increased, quotas established, or "adjustment assistance" given to harmed workers, firms, or communities.

Overall responsibility for promoting trade and assisting U.S. businesses entering international markets lies with the Department of Commerce. Its International Trade Administration, headed by an under secretary, runs a number of programs to publicize U.S. goods and advise firms.

Arms control

The Arms Control and Disarmament Agency is a quasi-independent body under the aegis of the State Department. It makes and carries out arms control programs and staffs U.S. negotiations with other nations. One such negotiation was the Strategic Arms Limitation Talks (SALT) with the Soviet Union. The director of the Arms Control and Disarmament Agency reports to the president through the secretary of state. Needless to say, this agency's status rises and falls with the administration's interest in arms negotiations. It is interesting, however, that when serious arms negotiations began under the Reagan administration, a special team of negotiators was chosen, most of them outside the agency.

THE DEFENSE ESTABLISHMENT

Military preparedness is a pivotal foreign policy resource. In times of crisis, it may push aside all other foreign policy considerations. In peacetime, it is a tool for bargaining with foreign powers.

The Department of Defense

Across the Potomac River from the nation's capital stands the Pentagon. This nerve center of the defense establishment houses some 24,000 employees. It is so huge that messengers ride electric carts along its 17 miles of corridors. Like the Pentagon, everything about the Department of Defense (DOD) is big. Its budget approaches $300 billion annually. It is the nation's largest employer, with 1 million civilian employees and more than 2 million military employees.

Overseas, the Pentagon supervises 359 U.S. military bases. The U.S. military presence in all corners of the world affects the global balance of power, both economic and military.

The DOD structure

Actually, DOD is a relatively young agency. After more than 150 years of separate existence, the uniformed services were brought under the control of a single secretary of defense by the National Security Act of 1947 (amended in 1949). The Office of the Secretary of Defense handles procurement, intelligence, personnel, research, logistics and installations, and financial and systems analysis. Its foreign policy arm is the Office of International Security Affairs (ISA). It also has two intelligence organizations, the Defense Intelligence Agency (DIA) and the National Security Agency (NSA).

Another portion of the central defense apparatus is the Joint Chiefs of Staff, appointed by the president for four-year terms. These include the chiefs of staff of the three armed services and the commandant of the Marine Corps. The chairman of the joint chiefs is appointed by the president to a two-year term, with one renewal. The staff is drawn equally from the various services.

The joint chiefs have two overall roles. One is giving military advice to the president, the secretary of defense, the National Security Council, and Congress. The other is supervising the four combatant commands—in readiness, capabilities, and planning. The challenge for the joint chiefs and their staff is to speak for the whole military and resist the strong pull of their individual services. Reformers would like to strengthen the joint chiefs and their staffs and underscore their independence from the individual services.

Interservice rivalries

Within DOD, the independent services are represented through separate Departments of the Army, Air Force, and Navy (including the Marine Corps). Each of these departments is headed by a civilian secretary and assistant secretaries. Military operations are the responsibility of the respective chiefs of staff.

The history of DOD has been a struggle to coordinate the various ser-

PRACTICE OF POLITICS

A Visit to the Pentagon

The Pentagon, the world's largest office building, stands across from the nation's capital in Virginia. It was begun in August 1941, on the eve of World War II. When Japan attacked Pearl Harbor four months later, construction was accelerated. Working three shifts around the clock, 10,000 workers had the first offices ready for occupancy on April 20, 1942. Because there was a war on, the building was never formally dedicated.

The Pentagon is still awesome, after nearly a half century. It covers 29 acres. It has 6.5 million square feet of floor space—three times that of the Empire State Building. The U.S. Capitol could be placed inside one of its five sections.

The building's 24,000 employees can choose among two restaurants, six cafeterias, nine beverage bars, and an outdoor snack bar. They can drink from 685 water fountains and check their schedule from 5,400 clocks. In the basement are a post office and a shopping mall.

All of this may sound excessive, yet the Defense Department is cramped for space. A massive Navy Department building sits on a hill overlooking the Pentagon. And scores of buildings around Washington house Defense Department workers, not to mention the workers of the department's thousands of private contractors.

Source: Adapted from Michael J. Brennan, "A Five-Star Tour of the Pentagon," *Washington Post*, February 5, 1988. See also the engaging account in David Brinkley, *Washington Goes to War* (New York: Alfred A. Knopf, 1988).

army and navy radio equipment was incompatible. In one instance, an army officer slipped into a phone booth and used his AT&T credit card to call on a civilian line to Fort Bragg, North Carolina, so that his request could be relayed to the navy. This was the most quoted story from the Grenadan operation.

With mounting evidence of inefficiency and increased pressure on defense spending, in 1986 the armed services panels on Capitol Hill passed a wide-ranging measure to reorganize the military chain of command. The Joint Chiefs of Staff would be strengthened, and the chairman would be the military adviser to the president, with authority to state his position whether or not the four services had reached unanimous agreement. Theater commanders (in the Atlantic and Pacific regions, for example) would have more authority to train and supervise their troops, regardless of which service they came from. And to counter horror stories about inefficient weapons buying, a weapons "czar" would be appointed to oversee procurement.

Military–civilian relations

Another aspect of DOD's structure is the relation between military officers and civilians. Our country is dedicated to civilian control, exercised by the president as commander in chief and transmitted through the secretary of defense and other presidential appointees.

Truman's dismissal of World War II hero General Douglas MacArthur for insubordination during the Korean War spectacularly illustrated this principle. At the time, surveys showed that twice as many people supported MacArthur as supported Truman. Early in his term, Jimmy Carter recalled and reassigned two army generals for making statements that went beyond administration policies.

Nevertheless, military officers are at the vortex of the defense establishment. They are, of course, experts in combat techniques and weapons capabilities. They are looked to as experienced military tacticians. An unmistakable mystique surrounds people who have fought an enemy on a battlefield and who display the brass and ribbons to prove it. Many armchair warriors in the Pentagon and in Congress are bedazzled by military brass. They sometimes adopt positions more favorable to the military than those advocated by the officers themselves. Service and veterans' groups also promote the military viewpoint within bureaucracy and in public arenas.

The Military–Industrial Complex

The vast bulk of defense spending goes for structural policies or programs. Defense has about $200 billion to spend on procurement each year—a figure that escalated in the 1980s. The rest of the defense budget goes mostly for personnel.

Defense spending, in other words, is tightly linked to the nation's economy. Supporters of such spending include firms with defense contracts, labor unions in defense industries, towns benefiting from contracts or installations, and congressmen from those locales. Competing interests are part of the reason for abuses in the Pentagon procurement system: cost overruns, $600 toilet seats, defective tank engines, and write-offs of excessive overhead and lobbying costs.

In his farewell speech, President Eisenhower, a five-star general himself, warned against the "unwarranted influence" of what he called the **military-industrial complex.** Said Eisenhower (1961: 616): "The conjunction of an immense military establishment and a large arms industry is new in the American experience. The total influence—economic, political, even spiritual—is felt in every city, every statehouse, every office of the federal government."

Defense influence has skyrocketed since then, fulfilling Eisenhower's fears that the enormity of the defense apparatus would embed itself in the nation's economic and political structure and voraciously consume the nation's resources. Military budgets, now several times what they were in the 1950s, carry an aura of urgency and necessity that makes them hard to oppose. After the Vietnam War, the defense share of the federal budget went down some. Lacking a "hot war," or fears brought on by the Cold War, military preparedness lost some of its urgency. By the 1980s, a bipartisan consensus favored defense spending hikes to close gaps and meet threats around the world; but President Reagan's hikes were so steep that many legislators, fearing the effect on deficits, forced somewhat slower growth. By the mid-1980s, the consensus for higher defense spending had dissipated.

THE INTELLIGENCE COMMUNITY

"Nothing is more necessary and useful for a general than to know the intentions and projects of the enemy," wrote Niccolò Machiavelli in *The Prince,* a 16th-century tract on politics. Covert efforts to pinpoint enemy plans and resources have always played a part in military strategy. Washington organized a spy system during the Revolutionary War; spies have been vital in every war since then. During World War II, President Roosevelt created the Office of Strategic Services (OSS). This cloak-and-dagger outfit performed a whole range of covert activities—espionage, sabotage, intelligence, and counterintelligence.

The Central Intelligence Agency

The Central Intelligence Agency (CIA), successor to the wartime OSS, was formed by the National Security Act of 1947, as amended in 1949. Its "charter," or mandate, was vague, an omission subsequently viewed as regrettable. It was planned to coordinate the various intelligence agencies, including those of State, Defense, and the Atomic Energy Commission.

The CIA's heyday

Under a series of tough-minded directors, the CIA became a prime instrument of the Cold War crusade against communism. As we now know, the agency was also conducting its own brand of foreign policy. At times, this was at variance with stated U.S. policy and outside the boundaries of the agency's charter.

The CIA employs about 15,000 people and spends perhaps $10 billion a year. Its headquarters stand in a wooded area near Langley, Virginia, across the Potomac from Washington. Its Intelligence Directorate conducts research and collects overt information. Its Operations Directorate collects information secretly (espionage). The CIA has also engaged in secret political warfare, which has brought it controversy and notoriety.

Central Intelligence Agency (CIA) headquarters, in Langley, Virginia, across the Potomac River from Washington, D.C. The CIA acted under minimal supervision for its first two decades, underwent criticism and review in the mid-1970s, and now seems to be flying high again.

The CIA enjoys unusual autonomy and freedom from outside scrutiny, even though it is responsible to the National Security Council and then to the president (who appoints the CIA's director and deputy director). Until the late 1970s, it was virtually exempt from congressional oversight. Irish and Frank (1975: 487) state: "From its inception, the CIA has operated on its own terms with minimum public exposure and congressional oversight. The agency does whatever it does silently and secretly. It never publicizes, admits, or denies the range of its activities. Its budget is buried in numerous departmental estimates, and its personnel are covertly dispersed through various front organizations."

Doubts and reversals

Nothing in the CIA's charter suggests that it was to intervene in affairs of foreign countries, much less conduct covert military operations. By the 1960s, however, spotty reports of its activities began to surface in the press. In some foreign countries, the CIA became a sinister symbol of U.S. power. Arthur M. Schlesinger, Jr. (1965: 427), wrote that by the mid-1960s the CIA budget exceeded that of the State Department by 50 percent; CIA operatives outnumbered State's in many embassies. "The root fear," explained Roger Hilsman (1967: 64–65), "was that the CIA represented . . . a state within a state, and certainly the basis for fear was there."

By the mid-1970s, revelations of CIA operations had damaged its credibility. It had sponsored a series of thrusts at foreign powers, including the overthrow of some regimes. Assassination plots against foreign leaders were uncovered. The CIA had also spied on American citizens at home. This violated its charter's prohibition of domestic activities. It had infiltrated antiwar and other dissident groups; it used dozens of foundations and private groups as fronts, subsidizing even the National Students Association (Wise, 1976).

It was further revealed that the CIA had helped a White House group later dubbed the "plumbers" (because they fixed leaks). The plumbers burglarized a psychiatrist's office to obtain records on Daniel Ellsberg, a former NSC aide who had turned against the Vietnam War and leaked the secret Pentagon Papers (detailing the Vietnam involvement) to the press. Later Nixon tried to enlist the CIA in his efforts to stop the FBI from probing the Watergate burglary, in which zealous Nixon operatives broke into Democratic headquarters during the 1972 presidential campaign.

These revelations, special inquiries by House and Senate committees, and a high-level executive report caused President Ford to revise the CIA's procedures in 1976. Two years later, President Carter sought to rehabilitate the agency by giving it a coordinating role within the intelligence community and permitting CIA spying. The latter was to be done only with specific approval.

New restrictions and reporting requirements were intended to focus the agency's mission and increase control. The agency, for example, is now required to keep the House and Senate Intelligence committees "fully and currently informed" about its activities. Apparently, this requirement is not always honored. As one Hill staffer remarked, the CIA director "wouldn't tell you if your coat was on fire—unless you asked him" (Lardner, 1984).

Unleashed again—and tethered

In the 1980s, the CIA's fortunes turned again. As the Cold War warmed up and U.S.-Soviet relations cooled off, concern over the nation's intelligence capacity grew. Stronger CIA directors were appointed; many of the 1970s restrictions on the CIA's activities were relaxed; its budget was tripled.

But the revitalized CIA was soon jolted by a new generation of setbacks (Walcott, 1987). A public furor greeted the disclosure that the CIA had helped mine harbors to aid the administration's drive against Nicaragua's leftist government. The agency's role in the Iran-*contra* fiasco came under fire. Failures to share information with the congressional intelligence panels had adverse effects. Finally, the intelligence community, like other government agencies, was forced to fight for funds during the budget crunch. Like other agencies, the CIA prospers or suffers with the political climate.

Other Agencies

The CIA is the keystone of the intelligence community, but it is by no means the only participant. In fact, 40 or more government agencies do intelligence work, with funding that has risen steadily and now amounts to some $24 billion a year (the figures are secret).

Under a 1978 reorganization, the 11 chief members of the intelligence community, in addition to the CIA, are the National Security Agency (NSA); the Defense Intelligence Agency (DIA); army, navy, and air force intelligence operations; the State Department's Bureau of Intelligence and Research; the Federal Bureau of Investigation; the Drug Enforcement Administration; and the Treasury and Energy departments.

Intelligence is a minor part of some of these organizations in dollars or personnel. Yet their intelligence concerns—from terrorism to nuclear safety to narcotics traffic—are important in terms of the government's overall responsibilities. The agencies are supposed to cooperate with one another; how much overlap or duplication results, no one knows for sure.

The Intelligence Dilemma

The exposés of recent years have not resolved the question of the proper scope of intelligence. The dilemma arises from conflicting goals.

On the one hand, most people concede that such intelligence is needed. The CIA was formed in part because policymakers wanted to avoid intelligence failures like the one that resulted in Pearl Harbor (Crabb and Holt, 1988: 25–26). In 1979, a sizable Soviet military force was belatedly found in Cuba; that same year, the United States (like most other countries) was caught by surprise when the Iranian monarchy fell.

Covert operations, on the other hand, are more controversial. Intelligence leaders, such as former CIA directors Allen Dulles and William Casey, argue that they are needed to protect the United States from a hostile world. Critics counter that they cause distrust of our policies at home and abroad and often do far more harm than good.

Secret agencies like the CIA have other drawbacks. Much of their information comes from conventional sources, but they are sometimes tempted to rely on tips from dissidents or spies in foreign countries. This puts them at the mercy of the people whose view of the world may be biased or distorted. For instance, reports from Cuban refugees led the CIA to tell Kennedy that an invasion of Cuba would trigger an anti-Castro uprising that would liberate the island. Partly on this basis, Kennedy in 1961 proceeded with the Eisenhower-planned Bay of Pigs invasion—an action he bitterly regretted.

A more serious problem for secret agencies is their "closed" character. They lack adequate review of their plans; obviously, no public debate is involved. Hence, leaders are prone to overshoot their missions; they launch shoddy or ill-advised projects of little value. Intelligence agencies are especially vulnerable to this form of "group think" (Janis, 1983). Their operatives (and the people with whom they deal) walk in a kind of political netherworld. They have their own biased picture of what makes the world tick.

FOREIGN POLICY IN A DEMOCRACY

The debate over intelligence activities points up a larger dilemma: Can foreign policy be carried on effectively by a free and open society?

Through history, affairs between nations were carried out by a small cadre of professional diplomats acting on behalf of their chiefs of state. Elites dominated international affairs. The reason was that matters of negotiation or information gathering could not involve large numbers of people. Such matters require speed, confidence, and coherence. Also, foreign policy can demand that national resources be diverted from consumption or services to other uses with less immediate benefits. A war can mean the sacrifice of a nation's treasure or the lives of its citizens.

Some people feel that foreign policy-making is not compatible with open, discursive policy debates. Diplomatic realists feel that broad discussion hampers leaders from pursuing the nation's best interests. Hence, few of them admire former President Woodrow Wilson's goal of "open covenants openly arrived at."

No one can prove or disprove these beliefs. They are matters of faith, not empirical propositions. The Vietnam War era was not, by and large, kind to elite theorists of foreign policy-making. The war itself was a failure; executive officers convinced themselves and each other of the correctness of their premises and the viability of their methods. In theory, policymakers should tap all relevant information and select rational options. In fact, decision makers are often prisoners of biased or false data, sometimes deliberately twisted to fit the aims of those in the top posts.

A good case can be made for "multiple advocacy" in foreign policy. Here, a variety of outlooks and specialized skills are brought to bear on tough problems (George, 1972). Closed decision systems are best suited for limited objectives that are fully agreed on. But broad foreign policy objectives are by no means self-evident or easily agreed on. The marketplace of ideas, in short, is a proper setting for foreign policy-making; the policies themselves are open to debate and contention.

CONCLUSIONS

In this chapter, we explained foreign and defense policies. We also identified the major policymakers. Foreign and defense policies are closely tied to domestic problems, though often thought to be remote from them. Also, many foreign and military issues are structural (distributive). They require allocations of personnel, money, and materials that

are not very different from the allocations required for domestic politics.

1. Foreign policy, which embraces this nation's dealings with other nations, involves the pursuit of national goals and the use of national resources. Whether or not the nation realizes its

goals depends on the abundance of its resources and on its willingness to use them. Some goals are so costly that they are out of even the richest nation's reach.

2. Presidents are the chief agents in foreign affairs; they conduct diplomatic negotiations and manage day-to-day relations with other powers; they are the commanders in chief of the armed forces. Their aides must distill the viewpoints of various foreign policy agencies into usable policy advice.

3. Congress shares foreign policy powers with the president. It advises and consents to appointments and treaties; it declares war; it provides funds; and it oversees executive activities. After a period of executive dominance, Congress has, since the Vietnam War, been more active in overseeing foreign and defense policies.

4. Makers of foreign policy work against a backdrop of public opinion, media coverage, interest-group activity, and electoral politics.

5. The State Department is the prime implementer of foreign policy. It lacks a vigorous domestic constituency. Moreover, it has the thankless job of conveying foreign powers' reactions to U.S. policies.

6. The defense establishment—mainly the services embraced by the Department of Defense—oversees our global military posture. It has many ties to powerful domestic groups—business, labor, and political officials. It is not a unified community, but its economic importance lends it irresistible political leverage.

7. Intelligence agencies carry out an alternative mode of foreign policy. Although most people agree that intelligence gathering is needed, many question the advisability of covert activities involving actual intervention abroad.

FURTHER READING

AMBROSE, STEPHEN E. (1980) *Rise to Globalism: American Foreign Policy, 1938–1980.* 2nd ed. New York: Penguin Books. A readable account of recent U.S. diplomatic history.

CRABB, CECIL V., JR., and PAT M. HOLT (1988) *Invitation to Struggle: Congress, the President and Foreign Policy.* 3rd ed. Washington, D.C.: Congressional Quarterly Press. An examination of recent presidential and congressional foreign policy-making, with case studies.

FALLOWS, JAMES (1981) *National Defense.* New York: Random House. A critical review of U.S. defense policy by a prominent neoliberal and former Carter speech writer.

FRANK, THOMAS, and EDWARD WEISBAND (1979) *Foreign Policy by Congress.* New York: Oxford University Press. A study of Congress's expanded role in foreign policy, emphasizing the 1973 War Powers Resolution, lobby groups, and congressional staff growth.

HADLEY, ARTHUR T. (1986) *The Straw Giant.* New York: Random House. A readable analysis of the defense muddle, by a journalist who has made a life's work of studying it.

LAQUEUR, WALTER (1985) *A World of Secrets: The Uses and Limits of Intelligence.* A scholarly history and analysis of intelligence, its organizational problems, and its limits in a democracy.

NATHAN, JAMES A., and JAMES K. OLIVER (1983) *Foreign Policymaking and the American Political System.* Boston: Little, Brown. A good standard treatment of the politics of foreign policy.

Chapter Twenty-One

A MORE PERFECT UNION?

A SILENT REVOLUTION

A RESPONSIVE GOVERNMENT

WHAT AMERICANS EXPECT OF A MORE PERFECT UNION

TOWARD A MORE PERFECT UNION—YOUR JOB

We are in the midst of change. In a changing world, constitutions, governments, politics change. The great philosopher Diogenes wisely said, "Nothing endures but change." Adaptations of governmental institutions and political processes to change provide the dynamic for political life and make it interesting. Nothing could be more tedious and dull than the boredom of an unchanging politics, a utopian perfection in which "the ever-whirling wheel of change" has come to rest. ✍

**A SILENT
REVOLUTION**

*I*n the preceding chapters, we have recounted many of the changes taking place in the American political system, drawing attention to those that most directly affect our governing institutions and processes and that are most comprehensible to us. Yet today changes are occurring in the Western world whose impact is not easy to assess with confidence.

Technological innovations are developing at a galloping pace; we live amid an information revolution precipitated by telecommunications and computer technology. The occupational structure of American society is undergoing a transformation; fewer and fewer Americans work as farmers or industrial workers, and more and more work in the service sector, as technicians, or in the so-called knowledge industry. Economic growth and affluence have escalated; high real incomes and growing welfare programs have dramatically reduced the proportion of Americans who must be primarily concerned with their material, physical security. Education levels among Americans have been increasing exponentially; in 1940, only a fourth of all Americans had completed high school, compared to two thirds who are high school graduates today—and nearly half of *all* Americans under 35 years old are now enrolled in school. Mass media of communication are evolving in such a way as to provide virtually instant and pervasive availability of information.

The new generation of Americans has grown up in a world that, for the majority, has been affluent and secure, a world generally free from economic privation and hardship and from the insecurity and fear of war and its destruction. These Americans, and many of their older fellow citizens as well, show signs of change in the priorities they give to values. They seem to give lower priority to economic and physical security and higher priority to values that emphasize the *quality* of life. This change in priorities is evidenced by rising concern about such values as human rights and protection of the environment.

In addition to the shift toward values emphasizing the quality of life, a notable shift is taking place in the distribution of political skills. A growing proportion of the electorate shows greater sophistication about, greater understanding of, and more interest in domestic and international politics. This increase in political skills makes for a more demanding public, a public more determined to participate in political decision making. Under some circumstances, it may make citizens less willing to accept political leadership and less susceptible to being mobilized by leaders. At some times, the public may be less governable, more rancorous and contentious.

These signs of value change and growth in political skills are not fully visible yet, and important countertendencies are still at play. But perceptible trends in the United States and other Western industrial nations portend the real possibility of a "silent revolution" among Western publics that may have far-reaching political effects. Some of these effects are discernible in today's politics. New moral stances, the role of women, adequate energy resources, environmental protection, and participation in political decision making are the rising political issues of our time, at least partly displacing the older issues of material well-being, such as employment, wages, working conditions, and other facets of economic security.

The social basis of politics has shifted, as is evidenced by the decline in class voting and in the social class differences between supporters of the two major American political parties. Older concerns, related to social class conflict in politics, are no longer so important. The "new politics" reflects a more radical politics of the middle class, radiating its postmaterialist lifestyles into political affairs, and a more conservative politics of the working class, holding tenaciously to traditional values.

Public expectations about government may be undergoing a lasting change. We are told that nowadays many Americans, even among political liberals, believe that too much was expected of government in the 1960s and 1970s. Indeed, the central feature of the Reagan-era rhetoric has been the belief that government's role must be curtailed. A growing number may feel that existing governmental institutions cannot create the good and perfect society and that expectations need to be lowered. A more demanding but less expectant public may become a more dissatisfied public, a more disappointed public. As a result, government may need to learn how to operate in a less supportive environment, with a more questioning and unaccepting public, with less goodwill, in a persistently low-level crisis of legitimacy.

We cannot say that the American tradition of liberal democracy will survive forever, that it will emerge unscathed from the transformations of mass publics that are likely to occur in the future of the Western world. If we are in the midst of a silent revolution, new challenges will confront our governing institutions. There are those who seriously fear that changes in value priorities and the emerging preeminence of technology and electronics—in the "technetronic era"—will greatly strain our ways of governing. A growing fascination with technology and efficiency and feelings of futility about the capacity of government to ensure economic, cultural, and racial justice may threaten our decentralized system of politics, undermining the federal system, the loosely organized party system, and the fragmented character of congressional decision making. We may well be in for a more centralized, more nationalized governing life. Such concerns as these deserve careful consideration even though they often grow out of immense pessimism about America's future.

In a future filled with more demands on government, more demanding citizens, and a worried sense of finite limits on what the governing process can accomplish, a responsive government is more vitally needed than ever—and more difficult to sustain. A responsive government can be expected to take action on matters that are widely viewed as public problems and as proper subjects for government intervention. A responsive government will be prompt, efficient, and effective when it does act. And,

A RESPONSIVE GOVERNMENT

finally, a responsive government will show respect for the people with whom it deals and use fair, open, and efficient procedures.

Of course, judgments about responsiveness, like judgments about other aspects of governing institutions and behavior, can be very political. Different standpoints and values result in different judgments about responsiveness. National public policies change only slowly, so that people who demand quick change are apt to see the government as unresponsive, whereas those who are content with current policies are apt to see it as responsive enough.

Government has a way of being more responsive in some policy arenas than in others. Slow change is most likely in the realm of domestic policies, especially distributive policies. Government aid tends to be given to a number of special publics without sudden change. Regulatory policy is most often shaped to reduce real competition in favor of peace between the government and the regulated interests. Protective regulatory policy moves by fits and starts. Occasional bursts of governmental action are commonly tempered by weakening amendments or interpretations almost as soon as the policy is enacted. Redistributive policy only rarely results in profound redistribution. So there is a blunting in the degree to which progressive federal income tax policy "soaks the rich" or provides relief to the poor. The lot of the "have-nots" is enhanced only marginally, though that margin may be very important.

In foreign and defense policy, governmental responsiveness varies. Changes in structural matters—for instance, in the structure of the armed services—are notoriously slow, as service interests and the drag of inertia affect responses to external realities. Changes in strategic matters are fitful, often requiring time for policymakers to adjust to new information or changes of course by rivals. Responses to crises are unpredictable and may or may not result in long-run policy changes.

A responsive government does not necessarily take immediate action. In a world of complex problems and events, governments prudently deliberate over the wisdom of alternatives. Besides, it is in the nature of large-scale governing institutions to maximize the amount of decision making in a way that minimizes the potential for profound changes in public policies. Most policy changes come in small steps, only after executive incubation, legislative deliberation, and bureaucratic rulemaking. When there is a crisis, governmental responsiveness comes under sharper than usual scrutiny, but once the emergency is over, response or lack of response by government tends to fade as a salient issue. In short, we live in a world of lumbering governmental response to change, and the responsiveness of government is itself likely to be a political issue.

To say that governmental responsiveness to policy demands is slow and deliberate is not to say that the government cannot respond quickly when necessary. The government has in the past responded quickly to external threats, as when the Japanese bombed Pearl Harbor in 1941 or when the Iranians threatened international shipping by laying mines in the Persian

Gulf in 1985. But it remains true that the responsiveness of governing institutions today is shaped by changes in American society in the 1980s, the value changes of the technetronic age, and the distribution of political skills.

No political system known to human experience is guaranteed perpetuation. The men who concocted the American constitutional system probably did not expect it to endure for two centuries. Thomas Jefferson thought that the nation would be lucky if the constitution lasted a single generation. He believed that governments tend to become autocratic, that the people have to rise up against governments from time to time to preserve their liberty, that "the tree of liberty must be refreshed from time to time with the blood of patriots and tyrants."

WHAT AMERICANS EXPECT OF A MORE PERFECT UNION

The longevity of our governing institutions encourages a more optimistic view. The fundamental features of the American system adapted well to the enormous growth of territory and population that occurred in the 19th century, survived one of the bloodiest civil wars in human history, endured massive industrialization, and adjusted to the world leadership role thrust upon the United States in the 20th century. Yet the ideals of the Constitution remain what they were at the beginning: to protect freedom, provide justice, ensure domestic tranquillity, and provide for the common defense. The founders of the nation did not form a more perfect union in vain, and there is reason to believe that our constitutional system can meet the challenges of the future.

Great political skill and ingenuity will be required to meet these challenges—growing population; scarcities of resources; escalating information technology; complex problems of economic planning, land utilization, and transportation; and international pressures. Our governing apparatus will meet them most effectively if political leaders and institutions are reasonably responsive to the needs and expectations of the American people and if the people themselves take part in politics, thereby contributing to their government's ability to respond to their changing priorities in a technologically different future.

A free government adapts to the changing expectations that its people have of what it should do and how it should do it. Americans have always demanded much from their government, and they should. What they should not do is expect that one particular set of human institutions and processes—governing institutions and processes—can solve all problems, relieve all anxieties, alleviate all misery, and abolish every unfairness of life. Surely, no one set of human institutions is capable of producing heaven on earth.

But the fact that we live under an imperfect government in an imperfect world does not mean that we need despair. Americans can, and usually do, expect to live in a political system that is *participatory*. Growing proportions of Americans of all races and creeds are capable of constructive

A fragile symbol of ever-fragile liberty. Ordered by the Pennsylvania Provincial Assembly, the Liberty Bell was cast in England and delivered to Philadelphia in 1752. It carries the biblical inscription "Proclaim liberty throughout all the land unto all the inhabitants thereof." The bell cracked when it was first tested; it cracked again in 1835 while tolling the death of Chief Justice John Marshall.

participation in their nation's political life. They can reasonably expect that their participation in politics will be encouraged and fostered and that it will carry weight.

Americans expect a political system worthy of *trust*. Both those who govern and the institutions within which they work must be viewed as proceeding free of corruption and in honorable and fair ways. Governing institutions need not be unflawed robots, never making mistakes or showing human failings, for a government to be generally honest and trustworthy. On the one hand, governments ought to perform so that citizens view them as right and proper—legitimate. On the other hand, in a perpetually imperfect union it is well for citizens to remember the advice that "eternal vigilance is the price of liberty."

We are entitled to be governed by leaders and institutions that are generally *competent*. No government encourages cynicism and hostility more than one led by fools or incompetents. In a democratic society, a competent government is responsive to citizens. A competent government does what its leaders promise, but they do not promise what it cannot deliver. A competent government does what it can do as effectively as possible.

WORDS AND IDEAS

A More Perfect Union

"I stand here today as the great-grandson of a slave presiding over the fifth-largest city in this country. It points out how far we have come in this country and how far our Constitution has indeed evolved."

Source: From a speech by Mayor W. Wilson Goode at Philadelphia's party for the 200th anniversary of the Constitutional Convention.

But it does not do *everything* it could do; it does not overreach the limits that have been set on its use of coercive power. It recognizes that for some public problems the solution is worse than the problem—that the coercive power needed to solve the problem is so great that living with the problem is preferable to solving it. We might be able to solve the problem of urban poverty and homelessness by forcibly removing people from core areas of the great cities to places where there is ample employment. Such a "solution" might befit a totalitarian dictatorship, but it would not befit a competent democratic government.

Americans are entitled to governmental policies that are *equitable*. Equality has a long and honorable place in the constellation of American political beliefs. The importance of equality as an ideal has grown immensely over the course of our history, and the practice of equality has grown monumentally as well. An overwhelming majority of Americans hold an unmistakable belief in equality of opportunity for education, for work, for status, for the benefits of government, for participation in politics, for health, and for a decent standard of living. Few countries in this world provide a more pervasive equality of opportunity for a good life for their people. Nevertheless, persistent gaps remain in the opportunities available to black persons, the poor, the poorly educated, Hispanics, women, and the aged. We will continue to evaluate our governing institutions on the basis of their success in erasing inequalities in opportunity to share in the abundance and promise of American life.

Americans must expect their governing institutions and processes to provide a wide latitude of individual *liberty*. Freedom is precious, a rare and delicate blessing. Individual liberty is pervasive in America, whose citizens can live where they wish and can enjoy freedom of expression and belief. Although freedom may be buttressed by claims to the natural rights that persons have simply because they are human—the inalienable rights with which their Creator has endowed them—in practical terms liberty is won and held by vigilant men and women who demand that it be protected by their government. We should evaluate the adequacy of American government by the degree to which it jealously guards our liberties.

Finally, Americans can expect their governing institutions to be *accommodating*. We live in a multiracial and multiethnic society, in which various kinds of religious beliefs abound, in which there are many and conflicting economic interests, in which a heterogeneous population is scattered over a great continent marked by lasting differences among states and regions. A monumental task of governing in such a society as ours is to work out accommodations among divergent interests and demands so that conflicts can be peaceably resolved and we can live and work together without fear, violence, or hatred. Politics is the high calling of leaders who succeed in effecting the compromises that make possible a prosperous and peaceful nation.

These are the standards by which Americans have evaluated and ought to continue to evaluate the character of their politics and the adequacy of their government. The capacity of the governing process to adapt to an uncertain future depends on meeting these standards and on the willingness of America's people to uphold them.

TOWARD A MORE PERFECT UNION— YOUR JOB

It may not be literally true that the government of a nation is only as good as its people or that people get the kind of government they deserve. In the short run, at least, government performance or the ethical standards of some leaders can be well below what people deserve. At the same time, good government does not happen by magic.

A more perfect union for America will depend on your engagement in politics. It needs your commitment. American democracy is not a golden egg laid by some munificent goose for us to enjoy without effort. Making our governing institutions more perfect will require your participation in politics, your intelligence, your good judgment, your watchfulness and commitment, your knowledge.

It will not do to say that Americans are free to hoard their talents and vision, their knowledge and ability, their beliefs and concerns in their private worlds. Nor will it do, in the face of an uncertain future and in a complex and imperfect world, for Americans to retreat into a world of private luxury and "self-realization," taking but never giving, carping and whining about political fallibility without engaging in politics themselves. A citizen has a collective responsibility, a duty to uphold and contribute to the public interest. In a free and democratic country, politics is a great challenge. There are great things to be done, great changes to be made, in order to build a more perfect union.

The framers of the Constitution faced great uncertainties, made many mistakes, felt many inadequacies, perceived abounding complexities. They

The Statue of Liberty, a major symbol of the Union's promise. A more perfect union needs work and commitment. Scaffolding rises around the Statue of Liberty in New York Harbor as renovation begins in 1984. President Grover Cleveland unveiled and dedicated the statue on October 28, 1886. France gave the United States the 225-ton, 152-foot-high statue to commemorate 100 years of U.S. independence. The statue was rededicated in 1986.

created the foundations of a great republic. It is a legacy in which we all share. The uncertainty of change makes governing institutions the vessel in which that legacy resides. Your job, and the job of all Americans, is to take politics and government seriously, to contribute to them, to mix your talents, judgment, and goodwill with that of others in order to sustain and perfect our national inheritance and to help construct a better world for yourself and for your posterity.

APPENDIXES

The Declaration of Independence in Congress, July 4, 1776

The unanimous Declaration of the thirteen united States of America,

When in the Course of human events, it becomes necessary for one people to dissolve the political bands which have connected them with another, and to assume among the Powers of the earth, the separate and equal station to which the Laws of Nature and Nature's God entitle them, a decent respect to the opinions of mankind requires that they should declare the causes which impel them to the separation.

We hold these truths to be self-evident, that all men are created equal, that they are endowed by their Creator with certain unalienable Rights, that among these are Life, Liberty and the pursuit of Happiness. That to secure these rights, Governments are instituted among Men, deriving their just powers from the consent of the governed. That whenever any Form of Government becomes destructive of these ends, it is the Right of the People to alter or to abolish it, and to institute new Government, laying its foundation on such principles and organizing its powers in such form, as to them shall seem most likely to effect their Safety and Happiness. Prudence, indeed, will dictate that Governments long established should not be changed for light and transient causes; and accordingly all experience hath shown, that mankind are more disposed to suffer, while evils are sufferable, than to right themselves by abolishing the forms to which they are accustomed. But when a long train of abuses and usurpations, pursuing invariably the same Object evinces a design to reduce them under absolute Despotism, it is their right, it is their duty, to throw off such Government, and to provide new Guards for their future security.—Such has been the patient sufferance of these Colonies; and such is now the necessity which constrains them to alter their former Systems of Government. The history of the present King of Great Britain is a history of repeated injuries and usurpations, all having in direct object the establishment of an absolute Tyranny over these States. To prove this, let Facts be submitted to a candid world.

He has refused his Assent to Laws, the most wholesome and necessary for the public good.

He has forbidden his Governors to pass Laws of immediate and pressing importance, unless suspended in their operation till his Assent should be obtained; and when so suspended, he has utterly neglected to attend to them.

He has refused to pass other Laws for the accommodation of large districts of people, unless those people would relinquish the right of Representation in the Legislature, a right inestimable to them and formidable to tyrants only.

He has called together legislative bodies at places unusual, uncomfortable, and distant from the depository of their Public Records, for the sole purpose of fatiguing them into compliance with his measures.

He has dissolved Representative Houses repeatedly,

for opposing with manly firmness his invasions on the rights of the people.

He has refused for a long time, after such dissolutions, to cause others to be elected; whereby the Legislative Powers, incapable of Annihilation, have returned to the People at large for their exercise; the State remaining in the mean time exposed to all the dangers of invasion from without, and convulsions within.

He has endeavoured to prevent the population of these States; for that purpose obstructing the Laws for Naturalization of Foreigners; refusing to pass others to encourage their migrations hither, and raising the conditions of new Appropriations of Lands.

He has obstructed the Administration of Justice, by refusing his Assent to Laws for establishing Judiciary Powers.

He has made Judges dependent on his Will alone, for the tenure of their offices, and the amount and payment of their salaries.

He has erected a multitude of New Offices, and sent hither swarms of Officers to harass our people, and eat out their substance.

He has kept among us, in times of peace, Standing Armies without the Consent of our legislatures.

He has affected to render the Military independent of and superior to the Civil Power.

He has combined with others to subject us to a jurisdiction foreign to our constitution, and unacknowledged by our laws; giving his Assent to their acts of pretended Legislation:

For quartering large bodies of armed troops among us:

For protecting them, by a mock Trial, from Punishment for any Murders which they should commit on the inhabitants of these States:

For cutting off our Trade with all parts of the world:

For imposing taxes on us without our Consent:

For depriving us in many cases, of the benefits of Trial by Jury:

For transporting us beyond Seas to be tried for pretended offences:

For abolishing the free System of English Laws in a neighbouring Province, establishing therein an Arbitrary government, and enlarging its Boundaries so as to render it at once an example and fit instrument for introducing the same absolute rule into these Colonies:

For taking away our Charters, abolishing our most valuable Laws, and altering fundamentally the Forms of our Governments:

For suspending our own Legislatures, and declaring themselves invested with Power to legislate for us in all cases whatsoever.

He has abdicated Government here, by declaring us out of his Protection and waging War against us.

He has plundered our seas, ravaged our Coasts, burnt our towns, and destroyed the lives of our people.

He is at this time transporting large armies of foreign mercenaries to compleat the works of death, desolation and tyranny, already begun with circumstances of Cruelty and perfidy scarcely paralleled in the most barbarous ages, and totally unworthy the Head of a civilized nation.

He has constrained our fellow Citizens taken Captive on the high Seas to bear Arms against their Country, to become the executioners of their friends and Brethren, or to fall themselves by their Hands.

He has excited domestic insurrections amongst us, and has endeavoured to bring on the inhabitants of our frontiers, the merciless Indian Savages, whose known rule of warfare, is an undistinguished destruction of all ages, sexes and conditions.

In every stage of these Oppressions We have Petitioned for Redress in the most humble terms: Our repeated Petitions have been answered only by repeated injury. A Prince, whose character is thus marked by every act which may define a Tyrant, is unfit to be the ruler of a free people.

Nor have We been wanting in attentions to our British brethren. We have warned them from time to time of attempts by their legislature to extend an unwarrantable jurisdiction over us. We have reminded them of the circumstances of our emigration and settlement here. We have appealed to their native justice and magnanimity, and we have conjured them by the ties of our common kindred to disavow these usurpations which, would inevitably interrupt our connections and correspondence. They too have been deaf to the voice of justice and of consanguinity. We must, therefore, acquiesce in the necessity, which denounces our Separation, and hold them, as we hold the rest of mankind, Enemies in War, in Peace Friends.

We, therefore, the Representatives of the United States of America, in General Congress, Assembled, appealing to the Supreme Judge of the world for the rectitude of our intentions, do, in the Name, and by authority of the good People of these Colonies, solemnly publish and declare, That these United Colonies are, and of Right ought to be Free and Independent States; that they are Absolved from all Allegiance to the British Crown, and that all political connection between them and the State of Great Britain, is and ought to be totally dissolved; and that as Free and Independent States, they have full power to levy War, conclude Peace, contract Alliances, establish Commerce, and to do all other Acts and Things which Independent States may of right do. And for the support of this Declaration, with a firm reliance on the Protection of Divine Providence, we mutually pledge to each other our Lives, our Fortunes and our sacred Honor.

The Constitution of the United States

We the People of the United States, In Order to form a more perfect Union, establish Justice, insure domestic Tranquility, provide for the common defense, promote the general Welfare, and secure the Blessings of Liberty to ourselves and our Posterity, do ordain and establish this Constitution for the United States of America.

ARTICLE I

Section 1. All legislative Powers herein granted shall be vested in a Congress of the United Sates, which shall consist of a Senate and House of Representatives.

Section 2. The House of Representatives shall be composed of members chosen every second Year by the People of the several States, and the Electors in each State shall have the Qualifications requisite for Electors of the most numerous Branch of the State Legislature.

No Person shall be a representative who shall not have attained to the Age of twenty five Years, and been seven Years a Citizen of the United States, and who shall not, when elected, be an Inhabitant of that State in which he shall be chosen.

Representatives and direct Taxes shall be apportioned among the several States which may be included within this union, according to their respective Numbers, which shall be determined by adding to the whole Number of free Persons, including those bound to Service for a Term of Years, and excluding Indians not taxed, three fifths of all other Persons. The actual Enumeration shall be made within three Years after the first Meeting of the Congress of the United States, and within every subsequent term of ten Years, in such Manner as they shall be Law direct. The Number of Representatives shall not exceed one for every thirty Thousand, but each State shall have at Least one Representative; and until such enumeration shall be made, the State of New Hampshire shall be entitled to chuse three, Massachusetts eight, Rhode-Island and Providence Plantations one, Connecticut five, New York six, New Jersey four, Pennsylvania eight, Delaware one, Maryland six, Virginia ten, North Carolina five, South Carolina five, and Georgia three.

When vacancies happen in the Representation from any State, the Executive Authority thereof shall issue Writs of Election to fill such Vacancies.

The House of Representatives shall chuse their speaker and other Officers; and shall have the sole Power of Impeachment.

Section 3. The Senate of the United States shall be composed of two Senators from each State, chosen by the

Legislature thereof, for six Years; and each Senator shall have one Vote.

Immediately after they shall be assembled in Consequence of the first Election, they shall be divided as equally as may be into three Classes. The Seats of the Senators of the first Class shall be vacated at the Expiration of the second Year, of the second Class at the Expiration of the fourth Year, and the third Class at the Expiration of the sixth Year, so that one third may be chosen every second Year; and if Vacancies happen by Resignation, or otherwise, during the Recess of the Legislature of any State, the Executive thereof may make temporary Appointments until the next Meeting of the Legislature, which shall then fill such Vacancies.

No Person shall be a Senator who shall not have attained to the Age of thirty Years, and been nine Years a Citizen of the United States, and who shall not, when elected, be an Inhabitant of that State for which he shall be chosen.

The Vice President of the United States shall be President of the Senate, but shall have no Vote, unless they be equally divided.

The Senate shall chuse their other Officers, and also a President pro tempore, in the Absence of the Vice President, or when he shall exercise the Office of the President of the United States.

The Senate shall have the sole Power to try all Impeachments. When sitting for that Purpose, they shall be on Oath of Affirmation. When the President of the United States is tried, the Chief Justice shall preside: And no Person shall be convicted without the Concurrence of two thirds of the Members present.

Judgment in Cases of Impeachment shall not extend further than to removal from Office, and disqualification to hold and enjoy any Office of honor, Trust or Profit under the United States: but the Party convicted shall nevertheless be liable and subject to Indictment, Trial, Judgment and Punishment, according to law.

Section 4. The Times, Places and Manner of holding Elections for Senators and Representatives shall be prescribed in each State by the Legislature thereof; but the Congress may at any time by Law make or alter such Regulations, except as to the Places of chusing Senators.

The Congress shall assemble at least once in every Year, and such Meeting shall be on the first Monday in December, unless they shall by Law appoint a different Day.

Section 5. Each House shall be the Judge of the Elections, Returns and Qualifications of its own Members, and a Majority of each shall constitute a Quorum to do Business; but a smaller Number may adjourn from day to day, and may be authorized to compel the Attendance of absent Members, in such Manner, and under such Penalties as each House may provide.

Each House may determine the Rules of its Proceedings, punish its Members for disorderly Behaviour, and, with the Concurrence of two thirds, expel a Member.

Each House shall keep a Journal of its Proceedings, and from time to time publish the same, excepting such Parts as may in their Judgment require Secrecy; and the Yeas and Nays of the Members of either House on any question shall, at the Desire of one fifth of those Present, be entered on the Journal.

Neither House, during the Session of Congress, shall, without the Consent of the other, adjourn for more than three days, nor to any other Place than that in which the two Houses shall be sitting.

Section 6. The Senators and Representatives shall receive a Compensation for their Services, to be ascertained by Law, and paid out of the Treasury of the United States. They shall in all Cases, except Treason, Felony and Breach of the Peace, be privileged from Arrest during their Attendance at the Session of their respective Houses, and in going to and returning from the same; and for any Speech or Debate in either House, they shall not be questioned in any other Place.

No Senator or Representative shall, during the Time for which he was elected, be appointed to any civil Office under the Authority of the United States, which shall have been created, or the Emoluments whereof shall have been encreased during such time; and no Person holding any Office under the United States, shall be a Member of either House during his Continuance in Office.

Section 7. All Bills for raising Revenue shall originate in the House of Representatives; but the Senate may propose or concur with Amendments as on other Bills.

Every Bill which shall have passed the House of Representatives and the Senate, shall, before it becomes a Law, be presented to the President of the United States; If he approve he shall sign it, but if not he shall return it, with his Objections to that House in which it shall have originated, who shall enter the Objections at large on their Journal, and proceed to reconsider it. If after such Reconsideration two thirds of that House shall agree to pass the Bill, it shall be sent, together with the Objections, to the other House, by which it shall likewise to reconsidered, and if approved by two thirds of that House, it shall become a Law. But in all such Cases the Votes of both Houses shall be determined by Yeas and Nays, and the Names of the Pesons voting for and against the Bill shall be entered on the Journal of each House respectively. If any Bill shall not be returned by the President within ten Days (Sundays excepted) after it shall have been presented to him, the Same shall be a Law, in like Manner as if he signed it, unless the Congress by their Adjournment prevent its Return, in which Case it shall not be a law.

Every Order, Resolution, or Vote to which the Concurrence of the Senate and House of Representatives may be necessary (except on a question of Adjournment) shall be presented to the President of the United States; and before the Same shall take Effect, shall be approved by two thirds of the Senate and House of Representatives, according to the Rules and Limitations prescribed in the Case of a Bill.

Section 8. The Congress shall have the Power To lay and collect Taxes, Duties, Imposts and Excises, to pay the Debts and provide for the common Defence and general Welfare of the United States; but all Duties, Imposts and Excises shall be uniform throughout the United States;

To borrow Money on the credit of the United States;

To regulate Commerce with foreign Nations, and among the several States, and with the Indian Tribes;

To establish an uniform Rule of Naturalization, and uniform Laws on the subject of Bankruptcies throughout the United States;

To coin Money, regulate the Value thereof, and of foreign Coin, and fix the Standard of Weights and Measures;

To provide for the Punishment of counterfeiting the Securities and current Coin of the United States;

To establish Post Offices and post Roads;

To promote the Progress of Science and useful Arts, by securing for limited Times to Authors and Inventors the exclusive Right to their respective Writings and Discoveries;

To constitute Tribunals inferior to the supreme Court;

To define and punish Piracies and Felonies committed on the high Seas, and Offences against the Law of Nations;

To declare War, grant Letters of Marque and Reprisal, and make Rules concerning Captures on Land and Water;

To raise and support Armies, but no Appropriation of Money to that Use shall be for a longer Term than two Years;

To provide and maintain a Navy;

To make Rules for the Government and Regulation of the land and naval Forces;

To provide for calling forth the Militia to execute the Laws of the Union, suppress Insurrections and repel Invasions;

To provide for organizing, arming, and disciplining, the Militia, and for governing such Part of them as may be employed in the Service of the United States, reserving to the States respectively, the Appointment of the Officers, and the Authority of training the Militia according to the discipline prescribed by Congress;

To exercise exclusive Legislation in all Cases whatsoever, over such District (not exceeding ten Miles square) as may, by Cession of particular States, and the Acceptance of Congress, become the Seat of the Government of the United States, and to exercise like Authority over all Places purchased by the Consent of the Legislature of the State in which the Same shall be for the Erection of Forts, Magazines, Arsenals, dock-Yards, and other needful Buildings;—And

To make all Laws which shall be necessary and proper for carrying into Execution the foregoing Powers, and all other Powers vested by this Constitution in the Government of the United States, or in any Department or Officer thereof.

Section 9. The Migration or Importation of such Persons as any of the States now existing shall think proper to admit, shall not be prohibited by the Congress prior to the Year one thousand eight hundred and eight, but a Tax or duty may be imposed on such Importation, not exceeding ten dollars for each Person.

The Privilege of the Writ of Habeas Corpus shall not be suspended, unless when in Cases of Rebellion or Invasion the public Safety may require it.

No Bill of Attainder or ex post facto Law shall be passed.

No Capitation, or other direct, Tax shall be laid, unless in Proportion to the Census or Enumeration herein before directed to be taken.

No Tax or Duty shall be laid on Articles exported from any State.

No Preference shall be given by any Regulation of Commerce or Revenue to the Ports of one State over those of another: nor shall Vessels bound to, or from, one State be obliged to enter, clear, or pay Duties in another.

No Money shall be drawn from the Treasury, but in Consequence of Appropriations made by Law; and a regular Statement and Account of the Receipts and Expenditures of all public Money shall be published from time to time.

No Title of Nobility shall be granted by the United States: And no Person holding any office of Profit or Trust under them, shall, without the Consent of the Congress, accept of any present, Emolument, Office, or Title, of any kind whatever, from any King, Prince, or foreign States.

Section 10. No State shall enter into any Treaty, Alliance, or Confederation; grant Letters of Marque or Reprisal; coin Money; emit Bills of Credit; make any Thing but gold and silver Coin a Tender in Payment of Debts; pass any Bill of Attainder, ex post facto Law, or Law impairing the Obligation of Contracts, or grant any Title of Nobility.

No State shall, without the Consent of the Congress, lay any Imposts or Duties on Imports or Exports, except what may be absolutely necessary for executing its inspection Laws: and the net Produce of all Duties and Imposts, laid by any State on Imports or Exports, shall be for the Use of the Treasury of the United States; and all such Laws shall be subject to Revision and Controul of the Congress.

No State shall, without the Consent of Congress, lay any Duty of Tonnage, keep Troops, or Ships of War in time of Peace, enter into any Agreement or Compact with another State, or with a foreign Power, or engage in War, unless actually invaded, or in such imminent Danger as will not admit of delay.

ARTICLE II

Section 1. The executive Power shall be vested in a President of the United States of America. He shall hold his Office during the Term of four Years, and, together with the Vice President, chosen for the same term, be elected, as follows.

Each State shall appoint, in such Manner as the Legislature thereof may direct, a Number of Electors, equal to the whole Number of Senators and Representatives to which the State may be entitled in the Congress: but no Senator or Representative, or Person holding an office of Trust or Profit under the United States, shall be appointed an Elector.

The Electors shall meet in their respective States, and vote by Ballot for two Persons, of whom one at least shall not be an Inhabitant of the same State with themselves. And they shall make a List of all the Persons voted for, and of the Number of Votes for each; which List they shall sign and certify, and transmit sealed to the Seat of the Government of the United States, directed to the President of the Senate. The President of the Senate shall, in the Presence of the Senate and House of Representatives, open all the Certificates, and the Votes shall then be counted. The Person having the greatest Number of Votes shall be the President, if such Number be a Majority of the whole Number of Electors appointed; and if there be more than one who have such Majority, and have an equal Number of Votes, then the House of Representatives shall immediately chuse by Ballot one of them for President: and if no Person have a Majority, then from the five highest on the List the said House shall in like Manner chuse the President. But in chusing the President, the Votes shall be taken by States, the Representation from each State having one Vote; a Quorum for this Purpose shall consist of a Member or Members from two thirds of the States, and a Majority of all the States shall be necessary to a Choice. In every Case, after the Choice of the President, the Person having the greatest Number of Votes of the Electors shall be the Vice President. But if there should remain two or more who have equal Votes, the Senate shall chuse from them by Ballot the Vice President.

The Congress may determine the Time of chusing the Electors and the Day on which they shall give their Votes; which Day shall be the same throughout the United States.

No Person except a natural born Citizen, or a Citizen of the United States, at the time of the Adoption of this Constitution, shall be eligible to the Office of President; neither shall any person be eligible to that Office who shall not have attained to the Age of thirty five Years, and been fourteen Years a Resident within the United States.

In Case of the Removal of the President from Office, or of his Death, Resignation, or Inability to discharge the Powers and Duties of the said Office, the Same shall devolve on the Vice President, and the Congress may by Law provide for the Case of Removal, Death, Resignation or Inability, both of the President and Vice President, declaring what Officer shall then act as President, and such Officer shall act accordingly, until the Disability be removed, or a President shall be elected.

The President shall, at stated Times, receive for his Services a Compensation, which shall neither be encreased nor diminished during the Period for which he shall have been elected, and he shall not receive within that Period any other Emolument from the United States, or any of them.

Before he enter on the Execution of his Office, he shall take the following Oath or Affirmation:— "I do solemnly swear (or affirm) that I will faithfully execute the Office of President of the United States, and will to the best of my Ability, preserve, protect and defend the Constitution of the United States."

Section 2. The President shall be Commander in Chief of the Army and Navy of the United States, and of the Militia of the several States, when called into the actual Service of the United States; he may require the Opinion, in writing, of the principal Officer in each of the executive Departments, upon any Subject relating to the Duties of their respective Offices, and he shall have power to grant Reprieves and Pardons for Offences against the United States, except in Cases of Impeachment.

He shall have Power, by and with the Advice and Consent of the Senate, to make Treaties, provided two thirds of the Senators present concur; and he shall nominate, and by and with the Advice and Consent of the Senate, shall appoint Ambassadors, other public Ministers and Consuls, Judges of the supreme Court, and all other Officers of the United States, whose Appointments are not herein otherwise provided for, and which shall be established by Law; but the Congress may by Law vest the Appointment of such inferior officers, as they think proper, in the President alone, in the Courts of Law, or in the Heads of Departments.

The President shall have Power to fill up all Vacancies that may happen during the Recess of the Senate, by granting Commissions which shall expire at the End of their next Session.

Section 3. He shall from time to time give to the Congress Information of the State of the Union, and recommend to their Consideration such Measures as he shall judge necessary and expedient; he may, on extraordinary Occasions, convene both Houses, or either of them, and in Case of Disagreement between them, with Respect to the Time of Adjournment, he may adjourn them to such Time as he shall think proper; he shall receive Ambassadors and other public Ministers; he shall take Care that the Laws be faithfully executed, and shall Commission all of the officers of the United States.

Section 4. The President, Vice President and all civil Officers of the United States, shall be removed from Office on Impeachment for, and Conviction of, Treason, Bribery, or other High Crimes and Misdemeanors.

ARTICLE III

Section 1. The judicial Power of the United States, shall be vested in one supreme Court, and in such inferior Courts as the Congress may from time to time ordain and establish. The Judges, both of the supreme and inferior Courts, shall hold their Offices during good Behaviour, and shall, at stated Times, receive for their Services, a Compensation, which shall not be diminished during their Continuance in Office.

Section 2. The judicial Power shall extend to all Cases, in Law and Equity, arising under this Constitution, the Laws of the United States, and Treaties made, or which shall be made, under their Authority;—to all Cases affecting Ambassadors, other public Ministers and Consuls;—to all Cases of admiralty and maritime Jurisdiction;—to Controversies to which the United States shall be a Party;—to Controversies between two or more States;—between Citizens of different States;—between Citizens of the same State claiming Lands under Grants of different States, and between a State, or the Citizens thereof, and foreign States, Citizens or Subjects

In all Cases affecting Ambassadors, other public Ministers and Consuls, and those in which a State shall be Party, the supreme Court shall have original Jurisdiction. In all the other Cases before mentioned, the supreme Court shall have appellate Jurisdiction, both as to Law and Fact, with such Exceptions, and under such Regulations as the Congress shall make.

The Trial of all Crimes, except in Cases of Impeachment, shall be by Jury; and such Trial shall be held in the State where the said Crimes shall have been committed; but when not committed within any State, the Trial shall be at such Place or Places as the Congress may by Law have directed.

Section 3. Treason against the United States, shall consist only in levying War against them, or in adhering to their Enemies, giving them Aid and Comfort. No Person shall be convicted of Treason unless on the Testimony of two Witnesses to the same overt Act, or on Confession in open Court.

The Congress shall have Power to declare the Punishment of Treason, but no Attainder of Treason shall work Corruption of Blood, or Forfeiture except during the Life of the Person attainted.

ARTICLE IV

Section 1. Full Faith and Credit shall be given in each State to the public Acts, Records, and judicial Proceedings of every other State. And the Congress may by general Laws prescribe the Manner in which such Acts, Records and Proceedings shall be proved, and the Effect thereof.

Section 2. The Citizens of each State shall be entitled to all Privileges and Immunities of Citizens in the several States.

A Person charged in any State with Treason, Felony, or other Crime, who shall flee from Justice, and be found in another State, shall on Demand of the executive Authority of the State from which he fled, be delivered up, to be removed to the State having Jurisdiction of the Crime.

No Person held to Service or Labour in one State, under the Laws thereof, escaping into another, shall, in Consequence of any Law or Regulation therein, be discharged from such Service or Labour, but shall be delivered up on Claim of the Party to whom such Service of Labour may be due.

Section 3. New States may be admitted by the Congress into this Union; but no new State shall be formed or erected within the Jurisdiction of any other State; nor any State be formed by the Junction of two or more States, or Parts of States, without the Consent of the Legislatures of the States concerned as well as of the Congress.

The Congress shall have Power to dispose of and make all needful Rules and Regulations respecting the Territory or other Property belonging to the United States; and nothing in this Constitution shall be so construed as to Prejudice any Claims of the United States, or of any particular State.

Section 4. The United States shall guarantee to every State in this Union a Republican Form of Government, and shall protect each of them against Invasion; and on Application of the Legislature, or of the Executive (when the Legislature cannot be convened) against domestic Violence.

ARTICLE V

The Congress, whenever two thirds of both Houses shall deem it necessary, shall propose Amendments to this Constitution, or, on the Application of the Legislatures of two thirds of the several States, shall call a Convention for proposing Amendments, which, in either Case, shall be valid to all Intents and Purposes, as Part of this Constitution, when ratified by the Legislatures in three fourths of the several States, or by Conventions in three fourths thereof, as the one or the other Mode of Ratification may be proposed by the Congress; Provided that no Amendment which may be made prior to the Year One thousand eight hundred and eight shall in any Manner affect the first and fourth Clauses in the Ninth Section of the first Article; and that no State, without its Consent, shall be deprived of its equal Suffrage in the Senate.

ARTICLE VI

All Debts contracted and Engagements entered into, before the Adoption of this Constitution, shall be as valid against the United States under this Constitution, as under the Confederation.

This Constitution, and the Laws of the United States which shall be made in Pursuance thereof; and all Treaties made, or which shall be made, under the Authority of the United States, shall be the supreme Law of the Land; and the Judges in every State shall be bound thereby, any Thing in the Constitution or Laws of any State to the Contrary notwithstanding.

The Senators and Representatives before mentioned, and the Members of the several State Legislatures, and all executive and judicial Officers, both of the United States and of the several States, shall be bound by Oath or Affirmation, to support this Constitution; but no religious Test shall ever be required as a Qualification to any Office or public Trust under the United States.

ARTICLE VII

The Ratification of the Conventions of nine States, shall be sufficient for the Establishment of this Constitution between the States so ratifying the Same.

Done in Convention by the Unanimous Consent of the States present the Seventeenth Day of September in the Year of our Lord one thousand seven hundred and Eighty seven and of the independence of the United States of America the Twelfth. In witness whereof We have hereunto subscribed our Names.

[The first 10 Amendments were ratified December 15, 1791, and form what is known as the Bill of Rights.]

Amendment 1

Congress shall make no law respecting an establishment of religion, or prohibiting the free exercise thereof; or abridging the freedom of speech, or of the press; or the right of the people peaceably to assemble, and to petition the Government for a redress of grievances.

Amendment 2

A well regulated Militia, being necessary to the security of a free State, the right of the people to keep and bear Arms, shall not be infringed.

Amendment 3

No Soldier shall, in time of peace be quartered in any house, without the consent of the Owner, nor in time of war, but in a manner to be prescribed by law.

Amendment 4

The right of the people to be secure in their persons, houses, papers, and effects, against unreasonable searches and seizures, shall not be violated, and no Warrants shall issue, but upon probable cause, supported by Oath or affirmation, and particularly describing the place to be searched and the persons or things to be seized.

Amendment 5

No person shall be held to answer for a capital, or otherwise infamous crime, unless on a presentment or indictment of a Grand Jury, except in cases arising in the land or naval forces, or in the Militia, when in actual service in time of War or public danger; nor shall any person be subject for the same offence to be twice put in jeopardy of life or limb; nor shall be compelled in any criminal case to be a witness against himself, nor be deprived of life, liberty, or property, without due process of law; nor shall private property be taken for public use, without just compensation.

Amendment 6

In all criminal prosecutions, the accused shall enjoy the right to a speedy and public trial, by an impartial jury of the State and district wherein the crime shall have been committed, which district shall have been previously ascertained by law, and to be informed of the nature and cause of the accusation; to be confronted with the witnesses against him; to have compulsory process for obtaining witnesses in his favor, and to have the Assistance of Counsel for his defence.

Amendment 7

In Suits at common law, where the value in controversy shall exceed twenty dollars, the right of trial by jury shall be preserved, and no fact tried by a jury, shall be otherwise re-examined in any Court of the United States, than according to the rules of the common law.

Amendment 8

Excessive bail shall not be required, nor excessive fines imposed, nor cruel and unusual punishments inflicted.

Amendment 9

The enumeration in the Constitution, of certain rights, shall not be construed to deny or disparage others retained by the people.

Amendment 10

The powers not delegated to the United States by the Constitution, nor prohibited by it to the States, are reserved to the States respectively, or to the people.

Amendment 11

[Ratified February 7, 1795]

The Judicial power of the United States shall not be construed to extend to any suit in law or equity, commenced or prosecuted against one of the United States by Citizens of another State, or by Citizens or Subjects of any Foreign State.

Amendment 12

[Ratified July 27, 1804]

The Electors shall meet in their respective states and vote by ballot for President and Vice-President, one of whom, at least, shall not be an inhabitant of the same state with themselves; they shall name in their ballots the person voted for as President, and in distinct ballots the person voted for as Vice-President, and they shall make distinct lists of all persons voted for as President, and of all persons voted for as Vice-President, and of the number of votes for each, which lists they shall sign and certify, and transmit sealed to the seat of the government of the United States, directed to the President of the Senate; The President of the Senate shall, in the presence of the Senate and House of Representatives, open all the certificates and the votes shall then be counted;—The person having the greatest number of votes for President, shall be the President, if such number be a majority of the whole number of Electors appointed; and if no person have such majority, then from the persons having the highest numbers not exceeding three on the list of those voted for President, the House of Representatives shall choose immediately, by ballot, the President. But in choosing the President, the votes shall be taken by states, the representation from each state having one vote; a quorum for this purpose shall consist of a member or members from two-thirds of the states, and a majority of all the states shall be necessary to a choice. And if the House of Representatives shall not choose a President whenever the right of choice shall devolve upon them, before the fourth day of March next following, the Vice-President shall act as President, as in the case of the death or other constitutional disability of the President.—The person having the greatest number of votes as Vice-President,

shall be the Vice-President, if such number be a majority of the whole number of Electors appointed, and if no person have a majority, then from the two highest numbers on the list, the Senate shall choose the Vice-President; a quorum for the purpose shall consist of two-thirds of the whole number of Senators, and a majority of the whole number shall be necessary to a choice. But no person constitutionally ineligible to the office of President shall be eligible to that of Vice-President of the United States.

Amendment 13

[Ratified December 6, 1865]

Section 1. Neither slavery nor involuntary servitude, except as a punishment for crime whereof the party shall have been duly convicted, shall exist within the United States, or any place subject to their jurisdiction.
Section 2. Congress shall have the power to enforce this article by appropriate legislation.

Amendment 14

[Ratified July 9, 1868]

Section 1. All persons born or naturalized in the United States, and subject to the jurisdiction thereof, are citizens of the United States and of the State wherein they reside. No State shall make or enforce any law which shall abridge the privileges or immunities of citizens of the United States; nor shall any State deprive any person of life, liberty, or property, without due process of law; nor deny to any person within its jurisdiction the equal protection of the laws.

Section 2. Representatives shall be appointed among the several States according to their respective numbers, counting the whole number of persons in each State, excluding Indians not taxed. But when the right to vote at any election for the choice of electors for President and Vice President of the United States, Representatives in Congress, the Executive and Judicial Officers of a State, or the members of the Legislature thereof, is denied to any of the male inhabitants of such State, being twenty-one years of age, and citizens of the United States, or in any way abridged, except for participation in rebellion, or other crime, the basis of representation therein shall be reduced in the proportion which the number of such male citizens shall bear to the whole number of male citizens twenty-one years of age in such State.

Section 3. No person shall be a Senator or Representative in Congress, or elector of President and Vice President, or hold any office, civil or military, under the United States, or under any State, who, having previously taken an oath, as a member of Congress, or as an officer of the United States, or as a member of any State legislature, or as an executive or judicial officer of any State, to support the Constitution of the United States, shall have engaged in insurrection or rebellion against the same, or given aid or comfort to the enemies thereof. But Congress may by a vote of two thirds in each House, remove such disability.

Section 4. The validity of the public debt of the United States, authorized by law, including debts incurred for payment of pensions and bounties for services in suppressing insurrection or rebellion, shall not be questioned. But neither the United States nor any State shall assume or pay any debt or obligation incurred in aid of insurrection or rebellion against the United States, or any claim for the loss or emancipation of any slave; but all such debts, obligations and claims shall be held illegal and void.

Section 5. The Congress shall have power to enforce, by appropriate legislation, the provisions of this article.

Amendment 15

[*Ratified February 3, 1870*]

Section 1. The right of citizens of the United States to vote shall not be denied or abridged by the United States or by any State on account of race, color, or previous condition of servitude.

Section 2. The Congress shall have power to enforce this article by appropriate legislation.

Amendment 16

[*Ratified February 3, 1913*]

The Congress shall have power to lay and collect taxes on incomes, from whatever source derived, without apportionment among the several States, and without regard to any census or enumeration.

Amendment 17

[*Ratified April 8, 1913*]

The Senate of the United States shall be composed of two Senators from each State, elected by the people thereof for six years; and each Senator shall have one vote. The electors in each State shall have the qualification requisite for electors of the most numerous branch of the State legislatures.

When vacancies happen in the representation of any State in the Senate, the executive authority of such State shall issue writs of election to fill such vacancies: *Provided,* That the legislature of any State may empower the executive thereof to make temporary appointments until the people fill the vacancies by election as the legislature may direct.

This amendment shall not be so construed as to affect the election or term of any Senator chosen before it becomes valid as part of the Constitution.

Amendment 18

[*Ratified January 16, 1919*]

Section 1. After one year from the ratification of this article the manufacture, sale, or transportation of intoxicating liquors within, the importation thereof into, or the exportation thereof from the United States and all territory subject to the jurisdiction thereof for beverage purposes is hereby prohibited.

Section 2. The Congress and the several States shall have concurrent power to enforce this article by appropriate legislation.

Section 3. This article shall be inoperative unless it shall have been ratified as an amendment to the Constitution by the legislatures of the several States, as provided in the Constitution, within seven years from the date of the submission hereof to the States by the Congress.

Amendment 19

[*Ratified August 18, 1920*]

The right of citizens of the United States to vote shall not be denied or abridged by the United States or by any State on account of sex. Congress shall have the power to enforce this article by appropriate legislation.

Amendment 20

[*Ratified January 23, 1933*]

Section 1. The terms of the President and Vice President shall end at noon on the 20th day of January, and the terms of Senators and Representatives at noon on the 3d day of January, of the years in which such terms would have ended if this article had not been ratified; and the terms of their successors shall then begin.

Section 2. The Congress shall assemble at least once in every year, and such meetings shall begin at noon on the 3d day of January, unless they shall by law appoint a different day.

Section 3. If, at the time fixed for the beginning of the term of the President, the President elect shall have died, the Vice President elect shall become President. If a President shall not have been chosen before the time fixed for the beginning of his term, or if the President elect shall have failed to qualify, then the Vice President elect shall act as President until a President shall have qualified; and the Congress may by law provide for the case wherein neither a President elect nor a Vice President elect shall have qualified, declaring who shall then act as President, or the manner in which one who is to act shall be selected, and such person shall act accordingly until a President or Vice President shall have qualified.

Section 4. The Congress may by law provide for the case of the death of any of the persons from whom the House of Representatives may choose a President whenever the right of choice shall have devolved upon them, and for the case of the death of any of the persons from whom the Senate may choose a Vice President whenever the right of choice shall have devolved upon them.

Section 5. Sections 1 and 2 shall take effect on the 15th day of October following the ratification of this article.

Section 6. This article shall be inoperative unless it shall have been ratified as an amendment to the Constitution by the legislatures of three-fourths of the several states within seven years from the date of its submission.

Amendment 21

[Ratified December 5, 1933]

Section 1. The eighteenth article of amendment to the Constitution of the United States is hereby repealed.

Section 2. The transportation or importation into any State, Territory, or Possession of the United States for delivery or use herein of intoxicating liquors, in violation of the laws thereof, is hereby prohibited.

Section 3. This article shall be inoperative unless it shall have been ratified as an amendment to the Constitution by conventions in several States, as provided in the Constitution, within seven years from the date of the submission hereof to the States by the Congress.

Amendment 22

[Ratified February 27, 1951]

Section 1. No person shall be elected to the office of the President more than twice, and no person who has held the office of President, or acted as President, for more than two years of a term to which some other person was elected President shall be elected to the office of the President more than once. But this Article shall not apply to any person holding the office of President when this Article was proposed by the Congress, and shall not prevent any person who may be holding the office of President, or acting as President, during the term within which this Article becomes operative from holding the office of President or acting as President during the remainder of such term.

Section 2. This article shall be inoperative unless it shall have been ratified as an amendment to the Constitution by the legislatures of three-fourths of the several States within seven years from the date of its submission to the States by the Congress.

Amendment 23

[Ratified March 29, 1961]

Section 1. The District constituting the seat of Government of the United States shall appoint in such manner as the Congress may direct:

A number of electors of President and Vice President equal to the whole number of Senators and Representatives in Congress to which the District would be entitled if it were a state, but in no event more than the least populous State; they shall be in addition to those appointed by the States, but they shall be considered, for the purposes of the election of President and Vice President, to be electors appointed by a State; and they shall meet in the District and perform such duties as provided by the twelfth article of amendment.

Section 2. The Congress shall have power to enforce this article by appropriate legislation.

Amendment 24

[Ratified January 23, 1964]

Section 1. The right of citizens of the United States to vote in any primary or other election for President or Vice President, for electors for President or Vice President, or for Senator or Representative in Congress, shall not be denied or abridged by the United States or by any State by reason or failure to pay any poll tax or other tax.

Section 2. The Congress shall have power to enforce this article by appropriate legislation.

Amendment 25

[Ratified February 10, 1967]

Section 1. In case of the removal of the President from office or of his death or resignation, the Vice President shall become President.

Section 2. Whenever there is a vacancy in the office of the Vice President, the President shall nominate a Vice President who shall take office upon confirmation by a majority vote of both House of Congress.

Section 3. Whenever the President transmits to the President pro tempore of the Senate and the Speaker of the House of Representatives his written declaration that he is unable to discharge the powers and duties of his office, and until he transmits to them a written declaration to the contrary, such powers and duties shall be discharged by the Vice President as Acting President.

Section 4. Whenever the Vice President and a majority of either the principal officers of the executive department or of such other body as Congress may by law provide, transmit to the President pro tempore of the Senate and the Speaker of the House of Representatives their written declaration that the President is unable to discharge the powers and duties of his office, the Vice President shall immediately assume the powers and duties of the office as Acting President.

Thereafter, when the President transmits to the President pro tempore of the Senate and the Speaker of the House of Representatives his written declaration that no inability exists, he shall resume the powers and duties of his office unless the Vice President and a majority of either the principal officers of the executive department or of such other body as Congress may by law provide, transmit within four days to the President pro tempore of the Senate and the Speaker of the House of Representatives their written declaration that the President is unable to discharge the powers and duties of his office. Thereupon Congress shall decide the issue, assembling within forty-eight hours for that purpose if not in session. If the Congress, within twenty-one days after receipt of the latter written declaration, or, if Congress is not in session, within twenty-one days after Congress is required to assemble, determines by two-thirds vote of both Houses that the President is unable to discharge the powers and duties of his office, the Vice President shall continue to discharge the same as Acting President; otherwise, the President shall resume the powers and duties of his office.

Amendment 26

[Ratified June 30, 1971]

Section 1. The right of citizens of the United States, who are eighteen years of age or older, to vote shall not be denied or abridged by the United States or by any State on account of age.

Section 2. The Congress shall have the power to enforce this article by appropriate legislation.

Equal Rights for Women

[Proposed March 22, 1972]

Section 1. Equality of rights under the law shall not be denied or abridged by the United States or by any State on account of sex.

Section 2. The Congress shall have power to enforce, by appropriate legislation, the provisions of this article.

Section 3. This amendment shall take effect two years after date of ratification.

District of Columbia Representation

[Proposed August 22, 1978]

Section 1. For purposes of representation in the Congress, election of the President and Vice President, and article V of this Constitution, the District constituting the seat of government of the United States shall be treated as though it were a State.

Section 2. The exercise of the rights and powers conferred under this article shall be by the people of the District constituting the seat of government, and as shall be provided by the Congress.

Section 3. The twenty-third article of amendment to the Constitution of the United States is hereby repealed.

Section 4. This article shall be inoperative, unless it shall have been ratified as an amendment to the Constitution by the legislatures of three-fourths of the several States within seven years from the date of its submission.

Presidents, Elections, and Congresses

Year	President	Vice president	Election year	Election opponent with most votes
1789–1797	George Washington	John Adams	1789	None
			1793	None
1797–1801	John Adams	Thomas Jefferson	1797	Thomas Jefferson
1801–1809	Thomas Jefferson	Aaron Burr (to 1805)	1801	John Adams
		George Clinton (to 1809)	1805	Charles C. Pinckney
1809–1817	James Madison	George Clinton (to 1813)	1809	Charles C. Pinckney
		Elbridge Gerry (to 1817)	1813	De Witt Clinton
1817–1825	James Monroe	Daniel D. Tompkins	1817	Rufus King
			1821	John Q. Adams
1825–1829	John Quincy Adams	John C. Calhoun	1824	Andrew Jackson
1829–1837	Andrew Jackson	John C. Calhoun (to 1833)	1828	John Q. Adams
		Martin Van Buren (to 1837)	1832	Henry Clay
1837–1841	Martin Van Buren	Richard M. Johnson	1836	William H. Harrison
1841	William H. Harrison	John Tyler	1840	Martin Van Buren
1841–1845	John Tyler	None	1840	Succeeded after death of Harrison
1845–1849	James K. Polk	George M. Dallas	1844	Henry Clay
1849–1850	Zachary Taylor	Millard Fillmore	1848	Lewis Cass
1850–1853	Millard Fillmore	None		Succeeded after death of Taylor
1853–1857	Franklin Pierce	William R. King	1852	Winfield Scott
1857–1861	James Buchanan	John C. Breckinridge	1856	John C. Fremont
1861–1865	Abraham Lincoln	Hannibal Hamlin (to 1865)	1860	Stephen Douglas
		Andrew Johnson (1865)	1864	George B. McClellan
1865–1869	Andrew Johnson	None		Succeeded after death of Lincoln
1869–1877	Ulysses S. Grant	Schuyler Colfax (to 1873)	1868	Horatio Seymour
		Henry Wilson (to 1877)	1872	Horace Greeley

Winner's popular vote percentage	Winner's electoral college vote percentage	Party of president	Congress	House		Senate	
				Majority party	Minority party	Majority party	Minority party
No popular vote	Not applicable	None	1st	38 Admin	26 Opp	17 Admin	9 Opp
			2nd	37 Fed	33 Dem-R	16 Fed	13 Dem-R
No popular vote	Not applicable		3rd	57 Dem-R	48 Fed	17 Fed	13 Dem-R
			4th	54 Fed	52 Dem-R	19 Fed	13 Dem-R
No popular vote	Not applicable	Fed	5th	58 Fed	48 Dem-R	20 Fed	12 Dem-R
			6th	64 Fed	42 Dem-R	19 Fed	13 Dem-R
No popular vote	Decided in House	Dem-R	7th	69 Dem-R	36 Fed	18 Dem-R	13 Fed
			8th	102 Dem-R	39 Fed	25 Dem-R	9 Fed
No popular vote	92.0		9th	116 Dem-R	25 Fed	27 Dem-R	7 Fed
			10th	118 Dem-R	24 Fed	28 Dem-R	6 Fed
No popular vote	69.7	Dem-R	11th	94 Dem-R	48 Fed	28 Dem-R	6 Fed
			12th	108 Dem-R	36 Fed	30 Dem-R	6 Fed
No popular vote	59.0		13th	112 Dem-R	68 Fed	27 Dem-R	9 Fed
			14th	117 Dem-R	65 Fed	25 Dem-R	11 Fed
No popular vote	84.3	Dem-R	15th	141 Dem-R	42 Fed	34 Dem-R	10 Fed
			16th	156 Dem-R	27 Fed	35 Dem-R	7 Fed
No popular vote	99.5		17th	158 Dem-R	25 Fed	44 Dem-R	4 Fed
			18th	187 Dem-R	26 Fed	44 Dem-R	4 Fed
39.1	Decided in House	Nat-R	19th	105 Admin	97 Dem-J	26 Admin	20 Dem-J
			20th	119 Dem-J	94 Admin	28 Dem-J	20 Admin
56.0	68.2	Dem	21st	139 Dem	74 Nat R	26 Dem	22 Nat R
			22nd	141 Dem	58 Nat R	25 Dem	21 Nat R
54.5	76.6		23rd	147 Dem	53 AntiMas	20 Dem	20 Nat R
			24th	145 Dem	98 Whig	27 Dem	25 Whig
50.9	57.8	Dem	25th	108 Dem	107 Whig	30 Dem	18 Whig
			26th	124 Dem	118 Whig	28 Dem	22 Whig
52.9	79.6	Whig					
52.9		Whig	27th	133 Whig	102 Dem	28 Whig	22 Dem
			28th	142 Dem	79 Whig	28 Whig	25 Dem
49.6	61.8	Dem	29th	143 Dem	77 Whig	31 Dem	25 Whig
			30th	115 Whig	108 Dem	36 Dem	21 Whig
47.3	56.2	Whig	31st	112 Dem	109 Whig	35 Dem	25 Whig
—	—	Whig	32nd	140 Dem	88 Whig	35 Dem	24 Whig
50.9	85.8	Dem	33rd	159 Dem	71 Whig	38 Dem	22 Whig
			34th	108 Rep	83 Dem	40 Dem	15 Rep
45.6	58.8	Dem	35th	118 Dem	92 Rep	36 Dem	20 Rep
			36th	114 Rep	92 Dem	36 Dem	26 Rep
39.8	59.4	Rep	37th	105 Rep	43 Dem	31 Rep	10 Dem
			38th	102 Rep	75 Dem	36 Rep	9 Dem
55.2	91.0						
—	—	Rep	39th	149 Union	42 Dem	42 Union	10 Dem
			40th	143 Rep	49 Dem	42 Rep	11 Dem
52.7	72.8	Rep	41st	149 Rep	63 Dem	56 Rep	11 Dem
			42nd	134 Rep	104 Dem	52 Rep	17 Dem
55.6	81.9		43rd	194 Rep	92 Dem	49 Rep	19 Dem
			44th	169 Rep	109 Dem	45 Rep	29 Dem

Year	President	Vice president	Election year	Election opponent with most votes
1877–1881	Rutherford B. Hayes	William A. Wheeler	1876	Samuel Tilden
1881	James A. Garfield	Chester A. Arthur	1880	Winfield S. Hancock
1881–1885	Chester A. Arthur	None		Succeeded after death of Garfield
1885–1889	Grover Cleveland	Thomas A. Hendricks	1884	James G. Blaine
1889–1893	Benjamin Harrison	Levi P. Morton	1888	Grover Cleveland
1893–1897	Grover Cleveland	Adlai E. Stevenson	1892	Benjamin Harrison
1897–1901	William McKinley	Garret A. Hobart (to 1901)	1896	William Jennings Bryan
		Theodore Roosevelt (1901)	1900	William Jennings Bryan
1901–1909	Theodore Roosevelt	(None, 1901–5)	1904	Succeeded after death of McKinley
		Charles W. Fairbanks (1905–9)		Alton B. Parker
1909–1913	William Howard Taft	James S. Sherman	1908	William Jennings Bryan
1913–1921	Woodrow Wilson	Thomas R. Marshall	1912	Theodore Roosevelt
			1916	Charles Evans Hughes
1921–1923	Warren G. Harding	Calvin Coolidge	1920	James Cox
1923–1929	Calvin Coolidge	(None, 1923–25)		Succeeded after death of Harding
		Charles G. Dawes (1925–29)	1924	John Davis
1929–1933	Herbert Hoover	Charles Curtis	1928	Alfred E. Smith
1933–1945	Franklin D. Roosevelt	John N. Garner (1933–41)	1932	Herbert Hoover
		Henry A. Wallace (1941–45)	1936	Alfred Landon
		Harry S Truman (1945)	1940	Wendell Willkie
			1944	Thomas Dewey
1945–1953	Harry S Truman	(None, 1945–49)		Succeeded after death of Roosevelt
		Alben W. Barkley	1948	Thomas Dewey
1953–1961	Dwight D. Eisenhower	Richard M. Nixon	1952	Adlai Stevenson
			1956	Adlai Stevenson
1961–1963	John F. Kennedy	Lyndon B. Johnson	1960	Richard M. Nixon

Winner's popular vote percentage	Winner's electoral college vote percentage	Party of president	Congress	House		Senate	
				Majority party	Minority party	Majority party	Minority party
47.9	50.1	Rep	45th	153 Dem	140 Rep	39 Rep	36 Dem
			46th	149 Dem	130 Rep	42 Dem	33 Rep
48.3	58.0	Rep	47th	147 Rep	135 Dem	37 Rep	37 Dem
—	—	Rep	48th	197 Dem	118 Rep	38 Rep	36 Dem
48.5	54.6	Dem	49th	183 Dem	140 Rep	43 Rep	34 Dem
			50th	169 Dem	152 Rep	39 Rep	37 Dem
47.8	58.1	Rep	51st	166 Rep	159 Dem	39 Rep	37 Dem
			52nd	235 Dem	88 Rep	47 Rep	39 Dem
46.0	62.3	Dem	53rd	218 Dem	127 Rep	44 Dem	38 Rep
			54th	244 Rep	105 Dem	43 Rep	39 Dem
51.0	60.6	Rep	55th	204 Rep	113 Dem	47 Rep	34 Dem
51.7	64.7		56th	185 Rep	163 Dem	53 Rep	26 Dem
—	—	Rep	57th	197 Rep	151 Dem	55 Rep	31 Dem
			58th	208 Rep	178 Dem	57 Rep	33 Dem
56.4	70.6		59th	250 Rep	136 Dem	57 Rep	33 Dem
			60th	222 Rep	164 Dem	61 Rep	31 Dem
51.6	66.4	Rep	61st	219 Rep	172 Dem	61 Rep	32 Dem
			62nd	228 Dem	161 Rep	51 Rep	41 Dem
41.9	81.9	Dem	63rd	291 Dem	127 Rep	51 Dem	44 Rep
			64th	230 Dem	196 Rep	56 Dem	40 Rep
49.3	52.2		65th	216 Dem	210 Rep	53 Dem	42 Rep
			66th	240 Rep	190 Dem	49 Rep	47 Dem
60.3	76.1	Rep	67th	301 Rep	131 Dem	59 Rep	37 Dem
—	—	Rep	68th	225 Rep	205 Dem	51 Rep	43 Dem
54.0	71.9		69th	247 Rep	183 Dem	56 Rep	39 Dem
			70th	237 Rep	195 Dem	49 Rep	46 Dem
58.2	83.6	Rep	71st	267 Rep	167 Dem	56 Rep	39 Dem
			72nd	220 Dem	214 Rep	48 Rep	47 Dem
57.4	88.9	Dem	73rd	310 Dem	117 Rep	60 Dem	35 Rep
			74th	319 Dem	103 Rep	69 Dem	25 Rep
60.8	98.5		75th	331 Dem	89 Rep	76 Dem	16 Rep
			76th	261 Dem	164 Rep	69 Dem	23 Rep
54.7	84.6		77th	268 Dem	162 Rep	66 Dem	28 Rep
			78th	218 Dem	208 Rep	58 Dem	37 Rep
53.4	81.4						
—	—	Dem	79th	242 Dem	190 Rep	56 Dem	38 Rep
			80th	245 Rep	188 Dem	51 Rep	45 Dem
49.5	57.1		81st	263 Dem	171 Rep	54 Dem	42 Rep
			82nd	234 Dem	199 Rep	49 Dem	47 Rep
55.1	83.2	Rep	83rd	221 Rep	211 Dem	48 Rep	47 Dem
			84th	232 Dem	203 Rep	48 Dem	47 Rep
57.4	86.1		85th	233 Dem	200 Rep	49 Dem	47 Rep
			86th	283 Dem	153 Rep	64 Dem	34 Rep
49.7	58.0	Dem	87th	263 Dem	174 Rep	65 Dem	35 Rep

Year	President	Vice president	Election year	Election opponent with most votes
1963–1969	Lyndon B. Johnson	(None, 1963–65)		Succeeded after death of Kennedy
		Hubert H. Humphrey (1965–69)	1964	Barry Goldwater
1969–1974	Richard M. Nixon	Spiro T. Agnew	1968	Hubert H. Humphrey
		Gerald R. Ford (appointed)	1972	George McGovern
1974–1977	Gerald R. Ford	Nelson A. Rockefeller		Succeeded after resignation of Nixon
1977–1981	Jimmy Carter	Walter Mondale	1976	Gerald R. Ford
1981–1989	Ronald Reagan	George Bush	1980	Jimmy Carter
			1984	Walter F. Mondale

Abbreviations:

Admin = Administration supporters **AntiMas** = Anti-Masonic party **Dem** = Democratic party **Dem-R** = Democratic = Republican party **Fed** = Federalist party **Dem-J** = Jacksonian Democrats party **Nat R** = National Republican party **Opp** = Opponents of administration **Rep** = Republican party **Union** = Unionist party

Winner's popular vote percentage	Winner's electoral college vote percentage	Party of president	Congress	House		Senate	
				Majority party	Minority party	Majority party	Minority party
—	—	Dem	88th	258 Dem	177 Rep	67 Dem	33 Rep
61.6	90.3		89th	295 Dem	140 Rep	68 Dem	32 Rep
			90th	247 Dem	187 Rep	64 Dem	36 Rep
43.4	55.9	Rep	91st	243 Dem	192 Rep	57 Dem	43 Rep
			92nd	254 Dem	180 Rep	54 Dem	44 Rep
60.7	96.7						
—	—	Rep	93rd	239 Dem	192 Rep	56 Dem	42 Rep
			94th	291 Dem	144 Rep	60 Dem	37 Rep
50.1	55.2	Dem	95th	292 Dem	143 Rep	61 Dem	38 Rep
			96th	280 Dem	155 Rep	58 Dem	41 Rep
50.7	90.9	Rep	97th	243 Dem	192 Rep	53 Rep	47 Dem
			98th	269 Dem	166 Rep	54 Rep	46 Dem
59.8	97.4		99th	253 Dem	182 Rep	53 Rep	47 Dem
			100th	257 Dem	177 Rep	54 Dem	46 Rep

THE 1988 PRESIDENTIAL ELECTION

The 1988 presidential election, pitting incumbent Republican Vice President George Bush and vice presidential candidate Daniel Quayle against Democratic challengers Michael S. Dukakis and George L. Bentsen, was an impressive win for Vice President Bush. He captured nearly 48 million popular votes (54 percent), while Dukakis won only 41 million (46 percent). Dukakis was able to garner the most popular votes in 10 states and the District of Columbia, winning 112 electoral votes. But Bush won the most popular votes in all the other states, and was accorded 426 electoral votes—far more than the minimum 270 electoral votes needed to capture the presidency. Table D–1 provides the state-by-state results, showing popular votes, percentages of popular votes, and electoral votes won by both presidential election tickets.

Bush won his largest majorities in the South and West. He captured the electoral votes of the Deep South states of Alabama, Florida, Georgia, Mississippi, South Carolina, and Virginia with 60 percent or more of the popular votes, and won substantial majorities in the others. Likewise, he garnered the electoral votes of western states—Arizona, Idaho, Nevada, Utah, Wyoming—with 60 percent or more of the popular votes. Bush also won less lopsided but more important contests in most of the large, urban, industrialized states—California, Illinois, Michigan, New Jersey, Ohio, and Pennsylvania—together giving him 155 electoral votes. Dukakis's largest electoral vote victory came in New York, where he won 52 percent of the popular vote. He also won by sizeable

margins in Hawaii, Iowa, Massachusetts, Minnesota, Oregon, Rhode Island, Washington, West Virginia, and Wisconsin. And, he garnered 86 percent of the popular vote in the District of Columbia to take its three electoral votes.

Although the election featured the contest between the Bush-Quayle and Dukakis-Bentsen tickets, other candidates' names appeared on the ballot, too. Former Republican Congressman Ron Paul of Texas ran for president on the Libertarian party ticket. A feisty New York City psychologist, Dr. Lenora B. Fulani, ran on the New Alliance party ticket, claiming to be the candidate of choice for followers of Rev. Jesse Jackson. Former Minnesota Democratic Senator Eugene J. McCarthy, now philosophical and poetic, accepted the standard of the Consumer party. There were other, lesser minor party candidates on the presidential ballot, as well. These minor party candidates added some interest to the election, but they attracted only a miniscule proportion of the presidential vote.

The Bush-Quayle ticket won majorities of voters in a variety of demographic categories, as Table D–2 shows. The major exceptions were blacks, 86 percent of whom voted for the Dukakis-Bentsen ticket, and Jews and Hispanics, about two-thirds of whom voted Democratic. Also, Dukakis won majority support among those with less than a high school education, in the lower-income categories, and among blue collar workers, students, teachers, and the unemployed. Bush made a poorer

TABLE D-1   1984 Presidential election results*

State	Bush-Quayle Republican			Dukakis-Bentsen Democratic		
	Popular Vote	*Percent of popular vote*	*Electoral vote*	*Popular Vote*	*Percent of popular vote*	*Electoral vote*
Alabama	809,663	60	9	547,347	40	—
Alaska	102,381	62	3	62,205	38	—
Arizona	694,379	61	7	447,272	39	—
Arkansas	463,574	57	6	344,991	43	—
California	4,756,490	52	47	4,448,393	48	—
Colorado	727,633	54	8	621,093	46	—
Connecticut	747,802	53	8	674,873	47	—
Delaware	130,581	57	3	99,479	43	—
District of Columbia	25,732	14	—	153,100	86	3
Florida	2,538,994	61	21	1,632,086	39	—
Georgia	1,070,089	60	12	715,635	40	—
Hawaii	158,625	45	—	192,364	55	4
Idaho	253,467	63	4	147,420	37	—
Illinois	2,298,648	51	24	2,180,657	49	—
Indiana	1,280,292	60	12	850,851	40	—
Iowa	541,540	45	—	667,085	55	8
Kansas	552,659	57	7	422,056	43	—
Kentucky	731,446	56	9	579,077	44	—
Louisiana	880,830	55	10	715,612	45	—
Maine	304,087	56	4	240,508	44	—
Maryland	834,202	51	10	793,939	49	—
Massachusetts	1,184,323	46	—	1,387,398	54	13
Michigan	1,941,440	54	20	1,670,883	46	—
Minnesota	958,199	46	—	1,106,975	54	10
Mississippi	551,745	60	7	360,892	40	—
Missouri	1,081,163	52	11	1,004,040	48	—
Montana	189,598	53	4	168,120	47	—
Nebraska	389,394	60	5	254,426	40	—
Nevada	205,942	60	4	132,716	38	—
New Hampshire	279,770	63	4	162,335	37	—
New Jersey	1,699,634	57	16	1,275,063	43	—
New Mexico	260,792	52	5	236,528	48	—
New York	2,974,190	48	—	3,227,518	52	36
North Carolina	1,232,132	58	13	890,034	42	—
North Dakota	165,517	57	3	127,081	43	—
Ohio	2,411,719	55	23	1,934,922	45	—
Oklahoma	678,244	58	8	483,373	42	—
Oregon	517,731	47	—	575,071	53	7
Pennsylvania	2,291,297	51	25	2,183,928	49	—
Rhode Island	169,730	44	—	216,668	56	4
South Carolina	599,871	62	8	367,511	38	—
South Dakota	165,516	53	3	145,632	47	—
Tennessee	939,434	58	11	677,715	42	—
Texas	3,014,007	56	29	2,331,286	44	—
Utah	426,858	67	5	206,853	33	—
Vermont	123,166	51	3	116,419	49	—
Virginia	1,305,131	60	12	860,767	40	—
Washington	800,182	49	—	844,554	51	10
West Virginia	307,824	48	—	339,112	52	6
Wisconsin	1,043,584	48	—	1,122,090	52	11
Wyoming	106,814	61	3	67,077	39	—
Total	47,917,341	54	426	41,013,030	46	112

*Unofficial returns.

Source: Gathered and reported by the Associated Press, from the *New York Times*, November 10, 1988, p. 17.

showing than Reagan had in 1984 in most demographic categories, but he held 80 percent of the 1984 Reagan voters and won about as heavily among conservatives as had Reagan in 1984. Dukakis did recover the support of about half of the so-called "Reagan Democrats"—those Democrats who voted for Reagan in 1984. In racial terms, almost all black Democrats voted for Dukakis; Bush won about a fifth of the votes of white Democrats, and gar-

nered his largest popular vote margins in the South.

The Bush sweep at the presidential level was countered by significant Democratic victories in congressional and state races. While losing the presidential election, the Democrats actually gained seats in the U.S. House of Representatives and Senate. They gained 5 House seats, giving them a 262–173 seat majority, the first time in nearly three decades that the party capturing the White

TABLE D–2   Portrait of the 1984 and 1988 presidential electorates*

Characteristic	Vote in 1984		Vote in 1988		Percent of 1988 Vote
	Reagan	Mondale	Bush	Dukakis	
All voters	59	41	54	46	100
Men	62	37	57	41	48
Women	56	44	50	49	52
Whites	64	35	59	40	85
Blacks	9	89	12	86	10
Hispanics	37	61	30	69	3
Married	62	38	57	42	69
Not married	52	46	46	53	31
18–29 years old	59	40	52	47	20
30–44 years old	57	42	54	45	35
45–59 years old	59	39	57	42	22
60 and older	60	39	50	49	22
Not a high school graduate	49	50	43	56	8
High school graduate	60	39	50	49	27
Some college	61	37	57	42	30
College graduate or more	58	41	56	43	35
White Protestant	72	27	66	33	48
Catholic	54	45	52	47	28
Jewish	31	67	35	64	4
White fundamentalist or evangelical Christian	78	22	81	18	9
Union household	46	53	42	57	25
Family income					
under $12,500	45	54	37	62	12
$12,500–$24,999	57	42	49	50	20
$25,000–$34,999	59	40	56	44	20
$35,000–$49,999	66	33	56	42	20
$50,000 and over	69	30	62	37	24
From the East	52	47	50	49	25
Midwest	58	40	52	47	28
South	64	36	58	41	28
West	61	38	52	46	19
Republicans	93	6	91	8	35
Democrats	24	75	17	82	37
Independents	63	35	55	43	26
White Democrats	29	70	21	79	27
Black Democrats	3	96	4	95	7

(continued)

TABLE D-2   *(concluded)*

Characteristic	Vote in 1984		Vote in 1988		Percent of 1988 Vote
	Reagan	*Mondale*	*Bush*	*Dukakis*	
Liberals	28	70	18	81	18
Moderates	63	47	49	50	45
Conservatives	82	17	80	19	33
Professional or manager	62	37	59	40	31
White collar worker	59	40	57	42	11
Blue collar worker	54	45	49	50	13
Full-time student	52	47	44	54	4
Teacher	51	48	47	51	5
Unemployed	32	67	37	62	5
Homemaker	61	38	58	41	10
Retired	60	40	50	49	16
1984 Reagan voters	100	0	80	19	56
1984 Democratic Reagan voters	100	0	48	51	9
1984 Mondale voters	0	100	7	92	28
First-time voters	61	38	51	47	7

*The 1988 *New York Times*/CBS News exit poll was based on questionnaires completed by voters as they left polling places throughout the United States on election day. The poll included 11,645 voters in 293 randomly selected voting precincts. The 1984 data come from similar exit polling in that year, based on questionnaires from 9,174 voters. Those who gave no answer are not shown.

Source: *New York Times,* November 10, 1988, p. 18.

House had lost seats in the House. And, the Democrats gained a Senate seat, to hold a 55–45 seat margin. In Connecticut, Virginia, Nebraska, and Nevada, senate seats switched from Republican to Democratic; in Montana, Louisiana, and Florida, Republicans captured former Democratic seats.

In the state governments, 1988 was largely a *status quo* election year. The Democrats won two new governorships—Evan Bayh became the first Democratic Indiana governor in 20 years, and Democratic businessman Gaston Caperton ousted incumbent West Virginia Governor Arch A. Moore, Jr. The Republicans captured a governorship from the Democrats in Montana; state senator Stan Stephens upset a reelection attempt by former governor Thomas Judge. After the election, 28 states had Democratic governors and 22 states had Republican governors, a net gain of one for the Democrats. Democrats retained control of both houses of the state legislatures in 27 states, and one Republican legislature (New Mexico) switched to a Democratic majority. The Republicans retained control of both houses in 8 states; none switched

from Democratic to Republican. The two parties divided control of the two houses in 13 states; and Nebraska's one-house legislature is nonpartisan.

Turnout in the presidential election was unusually low; only 50 percent of the voting age population cast ballots. Those who did vote carried a heavy burden of decision-making, required to make choices among a bewildering array of offices and batteries of propositions. At the extreme, voters in San Francisco had to choose among candidates for federal, state, and local offices, take sides on 29 state ballot propositions, and vote up or down on 24 municipal propositions! Many undoubtedly found voting too demanding, and many of those who went to the polls voted at the top of the ballot but suffered fatigue further down. And, many voters split their tickets, probably a record number, voting for one party's candidate for president and the other party's candidate for other offices. The record breaking ticket-splitting of the 1988 election indicates the volatility of the electorate, and foreshadows possible surprises for presidential elections in the 1990s.

A

Abscam   A 1979 FBI undercover operation in which agents posed as Arab businessmen seeking to bribe U.S. congressmen, seven of whom were eventually convicted of taking the bribes. The name "Abscam" derives from combining the words *Arab* and *scam.*

Absolute majority   More than 50 percent of those who are eligible to vote, regardless of how many potential voters are attending or voting. For example, to win the presidency, a candidate must win an absolute majority (270) of the 538 electoral votes.

Absolute rule   Government without limits on the exercise of power, under which the people have no protected or constitutional rights. Originally applied to the monarchs of 18th-century Europe.

Access   The ability of individuals or groups to have their points of view heard by those with the power to make decisions.

Administrative assistant (AA)   In congressional offices and other agencies, the person who serves as the key aide to the principal (senator, representative, administrator) and manages the office.

Advice and consent   The U.S. Senate's constitutional right (Article II, Section 2) to review and approve treaties and major presidential appointments.

Agencies   A generic term for the units of government in the executive branch; also called *bureaucracies.* Departments, bureaus, offices, commissions, authorities, administrations, and boards are among the designations that are often given to agencies.

Agenda setting   The stage of the policy process in which the government decides what problems to address.

Alienated   Those who feel estranged from their work, family, government, or society; alienation may mean dropping out of the political process, nonvoting, feelings of contempt for government.

Amicus curiae   Latin phrase meaning "friend of the court"; a person or party that, although not a party to a lawsuit, is permitted to participate, usually by filing a brief on behalf of one side or the other.

Apolitical   Being outside politics; not concerned with or interested in political affairs.

Appellate courts   Courts of law that hear appeals from the losing parties in trial court decisions.

Apportionment   The allocation of representatives to a legislative body (e.g., Congress or the state legislatures) from the various jurisdictions. The U.S. Constitution allots each state two senators and at least one member of the House of Representatives. Beyond this, each state is allocated additional representatives according to its population after each decennial census.

Aristocracy   Rule by a small elite group; more generally, a class of people with great wealth and status, usually inherited.

Articles of Confederation   The first constitution of the United States, in effect by 1781. It established a weak national government of the states that had been freed from British rule by the American Revolution, making no provision for a national executive or national courts. It was superseded in 1789 by the Constitution of the United States.

Atheist   A person who does not believe in God.

Attentive publics   Groups of citizens who are well informed, highly motivated, and often take an active stand on one or more public policy issues.

Australian ballot   The term for a secret ballot printed at government expense and employed at official polling stations under the supervision of election officials. This type of ballot replaced the nonsecret ballots distributed by political parties. First used in Australia, it was introduced in the United States as part of election reforms adopted in the 1880s.

Authoritarianism   A system of control in which leaders can compel people to obey their orders and can deny citizens their freedom.

B

Backgrounder   A meeting between a government official and the press in which the information conveyed cannot be directly attributed to the official.

Ballot position effect   The influence on the outcome of elections deriving from the location of the names of candidates on the ballot.

Benevolent leadership   A person who exercises power so as to enhance the welfare of his or her following and does this in such a way as to engender feelings of well-being.

Bicameral   A legislative body composed of two houses. The U.S. Congress is bicameral, consisting of the House of Representatives and the Senate.

Bill of attainder   A legislative act declaring a person or persons guilty of a crime without a trial and assessing punishment for that crime. Bills of attainder are prohibited in Article I, Sections 9 and 10 of the U.S. Constitution.

Bill of Rights The first 10 amendments to the U.S. Constitution, ratified in 1791. These amendments place restrictions on the national government's power, protecting the civil rights and liberties of individuals.

Bipartisanship A tradition, especially voiced in foreign affairs, whereby the two parties consult and cooperate under the theory that "politics stops at the water's edge."

Block grants Monetary grants-in-aid from the national government to states and localities for broad functional purposes, with lots of discretion about how to spend the money left to the states and localities.

Budget controllability The ability of the U.S. Congress or the president under existing law to control spending during a specific fiscal year. By this definition, much of the budget is uncontrollable.

Budget of the United States Government A multivolume document published in the winter of each year that contains the administration's request for congressional budgetary action for the fiscal year beginning the following October 1.

Bureaucracies Individual agencies in the bureaucracy. See *Agencies*.

Bureaucracy The totality of government agencies responsible for the day-to-day functioning of the government.

Bureaucrats Individuals employed by bureaucracies, or government agencies.

C

Cabinet The group of presidential advisers consisting of the heads of executive departments plus some others whom the president designates as having cabinet rank.

Campaigners Individuals who engage in activities designed to get a candidate elected to a political or governmental office.

Campaign strategy The plan for conducting a campaign for political party or public elective office, including fund-raising, recruiting and organizing a staff, establishing a campaign headquarters, preparing and executing a mass-media campaign, managing campaign travel, writing speeches, and planning direct mail efforts.

Candidate-centered campaigning Campaigning for elective office in which the major thrust of the campaign centers on the candidate rather than on the candidate's political party.

Catalytic group A coalition of groups established to coordinate their efforts on a particular lobbying project or issue concern. For example, the Leadership Coalition on Civil Rights combined civil rights, labor, and education organizations.

Categorical grants Federal grants-in-aid awarded to states or localities for a specific purpose, usually requiring matching funds, with little discretion about how to spend the money left to the states or localities.

Caucus A meeting of the members of a political party to conduct business, select candidates, or choose delegates to a state or national nominating convention.

Central clearance A function of the Office of Management and Budget (OMB) in which it analyzes and approves or disapproves legislative proposals emanating from executive departments and agencies according to their conformity with the president's policies and programs.

Centralization The process of drawing governing power and practice from lower units of government to higher ones.

Checks and balances The distribution of powers among separate branches of government so as to protect each branch from interference by the others.

Civic education A program of enlightenment intended to improve knowledge about public affairs, and perhaps also to ingrain commitment and loyalty to a political regime.

Civil service A collective term for all nonmilitary employees of a national, state, or local government.

Class action suits Lawsuits brought on behalf of an entire class of people who are in a similar legal position.

Clientele Individuals or groups that benefit from the services provided by a government agency; also called *clientele agency, clientele program*.

Closed primary See *Primary, closed*.

Closed rule A rule, proposed by the Rules Committee, that controls debate on the floor of the U.S. House of Representatives and permits no amendments to be presented during floor deliberation.

Cloture A formal process for ending extended debate in the U.S. Senate, requiring a motion signed by 16 senators followed by an affirmative vote of three fifths of all senators. See *Filibuster*.

Coalition A cluster of people and groups that can agree at least temporarily on a desirable outcome and work to achieve that outcome.

Coalition of minorities Term referring to the thesis that presidential popularity falls over time because of the accumulation of committed citizens' groups that are opposed to specific presidential decisions.

Cold War Hostile but noncombatant relations—marked by competition, arms buildups, and international tension—between the United States and the Soviet Union in the post–World War II period.

Commemorative measures Bills, resolutions, or laws providing for special recognition of individuals, places, things, or events (e.g., the naming of federal buildings; the issuance of special coins or medals; or the designation of special days, weeks, or months).

Commerce clause   The provision of Article I, Section 8 of the U.S. Constitution that empowers Congress to control trade among the states and with foreign countries. The commerce power is the basis for the national government's regulatory control over a wide range of activities affecting interstate and foreign commerce.

Committee of the whole   A legislative committee consisting of all the members of the legislature. In Congress, a Committee of the Whole House on the State of the Union is made up of the entire membership of the House of Representatives.

Committees of correspondence   Groups of citizens in the American colonies who organized themselves in the 1770s to exchange information and promote the overthrow of English rule.

Communist   A member of the Communist Party of the United States (CPUS); a believer in the Marxist doctrine that the class struggle in capitalist societies will end in socialist revolution, whereafter the Communist party will rule as the "vanguard of the proletariat."

Community activist   An individual who is active in public affairs in his or her community but is not necessarily involved in party or electoral politics. For example, the president of the community chest is a community activist who may not be involved in politics.

Competitive regulatory policies   Domestic policies that limit the number of people or groups that can supply or deliver certain goods and services.

Complete activist   A person who is involved in community social and political activity in a wide variety of ways.

Compound republic   See *Mixed government.*

Compulsory voting   A legal provision stipulating that citizens must vote in elections or pay a penalty. Such a provision has been adopted by a few democratic countries, including Australia, but has been ruled unconstitutional in the United States.

Concurrent powers   Governmental powers that may be exercised by both the national government and state governments. Taxation is good example of a concurrent power.

Conference committee   A committee comprising members of both houses of a bicameral legislature, whose purpose is to resolve differences in the versions of a bill or resolution passed by the two chambers.

Congressional liaison   Staffs in the White House and other executive agencies that are responsible for dealing with members of Congress, handling complaints, and lobbying for desired legislation.

Connecticut Compromise   The proposal advanced by the Connecticut delegation at the Constitutional Convention of 1787 to resolve differences between nationalism and state sovereignty by creating a bicameral Congress with a House of Representatives based on population and a Senate based on equal representation of the states.

Consent of the governed   The idea that government ought to be based on the will of the people.

Conservative   A political disposition to prefer the status quo and accept change only in moderation.

Conservative coalition   A bipartisan group of Republicans and conservative southern Democrats who vote together in Congress and who tended to dominate congressional politics from the late 1930s through the 1960s.

Conspiracy theories   Explanations of social, political, or economic events that emphasize secret deals, behind-the-scenes decision making, evil intentions, and plotting to engage in unlawful acts.

Constitutionalism   The tradition of limitations on the power of government, whose ultimate authority lies in the consent of the governed.

Converting election   An election in which a basic change in party support takes place but the normal majority party retains its dominant position.

Coordinated expenditures   Spending by political parties to support candidates (e.g., for polls, media production, consultants) that benefits specific candidates but does not involve direct financial contributions to a candidate's campaign committee.

Cracking   A technique of gerrymandering in which an area of strength for one political party is split between two or more districts so as to minimize that party's voting leverage.

Craft union   A labor organization whose membership is restricted to skilled craft workers, such as carpenters or bricklayers.

Crisis management   The process of handling a crisis situation by orchestrating the efforts of subordinates, reassuring the public, gathering accurate information, and handling press relations.

Crisis policies   Foreign and defense policies that are short-run responses to immediate problems that are perceived as serious, have burst on the agenda with little or no warning, and demand immediate action.

Critical election   An election that heralds a new political alignment, produces a new electoral majority, or indicates a secular shift in voting behavior.

Cross-cutting requirements   A form of regulatory federalism in which grant-in-aid recipients are required to comply with federal standards in matters not directly related to the aid.

Crossover sanctions A form of regulatory federalism in which sanctions are imposed on states or localities for failure to take actions imposed by the national government.

Cue giving The process of giving information or advice on voting or other behavior, as in a legislative body when leaders or well-informed members provide benchmarks for their colleagues.

D

Dark horse A long-shot candidate who is not given much chance to win a nomination or an election.

Dealignment Shifts in partisan allegiance in the electorate that dilute the influence that the major parties have over elections and voter attitudes.

Deficit The annual difference between government revenue and government spending if spending is larger than revenue.

Delegate role The role played by a legislator who acts as a conduit for constituent opinions and interests.

Democracy Rule by the people, or popular sovereignty. In a direct democracy, the people make laws directly; in a representative democracy, the people rule through elected representatives. The United States is a representative democracy.

Democratic party The national U.S. political party founded by Thomas Jefferson and James Madison as the Democratic-Republican party. The current name of the party was initiated in 1828 under Andrew Jackson's leadership.

Deviating election An election in which the system's basic electoral cleavages remain stable or unchanged, but the presidential candidate of the normal majority party suffers defeat.

Direct orders A form of regulatory federalism in which the national government gives direct orders to the states and localities.

Direct primary An election held to nominate the candidates of a political party.

Direct vote plan A proposal to abolish the electoral college system for electing the president and instead to choose the president through a direct popular election.

Discharge rule A legislative procedure through which a bill or resolution may be removed from a committee that has not acted on it.

Disenfranchisement Denial of the right to vote in elections. Millions of black Americans were disenfranchised in southern states after the Civil War and Reconstruction.

Distributive policies Domestic policies that provide governmental subsidies for private actions by individuals, groups, and corporations.

Divine right The notion that God has granted monarchs a right to rule. The Declaration of Independence flatly rejected this notion of the "divine right of kings."

Dual federalism The notion that the powers, functions, and responsibilities of the national and state governments are completely separate and distinct. Although this notion was widely held in the 19th century, it is no longer accepted.

Due process Protection against arbitrary action by government in violation of a person's civil rights or liberties, provided in the 5th and 14th amendments to the U.S. Constitution. Procedural due process concerns the fairness and propriety of the way in which legislative or administrative processes are executed. Substantive due process concerns the reasonableness and appropriateness of the subject matter or content of a law or an executive order.

E

Early money Campaign contributions that come to candidates early in an election effort; large early contributions may help a candidate "kill the money" for prospective opponents, thus crippling their candidacies.

Economic indicators Measures of economic activity that are published on a regular basis and are used by professional economists, politicians, the media, and the interested part of the public both to gauge the effect of government policies and to point toward needed future policies.

Electoral college system The system provided in the U.S. Constitution for the election of the president and vice president. Each state gets as many presidential electors as it has members of Congress; a presidential candidate must win an absolute majority of the electoral college vote to win.

Egalitarianism The view that all citizens should have an equal claim to the social, economic, or political rewards, benefits, or opportunities in the society.

Elastic clause The clause in Article I, Section 8 of the U.S. Constitution that empowers Congress to make all "necessary and proper" laws to carry out its enumerated powers.

Elitism Rule by the few.

Embassy A nation's major diplomatic staff, headed by an ambassador, in the capital of a foreign nation, established for the conduct of normal business between the two nations.

Entitlement program A government program that pays benefits to individuals, organizations, or other governments that meet the eligibility requirements set by law. The national government's largest entitlement program is Social Security; other entitlement programs of the national government include Medicare, Medicaid, unemployment insurance, and food stamps.

Enumerated powers The governmental powers that are explicitly spelled out in the U.S. Constitution, for example, the powers listed in Article I, Section 8.

Equality of opportunity The objective of public policies intended to assure that all persons in a similar class or category have the same chance to get what there is to get.

Equal protection The constitutional requirement that the government not treat people unequally on the basis of their race or religion. Equal protection of the laws is required by the 14th Amendment to the U.S. Constitution.

Establishment clause The clause in the 1st Amendment to the U.S. Constitution that says, "Congress shall make no law respecting an establishment of religion." See *Freedom of religion.*

Exclusive committee A committee so important that its members are supposed to hold no other standing committee assignment. In the U.S. House of Representatives, the exclusive committees are Appropriations, Rules, and Ways and Means.

Executive agreements International agreements or understandings entered into by a president without the advice and consent of the Senate.

Executive privilege The presidential claim that certain information may be withheld from Congress or the courts in order to maintain national security or preserve confidential communications and advice.

Exit polls Election surveys taken just as voters are leaving the voting booth.

Ex post facto law A retroactive criminal law. Under such a law, past actions are declared to be criminal even though they were not crimes when they were committed.

F

Faction The term James Madison used in *The Federalist,* No. 10, to describe "a number of citizens, whether amounting to a majority or minority of the whole, who are united and actuated by some common impulse of passion, or of interest."

Fairness doctrine A Federal Communications Commission policy, recently abandoned, that required radio and television stations to allow all sides on public issues fair access to the airwaves.

Faithless elector problem Arises when a presidential elector elected to cast a vote for one presidential candidate in fact votes for some other candidate. This problem has occurred only rarely.

Federalism The division of governmental powers between a national government and subnational units (states, provinces, regions, etc.).

***Federalist* papers** A series of essays written by James Madison, Alexander Hamilton, and John Jay in support of the ratification of the U.S. Constitution. Originally published in New York newspapers in 1788–89 under the name Publius, this collection of essays is a major statement of American political thought.

Federal supremacy The doctrine of the U.S. Constitution that, within its jurisdiction, the national government is supreme. Article VI says that the Constitution, laws, and treaties "shall be the supreme law of the land," indicating that national laws take precedence over state laws.

Federal system See *Federalism.*

Filibuster In the U.S. Senate, the practice of "extended debate" to delay or kill a piece of legislation or to force its sponsors to compromise.

Fiscal policy The manipulation of government finances by raising or lowering taxes or levels of government spending, or both.

Floor leader An elected legislative party leader who plays a crucial role in scheduling business and in persuading colleagues to vote with their party.

Formulation and legitimation The stage of the policy process in which the government formulates policy and program options and either legitimates one of them by adopting it or legitimates none by failing to act.

Fragment society A society whose members came from another society, bringing that society's culture, values, and political practices and then modifying these in the new societal situation. Early American settlers were a fragment of European society.

Freedom of expression Citizens' rights to free speech and press, freedom to assemble peaceably, freedom of belief, and freedom to petition the government. The First Amendment to the Constitution is the basic source of freedom of expression in the United States.

Freedom of religion The First Amendment to the Constitution prohibits Congress from passing laws that interfere with "the free exercise of religion" and from establishing a state church. The establishment clause is the basis for the separation of church and state in the United States.

Free elections Elections in which all adults have a right to elect political leaders of their own choosing. In the United States, few restrictions are placed on who may run for public offices and all persons over 18 years old may register and vote.

Front loading In the presidential nominating process, the inordinate influence of events early in the process, such as the Iowa caucuses or the New Hampshire primary.

Full faith and credit A provision of the U.S. Constitution requiring each state to recognize the civil rulings of other states as valid.

G

Gatekeeper In mass-media organizations, the editors, producers, and so on who decide what stories will be printed or broadcast.

General elections Elections held to select national, state, or local officials from among those nominated in primary elections, by conventions, or in caucuses.

General revenue sharing The sharing of the tax revenues of the national government among subnational levels of government. The Nixon administration started revenue sharing in 1972 to help financially pressed state and local governments, and the Reagan administration discontinued it in 1986; by then, many states showed budget surpluses, and a large federal deficit had accumulated.

General ticket system A system of elections in which candidates for offices run at large, as opposed to running only in particular districts.

Geopolitics A term referring to the extent to which a nation's physical territory, location, and resources determine its power and place in international affairs.

Gerrymandering The practice of drawing legislative district boundary lines for partisan political advantage.

GOP Grand Old Party; the Republican party.

Government The political institutions and processes, established by the Constitution, through which authoritative and binding decisions are made for the society.

Graft Taking advantage of public office for the purpose of self-enrichment; includes dishonesty, conflict of interest, bribery, blackmail, extortion, and other illegal techniques.

Grants-in-aid Payments by the national government to the states or local governments or payments by a state government to local governments. Usually, grants-in-aid carry with them prescriptions of standards and requirements.

Grass-roots democracy Free government by the rank and file, the voters in general.

Grass-roots lobbying A lobbying technique in which the public is mobilized behind a particular issue or measure, thus putting pressure on the elected decision maker to approve it.

Great Society The label for the domestic policies promulgated in the 1960s by President Lyndon B. Johnson and the huge Democratic party majorities in Congress. These policies were predicated on the belief that social and economic problems could be solved by adopting new federal programs and appropriating money. "The Great Society," said President Johnson, "demands an end to poverty and racial injustice."

Gross national product (GNP) The money value of all the goods and services produced in a nation in a particular year.

Gubernatorial powers Those powers that the governor of an American state may constitutionally exercise.

H

Home style The way in which legislators project themselves to their home constituencies, including their style of presentation, their use of the perquisites of office, and their explanation of legislative activity.

Homosexual A person who is sexually attracted to another person of the same sex.

Honeymoon period The brief period after taking office when an elected executive has uncritical public support and harmonious relations with the press, the legislature, and the public.

Horse-race coverage Media coverage of elections that focuses on the contest between the candidates rather than the issues.

Human rights Those rights to which all persons are entitled as human beings.

I

Ideologue One who believes intensely in a political ideology; a "true believer."

Ideology, political A comprehensive system of beliefs related to a program of political action (e.g., socialism, communism, fascism).

Impact The effect of government policies and programs on society or part of society. Impacts may be both intended and unintended.

Impeachment The power of Congress to remove the president, the vice president, federal judges, or other federal officials from office.

Imperial presidency The concept of a presidency grown too powerful in foreign affairs, wielding powers not granted by the Constitution.

Implementation The stage of the policy process in which the government takes concrete actions to reach its goals.

Implied powers The constitutional doctrine that the congressional power "to make all laws which shall be necessary and proper for carrying into execution the foregoing powers" (Article I, Section 8) implies that Congress can pass legislation on subjects not specifically listed in the Constitution. This doctrine was fully elaborated in the U.S. Supreme Court case of *McCulloch* v. *Maryland* (1819).

Inactives Individuals who are not involved in politics.

Incomes policy An economic policy that relies on direct controls of prices and wages by government.

Incorporation The judicial application of the protections of the U.S. Bill of Rights to the states, usually through the due process clause of the 14th Amendment.

Incumbency effect An incumbent is a current officeholder; the incumbency effect is the overwhelming advantage that incumbents have in winning reelection.

Independent spending The campaign contributions that organized groups or individuals make to political candidates insofar as these groups or individuals do not consult or coordinate with the candidate's campaign organization.

Individualistic political culture A political tradition in which politics is primarily a means through which individuals may improve themselves economically or socially.

Individual liberty The freedoms that individuals enjoy because they are protected by the Constitution and laws. In the United States, individual liberties are protected by the provisions of the Bill of Rights.

Industrial union A labor union that seeks to enroll all of the workers in a given industry—e.g., all autoworkers, all steelworkers, or all public employees.

Influence The ability of individuals or groups to help shape decisions.

Inherent powers Powers in foreign affairs arising from the status of the United States as a sovereign nation, necessarily engaged in external relations with other nations. These powers are not limited to express powers, such as the power to declare war or the power to make treaties.

Initiative and referendum Procedures through which citizens can vote on laws directly, dispensing with legislative deliberation. The initiative is a procedure in which a proposed new law is placed on an election ballot after the required number of signatures has been attained on a petition; fewer than half of the states provide for the initiative. The referendum is a procedure in which the legislature refers a proposal of law to the voters for ratification.

Insider strategy A strategy for winning the presidential nomination by obtaining support from party leaders and organized blocs within a party.

Interest group A group based on a common concern or interest that seeks to influence government agencies or policies.

Intergovernmental relations The political, programmatic, fiscal, and administrative processes by which higher units of government share revenues and other resources with lower units, usually if the lower units meet conditions established by the higher units.

Iran-*contra* affair A scheme within the Reagan administration during 1985 and 1986 in which arms were sold to Iran (to gain the release of American hostages) at high prices and the "profits" were transmitted to the *contras* fighting the Nicaraguan Sandinista regime.

Isolationism The policy of a nation to "go it alone" in world politics, to have as little as possible to do with other nations. This was the foreign policy of the United States during most of the 19th century.

Issue voting Voting for a candidate, not because of the candidate's political party affiliation, but because of his or her stand on issues.

Item veto The power of the executive to disapprove separate items in a bill. Many state governors have this constitutional power, but the president does not.

J

Judicial activism The theory and practice of judges who expand the role of courts in policy questions by interpreting laws broadly and questioning the policy choices of the legislative and executive branches.

Judicial restraint The theory and practice of judges who are reluctant to expand the role of courts in policy questions and therefore interpret laws narrowly and defer to the policy choices of the legislative and executive branches.

Judicial review The doctrine that allows the federal courts to declare unconstitutional actions of Congress, the executive branch, or the states, rendering those actions unenforceable. The U.S. Supreme Court renders the final court determination of constitutionality.

K

Keynesianism An economic theory whose essence is that government must intervene to adjust the level of demand for goods and services.

Kitchen cabinet A group of informal advisers of the chief executive. The term was first used to characterize advisers of Andrew Jackson who were said to meet in the kitchen because they were too disreputable to meet in the formal rooms of the White House.

L

Leaks Deliberate disclosures of information to the press in order to affect the outcome of a political controversy or debate.

Legislative assistant (LA) A staff aide to an elected legislator who specializes in the issues on which legislators must vote.

Legislative power   The constitutional power to make laws.

Legislative supremacy   The idea that the legislature's actions take precedence over executive or judicial power.

Legislative veto   A provision in a congressional statute that allows Congress, in one of a number of specific ways, to prevent specific programmatic actions proposed by the president or some unit in the executive branch. Such provisions were technically ruled unconstitutional in a 1983 U.S. Supreme Court decision, but existing legislative veto provisions have continued to be honored by both Congress and the executive branch and new legislative veto provisions have been enacted.

Legitimacy   The quality that gives political institutions not only the power to govern but also the right to do so. People obey legitimate authority because they regard it as rightful.

Libel   The creation or dissemination of written material that is false and malicious and that injures persons by subjecting them to ridicule or hatred.

Liberal   A person who favors government regulation of business in the public interest and government programs for education, welfare, medical care, and the like, on the ground that the masses of people would have little chance to enjoy freedom without government intervention on their behalf.

Liberal tradition   A long-standing practice of laissez-faire economic policies, individual freedom from interference by government, religious toleration, and the idea that individuals have natural rights that go beyond the rights that the government will protect.

Libertarian   An individual who thinks that government should not interfere in the lives of its citizens and that governing should involve little more than providing police protection and national security. Libertarians agree that "that government is best which governs least."

Liberty   A personal act that cannot be limited by government. See *Individual liberty*.

Limited government   The constitutional doctrine that sets limits on what the government can do. The U.S. Constitution, for example, sets limits on what the national and state governments can do.

Lobbyist   An individual or group that seeks to influence legislation or administrative action.

Local government   Any units of government that are clearly not national or state governments, including counties, cities, towns, townships, parishes, and special districts, such as school districts.

Louisiana Purchase   The territory extending from the Mississippi River to the Rocky Mountains and from the Gulf of Mexico to Canada, which the United States purchased from France in 1803, during Thomas Jefferson's presidency.

M

McCarthyism   Extreme and irresponsible anticommunism, epitomized by the behavior of U.S. Senator Joseph R. McCarthy (D-Wisc.), who flouted individual rights, recklessly charged that individuals were communists, and found people guilty by association in the congressional hearings that he conducted during the early 1950s. Ultimately, the U.S. Senate censured McCarthy for misconduct.

Machine politics   Control of a city, county, or state by a political boss who commands loyalty through patronage, favors, largess, intimidation, or affection.

Maintaining election   An election in which basic party loyalties in the electorate remain stable and the normal majority party wins.

Majority leader   The leader, elected by party colleagues, of the political party with a majority of the members of a legislative body.

Malapportionment   The drawing of legislative district boundary lines such that some segments of the population are greatly over- or underrepresented.

Marginal district   A legislative district in which the electoral outcome could go either way; usually defined as a legislative district in which the winning margin is no more than 55 or 60 percent.

Markup   A business meeting of a legislative committee in which a bill or resolution is worked on, amended, and prepared for reporting to the full legislative chamber.

Matthew effect   The general tendency of election systems to award majority political parties a larger share of the legislative seats than is warranted by their proportion of the popular vote. By the same token, minority parties tend to be awarded a smaller proportion of the legislative seats than is warranted by their proportion of the popular vote.

Midterm elections   The congressional elections that are held in the second year of a presidential term. Typically, the president's party loses congressional seats in midterm elections.

Military-industrial complex   A phrase that President Dwight Eisenhower used in his 1961 farewell address to characterize the undue concentration of power in the nation's armed forces and their industrial suppliers.

Mixed government   A system of government that divides the exercise of political power between a national government and component states and between legislative, executive, and judicial branches of government. The framers of the U.S. Constitution fashioned such a system, which Alexander Hamilton called a *compound republic*.

Momentum   In an election campaign, the boost given to a candidate by a favorable event, such as a primary victory or a favorable poll result, or simply by the assumption that the candidate is on the road to victory.

Monetarism An economic theory whose essence is that the market will produce the most efficient use of economic resources if the government keeps the money supply growing at the same rate as the growth of productivity in the economy.

Monetary policy Government actions that deal with the amount of money in circulation, interest rates (the cost of borrowing money), and the functioning of credit markets and the banking system.

Moralistic political culture A political tradition in which politics is conceived as an important public good, political office is viewed as a public trust, and political decision making is expected to be in the public interest.

Muckrakers The name that President Theodore Roosevelt gave to investigative journalists.

Multiple-member district A legislative constituency in which two or more seats are to be filled.

N

National identity The extent to which the citizens of a nation identify themselves with that nation. American national identity was well established at the time of the Revolution; today nearly all of the people living in the United States identify themselves as Americans.

Natural rights Rights of persons that derive from natural law and cannot be abrogated by government. The Declaration of Independence says that people are "endowed by their Creator with certain unalilenable rights."

New Deal coalition The political alignment of urban workers, farmers, ethnics, Southerners, and liberal intellectuals associated with the election of Franklin D. Roosevelt in 1932. The domestic policies and programs of the Roosevelt administration were known as the New Deal. The coalition that supported the New Deal made the Democratic party the dominant U.S. party for three decades, and debate about the status of this coalition continues. See *Coalition*.

New Jersey Plan The proposal that William Paterson of New Jersey advanced at the 1787 Constitutional Convention, which provided for equal representation of the states in a one-house Congress, a plural national executive apointed by Congress, and a judiciary appointed by the executive.

News hole The amount of space available for news stories, once advertising and features have been accounted for.

Nominating convention A party meeting, composed of delegates from local party organizations, to nominate candidates for public office.

Nonconformity Unwillingness to adhere to conventional standards or practices of politics, social behavior, or morality.

Nonpartisanship A system in which legislative activity or elections are carried on without political party labels or partisan loyalties. Many U.S. city officials are chosen in nonpartisan elections, and the Nebraska legislature is nonpartisan.

O

Office-bloc ballot An election ballot organized so that all of the candidates are listed under the office for which they are running.

Oligarchy Rule by a minority political elite; rule of the many by the few.

Open rule A rule governing debate in the U.S. House of Representatives, reported to the House floor by the Rules Committee, that permits amendments to be made on the floor.

Opinion leaders The political informed and interested minority of the population who share views with their friends and associates and thus help shape public opinion.

Outsider strategy A presidential nomination strategy that stresses mass public support, popularity in the polls, and effective use of the media.

Oversight A generic name for the various means by which Congress monitors the implementation of programs by executive-branch agencies and keeps Congress informed about such implementation.

P

Packing A gerrymandering strategem in which election district boundary lines are drawn to include as many of one party's voters as possible in election districts so as to make those districts safe for the incumbents or to waste the votes of the opposition party.

Pack journalism The tendency of reporters to read one another's work and shape their stories so that these are in agreement.

Parliamentarian The officer in a legislative body who interprets the rules, procedures, and precedents governing debate.

Partial preemption A form of regulatory federalism in which the national government sets the basic policies to be followed in a program, giving the states or local governments administrative responsibility if certain standards are met.

Party caucus See *Caucus*.

Party government A governing process in which political parties formulate programs, define alternatives for the voters, and have the power to implement their programs if elected.

Party identification Loyalty to a political party. The

vast majority of Americans identify themselves as either Democrats or Republicans, but a significant minority identify themselves as "independents."

Party platform A statement of party principles and proposals drawn up at election time, usually at the national party conventions.

Party unity votes According to *Congressional Quarterly,* a Washington-based reporting service, any legislative vote in which a majority of Republicans is aligned against a majority of Democrats. See *Party voting.*

Party voting Vote choices made on the basis of party identification; voting a straight ticket is a form of party voting. In a legislative body, a party vote is a vote along party lines, in which members of one party vote against members of the other party.

Party-centered campaigns Campaigns for public office that are managed and funded by the political party organization and its leadership.

Party-column ballot An election ballot organized so that all candidates are listed under their party designation.

Patronage The practice of rewarding party or political loyalists, friends, or supporters with jobs, contracts, or other favors.

Pigeonhole In legislative parlance, to kill a bill or resolution by allowing it to languish in committee.

Platform A statement of basic principles put forth by a political party.

Plurality vote The vote of a candidate for an elective office that, though larger than the votes of other candidates for the office, is not a majority.

Pocket veto The failure of a president to sign a bill into law that Congress passed when fewer than 10 days were left in the congressional session. The bill is thus lost.

Point of order A parliamentary objection that normal procedure is not being followed.

Policy The government's official statements about its goals and planned actions.

Political action committee (PAC) An organization whose purpose is to raise and distribute campaign funds to its favorite candidates for political office. First developed by labor unions, PACs are now most numerous among business and trade associations.

Political culture The pattern of beliefs, evaluations, and symbols associated with the political community, the constitutional system, and the government of the day.

Political cynicism Contemptuous distrust of political leaders, processes, and institutions, based on the belief that political conduct is motivated mainly by self-interest.

Political development The evolution of political and governing institutions so that they become stable, relatively complex, legitimate, responsive, and effective.

Political efficacy A citizen's belief that he or she can understand and participate in public affairs and that the political process is responsive to such participation.

Political equality A condition in which all citizens have equal political influence. In the American system of political representation, the prevailing "one person, one vote" doctrine is an attempt to achieve this condition. See *Equal protection.*

Political laboratories The states are laboratories in which politicians get occupational training and in which policymakers experiment with innovations in public policies.

Politically active subculture Those individuals and groups in a political system that are highly motivated to be involved in politics and public affairs.

Political party An organization whose primary purpose is to capture control of political offices by getting its leaders elected to them.

Political socialization The process through which political values, attitudes, beliefs, and symbols are transmitted from one generation to another.

Political trust The extent to which citizens have confidence in political institutions and the people running them.

Politico role A role adopted by legislators that is a pragmatic mixture of the delegate and trustee roles.

Poll tax A tax levied on citizens as a condition for voting in elections. In 1964, the 24th Amendment to the Constitution prohibited poll taxes in the United States.

Popular sovereignty Rule by the people. The U.S. Constitution enshrines popular sovereignty in its Preamble: "We the People of the United States, in order to form a more perfect union . . ."

Populist A person who believes in mobilizing the masses, or the poorer sectors of society, against the existing power structure. In the United States, populism grew out of the farmers' protest movement of the 1890s.

Position effect The advantage or disadvantage to a candidate for office stemming from his or her name's location on the ballot or voting machine.

Power elite Any group of political leaders who are in a position to exercise major power. See *Elitism.*

Power of the purse Control over the distribution of the money raised and spent by the government. Because the power to tax and spend public funds is explicitly given to congress in the U.S. Constitution, Congress is said to have "the power of the purse."

Preprimary convention A party convention that is held to reach agreement on a nominee for public office before the primary election, either to forestall the primary or to influence the primary's outcome.

Presidential electors The electors who compose the

electoral college, which elects the president and vice president of the United States. In the presidential election held every four years, voters in each state choose as many presidential electors as the state has U.S. senators and representatives. See *Electoral college system*.

Presidential veto   See *Veto*.

President pro tem   In the U.S. Senate and state senates, the officer who acts in place of the vice president or lieutenant governor in performing routine and ceremonial duties for the chamber.

Primary, blanket   A primary election that permits voters to choose candidates from more than one political party on the same day, e.g. by voting for a gubernatorial candidate of one party, a senatorial candidate of another party, a state legislative candidate of another party, and so on. The states of Alaska and Washington have blanket primaries.

Primary, closed   A primary election in which a voter must declare his or her political party affiliation and vote only the ballot of the party with which he or she is affiliated.

Primary, open   A primary election in which a voter may vote for the nomination of any party's candidate regardless of the voter's prior political party affiliation.

Primary election   An election held before the general election to nominate a political party's candidates for public offices.

Prior restraint   Prepublication censorship.

Private bill   A bill that deals with matters concerning an individual citizen.

Probability sampling   The method of drawing samples for public opinion polls so that every sampling unit (e.g., an individual or an area) has an equal probability of being selected.

Progressive tax   A tax in which people in each successively higher income bracket pay a progressively higher tax rate. The federal income tax is an example of progressive taxation.

Property rights   The constitutional rights of individuals to the protection of their property. The 5th Amendment says that Congress cannot pass laws depriving individuals of their "life, liberty, or property without due process of law," and the 14th Amendment applies these rights to the states.

Protective regulatory policies   Domestic policies that protect the public by setting conditions for various private activities. Some of these conditions ban or limit harmful activities; others require helpful activities.

Public funding   Government financing of presidential election campaign costs; which the Federal Elections Campaign Act provides for candidates who qualify and wish to accept a federal subsidy. Funds are provided from the presidential election campaign fund, to which taxpayers contribute by checking a box on their federal income tax returns.

Public interest group   An interest group that claims to represent a broad public good rather than a narrow economic or social interest.

Public law   A law enacted by a legislative body and signed by the executive; a law that deals, not with an individual, but with large classes of people.

Public opinion polls   Measurements of public opinion that use scientific sampling procedures and interviews.

Public presidency   A term referring to the efforts that modern presidents have made to "go public" by exploiting their visibility and media access to overcome the limitations imposed by checks and balances.

Q

Quorum   The number of a legislative body's members required to conduct business; usually majority of the body's elected members.

Quorum call   A call of the roll in a legislative body to determine whether a quorum is present.

R

Rally-round-the-flag   An upsurge of popularity experienced by presidents in times of crisis.

Ratification   The process of giving approval. The U.S. Constitution provided that it would take effect upon the ratification of nine states. Constitutional amendments must be ratified by conventions or legislatures in three fourths of the states.

Reagan doctrine   The idea that U.S. policy should encourage and support anticommunist movements throughout the world.

Realigning election   An election in which the basic party loyalties of voters change and the normal party majority is displaced.

Realignment   See Realigning election.

Realignment, split-level   A change in voter allegiances such that party realignment takes one form at the presidential level (e.g., favoring Republicans) and another at the congressional level (e.g., favoring Democrats).

Recall election   An election that allows citizens to vote officeholders out of office between regularly scheduled elections. A recall election can be called through a petition bearing the legally required number of voters' signatures.

Reconciliation bill   A bill under the congressional budget process that reconciles tax, spending, and debt levels with ceilings adopted earlier in a budget resolution.

Redistributive policies   Domestic policies that are perceived to transfer wealth, property rights, or some other value to one social class or racial group at the expense of another social class or racial group.

Reference group A group that serves as a positive or negative guidepost for many people who are not formal members.

Regime A system of government that is provided for in a nation's constitution; the constitutional system.

Regressive tax A tax placing a reduced burden on higher-income earners because the tax is a flat rate. Its effect is such that the percentage of income paid in taxes falls as the level of income increases. Sales taxes are often said to be regressive.

Regulatory federalism The national government's practice of using relationships with state and local governments as the basis for regulating individuals, organizations, and intergovernmental relations.

Representation, political A process in which a person speaks for, acts for, or symbolizes a constituency.

Representation, virtual A situation in which a group's interests are served by elected officials who are not members of the group.

Representative government A system of government in which legislatures representative of the people are chosen in free elections.

Republican government A system in which "government of the people, by the people, for the people" is carried out through elected representatives. The U.S. Constitution guarantees every state a "republican form of government."

Republican party The national U.S. political party founded in 1854 that first won major office with the election of Abraham Lincoln as president in 1860 and dominated American politics until the New Deal.

Reserved powers Powers not delegated to the national government, which the 10th Amendment declares are "reserved to the states . . . or to the people." These powers are not defined specifically; traditionally, they have included the states' police powers—to regulate the health, safety, and morals of the people.

Resulting powers Constitutional powers of the national government that arise out of two or more powers specifically enumerated in the U.S. Constitution.

Retrospective voting Voting in elections in which the voter bases his or her choice on an evaluation of the past performance of the incumbent officeholder, the incumbent administration, or the incumbent political party.

Revenue sharing See *General revenue sharing*.

Right A claim, backed by law and government action, to certain protections, guarantees, or benefits. See *Individual liberty*.

Rights of accused The constitutional rights accorded to persons accused of crimes, such as the right to a fair trial, the right to counsel, protection from self-incrimination, the right to bail, and protection against cruel and unusual punishment.

Rotation in office The practice, derived from Jacksonian democracy, of frequently changing the occupants of political offices so that they do not acquire the "arrogance of power."

Runoff primary A primary election that is held when no candidate wins a majority in an earlier primary.

S

Sampling error The error caused by generalizing the behavior of a population from a sample of that population that is not completely representative of the population as a whole.

Select committee A temporary investigative committee of a legislature, originally appointed by the presiding officer.

Senatorial courtesy The deference accorded senators by the executive and other senators with regard to nominations of persons from their state to executive or judicial posts.

Seniority system The traditional practice of selecting committee and subcommittee chairmen (and the minority party's ranking members) on the basis of continuous service on the committee or subcommittee.

Separation of powers The allocation of governmental powers among three separate branches of government—the legislative, executive, and judicial branches—to prevent a concentration of power in any one governing institution.

Single-member district An election district in which only one officeholder is elected. All members of the U.S. House of Representatives are elected from single-member districts.

Social class voting Voting in elections on the basis of social class identification. For the electorate as a whole, social class voting is indicated if a large proportion of the persons in one social class vote for one party and a large proportion of the persons in another social class vote for the other party, indicating social class polarization.

Social contract The philosophical idea that the mutual obligations between the citizen and the government are grounded in a contract that they have made with each other. If the government breaks the contract, revolution is justified. The framers of the U.S. Constitution regarded it as such a contract.

Socialism A system of government in which the government owns and operates many of the means of production and distribution and provides many human welfare needs. Socialism may or may not be democratic.

Socioeconomic status (SES) A person's location in the social structure, determined by his or her levels of education, occupational prestige, and income. Sometimes SES is based on objective measurements of these levels; sometimes it is indicated through the individual's subjective view of his position.

Special committee A temporary investigative committee of a legislature, originally selected from nominations of the party caucuses. In the U.S. Congress, there is currently no practical distinction between a select committee and a special committee.

Split-ticket voting A vote cast for candidates of different political parties for different offices in the same election. A voter who votes Democratic for president and also for a Republican congressional candidate casts a split ticket.

Spoils system A derisive term for the patronage practices of one's political opponents. The term derives from a claim made during the age of Jackson that the party winning an election was entitled to monopolize political jobs—"to the victor belongs the spoils."

Standing committee A legislative committee that is defined in the rules of the body and therefore considered more or less permanent.

State of the Union address The annual presidential message to a joint session of Congress, provided for in Article II, Section 3 of the Constitution, in which the president reports on current problems and proposes his legislative initiatives.

States' rights Constitutional rights that have neither been given to the national government nor forbidden to the states. States' rights arguments are sometimes used to oppose federal policies, most notably in opposition to federal civil rights legislation.

Stewardship theory The belief that the president of the United States, as a trustee of the people, may exercise any powers not specifically prohibited by the Constitution or laws. This notion of presidential power was most explicitly articulated in President Theodore Roosevelt's *Autobiography* (1913).

Straight-ticket voting The practice of voting for the candidates of the same political party for all the offices to be filled in a given election.

Stratarchy A term describing local, state, or national political party organizations that are layered but not hierarchical.

Strategic policies Foreign and defense policies that set the basic national military and foreign policy stance.

Structural policies Foreign and defense policies that procure, locate, and organize military personnel and matériel.

Subgovernment A small cluster of people who are linked by their intense interest in a specific policy or program and make most of the routine decisions on that policy or program. These people come from congressional subcommittees with jurisdiction over the policy or program, responsible executive bureaus, and interest groups.

Subpresidencies A term used to denote separate though interlocking presidential responsibilities in national security, macroeconomics, and domestic affairs.

Suffrage The right to vote in elections.

Superdelegates Delegates' positions to Democratic national presidential nominating conventions that are set aside for party officers and elected officials without regard to candidate loyalties.

Super Tuesday The clustering of Democratic presidential primaries, especially in southern and border states, on a single day (beginning in 1988) in order to maximize the influence of those states on the nomination process.

Supply-side economics An economic theory whose essence is that government should cut taxes and keep them low to encourage a steady flow of private investment, which will support the continuous growth of the economy.

Supremacy clause See *Federal supremacy*.

Suspension of the rules In parliamentary procedure, the act of temporarily setting aside the body's usual rules, usually by a two-thirds vote, in order to take a certain action, such as passing a popular bill.

T

Tax expenditures The losses of tax revenue attributable to provisions of the federal tax laws that allow special exclusions, exemptions, or deductions from gross income or that provide special tax credits, preferential tax rates, or deferrals of tax liability.

Think tank An oganization of scholars, researchers, or specialists that produces books, pamphlets, or articles on issues of public concern.

Third parties Splinter parties or political movements that attempt to attract votes from the two major parties or to alter those parties' agendas.

Three-fifths Compromise An agreement reached at the Constitutional Convention of 1787, necessary to win the support of southern delegates, whereby three fifths of a state's black slaves would be counted along with whites to determine the state's representation in the U.S. House of Representatives. Slavery was abolished in 1865 with the adoption of the 13th Amendment to the Constitution.

Tories In the American context, persons who remained loyal to the British Crown during the American Revolution.

Trade association An organization made up of firms in a given industry.

Traditionalistic political culture A political tradition in which politics is organized hierarchically and those at the top of the social structure play a distinctive and dominant role in political decision making.

Treaty A formal agreement among sovereign nations establishing rights and obligations among the parties. In the United States, treaties are proposed by the president and do not become valid until the Senate consents to them by a two-thirds vote.

Trial courts Courts of law that have original jurisdiction over cases and hear and try them for the first time.

Trustee role A role assumed by lawmakers that emphasizes decisions based, not on constituency considerations, but on information, judgment, or conscience. Sometimes termed a *Burkean role,* after the British statesman Edmund Burke (1729–97), who advocated such a position while a member of Parliament.

Two-party system A political system in which only two political parties have a reasonable chance to win major public offices. Although other political parties exist and run candidates for office in the United States, only the Democratic and Republican party candidates have much chance of capturing the presidency and most other offices.

Two-term tradition The historic tradition, established by the example of George Washington, that the president would serve for only two terms. This tradition was broken in 1940, when Franklin D. Roosevelt was elected to a third term. In 1951, the 22nd Amendment to the Constitution limited a president to two terms.

U

Umbrella groups Interest groups that embrace a wide variety of citizen issues or concerns.

Unanimous consent A request in a legislative body that something, usually a noncontroversial action or motion, be adopted "without objection."

Unanimous consent agreement In the U.S. Senate, an agreement formulated by party floor leaders to control debate, to schedule consideration of amendments, and sometimes even to set a time for voting.

Unicameral A legislature with only one house. Of the 51 national and state legislatures in the United States, only Nebraska's is unicameral; the others are bicameral.

Unitary system A constitutional system in which all political authority lies in the hands of the central government. Many countries are unitary systems; Great Britain, France, and Japan are good examples. Within their spheres, the states of the United States are unitary systems. The United States is a federal system.

Urban machines Historically, strong party organizations in big cities that maintained control of city government by herding masses of uneducated voters to the polls in exchange for jobs and services. See *machine politics.*

V

Veto The chief executive's constitutional power to refuse approval of legislation so that it cannot become law.

Vice presidency The second-highest elective office in the United States. The vice president, who is now elected on a slate with the president, succeeds to the presidency in the event of the president's death, removal, or resignation.

Virginia Plan The major proposal for a new national government made in 1787 at the Constitutional Convention. Although sometimes called the Randolph Plan because Edmund Randolph of Virginia submitted it, this proposal was mainly written by James Madison. The U.S. Constitution contains the most important provisions of the Virginia Plan.

Voter registration The requirement in every state except North Dakota that individuals be registered in order to vote in elections.

Voter turnout The number or percentage of persons of voting age who actually cast votes in elections.

Voting specialists Citizens whose participation in politics is limited to voting in elections.

W

War, declaration of An action reserved to Congress by Article I, Section 8 of the U.S. Constitution. The United States has engaged in five declared wars: the War of 1812, the Mexican War, the Spanish-American War, and World Wars I and II.

War powers The constitutional powers to make war, divided between Congress (declaration of war, power of the purse) and the president (commander in chief).

Watergate The name of the scandal that led to President Richard M. Nixon's resignation in 1974, so called because members of Nixon's reelection staff were caught burglarizing the Democratic National Committe headquarters located in the Watergate building in Washington, D.C.

Whips In legislatures, party officers who keep track of important legislation and try to have all of the party's legislators on hand for votes important to the party.

Winner-take-all election An election in which the candidate with a plurality or majority of the votes takes all of the delegates, electoral votes, or legislative seats. See *Winner-take-all rule.*

Winner-take-all rule A rule in election systems by which the candidate or party winning a plurality of the votes wins everything. In U.S. presidential elections, all of a state's electoral votes are awarded to the presidential candidate winning the most popular votes in that state.

Women's suffrage Women's right to vote in elections. Women were not granted the right to vote in national elections until the 19th Amendment was adopted in 1920, though state constitutions and laws enfranchised them earlier.

Written constitution The basic, or fundamental, written law of a sovereign entity. The United States is said to have the oldest written constitution in the world. The constitutions of some countries, notably Great Britain, are not written in a single document, as is that of the United States. The British constitution derives from various historic documents, laws, and practices.

CHAPTER 1

BAILYN, BERNARD (1968) *The Origins of American Politics*. New York: Vintage Books.

BURNETT, EDMUND CODY (1964) *The Continental Congress*. New York: W. W. Norton.

BURNHAM, WALTER DEAN (1965) "The Changing Shape of the American Political Universe." *American Political Science Review* 59: 7–28

BURNHAM, WALTER DEAN (1970) *Critical Elections and the Mainsprings of American Politics*. New York: W. W. Norton.

CHAMBERS, WILLIAM NISBET, and WALTER DEAN BURNHAM, eds. (1975) *The American Party Systems*. 2nd ed. New York: Oxford University Press.

CONVERSE, PHILIP E. (1972) "Change in the American Electorate." In *The Human Meaning of Social Change*, ed. Angus Campbell and Philip E. Converse. New York: Russell Sage Foundation, pp. 263–337.

DAVIDSON, ROGER H., and WALTER J. OLESZEK (1985) *Congress and Its Members*. 2nd ed. Washington, D.C.: Congressional Quarterly Press.

HARTZ, LOUIS (1955) *The Liberal Tradition in America*. New York: Harcourt Brace Jovanovich.

HARTZ, LOUIS (1964) *The Founding of New Societies*. New York: Harcourt Brace Jovanovich.

HENDERSON, H. JAMES (1974) *Party Politics in the Continental Congress*. New York: McGraw-Hill.

HENRETTA, JAMES A.; W. ELLIOT BROWNLEE; DAVID BRODY; and SUSAN WARE (1987) *America's History*. Chicago: Dorsey Press.

HOLCOMBE, ARTHUR N. (1950) *Our More Perfect Union*. Cambridge, Mass.: Harvard University Press.

HUNTINGTON, SAMUEL P. (1968) *Political Order in Changing Societies*. New Haven, Conn.: Yale University Press.

JEWELL, MALCOLM E., and SAMUEL C. PATTERSON (1986) *The Legislative Process in the United States*. 4th ed. New York: Random House.

KAMMEN, MICHAEL (1969) *Deputyes & Libertyes: The Origins of Representative Government in Colonial America*. New York: Alfred A. Knopf.

KURTZ, STEPHEN G., and JAMES H. HUTSON, eds. (1973) *Essays on the American Revolution*. Chapel Hill: University of North Carolina Press.

LASSWELL, HAROLD D. (1958) *Politics: Who Gets What, When, How*. New York: Meridian. (First published in 1936.)

LIPSET, SEYMOUR MARTIN (1963) *The First New Nation*. New York: Basic Books.

LOWI, THEODORE J. (1971) *The Politics of Disorder*. New York: Basic Books.

MAIN, JACKSON TURNER (1973) *Political Parties before the Constitution*. Chapel Hill: University of North Carolina Press.

MCCLOSKEY, ROBERT G. (1960) *The American Supreme Court*. Chicago: University of Chicago Press.

MORISON, SAMUEL ELIOT (1965) *The Oxford History of the American People*. New York: Oxford University Press.

PLUMB, J. H. (1963) *Men and Centuries*. Boston: Houghton Mifflin.

RANNEY, AUSTIN (1975) *Curing the Mischiefs of Faction*. Berkeley: University of California Press.

RIPLEY, RANDALL B. (1988) *Congress: Process and Policy*. 4th ed. New York: W. W. Norton.

ROOSEVELT, THEODORE (1927) *Theodore Roosevelt: An Autobiography*. New York: Charles Scribner's Sons.

SKOWRONEK, STEPHEN (1982) *Building a New American State*. Cambridge: Cambridge University Press.

STOHL, MICHAEL (1976) *War and Domestic Political Violence*. Beverly Hills, Calif.: Sage Publications.

WILLS, GARRY (1978) *Inventing America*. Garden City, N.Y.: Doubleday.

WOOD, GORDON S. (1969) *The Creation of the American Republic, 1776–1787*. New York: W. W. Norton.

YOUNG, JAMES S. (1966) *The Washington Community, 1800–1828*. New York: Columbia University Press.

CHAPTER 2

BERRY, MARY FRANCES (1986) *Why ERA Failed*. Bloomington: Indiana University Press.

BOLES, JANET K. (1979) *The Politics of the Equal Rights Amendment*. New York: Longman.

BOWEN, CATHERINE DRINKER (1966) *Miracle at Philadelphia*. Boston: Little, Brown.

COOPER, JAMES FENIMORE (1956) *The American*

Democrat. New York: Vintage Books. (First published in 1838.)

FARRAND, MAX (1913) *The Framing of the Constitution of the United States.* New Haven, Conn.: Yale University Press.

GARRATY, JOHN A., ed. (1975) *Quarrels That Have Shaped the Constitution.* New York: Harper Torchbooks.

GRAHAM, GEORGE J., and SCARLETT G. GRAHAM, eds. (1984) *Founding Principles of American Government.* Rev. ed. Chatham. N.J.: Chatham House Publishers.

HEALE, M. J. (1977) *The Making of American Politics.* New York: Longman.

HYNEMAN, CHARLES S., and GEORGE W. CAREY (1967) *A Second Federalist: Congress Creates a Government.* New York: Appleton-Century-Crofts.

JILLSON, CALVIN C. (1988) *Constitution Making: Conflict and Consensus in the Federal Convention of 1787.* New York: Agathon Press.

JILLSON, CALVIN C., and CECIL L. EUBANKS (1984) "The Political Structure of Constitution Making: The Federal Convention of 1787." *American Journal of Political Science* 28: 435–58.

KELLY, ALFRED H.; WINFRED A. HARBISON; and HERMAN BELZ (1983) *The American Constitution: Its Origin and Development.* 6th ed. New York: W. W. Norton.

LEWIS, JOHN D., ed. (1967) *Anti-Federalists versus Federalists.* San Francisco: Chandler Publishing.

MCDONALD, FORREST (1965) *The Formation of the American Republic, 1776–1790.* Baltimore: Penguin Books.

MADISON, JAMES (1893) *Journal of the Constitutional Convention,* ed. E. H. Scott. Chicago: Scott, Foresman. (First published in 1840.)

MANSBRIDGE, JANE J. (1986) *Why We Lost the ERA.* Chicago: University of Chicago Press.

ROCHE, JOHN P. (1961) "The Founding Fathers: A Reform Caucus in Action." *American Political Science Review* 55: 799–816.

SCHWARTZ, BERNARD (1977) *The Great Rights of Mankind.* New York: Oxford University Press.

SMITH, DAVID G. (1965) *The Convention and the Constitution.* New York: St. Martin's Press.

SUNDQUIST, JAMES L. (1986) *Constitutional Reform and Effective Government.* Washington, D.C.: Brookings Institution.

WILLS, GARRY (1981) *Explaining America: The Federalist.* New York: Penguin Books.

CHAPTER 3

ADVISORY COMMISSION ON INTERGOVERNMENTAL RELATIONS (1984) *Regulatory Federalism: Policy, Process, Impact, and Reform.* Washington, D.C.: Advisory Commission on Intergovernmental Relations.

ADVISORY COMMISSION ON INTERGOVERNMENTAL RELATIONS (1986) *Significant Features of Fiscal Federalism, 1985–86 Edition.* Washington, D.C.: Advisory Commission on Intergovernmental Relations.

ARONSON, J. RICHARD, and JOHN L. HILLEY (1986) *Financing State and Local Governments.* 4th ed. Washington, D.C.: Brookings Institution.

CHUBB, JOHN E. (1985) "Federalism and the Bias for Centralization." In *The New Direction in American Politics,* ed. John E. Chubb and Paul E. Peterson. Washington, D.C.: Brookings Institution pp. 273–306.

DERTHICK, MARTHA (1986) "Preserving Federalism: Congress, the States, and the Supreme Court." *Brookings Review* 4: 32–37.

ELAZAR, DANIEL J. (1984) *American Federalism: A View from the States.* 3rd ed. New York: Harper & Row.

GASTIL, RAYMOND D. (1975) *Cultural Regions of the United States.* Seattle: University of Washington Press.

GELFAND, LAWRENCE E., and ROBERT J. NEYMEYER, eds. (1985) *Changing Patterns in American Federal-State Relations during the 1950s, the 1960s, and the 1970s.* Iowa City, Iowa: Center for the Study of the Recent History of the United States.

GLENDENING, PARRIS N., and MAVIS MANN REEVES (1984) *Pragmatic Federalism.* 2nd ed. Pacific Palisades, Calif.: Palisades Publishers.

GOLONKA, SUSAN (1985) "Whatever Happened to Federalism? *Intergovernmental Perspective* 11 (Winter): 8–18.

NATHAN, RICHARD P.; FRED C. DOOLITTLE; and ASSOCIATES (1987) *Reagan and the States.* Princeton, N.J.: Princeton University Press.

REAGAN, MICHAEL D., and JOHN G. SANZONE (1981) *The New Federalism.* 2nd ed. New York: Oxford University Press.

WILLS, GARRY (1981) *Explaining America: The Federalist.* New York: Penguin Books.

WRIGHT, DEIL (1982) *Understanding Intergovernmental Relations.* 2nd ed. Monterey, Calif.: Brooks/Cole Publishing.

CHAPTER 4

ABRAMSON, PAUL R. (1983) *Political Attitudes in America.* San Francisco: W. H. Freeman.

ABRAMSON, PAUL R.; JOHN H. ALDRICH; and DAVID W. ROHDE (1986) *Change and Continuity in the 1984 Elections.* Washington, D.C.: Congressional Quarterly Press.

BEER, WILLIAM R. (1987) "The Wages of Discrimination." *Public Opinion* 10: 17–19, 58.

BRISCHETTO, ROBERT R., and RODOLFO O. DE LA GARZA (1985) *The Mexican American Electorate: Political Opinions and Behavior across Cultures in San Antonio.* San Antonio and Austin, Tex.: Southwest Voter Registration Education Project and Center for Mexican American Studies.

CAIN, BRUCE; JOHN FEREJOHN; and MORRIS FIORINA (1987) *The Personal Vote.* Cambridge, Mass.: Harvard University Press.

CEASER, JAMES (1987) "Saying Good-Bye to a Nice Affair: Thoughts on the Iran-Contra Hearings." *Public Opinion* 10: 7–8, 55–56.

CITRIN, JACK (1974) "The Political Relevance of Trust in Government," *American Political Science Review* 68: 973–88.

CLARKE, JAMES W. (1982) *American Assassins.* Princeton, N.J.: Princeton University Press.

CROTTY, WILLIAM J., ed. (1971) *Assassinations and the Political Order.* New York: Harper & Row.

CURRY, RICHARD O., and THOMAS M. BROWN, eds. (1972) *Conspiracy: The Fear of Subversion in American History.* New York: Holt, Rinehart & Winston.

DAWSON, RICHARD E.; KENNETH PREWITT; and KAREN S. DAWSON (1977) *Political Socialization.* 2nd ed. Boston: Little, Brown.

DELLI CARPINI, MICHAEL X. (1986) *Stability and Change in American Politics.* New York: New York University Press.

FLANIGAN, WILLIAM H., and NANCY H. ZINGALE (1983) *Political Behavior of the American Electorate.* 5th ed. Boston: Allyn & Bacon.

GARCIA, F. CHRIS (1973) *Political Socialization of Chicano Children.* New York: Praeger Publishers.

GREENBERG, BRADLEY S., and EDWIN B. PARKER, eds. (1965) *The Kennedy Assassination and the American Public.* Stanford, Calif.: Stanford University Press.

GREENBERG, EDWARD S. (1969) "Children and the Political Community: A Comparison across Racial Lines." *Canadian Journal of Political Science* 2: 471–92.

GREENSTEIN, FRED I. (1974) "What the President Means to Americans." In *Choosing the President*, ed. James D. Barber. Englewood Cliffs, N.J.: Prentice-Hall, pp. 121–47.

GREENSTEIN, FRED I. (1975) "The Benevolent Leader Revisited: Children's Images of Political Leaders in Three Democracies." *American Political Science Review* 69: 137–98.

HARRIS, LOUIS (1987) *Inside America.* New York: Vintage Books.

HESS, ROBERT D. and JUDITH V. TORNEY (1967) *The Development of Political Attitudes in Children.* Chicago: Aldine Publishing.

HOFSTADTER, RICHARD (1965) *The Paranoid Style in American Politics.* New York: Alfred A. Knopf.

HUCKFELDT, ROBERT (1986) *Politics in Context.* New York: Agathon Press.

HUNTINGTON, SAMUEL P. (1981) *American Politics: The Promise of Disharmony.* Cambridge, Mass.: Harvard University Press.

JACKMAN, ROBERT W. (1972) "Political Elites, Mass Publics, and Support for Democratic Principles." *Journal of Politics* 34: 753–73.

JAHODA, GUSTAV (1963) "The Development of Children's Ideas about Country and Nationality." *British Journal of Educational Psychology* 33: 143–53.

JENNINGS, M. KENT, and RICHARD G. NIEMI (1974) *The Political Character of Adolescence.* Princeton, N.J.: Princeton University Press.

JENNINGS, M. KENT, and RICHARD G. NIEMI (1981) *Generations and Politics.* Princeton, N.J.: Princeton University Press.

KIRKPATRICK, JEANE J. (1974) *Political Woman.* New York: Basic Books.

KLEIN, ETHEL (1984) *Gender Politics.* Cambridge, Mass.: Harvard University Press.

LANE, ROBERT E. (1962) *Political Ideology.* New York: Free Press.

LIEBMAN, ROBERT C., and ROBERT WUTHNOW (1983) *The New Christian Right.* Hawthorne, N.Y.: Aldine Publishing.

LIPSET, SEYMOUR MARTIN, and EARL RAAB (1970) *The Politics of Unreason.* New York: Harper & Row.

LIPSET, SEYMOUR MARTIN, and WILLIAM SCHNEIDER (1983) *The Confidence Gap.* New York: Free Press.

MCCLOSKY, HERBERT, and ALIDA BRILL

(1983) *Dimensions of Tolerance*. New York: Russell Sage Foundation.

MCCLOSKY, HERBERT, and JOHN ZALLER (1984) *The American Ethos*. Cambridge, Mass.: Harvard University Press.

NUNN, CLYDE Z.; HARRY J. CROCKETT, JR.; and J. ALLEN WILLIAMS, JR. (1978) *Tolerance for Nonconformity*. San Francisco: Jossey-Bass.

ORREN, KAREN, and PAUL PETERSON (1967) "Presidential Assassination: A Case Study in the Dynamics of Political Socialization." *Journal of Politics* 29: 388–404.

ORUM, ANTHONY M., and ROBERTA S. COHEN (1973) "The Development of Political Orientations among Black and White Children." *American Sociological Review* 38: 62–74.

SAPIRO, VIRGINIA (1983) *The Political Integration of Women*. Urbana: University of Illinois Press.

SMITH, TOM W., and PAUL B. SHEATSLEY (1984) "American Attitudes toward Race Relations." *Public Opinion* 7: 14–15, 50–53.

STOUFFER, SAMUEL A. (1955) *Communism, Conformity, and Civil Liberties*. New York: John Wiley & Sons.

VERBA, SIDNEY, and GARY R. OREN (1985) *Equality in America*. Cambridge, Mass.: Harvard University Press.

WOLFENSTEIN, MARTHA, and GILBERT KLIMAN, eds. (1965) *Children and the Death of a President*. Garden City, N.Y.: Doubleday.

WRIGHT, JAMES D. (1976) *The Dissent of the Governed*. New York: Academic Press.

CHAPTER 5

ALMOND, GABRIEL A., and SIDNEY VERBA (1963) *The Civic Culture*. Princeton, N.J.: Princeton University Press.

BAIN, HENRY M., and DONALD S. HECOCK (1957) *Ballot Position and Voter's Choice*. Detroit: Wayne State University Press.

BARNES, SAMUEL H., and MAX KAASE (1979) *Political Action: Mass Participation in Five Western Democracies*. Beverly Hill, Calif.: Sage Publications.

BRISCHETTO, ROBERT R., and RODOLFO O. DE LA GARZA (1983) *The Mexican American Electorate: Political Participation and Ideology*. San Antonio and Austin, Tex.: Southwest Voter Registration Education Project and Center for Mexican American Studies.

BRODY, RICHARD A. (1978) "The Puzzle of Political Participation in America." In *The New American Political System*, ed. Anthony King. Washington,

D.C.: American Enterprise Institute for Public Policy Research, pp. 287–324.

BROWNING, RUFUS P.; DALE ROGERS MARSHALL; and DAVID H. TABB (1984) *Protest Is Not Enough*. Berkeley: University of California Press.

BULLITT, STIMSON (1977) *To Be a Politician*. Rev. ed. New Haven, Conn.: Yale University Press.

BURNHAM, WALTER DEAN (1982) *The Current Crisis in American Politics*. New York: Oxford University Press.

CAMPBELL, ANGUS; PHILIP E. CONVERSE; WARREN E. MILLER; and DONALD E. STOKES (1960) *The American Voter*. New York: John Wiley & Sons.

CARROLL, SUSAN J. (1985) *Women as Candidates in American Politics*. Bloomington: Indiana University Press.

CASSEL, CAROL A. (1979) "Changes in Electoral Participation in the South." *Journal of Politics* 41: 907–17.

CROTTY, WILLIAM J. (1977) *Political Reform and the American Experiment*. New York: Thomas Y. Crowell.

GLASS, DAVID; PEVERILL SQUIRE; and RAYMOND WOLFINGER (1984) "Voter Turnout: An International Comparison." *Public Opinion* 6: 49–55.

GREEN, PAUL M. (1983) "Washington's Victory: Divide and Conquer." *Illinois Issues* 9: 15–20.

KATZ, DANIEL; BARBARA A. GUTEK; ROBERT L. KAHN; and EUGENIA BARTON (1975) *Bureaucratic Encounters*. Ann Arbor, Mich.: Institute for Social Research.

KIRKPATRICK, JEANE (1976) *The New Presidential Elite: Men and Women in National Politics*. New York: Russell Sage Foundation.

LANE, ROBERT E. (1959) *Political Life: Why People Get Involved in Politics*. Glencoe, Ill.: Free Press.

MILBRATH, LESTER W., and M. L. GOEL (1977) *Political Participation*. 2nd ed. Chicago: Rand McNally.

NIE, NORMAN H., and SIDNEY VERBA (1975) "Political Participation." In *Handbook of Political Science*, ed. Fred I. Greenstein and Nelson W. Polsby. Reading, Mass.: Addison-Wesley Publishing, vol. 4, pp. 1–74.

PATTERSON, SAMUEL C., and GREGORY A. CALDEIRA (1983) "Getting Out the Vote: Participation in Gubernatorial Elections." *American Political Science Review* 77: 675–89.

PHILLIPS, KEVIN P., and PAUL H. BLACKMAN (1975) *Electoral Reform and Voter Participation*. Washington, D.C.: American Enterprise Institute for Public Policy Research.

POWELL, G. BINGHAM (1986) "American Voter Turnout in Comparative Perspective." *American Political Science Review* 80: 17–43.

RUSK, JERROLD G. (1976) "The Effects of the Australian Ballot Reform on Split Ticket Voting: 1876–1980." In *Controversies in American Voting Behavior*, ed. Richard G. Niemi and Herbert F. Weisberg. San Francisco: W. H. Freeman, pp. 484–513.

SMOLKA, RICHARD G. (1977) *Election Day Registration.* Washington, D.C.: American Enterprise Institute for Public Policy Research.

VERBA, SIDNEY, and NORMAN H. NIE (1972) *Participation in America.* New York: Harper & Row.

WOLFINGER, RAYMOND E., and STEVEN J. ROSENSTONE (1980) *Who Votes?* New Haven, Conn.: Yale University Press.

ZUKERMAN, ALAN. S., and DARRELL M. WEST (1985) "The Political Bases of Citizen Contacting: A Cross-National Analysis." *American Political Science Review* 79: 117-31.

CHAPTER 6

AMERICAN ASSEMBLY (1982) *The Future of American Political Parties.* New York: American Assembly of Columbia University.

BIBBY, JOHN F. (1980) "Party Renewal in the National Republican Party." In *Party Renewal in America,* ed. Gerald M. Pomper. New York: Praeger Publishers, pp. 102–15.

BIBBY, JOHN F. (1987) *Politics, Parties, and Elections in America.* Chicago: Nelson-Hall.

BIBBY, JOHN F.; CORNELIUS P. COTTER; JAMES L. GIBSON; and ROBERT L. HUCKSHORN (1983) "Parties in State Politics." In *Politics in the American States*, ed. Virginia Gray, Herbert Jacob, and Kenneth N. Vines. 4th ed. Boston: Little, Brown, pp. 59–96.

BRODER, DAVID S. (1972) *The Party's Over.* New York: Harper and Row.

CAVANAGH, THOMAS E., and JAMES L. SUNDQUIST (1985) "The New Two-Party System." In *The New Direction in American Politics*, ed. John E. Chubb and Paul E. Peterson. Washington, D.C.: Brookings Institution.

CONVERSE, PHILIP E. (1966) "The Concept of the Normal Vote." In Angus Campbell et al. *Elections and the Political Order.* New York: John Wiley & Sons.

COOK, RHODES (1986) "Brushing Aside Complaints, DNC Approves Rules for 1988." *Congressional Quarterly Weekly Report* 44 (March 15): 627.

COTTER, CORNELIUS P., and JOHN F. BIBBY (1980) "Institutional Development of Parties and the Thesis of Party Decline." *Political Science Quarterly* 95 (Spring): 1–27.

COTTER, CORNELIUS P.; JAMES L. GIBSON; JOHN F. BIBBY; and ROBERT J. HUCKSHORN (1984) *Party Organization in American Politics.* New York: Praeger Publishers.

COTTER, CORNELIUS P., and BERNARD C. HENNESSY (1964) *Politics without Power: The National Party Committees.* New York: Atherton Press.

DEMOCRATIC NATIONAL COMMITTEE (1982) *Report on the Commission on Presidential Nomination, Adopted by the Democratic National Committee.* Washington, D.C.: Democratic National Committee.

DENNIS, JACK (1966) "Support for the Party System by the Mass Public." *American Political Science Review* 60: 600–615.

DOWNS, ANTHONY (1957) *An Economic Theory of Democracy.* New York: Harper & Row.

DUVERGER, MAURICE (1954) *Political Parties.* New York: John Wiley & Sons.

EHRENHALT, ALAN (1984) "How Not to Pick a Presidential Candidate." *Congressional Quarterly Weekly Report* 42 (January 28): 167.

ELDERSVELD, SAMUEL J. (1982) *Political Parties in American Society.* New York: Basic Books.

EPSTEIN, LEON D. (1967) *Political Parties in Western Democracies.* New York: Praeger Publishers.

EPSTEIN, LEON D. (1986) *Political Parties in the American Mold.* Madison: University of Wisconsin Press.

GIBSON, JAMES L.; CORNELIUS P. COTTER; and JOHN F. BIBBY (1983) "Assessing Party Organizational Strength." *American Journal of Political Science* 27 (May): 193–222.

GIBSON, JAMES L.; CORNELIUS P. COTTER; JOHN F. BIBBY; and ROBERT J. HUCKSHORN (1982) "Whither the Local Parties?" Paper delivered at the Western Political Science Association meeting (March).

JOHNSTON, MICHAEL (1979) "Patrons and Clients, Jobs and Machines: A Case Study of the Uses of Patronage." *American Political Science Review* 73 (June): 385–93.

KAYDEN, XANDRA, and EDDIE MAHE, JR. (1985) *The Party Goes On: The Persistence of the Two-Party System in the United States.* New York: Basic Books.

KETCHAM, RALPH (1984) *Presidents above Party: The First American Presidency, 1789–1829.* Chapel Hill: University of North Carolina Press.

KEY, V. O., JR. (1964) *Politics, Parties, and Pressure Groups.* 5th ed. New York: Thomas Y. Crowell.

LADD, EVERETT CARLL (1985) "Realignment." *Campaigns and Elections* 6 (Summer): 58–60.

LONGLEY, CHARLES H. (1980) "Party Reform and Nationalization: The Case of the Democrats." In *The Party Symbol*, ed. William J. Crotty. San Francisco: W. H. Freeman.

MAYHEW, DAVID R. (1966) *Party Loyalty among Congressmen.* Cambridge, Mass.: Harvard University Press.

MAYHEW, DAVID R. (1974) "Congressional Elections: The Case of the Vanishing Marginals." *Polity* 6 (Spring): 295–317.

MILLER, WARREN E., and M. KENT JENNINGS (1986) *Parties in Transition: A Longitudinal Study of Party Elites and Party Supporters.* New York: Russell Sage Foundation.

MOREHOUSE, SARAH MCCALLY (1980) "The Effect of Pre-primary Endorsements on State Party Strength." Paper presented at the American Political Science Association convention (August).

NIE, NORMAN H.; SIDNEY VERBA; and JOHN R. PETROCIK (1976) *The Changing American Voter.* Cambridge, Mass.: Harvard University Press.

NIEMI, RICHARD G., and HERBERT F. WEISBERG, eds. (1984) *Controversies in American Voting Behavior.* 2nd ed. Washington, D.C.: Congressional Quarterly Press.

PATTERSON, THOMAS E., and ROBERT D. MCCLURE (1976) *The Unseeing Eye.* New York: G. P. Putnam's Sons.

PLISSNER, MARTIN, and WARREN MITOFSKY (1981) "Political Elites." *Public Opinion* 4 (October–November): 47–50.

POLSBY, NELSON W. (1983) *Consequences of Party Reform.* Oxford: Oxford University Press.

POLSBY, NELSON W., and AARON WILDAVSKY (1984) *Presidential Elections.* 6th ed. New York: Charles Scribner's Sons.

POMPER, GERALD M., with SUSAN S. LEDERMAN (1980) *Elections in America.* 2nd ed. New York: Longman.

RANNEY, AUSTIN (1974) "Changing the Rules of the Nominating Game." In *Choosing the President*, ed. James D. Barber. Englewood Cliffs, N.J.: Prentice-Hall, pp. 71–93.

RANNEY, AUSTIN (1976) "Parties in State Politics." In *Politics in the American States*, ed. Herbert Jacobs and Kenneth Vines. 3rd ed. Boston: Little, Brown, pp. 61–99.

RANNEY, AUSTIN (1977) *Participation in American Presidential Nominations, 1976.* Washington, D.C.: American Enterprise Institute.

ROSENSTONE, STEVEN J.; ROY J. BEHR; and EDWARD LAZARUS (1984) *Third Parties in America.* Princeton, N.J.: Princeton University Press.

SABATO, LARRY J. (1988) *The Party's Just Begun.* Glenview, Ill.: Scott, Foresman/Little, Brown.

SHAFER, BYRON E. (1988) *Bifurcated Politics: Evolution and Reform in the National Party Conventions.* Cambridge: Harvard University Press.

SORAUF, FRANK J. (1984) *Party Politics in America.* 5th ed. Boston: Little, Brown.

SOUTHWELL, PRISCILLA (1986) "The 1984 Democratic Nominating Process." *American Politics Quarterly* 14 (January–April): 75–88.

TIMES MIRROR COMPANY (1987) *The People, Press, and Politics.* Study of the American electorate conducted by the Gallup Organization in September 1987.

TOURTELLOT, ARTHUR (1964) *The Presidents on the Presidency.* New York: Doubleday.

WATTENBERG, MARTIN D. (1986) *The Decline of American Political Parties, 1952–1984.* Cambridge, Mass.: Harvard University Press.

WEAVER, PAUL H. (1976) "Captives of Melodrama." *New York Times Magazine* (August 29): 6 ff.

WHITE, JOHN KENNETH, and DWIGHT MORRIS (1984) "Shattered Images: Political Parties in the 1984 Election." *Public Opinion* 6 (December–January): 44–48.

CHAPTER 7

BAUER, RAYMOND A.; ITHIEL DE SOLA POOL; and LEWIS ANTHONY DEXTER (1963) *American Business and Public Policy.* New York: Atherton Press.

BERRY, JEFFREY (1977) *Lobbying for the People.* Princeton, N.J.: Princeton University Press.

CIGLER, ALLAN J., and BURDETT A. LOOMIS (1983) "The Changing Nature of Interest Group Politics." In *Interest Group Politics*, ed. Allan J. Cigler and Burdett A. Loomis. Washington, D.C.: Congressional Quarterly Press, pp. 1–30.

COOK, MARY ETTA, and ROGER H. DAVIDSON (1985) "Deferral Politics." In *Public Policy and the Natural Environment*, ed. Helen Ingram. Greenwich, Conn.: JAI Press, pp. 47–76.

CORRIGAN, RICHARD (1986) "NRA, Using Members, Ads, and Money, Hits Police Line in Lobbying." *National Journal* (January 4): 8–14.

COSTAIN, ANNE N., and W. DOUGLAS COSTAIN (1983) "The Women's Lobby: Impact of a Movement on Congress." In *Interest Group Politics,* ed. Allan J. Cigler and Burdett A. Loomis. Washington, D.C.: Congressional Quarterly Press, pp. 191–216.

DERTHICK, MARTHA, and PAUL J. QUIRK (1985) *The Politics of Deregulation*. Washington, D.C.: The Brookings Institution.

HAIDER, DONALD H. (1974) *When Governments Come to Washington*. New York: Free Press.

HAMMOND, SUSAN WEBB; ARTHUR G. STEVENS, JR.; and DANIEL P. MULHOLLAN (1986) "Congressional Caucuses: Legislators as Lobbyists." In *Interest Group Politics*, ed. Allan J. Cigler and Burdett A. Loomis. 2nd ed. Washington, D.C.: Congressional Quarterly Press, pp. 275–97.

HAYES, MICHAEL T. (1981) *Lobbyists and Legislators*. New Brunswick, N.J.: Rutgers University Press.

HECLO, HUGH (1978) "Issue Networks and the Executive Establishment." In *The New American Political System*, ed. Anthony King. Washington, D.C.: American Enterprise Institute, pp. 87–124.

JOHNSON, LYNDON B. (1971) *The Vantage Point*. New York: Holt, Rinehart & Winston.

KELLER, BILL (1983) "Lowest Common Denominator Lobbying: Why the Banks Fought Withholding." *Washington Monthly* 15 (May): 32–39.

KINGDON, JOHN W. (1984) *Agendas, Alternatives, and Public Policies*. Boston: Little, Brown.

KLEIN, ETHEL (1984) *Gender Politics: From Consciousness to Mass Politics*. Cambridge, Mass.: Harvard University Press.

LIPSET, SEYMOUR M., et al. (1956) *Union Democracy*. Glencoe, Ill.: Free Press.

LIPSKY, MICHAEL (1968) "Protest as a Political Resource." *American Political Science Review* 62 (December): 1144–58.

LOWI, THEODORE, J. (1969) *The End of Liberalism*. New York: W. W. Norton.

MCCONNELL, GRANT (1967) *Private Power and American Democracy*. New York: Alfred A. Knopf.

MICHELS, ROBERT (1959) *Political Parties*. New York: Dover Publications. (First published in 1915.)

MILBRATH, LESTER, and M. L. GOEL (1977) *Political Participation*. 2nd. ed. Chicago: Rand McNally.

MOE, TERRY M. (1980) *The Organization of Interests*. Chicago: University of Chicago Press.

OLSON, MANCUR, JR. (1965) *The Logic of Collective Action*. Cambridge, Mass.: Harvard University Press.

OLSON, MANCUR, JR. (1987) "Why Some Minorities Get Nothing." *Washington Post* (May 21): A23.

ORNSTEIN, NORMAN J., and SHIRLEY ELDER (1978) *Interest Groups, Lobbying, and Policymaking*. Washington, D.C.: Congressional Quarterly Press.

PIKA, JOSEPH A. (1983) "Interest Groups and the Executive." In *Interest Group Politics*, ed. Allan J. Cigler and Burdett A. Loomis. Washington, D.C.: Congressional Quarterly Press, pp. 298–323.

RIGGS, FRED W. (1950) *Pressures on Congress: A Study of the Repeal of Chinese Exclusion*. New York: King's Crown Press.

SALISBURY, ROBERT H. (1983) "Interest Groups: Toward a New Understanding." In *Interest Group Politics*, ed. Allan J. Cigler and Burdett A. Loomis. Washington, D.C.: Congressional Quarterly Press, pp. 354–70.

SANSWEET, STEPHEN J. (1980) "Political-Action Units at Firms Are Assailed by Some over Tactics." *The Wall Street Journal* (July 24): 1.

SCHATTSCHNEIDER, E. E. (1942) *Party Government*. New York: Holt, Rinehart & Winston.

SCHATTSCHNEIDER, E. E. (1960) *The Semi-Sovereign People*. New York: Holt, Rinehart & Winston.

SCHOLZMAN, KAY LEHMAN, and JOHN T. TIERNEY (1983) "More of the Same: Washington Pressure Group Activity in a Decade of Change." *Journal of Politics* 45 (May): 351–377.

STEINBACH, CAROL F. (1987) "Women's Movement II." *National Journal* (August 29): 2145.

TRUMAN, DAVID B. (1971) *The Governmental Process*. 2nd ed. New York: Alfred A. Knopf.

U.S. HOUSE OF REPRESENTATIVES, COMMISSION ON ADMINISTRATIVE REVIEW (1977) *Final Report*. H. Doc. 95–272 (December 31), vol. 2.

VERBA, SIDNEY, and NORMAN H. NIE (1972) *Participation in America*. New York: Harper & Row.

WALKER, JACK L. (1983) "The Origins and Maintenance of Interest Groups in America." *American Political Science Review* 77 (June): 390–406.

ZEIGLER, L. HARMON, and G. WAYNE PEAK (1972) *Interest Groups in American Society*. 2nd ed. Englewood Cliffs, N.J.: Prentice-Hall.

CHAPTER 8

BAGDIKIAN, BEN H. (1971) *The Information Machines: Their Impact on Men and the Media*. New York: Harper & Row.

BERELSON, BERNARD; PAUL LAZARSFELD; and WILLIAM MCPHEE (1954) *Voting*. Chicago: University of Chicago Press.

BONAFEDE, DOM (1980) "The Press Makes News in Covering the 1980 Primary Election Campaign." *National Journal* 12 (July 12): 1132–35.

BRODER, DAVID S. (1981) "New Life for an Old Forum." *Washington Post* (February 4): A17.

BRODER, DAVID S. (1987) *Behind the Front Page: A Candid Look at How the News Is Made.* New York: Simon & Schuster.

CLANCEY, MAURA, and MICHAEL J. ROBINSON (1985) "The Media in Campaign '84." *Public Opinion* 7 (December–January): 49–54.

CROUSE, TIMOTHY (1973) *The Boys on the Bus.* New York: Ballantine.

DE FLEUR, MELVIN L., and SANDRA BALL-RO-KEACH (1975) *Theories of Mass Communication.* 3rd ed. New York: David McKay.

DE FRANK, THOMAS M. (1982) "Fine-Tuning the White House Press Conference." *Washington Journalism Review* 4 (October): 27–29.

DREW, ELIZABETH (1976) "A Reporter in Washington, D.C.: Winter Notes—II." *New Yorker* (May 31): 54–99.

ERICKSON, ROBERT S. (1976) "The Influence of Newspaper Endorsements in Presidential Elections: The Case of 1964." *American Journal of Political Science* 20 (May): 207–33.

FAGAN, RICHARD (1966) *Politics and Communication.* Boston: Little, Brown.

FRIENDLY, JONATHAN (1983) "Reporter's Notebook: Surprising Profile of a Journalist." *New York Times* (May 13): A16.

GRABER, DORIS (1984) *Mass Media and American Politics.* 2nd ed. Washington, D.C.: Congressional Quarterly Press.

GREY, DAVID C. (1968) *The Supreme Court and the News Media.* Evanston, Ill.: Northwestern University Press.

HEARD, ALEXANDER (1966) "The Organization and Functions of Campaigns." In *American Party Politics: Essays and Readings*, ed. Donald G. Herzberg and Gerald M. Pomper. New York: Holt, Rinehart & Winston, pp. 321–30.

HESS, STEPHEN (1981) *The Washington Reporters.* Washington, D.C.: Brookings Institution.

HESS, STEPHEN (1984) *The Government/Press Connection.* Washington, D.C.: Brookings Institution.

HESS, STEPHEN (1986) *The Ultimate Insiders.* Washington, D.C.: Brookings Institution.

KATZ, ELIHU (1957) "The Two-Step Flow of Communication: An Up-to-Date Report on an Hypothesis." *Public Opinion Quarterly* 21 (Spring): 61–78.

KATZ, ELIHU, and JACOB J. FELDMAN (1962) "The Debates in the Light of Research: A Survey of Surveys." In *The Great Debates*, ed. Sidney Krause. Bloomington: Indiana University Press.

KRAUS, SIDNEY, and DENNIS DAVIS (1976) *The Effects of Mass Communication on Political Behavior.* University Park: Pennsylvania State University Press.

LASSWELL, HAROLD D. (1948) "The Structure and Function of Communication in Society." In *The Communication of Ideas,* ed. L. Bryson. New York: Harper & Row, pp. 37–51.

LAZARSFELD, PAUL; BERNARD BERELSON; and HAZEL GAUDET (1944) *The People's Choice.* New York: Columbia University Press.

MCLUHAN, MARSHALL (1964) *Understanding Media.* New York: McGraw-Hill.

MINOW, NEWTON N.; JOHN BARTLOW MARTIN; and LEE M. MITCHELL (1973) *Presidential Television.* New York: Basic Books.

NADER, RALPH (1977) "The Labor Press: Let Them Eat Puffery." *Los Angeles Times* (October 6): II, 7.

NEW YORK TIMES (1986) "Suit Studies the Wages of Journalism." (July 20): 26.

PATTERSON, THOMAS E. (1980) *The Mass Media Election: How Americans Choose Their President.* New York: Praeger Publishers.

PATTERSON, THOMAS E., and ROBERT G. MCCLURE (1976) *The Unseeing Eye.* New York: G. P. Putnam's Sons.

RANDOLPH, ELEANOR (1987) "Network News Confronts Era of Limits." *Washington Post* (February 9): A1.

RANNEY, AUSTIN (1983) *Channels of Power: The Impact of Television on American Politics.* New York: Basic Books.

ROBINSON, JOHN P. (1977) *Changes in Americans' Use of Time, 1965–1975.* Cleveland: Cleveland State University Report.

ROBINSON, MICHAEL J. (1977) "The TV Primaries." *Wilson Quarterly* (Spring): 80–83.

ROBINSON, MICHAEL J., and MAURA CLANCEY (1984) "Teflon Politics." *Public Opinion* 7 (April–May): 14–18.

ROSHKO, BERNARD (1975) *Newsmaking.* Chicago: University of Chicago Press.

SCHWARTZ, TONY (1984) "The Major TV Networks' Dwindling Audiences." *New York Times* (January 14): C20.

SEARS, DAVID O. (1977) "The Debates in the Light of Research: An Overview of the Effects." Paper presented at the annual meeting of the American Political

Science Association, Washington, D.C. (September 1–4).

SHALES, TOM (1984) "Bringing Him Back Live." *Washington Post* (January 4): D1.

SHAW, DONALD L., and MAXWELL E. MCCOMBS (1977) *The Emergence of American Political Issues: The Agenda-Setting Function of the Press.* St. Paul, Minn.: West Publishing.

TOLCHIN, MARTIN (1985) "When Nothing Happens and They Call It News." *New York Times* (March 22): A14.

WASHINGTON POST WRITERS GROUP (1976) *Of the Press, by the Press, for the Press, and Others, Too.* Boston: Houghton Mifflin.

CHAPTER 9

ABRAMSON, PAUL R. (1975) *Generational Change in American Politics.* Lexington, Mass.: D.C. Heath.

ABRAMSON, PAUL R.; JOHN H. ALDRICH; and DAVID W. ROHDE (1982) *Change and Continuity in the 1980 Elections.* Washington, D.C.: Congressional Quarterly Press.

ASHER, HERBERT B. (1988) *Presidential Elections and American Politics.* 4th ed. Homewood, Ill.: Dorsey Press.

AXELROD, ROBERT (1972) "Where the Votes Come From: An Analysis of Electoral Coalitions, 1952–1968." *American Political Science Review* 66 (March): 11–20.

BEST, JUDITH (1975) *The Case against Direct Election of the President.* Ithaca, N.Y.: Cornell University Press.

BURNHAM, WALTER DEAN (1970) *Critical Elections and the Mainsprings of American Politics.* New York: W. W. Norton.

BURNHAM, WALTER DEAN (1982) *The Current Crisis in American Politics.* New York: Oxford University Press.

CAMPBELL, ANGUS; PHILIP E. CONVERSE; WARREN E. MILLER; and DONALD E. STOKES (1960) *The American Voter.* New York: John Wiley & Sons.

CONVERSE, PHILIP E. (1972) "Change in the American Electorate." In *The Human Meaning of Social Change,* ed. Angus Campbell and Philip E. Converse. New York: Russell Sage Foundation, pp. 263–337.

CROTTY WILLIAM J. (1977) *Political Reform and the American Experiment.* New York: Thomas Y. Crowell.

FIORINA, MORRIS P. (1981) *Retrospective Voting in American National Elections.* New Haven: Yale University Press.

GINSBERG, BENJAMIN, and ALAN STONE, eds. (1986) *Do Elections Matter?* Armonk, N.Y.: M. E. Sharpe, Inc.

GLENN, NORVAL D. (1972) "Sources of the Shift to Political Independence: Some Evidence from a Cohort Analysis." *Social Science Quarterly* 53 (December): 494–519.

GREEN, PAUL M. (1983) "Washington's Victory: Divide and Conquer." *Illinois Issues* 9 (April): 15–20.

JACKSON, BROOKS (1984) "Loopholes Allow Flood of Campaign Giving by Business, Fat Cats." *The Wall Street Journal* (July 5): 1.

JACOBSON, GARY C. (1980) *Money in Congressional Elections.* New Haven: Yale University Press.

JACOBSON, GARY C. (1984) "Money in the 1980 and 1982 Congressional Elections." In *Money and Politics in the United States,* ed. Michael J. Malbin. Chatham, N.J.: Chatham House Publishers, pp. 38–69.

KAYDEN, XANDRA (1978) *Campaign Organization.* Lexington, Mass.: D. C. Heath & Co.

KEY, V. O., JR. (1966) *The Responsible Electorate.* Cambridge, Mass.: Harvard University Press.

LONGLEY, LAWRENCE D., and ALAN G. BRAUN (1975) *The Politics of Electoral College Reform.* 2d ed. New Haven, Conn.: Yale University Press.

MALBIN, MICHAEL J., ed. (1984) *Money and Politics in the United States.* Chatham, N.J.: Chatham House Publishers.

MILLER, WARREN E., and TERESA A. LEVITIN (1976) *Leadership and Change: The New Politics and the American Electorate.* Cambridge, Mass.: Winthrop.

NIE, NORMAN H.; SIDNEY VERBA; and JOHN R. PETROCIK eds. (1979) *The Changing American Voter.* Enlarged ed. Cambridge, Mass.: Harvard University Press.

NIEME, RICHARD G., and HERBERT F. WEISBERG, eds. (1976) *Controversies in American Voting Behavior.* San Francisco: W. H. Freeman.

PEIRCE, NEAL R., and LAWRENCE D. LONGLEY (1981) *The People's President.* Rev. ed. New Haven, Conn.: Yale University Press.

PHILLIPS, KEVIN P., and PAUL H. BLACKMAN (1975) *Electoral Reform and Voter Participation.* Washington, D.C.: American Enterprise Institute for Public Policy Research.

POLSBY, NELSON W., and AARON WILDAVSKY

(1984) *Presidential Elections.* 6th ed. New York: Charles Scribner's Sons.

POMPER, GERALD M. (1975) *Voters' Choice: Varieties of American Electoral Behavior.* New York: Dodd, Mead.

POMPER, GERALD M., and SUSAN S. LEDERMAN (1980) *Elections in America,* 2nd ed. New York: Longman.

RUSK, JERROLD G. (1976) "The Effect of the Australian Ballot Reform on Split Ticket Voting: 1876–1980." In *Controversies in American Voting Behavior,* ed. Richard G. Niemi and Herbert F. Weisberg. San Francisco: W. H. Freeman, pp. 484–513.

SABATO, LARRY J. (1981) *The Rise of Political Consultants.* New York: Basic Books.

SALMORE, STEPHEN A. and BARBARA G. SALMORE (1985) *Candidates, Parties, and Campaigns.* Washington, D.C.: Congressional Quarterly Press.

SAYRE, WALLACE S., and JUDITH H. PARRIS (1970) *Voting for President: The Electoral College and the American Political System.* Washington, D.C.: Brookings Institution.

SHOGAN, ROBERT (1977) "Fund Raiser a Political Maverick—Brings Millions into Conservative Coffers." *Los Angeles Times* (December 19): II, 10.

SMOLKA, RICHARD G. (1977) *Election Day Registration.* Washington, D.C.: American Enterprise Institute for Public Policy Research.

TUFTE, EDWARD R. (1973) "The Relationship between Seats and Votes in Two-Party Systems." *American Political Science Review* 67 (June): 540–54.

WHITE, THEODORE H. (1961) *The Making of the President 1960.* New York: Atheneum.

YUNKER, JOHN H., and LAWRENCE D. LONGLEY (1976) "The Electoral College: Its Biases Newly Measured for the 1960s and 1970s." *Sage Professional Papers in American Politics 3,* 04-031. Beverly Hills, Calif.: Sage Publications.

CHAPTER 10

BULLOCK, CHARLES S. (1973) "Committee Transfers in the U.S. House of Representatives." *Journal of Politics* 35 (February): 85–117.

COLLIE, MELISSA P., and DAVID W. BRADY (1985) "The Decline of Partisan Voting Coalitions in the House of Representatives." In *Congress Reconsidered,* ed. Lawrence Dodd and Bruce I. Oppenheimer. 3rd ed. Washington, D.C.: Congressional Quarterly Press, pp. 272–87.

DAVIDSON, ROGER H. (1969) *The Role of the Congressman.* Indianapolis, Ind.: Bobbs-Merrill.

DAVIDSON, ROGER H., and WALTER J. OLESZEK (1985) *Congress and Its Members.* 2nd ed. Washington, D.C.: Congressional Quarterly Press.

EHRENHALT, ALAN (1981) "The 'Juniority' System in Congress." *Congressional Quarterly Weekly Report* 39 (March 21): 535.

EHRENHALT, ALAN, ed. (1987) *Politics in America: The 100th Congress.* Washington, D.C.: Congressional Quarterly Press.

FENNO, RICHARD F., JR. (1973) *Congressmen in Committees.* Boston: Little, Brown.

FENNO, RICHARD F., JR. (1978) *Home Style: House Members in Their Districts.* Boston: Little, Brown.

FIORINA, MORRIS, P. (1977) *Congress: Keystone of the Washington Establishment.* New Haven, Conn.: Yale University Press.

FROMAN, LEWIS A., and RANDALL B. RIPLEY (1965) "Conditions for Party Leadership." *American Political Science Review* 69 (March): 52–63.

GERTZOG, IRWIN N. (1984) *Congressional Women: Their Recruitment, Treatment, and Behavior.* New York: Praeger Publishers.

GREEN, MARK J.; J. M. FALLOWS; and DAVID R. ZWICK (1972) *Who Runs Congress?* New York: Bantam-Grossman.

HAMMOND, SUSAN WEBB; ARTHUR G. STEVENS, JR.; and DANIEL P. MULHOLLAN (1983) "Congressional Caucuses: Legislators as Lobbyists." In *Interest Group Politics,* ed. Allan J. Cigler and Burdett A. Loomis. Washington, D.C.: Congressional Quarterly Press, pp. 275–97.

HOUSE COMMISSION ON ADMINISTRATIVE REVIEW (1977) *Final Report.* 95th Congress, 1st session, H. Doc. 95–272.

HUITT, RALPH K. (1961) "The Outsider in the Senate: An Alternative Role." *American Political Science Review* 55: (September), pp. 566–575.

MALBIN, MICHAEL J. (1987) "Factions and Incentives in Congress." *Public Interest* 86: 91–108.

MATTHEWS, DONALD R. (1960) *U.S. Senators and Their World.* Chapel Hill: University of North Carolina Press.

MAYHEW, DAVID R. (1974) *Congress: The Electoral Connection.* New Haven, Conn.: Yale University Press.

MILLER, WARREN E., and DONALD E. STOKES (1963) "Constituency Influence in Congress." *American Political Science Review* 57: 45–56.

ORNSTEIN, NORMAN J.; ROBERT L. PEABODY; and DAVID W. ROHDE (1985) "The Senate through the 1980s: Cycles of Change." In *Congress Reconsidered*, ed. Lawrence C. Dodd and Bruce I. Oppenheimer. 3rd ed. Washington, D.C.: Congressional Quarterly Press, pp. 13–33.

PARKER, GLENN R. (1974) *Political Beliefs about the Structure of Government: Congress and the Presidency.* Sage Professional Papers in American Politics, vol. 2. Beverly Hills, Calif.: Sage Publications.

PARKER, GLENN R. (1986) *Homeward Bound: Explaining Changes in Congressional Behavior.* Pittsburgh, Pa.: University of Pittsburgh Press.

PARKER, GLENN R., and ROGER H. DAVIDSON (1979) "How Come We Love Our Congressmen So Much More than Our Congress?" *Legislative Studies Quarterly* 4 (February): 53–61.

POLSBY, NELSON W. (1968) "The Institutionalization of the U.S. House of Representatives." *American Political Science Review* 62 (March): 144–68.

RIPLEY, RANDALL B. (1967) *Party Leaders in the House of Representatives.* Washington, D.C.: Brookings Institution.

ROTHMAN, DAVID J. (1966) *Politics and Power: The United States Senate, 1869–1901).* Cambridge, Mass.: Harvard University Press.

SHEPSLE, KENNETH A. (1978) *The Giant Jigsaw Puzzle: Democratic Committee Assignments in the Modern House.* Chicago: University of Chicago Press.

SMITH, STEVEN S., and CHRISTOPHER J. DEERING (1984) *Committees in Congress.* Washington, D.C.: Congressional Quarterly Press.

TUFTE, EDWARD (1973) "The Relationship between Seats and Votes in Two-Party Systems." *American Political Science Review* 67 (June): 540–54.

WILSON, WOODROW (1980) *Congressional Government.* Baltimore: Johns Hopkins University Press. (First published in 1885.)

YOUNG, JAMES S. (1966) *The Washington Community, 1800–1828.* New York: Columbia University Press.

CHAPTER 11

DAVIDSON, ROGER H. (1986) "The Legislative Work of Congress." Paper delivered at annual meeting of the American Political Science Association (August).

FENNO, RICHARD F., JR. (1978) *Home Style: House Members in Their Districts.* Boston: Little, Brown.

GETTINGER, STEPHEN (1986) "Deficit Reduction Bill's Tortuous Journey Ends." *Congressional Quarterly Weekly Report* (April 5): 751–54.

HUNT, ALBERT R. (1980) "Teachers Tie Election

Cash to Single Issue." *The Wall Street Journal* (October 17): 33.

KINGDON, JOHN W. (1981) *Congressmen's Voting Decisions.* 2nd ed. New York: Harper & Row.

MANLEY, JOHN F. (1973) "The Conservative Coalition in Congress." *American Behavioral Scientist* 17: 223–47.

MATSUNAGA, SPARK M., and PING CHEN (1976) *Rulemakers of the House.* Urbana: University of Illinois Press.

OLESZEK, WALTER J. (1988) *Congressional Procedures and the Policy Process.* 3rd ed. Washington, D.C.: Congressional Quarterly Press.

RICHARDSON, SULA P. (1987) *National Observance and Other Commemorative Legislation.* CRS Report 87–878 (October 30).

SCHNEIDER, JERROLD E. (1979) *Ideological Coalitions in Congress.* Westport, Conn.: Greenwood Press.

SUNDQUIST, JAMES L. (1981) *The Decline and Resurgence of Congress.* Washington, D.C.: Brookings Institution.

WILSON, WOODROW (1980) *Congressional Government.* Baltimore: Johns Hopkins University Press. (First published in 1885.)

CHAPTER 12

BARBER, JAMES DAVID (1977) *Presidential Character.* 2nd ed. Englewood Cliffs, N.J.: Prentice-Hall.

CORWIN, EDWARD S. (1957) *The President: Office and Powers.* New York: New York University Press.

CRONIN, THOMAS E. (1980) *The State of the Presidency.* 2nd ed. Boston: Little, Brown.

FISHER, LOUIS (1975) *Presidential Spending Power.* Princeton, N.J.: Princeton University Press.

GAMAREKIAN, BARBARA (1988) "First Ladies Step Further Out of Shadows." *New York Times* (March 10): B5.

GREENFIELD, MEG (1986) "The Gilded Age of Ceremony." *Washington Post* (July 8): A15.

GREENHOUSE, LINUS (1988) "Reagan Nominee for Judgeship Urged to Withdraw." New York: New York University Press.

HECLO, HUGH (1977) *A Government of Strangers.* Washington, D.C.: Brookings Institution.

HESS, STEPHEN (1976) *Organizing the Presidency.* Washington, D.C.: Brookings Institution.

KAMEN, AL (1984) "Great Little Law Firm." *Washington Post* (September 4): A1.

KESSEL, JOHN (1975) *The Domestic Presidency.* North Scituate, Mass.: Duxbury Press.

LIGHT, PAUL C. (1984) *The Vice President*. Baltimore: Johns Hopkins University Press.

NATHAN, RICHARD P. (1983) *The Administrative Presidency*. New York: John Wiley & Sons.

PRITCHETT, C. HERMAN (1982) "The President's Constitutional Position." In *Rethinking the Presidency*, ed. Thomas E. Cronin. Boston: Little, Brown, pp. 177–38.

SCIGLIANO, ROBERT (1971) *The Supreme Court and the Presidency*. New York: Free Press.

Select Committee on *Secret Military Assistance to Iran and the Nicaraguan Opposition* (1987) Final Report (October).

SUNDQUIST, JAMES L. (1986) *Constitutional Reform and Effective Government*. Washington, D.C.: Brookings Institution.

CHAPTER 13

BARBER, JAMES DAVID (1977) *Presidential Character*. 2nd ed. Englewood Cliffs, N.J.: Prentice-Hall.

BONAFEDE, DOM (1987) " 'Thank You, Mr. President.' " *National Journal* 19 (May 2): 1067–71.

DAVIDSON, ROGER H., and WALTER J. OLESZEK (1985) *Congress and Its Members*. 2nd ed. Washington, D.C.: Congressional Quarterly Press.

EDWARDS, GEORGE C., III (1983) *The Public Presidency*. New York: St. Martin's Press.

FISHER, LOUIS (1975) *Presidential Spending Power*. Princeton, N.J.: Princeton University Press.

FORD, HENRY JONES (1967) *The Rise and Growth of American Politics*. New York: Da Capo Press. (First published in 1898.)

GREENSTEIN, FRED I. (1974) "What the President Means to Americans: Presidential 'Choice' between Elections," In *Choosing the President*, ed. James David Barber. Englewood Cliffs, N.J.: Prentice-Hall, pp. 121–47.

GROSSMAN, MICHAEL B., and MARTHA J. KUMAR (1981) *Portraying the President: The White House and the News Media*. Baltimore: Johns Hopkins University Press.

KERNELL, SAMUEL (1986) *Going Public: New Strategies of Presidential Leadership*. Washington, D.C.: Brookings Institution.

LIGHT, PAUL C. (1982) *The President's Agenda*. Baltimore: Johns Hopkins University Press.

MAYER, JANE (1986) "It Took Work to Get Reagan into Grenada for Four Hours Today." *Wall Street Journal* (February 20): 1, 15.

MINOW, NEWTON J.; JOHN BARTLOW MARTIN;

and LEE M. MITCHELL (1973) *Presidential Television*. New York: Basic Books.

MUELLER, JOHN E. (1973) *War, Presidents, and Public Opinion*. New York: John Wiley & Sons.

NATHAN, RICHARD P. (1983) *The Administrative Presidency*. New York: John Wiley & Sons.

NEUSTADT, RICHARD E. (1976) *Presidential Power: The Politics of Leadership*. Rev. ed. New York: John Wiley & Sons.

REEDY, GEORGE E. (1970) *The Twilight of the Presidency*. New York: New American Library.

REMPEL, WILLIAM C. (1987) "Channell Used White House as Bait for Fund Raising." *Los Angeles Times* (May 12): I, 16.

SCHLESINGER, ARTHUR M., JR. (1973) *The Imperial Presidency*. Boston, Mass.: Houghton Mifflin.

SCIGLIANO, ROBERT (1971) *The Supreme Court and the Presidency*. New York: Free Press.

STIMSON, JAMES A. (1976) "Public Support for American Presidents: A Cyclical Model." *Public Opinion Quarterly* 40 (Spring): 1–21.

WAYNE, STEPHEN J. (1982) "Expectations of the President." In *The President and the Public*, ed. Doris A. Graber. Philadelphia, Pa.: Institute for the Study of Human Issues, pp. 17–38.

WILSON, WOODROW (1961) *Constitutional Government in the United States*. New York: Columbia University Press. (First published in 1908.)

CHAPTER 14

ABERBACH, JOEL D.; ROBERT D. PUTNAM, and BERT A. ROCKMAN (1981) *Bureaucrats and Politicians in Western Democracies*. Cambridge, Mass.: Harvard University Press.

BERMAN, LARRY (1979) *The Office of Management and Budget and the Presidency, 1921–1979*. Princeton, N.J.: Princeton University Press.

BROWN, DAVID S. (1972) "The Management of Advisory Committees: An Assignment for the 70's." *Public Administration Review* 32 (July–August): 334–42.

COLE, RICHARD L., and DAVID A CAPUTO (1979) "Presidential Control of the Senior Civil Service: Assessing the Strategies of the Nixon Years." *American Political Science Review* 73 (June): 399–413.

DOWNS, ANTHONY (1967) *Inside Bureaucracy*. Boston: Little, Brown.

DREW, ELIZABETH B. (1970) "Dam Outrage: The Story of the Army Engineers." *Atlantic* (April): 541–62.

FENNO, RICHARD F., JR. (1966) *The Power of the*

Purse: Appropriations Politics in Congress. Boston: Little, Brown.

FIORINA, MORRIS P. (1977) *Congress—Keystone of the Washington Establishment.* New Haven, Conn.: Yale University Press.

FIORINA, MORRIS P. (1979) "Control of the Bureaucracy: A Mismatch of Incentives and Capabilities." In *The Presidency and the Congress: A Shifting Balance of Power,* ed. William Livingston, Lawrence Dodd, and Richard Schott. Austin, Tex.: Lyndon B. Johnson School of Public Affairs and Lyndon Baines Johnson Library.

FISHER, LOUIS (1985) "Judicial Misjudgments about the Lawmaking Process: The Legislative Veto Case." *Public Administration Review* 45 (November): 705–11.

FRIED, ROBERT C. (1976) *Performance in American Bureaucracy.* Boston: Little, Brown.

HECLO, HUGH (1975) "OMB and the Presidency—The Problem of 'Neutral Competence.' " *Public Interest* (Winter): 80–98.

HECLO, HUGH (1977) *A Government of Strangers.* Washington, D.C.: Brookings Institution.

JONES, CHARLES O. (1975) *Clean Air: The Policies and Politics of Pollution Control.* Pittsburgh, Pa.: University of Pittsburgh Press.

KAISER, FREDERICK M. (1980) "Congressional Action to Overturn Agency Rules: Alternatives to the 'Legislative Veto.' " *Administrative Law Review* 32 (Fall): 667–712.

KATZ, DANIEL; BARBARA A. GUTEK; ROBERT L. KAHN; and EUGENIA BARTON (1975) *Bureaucratic Encounters.* Ann Arbor, Mich.: Institute for Social Research.

KATZMANN, ROBERT A. (1980) *Regulatory Bureaucracy: The Federal Trade Commission and Antitrust Policy.* Cambridge, Mass.: Harvard University Press.

KAUFMAN, HERBERT (1976) *Are Government Organizations Immortal?* Washington, D.C.: Brookings Institution.

LEWIS, GREGORY B. (1986) "Race, Sex, and Supervisory Authority in Federal White-Collar Employment." *Public Administration Review* 46 (January–February): 25–30.

LOWI, THEODORE J. (1979) *The End of Liberalism.* 2nd ed. New York: W. W. Norton.

MEIER, KENNETH J. (1979) *Politics and the Bureaucracy: Policymaking in the Fourth Branch of Government.* North Scituate, Mass.: Duxbury Press.

MOE, RONALD C. (1975) "Senate Confirmation of Executive Appointments: The Nixon Era." In *Congress against the President,* ed. Harvey Mansfield. New York: Praeger Publishers, pp. 142–52.

MOSHER, LAWRENCE (1983) "Despite Setbacks. Watt is Succeeding in Opening Up Public Lands for Energy." *National Journal* (June 11): 1230–34.

NATHAN, RICHARD P. (1983) *The Administrative Presidency.* New York: John Wiley & Sons.

NEUSTADT, RICHARD E. (1973) "Politicians and Bureaucrats." In *Congress and America's Future,* ed. David B. Truman. 2nd ed. Englewood Cliffs, N.J.: Prentice-Hall, pp. 118–40

NEWLAND, CHESTER A. (1983) "A Mid-Term Appraisal—The Reagan Presidency: Limited Government and Political Administration." *Public Administration Review* 43 (January–February): 1–21.

OGUL, MORRIS S. (1976) *Congress Oversees the Bureaucracy: Studies in Legislative Supervision.* Pittsburgh, Pa.: University of Pittsburgh Press.

PETRACCA, MARK P. (1986) "Federal Advisory Committees, Interest Groups, and the Administrative State." *Congress and the Presidency* 13 (Spring): 83–114.

RIPLEY, RANDALL B., and GRACE A. FRANKLIN (1987) *Congress, the Bureaucracy, and Public Policy.* 4th ed. Chicago: Dorsey Press.

ROTHMAN, STANLEY, and S. ROBERT LICHTER (1983) "How Liberal Are Bureaucrats?" *Regulation* (November–December): 16–22.

ROURKE, FRANCIS E. (1976) *Bureaucracy, Politics, and Public Policy.* 2nd ed. Boston: Little, Brown.

RUBIN, IRENE S. (1985) *Shrinking the Federal Government: The Effect of Cutbacks on Five Federal Agencies.* New York: Longman.

SEIDMAN, HAROLD, and ROBERT GILMOUR (1986) *Politics, Position, and Power: From the Positive to the Regulatory State.* 4th ed. New York: Oxford University Press.

TAYLOR, TELFORD (1955) *Grand Inquest,* New York: Simon & Schuster.

WILENSKY, HAROLD L. (1967) *Organizational Intelligence.* New York: Basic Books.

WILSON, JAMES Q. (1975) "The Rise of the Bureaucratic State." *Public Interest* (Fall): 77–103.

WYNIA, BOB L. (1974) "Federal Bureaucrats; Attitudes toward a Democratic Ideology." *Public Administration Review* 34 (March–April): 156–62.

CHAPTER 15

ABRAHAM,, HENRY J. (1985) *Justices and Presidents: A Political History of Appointments to the Supreme Court.* 2nd ed. New York: Oxford University Press.

ABRAHAM, HENRY J. (1986) *The Judicial Process.* 5th ed. New York: Oxford University Press.

BALL, HOWARD (1980) *Courts and Politics: The Fed-*

eral Judicial System. Englewood Cliffs, N.J.: Prentice-Hall.

BARNUM, DAVID G. (1985) "The Supreme Court and Public Opinion: Judicial Decision Making in the Post–New Deal Period." *Journal of Politics* 47 (May): 652–66.

BAUM, LAWRENCE (1985) *The Supreme Court*. 2nd ed. Washington, D.C.: Congressional Quarterly Press.

BLACK, CHARLES L., JR. (1970) *Perspectives in Constitutional Law*. Rev. ed. Englewood Cliffs, N.J.: Prentice-Hall.

BOND, JON R., and CHARLES A. JOHNSON (1982) "Implementing a Permissive Policy: Hospital Abortion Services after *Roe* v. *Wade*." *American Journal of Political Science* 26 (February): 1–24.

CALDEIRA, GREGORY A., and JOHN R. WRIGHT (1987) "Organized Interests and Agenda-Setting in the Supreme Court." Unpublished paper.

CARP, ROBERT A., and C. K. ROWLAND (1983) *Policymaking and Politics in the Federal District Courts*. Knoxville: University of Tennessee Press.

CASPER, JONATHAN D. (1976) "The Supreme Court and National Policy Making." *American Political Science Review* 70 (March): 50–63.

COOK, BEVERLY B. (1977) "Public Opinion and Federal Judicial Policy." *American Journal of Political Science* 21 (August): 567–600.

COOK, BEVERLY B. (1979) "Judicial Policy: Change over Time." *American Journal of Political Science* 23 (February): 208–14.

DAHL, ROBERT A. (1957) "Decision-Making in a Democracy: The Supreme Court as a National Policy-Maker. *Journal of Public Law* 6 (Fall): 279–95.

EISENSTEIN, JAMES (1978) *Counsel for the United States*. Baltimore: Johns Hopkins University Press.

GILES, MICHEAL W., and THOMAS G. WALKER (1975) "Judicial Policy-Making and Southern School Segregation." *Journal of Politics* 37 (November): 917–36.

GLAZER, NATHAN (1975) "Towards an Imperial Judiciary?" *Public Interest* (Fall): 104–23.

GOLDMAN, SHELDON (1983) "Reagan's Judicial Appointments at Mid-Term: Shaping the Bench in His Own Image." *Judicature* 66 (March): 334–47.

GOLDMAN, SHELDON (1985) "Reaganizing the Judiciary: The First Term Appointments." *Judicature* 68 (April–May): 313–29.

GOLDMAN, SHELDON (1987) "Reagan's Second Term Judicial Appointments: The Battle at Midway." *Judicature* 70 (April–May): 324–39.

GOLDMAN, SHELDON, and THOMAS P. JAHNIGE (1985) *The Federal Courts as a Political System*. 3rd ed. New York: Harper & Row.

HEARST CORPORATION (1983) *The American Public, the Media, and the Judicial System*. New York: Hearst Corporation.

HOROWITZ, DONALD L. (1977) *The Courts and Social Policy*. Washington, D.C.: Brookings Institution.

JACOB, HERBERT (1984) *Justice in America: Courts, Lawyers, and the Judicial Process*. 4th ed. Boston: Little, Brown.

KRITZER, HERBERT M. (1979) "Federal Judges and Their Political Environments: The Influence of Public Opinion." *American Journal of Political Science* 23 (February): 194–207.

MCCLOSKEY, ROBERT G. (1960) *The American Supreme Court*. Chicago: University of Chicago Press.

MILNER, NEAL A. (1971) *The Court and Local Law Enforcement: The Impact of Miranda*. Beverly Hills, Calif.: Sage Publications.

MUIR, WILLIAM (1968) *Prayer in the Public Schools*. Chicago: University of Chicago Press.

MURPHY, BRUCE ALLEN (1982) *The Brandeis/Frankfurter Connection: The Secret Political Activities of Two Supreme Court Justices*. New York: Oxford University Press.

NAGEL, STUART S. (1961) "Political Party Affiliation and Judges' Decisions." *American Political Science Review* 55 (December): 843–50.

O'CONNOR, KAREN, and LEE EPSTEIN (1983) "The Rise of Conservative Interest Group Litigation." *Journal of Politics* 45 (May): 479–89.

REHNQUIST, WILLIAM H. (1976) "The Notion of a Living Constitution." *Texas Law Review* 54 (May): 693–706.

RICHARDSON, RICHARD J., and KENNETH N. VINES (1970) *The Politics of Federal Courts*. Boston: Little, Brown.

ROHDE, DAVID W., and HAROLD J. SPAETH (1976) *Supreme Court Decision Making*. San Francisco: W. H. Freeman.

ROWLAND, C. K., and ROBERT A. CARP (1980) "A Longitudinal Study of Party Effects on Federal District Court Policy Propensities." *American Journal of Political Science* 24 (May): 291–305.

SARAT, AUSTIN, and JOEL B. GROSSMAN (1975) "Courts and Conflict Resolution: Problems in the Mobilization of Adjudication." *American Political Science Review* 69 (December): 1200–17.

SCIGLIANO, ROBERT (1971) *The Supreme Court and the Presidency*. New York: Free Press.

SHAPIRO, MARTIN (1978) "The Supreme Court: From Warren to Burger." In *The New American Political System*, ed. Anthony King. Washington, D.C.: American Enterprise Institute for Public Policy Research.

SLOTNICK, ELLIOT E. (1979) "Who Speaks for the Court? Majority Opinion Assignment from Taft to Burger." *American Journal of Political Science* 23 (February): 60–77.

WASBY, STEPHEN L. (1976) *Small Town Police and the Supreme Court*. Lexington, Mass.: Lexington Books.

WOODWARD, BOB, and SCOTT ARMSTRONG (1979) *The Brethren: Inside the Supreme Court*. New York: Simon & Schuster.

CHAPTER 16

BEAM, DAVID R. (1984) "New Federalism, Old Realities: The Reagan Administration and Intergovernmental Reform." In *The Reagan Presidency and the Governing of America*, ed. Lester M. Salamon and Michael S. Lund. Washington, D.C.: Urban Institute, pp. 415–22.

CATER, DOUGLASS (1964) *Power in Washington*. New York: Random House.

CEASER, JAMES W. (1984) "The Theory of Governance and the Reagan Administration." In *The Reagan Presidency and the Governing of America*, ed. Lester M. Salamon and Michael S. Lund. Washington, D.C.: Urban Institute, pp. 57–87.

CHUBB, JOHN E. (1985) "Federalism and the Bias for Centralization." In *The New Direction in American Politics*, ed. John E. Chubb and Paul E. Peterson. Washington, D.C.: Brookings Institution, pp. 273–306.

COBB, ROGER W., and CHARLES D. ELDER (1983) *Participation in American Politics: The Dynamics of Agenda-Building*. 2nd ed. Baltimore: Johns Hopkins University Press.

DERTHICK, MARTHA (1970) *The Influence of Federal Grants: Public Assistance in Massachusetts*. Cambridge, Mass.: Harvard University Press.

DODD, LAWRENCE C. (1981) "Congress, the Constitution, and the Crisis of Legitimation." In *Congress Reconsidered*, ed. Lawrence C. Dodd and Bruce I. Oppenheimer. 2nd ed. Washington, D.C.: Congressional Quarterly Press, pp. 390–420.

INGRAM, HELEN (1977) "Policy Implementation through Bargaining: The Case of Federal Grants-in-Aid." *Public Policy* 25 (Fall): 499–526.

KETTL, DONALD F. (1983) *The Regulation of American Federalism*. Baton Rouge: Louisiana State University Press.

KINGDON, JOHN W. (1984) *Agendas, Alternatives, and Public Policies*. Boston: Little, Brown.

LEWIS, EUGENE (1977) *American Politics in a Bureaucratic Age: Citizens, Constituents, Clients, and Victims*. Cambridge, Mass.: Winthrop.

LINDBLOM, CHARLES E. (1959) "The Science of 'Muddling Through.'" *Public Administration Review* 19 (Spring): 79–88.

LOWI, THEODORE J. (1979) *The End of Liberalism*. 2nd ed. New York: W. W. Norton.

NATHAN, RICHARD P., and PAUL R. DOMMEL (1978) "Federal-Loan Relations under Block Grants." *Political Science Quarterly* 93 (Fall): 421–42.

NATHAN, RICHARD P., and FRED C. DOOLITTLE (1984a) "Overview: Effects of the Reagan Domestic Program on States and Localities." Unpublished paper. Princeton, N.J.: Urban and Regional Research Center, Woodrow Wilson School, Princeton University.

NATHAN, RICHARD P., and FRED C. DOOLITTLE (1984b) "The Untold Story of Reagan's 'New Federalism.'" *Public Interest* 77 (Fall): 96–105.

NELSON, BARBARA J. (1984) *Making an Issue of Child Abuse*. Chicago: University of Chicago Press.

PETERSON, GEORGE E. (1984a) "Federalism and the States: An Experiment in Decentralization." In *The Reagan Record*, ed. John L. Palmer and Isabel V. Sawhill. Cambridge, Mass.: Ballinger, pp. 217–51.

PETERSON, PAUL E. (1984b) "When Federalism Works." In *Emerging Issues in American Federalism: Papers Prepared for ACIR's 25th Anniversary*. Washington, D.C.: Advisory Commission on Intergovernmental Relations, pp. 13–25.

REAGAN, MICHAEL D., and JOHN G. SANZONE (1981) *The New Federalism*. 2nd ed. New York: Oxford University Press.

STEWART, RICHARD B. (1982) "The Legal Structure of Interstate Resource Conflicts." In *Regional Conflict and National Policy*, ed. Kent A. Price. Washington, D.C.: Resources for the Future, pp. 87–109.

VAN HORN, CARL E. (1979) *Policy Implementation in the Federal System*. Lexington, Mass.: Lexington Books.

VAN METER, DONALD S., and CARL E. VAN HORN (1975) "The Policy Implementation Process: A Conceptual Framework." *Administration and Society* 6 (February): 445–88.

WALKER, DAVID B. (1981) *Toward a Functioning Federalism*. Cambridge, Mass.: Winthrop.

WILLIAMS, WALTER (1980) *Government by Agency: Lessons from the Social Program Grants-in-Aid Experience*. New York: Academic Press.

CHAPTER 17

BAILEY, STEPHEN K., and EDITH K. MOSHER (1968) *ESEA: The Office of Education Administers a Law*. Syracuse, N.Y.: Syracuse University Press.

BAUMER, DONALD C., and CARL E. VAN HORN (1984) *The Politics of Unemployment*. Washington, D.C.: Congressional Quarterly Press.

BENDINER, ROBERT (1964) *Obstacle Course on Capitol Hill*. New York: McGraw-Hill.

BULLOCK, CHARLES S., III (1980) "The Office for Civil Rights and Implementation of Desegregation Programs in the Public Schools." *Policy Studies Journal* 8 (Special Issue no. 2): 547–616.

EIDENBERG, EUGENE, and ROY D. MOREY (1969) *An Act of Congress*. New York: W. W. Norton.

FRANKLIN, GRACE A., and RANDALL B. RIPLEY (1984) *CETA: Politics and Policy, 1973–1982*. Knoxville: University of Tennessee Press.

JANTSCHER, GERALD R. (1975) *Bread upon the Waters: Federal Aids to the Maritime Industries*. Washington, D.C.: Brookings Institution.

JONES, CHARLES O. (1984) *An Introduction to the Study of Public Policy*. 3rd ed. Monterey, Calif.: Brooks/Cole Publishing.

LAWRENCE, SAMUEL A. (1965) *United States Merchant Shipping Policies and Politics*. Washington, D.C.: Brookings Institution.

LAZIN, FREDERICK A. (1973) "The Failure of Federal Enforcement of Civil Rights Regulations in Public Housing, 1963–1971: The Co-optation of a Federal Agency by Its Local Constituency." *Policy Sciences* 4 (September): 263–73.

LEMAN, CHRISTOPHER (1979) "How to Get There from Here: The Grandfather Effect and Public Policy." *Policy Analysis* 6 (Winter): 99–116.

LOWI, THEODORE J. (1964) "American Business, Public Policy, Case-Studies, and Political Theory." *World Politics* 16 (July): 677–715.

MARMOR, THEODORE R. (1973) *The Politics of Medicare*. Rev. ed. Chicago: Aldine Publishing.

MENZEL, DONALD C. (1983) "Redirecting the Implementation of a Law: The Reagan Administration and Coal Surface Mining Regulation." *Public Administration Review* 43 (September–October): 411–20.

MIRENGOFF, WILLIAM, and LESTER RINDLER (1976) *The Comprehensive Employment and Training Act Impact on People, Places, Programs*. Washington, D.C.: National Academy of Sciences.

MUNGER, FRANK J., and RICHARD F. FENNO, JR. (1962) *National Politics and Federal Aid to Education*. Syracuse, N.Y.: Syracuse University Press.

MURPHY, JEROME T. (1971) "Title I of ESEA: The Politics of Implementing Federal Education Reform." *Harvard Educational Review* 41 (February): 35–63.

MURPHY, JEROME T. (1973) "The Education Bureaucracies Implement Novel Policy: The Politics of Title I of ESEA, 1965–72." In *Policy and Politics in America: Six Case Studies*, ed. Allan P. Sindler. Boston: Little, Brown, pp. 160–98.

NATHAN, RICHARD P.; ALLEN D. MANVEL; SUSANNAH E. CALKINS; and ASSOCIATES (1975) *Monitoring Revenue Sharing*. Washington, D.C.: Brookings Institution.

RABKIN, JEREMY (1980) "Office for Civil Rights." In *The Politics of Regulation*, ed. James Q. Wilson. New York: Basic Books.

REDMAN, ERIC (1973) *The Dance of Legislation*. New York: Simon & Schuster.

REID, T. R. (1980) *Congressional Odyssey: The Saga of a Senate Bill*. San Francisco: W. H. Freeman.

RIPLEY, RANDALL B., and GRACE A. FRANKLIN (1986) *Policy Implementation and Bureaucracy*. 2nd ed. Chicago: Dorsey Press.

RIPLEY, RANDALL B., and GRACE A. FRANKLIN (1987) *Congress, the Bureaucracy, and Public Policy*. 4th ed. Chicago: Dorsey Press.

SUNDQUIST, JAMES L. (1968) *Politics and Policy*. Washington, D.C.: Brookings Institution.

TALBOT, ROSS B., and DONALD F. HADWIGER (1968) *The Policy Process in American Agriculture*. San Francisco: Chandler Publishing.

VAN HORN, CARL E., and DONALD S. VAN METER (1976) "The Implementation of Intergovernmental Policy." In *Public Policy Making in a Federal System*, ed. Charles O. Jones and Robert D. Thomas. Beverly Hills, Calif.: Sage Publications, pp. 39–62.

CHAPTER 18

AARON, HENRY J., and others (1986) *Economic Choices, 1987*. Washington, D.C.: Brookings Institution.

BAILEY, STEPHEN K. (1950) *Congress Makes a Law: The Story behind the Employment Act of 1946*. New York: Columbia University Press.

BAUER, RAYMOND A.; ITHIEL DE SOLA POOL; and LEWIS A. DEXTER (1963) *American Business and Public Policy*. New York: Atherton Press.

BELL, DANIEL, and LESTER THUROW (1986) *The Deficits*. New York: New York University Press.

CAGAN, PHILLIP, ed. (1985) *Essays in Contemporary Economic Problems, 1985: The Economy in Deficit*. Washington, D.C.: American Enterprise Institute for Public Policy Research.

EISNER, ROBERT (1986) *How Real Is the Federal Deficit?* New York: Free Press.

HECLO, HUGH (1984) "Executive Budget Making." In *Federal Budget Policy in the 1980s*, ed. Gregory B. Mills and John L. Palmer. Washington, D.C.: Urban Institute, pp. 255–91.

HUITT, RALPH K. (1963) "Congressional Organization and Operations in the Field of Money and Credit." In *Fiscal and Debt Management Policies*. Englewood Cliffs, N.J.: Prentice-Hall, published for the Commission on Money and Credit, pp. 399–495.

KETTL, DONALD F. (1986) *Leadership at the Fed*. New Haven, Conn.: Yale University Press.

KIEWIET, D. RODERICK (1983) *Macroeconomics and Micropolitics: The Electoral Effects of Economic Issues*. Chicago: University of Chicago Press.

KOTLIKOFF, LAURENCE J. (1986) "Deficit Delusion." *Public Interest* 84 (Summer): 53–65.

LAWRENCE, ROBERT Z. (1984) *Can America Compete?* Washington, D.C.: Brookings Institution.

LELOUP, LANCE T. (1986 and 1988) *Budgetary Politics*. 3rd and 4th eds. Brunswick, Ohio: King's Court.

LEVY, FRANK, and RICHARD C. MICHEL (1983) "The Way We'll Be in 1984: Recent Changes in the Level and Distribution of Disposable Income." Discussion paper. Washington, D.C.: Urban Institute.

MANLEY, JOHN F. (1970) *The Politics of Finance*. Boston: Little, Brown.

MOON, MARILYN, and ISABEL V. SAWHILL (1984) "Family Incomes: Gainers and Losers." In *The Reagan Record*, ed. John L. Palmer and Isabel V. Sawhill. Cambridge, Mass.: Ballinger.

ORNSTEIN, NORMAN J. (1985) "The Politics of the Deficit." In *Essays in Contemporary Economic Problems, 1985: The Economy in Deficit*, ed. Phillip Cagan. Washington, D.C.: American Enterprise Institute for Public Policy Research.

PECHMAN, JOSEPH A. (1985) *Who Paid the Taxes, 1966–85?* Washington, D.C.: Brookings Institution.

PECHMAN, JOSEPH A. (1987) *Federal Tax Policy*. 5th ed. Washington, D.C.: Brookings Institution.

PETERSON, PAUL E. (1985) "The New Politics of Deficits." In *The New Direction in American Politics*, ed. John E. Chubb and Paul E. Peterson. Washington, D.C.: Brookings Institution, pp. 365–97.

REICH, ROBERT B. (1983) *The Next American Frontier: A Provocative Program for Economic Renewal*. New York: Times Books.

SCHICK, ALLEN (1980) *Congress and Money: Budgeting, Spending and Taxing*. Washington, D.C.: Urban Institute.

SCHICK, ALLEN (1984) "The Budget as an Instrument of Presidential Policy." In *The Reagan Presidency and the Governing of America*, ed. Lester M. Salamon and Michael S. Lund. Washington, D.C.: Urban Institute, pp. 91–125.

SCHULTZE, CHARLES L. (1983) "Industrial Policy: A Dissent." *Brookings Review* 2 (Fall): 3–12.

SMITH, STEVEN S. (1985) "New Patterns of Decisionmaking in Congress." In *The New Direction in American Politics*, ed. John E. Chubb and Paul E. Peterson. Washington, D.C.: Brookings Institution, pp. 203–33.

TUFTE, EDWARD R. (1978) *Political Control of the Economy*. Princeton, N.J.: Princeton University Press.

WILDAVSKY, AARON (1988) *The New Politics of the Budgetary Process*. Glenview, Ill.: Scott, Foresman.

WOOLLEY, JOHN T. (1984) *Monetary Politics: The Federal Reserve and the Politics of Monetary Policy*. Cambridge: Cambridge University Press.

CHAPTER 19

BULLOCK, CHARLES S., III (1980) "The Office for Civil Rights and Implementation of Desegregation Programs in the Public Schools." *Policy Studies Journal* 8 (Special Issue no. 2): 597–616.

DUCAT, CRAIG R., and HAROLD W. CHASE (1983) *Constitutional Interpretation: Cases—Essays—Materials*. 3rd ed. St. Paul, Minn.: West Publishing.

GARCIA, F. CHRIS, and RUDOLPH O. DE LA GARZA (1977) *The Chicano Political Experience*. North Scituate, Mass.: Duxbury Press.

GASTIL, RAYMOND D. (1982) *Freedom in the World*. New York: Freedom House.

GOLDSTEIN, LESLIE FRIEDMAN (1979) *The Constitutional Rights of Women*. New York: Longman.

GOLDSTEIN, LESLIE FRIEDMAN (1981) "The Constitutional Status of Women: The Burger Court and the Sexual Revolution in American Law." *Law and Policy Quarterly* 3 (January): 5–28.

GROSSMAN, JOEL B., and RICHARD S. WELLS (1980) *Constitutional Law and Judicial Policy Making*. 2nd ed. New York: John Wiley & Sons.

HANSEN, SUSAN B. (1980) "State Implementation of Supreme Court Decisions: Abortion Rates since *Roe v. Wade.*" *Journal of Politics* 42 (May): 372–95.

KICKINGBIRD, LYNN, and KIRKE KICKINGBIRD (1977) *Indians and the U.S. Government,* Washington, D.C.: Institute for the Development of Indian Law.

KLUGER, RICHARD (1976) *Simple Justice: The History of* Brown *v.* Board of Education *and Black America's Struggle for Equality.* New York: Alfred A. Knopf.

MCCLOSKY, HERBERT, and ALIDA BRILL (1983) *Dimensions of Tolerance: What Americans Believe about Civil Liberties.* New York: Russell Sage Foundation.

ORFIELD, GARY (1978) *Must We Bus?* Washington, D.C.: Brookings Institution.

RABKIN, JEREMY (1980) "Office for Civil Rights." In *The Politics of Regulation,* ed. James Q. Wilson, New York: Basic Books.

RODGERS, HARRELL R., JR., and CHARLES S. BULLOCK, III (1976) *Coercion to Compliance.* Lexington, Mass.: D. C. Heath.

SUNDQUIST, JAMES L. (1968) *Politics and Policy.* Washington, D.C.: Brookings Institution.

TAYLOR, CHARLES LEWIS, and MICHAEL C. HUDSON (1972) *World Handbook of Political and Social Indicators.* 2nd ed. New Haven, Conn.: Yale University Press.

CHAPTER 20

ALLISON, GRAHAM T. (1971) *The Essence of Decision: Explaining the Cuban Missile Crisis.* Boston: Little, Brown.

ALLISON, GRAHAM T., and MORTON H. HALPERIN (1972) "Bureaucratic Politics: A Paradigm and Some Policy Implications." *World Politics* 24 (supplement): 40–79.

ALMOND, GABRIEL (1960) *The American People and Foreign Policy.* New York: Praeger Publishers.

BAUER, RAYMOND A,; ITHIEL DE SOLA POOL; and LEWIS ANTHONY DEXTER (1963) *American Business and Public Policy: The Politics of Foreign Trade.* New York: Atherton Press.

BAX, FRANS R. (1977) "The Legislative-Executive Relationship in Foreign Policy: New Partnership or New Competition?" *Orbis* (Winter): 881–904.

BEDELL, SALLY (1982) "Why TV News Can't Be a Complete View of the World." *New York Times* (August 8): sec. 2, p. 1.

BERNSTEIN, RICHARD (1982) "An Elite Group in U.S. Policy Is Diversifying." *New York Times* (October 30): 29.

CARROLL, HOLBERT N. (1966) *The House of Representatives and Foreign Affairs.* Rev. ed. Boston: Little, Brown.

COHEN, BERNARD C. (1965) *The Press and Foreign Policy.* Princeton, N.J.: Princeton University Press.

CRABB, CECIL V., JR. (1983) *American Foreign Policy in the Nuclear Age.* 4th ed. New York: Harper & Row.

CRABB, CECIL V., JR., and PAT M. HOLT (1984) *Invitation to Struggle: Congress, the President, and Foreign Policy.* 2nd. ed. Washington, D.C.: Congressional Quarterly Press.

DESTLER, I. M. (1981) "Dateline Washington: Congress as Boss?" *Foreign Policy* 42 (Spring): 167–80.

DULLES, ALLEN (1963) *The Craft of Intelligence.* New York: Harper & Row.

EISENHOWER, DWIGHT D. (1961) *Public Papers of the Presidents.* Washington, D.C.: U.S. Government Printing Office.

FISHER, LOUIS (1985) *Constitutional Conflicts between Congress and the President.* Princeton, N.J.: Princeton University Press.

FULBRIGHT, J. WILLIAM (1966) *The Arrogance of Power.* New York: Random House.

GEORGE, ALEXANDER L. (1972) "The Case for Multiple Advocacy in Making Foreign Policy." *American Political Science Review* 66 (September): 751–85.

HILSMAN, ROGER (1967) *To Move a Nation: The Politics of Foreign Policy in the Administration of John F. Kennedy.* Garden City, N.Y.: Doubleday.

HUNTINGTON, SAMUEL, P. (1961) *The Common Defense.* New York: Columbia University Press.

HYMAN, HAROLD M. (1986) *Quiet Past and Stormy Present? War Powers in American History.* Washington, D.C.: American Historical Association Bicentennial Essays on the Constitution.

IRISH, MARIAN, and ELKE FRANK (1975) *U.S. Foreign Policy: Context, Conduct, Content.* New York: Harcourt Brace Jovanovich.

JANIS, IRVING L. (1983) *Groupthink.* Boston: Houghton Mifflin.

KATZ, DANIEL, et al., eds. (1954) *Public Opinion and Propaganda.* New York: Holt, Rinehart & Winston.

KENNAN, GEORGE F. (1952) *American Diplomacy, 1900–1950.* New York: New American Library.

LADD, EVERETT C. (1986) "The Foreign Policy Record: Reagan's Sphere of Influence." *Public Opinion* 9 (Summer): 3–5.

LARDNER, GEORGE, JR. (1984) "Will We Ever Harness Our Rogue Agency?" *Washington Post* (April 22): D5.

LEWIS, ANTHONY (1984) "Royal Prerogative (1)" *New York Times* (July 2): A15.

MATHIAS, CHARLES MCC., JR. (1981) "Ethnic Groups and Foreign Policy." *Foreign Affairs* 59 (Summer): 975–98.

MUELLER, JOHN E. (1973) *War, Presidents, and Public Opinion.* New York: John Wiley & Sons.

REILLY, JOHN E., ed. (1983) *American Public Opinion and U.S. Foreign Policy, 1983.* Chicago: Chicago Council on Foreign Relations.

ROBERTS, STEVEN B. (1986) "The Global Village: A Case in Point." *New York Times* (February 20): B8.

SAMPSON, ANTHONY (1977) *The Arms Bazaar: From Lebanon to Lockheed.* New York: Viking Press.

SCHLESINGER, ARTHUR M., JR. (1965) *A Thousand Days: John F. Kennedy in the White House.* Boston: Houghton Mifflin.

SCHLESINGER, ARTHUR M., JR. (1973) *The Imperial Presidency.* Boston: Houghton Mifflin.

SHALES, TOM (1986) "Islands in the Swirl of the Storm." *Washington Post* (February 24): D1–2.

SHAW, DAVID (1986) "Foreign Correspondents: It's On-the-Job Training." *Los Angeles Times* (July 2): I, 1 ff.

SPYKMAN, NICHOLAS J. (1942) *America's Strategy in World Politics.* New York: Harcourt Brace Jovanovich.

WALCOTT, JOHN (1987) "Revitalized for a Time, the CIA Is Now Jolted by Variety of Setbacks." *The Wall Street Journal* (January 22): 1.

WILLIAMS, JUAN (1983) "Reagan's Days Off Erupt in Crisis." *Washington Post* (October 24): A14.

WISE, DAVID (1976) *The American Police State.* New York: Random House.

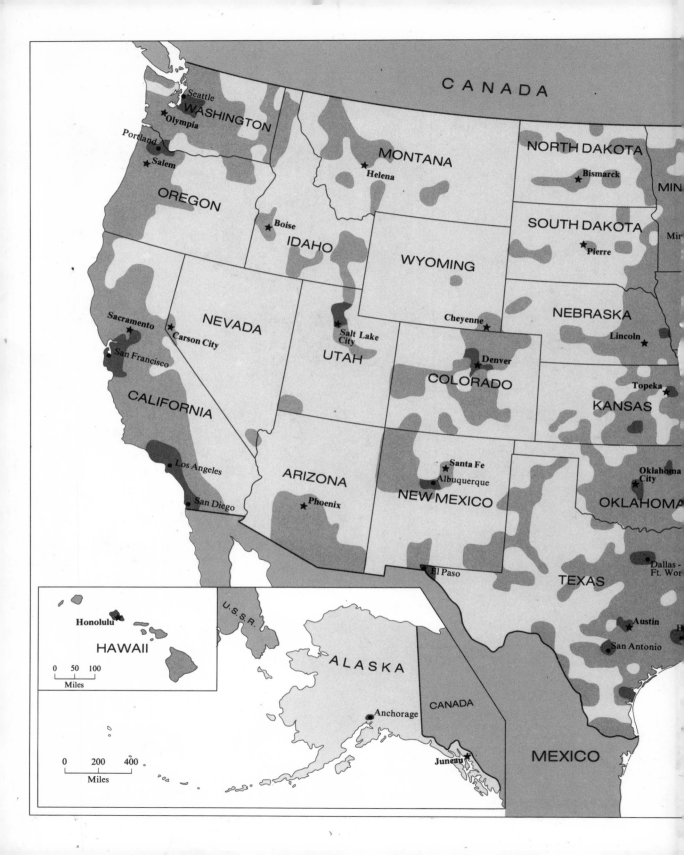